Brief Table of Contents

focus on . . . the Cover

How do you feel when you look at this cover? We hope the image on the book conveys a feeling of relaxation and overall peace of mind—both achieved, in part, by developing a solid financial plan. From cover to cover, this text's goal is to actively help you gain the financial literacy and personal finance skills you need to make sound financial decisions for life. Use this book as a tool to help you plan for a successful financial future!

focus on PERSONAL FINANCE

An Active Approach to Help You Develop Successful Financial Skills

KAPOOR | DLABAY | HUGHES

Focus on Personal Finance

An Active Approach to Help You Develop
Successful Financial Skills

THIRD EDITION

Jack R. Kapoor
COLLEGE OF DUPAGE

Les R. Dlabay
LAKE FOREST COLLEGE

Robert J. Hughes
DALLAS COUNTY COMMUNITY COLLEGES

McGraw-Hill Irwin

FOCUS ON PERSONAL FINANCE: AN ACTIVE APPROACH TO HELP YOU DEVELOP
SUCCESSFUL FINANCIAL SKILLS

Some ancillaries, including electronic and print components, may not be available to customers
outside the United States.

This book is printed on acid-free paper.

2 3 4 5 6 7 8 9 0 WCK/WCK 14 13 12 11 10

ISBN   978-0-07-338242-5
MHID 0-07-338242-6

Vice president and editor-in-chief: *Brent Gordon*
Publisher: *Douglas Reiner*
Executive editor: *Michele Janicek*
Director of development: *Ann Torbert*
Development editor: *Elizabeth Hughes*
Vice president and director of marketing: *Robin J. Zwettler*
Marketing director: *Sankha Basu*
Senior marketing manager: *Melissa S. Caughlin*
Vice president of editing, design and production: *Sesha Bolisetty*
Project manager: *Dana M. Pauley*
Production supervisor: *Gina Hangos*
Interior designer: *Cara Hawthorne, cara david DESIGN*
Lead media project manager: *Brian Nacik*
Cover design: *Cara Hawthorne, cara david DESIGN*
Interior design: *Cara Hawthorne, cara david DESIGN*
Typeface: *10/12 Times New Roman MT Std-Regular*
Compositor: *Laserwords Private Limited*
Printer: *Quebecor World Versailles Inc.*

Library of Congress Cataloging-in-Publication Data

Kapoor, Jack R., 1937-
    Focus on personal finance : an active approach to help you develop successful financial
skills / Jack R. Kapoor, Les R. Dlabay, Robert J. Hughes.—3rd ed.
      p. cm.—(The McGraw-Hill/Irwin series in finance, insurance, and real estate)
    Includes index.
    ISBN-13: 978-0-07-338242-5 (alk. paper)
    ISBN-10: 0-07-338242-6 (alk. paper)
    1. Finance, Personal. 2. Investments. I. Dlabay, Les R. II. Hughes, Robert James, 1946-
III. Title.
HG179.K368 2010
332.024'01—dc22

                                                                                2009021387

www.mhhe.com

To my father, Ram Kapoor, and the memory of my mother, Sheila; my wife, Theresa, and my children, Karen, Kathryn, and Dave

To the memory of my parents, Mary and Les Dlabay; to my wife, Linda, and my children, Carissa and Kyle

To my mother, Barbara Y. Hughes; and my wife, Peggy

Focus on . . . the Authors

Jack R. Kapoor, *College of DuPage*

Jack Kapoor is a professor of business and economics in the Business and Technology Division of the College of DuPage, Glen Ellyn, Illinois, where he has taught business and economics since 1969. He received his BA and MS from San Francisco State College and his EdD from Northern Illinois University. He previously taught at Illinois Institute of Technology's Stuart School of Management, San Francisco State University's School of World Business, and other colleges. Professor Kapoor was awarded the Business and Technology Division's Outstanding Professor Award for 1999–2000. He served as an assistant national bank examiner for the U.S. Treasury Department and has been an international trade consultant to Bolting Manufacturing Co., Ltd., Bombay, India.

Dr. Kapoor is known internationally as a co-author of several textbooks, including *Business: A Practical Approach* (Rand McNally), *Business* (Cengage Learning), *Business and Personal Finance* (Glencoe), and *Personal Finance* (McGraw-Hill). He served as a content consultant for the popular national television series *The Business File: An Introduction to Business* and developed two full-length audio courses in Business and Personal Finance. He has been quoted in many national newspapers and magazines, including *USA Today, U.S. News & World Report,* the *Chicago Sun-Times, Crain's Small Business,* the *Chicago Tribune,* and other publications.

Dr. Kapoor has traveled around the world and has studied business practices in capitalist, socialist, and communist countries.

Les R. Dlabay, *Lake Forest College*

Sharing resources with the less fortunate is an ongoing financial goal of Les Dlabay, professor of business at Lake Forest College, Lake Forest, Illinois. Through child sponsorship programs, world hunger organizations, and community service activities, he believes the extensive wealth in our society should be used to help others. In addition to writing several textbooks, Dr. Dlabay teaches various international business courses. His "hobbies" include collecting cereal packages from over 100 countries and paper currency from 200 countries, which are used to teach about economic, cultural, and political aspects of foreign business environments. Professor Dlabay also uses many field research activities with his students, conducting interviews, surveys, and observations of business activities.

Robert J. Hughes, *Dallas County Community Colleges*

Financial literacy! Only two words, but Bob Hughes, professor of business at Dallas County Community Colleges, believes that these two words can literally change people's lives. Whether you want to be rich or just manage the money you have, the ability to analyze financial decisions and gather financial information are skills that can always be improved. In addition to writing several textbooks, Dr. Hughes has taught personal finance, introduction to business, business math, small business management, small business finance, and accounting since 1972. He also served as a content consultant for two popular national television series, *It's Strictly Business* and *Dollars & Sense: Personal Finance for the 21st Century,* and is the lead author for a business math project utilizing computer-assisted instruction funded by the ALEKS Corporation. He received his BBA from Southern Nazarene University and his MBA and EdD from the University of North Texas. His hobbies include writing, investing, collecting French antiques, art, and travel.

Dear Personal Finance Professors and Personal Finance Students

It is both amazing and alarming how quickly the economy can change—we were in a much different economic state when we wrote the previous edition of this text just a few years ago. The economic meltdown that began in late 2007 rivals that of the "Great Depression" and has affected countries, companies, and individuals both in the United States and around the world.

Hopefully, by the time you read this material, the economy will be improving. Still, it is important to remember the old adage, "History is a great teacher." In order to avoid the problems that many people have experienced during the recent economic crisis, you must manage your money in order to obtain freedom from financial worries. That's what the new third edition of *Focus on Personal Finance* is all about. As authors, we wanted to provide you with the information you need to develop a financial plan that will enable you to achieve your financial goals.

For three editions, we have been keenly aware that our customers are instructors *and* students. With each revision, we have asked instructors for suggestions that would help professors teach better and help students learn more efficiently. And with each edition, we have incorporated these suggestions and ideas to create what has become a best-selling Personal Finance text. We are also proud to say that we have included extensive student feedback in our text and program features. We can only say *thank you* for your suggestions, ideas, and support. Without you—both instructors and students—we would have no reason to write a Personal Finance text.

Finally, a text should always be evaluated by the people who use it. We welcome your comments, suggestions, and questions. We invite you to examine the visual guide that follows to see how *Focus on Personal Finance* can help students obtain financial security and success in life.

Welcome to the new third edition of *Focus on Personal Finance!*

Jack Kapoor
kapoorj@cod.edu

Les Dlabay
dlabay@lakeforest.edu

Bob Hughes
bhughes@dcccd.edu

New to This Edition

The third edition of *Focus on Personal Finance* contains new and updated boxed features, exhibits and tables, articles, and end of chapter material. The following grid highlights some of the more significant content revisions made to *Focus*, 3e.

Chapter 1	• New material and exercises on "Personal Tactics for Surviving a Financial Crisis" • Addition of financial calculator key strokes in the Time Value of Money appendix
Chapter 2	• Extended material on avoiding debt and creating a successful money management plan
Chapter 5	• Discussion of micro lending organizations • New examples of home equity loans • Expanded discussion on avoiding credit card debt • Discussion of recent credit card legislation • Expanded bankruptcy coverage
Chapter 8	• New example box on how to decrease insurance premiums
Chapter 9	• Expanded discussion on group health insurance • New information on Health Savings Accounts (HSAs) • Expanded coverage on the need for disability income • Discussion of the Obama Administration's plan to cut health care costs
Chapter 11	• New section on surviving a financial crisis • Expanded market risk discussion with new information on the business cycle and the length of the typical economic crisis. • Updated information on Treasury securities
Chapter 12	• New information about the importance of the price-earnings (PE) ratio is included in the section "Why Corporate Earnings Are Important."
Chapter 13	• New material in the chapter introduction on the effect of the economic crisis on mutual fund investments. • Updated data on the importance of mutual fund investments in the section "Why Investors Purchase Mutual Funds." • Expanded discussion of different types of exchange-traded funds in the section "Characteristics of Funds." • Description of lifecycle funds
Chapter 14	• Revision and update of individual retirement accounts
Appendix A	• New material on career strategies in a weak job market

Focus on . . . Learning

GET INSIDE THE BOOK

Getting Personal

Fill it in and get personal! Each chapter starts with a personal assessment questionnaire focusing on your current personal financial habits. The quiz introduces you to topics in the upcoming chapter.

Objective References

Citations in the margins next to the relevant text refer to corresponding chapter objectives, listed at the beginning of each chapter.

Personal Financial Planning in Action

Getting Personal

What are your money habits? For each of the following statements, select "yes" or "no" to indicate your behavior regarding these financial planning activities:

	Yes	No
1. I usually have enough money for the things I need.	___	___
2. I owe less money today than I owed a year or two ago.	___	___
3. My written goals for the next year need revision due to changing financial situations in our society.	___	___
4. When making major financial decisions, I research them using a variety of information sources.	___	___
5. I am aware of various personal financial risks that can result from changing economic conditions.	___	___

After studying this chapter, you will be asked to reconsider your responses to these items.

Making Financial Decisions

OBJECTIVE 1

Identify social and economic influences on personal financial goals and decisions.

Money is a constant topic of conversation in our society. People everywhere talk about money.

Most people want to handle their finances so that they get full satisfaction from each available dollar. Typical financial goals may include buying a new car or a larger home, pursuing advanced career training, contributing to charity, traveling extensively, and ensuring self-sufficiency during working and retirement years. To achieve these and other goals, people need to identify and set priorities. Financial and personal

Objectives

Learning objectives highlight the goals of each chapter for easy reference. Throughout the book, in the end-of-chapter material, and even in the supplement materials, these objectives provide instructors with a valuable foundation for assessment.

Why Is This Important?

Understanding the significance of the chapter content and its potential impact on their lives motivates students to take an active approach to their learning.

Your Personal Financial Plan Sheets

A list of the *Your Personal Financial Plan* worksheets for each chapter is presented at the start of each chapter for easy reference.

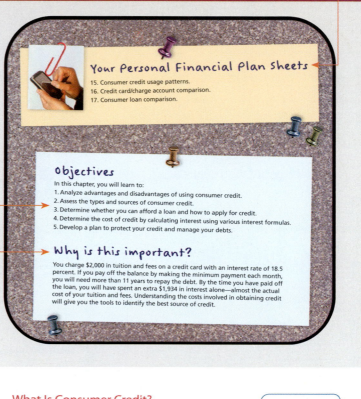

Your Personal Financial Plan Sheets

15. Consumer credit usage patterns.
16. Credit card/charge account comparison.
17. Consumer loan comparison.

objectives

In this chapter, you will learn to:
1. Analyze advantages and disadvantages of using consumer credit.
2. Assess the types and sources of consumer credit.
3. Determine whether you can afford a loan and how to apply for credit.
4. Determine the cost of credit by calculating interest using various interest formulas.
5. Develop a plan to protect your credit and manage your debts.

Why is this important?

You charge $2,000 in tuition and fees on a credit card with an interest rate of 18.5 percent. If you pay off the balance by making the minimum payment each month, you will need more than 11 years to repay the debt. By the time you have paid off the loan, you will have spent an extra $1,934 in interest alone—almost the actual cost of your tuition and fees. Understanding the costs involved in obtaining credit will give you the tools to identify the best source of credit.

What Is Consumer Credit?

Credit is an arrangement to receive cash, goods, or services now and pay for them in the future. **Consumer credit** refers to the use of credit for personal needs (except a home mortgage) by individuals and families, in contrast to credit used for business purposes.

Consumer credit is based on trust in people's ability and willingness to pay bills when due. It works because people by and large are honest and responsible. But how does consumer credit affect our economy, and how is it affected by our economy?

> **OBJECTIVE 1**
> Analyze advantages and disadvantages of using consumer credit.

credit An arrangement to receive cash, goods, or services now and pay for them in the future.

Key Terms

Key terms appear in bold type within the text and are defined in the margins. A list of key terms and page references is located at the end of each chapter.

Concept Checks

Concept Checks at the end of each major section provide fill-in-the-blank questions to help you assess your knowledge of the main ideas covered in that section. You'll know whether you have mastered the concepts and are ready to move on, or if you should stop and revisit certain topics.

Your Personal Financial Plan Sheet References

The integrated use of the *Your Personal Financial Plan* sheets is highlighted with an icon in the margin. This visual, near the text material needed to complete each worksheet, helps you better integrate this study resource into your learning process and continue to track your personal financial habits.

Sheet 4 Planning Your Career

CONCEPT CHECK 1–4

1 What actions might a person take to identify alternatives when making a financial decision?

_____

2 Why are career planning activities considered to be personal financial decisions?

_____

3 For the following situations, identify the type of risk being described.

_____ Not getting proper rest and exercise.

_____ Not being able to obtain cash from a certificate of deposit before the maturity date.

_____ Taking out a variable rate loan when rates are expected to rise.

_____ Training for a career field with low potential demand in the future.

4 For the following main sources of personal finance information, list a specific Web site, organization, or person whom you might contact in the future.

Type of information	Specific source	Contact information
Web site		
Financial institution		
Media source		
Financial specialist		

Apply Yourself!

Objective 4

Located at the end of each Concept Check, this feature contains activities relevant to the material giving students an immediate opportunity to apply what they have learned.

Exhibit **1–5** Financial Planning in Action

Exhibits and Tables

Throughout the text, exhibits and tables visually illustrate important personal finance concepts and processes.

Focus on . . . Personal Finance in Real Life

items have value, they may be difficult to convert to cash. You may decide to list your possessions on the balance sheet at their original cost. However, these values probably need to be revised over time, since a five-year-old television set, for example, is worth less now than when it was new. Thus you may wish to list your possessions at their current value (also referred to as *market value*).

4. *Investment assets* are funds set aside for long-term financial needs. The Scott family will use their investments for such things as financing their children's education, purchasing a vacation home, and planning for retirement. Since investment assets usually fluctuate in value, the amounts listed should reflect their value at the time the balance sheet is prepared.

did you know?

According to the Bureau of the Census, U.S. Department of Commerce, the assets most frequently held by households are motor vehicles, homes, savings accounts, U.S. savings bonds, certificates of deposit, mutual funds, stocks, corporate bonds, and retirement accounts.

STEP 2: DETERMINING AMOUNTS OWED After looking at the total assets of the Scott family, you might conclude that they have a strong financial position. However, their debts must also be considered. **Liabilities** are amounts owed to others but do not include items not yet due, such as next month's rent. A liability is a debt you owe now, not something you may owe in the future. Liabilities fall into two categories:

1. **Current liabilities** are debts you must pay within a short time, usually less than a year. These liabilities include such things as medical bills, tax payments, insurance premiums, cash loans, and charge accounts.
2. **Lo**ng-term lia**bilities** are debts you do not have to pay in full until more than a

liabilities Amounts owed to others.

current liabilities Debts that must be paid within a short time, usually less than a year.

Did You Know?

Each chapter contains several *did you know?* boxes. These notes contain fun facts, information, and financial planning assistance you can use in creating your personal financial plan.

New to this book is a twist on the popular *did you know?* feature. **Green** *did you know?* boxes recommend socially conscious financial activities for students interested in giving back to others.

From the Pages of . . . Kiplinger's Personal Finance

This one-page chapter feature presents a recent article from the well-known *Kiplinger's Personal Finance Magazine* related to a chapter topic. Each article presents a personal finance issue for you to debate and solve, using the questions at the bottom of the page. This is an excellent tool to develop critical thinking and writing skills!

Go to the online subscription page for access to even more Kiplinger's articles.

from the pages of . . . KIPLINGER'S PERSONAL FINANCE

LOWDOWN | To cope with a shrinking portfolio, we suggest that you set spending priorities, tune out the noise and keep your cool. *by laura cohn*

What You Need to know ABOUT FINANCIAL STRESS

1. This too will pass. Same thing Mom told you when you flunked your first driver's-license test. In the meantime, talk it out. Ari Kiev, a psychiatrist, stock-trading coach and author of *Mastering Trading Stress*, suggests building a network of friends and meeting regularly. Hire a facilitator to keep the conversation going. The outsider adds an element of objectivity—and makes the sessions less emotional. Plus, your concerns will get out into the open. If your worries stay locked up in your head, they can spin out of control.

2. Work it off. Dust off your running shoes or sign up for a yoga class. After all, none other than bond guru Bill Gross stays centered by practicing yoga five days a week.

3. Get in touch with your inner investor. If you understand how you're hardwired, you'll know what questions to fire at your financial adviser. To test what kind of investor you are, go to TransAmerica's retirement home page (www.securepathbytransamerica.com) and click on the link for

taking the "change profile" quiz. TransAmerica groups investors into four categories: Venturers, Adapters, Anchoreds and Pursuers. Each personality has its strengths and shortcomings. Venturers, for instance, may be so willing to try new things that they overestimate how prepared they are in uncertain economic times. Likewise, Adapters may be so focused on going with the flow that they don't maximize their returns.

4. Take a news break. There's no need to watch the Dow every minute of the day. And don't subject yourself to the 24-hour news cycle, says Chris Holman, senior executive coach at consulting firm Client-Wise LLC. Turn off the TV, shut off the radio and recognize that headlines are just fragments of the bigger picture. "Headlines are a lagging indicator, not a leading indicator," says Holman.

5. Curb your spending. Focus on what you can control by prioritizing your expenses. For example, if you take your family out to dinner every Sunday, maybe order in a pizza instead. If your kids

usually go to sleep-away camp, you might want to delay signing them up until later in the year. Your company may already be doing the same thing. Some 19% of employers have eliminated perks or plan to do so in the next year, according to a survey by consulting firm Watson Wyatt.

6. Unplug and play. Turn off the computer and put away the Wii. Spend time on inexpensive activities that bring you pleasure, such as hosting a potluck dinner for friends. Break out your favorite board game, or romp in the sandbox with your toddler. "Play connects you with other people and reminds you that, in the end, relationships are more important than money," says Lisa Kirchenbauer, president of Kirchenbauer Financial Management" Consulting.

SOURCE: Reprinted by permission from the February issue of *Kiplinger's Personal Finance*. Copyright © 2009 The Kiplinger Washington Editors, Inc.

1. Explain how these suggested actions might be applied to various financial planning decisions:

_____

2. Which of these actions might be most useful to you when considering various financial planning activities?

_____

3. What information is available at www.kiplinger.com that might be of value when making personal financial decisions?

_____

Personal Finance in Practice

These boxes offer information that can assist you if you are faced with special situations and unique financial planning decisions. They challenge you to apply the concepts you have learned to your life and record personal responses.

Figure It Out!

This boxed feature presents important mathematical applications relevant to personal finance situations and concepts.

Figure It Out!

> Annual Contributions to Achieve a Financial Goal

Achieving specific financial goals often requires regular deposits to a savings or investment account. By using time value of money calculations, you can determine the amount you should save or invest to achieve a specific goal for the future.

EXAMPLE 1
Jonie Emerson has two children who will start college in 10 years. She plans to set aside $1,500 a year for her children's college educations during that period and estimates she will earn an annual interest rate of 5 percent on her savings. What amount can Jonie expect to have available for her children's college educations when they start college?

CALCULATION:

$1,500 × Future value of a series of deposits, 5%, 10 years

EXAMPLE 2
Don Calder wants to accumulate $50,000 over the next 10 years as a reserve fund for his parents' retirement living expenses and health care. If he earns an average of 8 percent on his investments, what amount must he invest each year to achieve this goal?

CALCULATION:

$50,000 ÷ Future value of a series of deposits, 8%, 10 years
$50,000 ÷ 14.487 (Exhibit 1 − 3B) = $3,452.80

Don needs to invest approximately $3,450 a year for 10 years at 8 percent to achieve the desired financial goal.

Annotated Web Links

Web sites that are relevant to a section or concept in the text are presented in the margins.

disability insurance more than they need life insurance. Yet surveys reveal that most people have adequate life insurance but few have needed disability insurance.

Key Web Sites for Investing
www.fool.com
www.cbsmarketwatch.com

INVESTING Although many types of investments are available, people invest for two primary reasons. Those interested in *current income* select investments that pay regular dividends or interest. In contrast, investors who desire *long-term growth* choose stocks, mutual funds, real estate, and other investments with potential for increased value in the future. You can achieve investment diversification by including a variety of assets in your *portfolio*—these may include stocks, bond mutual funds, real estate, and collectibles such as rare coins.

Key Web Sites for Retirement and Estate Planning
www.ssa.gov
www.aarp.org/financial/

RETIREMENT AND ESTATE PLANNING Most people desire financial security upon completion of full-time employment. But retirement planning also involves thinking about your housing situation, your recreational activities, and possible part-time or volunteer work.

Transfers of money or property to others should be timed, if possible, to minimize the tax burden and maximize the benefits for those receiving the financial resources. Knowledge of property transfer methods can help you select the best course of action for funding current and future living costs, educational expenses, and retirement needs of dependents.

Focus on . . . Practice and Assessment

Back to Getting Personal

Now, what would you do differently? At the end of each chapter, you are asked to reconsider your initial responses to the chapter opening self-assessment, *Getting Personal*. Having read the chapter, you are now encouraged to rethink your personal financial habits and record what you'd do differently and why.

Chapter Summary

Organized by chapter objective, this concise content summary is a great study and self-assessment tool, located conveniently at the end of chapters.

Key Formulas

A list of *Key Formulas* and page references appears at the end of select chapters, grouped for easy reference.

Self-Test Problems

New to this book are *Self-Test Problems* and *Solutions*. These additional chapter problems are worked out step-by-step so that students can see how they were solved. This new user-friendly feature increases students' comprehension of the material and gives them the confidence to solve the rest of the end-of-chapter problems independently.

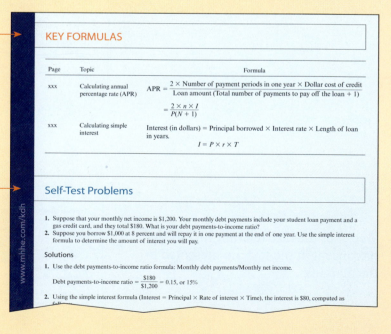

Problems

Problems

A variety of problems allow students to put their quantitative analysis of personal financial decisions to work. Each problem is tagged with a corresponding learning objective for easy assessment.

Problems

1. A few years ago, Michael Tucker purchased a home for $100,000. Today the home is worth $150,000. His remaining mortgage balance is $50,000. Assuming Michael can borrow up to 80 percent of the market value of his home, what is the maximum amount he can borrow? (Obj. 2)

2. Louise McIntyre's monthly gross income is $2,000. Her employer withholds $400 in federal, state, and local income taxes and $160 in Social Security taxes per month. Louise contributes $80 per month for her IRA. Her monthly credit payments for Visa, MasterCard, and Discover cards are $35, $30, and $20, respectively. Her monthly payment on an automobile loan is $285. What is Louise's debt payments-to-income ratio? Is Louise living within her means? Explain. (Obj. 3)

Questions

These questions test qualitative analysis of personal finance content.

Questions

1. In your opinion, what is the main benefit of wise financial planning?
2. What factors in an economy might affect the level of interest rates?
3. Describe risks that you might encounter when making financial decisions over the next few years.
4. What are possible drawbacks associated with seeking advice from a financial planning professional? How might these concerns be minimized?
5. Talk with several people about their career choices. How have their employment situations affected their financial planning activities?

Case in Point

Students can work through a hypothetical personal finance dilemma in order to practice concepts just learned from a chapter. A series of questions reinforces your successful mastery and application of these chapter topics.

Case in Point

NOW WHAT SHOULD I DO . . .?

When Nina opened the letter from her aunt, she discovered a wonderful surprise. "My aunt has given me a gift of $12,000!"

"Why would she do that?" mused Kevin.

"I guess her investments have increased in value by much more than she needs. She wants to share it with family members." Nina shrugged, still in a little bit of shock. "I wonder what I should do with the money?"

"Wow, I could easily use $100,000 instead of $12,000!" Nina laughed. "So what should I do?"

"Some financial advisers recommend not doing *anything* for at least six months," warned Kevin. "You might be tempted to buy on impulse instead of spending the money on things with lasting value."

"Well now I'm really not sure what to do!"

"Oh, I have some suggestions for you . . ." Kevin said.

Recovering herself, Nina teased, "Wait a minute! When did this become *our* money?"

Kevin threw his hands in the air, "Hey, I just thought I'd offer some ideas."

After some discussion, Nina considered the following uses for the money:

Credit card debt—use a portion of the money to pay off credit card bills from her last vacation.

Savings—set aside money for a down payment on a house.

Long-term investments—invest the money in a tax-deferred retirement account.

Career training—use the money for technology certification courses to enhance her earning power.

Community donations—contribute funds to a homeless shelter and a world hunger relief organization.

Questions

1. What additional information about Nina must be known before determining which areas of financial planning should be her top priority?
2. How might time value of money calculations be used by Nina in her decision-making process?
3. What actions do you recommend that Nina take before making a final decision about the use of these funds?

Continuing Case

Continuing Case

This revised feature allows students to apply course concepts in a life situation. It encourages students to evaluate the finances that affect a household and then respond to the resulting shift in needs, resources, and priorities through the questions at the end of each case.

Continuing Case

Vikki Rococo (age 22) graduated from college two months ago. She is currently living with her parents, Dave and Amy (ages 47 and 45), to save money and begin to pay off her student loans. She used most of her existing cash to purchase her used car (current value: $8000). Vikki is working at a local company processing 401(k) plan benefits and the experience has motivated her to immediately start investing for her retirement. She currently has a $15,000 student loan (at 6.8% annual interest) and $2,000 of credit card debt (at 21%). When she moved back home, Vikki signed a contract with her parents that states that she will pay them $200/month rent until she moves out in one year. Her dad's hours at work were recently cut and her parents are living on a limited income so they appreciate the rent money.

Vikki's financial statistics are shown below:

Assets	Income	Student loan $250
Checking account $1,500	Gross annual salary $40,000	Car loan $200
Car $8,000	(before taxes)	Credit card payments $40
401(k) balance $500	$2,333 monthly pay after-taxes	Entertainment $100
		Gas/repairs $150
Liabilities	*Monthly Expenses*	*Retirement savings*
Student loan $15,000	Rent $200	401(k) $500 per month, plus 50%
Credit card balance $2,000	Food $100	employer match on the first 7% of pay

Questions

1. Given her current situation, what do you think Vikki's short-term goals are? What about her long-term goals? How do they compare to her parent's goals?
2. What types of time value of money calculations would be helpful for Vikki?
3. What do you think is Vikki's most challenging part of the Financial Planning Process (Exhibit 1–4, p. 17)?
4. How can she use *Your Personal Financial Plan* sheets 1–4?

mhhe.com/kdh

Daily Spending Diary

Directions: Record every cent of your spending each day in the categories provided, or create your own format to monitor your spending. You can indicate the use of a credit card with (CR). Comments should reflect what you have learned about your spending patterns and desired changes you might want to make in your spending habits. (Note: As income is received, record in Date column.)

Month: _____ Amount available for spending: $ _____ Amount to be saved: $ _____

Date (Income)	Total Spending	Auto, Transportation	Housing, Utilities	Food (H) Home (A) Away	Health, Personal Care	Education	Recreation, Leisure	Donations, Gifts	Other (note item, amount)	Comments
Example	$83	$20 (gas) (CR)		$47 (H)		$2 (pen)	$4 (DVD rental)	$10 (church)		This takes time but it helps me control my spending
1										
2										
3										
4										
5										

Spending Diary

"I FIRST THOUGHT THIS PROCESS WOULD BE A WASTE OF TIME, BUT THE INFORMATION HAS HELPED ME BECOME MUCH MORE CAREFUL OF HOW I SPEND MY MONEY."

Nearly everyone who has made the effort to keep a daily spending diary has found it beneficial. While at first the process may seem tedious, after a while recording this information becomes easier and faster.

Directions

Using the Daily Spending Diary sheets provided at the end of the book, record *every cent* of your spending each day in the categories provided. Or you may create your own format to monitor your spending. You can indicate the use of a credit card

Daily Spending Diary

Do you buy a latte or a soda every day before class? Do you and your friends meet for a movie once a week? How much do you spend on gas for your car each month? Do you like to donate to your favorite local charity a couple of times a year?

These everyday spending activities might go largely unnoticed, yet they have a significant effect on the overall health of an individual's finances. The Daily Spending Diary sheets offer students a place to keep track of *every cent they spend* in any category. Careful monitoring and assessing of these noted daily spending habits can lead to better control and understanding of your personal finances.

Your Personal Financial Plan

The *Your Personal Financial Plan* sheets that correlate with sections of the text are conveniently located at the end of each chapter. The perforated worksheets ask students to work through the applications and record their own personal financial plan responses. These sheets apply concepts learned to your unique situation and serve as a road map to your personal financial future. Students can fill them out, rip them out, submit them for homework, and keep them filed in a safe spot for future reference. Excel spreadsheets for each of the *Your Personal Financial Plan* are available at www.mhhe.com/kdh.

Key Web sites are provided to help students research and devise their personal financial plan, and the "What's Next for Your Personal Financial Plan?" section at the end of each sheet challenges students to use their responses to plan the next level, as well as foreshadow upcoming concepts.

Look for one or more *Your Personal Financial Plan* icons next to most Concept Checks. The graphics direct students to the Personal Financial Plan sheet that corresponds with the preceding section.

Name: _____ Date: _____

Your Personal Financial Plan

2

Setting Personal Financial Goals

Financial Planning Activities: Based on personal and household needs and values, identify specific goals that require action for your life.

Suggested Web Sites: www.financialplan.about.com www.money.com

Short-Term Monetary Goals (less than two years)

Description	Amount needed	Months to achieve	Action to be taken	Priority
Example: pay off credit card debt	$850	12	Use money from pay raise	High

Intermediate and Long-Term Monetary Goals

Description	Amount needed	Months to achieve	Action to be taken	Priority

Nonmonetary Goals

Description	Time frame	Actions to be taken
Example: set up file for personal financial records and documents	next 2–3 months	locate all personal and financial records and documents; set up files for various spending, saving, borrowing categories

What's Next for Your Personal Financial Plan?

- Based on various financial goals, calculate the savings deposits necessary to achieve those goals.
- Identify current economic trends that might influence various saving, spending, investing, and borrowing decisions.

Online Support for Students and Instructors

Online Learning Center (OLC): www.mhhe.com/kdh

The Online Learning Center (OLC) contains additional Web-based study and teaching aids created for this text. OLCs can be delivered in multiple ways—through the textbook Web site (www.mhhe.com/kdh), through PageOut (see below), or within a course management system like Blackboard, WebCT, TopClass, and eCollege. Ask your campus representative for more details.

Few textbooks provide such innovative and practical instructional resources for both students and teachers. The comprehensive teaching–learning package for *Focus on Personal Finance* includes the following:

For Instructors

The Instructor's site on the OLC provides the instructor with one resource for all supplementary material, including:

- *Instructor's Manual:* Created and revised by the authors, this supplement includes a "Course Planning Guide" with instructional strategies, course projects, and supplementary resource lists. The "Chapter Teaching Materials" section of the *Instructor's Manual* provides a chapter overview, the chapter objectives with summaries, introductory activities, and detailed lecture outlines with teaching suggestions. This section also includes concluding activities, ready-to-duplicate quizzes, supplementary lecture materials and activities, and answers to concept checks, end-of-chapter questions, problems, and cases.
- *Test Bank,* revised by Lora Reinholz, Marquette University, consists of true–false, multiple-choice, problem-solving, and essay questions. These test items are organized by the learning objectives for each chapter. This resource also includes answers, page references, and an indication of difficulty level.
- *Computerized Testing Software,* McGraw-Hill's EZ Test is a flexible and easy-to-use electronic testing program. The program allows instructors to create tests from book-specific items. It accommodates a wide range of question types, and instructors may add their own questions. Multiple versions of the test can be created, and any test can be exported for use with course management systems such as WebCT, BlackBoard, or PageOut. EZ Test Online gives you a place to easily administer your EZ Test–created exams and quizzes online. The program is available for Windows and Macintosh environments.
- Chapter *PowerPoint Presentations* revised and enhanced by Lynn Kugele, The University of Mississippi, offer more than 300 visual presentations that may be edited and manipulated to fit a particular course format. If you choose to customize the slides, an online digital image library allows you to pick and choose from all of the figures and tables in the book.

Additional Cases

Video Cases—The chapter video cases have been moved to the OLC. Each case accompanies a 3–10 minute digital segment tied to topics within the chapter. Ten additional 30-minute videos help to visually illustrate important personal finance concepts in potential real-life situations. Developed by Coastline Community College, these videos can be used with multiple chapters at any time during the course. (DVD ISBN 0077245792)

New Continuing Case—A second continuing case with follow-up questions and answers is provided in the event you want to give your students even more real-world examples and problems or if you want to switch cases each semester.

For Students

Self-Study Quizzes

Quizzes consist of 10–15 self-grading multiple-choice questions on important chapter topics. They instantly reveal a score and hints to help students solve questions they answered incorrectly. Each chapter contains a chapter quiz so that students can thoroughly gauge their understanding of the material.

Narrated Student PowerPoint

Every student learns differently and the *Narrated Power Point* was created with that in mind! Revised and expanded by Brad Duerson, at Des Moines Area Community College, the interactive chapter presentations are part of the online premium content package and can be purchased. They guide students through understanding key topics and principles by presenting real-life examples based on chapter content. The slides are accompanied by an audio narration and can be viewed online or downloaded onto an iPod (see details below).

iPod Content

Harness the power of one of the most popular technology tools that students use today, the Apple® iPod. Our innovative approach enables students to download *Narrated PowerPoints,* quizzes, and videos right into their iPod or MP3 player for studying on the go!

And More!

Looking for more ways to study? Self-grading crossword puzzles and flashcards will help you learn the material. You can also access Excel templates for the Your Personal Financial Plan sheets and the Daily Spending Diary.

Personal Finance Telecourse

If you teach personal finance as a telecourse, this text is a perfect fit! A telecourse program is available from Coastline Community College titled *Dollars & Sense: Personal Finance for the 21st Century* that is based on the Kapoor, Dlabay, and Hughes text. The program includes 26 thirty-minute videotapes, which you purchase directly from Coast by contacting Lynn Dahnke, Marketing Director, Coast Learning Systems, 11460 Warner Ave., Fountain Valley, CA 92708, (800) 547-4748 or www.CoastLearning.org. The course also has a *Telecourse Study Guide* (ISBN 0073363944) available that connects the videos to the text. To make sure your students receive the text and telecourse study guide package, order through McGraw-Hill/Irwin.

Assurance of Learning

Many educational institutions today are focused on the notion of assurance of learning, an important element of some accreditation standards. *Focus on Personal Finance* is designed specifically to support your assurance of learning initiatives with a simple, yet powerful, solution.

Each test bank question for *Focus on Personal Finance* maps to a specific chapter learning outcome/objective listed in the text. You can use the test bank software to easily query for learning outcomes/objectives that directly relate to the learning objectives for your course. You can then use the reporting features of the software to aggregate student results in similar fashion, making the collection and presentation of assurance of learning data simple and easy.

McGraw-Hill's Connect and Connect Plus

McGraw-Hill *Connect Finance*

Less Managing. More Teaching. Greater Learning.
McGraw-Hill *Connect Finance* is an online assignment and assessment solution that connects students with the tools and resources they'll need to achieve success.

Connect helps prepare students for their future by enabling faster learning, more efficient studying, and higher retention of knowledge.

McGraw-Hill *Connect Finance* Features *Connect Finance* offers a number of powerful tools and features to make managing assignments easier, so faculty can spend more time teaching. With *Connect Finance*, students can engage with their coursework anytime and anywhere, making the learning process more accessible and efficient. *Connect Finance* offers you the features described below.

Simple assignment management With *Connect Finance*, creating assignments is easier than ever, so you can spend more time teaching and less time managing. The assignment management function enables you to:

- Create and deliver assignments easily with selectable end-of-chapter questions and test bank items.

- Streamline lesson planning, student progress reporting, and assignment grading to make classroom management more efficient than ever.
- Go paperless with the eBook and online submission and grading of student assignments.

Smart grading When it comes to studying, time is precious. *Connect Finance* helps students learn more efficiently by providing feedback and practice material when they need it, where they need it. When it comes to teaching, your time is also precious. The grading function enables you to:

- Have assignments scored automatically, giving students immediate feedback on their work and side-by-side comparisons with correct answers.
- Access and review each response; manually change grades or leave comments for students to review.
- Reinforce classroom concepts with practice tests and instant quizzes.

Instructor library The *Connect Finance* Instructor Library is your repository for additional resources to improve student engagement in and out of class. You can select and use any asset that enhances your lecture.

Student study center The *Connect Finance* Student Study Center is the place for students to access additional resources. The Student Study Center:

- Offers students quick access to lectures, practice materials, eBooks, and more.
- Provides instant practice material and study questions, easily accessible on the go.
- Gives students access to the Personalized Learning Plan described below.

Personalized Learning Plan The Personalized Learning Plan (PLP) connects each student to the learning resources needed for success in the course. For each chapter, students:

- Take a practice test to initiate the Personalized Learning Plan.
- Immediately upon completing the practice test, see how their performance compares to the chapter objectives to be achieved within each section of the chapters.
- Receive a Personalized Learning Plan that recommends specific readings from the text, supplemental study material, and practice work that will improve their understanding and mastery of each learning objective.

Student progress tracking *Connect Finance* keeps instructors informed about how each student, section,

and class is performing, allowing for more productive use of lecture and office hours. The progress-tracking function enables you to:

- View scored work immediately and track individual or group performance with assignment and grade reports.
- Access an instant view of student or class performance relative to learning objectives.

Lecture capture through Tegrity Campus—For an additional charge Lecture Capture offers new ways for students to focus on the in-class discussion, knowing they can revisit important topics later. This can be delivered through Connect or separately. See below for more details.

McGraw-Hill *Connect Plus Finance* McGraw-Hill reinvents the textbook learning experience for the modern student with *Connect Plus Finance*. A seamless integration of an eBook and *Connect Finance*, *Connect Plus Finance* provides all of the *Connect Finance* features plus the following:

- An integrated eBook, allowing for anytime, anywhere access to the textbook.
- Dynamic links between the problems or questions you assign to your students and the location in the eBook where that problem or question is covered.
- A powerful search function to pinpoint and connect key concepts in a snap.

In short, *Connect Finance* offers you and your students powerful tools and features that optimize your time and energies, enabling you to focus on course content, teaching, and student learning. *Connect Finance* also offers a wealth of content resources for both instructors and students. This state-of-the-art, thoroughly tested system supports you in preparing students for the world that awaits.

For more information about Connect, go to **www.mcgrawhillconnect.com,** or contact your local McGraw-Hill sales representative.

Tegrity Campus: Lectures 24/7

Tegrity Campus is a service that makes class time available 24/7 by automatically capturing every lecture in a searchable format for students to review when they study and complete assignments. With a simple one-click start-and-stop process, you capture all computer screens and corresponding audio. Students can replay any part of any class with easy-to-use browser-based viewing on a PC or Mac.

Educators know that the more students can see, hear, and experience class resources, the better they learn. In fact, studies prove it. With Tegrity Campus, students quickly recall key moments by using Tegrity Campus's unique search feature. This search helps students efficiently find what they need, when they need it, across an entire semester of class recordings. Help turn all your students' study time into learning moments immediately supported by your lecture.

To learn more about Tegrity watch a 2-minute Flash demo at **http://tegritycampus.mhhe.com**.

McGraw-Hill Customer Care Contact Information

At McGraw-Hill, we understand that getting the most from new technology can be challenging. That's why our services don't stop after you purchase our products. You can e-mail our Product Specialists 24 hours a day to get product-training online. Or you can search our knowledge bank of Frequently Asked Questions on our support website. For Customer Support, call **800-331-5094**, e-mail **hmsupport@mcgraw-hill.com**, or visit **www.mhhe.com/support**. One of our Technical Support Analysts will be able to assist you in a timely fashion.

Thank You!

We express our deepest appreciation for the efforts of the colleagues whose extensive feedback over the years has helped to shape and create this text.

Chris A. Austin, *Normandale Community College*
Gail H. Austin, *Rose State College*
Tom Bilyeu, *Southwestern Illinois College*
Ross Blankenship, *State Fair Community College*
William F. Blosel, *California University of Pennsylvania*
John Bockino, *Suffolk County Community College*
Karen Bonding, *University of Virginia*
Jennifer Brewer, *Butler County Community College*
Peg Camp, *University of Nebraska–Kearney*
Stephen Chambers, *Johnson County Community College*
It-Keong Chew, *University of Kentucky*
Julie Douthit, *Abilene Christian University*
Bill Dowling, *Savannah State University*
Dorsey Dyer, *Davidson County Community College*
John D. Farlin, *Ohio Dominican University*
Garry Fleming, *Roanoke College*
Paula G. Freston, *Merced College*
Robert Friederichs, *Alexandria Technical College*
Caroline S. Fulmer, *University of Alabama*
Dwight Giles, *Jefferson State Community College*
Michael Gordinier, *Washington University*
Shari Gowers, *Dixie State College*
Michael P. Griffin, *University of Massachusetts– Dartmouth*
Ward Hooker, *Orangeburg–Calhoun Tech College*
Ishappa S. Hullur, *Morehead State University*
Samira Hussein, *Johnson County Community College*
Dorothy W. Jones, *Northwestern State University*
Jeanette Klosterman, *Hutchinson Community College*
Robert Kozub, *University of Wisconsin–Milwaukee*
Margo Kraft, *Heidelberg College*
John Ledgerwood, *Bethune-Cookman College*
Richard "Lee" Kitchen, *Tallahassee Community College*
Marc LeFebvre, *Creighton University*
Nolan Lickey, *Utah Valley State College*
Joseph T. Marchese, *Monroe Community College*
Kenneth L. Mark, *Kansas City Kansas Community College*
Paul S. Marshall, *Widener University*
Jennifer Morton, *Ivy Tech Community College of Indiana*
Allan O'Bryan, *Rochester Community & Tech College*
Carl Parker, *Fort Hays State University*

David M. Payne, *Ohio University*
Aaron Phillips, *California State University–Bakersfield*
Padmaja Pillutla, *Western Illinois University*
Brenda Rice, *Ozarks Technical Community College*
Carla Rich, *Pensacola Junior College*
John Roberts, *Florida Metropolitan University*
Sammie Root, *Texas State University–San Marcos*
Joan Ryan, *Clackamas Community College*
Tim Samolis, *Pittsburgh Technical Institute*
Steven R. Scheff, *Florida Gulf Coast University*
James T. Schiermeyer, *Texas Tech University*
Joseph Simon, *Casper College*
Vernon Stauble, *San Bernardino Valley College*
Lea Timpler, *College of the Canyons*
Dick Verrone, *University of North Carolina–Wilmington*
Randall Wade, *Rogue Community College*
Kent Weilage, *McCook Community College*
Sally Wells, *Columbia College*
Micheline West, *New Hampshire Tech*
Bob Willis, *Rogers State University*
Glen Wood, *Broome Community College*

Many talented professionals at McGraw-Hill/Irwin have contributed to the development of *Focus on Personal Finance*. We are especially grateful to Michele Janicek, Elizabeth Hughes, Melissa Caughlin, Dana Pauley, Cara David, Michael McCormick, and Allison Souter.

In addition, Jack Kapoor expresses special appreciation to Theresa and Dave Kapoor, Kathryn Thumme, and Karen Tucker for their typing, proofreading, and research assistance. Finally, we thank our wives and families for their patience, understanding, encouragement, and love throughout this project.

A special thanks to the talented instructors who helped to develop and accuracy check the supplements for this edition: Lora Reinholz, Marquette University, Lynn Kugele, University of Mississippi, Brad Duerson, Des Moines Area Community College, Michelle Grant, Bossier Parish Community College, Barry Freeman, Bergen Community College, and Kenneth Mark, Kansas City Kansas Community College.

Contents

Focus on Personal Finance

An Active Approach to Help You Develop
Successful Financial Skills

THIRD EDITION

Personal Financial Planning in Action

Getting Personal

What are your money habits? For each of the following statements, select "yes" or "no" to indicate your behavior regarding these financial planning activities:

	Yes	No
1. I usually have enough money for the things I need.	____	____
2. I owe less money today than I owed a year or two ago.	____	____
3. My written goals for the next year need revision due to changing financial situations in our society.	____	____
4. When making major financial decisions, I research them using a variety of information sources.	____	____
5. I am aware of various personal financial risks that can result from changing economic conditions.	____	____

After studying this chapter, you will be asked to reconsider your responses to these items.

Making Financial Decisions

OBJECTIVE 1

Identify social and economic influences on personal financial goals and decisions.

Money is a constant topic of conversation in our society. People everywhere talk about money.

Most people want to handle their finances so that they get full satisfaction from each available dollar. Typical financial goals may include buying a new car or a larger home, pursuing advanced career training, contributing to charity, traveling extensively, and ensuring self-sufficiency during working and retirement years. To achieve these and other goals, people need to identify and set priorities. Financial and personal

Your Personal Financial Plan Sheets

1. Personal financial data.
2. Setting personal financial goals.
3. Achieving financial goals using time value of money.
4. Planning your career.

Objectives

In this chapter, you will learn to:

1. Identify social and economic influences on personal financial goals and decisions.
2. Develop personal financial goals.
3. Assess personal and financial opportunity costs associated with financial decisions.
4. Implement a plan for making personal financial and career decisions.

Why is this important?

Difficult economic times intensify the importance of wise personal financial decisions. Each year, more than a million people declare bankruptcy, and Americans lose more than $1.2 billion in fraudulent investments. Both of these common difficulties result from poor personal financial planning and incomplete information. Your ability to make wise money decisions is a foundation for your current and long-term well-being.

satisfaction are the result of an organized process that is commonly referred to as *personal money management* or *personal financial planning*.

Your Life Situation and Financial Planning

Personal financial planning is the process of managing your money to achieve personal economic satisfaction. This planning process allows you to control your financial situation. Every person, family, or household has a unique situation; therefore, financial decisions must be planned to meet specific needs and goals.

personal financial planning The process of managing your money to achieve personal economic satisfaction.

financial plan A formalized report that summarizes your current financial situation, analyzes your financial needs, and recommends future financial activities.

A comprehensive financial plan can enhance the quality of your life and increase your satisfaction by reducing uncertainty about your future needs and resources. A **financial plan** is a formalized report that summarizes your current financial situation, analyzes your financial needs, and recommends future financial activities. You can create this document on your own (by using the sheets at the end of each chapter) or you can seek assistance from a financial planner or use a money management software package.

Some of the advantages of personal financial planning include

- Increased effectiveness in obtaining, using, and protecting your financial resources throughout your life.
- Increased control of your financial affairs by avoiding excessive debt, bankruptcy, and dependence on others.
- Improved personal relationships resulting from well-planned and effectively communicated financial decisions.
- A sense of freedom from financial worries obtained by looking to the future, anticipating expenses, and achieving personal economic goals.

did you know?

According to a *Consumer Reports Money Adviser* reader survey, the worst money habits reported are too much low-interest savings, not monitoring investments, impulse spending, not enough savings, and too much credit card debt.

Many factors influence daily financial decisions, ranging from age and household size to interest rates and inflation. People in their 20s spend money differently from those in their 50s. Personal factors such as age, income, household size, and personal beliefs influence your spending and saving patterns. Your life situation or lifestyle is created by a combination of factors.

As our society changes, different types of financial needs evolve. Today people tend to get married at a later age, and more households have two incomes. Many households are headed by single parents. More than 2 million women provide care for both dependent children and parents. We are also living longer; over 80 percent of all Americans now living are expected to live past age 65.

adult life cycle The stages in the family situation and financial needs of an adult.

As Exhibit 1–1 shows, the **adult life cycle**—the stages in the family and financial needs of an adult—is an important influence on your financial activities and decisions. Your life situation is also affected by events such as graduation, dependent children leaving home, changes in health, engagement and marriage, divorce, birth or adoption of a child, retirement, a career change or a move to new area, or the death of a spouse, family member, or other dependent.

values Ideas and principles that a person considers correct, desirable, and important.

In addition to being defined by your family situation, you are defined by your **values**—the ideas and principles that you consider correct, desirable, and important. Values have a direct influence on such decisions as spending now versus saving for the future or continuing school versus getting a job.

Financial Planning in Our Economy

economics The study of how wealth is created and distributed.

Daily economic activities have a strong influence on financial planning. **Economics** is the study of how wealth is created and distributed. The economic environment includes various institutions, principally business, labor, and government, that work together to satisfy our needs and wants.

While various government agencies regulate financial activities, the Federal Reserve System, our nation's central bank, has significant responsibility in our economy. *The Fed,* as it is called, is concerned with maintaining an adequate money supply. It achieves this by influencing borrowing, interest rates, and the buying or selling of government securities. The Fed attempts to make adequate funds available for consumer

Exhibit 1–1   Financial Planning Influences, Goals, and Activities

Life Situation Factors Affect Financial Planning Activities

Age	Marital Status	Number and Age of Household Members	Employment Situation
• 18–24 • 25–34 • 35–44 • 45–54 • 55–64 • 65 and over	• single • married • separated/divorced • widowed	• no other household members • preschool children • elementary and secondary school children • college students • dependent adults • nondependent adults	• full-time student • not employed • full-time employment or volunteer work • part-time employment or volunteer work

TIME TO TAKE ACTION . . . COMMON FINANCIAL GOALS AND ACTIVITIES

- Obtain appropriae career training.
- Create an effective financial recordkeeping system.
- Develop a regular savings and investment program.

- Accumulate an appropriate emergency fund.
- Purchase appropriate types and amounts of insurance coverage.
- Create and implement a flexible budget.

- Evaluate and select appropriate investments.
- Establish and implement a plan for retirement goals.
- Make a will and develop an estate plan.

If this is your Life Situation, you should . . .	Specialized Financial Activities
Young, single (18–35)	• Establish financial independence. • Obtain disability insurance to replace income during prolonged illness. • Consider home purchase for tax benefit.
Young couple with children under 18	• Carefully manage the increased need for the use of credit. • Obtain an appropriate amount of life insurance for the care of dependents. • Use a will to name guardian for children.
Single parent with children under 18	• Obtain adequate amounts of health, life, and disability insurance. • Contribute to savings and investment fund for college. • Name a guardian for children and make other estate plans.
Young dual-income couple, no children	• Coordinate insurance coverage and other benefits. • Develop savings and investment program for changes in life situation (larger house, children). • Consider tax-deferred contributions to retirement fund.
Older couple (50+), no dependent children at home	• Consolidate financial assets and review estate plans. • Consider household budget changes several years prior to retirement. • Plan retirement housing, living expenses, recreational activities, and part-time work.
Mixed-generation household (elderly individuals and children under 18)	• Obtain long-term health care insurance and life/disability income for care of younger dependents. • Use dependent care service if needed. • Provide arrangements for handling finances of elderly if they become ill. • Consider splitting of investment cost, with elderly getting income while alive and principal going to surviving relatives.
Older (50+), single	• Arrange for long-term health care coverage. • Review will and estate plan. • Plan retirement living facilities, living expenses, and activities.

spending and business expansion while keeping interest rates and consumer prices at an appropriate level.

GLOBAL INFLUENCES The global economy can influence financial activities. The U.S. economy is affected by both foreign investors and competition from foreign companies. American businesses compete against foreign companies for the spending dollars of American consumers. When the level of exports of U.S.-made goods is lower than the level of imported goods, more U.S. dollars leave the country than the dollar value of foreign currency coming into the United States. This reduces the funds available for domestic spending and investment. Also, if foreign companies decide not to invest in the United States, the domestic money supply is reduced. This reduced money supply can cause higher interest rates.

INFLATION Most people are concerned with the buying power of their money. **Inflation** is a rise in the general level of prices. In times of inflation, the buying power of the dollar decreases. For example, if prices increased 5 percent during the last year, items that cost $100 then would now cost $105. This means more money is needed to buy the same amount of goods and services.

Inflation is most harmful to people living on fixed incomes. Due to inflation, retired people and others whose incomes do not change are able to afford fewer goods and services. Inflation can also adversely affect lenders of money. Unless an adequate interest rate is charged, amounts repaid by borrowers in times of inflation have less buying power than the money they borrowed.

Inflation rates vary. During the late 1950s and early 1960s, the annual inflation rate was in the 1 to 3 percent range. During the late 1970s and early 1980s, the cost of living increased 10 to 12 percent annually. At a 12 percent annual inflation rate, prices double (and the value of the dollar is cut in half) in about six years. To find out how fast prices (or your savings) will double, use the *rule of 72:* Just divide 72 by the annual inflation (or interest) rate.

> ### EXAMPLE: RULE OF 72
>
> An annual inflation rate of 4 percent, for example, means prices will double in 18 years (72 ÷ 4 = 18). Regarding savings, if you earn 6 percent, your money will double in 12 years (72 ÷ 6 = 12).

More recently, the reported annual price increase for goods and services as measured by the consumer price index has been in the 2 to 4 percent range. The *consumer price index (CPI)*, computed and published by the Bureau of Labor Statistics, is a measure of the average change in the prices urban consumers pay for a fixed "basket" of goods and services.

Inflation rates can be deceptive since the index is based on items calculated in a predetermined manner. Many people face *hidden* inflation since the cost of necessities (food, gas, health care), on which they spend the greatest proportion of their money, may rise at a higher rate than nonessential items, which could be dropping in price. This results in a reported inflation rate much lower than the actual cost-of-living increase being experienced by consumers.

INTEREST RATES In simple terms, interest rates represent the cost of money. Like everything else, money has a price. The forces of supply and demand influence interest

---

Key Web Sites for Global Business

www.businessweek .com/globalbiz

www.globalfinancialdata.com

inflation A rise in the general level of prices.

did you know?

Consumer prices can change by very significant amounts over time. The general price level in the United States between 1970 and 1980 nearly doubled. However, between 1990 and 2000, average consumer prices rose about 34 percent.

rates. When consumer saving and investing increase the supply of money, interest rates tend to decrease. However, as borrowing by consumers, businesses, and government increases, interest rates are likely to rise.

Interest rates can have a major effect on financial planning. The earnings you receive as a saver or an investor reflect current interest rates as well as a *risk premium* based on such factors as the length of time your funds will be used by others, expected inflation, and the extent of uncertainty about getting your money back. Risk is also a factor in the interest rate you pay as a borrower. People with poor credit ratings pay a higher interest rate than people with good credit ratings. Interest rates influence many financial decisions.

Financial Planning Activities

To achieve a successful financial situation, you must coordinate various components through an organized plan and wise decision making. Exhibit 1–2 presents an overview of the eight major personal financial planning areas.

OBTAINING You obtain financial resources from employment, investments, or ownership of a business. Obtaining financial resources is the foundation of financial planning, since these resources are used for all financial activities.

PLANNING Planned spending through budgeting is the key to achieving goals and future financial security. Efforts to anticipate expenses along with making certain financial decisions can help reduce taxes.

SAVING Long-term financial security starts with a regular savings plan for emergencies, unexpected bills, replacement of major items, and the purchase of special goods and services, such as a college education, a boat, or a vacation home. Once you have established a basic savings plan, you may use additional money for investments that offer greater financial growth.

BORROWING Maintaining control over your credit-buying habits will contribute to your financial goals. The overuse and misuse of credit may cause a situation in which

Key Web Sites for Economic Conditions

www.westegg.com/inflation

www.bls.gov

www.federalreserve.gov

www.bloomberg.com

Key Web Sites for Obtaining

www.rileyguide.com

www.monster.com

Key Web Sites for Planning

www.americasaves.org

www.irs.gov

Key Web Sites for Savings

www.bankrate.com

www.fdic.gov

Key Web Sites for Borrowing

www.finance-center.com

www.debtadvice.com

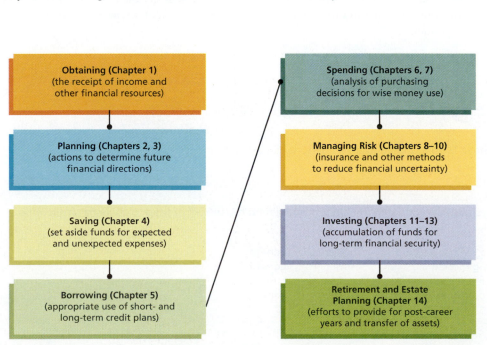

Exhibit 1–2

Components of Personal Financial Planning

bankruptcy A set of federal laws allowing you to either restructure your debts or remove certain debts.

Key Web Sites for Spending

www.consumer.gov

www.autoweb.com

Key Web Sites for Managing Risk

www.insure.com

www.insweb.com

Key Web Sites for Investing

www.fool.com

www.cbsmarketwatch.com

Key Web Sites for Retirement and Estate Planning

www.ssa.gov

www.aarp.org/financial/

a person's debts far exceed the resources available to pay those debts. **Bankruptcy** is a set of federal laws allowing you to either restructure your debts or remove certain debts. The people who declare bankruptcy each year may have avoided this trauma with wise spending and borrowing decisions. Chapter 5 discusses bankruptcy in detail.

SPENDING Financial planning is designed not to prevent your enjoyment of life but to help you obtain the items you want. Too often, however, people make purchases without considering the financial consequences. Some people shop compulsively, creating financial difficulties. You should detail your living expenses and your other financial obligations in a spending plan. Spending less than you earn is the only way to achieve long-term financial security.

MANAGING RISK Adequate insurance coverage is another component of personal financial planning. Certain types of insurance are commonly overlooked in financial plans. For example, the number of people who suffer disabling injuries or diseases at age 50 is greater than the number who die at that age, so people may need disability insurance more than they need life insurance. Yet surveys reveal that most people have adequate life insurance but few have needed disability insurance.

INVESTING Although many types of investments are available, people invest for two primary reasons. Those interested in *current income* select investments that pay regular dividends or interest. In contrast, investors who desire *long-term growth* choose stocks, mutual funds, real estate, and other investments with potential for increased value in the future. You can achieve investment diversification by including a variety of assets in your *portfolio*—these may include stocks, bond mutual funds, real estate, and collectibles such as rare coins.

RETIREMENT AND ESTATE PLANNING Most people desire financial security upon completion of full-time employment. But retirement planning also involves thinking about your housing situation, your recreational activities, and possible part-time or volunteer work.

Transfers of money or property to others should be timed, if possible, to minimize the tax burden and maximize the benefits for those receiving the financial resources. Knowledge of property transfer methods can help you select the best course of action for funding current and future living costs, educational expenses, and retirement needs of dependents.

 Sheet 1 Personal Financial Data

CONCEPT CHECK 1–1

1 What personal and economic factors commonly affect personal financial decisions?

2 For each of the following situations, indicate if the person would tend to "suffer" or tend to "benefit" from inflation. (Circle your answer)

A person with money in a savings account.	suffer	benefit
A person who is borrowing money.	suffer	benefit
A person who is lending money.	suffer	benefit
A person receiving a fixed income amount.	suffer	benefit

3 Listed here are the eight main components of personal financial planning. Circle one or more areas and describe an action that you might need to take in the next few months or years.

1. Obtaining	
2. Planning	
3. Saving	
4. Borrowing	

5. Spending	
6. Managing risk	
7. Investing	
8. Retirement estate planning	

Apply Yourself!

Objective 1

Using Web research and discussion with others, calculate the inflation rate that reflects the change in price for items frequently bought by you and your family.

Developing and Achieving Financial Goals

Why do so many Americans—living in one of the richest countries in the world—have money problems? The answer can be found in two main factors. The first is poor planning and weak money management habits in areas such as spending and the use of credit. The other factor is extensive advertising, selling efforts, and product availability that encourage overbuying. Achieving personal financial satisfaction starts with clear financial goals.

> **OBJECTIVE 2**
> Develop personal financial goals.

Types of Financial Goals

What would you like to do tomorrow? Believe it or not, that question involves goal setting, which may be viewed in three time frames:

- *Short-term goals* will be achieved within the next year or so, such as saving for a vacation or paying off small debts.
- *Intermediate goals* have a time frame of two to five years.
- *Long-term goals* involve financial plans that are more than five years off, such as retirement, money for children's college education, or the purchase of a vacation home.

Long-term goals should be planned in coordination with short-term and intermediate goals. Setting and achieving short-term goals is commonly the basis for moving toward success of long-term goals. For example, saving for a down payment to buy a house is a short-term goal that can be a foundation for a long-term goal: owning your own home.

A goal of obtaining increased career training is different from a goal of saving money to pay a semiannual auto insurance premium. *Consumable-product goals* usually

Personal Finance in Practice

> Developing Financial Goals

Based on your current situation or expectations for the future, create one or more financial goals based on this four-step process:

	STEP 1 Realistic goals for your life situation	STEP 2 State goals in measurable terms	STEP 3 Determine time frame	STEP 4 Action to be taken
SHORT-TERM GOALS (less than a year)	1.	2.	3.	4.
INTERMEDIATE GOALS (2 to 5 years)	1.	2.	3.	4.
LONG-TERM GOALS (more than 5 years)	1.	2.	3.	4.

occur on a periodic basis and involve items that are used up relatively quickly, such as food, clothing, and entertainment. *Durable-product goals* usually involve infrequently purchased, expensive items such as appliances, cars, and sporting equipment; these consist of tangible items. In contrast, many people overlook *intangible-purchase goals.* These goals may relate to personal relationships, health, education, community service, and leisure.

Goal-Setting Guidelines

An old saying goes, "If you don't know where you're going, you might end up somewhere else and not even know it." Goal setting is central to financial decision making. Your financial goals are the basis for planning, implementing, and measuring the progress of your spending, saving, and investing activities. Exhibit 1–1 on page 5 offers typical goals and financial activities for various life situations.

Effective financial goals should be:

- *Realistic,* based on your income and life situation. For example, if you are a full-time student, expecting to buy a new car each year is probably not realistic.
- *Stated in specific, measurable terms,* since having exact goals will help you create a plan to achieve them. For example, the goal of "accumulating $5,000 in an investment fund within three years" is a clearer guide to planning than the goal of "putting money into an investment fund."
- *Based on a time frame,* such as a goal to be achieved in three years. A time frame helps you measure your progress toward your financial goals.
- *Action oriented,* because your financial goals are the basis for the various financial activities you will undertake. For example, "reducing credit card debt" will likely mean a decreased use of credit.

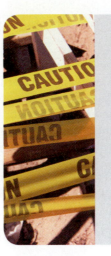

CAUTION! A survey conducted by the Consumer Federation of America (CFA) estimates that more than 60 million American households will probably fail to realize one or more of their major life goals largely due to a lack of a comprehensive financial plan. In households with annual incomes of less than $100,000, savers who say they have financial plans report about twice as much savings and investments as savers without plans.

Sheet 2 Setting Personal Financial Goals

CONCEPT CHECK 1–2

1 What are some examples of long-term goals?

_____

2 What are the main characteristics of useful financial goals?

_____

3 Match the following common goals to the life situation of the people listed.

a. Pay off student loans	_____ A young couple without children.
b. Start a college savings fund	_____ An older person living alone.
c. Increase retirement contributions	_____ A person who just completed college.
d. Finance long-term care	_____ A single mother with a preschool daughter.

Apply Yourself!

Objective 2

Ask friends, relatives, and others about their short-term and long-term financial goals. What are some of the common goals for various personal situations?

opportunity cost What a person gives up by making a choice.

Opportunity Costs and the Time Value of Money

Have you noticed that you always give up something when you make choices? In every financial decision, you sacrifice something to obtain something else that you consider more desirable. For example, you might forgo current buying to invest funds for future purchases or long-term financial security. Or you might gain the use of an expensive item now by making credit payments from future earnings.

Opportunity cost is what you give up by making a choice. This cost, commonly referred to as the *trade-off* of a decision, cannot always be measured in dollars. Opportunity costs should be viewed in terms of both personal and financial resources.

Personal Opportunity Costs

An important personal opportunity cost involves time that when used for one activity cannot be used for other activities. Time used for studying, working, or shopping will not be available for other uses. Other personal opportunity costs relate to health. Poor eating habits, lack of sleep, or avoiding exercise can result in illness, time away from school or work, increased health care costs, and reduced financial security. Like financial resources, your personal resources (time, energy, health, abilities, knowledge) require planning and wise management.

Financial Opportunity Costs

time value of money Increase in an amount of money as a result of interest earned.

You are constantly making choices among various financial decisions. In making those choices, you must consider the **time value of money,** the increases in an amount of money as a result of interest earned. Saving or investing a dollar instead of spending it today results in a future amount greater than a dollar. Every time you spend, save, invest, or borrow money, you should consider the time value of that money as an opportunity cost. Spending money from your savings account means lost interest earnings; however, what you buy with that money may have a higher priority than those earnings.

INTEREST CALCULATIONS Three amounts are used to calculate the time value of money for savings in the form of interest earned:

- The amount of the savings (commonly called the *principal*).
- The annual interest rate.
- The length of time the money is on deposit.

These three items are multiplied to obtain the amount of interest. Simple interest is calculated as follows:

For example, $500 on deposit at 6 percent for six months would earn $15 ($500 × 0.06 × $^6/_{12}$, or ½ year).

You can calculate the increased value of your money from interest earned in two ways: You can calculate the total amount that will be available later (future value), or you can determine the current value of an amount desired in the future (present value).

FUTURE VALUE OF A SINGLE AMOUNT Deposited money earns interest that will increase over time. **Future value** is the amount to which current savings will increase based on a certain interest rate and a certain time period. For example, $100 deposited in a 6 percent account for one year will grow to $106. This amount is computed as follows:

$$\text{Future value} = \$100 + (\$100 \times 0.06 \times 1 \text{ year}) = \$106$$

Original amount in savings   Amount of interest earned

future value The amount to which current savings will increase based on a certain interest rate and a certain time period; also referred to as *compounding*.

The same process could be continued for a second, third, and fourth year, but the computations would be time-consuming. Future value tables simplify the process (see Exhibit 1–3). To use a future value table, multiply the amount deposited by the factor for the desired interest rate and time period. For example, $650 at 8 percent for 10 years would have a future value of $1,403.35 ($650 × 2.159). The future value of an amount will always be greater than the original amount. As Exhibit 1–3A shows, all the future value factors are larger than 1. Future value computations may be referred to as *compounding,* since interest is earned on previously earned interest. Compounding allows the future value of a deposit to grow faster than it would if interest were paid only on the original deposit.

The sooner you make deposits, the greater the future value will be. Depositing $1,000 in a 5 percent account at age 40 will give you $3,387 at age 65. However, making the $1,000 deposit at age 25 would result in an account balance of $7,040 at age 65.

Key Web Sites for Time Value of Money

www.moneychimp.com/calculator

www.rbccentura.com/tools

www.dinkytown.net

FUTURE VALUE OF A SERIES OF DEPOSITS Many savers and investors make regular deposits. An *annuity* is a series of equal deposits or payments. To determine the future value of equal yearly savings deposits, use Exhibit 1–3B. For this table to be used, the deposits must earn a constant interest rate. If you deposit $50 a year at 7 percent for six years, starting at the end of the first year, you will have $357.65 at the end of that time ($50 × 7.153). The Figure It Out box on this page presents examples of using future value to achieve financial goals.

did you know?

If you invest $2,000 a year (at 9 percent) from ages 31 to 65, these funds will grow to $470,249 by age 65. However, if you save $2,000 a year (at 9 percent) for only 9 years (ages 22 to 30), at age 65 this fund will be worth $579,471! Most important: Start investing something now!

PRESENT VALUE OF A SINGLE AMOUNT Another aspect of the time value of money involves determining the current value of an amount desired in the future. **Present value** is the current value for a future amount based on a certain interest rate and a certain time period. Present value computations, also called *discounting,* allow you to determine how much to deposit now to obtain a desired total in the future. Present value tables (Exhibit 1–3C) can be used to make the computations. If you want $1,000 five years from now and you earn 5 percent on your savings, you need to deposit $784 ($1,000 × 0.784). The present value of the amount you want in the future will always be less than the future value. Note that all of the factors in Exhibit 1–3C are less than 1 and interest earned will increase the present value amount to the desired future amount.

present value The current value for a future amount based on a certain interest rate and a certain time period; also referred to as *discounting*.

Exhibit 1–3

Time Value of Money
Tables (condensed)

A. Future Value of $1 (single amount)

	PERCENT				
Year	5%	6%	7%	8%	9%
5	1.276	1.338	1.403	1.469	1.539
6	1.340	1.419	1.501	1.587	1.677
7	1.407	1.504	1.606	1.714	1.828
8	1.477	1.594	1.718	1.851	1.993
9	1.551	1.689	1.838	1.999	2.172
10	1.629	1.791	1.967	2.159	2.367

B. Future Value of a Series of Annual Deposits (annuity)

	PERCENT				
Year	5%	6%	7%	8%	9%
5	5.526	5.637	5.751	5.867	5.985
6	6.802	6.975	7.153	7.336	7.523
7	8.142	8.394	8.654	8.923	9.200
8	9.549	9.897	10.260	10.637	11.028
9	11.027	11.491	11.978	12.488	13.021
10	12.578	13.181	13.816	14.487	15.193

C. Present Value of $1 (single amount)

	PERCENT				
Year	5%	6%	7%	8%	9%
5	0.784	0.747	0.713	0.681	0.650
6	0.746	0.705	0.666	0.630	0.596
7	0.711	0.665	0.623	0.583	0.547
8	0.677	0.627	0.582	0.540	0.502
9	0.645	0.592	0.544	0.500	0.460
10	0.614	0.558	0.508	0.463	0.422

D. Present Value of a Series of Annual Deposits (annuity)

	PERCENT				
Year	5%	6%	7%	8%	9%
5	4.329	4.212	4.100	3.993	3.890
6	5.076	4.917	4.767	4.623	4.486
7	5.786	5.582	5.389	5.206	5.033
8	6.463	6.210	5.971	5.747	5.535
9	7.108	6.802	6.515	6.247	5.995
10	7.722	7.360	7.024	6.710	6.418

Note: See the appendix at the end of this chapter for more complete future value and present value tables.

Figure It Out!

> Annual Contributions to Achieve a Financial Goal

Achieving specific financial goals often requires regular deposits to a savings or investment account. By using time value of money calculations, you can determine the amount you should save or invest to achieve a specific goal for the future.

EXAMPLE 1

Jonie Emerson has two children who will start college in 10 years. She plans to set aside $1,500 a year for her children's college educations during that period and estimates she will earn an annual interest rate of 5 percent on her savings. What amount can Jonie expect to have available for her children's college educations when they start college?

CALCULATION:

$$\$1,500 \times \begin{array}{c} \text{Future value of a series of deposits,} \\ \text{5\%, 10 years} \end{array}$$

$$\$1,500 \times 12.578 \text{ (Exhibit 1 − 3B)} = \$18,867$$

EXAMPLE 2

Don Calder wants to accumulate $50,000 over the next 10 years as a reserve fund for his parents' retirement living expenses and health care. If he earns an average of 8 percent on his investments, what amount must he invest each year to achieve this goal?

CALCULATION:

$$\$50,000 \div \begin{array}{c} \text{Future value of a series of deposits,} \\ \text{8\%, 10 years} \end{array}$$

$$\$50,000 \div 14.487 \text{ (Exhibit 1 − 3B)} = \$3,452.80$$

Don needs to invest approximately $3,450 a year for 10 years at 8 percent to achieve the desired financial goal.

PRESENT VALUE OF A SERIES OF DEPOSITS You may also use present value computations to determine how much you need to deposit so that you can take a certain amount out of the account for a desired number of years. For example, if you want to take $400 out of an investment account each year for nine years and your money is earning an annual rate of 8 percent, you can see from Exhibit 1–3D that you would need to make a current deposit of $2,498.80 ($400 × 6.247).

The formulas for calculating future and present values, as well as tables covering additional interest rates and time periods, are presented in the appendix to this chapter. Computer programs and financial calculators may also be used for calculating time value of money.

Sheet 3 Achieving Financial Goals Using Time Value of Money

CONCEPT CHECK 1–3

1 What are some examples of personal opportunity costs?

2 What does time value of money measure?

3 Use the time value of money tables in Exhibit 1–3 to calculate the following:

 a.   The future value of $100 at 7 percent in 10 years.

 _____

 b.   The future value of $100 a year for six years earning 6 percent.

 _____

 c.   The present value of $500 received in eight years with an interest rate of 8 percent.

 _____

Apply Yourself!

Objective 3

What is the relationship between current interest rates and financial opportunity costs? Using time value of money calculations, state one or more goals in terms of an annual savings amount and the future value of this savings objective.

A Plan for Personal Financial Planning

> **OBJECTIVE 4**
>
> Implement a plan for making personal financial and career decisions.

We all make hundreds of decisions each day. Most of these decisions are quite simple and have few consequences. However, some are complex and have long-term effects on our personal and financial situations, as shown here:

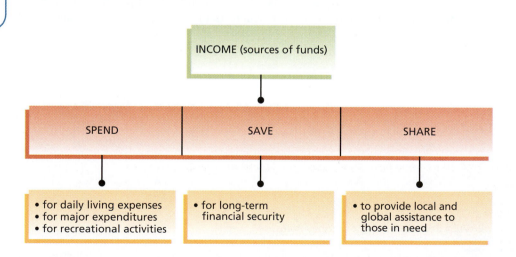

While everyone makes decisions, few people consider how to make better decisions. As Exhibit 1–4 shows, the financial planning process can be viewed as a six-step procedure that can be a adapted to any life situation.

Exhibit **1–4**

The Financial Planning Process

STEP 1: DETERMINE YOUR CURRENT FINANCIAL SITUATION

In this first step, determine your current financial situation regarding income, savings, living expenses, and debts. Preparing a list of current asset and debt balances and amounts spent for various items gives you a foundation for financial planning activities. The personal financial statements discussed in Chapter 2 will provide the information needed in this phase of financial decision making.

STEP 1 Example

Carla Elliot plans to complete her college degree in the next two years. She works two part-time jobs in an effort to pay her educational expenses. Currently, Carla has $700 in a savings account and existing debt that includes a $640 balance on her credit card and $2,300 in student loans. What additional information should Carla have available when planning her personal finances?

Example From Your Life

What actions have you taken to determine your current financial situation?

STEP 2: DEVELOP YOUR FINANCIAL GOALS

You should periodically analyze your financial values and goals. The purpose of this analysis is to differentiate your needs from your wants. Specific financial goals are vital to financial planning. Others can suggest financial goals for you; however, *you* must decide which goals to pursue. Your financial goals can range from spending all of your current income to developing an extensive savings and investment program for your future financial security.

STEP 2 Example

The main financial goals of Carla Elliot for the next two years are to complete her college degree and to maintain or reduce the amounts owed. What other goals might be appropriate for Carla?

(continued)

Example From Your Life

Describe some short-term or long-term goals that might be appropriate for your life situation.

_____

STEP 3: IDENTIFY ALTERNATIVE COURSES OF ACTION Developing alternatives is crucial when making decisions. Although many factors will influence the available alternatives, possible courses of action usually fall into these categories:

- *Continue the same course of action.* For example, you may determine that the amount you have saved each month is still appropriate.
- *Expand the current situation.* You may choose to save a larger amount each month.
- *Change the current situation.* You may decide to use a money market account instead of a regular savings account.
- *Take a new course of action.* You may decide to use your monthly saving budget to pay off credit card debts.

did you know?

According to the National Endowment for Financial Education, 70 percent of major lottery winners end up with financial difficulties. These winners often squander the funds awarded them, while others overspend and many end up declaring bankruptcy. Having more money does not automatically mean making better financial planning choices.

Not all of these categories will apply to every decision; however, they do represent possible courses of action. For example, if you want to stop working full time to go to school, you must generate several alternatives under the category "Take a new course of action." Creativity in decision making is vital to effective choices. Considering all of the possible alternatives will help you make more effective and satisfying decisions. For instance, most people believe they must own a car to get to work or school. However, they should consider other alternatives such as public transportation, carpooling, renting a car, shared ownership of a car, or a company car.

Remember, when you decide not to take action, you elect to "do nothing," which can be a dangerous alternative.

STEP 3 Example

To achieve her goals, Carla Elliot has several options available. She could reduce her spending, seek a higher-paying part-time job, or use her savings to pay off some of her debt. What additional alternatives might she consider?

_____

Example From Your Life

List various alternatives for achieving the financial goals you identified in the previous step.

_____

STEP 4: EVALUATE YOUR ALTERNATIVES You need to evaluate possible courses of action, taking into consideration your life situation, personal values, and current economic conditions. How will the ages of dependents affect your saving goals? How do you like to spend leisure time? How will changes in interest rates affect your financial situation?

CONSEQUENCES OF CHOICES Every decision closes off alternatives. For example, a decision to invest in stock may mean you cannot take a vacation. A decision to go to school full-time may mean you cannot work full-time. *Opportunity cost* is what you give up by making a choice. These *trade-offs* cannot always be measured in dollars. However, the resources you give up (money or time) have a value that is lost.

EVALUATING RISK Uncertainty is also a part of every decision. Selecting a college major and choosing a career field involve risk. What if you don't like working in this field or cannot obtain employment in it? Other decisions involve a very low degree of risk, such as putting money in an insured savings account or purchasing items that cost only a few dollars. Your chances of losing something of great value are low in these situations.

In many financial decisions, identifying and evaluating risk are difficult. Common risks to consider include:

- Inflation risk, due to rising or falling (deflation) prices that cause changes in buying power.
- Interest rate risk, resulting from changes in the cost of money, which can affect your costs (when you borrow) and benefits (when you save or invest).
- Income risk may result from a loss of a job or encountering illness.
- Personal risk involves tangible and intangible factors that create a less than desirable situation, such as health or safety concerns.
- Liquidity risk, when savings and investments that have potential for higher earnings are difficult to convert to cash or to sell without significant loss in value.

The best way to consider risk is to gather information based on your experience and the experiences of others and to use financial planning information sources.

FINANCIAL PLANNING INFORMATION SOURCES Relevant information is required at each stage of the decision-making process. In addition to this book, common sources available to help you with your financial decisions include (1) the Internet; (2) financial institutions, such as banks, credit unions, and investment companies; (3) media sources, such as newspapers, magazines, television, and radio; and (4) financial specialists, such as financial planners, insurance agents, investment advisers, credit counselors, lawyers, and tax preparers.

did you know?

More than 4 billion people around the world live on $2 or less a day. GlobalGiving is an online marketplace that connects potential donors to the causes in various countries. You select a project, make a tax-deductible donation, and get regular progress updates—so you can see the difference you are making. More than 450 prescreened local, community-based projects may be viewed at www.globalgiving.org.

STEP 4 Example

As Carla Elliot evaluates her alternative courses of action, she should consider both her short-term and long-term situations. What risks and trade-offs should Carla consider?

_____

Example From Your Life

In your life, what types of risks might be encountered when planning and implementing various personal financial activities?

_____

Personal Finance in Practice

Tactics for Surviving a Financial Crisis

Financial uncertainty can affect every aspect of our society. Everyone is concerned about the influence of weak economic prospects on personal financial actions. Most wise personal financial planning strategies advocated during strong economic times are equally valid during downturns. Fundamental personal economic decision making can serve individuals and households in all circumstances. For each of these recommended actions, consider an action you might take:

- Reduce your use of debt. While you may be tempted to pay for various items with a credit card, make every attempt to resist that action. Avoid additional debt in a time of economic uncertainty.

Actions you might take _____

- Reduce spending. Difficult times require difficult actions. Decide which budget items can be eliminated or reduced. This action will allow you to better control your short-term and long-term financial situation.

Actions you might take _____

- Review the safety of your savings. Make sure your accounts in banks and credit unions are within the limits covered by federal deposit insurance.

Actions you might take _____

- Evaluate insurance coverages. While you may be tempted to reduce spending by reducing insurance costs, be sure you have adequate coverage for life, health, home, and motor vehicles. Savings can be gained by comparing various insurance companies.

Actions you might take _____

- Avoid financial scams. People are desperate in poor economic times. This can make you more vulnerable to investment fraud, credit repair swindles, and other financial planning deceptions. Obtain complete information before taking action. Don't rush into a "too good to be true" situation.

Actions you might take _____

- Communicate with family members. Talking about the economic difficulties and financial uncertainty can reduce personal and household anxiety. These discussions can have benefits for the present as well as preparing children for financial situations they will likely encounter in their lifetime. Involve them in decisions that might be necessary to reduce family spending.

Actions you might take _____

Remember, these suggestions can be valid for every financial situation in every economic setting. Your ability to know and use wise personal finance strategies will serve you in every stage of your life and in every stage of the business cycle.

For additional suggestions for personal financial actions in difficult times, consider these sources:

"200+ Tools for Surviving the Economic Crisis" at http://mashable.com/2008/10/16/economic-crisis/

"Tips for Surviving a Recession with Your Personal Finances Intact" at www.yieldingwealth.com/tips-for-surviving-a-recession-with-your-personal-finances-intact/

Sources: "Your money: What to do now. Expert advice on how to ride out the financial storm," *Consumer Reports,* December 2008, pp. 16–19; "Talk Your Teen through Tough Economic Times" by Jennifer Barrett, *Money,* Feb 2009, p. 32.

STEP 5: CREATE AND IMPLEMENT YOUR FINANCIAL ACTION PLAN

You are now ready to develop an action plan to identify ways to achieve your goals. For example, you can increase your savings by reducing your spending or by increasing your income through extra time on the job. If you are concerned about year-end tax payments, you may increase the amount withheld from each paycheck, file quarterly tax payments, or shelter current income in a tax-deferred retirement program.

To implement your financial action plan, you may need assistance from others. For example, you may use the services of an insurance agent to purchase property insurance or the services of an investment broker to purchase stocks, bonds, or mutual funds. Exhibit 1–5 offers a framework for developing and implementing a financial plan, along with examples for several life situations.

Exhibit 1–5   Financial Planning in Action

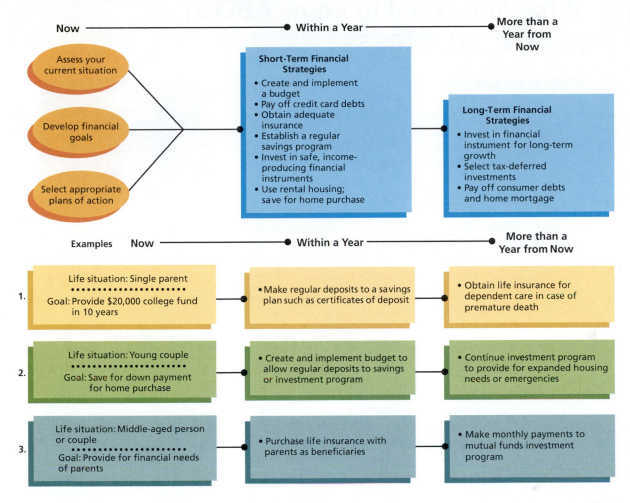

STEP 5 Example

Carla has decided to reduce her course load and work longer hours in an effort both to reduce her debt level and to increase the amount she has in savings. What are the benefits and drawbacks of this choice?

Example From Your Life

Describe the benefits and drawbacks of a financial situation you have encountered during the past year.

STEP 6: REVIEW AND REVISE YOUR PLAN Financial planning is a dynamic process that does not end when you take a particular action. You need to regularly assess your financial decisions. You should do a complete review of your finances at least once a year. Changing personal, social, and economic factors may require more frequent assessments.

LOWDOWN | To cope with a shrinking portfolio, we suggest that you set spending priorities, tune out the noise and keep your cool. *by laura cohn*

What You Need to know ABOUT FINANCIAL STRESS

1. This too will pass. Same thing Mom told you when you flunked your first driver's-license test. In the meantime, talk it out. Ari Kiev, a psychiatrist, stock-trading coach and author of *Mastering Trading Stress,* suggests building a network of friends and meeting regularly. Hire a facilitator to keep the conversation going. The outsider adds an element of objectivity— and makes the sessions less emotional. Plus, your concerns will get out into the open. If your worries stay locked up in your head, they can spin out of control.

2. Work it off. Dust off your running shoes or sign up for a yoga class. After all, none other than bond guru Bill Gross stays centered by practicing yoga five days a week.

3. Get in touch with your inner investor. If you understand how you're hardwired, you'll know what questions to fire at your financial adviser. To test what kind of investor you are, go to TransAmerica's retirement home page (www.securepathbytransamerica.com) and click on the link for

taking the "change profile" quiz. TransAmerica groups investors into four categories: Venturers, Adapters, Anchoreds and Pursuers. Each personality has its strengths and shortcomings. Venturers, for instance, may be so willing to try new things that they overestimate how prepared they are in uncertain economic times. Likewise, Adapters may be so focused on going with the flow that they don't maximize their returns.

4. Take a news break. There's no need to watch the Dow every minute of the day. And don't subject yourself to the 24-hour news cycle, says Chris Holman, senior executive coach at consulting firm Client-Wise LLC. Turn off the TV, shut off the radio and recognize that headlines are just fragments of the bigger picture. "Headlines are a lagging indicator, not a leading indicator," says Holman.

5. Curb your spending. Focus on what you can control by prioritizing your expenses. For example, if you take your family out to dinner every Sunday, maybe order in a pizza instead. If your kids

usually go to sleep-away camp, you might want to delay signing them up until later in the year. Your company may already be doing the same thing. Some 19% of employers have eliminated perks or plan to do so in the next year, according to a survey by consulting firm Watson Wyatt.

6. Unplug and play. Turn off the computer and put away the Wii. Spend time on inexpensive activities that bring you pleasure, such as hosting a potluck dinner for friends. Break out your favorite board game, or romp in the sandbox with your toddler. "Play connects you with other people and reminds you that, in the end, relationships are more important than money," says Lisa Kirchenbauer, president of Kirchenbauer Financial Management" Consulting.

1. Explain how these suggested actions might be applied to various financial planning decisions:

_____

2. Which of these actions might be most useful to you when considering various financial planning activities?

_____

3. What information is available at www.kiplinger.com that might be of value when making personal financial decisions?

_____

When life events affect your financial needs, this financial planning process will provide a vehicle for adapting to those changes. A regular review of this decision-making process will help you make priority adjustments that will bring your financial goals and activities in line with your current life situation.

STEP 6 Example

Over the next 6 to 12 months, Carla Elliot should reassess her financial, personal, and educational situation. What types of circumstances might occur that could require that Carla take a different approach to her personal finances?

_____

Example from Your Life

What factors in your life might affect your personal financial situation and decisions in the future?

_____

Career Choice and Financial Planning

Have you ever wondered why some people find great satisfaction in their work while others only put in their time? As with other personal financial decisions, career selection and professional growth require planning. The average person changes jobs seven times during a lifetime. Most likely, therefore, you will reevaluate your choice of a job on a regular basis. The lifework you select is a key to your financial well-being and personal satisfaction.

Like other decisions, career choice and professional development alternatives have risks and opportunity costs. In recent years, many people have placed family and personal fulfillment above monetary reward and professional recognition. Career choices require periodic evaluation of trade-offs related to personal, social, and economic factors.

In addition, changing personal and social factors will require you to continually assess your work situation. The steps of the financial planning process can provide an approach to career planning, advancement, and career change. Your career goals will affect how you use this process. If you desire more responsibility on the job, for example, you may decide to obtain advanced training or change career fields. Appendix A provides a plan for obtaining employment and professional advancement.

Your Career Planning Decisions

Based on the your current or future career situation, describe how you might use the Financial Planning Process (Exhibit 1–4, p. 17) to plan and implement an employment decision.

_____

_____

Sheet 4 Planning Your Career

CONCEPT CHECK 1–4

1 What actions might a person take to identify alternatives when making a financial decision?

_____

2 Why are career planning activities considered to be personal financial decisions?

_____

3 For the following situations, identify the type of risk being described.

_____ Not getting proper rest and exercise.

_____ Not being able to obtain cash from a certificate of deposit before the maturity date.

_____ Taking out a variable rate loan when rates are expected to rise.

_____ Training for a career field with low potential demand in the future.

4 For the following main sources of personal finance information, list a specific Web site, organization, or person whom you might contact in the future.

Type of information	Specific source	Contact information
Web site		
Financial institution		
Media source		
Financial specialist		

Apply Yourself!

Objective 4

Prepare a list of questions that might be asked of a financial planning professional by *(a)* a young person just starting out on his or her own, *(b)* a young couple planning for their children's education and for their own retirement, and *(c)* a person nearing retirement.

Back to... Getting Personal

Reconsider your responses to the "Getting Personal" questions at the beginning of the chapter. For more effective personal financial planning and goal setting:

- Consider information from several sources when making financial decisions, including various Web sites and Appendix B on page 510.
- Have specific, written financial goals that you review on a regular basis. To start (or continue) planning your financial goals, use the "Personal Finance in Practice: Developing Financial Goals" box on page 10.
- Use future value and present value computations to help you achieve personal financial goals. Calculators

are available at www.dinkytown.net, www.money-chimp.com/calculator, www.rbccentura.com/tools.

- Assess potential risks. Some risks are minor with limited consequences, others can have long-term effects. Inflation and interest rates will influence your financial decisions. Information on changing economic conditions is available at www.bls.gov, www.federalreserve.gov, and www.bloomberg.com.

What did you learn in this chapter that could help you make better personal financial planning decisions?

Chapter Summary

Objective 1 Financial decisions are affected by a person's life situation (income, age, household size, health), personal values, and economic factors (prices, interest rates, and employment opportunities). The major elements of financial planning are obtaining, planning, saving, borrowing, spending, managing risk, investing, and retirement and estate planning.

Objective 2 Financial goals should (1) be realistic; (2) be stated in specific, measurable terms; (3) have a time frame; and (4) indicate the type of action to be taken.

Objective 3 Every decision involves a trade-off with things given up. Personal opportunity costs include time,

effort, and health. Financial opportunity costs are based on the time value of money. Future value and present value calculations enable you to measure the increased value (or lost interest) that results from a saving, investing, borrowing, or purchasing decision.

Objective 4 Personal financial planning involves the following process: (1) determine your current financial situation; (2) develop financial goals; (3) identify alternative courses of action; (4) evaluate alternatives; (5) create and implement a financial action plan; and (6) review and revise the financial plan.

Key Terms

adult life cycle 4

bankruptcy 8

economics 4

financial plan 4

future value 13

inflation 6

opportunity cost 12

personal financial planning 3

present value 13

time value of money 12

values 4

Self-Test Problems

1. The Rule of 72 provides a guideline for determining how long it takes your money to double. This rule can also be used to determine your earning rate. If your money is expected to double in 12 years, what is your rate of return?

2. If you desire to have $10,000 in savings eight years from now, what amount would you need to deposit in an account that earns 5 percent?

Self-Test Solutions

1. Using the Rule of 72, if your money is expected to double in 12 years, you are earning approximately 6 percent (72 ÷ 12 years = 6 percent).
2. To calculate the present value of $10,000 for eight years at 5 percent, use Exhibit 1-3C, p. 14 (or Exhibit 1-C, p. 42): $10,000 × 0.677 = $6,770

Problems

(Note: Some of these problems require the use of the time value of money tables in the chapter appendix.)

1. Using the rule of 72, approximate the following amounts. (Obj. 1)

   a. If the value of land in an area is increasing 6 percent a year, how long will it take for property values to double?
   b. If you earn 10 percent on your investments, how long will it take for your money to double?
   c. At an annual interest rate of 5 percent, how long will it take for your savings to double?

2. In the early 2000s, selected automobiles had an average cost of $15,000. The average cost of those same automobiles is now $18,000. What was the rate of increase for these automobiles between the two time periods? (Obj. 1)

3. A family spends $34,000 a year for living expenses. If prices increase by 4 percent a year for the next three years, what amount will the family need for their living expenses after three years? (Obj. 1)

4. Ben Collins plans to buy a house for $120,000. If that real estate is expected to increase in value by 5 percent each year, what will its approximate value be seven years from now? (Obj. 1)

5. What would be the yearly earnings for a person with $6,000 in savings at an annual interest rate of 5.5 percent? (Obj. 3)

6. Using time value of money tables (Exhibit 1–3 or chapter appendix tables), calculate the following. (Obj. 3)

   a. The future value of $450 six years from now at 7 percent.
   b. The future value of $800 saved each year for 10 years at 8 percent.
   c. The amount a person would have to deposit today (present value) at a 6 percent interest rate to have $1,000 five years from now.
   d. The amount a person would have to deposit today to be able to take out $500 a year for 10 years from an account earning 8 percent.

7. If you desire to have $10,000 for a down payment for a house in five years, what amount would you need to deposit today? Assume that your money will earn 5 percent. (Obj. 3)

8. Pete Morton is planning to go to graduate school in a program of study that will take three years. Pete wants to have $10,000 available each year for various school and living expenses. If he earns 4 percent on his money, how much must he deposit at the start of his studies to be able to withdraw $10,000 a year for three years? (Obj. 3)

9. Carla Lopez deposits $3,000 a year into her retirement account. If these funds have an average earning of 8 percent over the 40 years until her retirement, what will be the value of her retirement account? (Obj. 3)

10. If a person spends $10 a week on coffee (assume $500 a year), what would be the future value of that amount over 10 years if the funds were deposited in an account earning 4 percent? (Obj. 3)

11. A financial company that advertises on television will pay you $60,000 now for annual payments of $10,000 that you are expected to receive for a legal settlement over the next 10 years. If you estimate the time value of money at 10 percent, would you accept this offer? (Obj. 3)

12. Tran Lee plans to set aside $1,800 a year for the next six years, earning 4 percent. What would be the future value of this savings amount? (Obj. 3)

13. If you borrow $8,000 with a 5 percent interest rate to be repaid in five equal payments at the end of the next five years, what would be the amount of each payment? (Note: Use the present value of an annuity table in the chapter appendix.) (Obj. 3)

Questions

1. In your opinion, what is the main benefit of wise financial planning?

2. What factors in an economy might affect the level of interest rates?

3. Describe risks that you might encounter when making financial decisions over the next few years.

4. What are possible drawbacks associated with seeking advice from a financial planning professional? How might these concerns be minimized?

5. Talk with several people about their career choices. How have their employment situations affected their financial planning activities?

Case in Point

NOW WHAT SHOULD I DO . . .?

When Nina opened the letter from her aunt, she discovered a wonderful surprise. "My aunt has given me a gift of $12,000!"

"Why would she do that?" mused Kevin.

"I guess her investments have increased in value by much more than she needs. She wants to share it with family members." Nina shrugged, still in a little bit of shock. "I wonder what I should do with the money?"

"Wow, I could easily use $100,000 instead of $12,000!" Nina laughed. "So what should I do?"

"Some financial advisers recommend not doing *anything* for at least six months," warned Kevin. "You might be tempted to buy on impulse instead of spending the money on things with lasting value."

"Well now I'm really not sure what to do!"

"Oh, I have some suggestions for you . . ." Kevin said.

Recovering herself, Nina teased, "Wait a minute! When did this become *our* money?"

Kevin threw his hands in the air, "Hey, I just thought I'd offer some ideas."

After some discussion, Nina considered the following uses for the money:

Credit card debt—use a portion of the money to pay off credit card bills from her last vacation.

Savings—set aside money for a down payment on a house.

Long-term investments—invest the money in a tax-deferred retirement account.

Career training—use the money for technology certification courses to enhance her earning power.

Community donations—contribute funds to a homeless shelter and a world hunger relief organization.

Questions

1. What additional information about Nina must be known before determining which areas of financial planning should be her top priority?

2. How might time value of money calculations be used by Nina in her decision-making process?

3. What actions do you recommend that Nina take before making a final decision about the use of these funds?

Continuing Case

Vikki Rococo (age 22) graduated from college two months ago. She is currently living with her parents, Dave and Amy (ages 47 and 45), to save money and begin to pay off her student loans. She used most of her existing cash to purchase her used car (current value: $8000). Vikki is working at a local company processing 401(k) plan benefits and the experience has motivated her to immediately start investing for her retirement. She currently has a $15,000 student loan (at 6.8% annual interest) and $2,000 of credit card debt (at 21%). When she moved back home, Vikki signed a contract with her parents that states that she will pay them $200/month rent until she moves out in one year. Her dad's hours at work were recently cut and her parents are living on a limited income so they appreciate the rent money.

Vikki's financial statistics are shown below:

Assets	*Income*	Student loan $250
Checking account $1,500	Gross annual salary $40,000	Car loan $200
Car $8,000	(before taxes)	Credit card payments $40
401(k) balance $500	$2,333 monthly pay after-taxes	Entertainment $100
		Gas/repairs $150
Liabilities	*Monthly Expenses*	
Student loan $15,000	Rent $200	*Retirement savings*
Credit card balance $2,000	Food $100	401(k) $500 per month, plus 50% employer match on the first 7% of pay

Questions

1. Given her current situation, what do you think Vikki's short-term goals are? What about her long-term goals? How do they compare to her parent's goals?
2. What types of time value of money calculations would be helpful for Vikki?
3. What do you think is Vikki's most challenging part of the Financial Planning Process (Exhibit 1–4, page 17)?
4. How can she use *Your Personal Financial Plan* sheets 1–4?

Spending Diary

"I FIRST THOUGHT THIS PROCESS WOULD BE A WASTE OF TIME, BUT THE INFORMATION HAS HELPED ME BECOME MUCH MORE CAREFUL OF HOW I SPEND MY MONEY."

Nearly everyone who has made the effort to keep a daily spending diary has found it beneficial. While at first the process may seem tedious, after a while recording this information becomes easier and faster.

Directions

Using the Daily Spending Diary sheets provided at the end of the book, record *every cent* of your spending each day in the categories provided. Or you may create your own format to monitor your spending. You can indicate the use of a credit card with (CR). This experience will help you better understand your spending patterns and identify desired changes you might want to make in your spending habits.

Questions

1. What did your daily spending diary reveal about your spending habits? What areas of spending might you consider changing?

2. How might your daily spending diary assist you when identifying and achieving financial goals?

The Daily Spending Diary sheets are located in Appendix C at the end of the book and on the student Web site, www.mhhe.com/kdh.

Personal Financial Data

Financial Planning Activities: Complete the information request to provide a quick reference for vital household data.

Suggested Web Sites: www.money.com   www.kiplinger.com

Name	_____	_____
Birthdate	_____	_____
Marital Status	_____	_____
Address	_____	_____
Phone	_____	_____
e-mail	_____	_____
Social Security No.	_____	_____
Drivers License No.	_____	_____
Place of Employment	_____	_____
Address	_____	_____
Phone	_____	_____
Position	_____	_____
Length of Service	_____	_____
Checking Acct. No.	_____	_____
Financial Inst.	_____	_____
Address	_____	_____
Phone	_____	_____

Dependent Data

Name	Birthdate	Relationship	Social Security No.
_____	_____	_____	_____
_____	_____	_____	_____
_____	_____	_____	_____
_____	_____	_____	_____

What's Next for Your Personal Financial Plan?

- Identify financial planning experts (insurance agent, banker, investment adviser, tax preparer, others) you might contact for financial planning information or assistance.
- Discuss with other household members various financial planning priorities.

Name: _____ **Date:** _____

Setting Personal Financial Goals

Financial Planning Activities: Based on personal and household needs and values, identify specific goals that require action for your life.

Suggested Web Sites: www.financialplan.about.com   www.money.com

Short-Term Monetary Goals (less than two years)

Description	Amount needed	Months to achieve	Action to be taken	Priority
Example: pay off credit card debt	$850	12	Use money from pay raise	High

Intermediate and Long-Term Monetary Goals

Description	Amount needed	Months to achieve	Action to be taken	Priority

Nonmonetary Goals

Description	Time frame	Actions to be taken
Example: set up file for personal financial records and documents	next 2–3 months	locate all personal and financial records and documents; set up files for various spending, saving, borrowing categories

What's Next for Your Personal Financial Plan?

- Based on various financial goals, calculate the savings deposits necessary to achieve those goals.
- Identify current economic trends that might influence various saving, spending, investing, and borrowing decisions.

Achieving Financial Goals Using Time Value of Money

Financial Planning Activities: Calculate future and present value amounts related to specific financial goal using time value of money tables, a financial calculator, spreadsheet software, or an online calculator.

Suggested Web Sites: www.moneychimp.com/calculator   www.rbccentura.com/tools

Future Value of a Single Amount

1. To determine future value of a single amount
2. To determine interest lost when cash purchases are made

(Use Exhibit 1–A in Chapter 1 appendix.)

current amount	times	future value factor	equals	future value amount
$ _____	×	$ _____	=	$ _____

Future Value of a Series of Deposits

1. To determine future values of regular savings deposits
2. To determine future value of regular retirement deposits

(Use Exhibit 1–B in Chapter 1 appendix.)

regular deposit amount	times	future value of annuity factor	equals	future value amount
$ _____	×	$ _____	=	$ _____

Present Value of a Single Amount

1. To determine an amount to be deposited now that will grow to desired amount

(Use Exhibit 1–C in Chapter 1 appendix.)

future amount desired	times	present value factor	equals	present value amount
$ _____	×	$ _____	=	$ _____

Present Value of a Series of Deposits

1. To determine an amount that can be withdrawn on a regular basis

(Use Exhibit 1–D in Chapter 1 appendix.)

regular amount to be withdrawn	times	present value of annuity factor	equals	present value amount
$ _____	×	$ _____	=	$ _____

What's Next for Your Personal Financial Plan?

- Describe some situations in which you could use time value of money calculations for achieving various personal financial goals.
- What specific actions are you taking to achieve various financial goals?

Name: _____   **Date:** _____

Planning Your Career

Financial Planning Activities: Research and plan various actions related to obtaining employment.

Suggested Web Sites: www.monster.com   www.careerjournal.com

Career area, job titles	
Useful career information sources—Web sites, books	
Career contacts (name, title, organization, address, phone, e-mail, organization Web site)	
Informational interview questions about the career field, industry	1. 2. 3.
Key items to include in my résumé	1. 2. 3.
Key points to emphasize in my cover letters	1. 2.
Interview questions I should practice answering	1. 2. 3.
Interview questions to ask the organization	1. 2.
Other career planning, job search ideas	

What's Next for Your Personal Financial Plan?

- Talk with various people who have worked in the career fields of interest to you.
- Outline a plan for long-term professional development and career advancement.

Time Value of Money Appendix

- "If I deposit $10,000 today, how much will I have for a down payment on a house in five years?"
- "Will $2,000 saved each year give me enough money when I retire?"
- "How much must I save today to have enough for my children's college education?"

The *time value of money,* more commonly referred to as *interest,* is the cost of money that is borrowed or lent. Interest can be compared to rent, the cost of using an apartment or other item. The time value of money is based on the fact that a dollar received today is worth more than a dollar that will be received one year from today, because the dollar received today can be saved or invested and will be worth more than a dollar a year from today. Similarly, a dollar that will be received one year from today is currently worth less than a dollar today.

The time value of money has two major components: future value and present value. *Future value* computations, which are also referred to as *compounding,* yield the amount to which a current sum will increase based on a certain interest rate and period of time. *Present value,* which is calculated through a process called *discounting,* is the current value of a future sum based on a certain interest rate and period of time.

In future value problems, you are given an amount to save or invest and you calculate the amount that will be available at some future date. With present value problems, you are given the amount that will be available at some future date and you calculate the current value of that amount. Both future value and present value computations are based on basic interest rate calculations.

Interest Rate Basics

Simple interest is the dollar cost of borrowing or earnings from lending money. The interest is based on three elements:

- The dollar amount, called the *principal.*
- The *rate of interest.*
- The amount of *time.*

The formula for computing interest is

$$\text{Interest} = \text{Principal} \times \text{Rate of interest} \times \text{Time}$$

Formula	Financial Calculator*
The interest rate is stated as a percentage for a year. For example, you must convert 12 percent to either 0.12 or 12/100 before doing your calculations. The time element must also be converted to a decimal or fraction. For example, three months would be shown as 0.25, or 1/4 of a year. Interest for 2½ years would involve a time period of 2.5.	
Example A: Suppose you borrow $1,000 at 5 percent and will repay it in one payment at the end of one year. Using the simple interest calculation, the interest is $50, computed as follows:	
$50 = $1,000 × 0.05 × 1 (year)	
Example B: If you deposited $750 in a savings account paying 8 percent, how much interest would you earn in nine months? You would compute this amount as follows:	
Interest = $750 × 0.08 × 3/4 (or 0.75 of a year) = $45	−750 PV, 8 I/Y, 9/12 = .75 N, 0 PMT, CPT FV 795. 795 − 750 = 45

*Note: These financial calculator notations may require slightly different keystrokes when using various brands and models.

Sample Problem 1

How much interest would you earn if you deposited $300 at 6 percent for 27 months? .

(Answers to sample problems are on page 38.)

Sample Problem 2

How much interest would you pay to borrow $670 for eight months at 12 percent?

Future Value of a Single Amount

The future value of an amount consists of the original amount plus compound interest. This calculation involves the following elements:

$$FV = \text{Future value}$$
$$PV = \text{Present value}$$
$$i = \text{Interest rate}$$
$$n = \text{Number of time periods}$$

The formula and financial calculator computations are as follows:

Future Value of a Single Amount		
Formula	**Table**	**Financial Calculator**
$FV = PV(1 + i)^n$	$FV = PV \text{ (Table factor)}$	PV , I/Y , N , PMT , CPT FV
Example C: The future value of $1 at 10 percent after three years is $1.33. This amount is calculated as follows:		
$\$1.33 = \$(1.001 + 0.10)^3$	Using Exhibit 1–A: $\$1.33 = \$1.00(1.33)$	1 PV , 10 I/Y , 3 N , 0 PMT , CPT FV 1.33

Future value tables are available to help you determine compounded interest amounts (see Exhibit 1–A on page 40). Looking at Exhibit 1–A for 10 percent and three years, you can see that $1 would be worth $1.33 at that time. For other amounts, multiply the table factor by the original amount. This process may be viewed as follows:

Future value (rounded)	$1		$1.10		$1.21		$FV = \$1.33$
		Interest $0.10		Interest $0.11		Interest $0.12	
After year	0		1		2		3

Example D: If your savings of $400 earns 12 percent, compounded *monthly,* over a year and a half, use the table factor for 1 percent for 18 time periods; the future value would be:

$\$478.46 = \$400(1 + 0.01)^{18}$	$\$478.40 = \$400(1.196)$	400 PV , 12/12 = 1 I/Y , 1.5 × 12 = 18 N , 0 PMT , CPT FV 478.46

Sample Problem 3

What is the future value of $800 at 8 percent after six years?

Sample Problem 4

How much would you have in savings if you kept $200 on deposit for eight years at 8 percent, compounded *semiannually?*

Future Value of a Series of Equal Amounts (an Annuity)

Future value may also be calculated for a situation in which regular additions are made to savings. The formula and financial calculator computations are as follows:

Future Value of a Series of Payments		
Formula	**Table**	**Financial Calculator**
$FV = Annuity \dfrac{(1 + i)^n - 1}{i}$	Using Exhibit 1–B: Annuity × Table Factor	PMT, N, I/Y, PV, CPT FV
This calculation assumes that (1) each deposit is for the same amount, (2) the interest rate is the same for each time period, and (3) the deposits are made at the end of the each time period.		
Example E: The future value of three $1 deposits made at the end of the next three years, earning 10 percent interest, is $3.31. This is calculated as follows:		
$\$3.31 = \$1 \dfrac{(1 + 0.10)^3 - 1}{0.10}$	Using Exhibit 1–B: $\$3.31 = \$1 \times 3.31$	−1 PMT, 3 N, 10 I/Y, 0 PV, CPT FV 3.31

This may be viewed as follows:

Future value (rounded)		$1		$2.10	FV = $3.31
	Deposit $1 Interest 0		Deposit $1 Interest $0.10		Deposit $1 Interest $0.21
After year 0		1		2	3

Example F: If you plan to deposit $40 a year for 10 years, earning 8 percent compounded annually, the future value of this amount is:		
$\$579.46 = \dfrac{\$40(1 + 0.08)^{10} - 1}{0.08}$	Using Exhibit 1–B $\$579.48 = \$40(14.487)$	−40 PMT, 10 N, 10 I/Y, 0 PV, CPT FV 579.46

Sample Problem 5

What is the future value of an annual deposit of $230 earning 6 percent for 15 years?

Sample Problem 6

What amount would you have in a retirement account if you made annual deposits of $375 for 25 years earning 12 percent, compounded annually?

Present Value of a Single Amount

If you want to know how much you need to deposit now to receive a certain amount in the future, the formula and financial calculator computations are as follows:

	Present Value of a Single Amount	
Formula	**Table**	**Financial Calculator**
$PV = \dfrac{FV}{(1 + i)^n}$	Using Exhibit 1–C: PV = FV(Table Factor)	FV, N, I/Y, PMT, CPT PV
Example G: The present value of $1 to be received three years from now based on a 10 percent interest rate is calculated as follows:		
$\$0.75 = \dfrac{\$1}{(1 + 0.10)^3}$	Using Exhibit 1–C: $0.75 = $1(0.751)	1 FV, 3 N, 10 I/Y, 0 PMT, CPT PV – .75131

This may be viewed as follows:

Future value $0.75	$0.83	$0.91	$1
(rounded)	Discount (interest)	Discount (interest)	Discount (interest)
	$0.075	$0.0825	$0.0905
After year 0	1	2	3

Present value tables are available to assist you in this process (see Exhibit 1–C on page 42). Notice that $1 at 10 percent for three years has a present value of $0.75. For amounts other than $1, multiply the table factor by the amount involved.

Example H: If you want to have $300 seven years from now and your savings earn 10 percent, compounded *semiannually* (which would be 5 percent for 14 time periods), finding how much you would have to deposit today is calculated as follows:

$\$151.52 = \dfrac{\$300}{(1 + 0.05)^{14}}$	Using Exhibit 1–C: $151.50 = $300(0.505)	300 FV, 7 × 2 = 14 N, 10/2 = 5 I/Y, 0 PMT, CPT PV – 151.52

Sample Problem 7

What is the present value of $2,200 earning 15 percent for eight years?

Sample Problem 8

To have $6,000 for a child's education in 10 years, what amount should a parent deposit in a savings account that earns 12 percent, compounded *quarterly?*

Present Value of a Series of Equal Amounts (an Annuity)

The final time value of money situation allows you to receive an amount at the end of each time period for a certain number of periods. The formula and financial calculator computations are as follows:

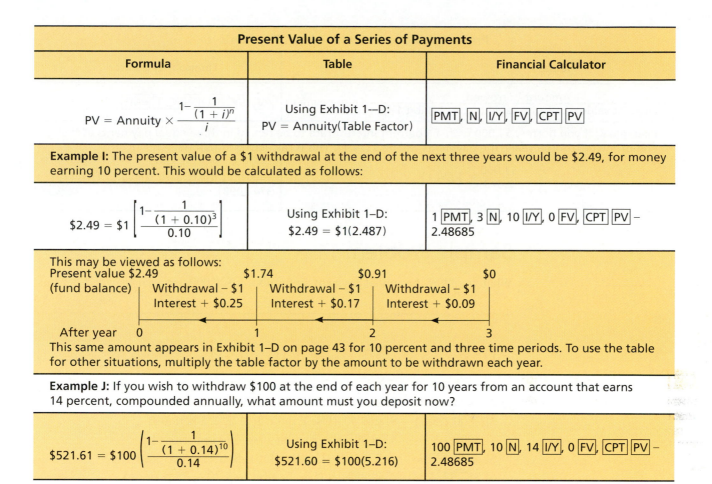

Present Value of a Series of Payments		
Formula	**Table**	**Financial Calculator**
$PV = Annuity \times \dfrac{1 - \dfrac{1}{(1+i)^n}}{i}$	Using Exhibit 1–D: PV = Annuity(Table Factor)	PMT, N, I/Y, FV, CPT PV

Example I: The present value of a $1 withdrawal at the end of the next three years would be $2.49, for money earning 10 percent. This would be calculated as follows:

$\$2.49 = \$1\left[\dfrac{1 - \dfrac{1}{(1+0.10)^3}}{0.10}\right]$	Using Exhibit 1–D: $2.49 = $1(2.487)	1 PMT, 3 N, 10 I/Y, 0 FV, CPT PV – 2.48685

This may be viewed as follows:

Present value $2.49 $1.74 $0.91 $0

(fund balance) | Withdrawal – $1 | Withdrawal – $1 | Withdrawal – $1 |
Interest + $0.25 | Interest + $0.17 | Interest + $0.09 |

After year   0   1   2   3

This same amount appears in Exhibit 1–D on page 43 for 10 percent and three time periods. To use the table for other situations, multiply the table factor by the amount to be withdrawn each year.

Example J: If you wish to withdraw $100 at the end of each year for 10 years from an account that earns 14 percent, compounded annually, what amount must you deposit now?

$\$521.61 = \$100\left(\dfrac{1 - \dfrac{1}{(1+0.14)^{10}}}{0.14}\right)$	Using Exhibit 1–D: $521.60 = $100(5.216)	100 PMT, 10 N, 14 I/Y, 0 FV, CPT PV – 2.48685

Sample Problem 9

What is the present value of a withdrawal of $200 at the end of each year for 14 years with an interest rate of 7 percent?

Sample Problem 10

How much would you have to deposit now to be able to withdraw $650 at the end of each year for 20 years from an account that earns 11 percent?

Using Present Value to Determine Loan Payments

Present value tables (Exhibit 1–D) can also be used to determine installment payments for a loan as follows:

Present Value to Determine Loan Payments	
Table	**Financial Calculator**
$\dfrac{\text{Amount borrowed}}{\text{Present value of a series table factor (Exhibit 1–D)}} = \text{Loan payment}$	$\boxed{\text{PV}}, \boxed{\text{I/Y}}, \boxed{\text{N}}, \boxed{\text{FV}}, \boxed{\text{CPT}}\,\boxed{\text{PMT}}$

Example K: If you borrow $1,000 with a 6 percent interest rate to be repaid in three equal payments at the end of the next three years, the payments will be $374.11. This is calculated as follows:

$$\frac{\$1,000}{2.673} = \$374.11$$

$1000\ \boxed{\text{PV}},\ 6\ \boxed{\text{I/Y}},\ 3\ \boxed{\text{N}},\ 0\ \boxed{\text{FV}},\ \boxed{\text{CPT}}\ \boxed{\text{PMT}}\ -374.10981$

Sample Problem 11

What would be the annual payment amount for a $20,000, ten-year loan at 7 percent?

Answers to Sample Problems

1} $300 × 0.06 × 2.25 years (27 months) = $40.50.
2} $670 × 0.12 × 2/3 (of a year) = $53.60.
3} $800(1.587) = $1,269.60. (Use Exhibit 1–A, 8%, 6 periods.)
4} $200(1.873) = $374.60. (Use Exhibit 1–A, 4%, 16 periods.)
5} $230(23.276) = $5,353.48. (Use Exhibit 1–B, 6%, 15 periods.)
6} $375(133.33) = $49,998.75. (Use Exhibit 1–B, 12%, 25 periods.)
7} $2,200(0.327) = $719.40. (Use Exhibit 1–C, 15%, 8 periods.)
8} $6,000(0.307) = $1,842. (Use Exhibit 1–C, 3%, 40 periods.)
9} $200(8.745) = $1,749. (Use Exhibit 1–D, 7%, 14 periods.)
10} $650(7.963) = $5,175.95. (Use Exhibit 1–D, 11%, 20 periods.)
11} $20,000/7.024 = $2,847.38. (Use Exhibit 1–D, 7%, 10 periods.)

Time Value of Money Application Exercises

1} **(Present value of an annuity)** You wish to borrow $18,000 to buy a new automobile. Rate is 8.6% over five four years with monthly payments. Find monthly the payment. (Answer: $444.52)
2} **(Present value of an annuity)** How much money must your rich uncle give you now to finance four years of college, assuming an annual cost of $48,000 and an interest rate of 6% (applied to the principal until disbursed)? (Answer: $166,325.07)
3} **(Present value of a single amount)** How much money must you set aside at age 20 to accumulate retirement funds of $100,000 at age 65, assuming a rate of interest of 7%? (Answer: $4,761.35)
4} **(Future value of a single amount)** If you deposit $2,000 in a 5-year certificate of deposit at 5.2%, how much will it be worth in five years? (Answer: $2,576.97)
5} **(Future value of a single amount)** If you deposit $2,000 in a 5-year certificate of deposit at 5.2% with quarterly compounding, how much will it be worth in five years? (Answer: $2,589.52)

6} **(Future value of an annuity)** You choose to invest $50/month in a 401(k) that invests in an international stock mutual fund. Assuming an annual rate of return of 9%, how much will this fund worth if retiring in 40 years? (Answer: $234,066.01)

7} **(Future value of an annuity)** If, instead, you invest $600/year in a 401(k) that invests in an international stock mutual fund. Assuming an annual rate of return of 9%, how much will this fund worth if retiring in 40 years? (Answer: $202,729.47)

Time Value of Money Calculation Methods: A Summary

The time value of money may be calculated using a variety of techniques. When achieving specific financial goals requires regular deposits to a savings or investment account, the computation may occur in one of several ways. For example, Jonie Emerson plans to deposit $10,000 in an account for the next 10 years. She estimates these funds will earn an annual rate of 5 percent. What amount can Jonie expect to have available after 10 years?

Method	Process, Results
Formula Calculation The most basic method of calculating the time value of money involves using a formula.	For this situation, the formula would be: $$PV(1 + i)^n = FV$$ The result should be $$\$10{,}000\,(1 + 0.05)^{10} = \$16{,}288.95$$
Time Value of Money Tables Instead of calculating with a formula, time value of money tables are available. The numeric factors presented ease the computational process.	Using the table in Exhibit 1–A: $10,000 × Future value of $1, 5%, 10 years $10,000 × 1.629 = $16,290
Financial Calculator A variety of financial calculators are programmed with various financial functions. Both future value and present value calculations may be performed using the appropriate keystrokes.	Using a financial calculator, the keystrokes would be: Amount −10000 $\boxed{\text{PV}}$ Time periods 10 $\boxed{\text{N}}$ Interest rate 5 $\boxed{\text{I}}$ Result $\boxed{\text{FV}}$ $16,288.94
Spreadsheet Software Excel and other software programs have built-in formulas for various financial computations, including time value of money.	When using a spreadsheet program, this type of calculation would require this format: $= FV$(rate, periods, amount per period, single amount) The results of this example would be: $= FV$(0.05, 10, 0, −10000) = $16,288.95
Time Value of Money Web Sites Many time-value-of-money calculators are also available online. These Web-based programs perform calculations for the future value of savings as well as determining amounts for loan payments.	Some easy-to-use calculators for computing the time value of money and other financial computations are located at • www.kiplinger.com/tools • www.dinkytown.net • www.rbccentura.com/tools • cgi.money.cnn.com/tools

Note: The slight differences in answers are the result of rounding.

Exhibit 1-A   Future Value (Compounded Sum) of $1 after a Given Number of Time Periods

Period	1%	2%	3%	4%	5%	6%	7%	8%	9%	10%	11%
1	1.010	1.020	1.030	1.040	1.050	1.060	1.070	1.080	1.090	1.100	1.110
2	1.020	1.040	1.061	1.082	1.103	1.124	1.145	1.166	1.188	1.210	1.232
3	1.030	1.061	1.093	1.125	1.158	1.191	1.225	1.260	1.295	1.331	1.368
4	1.041	1.082	1.126	1.170	1.216	1.262	1.311	1.360	1.412	1.464	1.518
5	1.051	1.104	1.159	1.217	1.276	1.338	1.403	1.469	1.539	1.611	1.685
6	1.062	1.126	1.194	1.265	1.340	1.419	1.501	1.587	1.677	1.772	1.870
7	1.072	1.149	1.230	1.316	1.407	1.504	1.606	1.714	1.828	1.949	2.076
8	1.083	1.172	1.267	1.369	1.477	1.594	1.718	1.851	1.993	2.144	2.305
9	1.094	1.195	1.305	1.423	1.551	1.689	1.838	1.999	2.172	2.358	2.558
10	1.105	1.219	1.344	1.480	1.629	1.791	1.967	2.159	2.367	2.594	2.839
11	1.116	1.243	1.384	1.539	1.710	1.898	2.105	2.332	2.580	2.853	3.152
12	1.127	1.268	1.426	1.601	1.796	2.012	2.252	2.518	2.813	3.138	3.498
13	1.138	1.294	1.469	1.665	1.886	2.133	2.410	2.720	3.066	3.452	3.883
14	1.149	1.319	1.513	1.732	1.980	2.261	2.579	2.937	3.342	3.797	4.310
15	1.161	1.346	1.558	1.801	2.079	2.397	2.759	3.172	3.642	4.177	4.785
16	1.173	1.373	1.605	1.873	2.183	2.540	2.952	3.426	3.970	4.595	5.311
17	1.184	1.400	1.653	1.948	2.292	2.693	3.159	3.700	4.328	5.054	5.895
18	1.196	1.428	1.702	2.026	2.407	2.854	3.380	3.996	4.717	5.560	6.544
19	1.208	1.457	1.754	2.107	2.527	3.026	3.617	4.316	5.142	6.116	7.263
20	1.220	1.486	1.806	2.191	2.653	3.207	3.870	4.661	5.604	6.727	8.062
25	1.282	1.641	2.094	2.666	3.386	4.292	5.427	6.848	8.623	10.835	13.585
30	1.348	1.811	2.427	3.243	4.322	5.743	7.612	10.063	13.268	17.449	22.892
40	1.489	2.208	3.262	4.801	7.040	10.286	14.974	21.725	31.409	45.259	65.001
50	1.645	2.692	4.384	7.107	11.467	18.420	29.457	46.902	74.358	117.390	184.570

Period	12%	13%	14%	15%	16%	17%	18%	19%	20%	25%	30%
1	1.120	1.130	1.140	1.150	1.160	1.170	1.180	1.190	1.200	1.250	1.300
2	1.254	1.277	1.300	1.323	1.346	1.369	1.392	1.416	1.440	1.563	1.690
3	1.405	1.443	1.482	1.521	1.561	1.602	1.643	1.685	1.728	1.953	2.197
4	1.574	1.630	1.689	1.749	1.811	1.874	1.939	2.005	2.074	2.441	2.856
5	1.762	1.842	1.925	2.011	2.100	2.192	2.288	2.386	2.488	3.052	3.713
6	1.974	2.082	2.195	2.313	2.436	2.565	2.700	2.840	2.986	3.815	4.827
7	2.211	2.353	2.502	2.660	2.826	3.001	3.185	3.379	3.583	4.768	6.276
8	2.476	2.658	2.853	3.059	3.278	3.511	3.759	4.021	4.300	5.960	8.157
9	2.773	3.004	3.252	3.518	3.803	4.108	4.435	4.785	5.160	7.451	10.604
10	3.106	3.395	3.707	4.046	4.411	4.807	5.234	5.696	6.192	9.313	13.786
11	3.479	3.836	4.226	4.652	5.117	5.624	6.176	6.777	7.430	11.642	17.922
12	3.896	4.335	4.818	5.350	5.936	6.580	7.288	8.064	8.916	14.552	23.298
13	4.363	4.898	5.492	6.153	6.886	7.699	8.599	9.596	10.699	18.190	30.288
14	4.887	5.535	6.261	7.076	7.988	9.007	10.147	11.420	12.839	22.737	39.374
15	5.474	6.254	7.138	8.137	9.266	10.539	11.974	13.590	15.407	28.422	51.186
16	6.130	7.067	8.137	9.358	10.748	12.330	14.129	16.172	18.488	35.527	66.542
17	6.866	7.986	9.276	10.761	12.468	14.426	16.672	19.244	22.186	44.409	86.504
18	7.690	9.024	10.575	12.375	14.463	16.879	19.673	22.091	26.623	55.511	112.460
19	8.613	10.197	12.056	14.232	16.777	19.748	23.214	27.252	31.948	69.389	146.190
20	9.646	11.523	13.743	16.367	19.461	23.106	27.393	32.429	38.338	86.736	190.050
25	17.000	21.231	26.462	32.919	40.874	50.658	62.669	77.388	95.396	264.700	705.640
30	29.960	39.116	50.950	66.212	85.850	111.070	143.370	184.680	237.380	807.790	2,620.000
40	93.051	132.780	188.880	267.860	378.720	533.870	750.380	1,051.700	1,469.800	7,523.200	36,119.000
50	289.000	450.740	700.230	1,083.700	1,670.700	2,566.200	3,927.400	5,998.900	9,100.400	70,065.000	497,929.000

Exhibit 1–B Future Value (Compounded Sum) of $1 Paid In at the End of Each Period for a Given Number of Time Periods (an Annuity)

Period	1%	2%	3%	4%	5%	6%	7%	8%	9%	10%	11%
1	1.000	1.000	1.000	1.000	1.000	1.000	1.000	1.000	1.000	1.000	1.000
2	2.010	2.020	2.030	2.040	2.050	2.060	2.070	2.080	2.090	2.100	2.110
3	3.030	3.060	3.091	3.122	3.153	3.184	3.215	3.246	3.278	3.310	3.342
4	4.060	4.122	4.184	4.246	4.310	4.375	4.440	4.506	4.573	4.641	4.710
5	5.101	5.204	5.309	5.416	5.526	5.637	5.751	5.867	5.985	6.105	6.228
6	6.152	6.308	6.468	6.633	6.802	6.975	7.153	7.336	7.523	7.716	7.913
7	7.214	7.434	7.662	7.898	8.142	8.394	8.654	8.923	9.200	9.487	9.783
8	8.286	8.583	8.892	9.214	9.549	9.897	10.260	10.637	11.028	11.436	11.859
9	9.369	9.755	10.159	10.583	11.027	11.491	11.978	12.488	13.021	13.579	14.164
10	10.462	10.950	11.464	12.006	12.578	13.181	13.816	14.487	15.193	15.937	16.722
11	11.567	12.169	12.808	13.486	14.207	14.972	15.784	16.645	17.560	18.531	19.561
12	12.683	13.412	14.192	15.026	15.917	16.870	17.888	18.977	20.141	21.384	22.713
13	13.809	14.680	15.618	16.627	17.713	18.882	20.141	21.495	22.953	24.523	26.212
14	14.947	15.974	17.086	18.292	19.599	21.015	22.550	24.215	26.019	27.975	30.095
15	16.097	17.293	18.599	20.024	21.579	23.276	25.129	27.152	29.361	31.772	34.405
16	17.258	18.639	20.157	21.825	23.657	25.673	27.888	30.324	33.003	35.950	39.190
17	18.430	20.012	21.762	23.698	25.840	28.213	30.840	33.750	36.974	40.545	44.501
18	19.615	21.412	23.414	25.645	28.132	30.906	33.999	37.450	41.301	45.599	50.396
19	20.811	22.841	25.117	27.671	30.539	33.760	37.379	41.446	46.018	51.159	56.939
20	22.019	24.297	26.870	29.778	33.066	36.786	40.995	45.762	51.160	57.275	64.203
25	28.243	32.030	36.459	41.646	47.727	54.865	63.249	73.106	84.701	98.347	114.410
30	34.785	40.588	47.575	56.085	66.439	79.058	94.461	113.280	136.310	164.490	199.020
40	48.886	60.402	75.401	95.026	120.800	154.760	199.640	259.060	337.890	442.590	581.830
50	64.463	84.579	112.800	152.670	209.350	290.340	406.530	573.770	815.080	1,163.900	1,668.800

Period	12%	13%	14%	15%	16%	17%	18%	19%	20%	25%	30%
1	1.000	1.000	1.000	1.000	1.000	1.000	1.000	1.000	1.000	1.000	1.000
2	2.120	2.130	2.140	2.150	2.160	2.170	2.180	2.190	2.200	2.250	2.300
3	3.374	3.407	3.440	3.473	3.506	3.539	3.572	3.606	3.640	3.813	3.990
4	4.779	4.850	4.921	4.993	5.066	5.141	5.215	5.291	5.368	5.766	6.187
5	6.353	6.480	6.610	6.742	6.877	7.014	7.154	7.297	7.442	8.207	9.043
6	8.115	8.323	8.536	8.754	8.977	9.207	9.442	9.683	9.930	11.259	12.756
7	10.089	10.405	10.730	11.067	11.414	11.772	12.142	12.523	12.916	15.073	17.583
8	12.300	12.757	13.233	13.727	14.240	14.773	15.327	15.902	16.499	19.842	23.858
9	14.776	15.416	16.085	16.786	17.519	18.285	19.086	19.923	20.799	25.802	32.015
10	17.549	18.420	19.337	20.304	21.321	22.393	23.521	24.701	25.959	33.253	42.619
11	20.655	21.814	23.045	24.349	25.733	27.200	28.755	30.404	32.150	42.566	56.405
12	24.133	25.650	27.271	29.002	30.850	32.824	34.931	37.180	39.581	54.208	74.327
13	28.029	29.985	32.089	34.352	36.786	39.404	42.219	45.244	48.497	68.760	97.625
14	32.393	34.883	37.581	40.505	43.672	47.103	50.818	54.841	59.196	86.949	127.910
15	37.280	40.417	43.842	47.580	51.660	56.110	60.965	66.261	72.035	109.690	167.290
16	42.753	46.672	50.980	55.717	60.925	66.649	72.939	79.850	87.442	138.110	218.470
17	48.884	53.739	59.118	65.075	71.673	78.979	87.068	96.022	105.930	173.640	285.010
18	55.750	61.725	68.394	75.836	84.141	93.406	103.740	115.270	128.120	218.050	371.520
19	63.440	70.749	78.969	88.212	98.603	110.290	123.410	138.170	154.740	273.560	483.970
20	72.052	80.947	91.025	102.440	115.380	130.030	146.630	165.420	186.690	342.950	630.170
25	133.330	155.620	181.870	212.790	249.210	292.110	342.600	402.040	471.980	1,054.800	2,348.800
30	241.330	293.200	356.790	434.750	530.310	647.440	790.950	966.700	1,181.900	3,227.200	8,730.000
40	767.090	1,013.700	1,342.000	1,779.100	2,360.800	3,134.500	4,163.210	5,529.800	7,343.900	30,089.000	120,393.000
50	2,400.000	3,459.500	4,994.500	7,217.700	10,436.000	15,090.000	21,813.000	31,515.000	45,497.000	80,256.000	165,976.000

Exhibit 1–C Present Value of $1 to be Received at the End of a Given Number of Time Periods

Period	1%	2%	3%	4%	5%	6%	7%	8%	9%	10%	11%	12%
1	0.990	0.980	0.971	0.962	0.952	0.943	0.935	0.926	0.917	0.909	0.901	0.893
2	0.980	0.961	0.943	0.925	0.907	0.890	0.873	0.857	0.842	0.826	0.812	0.797
3	0.971	0.942	0.915	0.889	0.864	0.840	0.816	0.794	0.772	0.751	0.731	0.712
4	0.961	0.924	0.885	0.855	0.823	0.792	0.763	0.735	0.708	0.683	0.659	0.636
5	0.951	0.906	0.863	0.822	0.784	0.747	0.713	0.681	0.650	0.621	0.593	0.567
6	0.942	0.888	0.837	0.790	0.746	0.705	0.666	0.630	0.596	0.564	0.535	0.507
7	0.933	0.871	0.813	0.760	0.711	0.665	0.623	0.583	0.547	0.513	0.482	0.452
8	0.923	0.853	0.789	0.731	0.677	0.627	0.582	0.540	0.502	0.467	0.434	0.404
9	0.914	0.837	0.766	0.703	0.645	0.592	0.544	0.500	0.460	0.424	0.391	0.361
10	0.905	0.820	0.744	0.676	0.614	0.558	0.508	0.463	0.422	0.386	0.352	0.322
11	0.896	0.804	0.722	0.650	0.585	0.527	0.475	0.429	0.388	0.350	0.317	0.287
12	0.887	0.788	0.701	0.625	0.557	0.497	0.444	0.397	0.356	0.319	0.286	0.257
13	0.879	0.773	0.681	0.601	0.530	0.469	0.415	0.368	0.326	0.290	0.258	0.229
14	0.870	0.758	0.661	0.577	0.505	0.442	0.388	0.340	0.299	0.263	0.232	0.205
15	0.861	0.743	0.642	0.555	0.481	0.417	0.362	0.315	0.275	0.239	0.209	0.183
16	0.853	0.728	0.623	0.534	0.458	0.394	0.339	0.292	0.252	0.218	0.188	0.163
17	0.844	0.714	0.605	0.513	0.436	0.371	0.317	0.270	0.231	0.198	0.170	0.146
18	0.836	0.700	0.587	0.494	0.416	0.350	0.296	0.250	0.212	0.180	0.153	0.130
19	0.828	0.686	0.570	0.475	0.396	0.331	0.277	0.232	0.194	0.164	0.138	0.116
20	0.820	0.673	0.554	0.456	0.377	0.312	0.258	0.215	0.178	0.149	0.124	0.104
25	0.780	0.610	0.478	0.375	0.295	0.233	0.184	0.146	0.116	0.092	0.074	0.059
30	0.742	0.552	0.412	0.308	0.231	0.174	0.131	0.099	0.075	0.057	0.044	0.033
40	0.672	0.453	0.307	0.208	0.142	0.097	0.067	0.046	0.032	0.022	0.015	0.011
50	0.608	0.372	0.228	0.141	0.087	0.054	0.034	0.021	0.013	0.009	0.005	0.003

Period	13%	14%	15%	16%	17%	18%	19%	20%	25%	30%	35%	40%	50%
1	0.885	0.877	0.870	0.862	0.855	0.847	0.840	0.833	0.800	0.769	0.741	0.714	0.667
2	0.783	0.769	0.756	0.743	0.731	0.718	0.706	0.694	0.640	0.592	0.549	0.510	0.444
3	0.693	0.675	0.658	0.641	0.624	0.609	0.593	0.579	0.512	0.455	0.406	0.364	0.296
4	0.613	0.592	0.572	0.552	0.534	0.515	0.499	0.482	0.410	0.350	0.301	0.260	0.198
5	0.543	0.519	0.497	0.476	0.456	0.437	0.419	0.402	0.320	0.269	0.223	0.186	0.132
6	0.480	0.456	0.432	0.410	0.390	0.370	0.352	0.335	0.262	0.207	0.165	0.133	0.088
7	0.425	0.400	0.376	0.354	0.333	0.314	0.296	0.279	0.210	0.159	0.122	0.095	0.059
8	0.376	0.351	0.327	0.305	0.285	0.266	0.249	0.233	0.168	0.123	0.091	0.068	0.039
9	0.333	0.300	0.284	0.263	0.243	0.225	0.209	0.194	0.134	0.094	0.067	0.048	0.026
10	0.295	0.270	0.247	0.227	0.208	0.191	0.176	0.162	0.107	0.073	0.050	0.035	0.017
11	0.261	0.237	0.215	0.195	0.178	0.162	0.148	0.135	0.086	0.056	0.037	0.025	0.012
12	0.231	0.208	0.187	0.168	0.152	0.137	0.124	0.112	0.069	0.043	0.027	0.018	0.008
13	0.204	0.182	0.163	0.145	0.130	0.116	0.104	0.093	0.055	0.033	0.020	0.013	0.005
14	0.181	0.160	0.141	0.125	0.111	0.099	0.088	0.078	0.044	0.025	0.015	0.009	0.003
15	0.160	0.140	0.123	0.108	0.095	0.084	0.074	0.065	0.035	0.020	0.011	0.006	0.002
16	0.141	0.123	0.107	0.093	0.081	0.071	0.062	0.054	0.028	0.015	0.008	0.005	0.002
17	0.125	0.108	0.093	0.080	0.069	0.060	0.052	0.045	0.023	0.012	0.006	0.003	0.001
18	0.111	0.095	0.081	0.069	0.059	0.051	0.044	0.038	0.018	0.009	0.005	0.002	0.001
19	0.098	0.083	0.070	0.060	0.051	0.043	0.037	0.031	0.014	0.007	0.003	0.002	0
20	0.087	0.073	0.061	0.051	0.043	0.037	0.031	0.026	0.012	0.005	0.002	0.001	0
25	0.047	0.038	0.030	0.024	0.020	0.016	0.013	0.010	0.004	0.001	0.001	0	0
30	0.026	0.020	0.015	0.012	0.009	0.007	0.005	0.004	0.001	0	0	0	0
40	0.008	0.005	0.004	0.003	0.002	0.001	0.001	0.001	0	0	0	0	0
50	0.002	0.001	0.001	0.001	0	0	0	0	0	0	0	0	0

Exhibit **1–D** Present Value of $1 Received at the End of Each Period for a Given Number of Time Periods (an Annuity)

Period	1%	2%	3%	4%	5%	6%	7%	8%	9%	10%	11%	12%
1	0.990	0.980	0.971	0.962	0.952	0.943	0.935	0.926	0.917	0.909	0.901	0.893
2	1.970	1.942	1.913	1.886	1.859	1.833	1.808	1.783	1.759	1.736	1.713	1.690
3	2.941	2.884	2.829	2.775	2.723	2.673	2.624	2.577	2.531	2.487	2.444	2.402
4	3.902	3.808	3.717	3.630	3.546	3.465	3.387	3.312	3.240	3.170	3.102	3.037
5	4.853	4.713	4.580	4.452	4.329	4.212	4.100	3.993	3.890	3.791	3.696	3.605
6	5.795	5.601	5.417	5.242	5.076	4.917	4.767	4.623	4.486	4.355	4.231	4.111
7	6.728	6.472	6.230	6.002	5.786	5.582	5.389	5.206	5.033	4.868	4.712	4.564
8	7.652	7.325	7.020	6.733	6.463	6.210	5.971	5.747	5.535	5.335	5.146	4.968
9	8.566	8.162	7.786	7.435	7.108	6.802	6.515	6.247	5.995	5.759	5.537	5.328
10	9.471	8.983	8.530	8.111	7.722	7.360	7.024	6.710	6.418	6.145	5.889	5.650
11	10.368	9.787	9.253	8.760	8.306	7.887	7.499	7.139	6.805	6.495	6.207	5.938
12	11.255	10.575	9.954	9.385	8.863	8.384	7.943	7.536	7.161	6.814	6.492	6.194
13	12.134	11.348	10.635	9.986	9.394	8.853	8.358	7.904	7.487	7.103	6.750	6.424
14	13.004	12.106	11.296	10.563	9.899	9.295	8.745	8.244	7.786	7.367	6.982	6.628
15	13.865	12.849	11.939	11.118	10.380	9.712	9.108	8.559	8.061	7.606	7.191	6.811
16	14.718	13.578	12.561	11.652	10.838	10.106	9.447	8.851	8.313	7.824	7.379	6.974
17	15.562	14.292	13.166	12.166	11.274	10.477	9.763	9.122	8.544	8.022	7.549	7.102
18	16.398	14.992	13.754	12.659	11.690	10.828	10.059	9.372	8.756	8.201	7.702	7.250
19	17.226	15.678	14.324	13.134	12.085	11.158	10.336	9.604	8.950	8.365	7.839	7.366
20	18.046	16.351	14.877	13.590	12.462	11.470	10.594	9.818	9.129	8.514	7.963	7.469
25	22.023	19.523	17.413	15.622	14.094	12.783	11.654	10.675	9.823	9.077	8.422	7.843
30	25.808	22.396	19.600	17.292	15.372	13.765	12.409	11.258	10.274	9.427	8.694	8.055
40	32.835	27.355	23.115	19.793	17.159	15.046	13.332	11.925	10.757	9.779	8.951	8.244
50	39.196	31.424	25.730	21.482	18.256	15.762	13.801	12.233	10.962	9.915	9.042	8.304

Period	13%	14%	15%	16%	17%	18%	19%	20%	25%	30%	35%	40%	50%
1	0.885	0.877	0.870	0.862	0.855	0.847	0.840	0.833	0.800	0.769	0.741	0.714	0.667
2	1.668	1.647	1.626	1.605	1.585	1.566	1.547	1.528	1.440	1.361	1.289	1.224	1.111
3	2.361	2.322	2.283	2.246	2.210	2.174	2.140	2.106	1.952	1.816	1.696	1.589	1.407
4	2.974	2.914	2.855	2.798	2.743	2.690	2.639	2.589	2.362	2.166	1.997	1.849	1.605
5	3.517	3.433	3.352	3.274	3.199	3.127	3.058	2.991	2.689	2.436	2.220	2.035	1.737
6	3.998	3.889	3.784	3.685	3.589	3.498	3.410	3.326	2.951	2.643	2.385	2.168	1.824
7	4.423	4.288	4.160	4.039	3.922	3.812	3.706	3.605	3.161	2.802	2.508	2.263	1.883
8	4.799	4.639	4.487	4.344	4.207	4.078	3.954	3.837	3.329	2.925	2.598	2.331	1.922
9	5.132	4.946	4.772	4.607	4.451	4.303	4.163	4.031	3.463	3.019	2.665	2.379	1.948
10	5.426	5.216	5.019	4.833	4.659	4.494	4.339	4.192	3.571	3.092	2.715	2.414	1.965
11	5.687	5.453	5.234	5.029	4.836	4.656	4.486	4.327	3.656	3.147	2.752	2.438	1.977
12	5.918	5.660	5.421	5.197	4.988	4.793	4.611	4.439	3.725	3.190	2.779	2.456	1.985
13	6.122	5.842	5.583	5.342	5.118	4.910	4.715	4.533	3.780	3.223	2.799	2.469	1.990
14	6.302	6.002	5.724	5.468	5.229	5.008	4.802	4.611	3.824	3.249	2.814	2.478	1.993
15	6.462	6.142	5.847	5.575	5.324	5.092	4.876	4.675	3.859	3.268	2.825	2.484	1.995
16	6.604	6.265	5.954	5.668	5.405	5.162	4.938	4.730	3.887	3.283	2.834	2.489	1.997
17	6.729	6.373	6.047	5.749	5.475	5.222	4.988	4.775	3.910	3.295	2.840	2.492	1.998
18	6.840	6.467	6.128	5.818	5.534	5.273	5.033	4.812	3.928	3.304	2.844	2.494	1.999
19	6.938	6.550	6.198	5.877	5.584	5.316	5.070	4.843	3.942	3.311	2.848	2.496	1.999
20	7.025	6.623	6.259	5.929	5.628	5.353	5.101	4.870	3.954	3.316	2.850	2.497	1.999
25	7.330	6.873	6.464	6.097	5.766	5.467	5.195	4.948	3.985	3.329	2.856	2.499	2.000
30	7.496	7.003	6.566	6.177	5.829	5.517	5.235	4.979	3.995	3.332	2.857	2.500	2.000
40	7.634	7.105	6.642	6.233	5.871	5.548	5.258	4.997	3.999	3.333	2.857	2.500	2.000
50	7.675	7.133	6.661	6.246	5.880	5.554	5.262	4.999	4.000	3.333	2.857	2.500	2.000

2 Money Management Skills

Getting Personal

What are your money management habits? For each of the following statements, circle the choice that best describes your current situation:

1. In difficult economic times, my money management strategy is to:
   a. continue spending as I usually do.
   b. monitor spending habits more closely.
   c. make use of my past savings to pay necessary bills.

2. My system for organizing personal financial records could be described as
   a. Nonexistent . . . I have documents that are missing in action!
   b. Basic . . . I can find most stuff when I need to!
   c. Very efficient . . . better than the Library of Congress!

3. The details of my cash flow statement are
   a. Simple . . . "money coming in" and "money going out."
   b. Appropriate for my needs . . . enough information for me.
   c. Very informative . . . I know where my money goes.

4. My budgeting activities could be described as
   a. "I don't have enough money to worry about where it goes."
   b. "I keep track of my spending using my debit card summary."
   c. "I have a written plan for spending and paying my bills on time."

After studying this chapter, you will be asked to reconsider your responses to these items.

OBJECTIVE 1

Identify the main components of wise money management.

A Successful Money Management Plan

"Each month, I have too many days and not enough money. If the month were only 20 days long, budgeting would be easy."

Daily spending and saving decisions are at the center of your financial planning activities. You must coordinate these decisions with your needs, goals, and personal

Your Personal Financial Plan Sheets

5. Financial documents and records.
6. Creating a personal balance sheet.
7. Creating a personal cash flow statement.
8. Developing a personal budget.

Objectives

In this chapter, you will learn to:
1. Identify the main components of wise money management.
2. Create a personal balance sheet and cash flow statement.
3. Develop and implement a personal budget.
4. Connect money management activities with saving for personal financial goals.

Why is this important?

When difficult economic conditions occur, people will often need to draw upon past savings. The average person in the United States saves less than three cents of every dollar earned. This lack of saving results in not having adequate funds for financial emergencies and long-term financial security. Effectively planning your spending and saving decisions provides a foundation for wise money management today and financial prosperity in the future.

situation. Maintaining financial records and planning your spending are essential skills for successful personal financial management. The time and effort you devote to these activities will yield many benefits. **Money management** refers to the day-to-day financial activities necessary to manage current personal economic resources while working toward long-term financial security.

money management Day-to-day financial activities necessary to manage current personal economic resources while working toward long-term financial security.

Components of Money Management

As shown here, three major money management activities are interrelated:

3. Creating and implementing a plan for spending and saving (budgeting)

2. Creating personal financial statements (balance sheets and cash flow statements of income and outflows)

1. Storing and maintaining personal financial records and documents

First, personal financial records and documents are the foundation of systematic resource use. These provide written evidence of business transactions, ownership of property, and legal matters. Next, personal financial statements enable you to measure and assess your financial position and progress. Finally, your spending plan, or *budget,* is the basis for effective money management.

Money Management Troubles and Debt

Difficult economic conditions often create difficult personal financial situations. These troubles are often in the form of increased debt and an inability to make credit payments. The process of getting out of debt can be viewed in a series of actions. While these steps may not all be possible immediately, consideration should be given to each to better address your daily money management situation[1]:

- *Evaluate your credit situation.* A list of amounts owed, the annual percentage rate (APR), and minimum monthly payment will help you see where you are, and what actions you might take. Your updated list will also show your progress.
- *Track your spending.* Complete information on where all your money goes will allow you to better plan how to budget for credit payments. (See the "Daily Spending Diary" sheets in Appendix C or online at www.mhhe.com/kdh.)
- *Plan to make payments on time.* While you make have to cut back on other spending items, maintaining a strong credit status will serve you well over time. Missed payments can result in late fees, penalties, and greater difficulty obtaining credit in the future. Consider using online banking for automatically making payments on time.

---

[1]"5 Ways to Dig Yourself Out of Trouble," *Kiplinger's Personal Finance,* November, 2008, p. 86.

- *Consider other income sources.* Working overtime, doing part-time work, consulting, and seeking other income sources can provide a short-term solution to paying off loans. However, over time other actions might require a higher paying job or a reduction to your spending patterns.
- *If appropriate, seek assistance.* Always contact your creditors before missing a payment to determine what alternatives you might have. Also, a variety of credit counseling agencies can help those who are overwhelmed by debt. Two organizations to consider are the National Foundation for Credit Counseling (www.nfcc.org) and the Association of Independent Consumer Credit Counseling Agencies (www.aiccca.org). Be very wary of debt consolidation, credit-repair, and other "too-good-to-be-true" credit assistance offers.

Your ability to avoid debt troubles and practice wise money management also requires a system for storing and locating financial documents.

A System for Personal Financial Records

Invoices, credit card statements, insurance policies, and tax forms are the basis of financial recordkeeping and personal economic choices. An organized system of financial records provides a basis for (1) handling daily business activities, such as bill paying; (2) planning and measuring financial progress; (3) completing required tax reports; (4) making effective investment decisions; and (5) determining available resources for current and future spending.

As Exhibit 2–1 shows, most financial records are kept in one of three places: a home file, a safe deposit box, or a home computer. A home file should be used to keep records for current needs and documents with limited value. Your home file may be a series of folders, a cabinet with several drawers, or even a box. Whatever method you use, it is most important that your home file be organized to allow quick access to needed documents and information.

Important financial records and valuable articles should be kept in a location that provides better security than a home file. A **safe deposit box** is a private storage area at a financial institution with maximum security for valuables and difficult-to-replace documents. Items commonly kept in a safe deposit box include an annual stock investment statement, contracts, a list of insurance policies, and valuables such as rare coins and stamps.

safe deposit box A private storage area at a financial institution with maximum security for valuables.

The number of financial records and documents may seem overwhelming; however, they can easily be organized into 10 categories (see Exhibit 2–1). These groups correspond to the major topics covered in this book. You may not need to use all of these records and documents at present. As your financial situation changes, you will add others.

How long should you keep personal finance records? Records such as birth certificates, wills, and Social Security data should be kept permanently. Records on property and investments should be kept as long as you own these items. Federal tax laws dictate the length of time you should keep tax-related information. Copies of tax returns and supporting data should be saved for seven years. Normally, an audit will go back only three years; however, under certain circumstances, the Internal Revenue Service may request information from further back. Financial experts also recommend keeping documents related to the purchase and sale of real estate indefinitely.

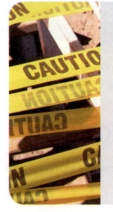

CAUTION! In the United States, people keep various documents and valuables in 30 million safe deposit boxes in banks and other financial institutions. While these boxes are usually very safe, each year a few people lose the contents of their safe deposit boxes through theft, fire, or natural disasters. Such losses are usually, but not always, covered by the financial institution's insurance.

Figure It Out!

Financial ratios provide guidelines for measuring the changes in your financial situation. These relationships can indicate progress toward an improved financial position.

Ratio	Calculation	Example	Interpretation
Debt ratio	Liabilities divided by net worth	$25,000/$50,000 = 0.5	Shows relationship between debt and net worth; a low debt ratio is best.
Current ratio	Liquid assets divided by current liabilities	$4,000/$2,000 = 2	Indicates $2 in liquid assets for every $1 of current liabilities; a high current ratio is desirable to have cash available to pay bills.
Liquidity ratio	Liquid assets divided by monthly expenses	$10,000/$4,000 = 2.5	Indicates the number of months in which living expenses can be paid if an emergency arises; a high liquidity ratio is desirable.
Debt-payments ratio	Monthly credit payments divided by take-home pay	$540/$3,600 = 0.15	Indicates how much of a person's earnings goes for debt payments (excluding a home mortgage); most financial advisers recommend a debt/payments ratio of less than 20 percent.
Savings ratio	Amount saved each month divided by gross income	$648/$5,400 = 0.12	Financial experts recommend monthly savings of 5–10 percent.

Based on the following information, calculate the ratios requested:

- Liabilities $12,000
- Liquid assets $2,200
- Monthly credit payments $150
- Monthly savings $130

- Net worth $36,000
- Current liabilities $550
- Take-home pay $900
- Gross income $1,500

(1) Debt ratio _____

(2) Debt-payments ratio _____

(3) Current ratio _____

(4) Savings ratio _____

Your Cash Flow Statement: Inflows and Outflows

cash flow The actual inflow and outflow of cash during a given time period.

Each day, financial events can affect your net worth. When you receive a paycheck or pay living expenses, your total assets and liabilities change. **Cash flow** is the actual inflow and outflow of cash during a given time period. Income from employment will probably represent your most important *cash inflow;* however, other income, such as interest earned on a savings account, should also be considered. In contrast, payments for items such as rent, food, and loans are *cash outflows.*

A **cash flow statement,** also called a *personal income and expenditure statement* (Exhibit 2–3), is a summary of cash receipts and payments for a given period, such as a month or a year. This report provides data on your income and spending patterns, which will be helpful when preparing a budget.

A checking account can provide information for your cash flow statement. Deposits to the account are your *inflows;* checks written, cash withdrawals, and debit card payments are your *outflows.* Of course, in using this system, when you do not deposit entire amounts received, you must also note the spending of these nondeposited amounts in your cash flow statement.

The process for preparing a cash flow statement involves three steps:

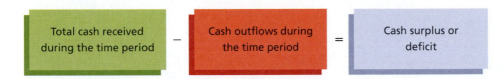

STEP 1: RECORD INCOME To create a cash flow statement, start by identifying the funds received. **Income** is the inflows of cash for an individual or a household. For most people, the main source of income is money received from a job. Other common income sources include commissions, self-employment income, interest, dividends, gifts, grants, scholarships, government payments, pensions, retirement income, alimony, and child support.

In Exhibit 2–3, notice that Kim Walker's monthly salary (or *gross income*) of $4,350 is her main source of income. However, she does not have use of the entire amount. **Take-home pay,** also called *net pay,* is a person's earnings after deductions for taxes and other items. Kim's deductions for federal, state, and Social Security taxes are $1,250. Her take-home pay is $3,100. This amount, plus earnings from savings and investments, is the income she has available for use during the current month.

Take-home pay is also called *disposable income,* the amount a person or household has available to spend. **Discretionary income** is money left over after paying for housing, food, and other necessities. Studies report that discretionary income ranges from less than 5 percent for people under age 25 to more than 40 percent for older people.

STEP 2: RECORD CASH OUTFLOWS Cash payments for living expenses and other items make up the second component of a cash flow statement. Kim Walker divides her cash outflows into two major categories: fixed expenses and variable expenses. Every individual and household has different cash outflows, but these main categories, along with the subcategories Kim uses, can be adapted to most situations.

1. *Fixed expenses* are payments that do not vary from month to month. Rent or mortgage payments, installment loan payments, cable television service fees, and a monthly train ticket for commuting to work are examples of constant or fixed cash outflows. For Kim, another type of fixed expense is the amount she sets aside each month for payments due once or twice a year. For example, Kim pays $384 every March for life insurance. Each month, she records a fixed outflow of $32 for deposit in a special savings account so that the money will be available when her insurance payment is due.

cash flow statement A financial statement that summarizes cash receipts and payments for a given period; also called a *personal income and expenditure statement.*

income Inflows of cash to an individual or a household.

take-home pay Earnings after deductions for taxes and other items; also called *disposable income.*

discretionary income Money left over after paying for housing, food, and other necessities.

did you know?

When there is not enough in savings for emergencies, people most often use a home equity loan or credit cards, borrow from relatives or against a retirement account, or sell some unneeded assets.

Exhibit 2–3   Creating a Cash Flow Statement

<table>
<tr><td></td><td colspan="4" align="center">**Kim Walker**
Cash Flow Statement for the Month Ended September 30, 2011</td></tr>
<tr><td></td><td colspan="4" align="center">**Income (cash inflows)**</td></tr>
</table>

Step 1

For a set time period (such as a month), record your income from various sources, such as wages, salary, interest, and payments from the government.

Salary (gross)		$4,350	
Less deductions			
Federal income tax	$810		
State income tax	108		
Social Security	332		
Total deductions	$1,250	$3,100	
Interest earned on savings		34	
Earnings from investments		62	
Total income		$3,196	

Cash Outflows

Fixed Expenses

Rent	$1,150	
Loan payment	216	
Cable television	52	
Monthly train ticket	196	
Life insurance	32	
Apartment insurance	23	
Total fixed outflows		$1,669

Step 2

Develop categories and record cash payments for the time period covered by the cash flow statement.

Variable Expenses

Food at home	260	
Food away from home	168	
Clothing	150	
Telephone	52	
Electricity	48	
Personal care (dry cleaning,		
laundry, cosmetics)	66	
Medical expenses	85	
Recreation/entertainment	100	
Gifts	70	
Donations	80	
Total variable outflows	1,079	
Total outflows		$2,748
Cash surplus + (or deficit −)		+$448

Step 3

Subtract the total outflows from the total inflows. A positive number (surplus) represents the amount available for saving and investing. A negative number (deficit) represents the amount that must be taken out of savings or borrowed.

Allocation of Surplus

Emergency fund savings	168
Savings for short-term/intermediate	
financial goals	80
Savings/investing for long-term	
financial security	200
Total surplus	$448

2. *Variable expenses* are flexible payments that change from month to month. Common examples of variable cash outflows are food, clothing, utilities (such as electricity and telephone), recreation, medical expenses, gifts, and donations. The use of a checkbook or some other recordkeeping system is necessary for an accurate total of cash outflows.

STEP 3: DETERMINE NET CASH FLOW The difference between income and outflows can be either a positive (*surplus*) or a negative (*deficit*) cash flow. A deficit exists if more cash goes out than comes in during a given month. This amount must be made up by withdrawals from savings or by borrowing.

When you have a cash surplus, as Kim did (Exhibit 2–3), this amount is available for saving, investing, or paying off debts. Each month, Kim sets aside money for her *emergency fund* in a savings account that she would use for unexpected expenses or to pay living costs if she did not receive her salary. She deposits the rest of the surplus in savings and investment plans that have two purposes. The first is the achievement of short-term and intermediate financial goals, such as a new car, a vacation, or reenrollment in school; the second is long-term financial security—her retirement. A cash flow statement provides the foundation for preparing and implementing a spending, saving, and investment plan.

Sheet 6 Creating a Personal Balance Sheet

Sheet 7 Creating a Personal Cash Flow Statement

CONCEPT CHECK 2–2

1 What are the main purposes of personal financial statements?

_____

2 What does a personal balance sheet tell you about your financial situation?

_____

3 For the following items, identify each as an asset (A), liability (L), cash inflow (CI), or cash outflow (CO):

_____ monthly rent   _____ automobile loan

_____ interest on savings account   _____ collection of rare coins

_____ retirement account   _____ mortgage amount

_____ electric bill   _____ market value of automobile

4 Jan Franks has liquid assets of $6,300 and monthly expenses of $2,100. Based on the liquidity ratio, she has _____ months in which living expenses could be paid if an emergency arises.

Apply Yourself!

Objective 2

Use the Web or library research to obtain information about the assets commonly held by households in the United States. How have the values of assets, liabilities, and net worth of U.S. consumers changed in recent years?

A Plan for Effective Budgeting

A **budget**, or *spending plan,* is necessary for successful financial planning. The common financial problems of overusing credit, lacking a regular savings program, and failing to ensure future financial security can be minimized through budgeting. The main purposes of a budget are to help you live within your income, spend your money wisely, reach your financial goals, prepare for financial emergencies, and develop wise financial management habits. Budgeting may be viewed in seven main steps.

Step 1: Set Financial Goals

Future plans are an important dimension for deciding your financial direction. Financial goals are plans for activities that require you to plan your spending, saving, and investing. As discussed in Chapter 1 , financial goals should (1) be realistic; (2) be

> **OBJECTIVE 3**
>
> Develop and implement a personal budget.

budget A specific plan for spending income; also called a *spending plan.*

Exhibit **2–4** Common Financial Goals

Personal Situation	Short-Term Goals (less than 2 years)	Intermediate Goals (2–5 years)	Long-Term Goals (over 5 years)
Single person	• Complete college • Pay off auto loan	• Take a vacation to Europe • Pay off education loan • Attend graduate school	• Buy a vacation home in the mountains • Provide for retirement income
Married couple (no children)	• Take an annual vacation • Buy a new car	• Remodel home • Build a stock portfolio	• Buy a retirement home • Provide for retirement income
Parent (young children)	• Increase life insurance • Increase savings	• Increase investments • Buy a new car	• Accumulate a college fund for children • Move to a larger home

stated in measurable terms; (3) have a definite time frame; and (4) imply the type of action to be taken. Exhibit 2–4 gives examples of common financial goals based on life situation and time.

Step 2: Estimate Income

As Exhibit 2–5 shows, after setting goals, you need to estimate available money for a given time period. A common budgeting period is a month, since many payments, such as rent or mortgage, utilities, and credit cards, are due each month. In determining available income, include only money that you are sure you'll receive. Bonuses, gifts, or unexpected income should not be considered until the money is actually received.

Budgeting income may be difficult if your earnings vary by season or your income is irregular, as with sales commissions. In these situations, estimate your income on the low side to help avoid overspending and other financial difficulties.

Step 3: Budget an Emergency Fund and Savings

To set aside money for unexpected expenses as well as future financial security, the Robinsons have budgeted several amounts for savings and investments (see Exhibit 2–5). Financial advisers suggest that an emergency fund representing three to six months of living expenses be established for use in periods of unexpected financial difficulty. This amount will vary based on a person's life situation and employment stability.

The Robinsons also set aside an amount each month for their automobile insurance payment, which is due every six months. Both this amount and the emergency fund are put into a savings account.

A frequent budgeting mistake is to save the amount you have left at the end of the month. When you do that, you often have *nothing* left for savings. Since saving is vital for long-term financial security, remember to always "pay yourself first."

did you know?

According to Lynnette Khalfani (www.themoneycoach.net), LIFE is the major budget buster:

L is "Listed" expenses (housing, utilities, food, clothing) that are underestimated.

I involves "Impulse buying," whether in stores or online.

F are "Forgotten" bills, such as annual insurance payments.

E are "Emergencies," such as unexpected auto or home repairs.

Exhibit 2–5 Developing a Monthly Budget

Step 1
Set financial goals.

Step 2
Estimate expected income from all sources; this amount is to be allocated among various outflow categories.

Step 3
Budget amount for an emergency fund, periodic expenses, and financial goals.

Step 4
Budget set amounts that you are obligated to pay.

Step 5
Budget estimated amounts to be spent for various household and living expenses.

Step 6
Record actual amounts for inflows and outflows. Compare actual amounts with budgeted amounts to determine variances.

Step 7
Evaluate whether revisions are needed in your spending and savings plan.

Monthly Budget for the Robinson Family

Financial goals

	Budgeted Amounts (dollars)	(percent)	Actual Amounts	Variance
Projected Inflows (income)				
Salary	2874	100	2874	—
Projected Outflows (disbursements)				
Emergency Fund and Savings:				
Emergency fund savings	115	4	115	—
Savings for auto insurance	29	1	29	—
Savings for vacation	57	2	57	—
Savings for investments	57	2	57	—
Total savings	258	9	258	—
Fixed Expenses				
Mortgage payment	518	18	518	—
Property taxes	115	4	115	—
Auto loan payment	144	5	144	—
Life insurance	29	1	29	—
Total fixed expenses	806	28	806	—
Variable expenses				
Food	402	14	417	−15
Utilities (telephone, heat, electric, water)	172	6	164	+8
Clothing	116	4	93	+23
Transportation (automobile operation, repairs, public transportation)	460	16	471	−11
Personal and health care	172	6	163	+9
Entertainment	172	6	201	−29
Reading, education	86	3	78	+8
Gifts, donations	144	5	150	−6
Personal allowances, miscellaneous expenses	86	3	90	−4
Total variable expenses	1810	63	1827	−17
Total outflow	2874	100	2891	−17

Step 4: Budget Fixed Expenses

Definite obligations make up this portion of a budget. As Exhibit 2–5 shows, the Robinsons have fixed expenses for housing, taxes, and loan payments. They make a monthly payment of $29 for life insurance. The budgeted total for their fixed expenses is $806, or 28 percent of estimated available income.

Assigning amounts to spending categories requires careful consideration. The amount you budget for various items will depend on your current needs and plans for the future. Exhibit 2–6 suggests budget allocations for different life situations. Although this information can be of value when creating budget categories, maintaining a detailed record of your spending for several months is a better source for your personal situation. However, don't become discouraged. Use a simple system, such as a notebook or your checkbook. This "spending diary" will help you know where your money is going.

Step 5: Budget Variable Expenses

Planning for variable expenses is not as easy as budgeting for savings or fixed expenses. Variable expenses will fluctuate by household situation, time of year, health, economic conditions, and a variety of other factors. A major portion of the Robinsons' planned spending—over 60 percent of their budgeted income—is for variable living

Exhibit 2–6 Typical After-Tax Budget Allocations

Budget Category	Student	Working Single (no dependents)	Couple (children under 18)	Single Parent (young children)	Parents (children over 18 in college)	Couple (over 55, no dependent children)
Housing (rent or mortgage payment; utilities; furnishings and appliances)	0–25%	30–35%	25–35%	20–30%	25–30%	25–35%
Transportation	5–10	15–20	15–20	10–18	12–18	10–18
Food (at home and away from home)	15–20	15–25	15–25	13–20	15–20	18–25
Clothing	5–12	5–15	5–10	5–10	4–8	4–8
Personal and health care (including child care)	3–5	3–5	4–10	8–12	4–6	6–12
Entertainment and recreation	5–10	5–10	4–8	4–8	6–10	5–8
Reading and education	10–30	2–4	3–5	3–5	6–12	2–4
Personal insurance and pension payments	0–5	4–8	5–9	5–9	4–7	6–8
Gifts, donations, and contributions	4–6	5–8	3–5	3–5	4–8	3–5
Savings	0–10	4–15	5–10	5–8	2–4	3–5

SOURCES: Bureau of Labor Statistics (http://stats.bls.gov); *American Demographics; Money; The Wall Street Journal.*

costs. They base their estimates on past spending as well as expected changes in their cost of living.

Step 6: Record Spending Amounts

After having established a spending plan, you will need to keep track of your actual income and expenses. This process is similar to preparing a cash flow statement. In Exhibit 2–5, notice that the Robinsons estimated specific amounts for income and expenses. These are presented under "Budgeted Amounts." The family's actual spending was not always the same as planned. A **budget variance** is the difference between the amount budgeted and the actual amount received or spent. The total variance for the Robinsons was a $17 **deficit,** since their actual spending exceeded their planned spending by this amount. They would have had a **surplus** if their actual spending had been less than they had planned.

Variances for income should be viewed as the opposite of variances for expenses. Less income than expected would be a deficit, whereas more income than expected would be a surplus. Spending more than planned for an item may be justified by reducing spending for another item or putting less into savings. However, revising your budget and financial goals may be necessary.

budget variance The difference between the amount budgeted and the actual amount received or spent.

deficit The amount by which actual spending exceeds planned spending.

surplus The amount by which actual spending is less than planned spending.

Step 7: Review Spending and Saving Patterns

Like most decision-making activities, budgeting is a circular, ongoing process. You will need to review and perhaps revise your spending plan on a regular basis.

REVIEW YOUR FINANCIAL PROGRESS The results of your budget may be obvious: having extra cash in checking or falling behind in your bill payments. However, such obvious results may not always be present. Occasionally, you will have to review areas where spending has been more or less than expected. You can prepare an annual summary to compare actual spending with budgeted amounts for each month. A spreadsheet program can be useful for this purpose. This summary will help you see areas where changes in your budget may be necessary. This review process is vital to both successful short-term money management and long-term financial security.

REVISE YOUR GOALS AND BUDGET ALLOCATIONS What should you cut first when a budget shortage occurs? This question doesn't have easy answers, and answers will vary for different households. The most common overspending areas are entertainment and food, especially away-from-home meals. Purchasing less expensive brand items, buying quality used products, and avoiding credit card purchases are common budget adjustment techniques. When household budgets must be cut, spending is most frequently reduced for vacations, dining out, cleaning and lawn *services, cable/Internet service, and charitable* donations.

At this point in the budgeting process, you may also revise your financial goals. Are you making progress toward achieving your objectives? Have changes in personal or economic conditions affected the desirability of certain goals? Have new goals surfaced that should be given a higher priority? Addressing these issues while creating an effective saving method will help ensure accomplishment of your financial goals.

did you know?

Most households can have an additional $500 or more a month available by not receiving a tax refund, by cutting insurance costs, by wiser food shopping, by using less energy, by having a less expensive phone and cable plan, and by not being in debt.

Personal Finance in Practice

> Selecting a Budgeting System

Although your checkbook will give you a fairly complete record of your expenses, it does not serve the purpose of planning for spending. A budget requires that you outline how you will spend available income. Described below are various budgeting systems. For each, list a benefit and concern of this method, and explain who might use this system.

Type of budgeting system	What are the benefits? What are the concerns?	Who might use this system?
A *mental budget* exists only in a person's mind. This simple system may be appropriate if you have limited resources and minimal financial responsibilities.		
A *physical budget* involves envelopes, folders, or containers to hold the money or slips of paper. Envelopes would contain the amount of cash or a note listing the amount to be used for "Food," "Rent," "Auto Payment," and other expenses.		
A *written budget* can be kept on notebook paper or on specialized budgeting paper available in office supply stores.		
Computerized budgeting systems use a spread-sheet program or specialized software such as Microsoft Money (www.msn.com/money) or Quicken (www.quicken.com).		

What would you do? Describe your current budgeting system. Are there any recordkeeping activities you might do differently?

CHARACTERISTICS OF SUCCESSFUL BUDGETING Having a spending plan will not eliminate financial worries. A budget will work only if you follow it. Changes in income, living expenses, and goals will require changes in your spending plan. Successful budgets are commonly viewed as being:

- *Well planned.* A good budget takes time and effort to prepare and should involve everyone affected by it.
- *Realistic.* If you have a moderate income, don't immediately expect to save enough money for an expensive car. A budget is designed not to prevent you from enjoying life but to help you achieve what you want most.
- *Flexible.* Unexpected expenses and life situation changes will require a budget that you can easily revise.
- *Clearly communicated.* Unless you and others involved are aware of the spending plan, it will not work. The budget should be written and available to all household members.

Sheet 8 Developing a Personal Budget

CONCEPT CHECK 2–3

1 What are the main purposes of a budget?

_____

_____

2 How does a person's life situation affect goal setting and amounts allocated for various budget categories?

_____

_____

3 For each of the following household expenses, indicate if the item is a FIXED or a VARIABLE expense.

_____ food away from home   _____ cable television

_____ rent   _____ electricity

_____ health insurance premium   _____ auto repairs

4 The Nollin family has budgeted expenses for a month of $4,560 and actual spending of $4,480. This would result in a budget SURPLUS or DEFICIT (circle one) of $_____.

Apply Yourself!

Objective 3

Ask two or three friends or relatives about their budgeting systems. Obtain information on how they maintain their spending records. Create a visual presentation (video or slide presentation) that communicates wise budgeting techniques.

Money Management and Achieving Financial Goals

Your personal financial statements and budget allow you to achieve your financial goals with

1. Your balance sheet: reporting your current financial position—where you are now.
2. Your cash flow statement: telling you what you received and spent over the past month.
3. Your budget: planning spending and saving to achieve financial goals.

Many people prepare a balance sheet on a periodic basis, such as every three or six months. Between those points in time, your budget and cash flow statement help you plan and measure spending and saving activities. For example, you might prepare a balance sheet on January 1, June 30, and December 31. Your budget would serve to

> **OBJECTIVE 4**
>
> Connect money management activities with saving for personal financial goals.

INTERVIEW | *Professor Michael Sherraden is director of the Center for Social Development at Washington University in St. Louis. He'd like every baby in the U.S. to get a tax-advantaged savings account, seeded by Uncle Sam, an idea that has bipartisan support in Congress.*

SAVINGS ACCOUNTS **FROM** DAY ONE
A Social Scientist Says We'll Have A Stronger Middle Class When We Give Savings Accounts To Babies

How would your savings plan work? I think there should be a lifelong system of accounts for everybody to save for important life goals—post-secondary education, homeownership, additional job training. Eventually, money in the accounts would provide retirement security. There's a strong rationale for making the accounts progressive, with low-income kids getting a slightly larger initial deposit because most of the tax benefits of college and retirement-savings plans now go to upper- and middle-income families. One bill in Congress calls for $500 for all children and an additional $500 for the poorest.

Where would the money come from? There are four million babies born every year. In an annual federal budget of $3 trillion, even at a cost of $4 billion, I wouldn't call it a large sum.

And who would manage it? The savings plans would be offered by the major asset managers. Good plan features would be simple investment options and low costs.

Will these accounts turn us into a nation of savers? There's at least some encouragement for everyone to save. Family members would get tax benefits for making additional deposits, although there would be caps on tax-deductible contributions. As with some trial programs already under way, matching funds could come from the government, charities or more-creative sources. For example, a corporation might want to "adopt" kids in a particular school district, matching their savings.

Even with compound interest, would these accounts generate enough to make a dent in college or retirement costs? For now, I'm focused on post-secondary education, which has a huge impact on lifetime earnings. Having $10,000 to $15,000 in an account for college

would have an impact on tens of millions of young people.

Will the recent market downturn diminish the accounts' appeal? If I paid attention to bear markets, I'd be distracted. I don't know whether we'll have accounts this year, but 10 to 15 years from now, we'll have an account for every child.

SOURCE: Reprinted by permission from the June issue of *Kiplinger's Personal Finance*. Copyright © 2008 The Kiplinger Washington Editors, Inc.

1. What are the benefits of this proposed savings plan for individual and society?

_____

2. Describe possible objections to this program.

_____

3. How would you modify this proposed savings program to better achieve the desired goals?

_____

plan your spending and saving between these points in time, and your cash flow statement of income and outflows would document your actual spending and saving. This relationship may be illustrated in this way:

Changes in your net worth result from cash inflows and outflows. In periods when your outflows exceed your inflows, you must draw on savings or borrow (buy on credit). When this happens, lower assets (savings) or higher liabilities (due to the use of credit) result in a lower net worth. When inflows exceed outflows, putting money into savings or paying off debts will result in a higher net worth.

Selecting a Saving Technique

Traditionally, the United States ranks low among industrial nations in savings rate. Low savings affect personal financial situations. Studies reveal that the majority of Americans do not set aside an adequate amount for emergencies.

Since most people find saving difficult, financial advisers suggest these methods to make it easier:

1. Write a check each payday and deposit it in a savings account not readily available for regular spending. This savings deposit can be a percentage of income, such as 5 or 10 percent, or a specific dollar amount.
2. *Payroll deduction* is available at many places of employment. Under a *direct deposit* system, an amount is automatically deducted from your salary and deposited in savings.
3. Saving coins or spending less on certain items can help you save. Each day, put your change in a container. You can also increase your savings by taking a sandwich to work instead of buying lunch or by refraining from buying snacks or magazines.

did you know?

For years, co-workers were amused by a woman who carried a brown bag to lunch each day. That woman later retired in financial comfort and lived her later years in beachfront property. A daily coffee and muffin can add up to over $1,300 a year.

How you save is far less important than making regular periodic savings deposits that will help you achieve financial goals. Small amounts of savings can grow faster than most people realize.

Calculating Savings Amounts

To achieve your financial objectives, you should convert your savings goals into specific amounts. Your use of a savings or investment plan is vital to the growth of your money. As Exhibit 2–7 shows, using the time value of money calculations, introduced in Chapter 1 , can help you calculate progress toward achieving your financial goals.

Exhibit 2–7

Using Savings to Achieve Financial Goals

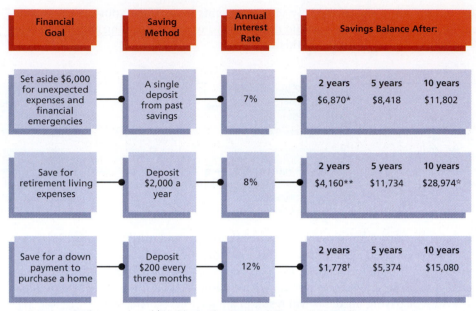

Financial Goal	Saving Method	Annual Interest Rate	Savings Balance After:		
			2 years	**5 years**	**10 years**
Set aside $6,000 for unexpected expenses and financial emergencies	A single deposit from past savings	7%	$6,870*	$8,418	$11,802
Save for retirement living expenses	Deposit $2,000 a year	8%	$4,160**	$11,734	$28,974☆
Save for a down payment to purchase a home	Deposit $200 every three months	12%	$1,778†	$5,374	$15,080

* Based on the future value of $1 tables in Chapter 1 and Chapter 1 Appendix.
** Based on the future value of a series of deposits tables in Chapter 1 and Chapter 1 Appendix.
☆ With annual $2,000 deposits, this same retirement account would grow to over $500,000 in 40 years.
† Based on quarterly compounding, explained in Chapter 4.

CONCEPT CHECK 2–4

1 What relationship exists among personal financial statements, budgeting, and achieving financial goals?

_____

2 What are some suggested methods to make saving easy?

_____

3 If you wanted to obtain the following types of information, check the box for the document that you would find most useful.

Financial information needed	Balance sheet	Cash flow statement	Budget
Amounts owed for medical expenses			
Spending patterns for the past few months			
Planned spending patterns for the next month			
Current value of investment accounts			
Amounts to deposit in savings accounts			

Apply Yourself!

Objective 4

Interview a young single person, a young couple, and a middle-aged person about their financial goals and savings habits. What actions do they take to determine and achieve various financial goals?

Back to … Getting Personal

Reconsider your responses to the "Getting Personal" questions at the beginning of the chapter. For more effective money management and budgeting:

- Develop a recordkeeping system for your financial documents as shown in Exhibit 2–1 on page 48.
- Prepare a balance sheet and a cash flow statement on a regular basis to monitor your financial situation and progress (see pages 49–54).
- Consider using online budgeting programs for your money management activities. Several are available. Use a Web search to locate one that fits your needs.

- Develop a regular savings plan to set aside some amount each week. Start small … but save something. For savings ideas go to www.americasaves.org or www.choosetosave.org.

What did you learn in this chapter that could help you with your daily money management actions?

Chapter Summary

Objective 1   Successful money management requires a coordination of personal financial records, personal financial statements, and budgeting activities. An organized system of financial records and documents should provide ease of access as well as security for financial documents that may be impossible to replace.

Objective 2   A personal balance sheet, also known as a *net worth statement,* is prepared by listing all items of value (assets) and all amounts owed to others (liabilities). The difference between your total assets and your total liabilities is your net worth. A cash flow statement, also called a *personal income and expenditure statement,* is a summary of cash receipts and payments for a given period, such as a month or a year.

Objective 3   The budgeting process consists of seven steps: (1) set financial goals; (2) estimate income; (3) budget an emergency fund and savings; (4) budget fixed expenses; (5) budget variable expenses; (6) record spending amounts; and (7) review spending and saving patterns.

Objective 4   The relationship among the personal balance sheet, cash flow statement, and budget provides the basis for achieving long-term financial security. Future value and present value calculations may be used to compute the increased value of savings for achieving financial goals.

Key Terms

assets 50
balance sheet 49
budget 55
budget variance 59
cash flow 52
cash flow statement 53
current liabilities 51

deficit 59
discretionary income 53
income 53
insolvency 51
liabilities 51
liquid assets 50
long-term liabilities 51

money management 45
net worth 51
safe deposit box 47
surplus 59
take-home pay 53

Key Formulas

Page	Topic	Formula
51	Net worth	Net worth = Total assets − Total liabilities *Example:* = $125,000 − $53,000 = $72,000
52	Debt ratio	Debt ratio = Liabilities/Net worth *Example:* = $7,000/$21,000 = 0.33
52	Current ratio	Current ratio = Liquid assets/Current liabilities *Example:* = $8,500/$4,500 = 1.88
52	Liquidity ratio	Liquidity ratio = Liquid assets/Monthly expenses *Example:* = $8,500/$3,500 = 2.4
52	Debt-payments ratio	Debt-payments ratio = Monthly credit payments/Take-home pay *Example:* = $760/$3,800 = 0.20
52	Savings ratio	Savings ratio = Amount saved per month/Gross monthly income *Example:* = $460/$3,800 = 0.12
54	Cash surplus (or deficit)	Cash surplus (or deficit) = Total inflows − Total outflows *Example:* = $5,600 − $4,970 = $630 (surplus)

Self-Test Problems

1. The Hamilton household has $145,000 is assets and $63,000 in liabilities. What is the family's net worth?
2. Harold Daley budgeted $210 for food for the month of July. He spent $227 on food during July. Does he have a budget surplus or deficit, and what amount?

Self-Test Solutions

1. Net worth is computed determined by assets ($145,000) minus liabilities ($63,000) resulting in $82,000.
2. The budget *deficit* of $17 is calculated by subtracting the actual spending ($227) from the budgeted amount ($210).

Problems

1. Based on the following data, determine the amount of total assets, total liabilities, and net worth. (Obj. 2)

Liquid assets, $3,670   Investment assets, $8,340
Current liabilities, $2,670   Household assets, $89,890
Long-term liabilities, $76,230

a. Total assets $_____

b. Total liabilities $_____

c. Net worth $_____

2. Using the following balance sheet items and amounts, calculate the total liquid assets and total current liabilities: (Obj 2)

Money market account $2,600   Medical bills $232

Mortgage $158,000   Checking account $780

Retirement account $86,700   Credit card balance $489

a. Total liquid assets $_____

b. Total current liabilities $_____

3. Use the following items to determine the total assets, total liabilities, net worth, total cash inflows, and total cash outflows.   (Obj 2)

Rent for the month, $650   Monthly take-home salary, $1,950

Spending for food, $345   Cash in checking account, $450

Savings account balance, $1,890   Balance of educational loan, $2,160

Current value of automobile, $7,800   Telephone bill paid for month, $65

Credit card balance, $235   Loan payment, $80

Auto insurance, $230   Household possessions, $3,400

Stereo equipment, $2,350   Payment for electricity, $90

Lunches/parking at work, $180   Donations, $70

Home computer, $1,500   Value of stock investment, $860

Clothing purchase, $110   Restaurant spending, $130

a. Total assets $_____

b. Total liabilities $_____

c. Net worth $_____

d. Total cash inflows $_____

e. Total cash outflows $_____

4. For each of the following situations, compute the missing amount.   (Obj. 2)

a. Assets $45,000; liabilities $16,000; net worth $_____

b. Assets $76,500; liabilities $_____; net worth $18,700

c. Assets $34,280; liabilities $12,965; net worth $_____

d. Assets $_____; liabilities $38,345; net worth $52,654

5. Based on this financial data, calculate the ratios requested: (Obj. 2)

Liabilities, $8,000   Net worth, $58,000

Liquid assets, $4,600   Current liabilities, $1,300

Monthly credit payments, $640   Take-home pay, $2,600

Monthly savings, $130   Gross income, $2,850

a. Debt ratio _____

b. Current ratio _____

c. Debt-payments ratio _____

d. Savings ratio _____

6. The Fram family has liabilities of $128,000 and a net worth of $340,000. What is the debt ratio? How would you assess this?   (Obj. 2)

7. Carl Lester has liquid assets of $2,680 and current liabilities of $2,436. What is his current ratio? What comments do you have about this financial position?   (Obj. 2)

8. For the following situations, calculate the cash surplus or deficit: (Obj. 2)

Cash inflows	Cash Outflows	Difference (surplus or deficit)
$3,400	$3,218	$_____ _____
4,756	4,833	$_____ _____
4,287	4,218	$_____ _____

9. The Brandon household has a monthly income of $5,630 on which to base their budget. They plan to save 10 percent and spend 32 percent on fixed expenses and 56 percent on variable expenses. (Obj. 3)

a. What amount do they plan to set aside for each major budget section?

Savings	$_____
Fixed expenses	$_____
Variable expenses	$_____

b. After setting aside these amounts, what amount would remain for additional savings or for paying off debts?

10. Fran Powers created the following budget and reported the actual spending listed. Calculate the variance for each of these categories, and indicate whether it was a *deficit* or a *surplus*. (Obj. 3)

Item	Budgeted	Actual	Variance	Deficit/Surplus
Food	$350	$298	_____	_____
Transportation	320	337	_____	_____
Housing	950	982	_____	_____
Clothing	100	134	_____	_____
Personal	275	231	_____	_____

11. Ed Weston recently lost his job. Before unemployment occurred, the Weston household (Ed; wife, Alice; two children, ages 12 and 9) had a monthly take-home income of $3,165. Each month, the money went for the following items: $880 for rent, $180 for utilities, $560 for food, $480 for automobile expenses, $300 for clothing, $280 for insurance, $250 for savings, and $235 for personal and other items. After the loss of Ed's job, the household's monthly income is $1,550, from his wife's wages and his unemployment benefits. The Westons also have savings accounts, investments, and retirement funds of $28,000. (Obj. 3)

a. What budget items might the Westons consider reducing to cope with their financial difficulties?
b. How should the Westons use their savings and retirement funds during this financial crisis? What additional sources of funds might be available to them during this period of unemployment?

12. Use future value and present value calculations (see tables in the appendix for Chapter 1) to determine the following: (Obj. 4)

a. The future value of a $500 savings deposit after eight years at an annual interest rate of 7 percent.
b. The future value of saving $1,500 a year for five years at an annual interest rate of 8 percent.
c. The present value of a $2,000 savings account that will earn 6 percent interest for four years.

13. Brenda plans to reduce her spending by $50 a month. What would be the future value of this reduced saving over the next 10 years? (Assume an annual deposit to her savings account, and an annual interest rate of 5 percent.) (Obj. 4)

14. Kara George received a $10,000 gift for graduation for her uncle. If she deposits this in a account paying 4 percent, what will be the value of this gift in 15 years? (Obj. 4)

Questions

1. Describe some common money management mistakes that can cause long-term financial concerns.

2. What do you believe to be the major characteristics of an effective system to keep track of financial documents and records?

3. How might financial ratios be used when planning and implementing financial activities?

4. Discuss with several people how a budget might be changed if a household faced a decline in income. What spending areas might be reduced first?

5. What are long-term effects of low savings for both individuals and the economy of a country?

Case in Point

A LITTLE BECOMES A LOT

Can you imagine saving 25 cents a week and having it grow to more than $30,000?

As hard as that may be to believe, that's exactly what Ken Lopez was able to do. Putting aside a quarter a week starting in second grade, he built up a small savings account. These funds were then invested in various stocks and mutual funds. While in college, Ken was able to pay for his education while continuing to save between $50 and $100 a month. He closely monitored spending. Ken realized that the few dollars here and there for snacks and other minor purchases quickly add up.

Today, at age 27, Ken works as a customer service manager for an online sales division of a retailing company. He lives with his wife, Alicia, and their two young children. The family's spending plan allows for all their needs and also includes regularly saving and investing for the children's education and for retirement. Recently, Ken was asked by a co-worker, Brian, "How come you and Alicia never seem to have financial stress in your household?"

Ken replied, "Do you know where your money is going each month?"

"Not really," was Brian's response.

"You'd be surprised by how much is spent on little things you might do without," Ken responded.

"I guess so, I just don't want to have to go around with a notebook writing down every amount I spend," Brian said in a troubled voice.

"Well, you have to take some action if you want your financial situation to change," Ken said in an encouraging voice.

Brian conceded with, "All right, what would you recommend?"

Questions

1. What money management behaviors did Ken practice that most people neglect?
2. Based on information at www.kiplinger.com, www.money. com, or www.asec.org, describe money management and financial planning advice that would be appropriate for Brian.
3. What additional goals might be appropriate for Ken, Alicia, and their children?

Continuing Case

Vikki Rococo (age 22) is living with her parents for one year while she begins to pay off her student loans and prepares to move into her own apartment. She has been working at a local company processing 401(k) plan benefits, and her manager just sent her to a training course called "Year-End—What you need to know for your clients." The training emphasized the importance of keeping information organized so that reports can be created and accessed quickly. Vikki finds the session valuable and decides that she really should improve the organization of her own financial files at home. To her dismay, she realizes that she has much more work to do than she originally thought. Her pay stubs, credit card statements, receipts, 401(k) statements, and a bunch of other work benefit envelopes and files had all been thrown together into a shoebox on the floor of her closet. She admits that she needs a much better system.

Vikki's financial statistics are shown below

Assets	Liabilities	Income
Checking account $3,500	Student loan $14,000	Gross annual salary $40,000
Car $7,500	Credit card balance $1,850	(before taxes)
401(k) balance $2,500		$2,333 monthly pay after-taxes

Monthly Expenses
Rent $200
Food $100
Student loan $250

Liabilities(continued)
Car loan $200
Credit card payments $40
Entertainment $100
Gas/repairs $150

Retirement savings
401(k) $500 per month, plus 50% employer match on the first 7% of pay

Questions

1. What recommendations do you have for Vikki's recordkeeping system?
2. What expenses should she include in her budget if she moves out?
3. How much should she have in an emergency fund? What steps should she take to reach this amount?
4. How can she use *Your Personal Financial Plan* sheets 5–8?

Spending Diary

"I AM AMAZED HOW LITTLE THINGS CAN ADD UP . . . HOWEVER, SINCE KEEPING TRACK OF ALL MY SPENDING, I REALIZE THAT I NEED TO CUT DOWN ON SOME ITEMS SO I CAN PUT SOME MONEY AWAY INTO SAVINGS."

Directions

Continue or start using the Daily Spending Diary sheets provided at the end of the book, or create your own format, to record *every cent* of your spending in the categories provided. This experience will help you better understand your spending patterns and help you plan for achieving financial goals. The Daily Spending Diary sheets are located in Appendix C at the end of the book and on the student Web site, www.mhhe.com/kdh.

Questions

1. What information from your daily spending diary might encourage you to reconsider various money management actions?

2. How can your daily spending diary assist you when planning and implementing a budget?

Financial Documents and Records

Financial Planning Activities: Indicate the location of the following records, and create files for the eight major categories of financial documents.

Suggested Web Sites: www.money.com www.kiplinger.com

Item	Home file	Safe deposit box	Other (specify)
1. *Money management records*			
• budget, financial statements			
2. Personal/employment records			
• current résumé, social security card			
• educational transcripts			
• birth, marriage, divorce certificates			
• citizenship, military papers			
• adoption, custody papers			
3. *Tax records*			
4. Financial services/consumer credit records			
• unused, canceled checks			
• savings, passbook statements			
• savings certificates			
• credit card information, statements			
• credit contracts			
5. Consumer purchase, housing, and automobile records			
• warranties, receipts			
• owner's manuals			
• lease or mortgage papers, title deed, property tax info			
• automobile title			
• auto registration			
• auto service records			
6. *Insurance records*			
• insurance policies			
• home inventory			
• medical information (health history)			
7. *Investment records*			
• broker statements			
• dividend reports			
• stock/bond certificates			
• rare coins, stamps, and collectibles			
8. Estate planning and retirement			
• will			
• pension, social security info			

What's Next for Your Personal Financial Plan?

- Select a location or computer program for storing your financial documents and records.
- Decide if various documents may no longer be needed.

5

Your Personal Financial Plan

Name: _____   Date: _____

Creating a Personal Balance Sheet

Financial Planning Activities: List current values of the assets; amounts owed for liabilities; subtract total liabilities from total assets to determine net worth.

Suggested Web Sites: www.kiplinger.com   www.money.com

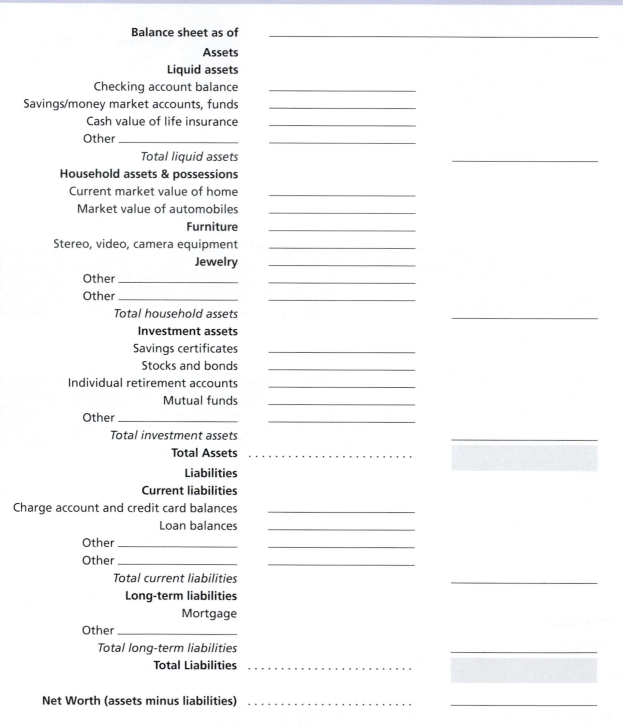

Balance sheet as of	_____	
Assets		
Liquid assets		
Checking account balance	_____	
Savings/money market accounts, funds	_____	
Cash value of life insurance	_____	
Other _____	_____	
Total liquid assets		_____
Household assets & possessions		
Current market value of home	_____	
Market value of automobiles	_____	
Furniture	_____	
Stereo, video, camera equipment	_____	
Jewelry	_____	
Other _____	_____	
Other _____	_____	
Total household assets		_____
Investment assets		
Savings certificates	_____	
Stocks and bonds	_____	
Individual retirement accounts	_____	
Mutual funds	_____	
Other _____	_____	
Total investment assets		_____
Total Assets		
Liabilities		
Current liabilities		
Charge account and credit card balances	_____	
Loan balances	_____	
Other _____	_____	
Other _____	_____	
Total current liabilities		_____
Long-term liabilities		
Mortgage	_____	
Other _____		
Total long-term liabilities		_____
Total Liabilities		
Net Worth (assets minus liabilities)		_____

What's Next for Your Personal Financial Plan?

- Compare your net worth to previous balance sheets.
- Decide how often you will prepare a balance sheet.

Creating a Personal Cash Flow Statement

Financial Planning Activities: Record inflows and outflows of cash for a one- (or three-) month period.

Suggested Web Sites: www.americasaves.org   www.money.com

For month ending _____

Cash Inflows
Salary (take-home)   _____
Other income: _____
Other income: _____
Total Income . . . .   _____

Cash Outflows
Fixed expenses
Mortgage or rent   _____
Loan payments   _____
Insurance   _____
Other _____   _____
Other _____   _____
Total fixed outflows . . . .   _____
Variable expenses   _____
Food   _____
Clothing   _____
Electricity   _____
Telephone   _____
Water   _____
Transportation   _____
Personal care   _____
Medical expenses   _____
Recreation/entertainment   _____
Gifts   _____
Donations   _____
Other _____   _____
Other _____   _____
Total variable outflows . . . .   _____
Total Outflows . . . .   _____
Surplus/Deficit . . . .   _____

Allocation of surplus
Emergency fund savings   _____
Financial goals savings   _____
Other savings _____   _____

What's Next for Your Personal Financial Plan?

- Decide which areas of spending need to be revised.
- Evaluate your spending patterns for preparation of a budget.

Name: _____   Date: _____

Developing a Personal Budget

Financial Planning Activities: Estimate projected spending based on your cash flow statement, and maintain records for actual spending for these same budget categories.

Suggested Web Sites: www.betterbudgeting.com   www.asec.org

	Budgeted amounts		Actual amounts	Variance
Income	Dollar	Percent		
Salary				
Other _____				
Total income		100%		
Expenses				
Fixed expenses Mortgage or rent				
Property taxes				
Loan payments				
Insurance				
Other _____				
Total fixed expenses				
Emergency fund/savings Emergency fund				
Savings for _____				
Savings for _____				
Total savings				
Variable expenses Food				
Utilities				
Clothing				
Transportation costs				
Personal care				
Medical and health care				
Entertainment				
Education				
Gifts/donations				
Miscellaneous				
Other _____				
Other _____				
Total variable expenses				
Total expenses		100%		

What's Next for Your Personal Financial Plan?

- Evaluate the appropriateness of your budget for your life situation.
- Assess whether your budgeting activities are helping you achieve your financial goals.

3 Taxes in Your Financial Plan

Getting Personal

For each of the following statements, select "agree" or "disagree" to reflect your current behavior regarding these tax planning activities:

	Agree	Disagree
1. My tax records are organized to allow me to easily find needed information.	_____	_____
2. I have an extra amount withheld from my pay to make sure I get a refund every year—instead of having those funds put into my savings.	_____	_____
3. I am able to file my taxes on time each year.	_____	_____
4. My tax returns have never been questioned by the Internal Revenue Service.	_____	_____
5. I stay informed on proposed tax changes being considered related to current economic conditions.	_____	_____

After studying this chapter, you will be asked to reconsider your responses to these items.

Taxes in Your Financial Plan

OBJECTIVE 1

Identify the major taxes paid by people in our society.

Taxes are an everyday financial fact of life. You pay taxes when you get a paycheck or make a purchase. However, most people concern themselves with taxes only immediately before April 15.

Planning Your Tax Strategy

Each year, the Tax Foundation determines how long the average person works to pay taxes. In recent years, "Tax Freedom Day" came in early May. This means that the

Objectives

In this chapter, you will learn to:
1. Identify the major taxes paid by people in our society.
2. Calculate taxable income and the amount owed for federal income tax.
3. Prepare a federal income tax return.
4. Select appropriate tax strategies for various life situations.

Why is this important?

Changing economic and political environments often result in new tax regulations, some of which may be favorable for you while others are not. An important element of tax planning is your refund. Each year, more than 90 million American households receive an average tax refund of over $1,600 for a total of over $144 billion. Invested at 5 percent for a year, these refunds represent about $7.2 billion in lost earnings. By having less withheld and obtaining a smaller refund, you can save and invest these funds for your benefit during the year.

time that elapsed from January 1 until late April represents the portion of the year people work to pay their taxes.

Tax planning starts with knowing current tax laws. Next, maintain complete and appropriate tax records. Then, make purchase and investment decisions that can reduce your tax liability. Your primary goal should be to pay your fair share of taxes while taking advantage of appropriate tax benefits.

Types of Tax

Most people pay taxes in four major categories: taxes on purchases, taxes on property, taxes on wealth, and taxes on earnings.

excise tax A tax imposed on specific goods and services, such as gasoline, cigarettes, alcoholic beverages, tires, and air travel.

estate tax A tax imposed on the value of a person's property at the time of death.

inheritance tax A tax levied on the value of property bequeathed by a deceased person.

TAXES ON PURCHASES You probably pay *sales tax* on many purchases. Many states exempt food and drugs from sales tax to reduce the financial burden on low-income households. In recent years, all but five states (Alaska, Delaware, Montana, New Hampshire, and Oregon) had a general sales tax. An **excise tax** is imposed by the federal and state governments on specific goods and services, such as gasoline, cigarettes, alcoholic beverages, tires, air travel, and telephone service.

TAXES ON PROPERTY *Real estate property tax* is a major source of revenue for local governments. This tax is based on the value of land and buildings. Some areas impose a *personal property tax* on the value of automobiles, boats, furniture, and farm equipment.

TAXES ON WEALTH An **estate tax** is imposed on the value of a person's property at the time of death. This federal tax is based on the fair market value of the deceased person's investments, property, and bank accounts less allowable deductions and other taxes.

Money and property passed on to heirs may be subject to a state tax. An **inheritance tax** is levied on the value of property bequeathed by a deceased person. This tax is paid for the right to acquire the inherited property.

Individuals are allowed to give money or items valued at $13,000 or less in a year to a person without being subject to taxes. Gift amounts greater than $13,000 are subject to federal tax. Amounts given for tuition payments or medical expenses are not subject to gift taxes.

did you know?

According to the Tax Foundation (www.taxfoundation.org), Alaska, New Hampshire, Tennessee, Delaware, and Alabama were the most "tax-friendly" states. In contrast, Maine, New York, Rhode Island, Vermont, and Ohio had the highest taxes as a percentage of income.

TAXES ON EARNINGS The two main taxes on wages and salaries are Social Security and income taxes. The Federal Insurance Contributions Act (FICA) created the Social Security tax to fund the old-age, survivors, and disability insurance portion of the Social Security system and the hospital insurance portion (Medicare).

Income tax is a major financial planning factor for most people. Some workers are subject to federal, state, and local income taxes. Currently, only seven states do not have a state income tax.

Throughout the year, your employer will withhold income tax payments from your paycheck, or you may be required to make estimated tax payments if you own your own business. Both types of payments are only estimates; you may need to pay an additional amount, or you may get a tax refund. The following sections will assist you in preparing your federal income tax return and planning your future tax strategies.

CONCEPT CHECK 3–1

1 What are the four major categories of taxes?

_____

_____

2 For each of the following situations, list the type of tax that is being described.

Financial planning situation	Type of tax
a. A tax on the value of a person's house.	
b. The additional charge for gasoline and air travel.	
c. Payroll deductions for federal government retirement benefits.	
d. Amount owed on property received from a deceased person.	
e. Payroll deductions for a direct tax on earnings.	

Apply Yourself!

Objective 1

Prepare a list of taxes that people commonly encounter in your geographic region.

OBJECTIVE 2

Calculate taxable income and the amount owed for federal income tax.

The Basics of Federal Income Tax

Each year, millions of Americans are required to pay their share of income taxes to the federal government. As shown in Exhibit 3–1, this process involves several steps.

Step 1: Determining Adjusted Gross Income

This process starts with steps to determine **taxable income,** which is the net amount of income, after allowable deductions, on which income tax is computed.

TYPES OF INCOME Most, but not all, income is subject to taxation. Your gross, or total, income can consist of three main components:

1. **Earned income** is usually in the form of wages, salary, commission, fees, tips, or bonuses.
2. **Investment income** (sometimes referred to as *portfolio income*) is money received in the form of dividends, interest, or rent from investments.
3. **Passive income** results from business activities in which you do not actively participate, such as a limited partnership.

Other types of income subject to federal income tax include alimony, awards, lottery winnings, and prizes. For example, cash and prizes won on television game shows are subject to both federal and state taxes.

Total income is also affected by exclusions. An **exclusion** is an amount not included in gross income. For example, the foreign income exclusion allows U.S. citizens working and living in another country to exclude a certain portion ($80,000) of their income from federal income taxes.

Exclusions may also be referred to as **tax-exempt income,** or income that is not subject to tax. For example, interest earned on most state and city bonds is exempt from federal income tax. **Tax-deferred income** is income that will be taxed at a later date.

taxable income The net amount of income, after allowable deductions, on which income tax is computed.

earned income Money received for personal effort, such as wages, salary, commission, fees, tips, or bonuses.

investment income Money received in the form of dividends, interest, or rent from investments; also called *portfolio income.*

passive income Income resulting from business activities in which you do not actively participate.

exclusion An amount not included in gross income.

tax-exempt income Income that is not subject to tax.

tax-deferred income Income that will be taxed at a later date.

Exhibit 3–1 Computing Taxable Income and Your Tax Liability

Step 1: Determining Adjusted Gross Income . . . .

Gross Income
- Wages and salaries
- Profits from business or profession
- Commissions, fees
- Employee awards
- Interest
- Gains or losses on sale of investments
- Alimony
- Royalties
- Dividends
- Property rental
- Pensions
- Tips, bonuses
- Prizes, gambling winnings

Less: Adjustments to income

Equals: Adjusted gross income

Step 2: Computing Taxable Income . . . . . .

Less: Standard deduction and exemptions   . . . . or . . . .   Less: Itemized deductions and exemptions

Equals: Taxable income

Step 3: Calculating Taxes Owed . . . .

Tax based on tax tables or tax schedules

Less: Tax credits

Plus: Other taxes

Equals: Total tax due

adjusted gross income (AGI) Gross income reduced by certain adjustments, such as contributions to an individual retirement account (IRA) and alimony payments.

ADJUSTMENTS TO INCOME **Adjusted gross income (AGI)** is gross income after certain reductions have been made. These reductions, called *adjustments to income,* include contributions to an IRA or a Keogh retirement plan, penalties for early withdrawal of savings, and alimony payments. Adjusted gross income is used as the basis for computing various income tax deductions, such as medical expenses.

Step 2: Computing Taxable Income

DEDUCTIONS A **tax deduction** is an amount subtracted from adjusted gross income to arrive at taxable income. Every taxpayer receives at least the **standard deduction,** a set amount on which no taxes are paid. As of 2008, single people receive a standard deduction of $5,450 (married couples filing jointly receive $10,900). Blind people and individuals 65 and older receive higher standard deductions.

Many people qualify for more than the standard deduction. **Itemized deductions** are expenses a taxpayer is allowed to deduct from adjusted gross income. Common itemized deductions include:

- *Medical and dental expenses*—physician fees, prescription medications, hospital expenses, medical insurance premiums, hearing aids, eyeglasses, and medical travel that has not been reimbursed or paid by others. The amount of this deduction is the medical and dental expenses that exceed 7.5 percent (as of 2009) of adjusted gross income.
- *Taxes*—state and local income tax, real estate property tax, and state or local personal property tax.
- *Interest*—mortgage interest, home equity loan interest, and investment interest expense up to an amount equal to investment income.
- *Contributions*—cash or property donated to qualified charitable organizations. Contribution totals greater than 20 percent of adjusted gross income are subject to limitations.
- *Casualty and theft losses*—financial losses resulting from natural disasters, accidents, or unlawful acts.
- *Moving expenses*—costs incurred for a change in residence associated with a new job that is at least 50 miles farther from your former home than your old main job location.
- *Job-related and other miscellaneous expenses*—unreimbursed job travel, union dues, required continuing education, work clothes or uniforms, investment expenses, tax preparation fees, safe deposit box rental (for storing investment documents), and so on. The total of these expenses must exceed 2 percent of adjusted gross income to qualify as a deduction.

tax deduction An amount subtracted from adjusted gross income to arrive at taxable income.

standard deduction A set amount on which no taxes are paid.

itemized deductions Expenses that can be deducted from adjusted gross income, such as medical expenses, real estate property taxes, home mortgage interest, charitable contributions, casualty losses, and certain work-related expenses.

CAUTION! Each year, taxpayers are deceived with bogus opportunities such as a home-based business to qualify for a "home office" deduction, increased refunds for a "tax consultant" fee, prepayment for prizes you have won, and an offer to obtain a refund of Social Security taxes paid during your lifetime for a "paperwork" fee of $100. Information on these and other tax frauds are available at www.ustreas.gov/tigta.

The standard deduction *or* total itemized deductions, along with the value of your exemptions (see next section), are subtracted from adjusted gross income to obtain your taxable income.

Exhibit **3–2**   A Tax Recordkeeping System

Tax Forms and Tax Filing Information
- Current tax forms and instruction booklets
- Reference books on current tax laws and tax-saving techniques
- Social Security numbers of household members
- Copies of federal tax returns from previous years

Income Records
- W-2 forms reporting salary, wages, and taxes withheld
- W-2P forms reporting pension income
- 1099 forms reporting interest, dividends, and capital gains and losses from savings and investments
- 1099 forms for self-employment income, royalty income, and lump-sum payments from pension or retirement plans

Expense Records
- Receipts for medical, dependent care, charitable donations, and job-related expenses
- Mortgage interest (Form 1098) and other deductible interest
- Business, investment, and rental-property expense documents

Personal Finance in Practice

> Is It Taxable Income? Is It Deductible?

Certain financial benefits individuals receive are not subject to federal income tax. Indicate whether each of the following items would or would not be included in taxable income when you compute your federal income tax.

Indicate whether each of the following items would or would not be deductible when you compute your federal income tax.

Is it taxable income . . . ?	Yes	No
1. Lottery winnings	___	___
2. Child support received	___	___
3. Worker's compensation benefits	___	___
4. Life insurance death benefits	___	___
5. Municipal bond interest earnings	___	___
6. Bartering income	___	___

Is it deductible . . . ?	Yes	No
7. Life insurance premiums	___	___
8. Cosmetic surgery for improved looks	___	___
9. Fees for traffic violations	___	___
10. Mileage for driving to volunteer work	___	___
11. An attorney's fee for preparing a will	___	___
12. Income tax preparation fee	___	___

Note: These taxable income items and deductions are based on the 2009 tax year and may change due to changes in the tax code.

Answers: 1, 6, 10, 12—yes; 2, 3, 4, 5, 7, 8, 9, 11—no.

---

did you know?

The most frequently overlooked tax deductions are state sales taxes, reinvested dividends, out-of-pocket charitable contributions, student loan interest paid by parents, moving expense to take first job, military reservists' travel expenses, child care credit, estate tax on income in respect of a decedent, state tax you paid last spring, refinancing points, and jury pay paid to employer.

exemption A deduction from adjusted gross income for yourself, your spouse, and qualified dependents.

You are required to maintain records to document tax deductions, such as a home filing system (Exhibit 3–2). Canceled checks and receipts serve as proof of payment for deductions such as charitable contributions, medical expenses, and business-related expenses. Travel expenses can be documented in a daily log with records of mileage, tolls, parking fees, and away-from-home costs.

Generally, you should keep tax records for three years from the date you file your return. However, you may be held responsible for providing back documentation up to six years. Records such as past tax returns and housing documents should be kept indefinitely.

EXEMPTIONS An **exemption** is a deduction from adjusted gross income for yourself, your spouse, and qualified dependents. A dependent must not earn more than a set amount unless he or she is under age 19 or is a full-time student under age 24; you must provide more than half of the dependent's support; and the dependent must reside in your home or be a specified relative and must meet certain citizenship requirements. For 2008, taxable income was reduced by $3,500 for each exemption claimed. After deducting the amounts for exemptions, you obtain your taxable income, which is the amount used to determine taxes owed.

Step 3: Calculating Taxes Owed

Your taxable income is the basis for computing the amount of tax owed.

Figure It Out!

> Tax Credits versus Tax Deductions

Many people confuse *tax credits* with *tax deductions.* Is one better than the other? A tax *credit,* such as eligible child care or dependent care expenses, results in a dollar-for-dollar reduction in the amount of taxes owed. A tax *deduction,* such as an itemized deduction in the form of medical expenses, mortgage interest, or charitable contributions, reduces the taxable on which your taxes are based.

Here is how a $100 tax credit compares with a $100 tax deduction:

As your might expect, tax credits are less readily available than tax deductions. To qualify for a $100 child care tax credit, you may have to spend $500 in child care expenses. In some situations, spending on deductible items may be more beneficial than qualifying for a tax credit. A knowledge of tax law and careful financial planning will help you use both tax credits and tax deductions to maximum advantage.

$100 Tax Credit

Reduces your taxes by $100.

$100 Tax Deduction

Reduces your taxable income by $100. The amount of your tax reduction depends on your tax bracket. Your taxes will be reduced by $15 if you are in the 15 percent tax bracket and by $28 if you are in the 28 percent tax bracket.

CALCULATIONS

1. If a person in a 28 percent tax bracket received a $1,000 tax *deduction,* how much would the person's taxes be reduced? $ _____

2. If a person in a 33 percent tax bracket received a $200 tax *credit,* how much would the person's taxes be reduced? $ _____

TAX RATES   Use your taxable income in conjunction with the appropriate tax table or tax schedule. For 2008, the six-rate system for federal income tax was as follows:

Rate on Taxable Income	Single Taxpayers	Married Taxpayers Filing Jointly	Head of Households
10%	Up to $8,025	Up to $16,050	Up to $11,450
15	$8,025–$32,550	$16,050–$65,100	$11,450–$43,650
25	$32,550–$78,850	$65,100–$131,450	$43,650–$112,650
28	$78,850–$164,550	$131,450–$200,300	$112,650–$182,400
33	$164,550–$357,700	$200,300–$357,700	$182,400–$357,700
35	Over $357,700	Over $357,700	Over $357,700

A separate tax rate schedule also exists for married persons who file separate income tax returns.

The 10, 15, 25, 28, and 35 percent rates are referred to as **marginal tax rates.** These rates are used to calculate tax on the last (and next) dollar of taxable income. After deductions and exemptions, a person in the 35 percent tax bracket pays 35 cents in taxes for every dollar of taxable income in that bracket.

marginal tax rate   The rate used to calculate tax on the last (and next) dollar of taxable income.

83

average tax rate Total tax due divided by taxable income.

In contrast, the **average tax rate** is based on the total tax due divided by taxable income. Except for taxpayers in the 10 percent bracket, this rate is less than a person's marginal tax rate. For example, a person with taxable income of $40,000 and a total tax bill of $4,200 would have an average tax rate of 10.5 percent ($4,200 ÷ $40,000).

Taxpayers with high amounts of certain deductions and various types of income may be subject to an additional tax. The *alternative minimum tax (AMT)* is designed to ensure that those who receive tax breaks also pay their fair share of taxes. The AMT was originally designed to prevent those with high incomes from using special tax breaks to pay little in taxes. However, in recent years, this tax is affecting many taxpayers. Some of the tax situations that can result in a person paying the AMT include high levels of deductions for state and local taxes, interest on second mortgages, medical expenses, and other deductions. Other items that can trigger the AMT are incentive stock options, long-term capital gains, and tax-exempt interest. Additional information about the AMT may be obtained at www.irs.gov.

tax credit An amount subtracted directly from the amount of taxes owed.

TAX CREDITS The tax owed may be reduced by a **tax credit,** an amount subtracted directly from the amount of taxes owed. One example of a tax credit is the credit given for child care and dependent care expenses. Another tax credit for low-income workers is the *earned-income credit (EIC),* for working parents with taxable income under a certain amount. Families that do not earn enough to owe federal income taxes are also eligible for the EIC and receive a check for the amount of their credit. A *tax credit* differs from a deduction in that a tax credit has a full dollar effect in lowering taxes, whereas a *deduction* reduces the taxable income on which the tax liability is computed.

Recent tax credits also included:

- Foreign tax credit to avoid double taxation on income taxes paid to another country.
- Retirement tax credit to encourage investment contributions to individual and employer-sponsored retirement plans by low- and middle-income taxpayers.
- Adoption tax credit to cover expenses when adopting a child under age 18.
- Hope Scholarship and Lifetime Learning tax credits to help offset college education expenses.

Step 4: Making Tax Payments

did you know?

Each year more than 90,000 taxpayers do not receive their refunds. The undeliverable checks total over $60 million, an average of more than $600 per check. These refund checks were returned by the post office because it was unable to deliver them. Taxpayers due a refund may contact the IRS at 1-800-829-1040.

You pay federal income taxes through either payroll withholding or estimated tax payments.

WITHHOLDING The pay-as-you-go system requires an employer to deduct federal income tax from your pay. The withheld amount is based on the number of exemptions and the expected deductions claimed. For example, a married person with children would have less withheld than a single person with the same salary, since the married person will owe less tax.

After the end of the year, you will receive a W-2 form, which reports your annual earnings and the amounts deducted for taxes. The difference between the amount withheld and the tax owed is either the additional amount to pay or your refund. Students and low-income individuals may file for exemption from withholding if they paid no federal income tax last year and do not expect to pay any in the current year.

Many taxpayers view an annual tax refund as a "windfall," extra money they count on each year. These taxpayers are forgetting the opportunity cost of withholding excessive amounts. Others view their extra tax withholding as "forced savings." However, a payroll deduction plan for savings could serve the same purpose while also earning interest on your funds.

ESTIMATED PAYMENTS Income from savings, investments, independent contracting, royalties, and pension payments is reported on Form 1099. People who receive such income may be required to make tax payments during the year (April 15, June 15, September 15, and January 15 as the last payment for the previous tax year). These payments are based on an estimate of taxes due at year-end. Underpayment or failure to make estimated payments can result in penalties and interest charges.

Step 5: Watching Deadlines and Avoiding Penalties

Most people are required to file a federal income tax return by April 15. If you are not able to file on time, you can use Form 4868 to obtain an automatic six-month extension.

This extension is for the 1040 form and other documents, but it does not delay your payment liability. You must submit the estimated amount owed along with Form 4868 by April 15. Failure to file on time can result in a penalty for being just one day late. Underpayment of quarterly estimated taxes may require paying interest on the amount you should have paid. Underpayment due to negligence or fraud can result in penalties of 50 to 75 percent.

The good news is that if you claim a refund several months or years late, the IRS will pay you interest. However, refunds must be claimed within three years of filing the return or within two years of paying the tax.

Sheet 9 Federal Income Tax Estimate

CONCEPT CHECK 3–2

1 How does tax-exempt income differ from tax-deferred income?

2 When would you use the standard deduction instead of itemized deductions?

3 What is the difference between your marginal tax rate and your average tax rate?

4 For each of the following, indicate if the item is a *tax deduction* or a *tax credit*.

Check the appropriate box to indicate if this is . . .	a tax deduction or . . .	a tax credit.
a. State personal income taxes paid		
b. Charitable donations		
c. Child care costs		
d. Moving expenses		

OBJECTIVE 3

Prepare a federal income tax return.

Filing Your Federal Income Tax Return

As you prepare to do your taxes, you must first determine whether you are required to file a return. Next, you need to decide which tax form best serves you and if you are required to submit supplementary schedules or forms.

Who Must File?

Every citizen or resident of the United States and every U.S. citizen who is a resident of Puerto Rico is required to file a federal income tax return if his or her income is above a certain amount. The amount is based on the person's *filing status* and other factors such as age. For example, single persons under 65 had to file a return on April 15, 2009 (for tax year 2008) if their gross income exceeded $8,950. If your gross income is less than this amount but taxes were withheld, you should file a return to obtain your refund.

Your filing status is affected by marital status and dependents. The five filing status categories are:

- *Single*—never-married, divorced, or legally separated individuals with no dependents.
- *Married, filing joint return*—combines the spouses' incomes.
- *Married, filing separate returns*—each spouse is responsible for his or her own tax. Under certain conditions, a married couple can benefit from this filing status.
- *Head of household*—an unmarried individual or a surviving spouse who maintains a household (paying for more than half of the costs) for a child or a dependent relative.
- *Qualifying widow or widower*—an individual whose spouse died within the past two years and who has a dependent; this status is limited to two years after the death of the spouse.

In some situations, you may have a choice of filing status. In such cases, compute your taxes under the alternatives to determine the most advantageous filing status.

did you know?

The Internal Revenue Service oversees more than 17,000 pages of laws and regulations with about 500 different tax forms.

Which Tax Form Should You Use?

Although about 400 federal tax forms and schedules exist, you have a choice of three basic forms when filing your income tax (see "Personal Finance in Practice" following). Recently about 20 percent of taxpayers used Form 1040EZ or Form 1040A; about 60 percent

Personal Finance in Practice

FORM 1040EZ

You may use Form 1040EZ if:

- You are single or married filing a joint return, under age 65, and claim no dependents.

- Your income consisted only of wages, salaries, and tips and not more than $1,500 of taxable interest.

- Your taxable income is less than $100,000.

- You do not itemize deductions or claim any adjustments to income or any tax credits.

Form 1040EZ — Income Tax Return for Single and Joint Filers With No Dependents (99) 2008. Department of the Treasury—Internal Revenue Service. OMB No. 1545-0074.

FORM 1040A

This form would be used by people who have less that $100,000 in taxable income from wages, salaries, tips, unemployment compensation, interest, or dividends and use the standard deduction. With Form 1040A, you can also take deductions for individual retirement account (IRA) contributions and a tax credit for child care and dependent care expenses. If you qualify for either Form 1040EZ or Form 1040A, you may wish to use one of them to simplify filing your tax return. You may not want to use either the Form 1040EZ or Form 1040A if Form 1040 allows you to pay less tax.

Form 1040A — U.S. Individual Income Tax Return (99) 2008. Department of the Treasury—Internal Revenue Service. OMB No. 1545-0074.

FORM 1040

Form 1040 is an expanded version of Form 1040A that includes sections for all types of income. You are required to use this form if your income is over $50,000 or if you can be claimed as a dependent on your parents return *and* you had interest or dividends over a set limit.

Form 1040 allows you to itemize your deductions. You can list various allowable expenses (medical costs, home mortgage interest, real estate property taxes) that will reduce taxable income and the amount you owe the government. You should learn about all the possible adjustments to income, deductions, and tax credits for which you may qualify.

Form 1040 — U.S. Individual Income Tax Return 2008. Department of the Treasury—Internal Revenue Service. OMB No. 1545-0074.

FORM 1040X

This form is used to amend a previously filed tax return. If you discover income that was not reported, or if you find additional deductions, you should file Form 1040X to pay the additional tax or obtain a refund.

used the regular Form 1040. Your decision in this matter will depend on your type of income, the amount of your income, the number of your deductions, and the complexity of your tax situation. Most tax preparation software programs will guide you in selecting the appropriate 1040 form.

What Is the Process for Completing the Federal Income Tax Return?

The major sections of Form 1040 (see Exhibit 3–3) correspond to tax topics discussed in the previous sections of this chapter:

1. *Filing status and exemptions.* Your tax rate is determined by your filing status and allowances for yourself, your spouse, and each person you claim as a dependent.

2. *Income.* Earnings from your employment (as reported by your W-2 form) and other income, such as savings and investment income, are reported in this section of Form 1040.

3. *Adjustments to income.* As discussed later in the chapter, if you qualify, you may deduct contributions (up to a certain amount) to an individual retirement account (IRA) or other qualified retirement program.

4. *Tax computation.* In this section, your adjusted gross income is reduced by your itemized deductions (see Exhibit 3–4) or by the standard deduction for your tax situation. In addition, an amount is deducted for each exemption to arrive at

Exhibit 3–3 Federal Income Tax Return—Form 1040

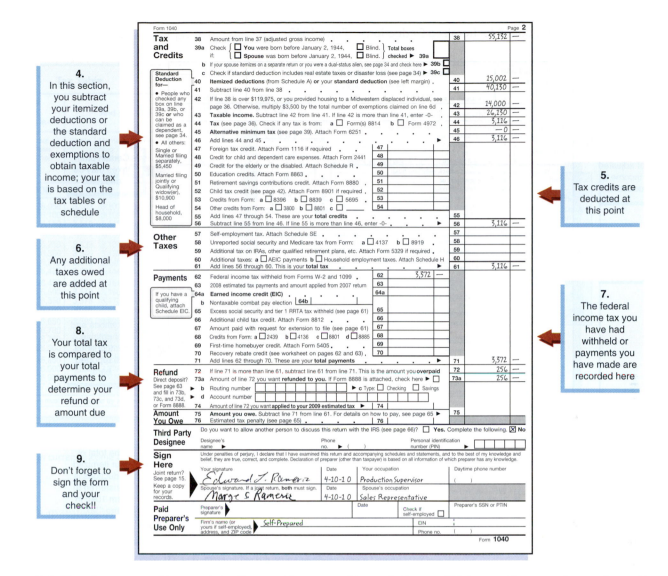

Note: These forms were used in a recent year; the current forms may not be exactly the same. Obtain current income tax forms and current tax information from your local IRS office, post office, public library, or at www.irs.gov.

your taxable income. That income is the basis for determining the amount of your tax (see Exhibit 3–5).

5. *Tax credits.* Any tax credits for which you qualify are subtracted at this point.

6. *Other taxes.* Any special taxes, such as self-employment tax, are included at this point.

7. *Payments.* Your total withholding and other payments are indicated in this section.

8. *Refund or amount you owe.* If your payments exceed the amount of income tax you owe, you are entitled to a refund. If the opposite is true, you must make an additional payment. Taxpayers who want their refunds sent directly to a bank can provide the necessary account information directly on Form 1040, 1040A, or 1040EZ.

9. *Your signature.* Forgetting to sign a tax return is one of the most frequent filing errors.

How Do I File My State Tax Return?

All but seven states (Alaska, Florida, Nevada, South Dakota, Texas, Washington, and Wyoming) have a state income tax. In most states, the tax rate ranges from 1 to 10

Exhibit 3–6

Tax-Planner Calendar

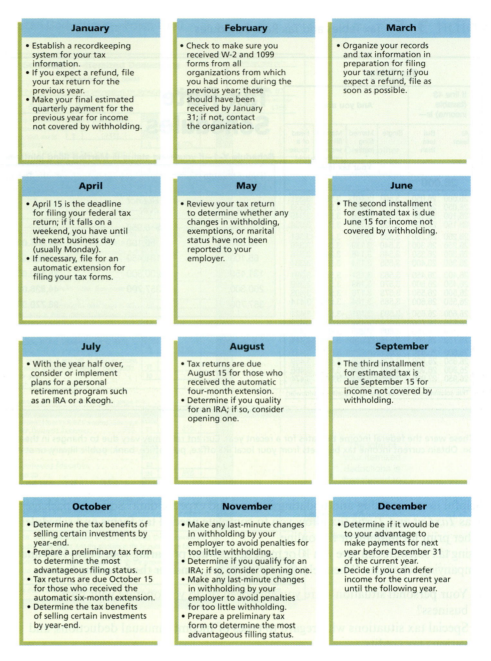

January	February	March
• Establish a recordkeeping system for your tax information. • If you expect a refund, file your tax return for the previous year. • Make your final estimated quarterly payment for the previous year for income not covered by withholding.	• Check to make sure you received W-2 and 1099 forms from all organizations from which you had income during the previous year; these should have been received by January 31; if not, contact the organization.	• Organize your records and tax information in preparation for filing your tax return; if you expect a refund, file as soon as possible.

April	May	June
• April 15 is the deadline for filing your federal tax return; if it falls on a weekend, you have until the next business day (usually Monday). • If necessary, file for an automatic extension for filing your tax forms.	• Review your tax return to determine whether any changes in withholding, exemptions, or marital status have not been reported to your employer.	• The second installment for estimated tax is due June 15 for income not covered by withholding.

July	August	September
• With the year half over, consider or implement plans for a personal retirement program such as an IRA or a Keogh.	• Tax returns are due August 15 for those who received the automatic four-month extension. • Determine if you quality for an IRA; if so, consider opening one.	• The third installment for estimated tax is due September 15 for income not covered by withholding.

October	November	December
• Determine the tax benefits of selling certain investments by year-end. • Prepare a preliminary tax form to determine the most advantageous filing status. • Tax returns are due October 15 for those who received the automatic six-month extension. • Determine the tax benefits of selling certain investments by year-end.	• Make any last-minute changes in withholding by your employer to avoid penalties for too little withholding. • Determine if you qualify for an IRA; if so, consider opening one. • Make any last-minute changes in withholding by your employer to avoid penalties for too little withholding. • Prepare a preliminary tax form to determine the most advantageous filling status.	• Determine if it would be to your advantage to make payments for next year before December 31 of the current year. • Decide if you can defer income for the current year until the following year.

Note: Children born before the end of the year give you a full-year exemption, so plan accordingly!

Step 2 Determine your eligibility with a particular company. A brief description of the criteria for each is provided. Some companies limit service to taxpayers in certain states; others target filers by age (younger than 21 or older than 61). Many of the services are limited to lower-income taxpayers, and some offer: "No restrictions. Everyone qualifies." A "Guide Me to a Service" option is available to help you narrow down the possible companies offering free preparation and e-filing for you.

Step 3 Next, connect to the company's Web site to begin the preparation of your tax return.

Step 4 Finally, use the company's online software to prepare your return. Your federal tax return is then filed electronically and your tax data is stored at the vendor's site. Taxpayers who do not qualify for the Free File Alliance program may still be able to file online for a nominal fee. You don't have to purchase the software; simply go to the software company's Internet site and pay a fee to use the tax program.

Taxpayers who use the Free File Alliance are cautioned to be careful consumers. A company may attempt to sell other financial products to inexperienced taxpayers, such as expensive refund anticipation loans. Also, taxpayers using the free file service must be aware that their state tax return might not be included in the free program.

Telefile is a file-by-phone system that has been tested in various geographic areas. It allows taxpayers to call a toll-free number, using a touch-tone phone, to file their tax returns. A follow-up written or voice "signature" confirmation is required.

What Tax Assistance Sources Are Available?

As with other aspects of personal financial planning, many tax resources are available to assist you.

IRS SERVICES If you prepare your own tax return or desire tax information, the IRS can assist in four ways:

1. *Publications.* The IRS offers hundreds of free booklets and pamphlets that can be obtained at a local IRS office, by mail request, or by telephone. Especially helpful is *Your Federal Income Tax* (IRS Publication 17). IRS publications and tax forms are available by phone at 1-800-TAX-FORM, online at www.irs.gov, or by fax at 703-368-9694.
2. *Recorded messages.* The IRS Tele-Tax system gives you 24-hour access to about 150 recorded tax tips at 1-800-829-4477.
3. *Phone hot line.* Information about specific problems is available through an IRS-staffed phone line at 1-800-829-1040.
4. *Walk-in service.* You can visit a local IRS office (400 are available) to obtain tax assistance.

did you know?

An IRS study of visits to its tax assistance centers found that 19 of 26 tax returns (83 percent) had been incorrectly prepared by IRS employees. The agency reported that 17 of the 19 inaccurately prepared fictitious returns would have resulted in incorrect refunds totaling nearly $32,000.

TAX PUBLICATIONS Each year, several tax guides are published and offered for sale. Publications such as *J. K. Lasser's Your Income Tax* and *The Ernst & Young Tax Guide* can be purchased online or at local stores.

THE INTERNET As with other personal finance topics, extensive information may be found on Web sites such as those mentioned earlier.

Tax Preparation Services

Over 40 million U.S. taxpayers pay someone to do their income taxes. The fee for this service can range from $40 at a tax preparation service for a simple return to more than $2,000 to a certified public accountant for a complicated return.

TYPES OF TAX SERVICES Doing your own taxes may not be desirable, especially if you have sources of income other than salary. The sources available for professional tax assistance include the following:

- Tax services range from local, one-person operations to national firms with thousands of offices, such as H&R Block.
- Enrolled agents—government-approved tax experts—prepare returns and provide tax advice. You may contact the National Association of Enrolled Agents at 1-800-424-4339 for information about enrolled agents in your area.

- Many accountants offer tax assistance along with other business services. A certified public accountant (CPA) with special training in taxes can help with tax planning and the preparation of your annual tax return.
- Attorneys usually do not complete tax returns; however, you can use an attorney's services when you are involved in a tax-related transaction or when you have a difference of opinion with the IRS.

EVALUATING TAX SERVICES   When planning to use a tax preparation service, consider these factors:

- What training and experience does the tax professional possess?
- How will the fee be determined? (Avoid preparers who earn a percentage of your refund.)
- Does the preparer suggest you report various deductions that might be questioned?
- Will the preparer represent you if your return is audited?
- Is tax preparation the main business activity, or does it serve as a front for selling other financial products and services?

Additional information about tax preparers may be obtained at the Web sites for the National Association of Enrolled Agents (www.naea.org) and the National Association of Tax Professionals (www.natptax.com).

TAX SERVICE WARNINGS   Even if you hire a professional tax preparer, you are responsible for supplying accurate and complete information. Hiring a tax preparer will not guarantee that you pay the *correct* amount. A study conducted by *Money* magazine of 41 tax preparers reported fees ranging from $375 to $3,600, with taxes due ranging from $31,846 to $74,450 for the same fictional family. If you owe more tax because your return contains errors or you have made entries that are not allowed, you are responsible for paying that additional tax, plus any interest and penalties.

Beware of tax preparers and other businesses that offer your refund in advance. These "refund anticipation loans" frequently charge very high interest rates for this type of consumer credit. Studies reveal interest rates sometimes exceeding 300 percent (on an annualized basis).

What If Your Return Is Audited?

tax audit A detailed examination of your tax return by the Internal Revenue Service.

The Internal Revenue Service reviews all returns for completeness and accuracy. If you make an error, your tax is automatically refigured and you receive either a bill or a refund. If you make an entry that is not allowed, you will be notified by mail. A **tax audit** is a detailed examination of your tax return by the IRS. In most audits, the IRS requests more information to support your tax return. Be sure to keep accurate records. Receipts, canceled checks, and other evidence can verify amounts that you claim. Avoiding common filing mistakes helps to minimize your chances of an audit (see Exhibit 3–7).

WHO GETS AUDITED?   About 0.6 percent of all tax filers—fewer than 1 million people—are audited each year. Although the IRS does not reveal its basis for auditing returns, several indicators are evident. People who claim large or unusual deductions increase their chances of an audit. Tax advisers suggest including a brief explanation or a copy of receipts for deductions that may be questioned.

TYPES OF AUDITS   The simplest and most frequent type of audit is the *correspondence audit*. This mail inquiry requires you to clarify or document minor questions.

Exhibit **3-7**   How to Avoid Common Filing Errors

- Organize all tax-related information for easy access.
- Follow instructions carefully. Many people deduct total medical and dental expenses rather than the amount of these expenses that exceeds 7.5 percent of adjusted gross income.
- Use the proper tax rate schedule or tax table column.
- Be sure to claim the correct number of exemptions and correct amounts of standard deductions.
- Consider the alternative minimum tax that may apply to your situation. Be sure to pay self-employment tax and tax on early IRA withdrawals.
- Check your arithmetic several times.
- Sign your return (both spouses must sign a joint return), or the IRS won't process it.
- Be sure to include the correct Social Security number(s) and to record amounts on the correct lines.
- Attach necessary documentation such as your W-2 forms and required supporting schedules.
- Make the check payable to "United States Treasury."
- Put your Social Security number, the tax year, and a daytime telephone number on your check—and be sure to sign the check!
- Keep a photocopy of your return.
- Put the proper postage on your mailing envelope.
- Finally, check everything again—and file on time!

The *office audit* requires you to visit an IRS office to clarify some aspect of your tax return.

The *field audit* is more complex. An IRS agent visits you at your home, your business, or the office of your accountant to have access to your records. A field audit may be done to verify whether an individual has a home office if this is claimed.

The IRS also conducts more detailed audits for about 50,000 taxpayers. These range from random requests to document various tax return items to line-by-line reviews by IRS employees.

YOUR AUDIT RIGHTS When you receive an audit notice, you have the right to request time to prepare. Also, you can ask the IRS for clarification of items being questioned. When audited, follow these suggestions:

- Decide whether you will bring your tax preparer, accountant, or lawyer.
- Be on time for your appointment; bring only relevant documents.
- Present tax evidence in a logical, calm, and confident manner; maintain a positive attitude.
- Make sure the information you present is consistent with the tax law.
- Keep your answers aimed at the auditor's questions. Answer questions clearly and completely. Be as brief as possible. The five best responses to questions during an audit are "Yes," "No," "I don't recall," "I'll have to check on that," and "What specific items do you want to see?"

If you disagree with the results of an audit, you may request a conference at the Regional Appeals Office. Although most differences of opinion are settled at this stage, some taxpayers take their cases further. A person may go to the U.S. tax court, the U.S. claims court, or the U.S. district court. Some tax disputes have gone to the U.S. Supreme Court.

CONCEPT CHECK 3–3

1 In what ways does your filing status affect preparation of your federal income tax return?

_____

_____

2 What are the main sources available to help people prepare their taxes?

_____

_____

3 What actions can reduce the chances of an IRS audit?

_____

_____

4 Which 1040 form should each of the following individuals use? (Check one for each situation.)

Tax situation	1040EZ	1040A	1040
a. A high school student with an after-school job and interest earnings of $480 from savings accounts.			
b. A college student who, because of ownership of property, is able to itemize deductions rather than take the standard deduction.			
c. A young, entry-level worker with no dependents and income only from salary.			

Apply Yourself!

Objective 3

Create a visual presentation (video or slide presentation) that demonstrates actions a person might take to reduce errors when filing a federal tax return.

Using Tax Planning Strategies

OBJECTIVE 4

Select appropriate tax strategies for various life situations.

tax avoidance The use of legitimate methods to reduce one's taxes.

tax evasion The use of illegal actions to reduce one's taxes.

For people to pay their fair share of taxes—no more, no less—they should practice **tax avoidance,** the use of legitimate methods to reduce one's taxes. In contrast, **tax evasion** is the use of illegal actions to reduce one's taxes. To minimize taxes owed, follow these guidelines:

- If you expect to have the *same* or a *lower* tax rate next year, *accelerate deductions* into the current year. Pay real estate property taxes or make charitable donations by December 31.
- If you expect to have a *lower* or the *same* tax rate next year, *delay the receipt of income* until next year so the funds will be taxed at a lower rate or at a later date.

Figure It Out!

> Short-Term and Long-Term Capital Gains

You will pay a lower tax rate on the profits from stocks and other investments if you hold the asset for more than 12 months. As of 2009, a taxpayer in the 28 percent tax bracket would pay $280 in taxes on a $1,000 short-term capital gain (assets held for one year or less). However, that same taxpayer would pay only $150 on the $1,000 (a 15 percent capital gains tax) If the investment were held for more than a year.

	Short-Term Capital Gain (Assets held for one year or less)	Long-Term Capital Gain (Assets held for more than one year)
Capital Gain	$1,000	$1,000
Capital Gains Tax Rate	28%	15%
Capital Gains Tax	$ 280	$ 150
Tax Savings	—	$ 130

- If you expect to have a *higher* tax rate next year, consider *delaying deductions,* since they will have a greater benefit. A $1,000 deduction at 25 percent lowers your taxes $250; at 28 percent, your taxes are lowered $280.
- If you expect to have a *higher* tax rate next year, *accelerate the receipt of income* to have it taxed at the current lower rate.

When considering financial decisions in relation to your taxes, remember that purchasing, investing, and retirement planning are the areas most heavily affected by tax laws.

Consumer Purchasing

The buying decisions most directly affected by taxes are the purchase of a residence, the use of credit, and job-related expenses.

PLACE OF RESIDENCE Owning a home is one of the best tax shelters. Both real estate property taxes and interest on the mortgage are deductible (as itemized deductions) and thus reduce your taxable income.

CONSUMER DEBT Current tax laws allow homeowners to borrow for consumer purchases. You can deduct interest on loans (of up to $100,000) secured by your primary or secondary home up to the actual dollar amount you have invested in it— the difference between the market value of the home and the amount you owe on it. These *home equity loans,* which are *second mortgages,* allow you to use that line of credit for various purchases. Some states place restrictions on home equity loans.

JOB-RELATED EXPENSES As previously mentioned, certain work expenses, such as union dues, some travel and education costs, business tools, and job search expenses, may be included as itemized deductions.

HEALTH CARE EXPENSES *Flexible spending accounts (FSAs),* also called *health savings accounts* and expense reimbursement accounts, allow you to reduce your taxable income when paying for medical expenses or child care costs. Workers are allowed to put pretax dollars into these employer-sponsored programs. These "deposits" result in a lower taxable income. Then, the funds in the FSA may be used to pay for various medical expenses and dependent care costs.

Investment Decisions

A major area of tax planning involves decisions related to investing.

TAX-EXEMPT INVESTMENTS Interest income from municipal bonds, which are issued by state and local governments, and other tax-exempt investments is not subject to federal income tax. Although municipal bonds have lower interest rates than other investments, the *after-tax* income may be higher. For example, if you are in the 27 percent tax bracket, earning $100 of tax-exempt income would be worth more to you than earning $125 in taxable investment income. The $125 would have an after-tax value of $91—$125 less $34 (27 percent of $125) for taxes.

TAX-DEFERRED INVESTMENTS Although tax-deferred investments, with income taxed at a later date, are less beneficial than tax-exempt investments, they give you the advantage of paying taxes in the future rather than now. Examples of tax-deferred investments include:

- *Tax-deferred annuities,* usually issued by insurance companies. These investments are discussed in Chapter 10.
- *Section 529 savings plans* are state-run, tax-deferred plans to set aside money for a child's education. The 529 is like a prepaid tuition plan in which you invest to cover future education costs. The 529 plans differ from state to state.
- *Retirement plans* such as IRA, Keogh, or 401(k) plans. The next section discusses the tax implications of these plans.

capital gains Profits from the sale of a capital asset such as stocks, bonds, or real estate.

Capital gains, profits from the sale of a capital asset such as stocks, bonds, or real estate, are also tax deferred; you do not have to pay the tax on these profits until the asset is sold. In recent years, *long-term* capital gains (on investments held more than a year) have been taxed at a lower rate.

The sale of an investment for less than its purchase price is, of course, a *capital loss.* Capital losses can be used to offset capital gains and up to $3,000 of ordinary income. Unused capital losses may be carried forward into future years to offset capital gains or ordinary income up to $3,000 per year.

SELF-EMPLOYMENT Owning your own business can have tax advantages. Self-employed persons may deduct expenses such as health and certain life insurance as business costs. However, business owners have to pay self-employment tax (Social Security) in addition to the regular tax rate.

CHILDREN'S INVESTMENTS A child under 14 with investment income of more than $1,500 is taxed at the parent's top rate. For investment income under $1,500, the child receives a deduction of $750 and the next $750 is taxed at his or her own rate, which is probably lower than the parent's rate. This restriction does not apply to children 14 and older.

Retirement Plans

A major tax strategy of benefit to working people is the use of tax-deferred retirement plans such as individual retirement arrangements (IRAs), Keogh plans, and 401(k) plans.

TRADITIONAL IRA The regular IRA deduction is available only to people who do not participate in employer-sponsored retirement plans or who have an adjusted gross income under a certain amount. As of 2007, the IRA contribution limit was $4,000. Older workers, age 50 and over, were allowed to contribute up to $4,500 as a "catch up" to make up for lost time saving for retirement.

In general, amounts withdrawn from deductible IRAs are included in gross income. An additional 10 percent penalty is usually imposed on withdrawals made before age 59½ unless the withdrawn funds are on account of death or disability, for medical expenses, or for qualified higher education expenses.

ROTH IRA The Roth IRA also allows a $5,000 annual contribution, which is not tax deductible; however, the earnings on the account are tax free after five years. The funds from the Roth IRA may be withdrawn before age 59½ if the account owner is disabled, or for the purchase of a first home ($10,000 maximum). Like the regular IRA, the Roth IRA is limited to people with an adjusted gross income under a certain amount.

Deductible IRAs provide tax relief up front as contributions reduce current taxes. However, taxes must be paid when the withdrawals are made from the deductible IRA. In contrast, the Roth IRA does not have immediate benefits, but the investment grows in value on a tax-free basis. Withdrawals from the Roth IRA are exempt from federal and state taxes.

EDUCATION IRA The Education Savings Account is designed to assist parents in saving for the college education of their children. Once again, the annual contribution (limited to $2,000) is not tax deductible and is limited to taxpayers with an adjusted gross income under a certain amount. However, as with the Roth IRA, the earnings accumulate tax free.

KEOGH PLAN If you are self-employed and own your own business, you can establish a Keogh plan. This retirement plan, also called an HR10 plan, may combine a profit-sharing plan and a pension plan of other investments purchased by the employee. In general, with a Keogh, people may contribute 25 percent of their annual income, up to a maximum of $30,000, to this tax-deferred retirement plan.

401(K) PLAN The part of the tax code called 401(k) authorizes a tax-deferred retirement plan sponsored by an employer. This plan allows you to contribute a greater tax-deferred amount ($16,500 in 2009) than you can contribute to an IRA. Older workers, age 50 and over, may be allowed to contribute an additional $5,500 if their employer allows. However, most companies set a limit on your contribution, such as 15 percent of your salary. Some employers provide a matching contribution in their 401(k) plans. For example, a company may contribute 50 cents for each $1 contributed by an employee. This results in an immediate 50 percent return on your investment.

Tax planners advise people to contribute as much as possible to a Keogh or 401(k) plan since (1) the increased value of the investment accumulates on a tax-free basis until the funds are withdrawn and (2) contributions reduce your adjusted gross income for computing your current tax liability.

Changing Tax Strategies

Debate over what types of tax reform would allow the U.S. economy to recover from current economic difficulties is ongoing. Congress frequently passes legislation that changes the tax code. These changes require that you regularly determine how to take best advantage of the tax laws for personal financial planning.

What tax actions should the federal government take to stimulate economic growth? Lower rates? Higher rates? Tax credit? Rebates? Recently, tax changes have included:

- Payroll tax credit for individuals, which allows lower withholding amounts to provide workers with funds that will hopefully simulate economic activity.
- Increased Hope Credit for college costs, to reduce educational costs.
- First-time home buyers' credit, to encourage home ownership and stimulate housing-related jobs.
- Home-energy tax credit, to cover energy-efficient skylights, windows, outer doors, water heaters, central air conditioners, and biomass stoves.
- Increased earned income credit, to assist low-income taxpayers.

In addition to these and other recent tax changes, the IRS usually modifies the tax form and filing procedures yearly, so be sure to carefully consider changes in your personal situation and your income level. Well-informed taxpayers monitor their personal tax strategies to best serve daily living needs and to achieve long-term financial goals.

Sheet 10 Tax Planning Activities

CONCEPT CHECK 3–4

1 How does tax avoidance differ from tax evasion?

_____

_____

2 What common tax-saving methods are available to most individuals and households?

_____

_____

3 For the following tax situations, indicate if this item refers to tax-exempt income or tax-deferred income.

	Tax-exempt	Tax-deferred
a. Interest earned on municipal bonds		
b. Earnings on an individual retirement account		
c. Education IRA earnings used for college expenses		
d. Income of U.S. citizens working in another country		

Apply Yourself!

Objective 4

Survey friends and relatives about their tax planning strategies. Do most people get a federal tax refund or owe taxes each year? Is their situation (refund or payment) planned?

Make the most of changes designed to give you a break on your 2008 tax bill.
By Mary Beth Franklin

LAST-MINUTE TAX SAVING TIPS

In this rocky economy, a tax refund can provide welcome relief. Congress approved more than 500 changes to the tax code in 2008 in response to the housing collapse, stock-market implosion and several natural disasters. And the passage of a new economic-stimulus package means that more breaks are on the way.

Niki Roberts, a graphic designer in Seattle, is one beneficiary of the tax-relief measures. Roberts, 35, thought that as a single woman she would never be able to afford to buy a home. But as housing prices continued to plummet, she decided to take the plunge. "I wanted to take advantage of this great opportunity," she says. Last summer, Roberts bought a two-bedroom, ranch-style house, complete with a fenced-in yard for her dog, Maggie. Now she's able to cash in on a slew of tax breaks—including a new $7,500 credit for first-time home buyers, as well as deductions for real estate taxes, mortgage interest and private mortgage insurance—that will result in a juicy refund check this spring.

Home Sweet Tax Break The new tax credit for first-time home buyers is actually a tax-free loan that must be paid back to the government over 15 years—starting two years after the year the credit is claimed. If you sell the home before you finish paying back the loan, the balance is due in full in the year of the sale. Here's how it works: You can claim a tax credit equal to 10% of the purchase price—up to $7,500—if you bought a principal residence after April 8, 2008. Because a tax credit reduces your tax bill dollar for dollar, it is more valuable than a deduction, which reduces the amount of your income that is taxed.

If you buy a home between January 1 and November 30, 2009, you can claim the first-time home-buyer credit on your 2008 or 2009 return. (The stimulus package raised the credit to $8,000 and eliminated the payback provisions for homes purchased in 2009 as long as you remain in the house for at least three years.) Use Form 1040X to amend your tax return if you have already filed or Form 4868

to delay your filing deadline until October 15. (An extension delays the deadline for filing forms but not for any payment you owe.)

Choose Your Deduction
Roberts will also benefit from a tax break that Congress renewed for 2008 that allows taxpayers to choose between deducting state income taxes and state sales taxes. Because Roberts lives in Washington, which has no state income tax, it's an easy choice. She can use the IRS's sales-tax calculator to determine the appropriate deduction based on her income, state and local sales-tax rates, and single filing status (she's eligible to write off $837). Or she can tally actual receipts if it would result in a bigger deduction.

1. How does a tax credit differ from a tax deduction?

_____

2. How do various tax law changes reflect economic conditions?

_____

3. Which of the tax-savings tips discussed may be value to you now or in the near future?

_____

Back to ... *Getting Personal*

Reconsider your responses to the "Getting Personal" questions at the beginning of the chapter. For more effective tax planning:

- Consider developing a system for organizing your tax records. See Exhibit 3–2 on page 81.
- Become aware of what is taxable income and what is deductible by using "Personal Finance in Practice" on page 82.
- Obtain the latest federal income tax forms and instructions, which are available at www.irs.org. Information about state income taxes may be obtained at www.taxadmin.org.

- Continually update your knowledge of income taxes to help you make better informed financial decisions. Ask several people about the actions they take to stay informed and to reduce the amount paid in taxes.

What did you learn in this chapter that could help you make wiser choices related to tax planning decisions?

Chapter Summary

Objective 1   Tax planning can influence spending, saving, borrowing, and investing decisions. An awareness of income taxes, sales taxes, excise taxes, property taxes, estate taxes, inheritance taxes, gift taxes, and Social Security taxes is vital for successful financial planning.

Objective 2   Taxable income is determined by subtracting adjustments to income, deductions, and allowances for exemptions from gross income. Your total tax liability is based on the published tax tables or tax schedules, less any tax credits.

Objective 3   The major sections of Form 1040 provide the basic framework for filing your federal income tax return.

The main sources of tax assistance are IRS services and publications, other publications, the Internet, computer software, and professional tax preparers such as commercial tax services, enrolled agents, accountants, and attorneys.

Objective 4   You may reduce your tax burden through careful planning and making financial decisions related to consumer purchasing, and the use of debt, investments, and retirement planning.

Key Terms

adjusted gross income (AGI) 80
average tax rate 84
capital gains 98
earned income 79
estate tax 78
excise tax 78
exclusion 79
exemption 82

inheritance tax 78
investment income 79
itemized deductions 81
marginal tax rate 88
passive income 79
standard deduction 81
taxable income 79
tax audit 94

tax avoidance 96
tax credit 84
tax deduction 81
tax-deferred income 79
tax evasion 96
tax-exempt income 79

Self-Test Problems

1. A person had $2,345 withheld for federal income taxes and had a tax liability of $2,410. Would this be a refund or an additional amount due for what amount?
2. Based on the following information, what is the amount of taxable income?

   Gross salary, $37,400   Interest earnings, $320
   Dividend income, $160   One personal exemption, $3,500
   Itemized deductions, $4,730

Solutions

1. To determine the amount of refund or additional tax due, compare the amount of tax liability with the amount withheld. The $2,410 tax liability minus the $2,345 would result in an additional tax due of $65.
2. Taxable income is calculated by adding salary, income, and dividends, and then subtracting itemized deductions and exemptions:

$$\$37,400 + \$320 + \$160 - \$3,500 - \$4,730 = \$29,650$$

Problems

1. Thomas Franklin arrived at the following tax information:

   Gross salary, $41,780   Interest earnings, $225
   Dividend income, $80   One personal exemption, $2,650
   Itemized deductions, $3,890   Adjustments to income, $1,150

   What amount would Thomas report as taxable income? (Obj. 2)

2. If Lola Harper had the following itemized deductions, should she use Schedule A or the standard deduction? The standard deduction for her tax situation is $6,050.

   Donations to church and other charities, $1,980
   Medical and dental expenses exceeding 7.5 percent of adjusted gross income, $430
   State income tax, $690
   Job-related expenses exceeding 2 percent of adjusted gross income, $1,610   (Obj. 2)

3. What would be the average tax rate for a person who paid taxes of $4,864.14 on a taxable income of $39,870? (Obj. 2)

4. Based on the following data, would Ann and Carl Wilton receive a refund or owe additional taxes? (Obj. 2)

   Adjusted gross income, $43,190   Itemized deductions, $11,420
   Child care tax credit, $80   Federal income tax withheld, $6,784
   Amount for personal exemptions, $7,950 Tax rate on taxable income, 15 percent

5. If $3,432 was withheld during the year and taxes owed were $3,316, would the person owe an additional amount or receive a refund? What is the amount? (Obj. 2)

6. If 400,000 people each receive an average refund of $1,900, based on an interest rate of 4 percent, what would be the lost annual income from savings on those refunds? (Obj. 2)

7. Using the tax table in Exhibit 3–5 (p. 91), determine the amount of taxes for the following situations: (Obj. 3)

   a. A head of household with taxable income of $26,210.
   b. A single person with taxable income of $26,888.
   c. A married person filing a separate return with taxable income of $26,272.

8. Elaine Romberg prepares her own income tax return each year. A tax preparer would charge her $60 for this service. Over a period of 10 years, how much does Elaine gain from preparing her own tax return? Assume she can earn 3 percent on her savings. (Obj. 3)

9. Each year, the Internal Revenue Service adjusts the value of an exemption based on inflation (and rounded to the nearest $50). If the exemption in a recent year was worth $3,100 and inflation was 4.7 percent, what would be the amount of the exemption for the upcoming tax year? (Obj. 3)

10. Would you prefer a fully taxable investment earning 10.7 percent or a tax-exempt investment earning 8.1 percent? Why? (Assume a 28 percent tax rate.) (Obj. 4)

11. On December 30, you decide to make a $1,000 charitable donation. (Obj. 4)

    a. If you are in the 27 percent tax bracket, how much will you save in taxes for the current year?
    b. If you deposit that tax savings in a savings account for the next five years at 8 percent, what will be the future value of that account?

12. Jeff Perez deposits $2,000 each year in a tax-deferred retirement account. If he is in a 27 percent tax bracket, what amount would his tax be reduced over a 20-year time period? (Obj. 4)

13. If a person with a 30 percent tax bracket makes a deposit of $4,000 to a tax-deferred retirement account, what amount would be saved on current taxes? (Obj. 4)

Questions

1. What factors might be considered when creating a tax that is considered fair by most people in a society?

2. How might tax-exempt income and tax credits be used by government to stimulate economic growth?

3. What tax information sources would you be most likely to use? Why?

4. Use IRS publications and other reference materials to answer a specific tax question. Contact an IRS office to obtain an answer for the same question. What differences, if any, exist between the information sources?

5. What are some tax advantages and disadvantages of owning your own business?

Case in Point

A SINGLE FATHER'S TAX SITUATION

Ever since his wife's death, Eric Stanford has faced difficult personal and financial circumstances. His job provides him with a fairly good income but keeps him away from his daughters, ages 8 and 10, nearly 20 days a month. This requires him to use in-home child care services that consume a major portion of his income. Since the Stanfords live in a small apartment, this arrangement has been very inconvenient.

Due to the costs of caring for his children, Eric has only a minimal amount withheld from his salary for federal income taxes. Thus more money is available during the year, but for the last few years he has had to make a payment in April—another financial burden.

Although Eric has created an investment fund for his daughters' college education and for his retirement, he has not sought to select investments that offer tax benefits. Overall, he needs to look at several aspects of his tax planning activities to find strategies that will best serve his current and future financial needs.

Eric has assembled the following information for the current tax year:

Earnings from wages, $42,590

Interest earned on savings, $125

IRA deduction, $2,000

Checking account interest, $65

Three exemptions at $2,750 each

Current standard deduction for filing status, $6,350

Amount withheld for federal income tax, $3,178

Tax credit for child care, $400

Filing status: head of household

Questions

1. What are Eric's major financial concerns in his current situation?

2. In what ways might Eric improve his tax planning efforts?
3. Calculate the following:
   a. What is Eric's taxable income? (Refer to Exhibit 3–1, page 80.)
   b. What is his total tax liability? (Use Exhibit 3–5, page 91.) What is his average tax rate?
   c. Based on his withholding, will Eric receive a refund or owe additional tax? What is the amount?

Continuing Case

Vikki Rococo (age 23) has been working at a local company processing 401(k) plan benefits for six months and she just received her W-2 from work, her 1099 from her bank, and her year-end statement for her 401(k) plan. Her parents, Dave and Amy (ages 48 and 46) received their property tax bill and year end statement for their mortgage.

Since she is living with her parents, Vikki wants to discuss her tax preparation with them. Her mom suggests that she organize her materials and plan to file online using Form 1040EZ. As Vikki begins to input her income, she takes a closer look at her W-2 from her employer and is surprised to see how much money has been deducted from her pay for the six months she has been working. The deductions for taxes plus her 401(k) plan are more than she earned last year as a student! She is worried about how much will be deducted next year, when she has worked for a full year. She wonders if she having too much federal income tax withheld from her paycheck.

Vikki's financial statistics are shown below:

Assets:

Checking account* $5,500 (interest received last year: $50)
  *including her emergency fund
Car $7,500
401(k) balance $3,000

Liabilities:

Student loan balance $13,700 (interest paid last year: $480)

Credit card balance $1,880 (interest paid last year: $120)

Income:
Gross salary received last year: $20,000 (for 6 months, before-tax). After-tax monthly salary: $2,333

Monthly Expenses:
Rent $200
Food $100

Student loan $250
Car loan $200
Credit card payments $40
Entertainment $100
Gas/repairs $150

Retirement Savings:
401(k) $500 per month, plus 50% employer match on first 7% of pay (contributions for last year: $3,000)

Questions

1. What types of taxes will Vikki need to pay? What taxes will her parents pay?
2. Using *Your Personal Financial Plan* sheet 9 and tax rates in the text, calculate Vikki's estimated federal income tax liability.
3. What is the difference between a tax credit and a tax deduction? Which is better?
4. What tax planning strategies should she consider? What strategies should her parents consider?
5. How can she use *Your Personal Financial Plan* sheet 10?

Spending Diary

"SALES TAX ON VARIOUS PURCHASES CAN REALLY INCREASE THE AMOUNT OF MY TOTAL SPENDING."

Directions

Continue your Daily Spending Diary to record and monitor your spending in various categories. Your comments should reflect what you have learned about your spending patterns and help you consider possible changes you might want to make in your spending habits. The Daily Spending Diary sheets are located in Appendix C at the end of the book and on the student Web site at www.mhhe.com/kdh.

Questions

1. What taxes do you usually pay that are reflected (directly or indirectly) in your daily spending diary?

2. How might your spending habits be revised to better control or reduce the amount you pay in taxes?

Name: _____ Date: _____

Federal Income Tax Estimate

Financial Planning Activities: Based on last year's tax return, estimates for the current year, and current tax regulations and rates, estimate your current tax liability.

Suggested Web Sites: www.irs.gov   www.taxlogic.com   www.walletpop.com/taxes

Gross income (wages, salary, investment income, and other ordinary income		$
Less Adjustments to income (see current tax regulations)		− $
Equals Adjusted gross income		= $
Less Standard deduction or	Itemized deduction	
	medical expenses (exceeding 7.5% of AGI)	$
	state/local income, property taxes	$
	mortgage, home equity loan	$
	interest	$
	contributions	$
	casualty and theft losses	$
	moving expenses, job-related and miscellaneous expenses (exceeding 2% of AGI)	$
Amount −$	**Total**	−$
Less Personal exemptions		−$
Equals Taxable income		= $
Estimated tax (based on current tax tables or tax schedules)		$
Less Tax credits		−$
Plus Other taxes		+$
Equals Total tax liability		= $
Less Estimated withholding and payments		−$
Equals Tax due (or refund)		= $

What's Next for Your Personal Financial Plan?

- Develop a system for filing and storing various tax records related to income, deductible expenses, and current tax forms.
- Using the IRS and other Web sites, identify recent changes in tax laws that may affect your financial planning decisions.

Name: _____ **Date:** _____

Tax Planning Activities

Financial Planning Activities: To determine which of the following actions are appropriate for your tax situation to prevent penalties and obtain tax savings.

Suggested Web Sites: www.turbotax.com   http://taxes.about.com

	Action to be taken (if applicable)	Completed
Filing status/withholding		
• Change filing status or exemptions due to changes in life situation		
• Change amount of withholding due to changes in tax situations		
• Plan to make estimated tax payments (due the 15th of April, June, September, and January)		
Tax records/documents		
• Organize home files for ease of maintaining and retrieving data		
• Send current mailing address and correct Social Security number to IRS, place of employment, and other income sources		
Annual tax activities		
• Be certain all needed data and current tax forms are available well before deadline		
• Research tax code changes and uncertain tax areas		
Tax-savings actions		
• Consider tax-exempt and tax-deferred investments		
• If you expect to have the same or lower tax rate next year, accelerate deductions into the current year		
• If you expect to have the same or lower tax rate next year, delay the receipt of income until next year		
• If you expect to have a higher tax rate next year, delay deductions since they will have a greater benefit		
• If you expect to have a higher tax rate next year, accelerate the receipt of income to have it taxed at the current lower rate		
• Start or increase use of tax-deferred retirement plans		
• Other		

What's Next for Your Personal Financial Plan?

- Identify saving and investing decisions that would minimize future income taxes.
- Develop a plan for actions to take related to your current and future tax situation.

4 Savings and Payment Services

Getting Personal

What are your attitudes toward financial services? For each of the following statements, circle the choice that best describes your current situation.

1. The financial service about which I'm least informed is
   a. Online banking.
   b. Certificates of deposit and other savings plans.
   c. Checking accounts and other payment methods.

2. My primary financial service activities involve the use of
   a. A bank or credit union.
   b. Online payments and ATMs.
   c. A check-cashing outlet.

3. When selecting a savings plan, my main concern is
   a. Bank location and availability of cash machines.
   b. Federal deposit insurance coverage.
   c. Rate of return.

4. My checking account records are
   a. Updated by me after every check written and deposit made.
   b. Based on a rough estimate in my checkbook.
   c. Known only by my financial institution.

After studying this chapter, you will be asked to reconsider your responses to these items.

What Financial Services Do You Need?

OBJECTIVE 1

Identify commonly used financial services.

More than 20,000 banks, savings and loan associations, credit unions, and other financial institutions provide various payment, savings, and credit services. Today a trip to "the bank" may mean a visit to a credit union, a stop at an ATM at the mall, or a transfer of funds online. While some financial decisions relate directly to goals, your daily activities require different financial services. Exhibit 4–1 is an overview of financial services for managing cash flows and moving toward specific financial goals.

Your Personal Financial Plan Sheets

11. Planning the use of financial services.
12. Comparing savings plans.
13. Using savings plans to achieve financial goals.
14. Comparing payment methods; bank reconciliation.

Objectives

In this chapter, you will learn to:
1. Identify commonly used financial services.
2. Compare the types of financial institutions.
3. Assess various types of savings plans.
4. Evaluate different types of payment methods.

Why is this important?

Although many financial institutions face economic difficulties, banking costs for consumers continue to remain high. ATM fees can range from nothing to as high as $3 per cash withdrawal. If you are charged two $1 transaction fees a week and could invest your money at 5 percent, this convenience will cost you more than $570 over a five-year period.

Meeting Daily Money Needs

Buying groceries, paying the rent, and completing other routine spending activities require a cash management plan. Cash, check, credit card, and debit card are the common payment choices. Mistakes made frequently when managing current cash needs include (1) overspending as a result of impulse buying and using credit; (2) having insufficient liquid assets to pay current bills; (3) using savings or borrowing to pay for current expenses; (4) failing to put unneeded funds in an interest-earning savings account or investment plan.

Exhibit **4–1**   Financial Services for Managing Cash Flow and Reaching Financial Goals

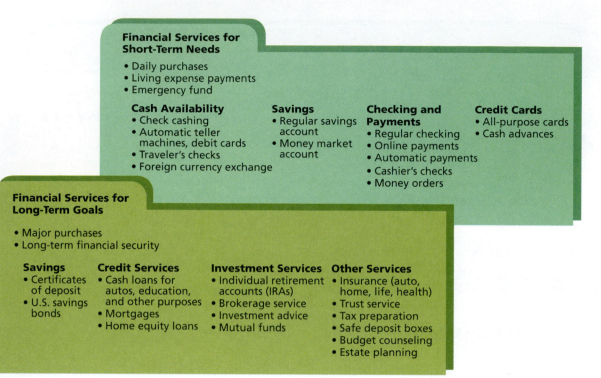

Sources of Quick Cash

No matter how carefully you manage your money, at some time you will need more cash than you have available. To cope in that situation, you have two basic choices: liquidate savings or borrow. A savings account, certificate of deposit, mutual fund, or other investment may be accessed when you need funds. Or a credit card cash advance or a personal loan may be appropriate. Remember, however, that both using savings and increasing borrowing reduce your net worth and your potential to achieve long-term financial security.

Types of Financial Services

Banks and other financial institutions offer services to meet a variety of needs. These services may be viewed in into four main categories:

1. *Savings* provides safe storage of funds for future use. Commonly referred to as *time deposits,* money in savings accounts and certificates of deposit are examples of savings plans.
2. *Payment services* offer an ability to transfer money to others for daily business activities. Checking accounts and other payment methods are generally called *demand deposits.*
3. *Borrowing* is used by most people at some time during their lives. Credit alternatives range from short-term accounts, such as credit cards and cash loans, to long-term borrowing, such as a home mortgage.
4. *Other financial services* include insurance, investments, tax assistance, and financial planning. A **trust** is a legal agreement that provides for the management

trust A legal agreement that provides for the management and control of assets by one party for the benefit of another.

and control of assets by one party for the benefit of another. This type of arrangement is usually created through a commercial bank or a lawyer. Parents who want to set aside certain funds for their children's education may use a trust.

To simplify financial services, many financial businesses offer all-purpose accounts. An **asset management account,** also called a *cash management account,* provides a complete financial services program for a single fee. Investment companies and others offer this type of account, with checking, an ATM card, a credit card, online banking, and a line of credit as well as access for buying stocks, bonds, mutual funds, and other investments.

asset management account An all-in-one account that includes savings, checking, borrowing, investing, and other financial services for a single fee; also called a *cash management account.*

Electronic and Online Banking

Banking online and through electronic systems continues to expand (see Exhibit 4–2). While most traditional financial institutions offer online banking services, Web-only banks have also become strong competitors. For example, E*Trade Bank operates online while also providing customers with access to ATMs. These "e-banks" and "e-branches" provide nearly every needed financial service:

Category	Online Services Available	Sample Providers
Savings plans	• Deposits to savings accounts, money market accounts, certificates of deposit (CDs), and retirement accounts • Direct deposit of paychecks and government payments	www.Netbank.com www.INGdirect.com www.hsbcdirect.com
Payment services and cash access	• Online payments including automatic transfers funds for rent, mortgage, utilities, loans, and investment deposits • ATM (cash machine) access for various banking activities • Payments for online purchases	www.usbank.com www.etradebank.com www.paypal.com www.paytrust.com
Borrowing	• Comparison of current loan rates • Online application and approval for auto loans, credit cards, mortgages, and other loans	www.eloan.com www.chase.com www.citibankdirect.com
Other services	• Online rates and applications for various types of insurance coverage • Buy, sell, monitor investments (stocks, bonds, mutual funds, and other securities)	www.insure.com www.wachovia.com www.etrade.com www.schwab.com

An **automatic teller machine (ATM),** also called a *cash machine,* provides various banking activities and other types of transactions such as buying transit passes, postage stamps, and gift certificates. To minimize ATM fees, compare several financial institutions. Use your own bank's ATM to avoid surcharges, and withdraw larger amounts to avoid fees on several small transactions.

The **debit card,** or *cash card,* that activates ATM transactions may also be used to make purchases. A debit card is in contrast to a *credit card,* since you are spending your own funds rather than borrowing additional money. A lost or stolen debit card can be expensive. If you notify the financial institution within two days of the lost card, your liability for unauthorized use is $50. After that, you can be liable for up to $500 of unauthorized use for up to 60 days. Beyond that, your liability is unlimited. However, some card issuers use the same rules for lost or stolen debit cards as for credit cards: a $50 maximum. Of course, you are not liable for unauthorized use, such as a con artist using your account number to make a purchase. Remember to report

automatic teller machine (ATM) A computer terminal used to conduct banking transactions; also called a *cash machine.*

debit card A plastic access card used in computerized banking transactions; also called a *cash card.*

Exhibit **4–2**

Electronic Banking
Services

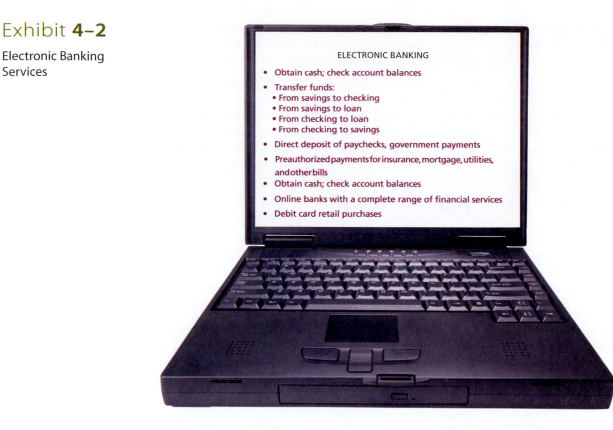

ELECTRONIC BANKING

- Obtain cash; check account balances
- Transfer funds:
  - From savings to checking
  - From savings to loan
  - From checking to loan
  - From checking to savings
- Direct deposit of paychecks, government payments
- Preauthorized payments for insurance, mortgage, utilities, and other bills
- Obtain cash; check account balances
- Online banks with a complete range of financial services
- Debit card retail purchases

the fraud within 60 days of receiving your statement to protect your right not to be charged for the transaction.

Other factors to consider when planning your online banking activities include:

Online Banking Benefits	Online Banking Concerns
• Time and money savings	• Potential privacy, security violations
• Convenience for transactions, comparing rates	• ATM fees can become costly
• No paper trail for identity thieves	• Difficulty depositing cash, checks
• Transfer access for loans, investments	• Overspending due to ease of access
• E-mail notices of due dates	• Online scams, "phishing," and e-mail spam

CAUTION! "Phishing" is a scam that uses e-mail spam or pop-up messages to deceive you into revealing your credit card number, bank account information, Social Security number, passwords, or other private information. These e-mails usually look official, like they are coming from a legitimate bank or other financial institution. Never disclose personal data online or by phone to a questionable source.

Financial Services and Economic Conditions

Changing interest rates, rising consumer prices, and other economic factors influence financial services. For successful financial planning, be aware of the current trends and future prospects for interest rates (see Exhibit 4–3). You can learn about these trends and prospects by reading *The Wall Street Journal* (www.wsj.com), *The Financial Times* (www.ft.com), the business section of daily newspapers, and business periodicals

Exhibit **4–3**

Changing Interest Rates and Financial Service Decisions

When interest rates are rising...

- Use long-term loans to take advantage of current low rates.
- Select short-term savings instruments to take advantage of higher rates when they mature.

- Use short-term loans to take advantage of lower rates when you refinance the loans.
- Select long-term savings instruments to "lock in" earnings at current high rates.

When interest rates are falling...

such as *BusinessWeek* (www.businessweek.com), *Forbes* (www.forbes.com), and *Fortune* (www.fortune.com).

Sheet 11 Planning the Use of Financial Services

CONCEPT CHECK 4–1

1 What are the major categories of financial services?

_____

_____

2 What financial services are available through electronic banking systems?

_____

_____

3 How do changing economic conditions affect the use of financial services?

_____

_____

Apply Yourself!

Objective 1

Survey several people to determine awareness and use of various financial services such as online banking.

Sources of Financial Services

Many types of businesses, including insurance companies, investment brokers, and credit card companies, offer financial services that were once exclusive to banks. Companies such as General Motors, Sears, and AT&T issue credit cards. Banks have also expanded their activities to provide investments, insurance, and real estate services.

OBJECTIVE 2

Compare the types of financial institutions.

Comparing Financial Institutions

The basic questions to ask when selecting a financial service provider are simple:

- Where can I get the best return on my savings?
- How can I minimize the cost of checking and payments services?
- Will I be able to borrow money if I need it?

As you use financial services, decide what you want from the organization that will serve your needs. With the financial marketplace constantly changing, plan to continually consider various factors before selecting an organization.

The services offered by the financial institution will likely be a major factor. In addition, personal service may be important to you. Convenience may take the form of branch office and ATM locations as well as online services. Remember, convenience and service have a cost; be sure to compare fees and other charges at several financial institutions.

Finally, also consider safety and rates. Obtain information about earnings you will receive on savings and checking accounts and the rate you will pay for borrowed funds. Most financial institutions have deposit insurance to protect customers against losses; however, not all of them are insured by federal government programs.

Types of Financial Institutions

Despite changes in the banking environment, many familiar financial institutions still serve your needs. As shown in Exhibit 4–4, some organizations (such as banks and credit unions) offer a wide range of services, while others provide specialized assistance, such as home loans. Be aware that distinctions among the various types of financial institutions are disappearing. For example, today, people can buy investments through their bank and credit union as well as from an investment company or brokerage firm.

Deposit institutions serve as intermediaries between suppliers (savers) and users (borrowers) of funds. The most common of these traditional organizations are:

commercial bank A financial institution that offers a full range of financial services to individuals, businesses, and government agencies.

- **Commercial banks,** which offer a full range of financial services, including checking, savings, lending, and most other services. Commercial banks are organized as corporations, with investors (stockholders) contributing the needed capital to operate.

savings and loan association (S&L) A financial institution that traditionally specialized in savings accounts and mortgage loans.

- **Savings and loan associations (S&Ls),** which traditionally specialized in savings accounts and mortgages. Today, many of these organizations have expanded to offer financial services comparable to those of a bank.

mutual savings bank A financial institution that is owned by depositors and specializes in savings accounts and mortgage loans.

- **Mutual savings banks,** which are owned by depositors, also specialize in savings and mortgages. Located mainly in the northeastern United States, the profits of a mutual savings bank go to the depositors through higher rates on savings.

credit union A user-owned, nonprofit, cooperative financial institution that is organized for the benefit of its members.

- **Credit unions,** which are user-owned, nonprofit, cooperative organizations. Although members traditionally had a common bond such as work location, church, or community affiliation, credit union membership today is more flexible, with more than 80 million people belonging to one. Annual banking studies consistently report lower fees and lower loan rates with higher satisfaction levels for credit unions compared to other financial institutions.

Nondeposit institutions offer various financial services. These institutions include:

- Life insurance companies, which provide financial security for dependents with various life insurance policies, some containing savings and investment

Exhibit **4–4**   Who Provides Financial Services?

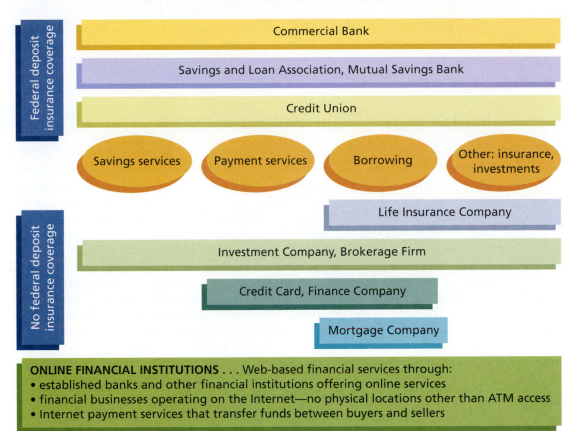

Note: The actual services offered by specific organizations may vary.

features. Expanded activities of life insurance companies include investment and retirement planning services.

- Investment companies, also called *mutual funds,* which offer a **money market fund**—a combination savings–investment plan. The company uses the money from many investors to purchase a variety of short-term financial instruments. However, unlike accounts at most deposit institutions, investment company accounts are not covered by federal deposit insurance.

- Brokerage firms, which often employ investment advisers, serve as an agent between the buyer and seller for stocks, bonds, and other investment securities. These companies obtain their earnings through the commissions and fees charged for various services.

- Credit card companies, which specialize in funding short-term retail lending. However, these networks, including VISA, MasterCard, and Discover, have also expanded into various other banking and investing services.

- Finance companies, which provide loans to consumers and small businesses. These loans have short and intermediate terms with higher rates than most other lenders charge. Most finance companies also offer other financial planning services.

money market fund A savings–investment plan offered by investment companies, with earnings based on investments in various short-term financial instruments.

did you know?

Bankrate.com suggests these actions to minimize fees; (1) avoid overdraft charges of nearly $30 each by linking your checking account to savings; (2) use ATMs that are in your bank's system; (3) search for true "free" checking accounts with a low minimum balance requirement; and (4) consider doing your banking at a credit union, where lower fees, lower borrowing rates, and higher rates for savings are usually offered.

- Mortgage companies, which are organized primarily to provide loans for home purchases. The services of mortgage companies are presented in Chapter 7.

These and other types of financial institutions compete for your business. More and more of these companies are offering a combination of services (saving, checking, credit, insurance, investments) from one source. These one-stop financial service operations are sometimes referred to as *financial supermarkets.*

Problematic Financial Businesses

Would you pay $8 to cash a $100 check? Or pay $20 to borrow $100 for two weeks? Many people without ready access to financial services (especially low-income consumers) use pawnshops, check-cashing outlets, loan stores, and rent-to-own centers.

PAWNSHOPS Pawnshops make loans based on the value of tangible possessions such as jewelry or other valuable items. Many low- and moderate-income families use these organizations to obtain cash loans quickly. Pawnshops charge higher fees than other financial institutions. Thousands of consumers are increasingly in need of small loans—usually $50 to $75, to be repaid in 30 to 45 days. Pawnshops have become the "neighborhood bankers" and the "local shopping malls," since they provide both lending and retail shopping services, selling items that owners do not redeem. While states regulate the interest rates charged by pawnshops, 3 percent a month or higher is common.

did you know?

"Switch kits" are often available to make changing banks easier. These forms and authorization letters facilitate a smooth transition of direct deposits and automatic payments from one financial institution to another.

CHECK-CASHING OUTLETS Most financial institutions will not cash a check unless you have an account. The more than 6,000 check-cashing outlets (CCOs) charge anywhere from 1 to 20 percent of the face value of a check; the average cost is 2 to 3 percent. However, for a low-income family, that can be a significant portion of the total household budget. CCOs, sometimes called a currency exchanges, also offer services, including electronic tax filing, money orders, private postal boxes, utility bill payment, and the sale of transit tokens. A person can usually obtain most of these services for less at other locations.

PAYDAY LOANS Many consumer organizations caution against using payday loans, also referred to as *cash advances, check advance loans, post-dated check loans,* and *delayed deposit loans.* Desperate borrowers pay annual interest rates of as much as 780 percent and more to obtain needed cash from payday loan companies. These enterprises have increased to more than 8,000. The most frequent users of payday loans are workers who have become trapped by debts or who have been driven into debt by misfortune.

In a typical payday loan, a consumer writes a personal check for $115 to borrow $100 for 14 days. The payday lender agrees to hold the check until the next payday. This $15 finance charge for the 14 days translates into an annual percentage rate of 391 percent. Some consumers "roll over" their loans, paying another $15 for the $100 loan for the next 14 days. After a few rollovers, the finance charge can exceed the amount borrowed. The Chicago Department of Consumer Services has reported annual rates ranging from 659 to 1,300 percent for some payday loans.

RENT-TO-OWN CENTERS Years ago, people who rented furniture and appliances found few deluxe items available. Today rental businesses offer big-screen televisions, seven-piece cherrywood bedroom sets, and personal computers. The rent-to-purchase industry is defined as stores that lease products to consumers who can own the item if they complete a certain number of monthly or weekly payments.

In Wisconsin, more than 10,000 customers of the Rent-A-Center chain became part of a class action lawsuit seeking refunds of finance charges for rented merchandise. The suit accused the rental chain of illegally charging interest rates as high as 100 percent to rent televisions and other appliances, often to customers in low-income areas.

CONCEPT CHECK 4–2

1 What factors do consumers usually consider when selecting a financial institution to meet their saving and checking needs?

_____

_____

2 What are examples of deposit-type financial institutions?

_____

_____

3 Match the following descriptions with the appropriate financial institution.

a. commercial bank   _____ Commonly used by people without a bank account.

b. credit union   _____ Investment services accompany main business focus.

c. life insurance company _____ Traditionally provides widest range of financial services.

d. check-cashing outlet   _____ Offers lower fee costs for members.

Apply Yourself!

Objective 2

Using the Web site for the Credit Union National Association (www.cuna.org) or other sources, obtain information about joining a credit union and the services offered by this type of financial institution.

Comparing Savings Plans

A savings plan is vital to attain financial goals. A range of savings alternatives exist (Exhibit 4–5). The many types of savings plans can be grouped into the following main categories.

> **OBJECTIVE 3**
>
> Assess various types of savings plans.

Regular Savings Accounts

Regular savings accounts, also called *passbook* or *statement accounts,* usually involve a low or no minimum balance and allow you to withdraw money as needed. Banks, savings and loan associations, and other financial institutions offer regular savings accounts. At a credit union, these savings plans are called *share accounts.*

Exhibit **4–5** Savings Alternatives

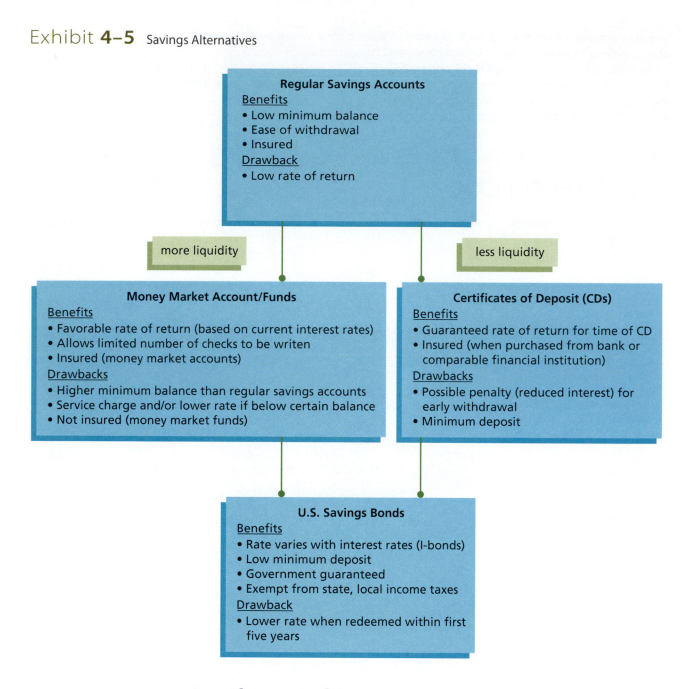

Regular Savings Accounts
Benefits
- Low minimum balance
- Ease of withdrawal
- Insured
Drawback
- Low rate of return

more liquidity

less liquidity

Money Market Account/Funds
Benefits
- Favorable rate of return (based on current interest rates)
- Allows limited number of checks to be writen
- Insured (money market accounts)
Drawbacks
- Higher minimum balance than regular savings accounts
- Service charge and/or lower rate if below certain balance
- Not insured (money market funds)

Certificates of Deposit (CDs)
Benefits
- Guaranteed rate of return for time of CD
- Insured (when purchased from bank or comparable financial institution)
Drawbacks
- Possible penalty (reduced interest) for early withdrawal
- Minimum deposit

U.S. Savings Bonds
Benefits
- Rate varies with interest rates (I-bonds)
- Low minimum deposit
- Government guaranteed
- Exempt from state, local income taxes
Drawback
- Lower rate when redeemed within first five years

Certificates of Deposit

certificate of deposit (CD) A savings plan requiring that a certain amount be left on deposit for a stated time period to earn a specified interest rate.

Higher earnings are available to savers when they leave money on deposit for a set time period. A **certificate of deposit (CD)** is a savings plan requiring that a certain amount be left on deposit for a stated time period (ranging from 30 days to five or more years) to earn a specific rate of return. These time deposits can be an attractive and a safe savings alternative. However, most financial institutions impose a penalty for early withdrawal of CD funds.

TYPES OF CDS Financial institutions offer certificates of deposit with various features:

- *Rising-rate* or *bump-up CDs* have higher rates at various intervals. However, this rate may be in effect for only a couple of months.

- *Stock-indexed CDs* have earnings based on the stock market with higher earnings in times of strong stock performance. At other times, you may earn no interest and may even lose part of your savings.
- *Callable CDs* start with higher rates and long-term maturities. However, the bank may "call" the account after a stipulated period, such as one or two years, if interest rates drop. When the call option is exercised, the saver receives the original investment principal and any interest that has been earned.
- *Promotional CDs* attempt to attract savers with gifts or special rates. A Boulder, Colorado, bank offered Rolex watches, archery equipment, and Zodiac inflatable boats in lieu of interest. Compare the value of the item to the lost interest.

MANAGING CDS When first buying or *rolling over* a CD (buying a new one at maturity), investigate potential earnings and costs. Do not allow your financial institution to automatically roll over your money into another CD for the same term. If interest rates have dropped, you might consider a shorter maturity. Or if you believe rates are at a peak and you won't need the money for some time, obtain a CD with a longer term.

Consider creating a CD *portfolio* with CDs maturing at different times, for example, $2,000 in a three-month CD, $2,000 in a six-month CD, $2,000 in a one-year CD, and $2,000 in a two-year CD. This will give you some degree of liquidity and flexibility when you reinvest your funds.

Interest-Earning Checking Accounts

Checking accounts frequently have a savings feature. These interest-earning accounts usually pay a low interest rate.

Money Market Accounts and Funds

To provide savers with higher interest rates, a savings plan with a floating interest rate was created. A **money market account** is a savings account that requires a minimum balance and has earnings based on the changing market level of interest rates. Money market accounts may allow a limited number of checks to be written and generally impose a fee when the account balance goes below the required minimum, usually $1,000.

Both money market accounts and money market funds offer earnings based on current interest rates, and both have minimum-balance restrictions and allow check writing. The major difference is in safety. Money market *accounts* at banks and savings and loan associations are covered by federal deposit insurance. This is not true of money market *funds,* which are a product of investment and insurance companies. Since money market funds invest mainly in short-term (less than a year) government and corporate securities, however, they are usually quite safe.

money market account A savings account offered by banks, savings and loan associations, and credit unions that requires a minimum balance and has earnings based on market interest rates.

U.S. Savings Bonds

Years ago, the low return on savings bonds made their purchase a patriotic act rather than a wise saving choice. In recent years, however, the Treasury Department has offered various programs to make buying savings bonds more attractive.

EE BONDS Series EE bonds (called Patriot Bonds after the September 11, 2001, terrorist attacks) may be purchased for amounts ranging from $25 to $5,000 (face values of $50 to $10,000, respectively). Electronic EE bonds are purchased at face value; for

LOWDOWN | Federal insurance is comforting, but so far it's temporary and it doesn't cover deposits after September 19. *By Robert Frick*

What You Need to Know About Your
MONEY-MARKET FUND

1. Don't confuse your money-market fund with cash. Many of us had gotten used to thinking of money-market funds as cash in the bank—until we got a wake-up call in September when one faltered and the government had to step in and offer funds insurance. Although money funds are cash-*like,* they're actually mutual funds that hold short-term debt.

The most conservative money funds hold only U.S. Treasury securities. These are bulletproof bills and notes backed by the U.S. government. More common are government-only funds, which own Treasuries but also hold government-backed securities from other issuers. Many funds also hold large amounts of commercial paper, short-term debt from companies.

2. And don't confuse the money-fund insurance with bank insurance. The government recently said it would insure money-market funds—about the same time it upped the insurance on your bank accounts from $100,000 to $250,000. Both moves were intended to halt massive withdrawals, which threatened to worsen the credit crisis. But while the extra bank insurance lasts through next year and all banks get it automatically, the money-fund insurance is more

short-term and companies have to apply for it.

3. Your coverage is limited. The feds are guaranteeing that the value of your money-market deposits won't drop below $1 a share through December 18. But they're covering only the balance you held at the close of business on September 19; if you've added to the fund since that cutoff date, the new deposits are not covered by the guarantee. But your previous balance is covered no matter how many times you withdraw or add money.

4. Make sure you're covered. Money funds were required to apply for the government insurance and pay a small fee. According to Crane Data, 95% of the $3.4 trillion in money-market assets is covered by the government program; most of the remainder is in Treasury-only and government-only funds, which are presumed to be safe. Don't assume your fund holds only Treasury debt. Less than 10% of funds own Treasury assets exclusively. Funds from Vanguard, Fidelity, Schwab and T. Rowe Price are insured, but it's a smart idea to call your fund or check its Web site to make sure it has the insurance.

5. There's a price to be paid for paranoia. You may be tempted to go with a supersafe,

Treasury-only fund, but you might as well put your money under the mattress. The average seven-day yield for Treasury-only funds is less than 1%. Have a little faith that Uncle Sam won't let money funds "break the buck" and consider general funds, which now pay 2.5% and even a percentage point or two higher. And here's a quirk that probably won't last long: Tax-free money-market funds now pay 3% or more because government entities that need to borrow money have to offer higher-than-average rates.

6. Expect the insurance option to continue past december. If the money-funds situation is still shaky, it's a sure bet the program will be extended past the December 18 limit. Moreover, the government is so worried that the buying and selling of commercial paper, which lubricates the credit markets, will freeze up that it started a new program in October to buy these short-term loans directly from issuers.

1. How do money-market funds differ from bank accounts?

_____

2. Describe actions you might take to ensure the safety of your various savings programs.

_____

3. Go to www.kiplinger.com to obtain updated information on money-market safety.

_____

example, you pay $50 for a $50 bond. These bonds may be purchased in amounts of $25 or more.

EE bonds increase in value every month as interest accrues monthly and compounds semiannually. If you redeem EE bonds before five years, you forfeit the latest three months of interest; after five years, you are not penalized. A bond must be held for one year before it can be cashed.

EE bonds purchased between May 1997 and April 30, 2005, earned market-based interest. Since that time, a fixed interest rate has been paid. Series EE bonds continue to earn interest for 30 years, well beyond the time at which the face value is reached. The main tax advantages of Series EE bonds are that (1) the interest earned is exempt from state and local taxes and (2) you do not have to pay federal income tax on earnings until the bonds are redeemed.

Redeemed Series EE bonds may be exempt from federal income tax if the funds are used to pay tuition and fees at a college, university, or qualified technical school for yourself or a dependent. The bonds must be purchased by an individual who is at least 24 years old, and they must be issued in the names of one or both parents. These provisions have been designed to assist low- and middle-income households; people whose incomes exceed a certain amount do not qualify for the exemption.

HH BONDS Series HH bonds are *current-income* bonds, which earn interest every six months. The interest is deposited electronically to your bank account. This interest is taxed as current income. The semiannual interest payments of HH bonds make them a popular source of retirement income.

You can redeem your HH bonds at any time after six months from the issue date. The value of HH bonds doesn't change, so when redeemed, you get back your original investment. HH bonds were available in denominations of $500, $1,000, $5,000, and $10,000. As of 2004, investors are no longer able to reinvest HH bonds or exchange EE bonds for HH bonds.

I BONDS The I bond earns a combined rate consisting of (1) a fixed rate for the life of the bond, and (2) an inflation rate that changes twice a year. Every six months a new, fixed base rate is set for new bonds. The additional interest payment is recalculated twice a year, based on the current annual inflation rate. I bonds are sold in the same denominations as EE bonds, but are purchased at face value, not discount. Also, as with EE bonds, the minimum holding period is one year.

A person may purchase up to $15,000 ($30,000 maturity face) of U.S. savings bonds a year. This amount applies to any person, so parents may buy an additional $15,000 in each child's name. Banks and other financial institutions sell U.S. savings bonds; they may also be purchased online. Lost, stolen, or destroyed savings bonds will be replaced by the government free of charge. Additional information and current value calculations for savings bonds' values may be obtained at www.savingsbonds.gov, where you can maintain an online savings bond account.

Evaluating Savings Plans

Selection of a savings plan is usually influenced by the rate of return, inflation, tax considerations, liquidity, safety, restrictions, and fees (see Exhibit 4–6).

RATE OF RETURN Earnings on savings can be measured by the **rate of return,** or *yield,* the percentage of increase in the value of your savings from earned interest.

---

did you know?

Most of the world's population has no access to basic financial services. The Grameen Bank makes loans to the poorest of the poor in Bangladesh, without collateral. These loans, based on mutual trust and community participation, are designed to fight poverty and enhance community development. The Grameen Bank, created by Professor Muhammad Yunus, has inspired similar activities in more than 40 countries. Indeed, Professor Yunus and the Grameen Bank shared the 2006 *Nobel Peace Prize.* Further information at www.grameen-info.org.

Key Web Site for Savings Bonds
www.savingsbonds.gov.

rate of return The percentage of increase in the value of savings as a result of interest earned; also called *yield*.

Exhibit **4–6**

Selecting a Savings Plan

For example, a $100 savings account that earned $5 after a year would have a rate of return, or yield, of 5 percent. This rate of return was determined by dividing the interest earned ($5) by the amount in the savings account ($100). The yield on your savings usually will be greater than the stated interest rate.

compounding A process that calculates interest based on previously earned interest.

Compounding refers to interest that is earned on previously earned interest. Each time interest is added to your savings, the next interest amount is computed on the new balance in the account. The more frequent the compounding, the higher your rate of return will be. For example, $100 in a savings account that earns 6 percent compounded annually will increase $6 after a year. But the same $100 in a 6 percent account compounded daily will earn $6.19 for the year. Although this difference may seem slight, large amounts held in savings for long periods of time will result in far higher differences (see Exhibit 4–7).

Exhibit **4–7**

Compounding Frequency Affects the Saving Yield

Shorter compounding periods result in higher yields. This chart shows the growth of $10,000, earning a rate of 8 percent, but with different compounding methods.

End of year	COMPOUNDING METHOD			
	Daily	Monthly	Quarterly	Annually
1	$10,832.78	$10,830.00	$10,824.32	$10,800.00
2	11,743.91	11,728.88	11,716.59	11,664.00
3	12,712.17	12,702.37	12,682.41	12,597.12
4	13,770.82	13,756.66	13,727.85	13,604.89
5	14,917.62	14.898.46	14,859.46	14,693.28
Annual yield	8.33%	8.30%	8.24%	8.00%

The *Truth in Savings Act* requires financial institutions to disclose the following information on savings account plans: (1) fees on deposit accounts; (2) the interest rate; (3) the annual percentage yield (APY); and (4) other terms and conditions of the savings plan. Truth in Savings (TIS) defines **annual percentage yield (APY)** as the percentage rate expressing the total amount of interest that would be received on a $100 deposit based on the annual rate and frequency of compounding for a 365-day period. APY reflects the amount of interest a saver should expect to earn.

annual percentage yield (APY) The percentage rate expressing the total amount of interest that would be received on a $100 deposit based on the annual rate and frequency of compounding for a 365-day period.

Example

When the number of days in the term is 365 (that is, where the stated maturity is 365 days) or where the account does not have a stated maturity, the APY formula is simply

$$APY = 100 \left(\frac{Interest}{Principal} \right)$$

$$= 100 \left(\frac{66}{1,200} \right)$$

$$= 100 \ (0.055) = 5.5\%$$

INFLATION The rate of return you earn on your savings should be compared with the inflation rate. When inflation was over 10 percent, people with money in savings accounts earning 5 or 6 percent were experiencing a loss in the buying power of that money. In general, as the inflation rate increases, the interest rates offered to savers also increase.

TAXES Like inflation, taxes reduce interest earned on savings. For example, a 10 percent return for a saver in a 28 percent tax bracket means a real return of 7.2 percent (the Figure It Out box shows how to compute the after-tax savings rate of return). As discussed in Chapter 3 , several tax-exempt and tax-deferred savings plans and investments can increase your real rate of return.

LIQUIDITY *Liquidity* allows you to withdraw your money on short notice without a loss of value or fees. Some savings plans impose penalties for early withdrawal or have other restrictions. With certain types of savings certificates and accounts, early withdrawal may be penalized by a loss of interest or a lower earnings rate. Consider the degree of liquidity you desire in relation to your savings goals. To achieve long-term financial goals, many people trade off liquidity for a higher return.

SAFETY Most savings plans at banks, savings and loan associations, and credit unions are insured by agencies affiliated with the federal government. This protection prevents a loss of money due to the failure of the insured institution. While a few financial institutions have failed in recent years, savers with deposits covered by federal insurance have not lost any money. Depositors of failed organizations either have been paid the amounts in their accounts or have had the accounts taken over by a financially stable institution.

The Federal Deposit Insurance Corporation (FDIC) administers separate insurance funds: the Bank Insurance Fund and the Savings Association Insurance Fund (SAIF). Credit unions may obtain deposit insurance through the National Credit Union Association (NCUA). Some state-chartered credit unions have opted for a private insurance program.

Figure It Out!

> After-Tax Savings Rate of Return

The taxability of interest on your savings reduces your real rate of return. In other words, you lose some portion of your interest to taxes. This calculation consists of the following steps:

1. Determine your top tax bracket for federal income taxes.

2. Subtract this rate, expressed as a decimal, from 1.0.

3. Multiply the result by the yield on your savings account.

4. This number, expressed as a percentage, is your after-tax rate of return.

For example,

1. You are in the 28 percent tax bracket.

2. $1.0 - 0.28 = 0.72$.

3. If the yield on your savings account is 6.25 percent, $0.0625 \times 0.72 = 0.045$.

4. Your after-tax rate of return is 4.5 percent.

You may use the same procedure to determine the *real rate of return* on your savings based on inflation. For example, if you are earning 6 percent on savings and inflation is 5 percent, your real rate of return (after inflation) is 5.7 percent: $0.06 \times (1 - 0.05) = 0.057$.

CALCULATIONS

1. What would be the after-tax return for a person who is receiving 4 percent on savings and is in a 15 percent tax bracket? _____ %

2. What would be the after-tax value of $100 earned in interest for a person who is in a 31 percent tax bracket? $_____

While the FDIC insures amounts of up to $100,000 (recently raised to $250,000 temporarily) per depositor per insured financial institution, a person may qualify for additional coverage if accounts in different ownership categories are used.

By using individual, joint, and trust accounts, you will be able to have federal deposit insurance amounts that exceed the coverage limit. However, for example, if you have a $70,000 individual account and a $240,000 joint account with a relative in the same financial institution, $20,000 of your savings will not be covered by federal deposit insurance (one-half of the $240,000 exceeds the $100,000 limit). Also, remember that different branch offices count as the same institution, which could affect your coverage limit. And, mergers in the financial service industry may bring accounts from different banks together.

As of April 2006, the Federal Deposit Insurance Corporation (FDIC) and the National Credit Union Administration (NCUA) increased deposit coverage for certain retirement accounts from $100,000 to $250,000. The higher insurance coverage applies to traditional and Roth IRAs, Simplified Employee Pension (SEP) IRAs, and Savings Incentive Match Plans for Employees (SIMPLE) IRAs. Also included are self-directed Keogh accounts and various plans for state government employees. This coverage applies only to retirement accounts in financial institutions insured by the FDIC and NCUA.

RESTRICTIONS AND FEES Other limitations can affect your choice of a savings program. For example, there may be a delay between the time interest is earned and the time it is added to your account. This means the interest will not

did you know?

In October 2008, the FDIC announced the temporary Transaction Account Guarantee Program to provide full coverage for non-interest (checking) accounts at FDIC-insured institutions agreeing to participate in this program. This unlimited insurance coverage expires in December 2009. For all other accounts, the FDIC increased the coverage for insured institutions to $250,000 per depositor, also until December 31, 2009. After that, deposit insurance will return to the $100,000 limit, except for certain retirement accounts, which are covered to $250,000. Go to www.fdic.gov for the latest details on deposit insurance.

be available for your immediate use. Also, some institutions charge a transaction fee for each deposit or withdrawal. Some financial institutions offer a "free gift" when a certain savings amount is deposited. To receive this gift, you have to leave your money on deposit for a certain time period, or you may receive less interest, since some of the earnings are used to cover the cost of the "free" items.

Sheet 12 Comparing Savings Plans

Sheet 13 Using Savings Plans to Achieve Financial Goals

CONCEPT CHECK 4–3

1 What are the main types of savings plans offered by financial institutions?

_____

_____

2 How does a money market *account* differ from a money market *fund?*

_____

_____

3 What are the benefits of U.S. savings bonds?

_____

4 How do inflation and taxes affect earnings on savings?

_____

_____

5 In the following financial situations, check the box that is the major influence for the person when selecting a savings plan:

Financial planning situation	Rate of return	Inflation	Taxes	Liquidity	Safety
a. An older couple needs easy access to funds for living expenses.					
b. A person is concerned with loss of buying power of funds on deposit.					
c. A saver desires to maximize earnings from the savings plan.					
d. A middle-aged person wants assurance that the funds are safe.					

Apply Yourself!

Objective 3

Conduct online research to obtain past and current data on various interest rates (such as prime rate, T-bill rate, mortgage rate, corporate bond rate, and six-month CD rate). Information may be obtained at www.federalreserve.gov and other Web sites. How do these rates affect various personal financial decisions?

Comparing Payment Methods

OBJECTIVE 4

Evaluate different types of payment methods.

Each year, paper checks account for a smaller and smaller portion of payments in our society. While check writing is being used less, checking accounts are still the common source for most debit card transactions and online payments. As shown in Exhibit 4–8, payment alternatives may be viewed in three main categories.

Electronic Payments

Transactions not involving cash, checks, or credit cards have expanded with technology, improved security, and increased consumer acceptance.

DEBIT CARD TRANSACTIONS Most retail stores, restaurants, and other businesses accept debit cards, also called check cards, issued by Visa and MasterCard. When the debit card transaction is processed, the amount of the purchase is deducted from your checking account. Most debit cards can be used two ways: (1) with your signature, like a credit card, or (2) with your personal identification number (PIN), like an ATM card.

ONLINE PAYMENTS Banks and Internet companies are serving as third parties to facilitate online bill payments. Some of these Internet companies are www.paypal.com, www.mycheckfree.com, and www.paytrust.com. When using these services, be sure to consider the monthly charge as well as online security and customer service availability. Also on the Web are "cyber cash" services creating their own *e-money* that serves as a medium of exchange for online transactions.

STORED-VALUE CARDS Prepaid cards for telephone service, transit fares, highway tolls, laundry service, and school lunches are common. Some of these stored-value cards are disposable; others can be reloaded with an additional amount.

SMART CARDS These "electronic wallets" are similar to other ATM cards. However, the imbedded microchip stores prepaid amounts as well as information with account balances, transaction records, insurance information, and medical history.

did you know?

Mobile payment systems through cell phones and other wireless devices are expanding. This usually occurs through an existing bank account. Most banking activities accessed by computer will soon also occur via cell phone. Some future transactions may bypass banks with charges directly on your phone bill.

Checking Accounts

Despite increased use of electronic payment systems, a checking account is still a necessity for most people. Checking accounts fall into three major categories: regular checking accounts, activity accounts, and interest-earning checking accounts.

Exhibit 4–8

Payment Alternatives

Electronic Payments	Checking Accounts	Other Payment Methods
Debit (cash) and credit cards	Regular checking account	Certified check
Online payments, transfer	Activity checking account	Cashier's check
Smart cards ("electronic wallet")	Interest-earning account	Traveler's checks
Stored-value (prepaid) cards		Money order

REGULAR CHECKING ACCOUNTS *Regular checking accounts* usually have a monthly service charge that you may avoid by keeping a minimum balance in the account. Some financial institutions will waive the monthly fee if you keep a certain amount in savings. Avoiding the monthly service charge can be beneficial. For example, a monthly fee of $7.50 results in $90 a year. However, you lose interest on the minimum-balance amount in a non-interest-earning account.

ACTIVITY ACCOUNTS *Activity accounts* charge a fee for each check written and sometimes a fee for each deposit in addition to a monthly service charge. However, you do not have to maintain a minimum balance. An activity account is most appropriate for people who write only a few checks each month and are unable to maintain the required minimum balance.

INTEREST-EARNING CHECKING *Interest-earning checking accounts* usually require a minimum balance. If the account balance goes below this amount, you may not earn interest and will likely incur a service charge. These are called *share draft accounts* at credit unions.

Evaluating Checking and Payment Accounts

Would you rather have a checking account that pays interest and requires a $1,000 minimum balance or an account that doesn't pay interest and requires a $300 minimum balance? This decision requires evaluating factors such as restrictions, fees and charges, interest, and special services (see Exhibit 4–9).

Exhibit 4–9

Checking Account Selection Factors

CHECKING ACCOUNT SELECTION FACTORS

Special Services
- Direct deposit of payroll and government checks
- 24-hour teller machines
- Overdraft protection
- Banking-at-home
- Discounts or free checking for certain groups (students, senior citizens, employees of certain companies)
- Free or discounted services, such as traveler's checks

Restrictions
- Minimum balance
- Federal deposit insurance
- Hours and location of branch offices
- Holding period for deposited checks

Fees and Charges
- Monthly fee
- Fees for each check or deposit
- Printing of checks
- Fee to obtain canceled check copy
- Overdraft, stop-payment order, certified check fee
- Fees for preauthorized bill payment, fund transfer, or home banking activity

Interest
- Interest rate
- Minimum deposit to earn interest
- Method of compounding
- Portion of balance used to compute interest
- Fee charged for falling below necessary balance to earn interest

RESTRICTIONS The most common limitation on a checking account is the required amount that must be kept on deposit to earn interest or avoid a service charge. In the past, financial institutions placed restrictions on the holding period for deposited checks. A waiting period was usually required before you could access the funds. The Check Clearing for the 21st Century Act (known as Check 21) shortens the processing time. This law establishes the *substitute check,* which is a digital reproduction of the original paper check, and is considered a legal equivalent of the original check.

CAUTION! A bounced check may result in not only a fee of $30 or more but also restrictions on the acceptance of your checks in the future. Some check-approval systems may keep your name on a "restricted" list for a period of six months to five years.

FEES AND CHARGES Nearly all financial institutions require a minimum balance or impose service charges for checking accounts. When using an interest-bearing checking account, compare your earnings with any service charge or fee. Also, consider the cost of lost or reduced interest resulting from maintaining the minimum balance. Checking account fees have increased in recent years. Items such as check printing, overdraft fees, and stop-payment orders have doubled or tripled in price at some financial institutions.

INTEREST The interest rate, the frequency of compounding, and the interest computation method will affect the earnings on your checking account.

SPECIAL SERVICES As financial institutions attempt to reduce paper and postage costs, canceled checks are no longer returned. Bank customers are provided with more detailed monthly statements and will likely have online access to view and print checks that have been paid.

Overdraft protection is an automatic loan made to checking customers for checks written in excess of their balance. This service is convenient but costly. Most overdraft plans make loans based on $50 or $100 increments. An overdraft of just $1 might trigger a $50 loan and corresponding finance charges of perhaps 18 percent. But overdraft protection can be less costly than the fee charged for a check you write when you do not have enough money on deposit to cover it. That fee may be $30 or more. Many financial institutions will allow you to cover checking account overdrafts with an automatic transfer from a savings account for a nominal fee.

overdraft protection An automatic loan made to checking account customers to cover the amount of checks written in excess of the available balance in the checking account.

Beware of checking accounts packaged with several services (safe deposit box, traveler's checks, low-rate loans, and travel insurance) for a single monthly fee. This may sound like a good value; however, financial experts observe that only a small group of people make use of all services in the package.

did you know?

"Remote deposit" allows a person to deposit checks into a bank account from home or office without having to present the actual check. The process begins with a scanner capturing a digital image of the check. Then, the image is transmitted online. Although mainly used by businesses, the system may also be used by individuals.

Other Payment Methods

A *certified check* is a personal check with guaranteed payment. The amount of the check is deducted from your balance when the financial institution certifies the check. A *cashier's check* is a check of a financial institution. You may purchase one by paying the amount of the check plus a fee. You may purchase a *money order* in a similar manner from financial institutions, post offices, and stores. Certified checks, cashier's checks, and money orders allow you to make a payment that the recipient knows is valid.

Traveler's checks allow you to make payments when you are away from home. This payment form requires you to sign each check twice. First, you sign the traveler's checks when you purchase them. Then, to identify you as the authorized person, you sign them again as you cash them. Electronic traveler's checks, in the form of a pre-paid travel card, are also available. The card allows travelers visiting other nations to get local currency from an ATM.

Managing Your Checking Account

Obtaining and using a checking account involves several activities.

OPENING A CHECKING ACCOUNT First, decide who the owner of the account is. Only one person is allowed to write checks on an *individual account.* A *joint account* has two or more owners. Both an individual account and a joint account require a signature card. This document is a record of the official signatures of the person or persons authorized to write checks on the account.

MAKING DEPOSITS A *deposit ticket* is used for adding funds to your checking account. On this document, you list the amounts of cash and checks being deposited. Each check you deposit requires an *endorsement*—your signature on the back of the check—to authorize the transfer of the funds into your account. The three common endorsement forms are:

- A *blank endorsement* is just your signature, which should be used only when you are actually depositing or cashing a check, since a check may be cashed by anyone once it has been signed.
- A *restrictive endorsement* consists of the words *for deposit only,* followed by your signature, which is especially useful when you are depositing checks.
- A *special endorsement* allows you to transfer a check to someone else with the words *pay to the order of* followed by the name of the other person and then your signature.

WRITING CHECKS Before writing a check, record the information in your check register and deduct the amount of the check from your balance. Many checking account customers use duplicate checks to maintain a record of their current balance.

The procedure for proper check writing has the following steps: (1) record the date; (2) write the name of the person or organization receiving the payment; (3) record the amount of the check in numerals; (4) write the amount of the check in words; checks for less than a dollar should be written as "only 79 cents," for example, and cross out the word *dollars* on the check; (5) sign the check; (6) note the reason for payment.

A *stop-payment order* may be necessary if a check is lost or stolen. Most banks do not honor checks with "stale" dates, usually six months old or older. The fee for a stop-payment commonly ranges from $20 to more than $30. If several checks are missing or you lose your checkbook, closing the account and opening a new one is likely to be less costly than paying several stop-payment fees.

RECONCILING YOUR CHECKING ACCOUNT Each month you will receive a *bank statement* summarizing deposits, checks paid, ATM withdrawals, interest earned, and fees such as service charges and printing of checks. The balance reported on the statement will usually differ from the balance in your checkbook. Reasons for a difference may include checks that have not yet cleared, deposits not received by the bank, and interest earned.

To determine the correct balance, prepare a *bank reconciliation,* to account for differences between the bank statement and your checkbook balance. This process involves the following steps:

1. Compare the checks written with those reported as paid on the statement. Use the canceled checks, or compare your check register with the check numbers

Personal Finance in Practice

> Are You Avoiding Identity Theft?

People who put their Social Security and driver's license numbers on their checks are making identity theft fairly easy. With one check, a con artist could know your Social Security, driver's license, and bank account numbers as well as your address, phone number, and perhaps even a sample of your signature.

An attorney had his wallet stolen. Within a week, the thieves ordered an expensive monthly cell phone package, applied for a Visa credit card, had a credit line approved to buy a Gateway computer, and received a PIN number from the Department of Motor Vehicles to change his driving record information online.

Identity fraud can range from passing bad checks and using stolen credit cards to theft of another person's total financial existence. The following quiz can help you avoid becoming one of the more than 1,000 people who each day have their identities stolen by con artists.

If you are a victim of identity theft, take the following actions:

- File a police report immediately in the area where the item was stolen. This proves you were diligent and is a first step toward an investigation (if there ever is one).

- Call the three national credit reporting organizations *immediately* to place a fraud alert on your name and Social Security number. The numbers are: Equifax, 1-800-525-6285; Experian (formerly TRW), 1-888-397-3742; and Trans Union, 1-800-680-7289.

- Contact the Social Security Administration fraud line at 1-800-269-0271.

Additional information on financial privacy and identity theft is available at www.identitytheft.org, www.idfraud.org, www.privacyrights.org.

Which of the following actions have you taken to avoid identity theft?	Yes	No	Action needed
1. I have only my initials and last name on my checks so a person will not know how I sign my checks.			
2. I do not put the full account number on my checks when paying a bill; I put only the last four numbers.			
3. I have my work phone and a P.O. box (if applicable) on my checks instead of home information.			
4. I don't put my Social Security number on any document unless it is legally required.			
5. I shred or burn financial information containing account or Social Security numbers.			
6. I use passwords other than maiden names.			
7. I do not mail bills from my home mailbox, especially if it is out by the street.			
8. I check my credit report yearly with all three major credit reporting agencies once or twice a year to make sure it is correct.			
9. I ask to have my name removed from mailing lists operated by credit agencies and companies offering credit promotions.			
10. I have a photocopy of the contents of my wallet (both sides of each item) as a record to cancel accounts if necessary.			

reported on the bank statement. *Subtract* from the *bank statement balance* the total of the checks written but not yet cleared.

2. Determine whether any deposits made are not on the statement; *add* the amount of the outstanding deposits to the *bank statement balance*.

3. *Subtract* fees or charges on the bank statement and ATM withdrawals from your *checkbook balance.*

4. *Add* any interest earned to your *checkbook balance.*

At this point, the revised balances for both the checkbook and the bank statement should be the same. If the two do not match, check your math; make sure every check and deposit was recorded correctly.

Example

To determine the true balance in your checking account:

Bank Statement		Your Checkbook	
Bank balance..............................	$920	Checkbook balance................	$1,041
Subtract: Outstanding checks ...	−187	Subtract: Fees, ATM withdrawals................	−271
Add: Deposit in transit.............	+200	Add: Interest earned, direct deposits.....................	+163
Adjusted bank statement balance................	933	Adjusted checkbook balance................................	933

Sheet 14 Comparing Payment Methods; Bank Reconciliation

CONCEPT CHECK 4–4

1 Are checking accounts that earn interest preferable to regular checking accounts? Why or why not?

_____

_____

2 What factors are commonly considered when selecting a checking account?

_____

_____

3 For the following situations, select and describe a payment method that would be appropriate for the needs of the person.

Payment situation	Suggested payment method
a. A need to send funds for a purchase from an organization that requires guaranteed payment.	
b. Traveling to Asia, you desire to be able to access funds in the local currencies of various countries.	
c. A desire to pay bills using your home computer instead of writing checks.	
d. You write only a few checks a month and you want to minimize your costs.	

4 Based on the following information, determine the true balance in your checking account.

Balance in your checkbook, $356   Balance on bank statement, $472

Service charge and other fees, $15   Interest earned on the account, $4

Total of outstanding checks, $187   Deposits in transit, $60

Apply Yourself!

Objective 4

Observe customers making payments in a retail store. How often are cash, checks, credit cards, or debit cards used?

Back to ... Getting Personal

Reconsider your responses to the "Getting Personal" questions at the beginning of the chapter. For making better financial choices related to financial services:

- Conduct a Web search of online banks to obtain information on services that might be of value to you now or in the future. Consider how changing interest rates might affect your decision to use various types of financial services.
- Consider various sources of financial services. Credit unions consistently offer a low-cost alternative for financial services. For additional information about

credit unions, go to www.cuna.org and www.creditunion.coop.
- Obtain current interest rates for CDs and other savings plans at www.bankrate.com. For the latest rates and information on U.S. savings bonds, go to www.savingsbonds.gov.
- Become better informed on the safety of savings plans and federal deposit insurance at www.fdic.gov.

What did you learn in this chapter that could help you make wiser choices when using financial services?

Chapter Summary

Objective 1   Financial products such as savings plans, checking accounts, loans, trust services, and electronic banking are used for managing daily financial activities.

Objective 2   Commercial banks, savings and loan associations, mutual savings banks, credit unions, life insurance companies, investment companies, finance companies, mortgage companies, pawnshops, and check-cashing outlets may be compared on the basis of services offered, rates and fees, safety, convenience, and special programs available to customers.

Objective 3   Commonly used savings plans include regular savings accounts, certificates of deposit, interest-earning checking accounts, money market accounts, money market funds, and U.S. savings bonds. Savings plans may be evaluated on the basis of rate of return, inflation, tax considerations, liquidity, safety, restrictions, and fees.

Objective 4   Debit cards, online payment systems, and stored-value cards are increasing in use for payment activities. Regular checking accounts, activity accounts, and interest-earning checking accounts can be compared with regard to restrictions (such as a minimum balance), fees and charges, interest, and special services.

Key Terms

annual percentage yield (APY) 123
asset management account 111
automatic teller machine
   (ATM) 111
certificate of deposit (CD) 118
commercial bank 114

compounding 122
credit union 114
debit card 111
money market account 119
money market fund 115
mutual savings bank 114

overdraft protection 128
rate of return 121
savings and loan association
   (S&L) 114
trust 110

Key Formulas

Page	Topic	Formula
123	Annual percentage yield (APY)	$APY = 100 \left[\left(1 + \dfrac{\text{Interest}}{\text{Principal}} \right)^{365/\text{days in term}} - 1 \right]$
		Principal = Amount of funds on deposit
		Interest = Total dollar amount earned on the principal
		Days in term = Actual number of days in the term of the account
	When the number of days in the term is 365 or where the account does not have a stated maturity, the APY formula is simply	$APY = 100 \left(\dfrac{\text{Interest}}{\text{Principal}} \right)$
		Example:
		$100 \left[\left(1 + \dfrac{\$56.20}{\$1,000} \right)^{\frac{365}{365}} - 1 \right] = 0.0562 = 5.62\%$
124	After-tax rate of return	Interest rate $\times$ (1 − Tax rate)
		Example:
		$0.05 \times (1 - 0.28) = 0.036 = 3.6\%$

Self-Test Problems

1. What would be the annual percentage yield (APY) for a savings account that earned $174 on a balance of $3,250 over the past 365 days?
2. If you earned a 4.2 percent return on your savings, with a 15 percent tax rate, what is the after-tax rate of return?

Solutions

1. To calculate the APY when the number of days in the term is 365, use this formula:

$$\text{APY} = 100\left(\frac{\text{Interest}}{\text{Principal}}\right)$$

$$= 100\left(\frac{174}{3250}\right)$$

$$= 100\,(0.0535) = 5.35\%$$

2. To calculate the after-tax rate of return use

Interest rate $\times$ (1 − Tax rate)

$0.042 \times (1 - 0.15) = 0.042\,(0.85) = 0.0357 = 3.57\%$

Problems

1. An ATM with a service fee of $2 is used by a person 100 times in a year. What would be the future value in 10 years (use a 4 percent rate) of the annual amount paid in ATM fees? (Obj. 1)

2. If a person has ATM fees each month of $22 for eight years, what would be the total cost of those banking fees? (Obj. 1)

3. A payday loan company charges 4 percent interest for a two-week period. What would be the annual interest rate from that company? (Obj. 2)

4. For each of these situations, determine the savings amount. Use the time value of money tables in Chapter 1 (Exhibit 1–3) or in the Chapter 1 appendix. (Obj. 3)

   a. What would be the value of a savings account started with $500, earning 6 percent (compounded annually) after 10 years?
   b. Brenda Young desires to have $10,000 eight years from now for her daughter's college fund. If she will earn 7 percent (compounded annually) on her money, what amount should she deposit now? Use the present value of a single amount calculation.
   c. What amount would you have if you deposited $1,500 a year for 30 years at 8 percent (compounded annually)?

5. What would be the annual percentage yield for a savings account that earned $56 in interest on $800 over the past 365 days? (Obj. 3)

6. With a 28 percent marginal tax rate, would a tax-free yield of 7 percent or a taxable yield of 9.5 percent give you a better return on your savings? Why? (Obj. 3)

7. Janie has $70,000 in a single ownership money market account, $30,000 in a single ownership savings certificate, and has a joint account with her mother with a balance of $214,000. Based on $100,000 of Federal Deposit Insurance Corporation coverage, what amount of Janie's savings would not be covered by deposit insurance? (Obj. 3)

8. A certificate of deposit will often result in a penalty for withdrawing funds before the maturity date. If the penalty involves two months of interest, what would be the amount for early withdrawal on a $20,000, 6 percent CD? (Obj. 3)

9. What might be a savings goal for a person who buys a five-year CD paying 4.67 percent instead of an 18-month savings certificate paying 3.29 percent? (Obj. 4)

10. What is the annual *opportunity cost* of a checking account that requires a $350 minimum balance to avoid service charges? Assume an interest rate of 3 percent. (Obj. 4)

11. Compare the costs and benefits of these two checking accounts: (Obj. 4)
    Account 1: A regular checking account with a monthly fee of $6 when the balance goes below $300.

    Account 2: An interest-earning checking account (paying 1.2 percent), with a monthly charge of $3 if the balance goes below $100.

12. A bank that provides overdraft protection charges 12 percent for each $100 (or portion of $100) borrowed when an overdraft occurs. (Obj. 4)

    a. What amount of interest would the customer pay for a $188 overdraft? (Assume the interest is for the full amount borrowed for whole year.)
    b. How much would be saved by using the overdraft protection loan if a customer has three overdraft charges of $30 each during the year?

13. What would be the net *annual* cost of the following checking accounts? (Obj. 4)

    a. Monthly fee, $3.75; processing fee, 25 cents per check; checks written, an average of 14 a month.
    b. Interest earnings of 4 percent with a $500 minimum balance; average monthly balance, $600; monthly service charge of $15 for falling below the minimum balance, which occurs three times a year (no interest earned in these months).

Questions

1. How has online banking changed the way consumers select and use various financial services?

2. What relationship exists between changing interest rates and the rates of return for various savings accounts, money market accounts, and certificates of deposit of various lengths?

3. What actions would you recommend to someone who was considering using the services of a pawnshop, check-cashing outlet, or payday loan company?

4. What fees and deductions may be overlooked when balancing your checking account?

5. a. What are potential benefits of an overdraft protection service for your checking account?

   b. What costs should a person consider before deciding to use the overdraft protection service?

Case in Point

BEWARE OF HIDDEN BANKING FEES

"Wow! My account balance is a little lower than I expected," commented Lisa Cross as she reviewed her monthly bank statement. "Wait a minute! There's nearly $20 in fees for ATM withdrawals and other service charges," she cried out.

Many people do not realize the amount they pay each month for various bank fees. These charges result from various services that give customers convenience, reliability, and safety.

"Oh no! I also went below the minimum balance required for my *free* checking account," Lisa groaned. "That cost me $7.50!"

Lisa is not alone in her frustration with fees paid for financial services. While careless money management caused many of these charges, others could be reduced or eliminated by comparing costs at various financial institutions.

5 Consumer Credit: Advantages, Disadvantages, Sources, and Costs

Getting Personal

Do you know how to use credit wisely? For each of the following statements, select the letter to indicate your answers regarding these statements:

1. I pay any bills I have when they are due ____.
   a. always
   b. most of the time
   c. sometimes

2. If I need more money for my expenses, I borrow it ____.
   a. never
   b. sometimes
   c. often

3. If I want to see a copy of my credit report, I can contact ____.
   a. a credit reporting agency
   b. a bank
   c. the principal of my school

4. If I default (do not repay) on a loan, it will stay on my credit report for ____.
   a. 7 years
   b. 2 years
   c. 6 months

5. If I have serious credit problems, I should ____.
   a. contact my creditors to explain the problem
   b. contact only the most persistent creditors
   c. not contact my creditors and hope they will forget about me

6. I can begin building a good rating by ____.
   a. opening a savings account and making regular monthly deposits
   b. paying most of my bills on time
   c. opening a checking account and bouncing checks

Source: *How to Be Credit Smart* (Washington, DC: Consumer Education Foundation, 1994).

Scoring: Give yourself 3 points for each a, 2 points for each b, and 1 point for each c. Add up the number of points. If you scored 6–9 points, you might want to take a closer look at how credit works before you get over your head in debt. If you scored 10–13 points, you are off to a good start, but be sure you know the pitfalls of opening a credit account.

Your Personal Financial Plan Sheets

15. Consumer credit usage patterns.
16. Credit card/charge account comparison.
17. Consumer loan comparison.

Objectives

In this chapter, you will learn to:

1. Analyze advantages and disadvantages of using consumer credit.
2. Assess the types and sources of consumer credit.
3. Determine whether you can afford a loan and how to apply for credit.
4. Determine the cost of credit by calculating interest using various interest formulas.
5. Develop a plan to protect your credit and manage your debts.

Why is this important?

You charge $2,000 in tuition and fees on a credit card with an interest rate of 18.5 percent. If you pay off the balance by making the minimum payment each month, you will need more than 11 years to repay the debt. By the time you have paid off the loan, you will have spent an extra $1,934 in interest alone—almost the actual cost of your tuition and fees. Understanding the costs involved in obtaining credit will give you the tools to identify the best source of credit.

What Is Consumer Credit?

Credit is an arrangement to receive cash, goods, or services now and pay for them in the future. **Consumer credit** refers to the use of credit for personal needs (except a home mortgage) by individuals and families, in contrast to credit used for business purposes.

Consumer credit is based on trust in people's ability and willingness to pay bills when due. It works because people by and large are honest and responsible. But how does consumer credit affect our economy, and how is it affected by our economy?

OBJECTIVE 1

Analyze advantages and disadvantages of using consumer credit.

credit An arrangement to receive cash, goods, or services now and pay for them in the future.

consumer credit The use of credit for personal needs (except a home mortgage).

The Importance of Consumer Credit in Our Economy

Consumer credit dates back to colonial times. Although credit was originally a privilege of the affluent, farmers came to use it extensively. No direct finance charges were imposed; instead, the cost of credit was added to the prices of goods. With the advent of the automobile in the early 1900s, installment credit, in which the debt is repaid in equal installments over a specified period of time, exploded on the American scene.

All economists now recognize consumer credit as a major force in the American economy. Any forecast or evaluation of the economy includes consumer spending trends and consumer credit as a sustaining force. To paraphrase an old political expression, as the consumer goes, so goes the U.S. economy.

Uses and Misuses of Credit

Using credit to purchase goods and services may allow consumers to be more efficient or more productive or to lead more satisfying lives. Many valid reasons can be found for using credit. A medical emergency may leave a person strapped for funds. A homemaker returning to the workforce may need a car. An item may cost less money now than it will cost later. Borrowing for a college education is another valid reason. But borrowing for everyday living expenses or financing a Corvette on credit when a Ford Escort is all your budget allows is probably not reasonable.

Using credit increases the amount of money a person can spend to purchase goods and services now. But the trade-off is that it decreases the amount of money that will be available to spend in the future. However, many people expect their incomes to increase and therefore expect to be able to make payments on past credit purchases and still make new purchases.

Here are some questions you should consider before you decide how and when to make a major purchase, for example, a car:

- Do I have the cash I need for the down payment?
- Do I want to use my savings for this purchase?
- Does the purchase fit my budget?
- Could I use the credit I need for this purchase in some better way?
- Could I postpone the purchase?
- What are the opportunity costs of postponing the purchase (alternative transportation costs, a possible increase in the price of the car)?
- What are the dollar costs and the psychological costs of using credit (interest, other finance charges, being in debt and responsible for making a monthly payment)?

If you decide to use credit, make sure the benefits of purchasing now (increased efficiency or productivity, a more satisfying life, etc.) outweigh the costs (financial and psychological) of using credit. Thus, credit, when effectively used, can help you have more and enjoy more. When misused, credit can result in default, bankruptcy, and loss of creditworthiness.

Advantages of Credit

Consumer credit enables people to enjoy goods and services now—a car, a home, an education, emergencies—and pay for them through payment plans based on future income.

Credit cards permit the purchase of goods even when funds are low. Customers with previously approved credit may receive other extras, such as advance notice of sales and the right to order by phone or to buy on approval. In addition, many shoppers believe that returning merchandise purchased on account is easier than returning cash purchases. Credit cards also provide shopping convenience and the efficiency of paying for several purchases with one monthly payment.

Credit is more than a substitute for cash. Many of the services it provides are taken for granted. Every time you turn on the water tap, click the light switch, or telephone a friend, you are using credit.

Using credit is safe, since charge accounts and credit cards let you shop and travel without carrying a large amount of cash. It offers convenience, since you need a credit card to make a hotel reservation, rent a car, and shop by phone or Internet. You may also use credit cards for identification when cashing checks, and the use of credit provides you with a record of expenses.

The use of credit cards can provide up to a 50-day "float," the time lag between when you make the purchase and when the lender deducts the balance from your checking account when payment is due. This float, offered by many credit card issuers, includes a grace period of 20 to 25 days. During the grace period, no finance charges are assessed on current purchases if the balance is paid in full each month within 25 days after billing.

Some corporations, such as General Electric Company and General Motors Corporation, issue their own Visa and MasterCard and offer rebates on purchases. In the late 1990s, however, some corporations began to eliminate these cards.

Finally, credit indicates stability. The fact that lenders consider you a good risk usually means you are a responsible individual. However, if you do not repay your debts in a timely manner, you will find that credit has many disadvantages.

Disadvantages of Credit

Perhaps the greatest disadvantage of using credit is the temptation to overspend, especially during periods of inflation. Buying today and paying tomorrow, using cheaper dollars, seems ideal. But continual overspending can lead to serious trouble.

Whether or not credit involves *security*—something of value to back the loan—failure to repay a loan may result in loss of income, valuable property, and your good reputation. It can even lead to court action and bankruptcy. Misuse of credit can create serious long-term financial problems, damage to family relationships, and a slowing of progress toward financial goals. Therefore, you should approach credit with caution and avoid using it more extensively than your budget permits.

Although credit allows immediate satisfaction of needs and desires, it does not increase total purchasing power. Credit purchases must be paid for out of future income; therefore, credit ties up the use of future income. Furthermore, if your income does not increase to cover rising costs, your ability to repay credit commitments will diminish. Before buying goods and services on credit, consider whether they will have lasting value, whether they will increase your personal satisfaction during present and future income periods, and whether your current income will continue or increase.

Finally, credit costs money. It is a service for which you must pay. Paying for purchases over a period of time is more costly than paying for them with cash. Purchasing with credit rather than cash involves one obvious trade-off: The items purchased will cost more due to monthly finance charges and the compounding effect of interest on interest.

Key Web Sites for Money Management

www.moneymanagement.com

www.moneypage.com

Key Web Sites for Consumer Credit

www.abcguides.com

www.lendingtree.com

CONCEPT CHECK 5–1

1 What is consumer credit?

_____

_____

2 Why is consumer credit important to our economy?

_____

_____

3 For each of following situations, check "yes" if a valid reason to borrow, or "no" if not.

	Yes	No
a. A medical emergency.	_____	_____
b. Borrowing for college education.	_____	_____
c. Borrowing for everyday living expenses.	_____	_____
d. Borrowing to finance a luxury car.	_____	_____

4 For each of the following statements, check "yes" if an advantage, "no" if a disadvantage of using credit.

	Yes	No
a. It is easier to return merchandise if it is purchased on credit.	_____	_____
b. Credit cards provide shopping convenience.	_____	_____
c. Credit tempts people to overspend.	_____	_____
d. Failure to repay a loan may result in loss of income.	_____	_____

Apply Yourself!

Objective 1

Using Web research and discussion with family members and friends, prepare a list of advantages and disadvantages of using credit.

Types of Credit

OBJECTIVE 2

Assess the types and sources of consumer credit.

Two basic types of consumer credit exist: closed-end and open-end credit. With **closed-end credit,** you pay back one-time loans in a specified period of time and in payments of equal amounts. With **open-end credit,** loans are made on a continuous basis and you are billed periodically for at least partial payment. Exhibit 5–1 shows examples of closed-end and open-end credit.

Closed-End Credit	Open-End Credit
• Mortgage loans • Automobile loans • Installment loans (installment sales contract, installment cash credit, single lump-sum credit)	• Cards issued by department stores, bank cards (Visa, MasterCard) • Travel and Entertainment (T&E) (American Express, Diners Club) • Overdraft protection

Exhibit **5–1**

Examples of Closed-End and Open-End Credit

Closed-End Credit

Closed-end credit is used for a specific purpose and involves a specified amount. Mortgage loans, automobile loans, and installment loans for purchasing furniture or appliances are examples of closed-end credit. Generally, the seller holds title to the merchandise until the payments have been completed.

The three most common types of closed-end credit are installment sales credit, installment cash credit, and single lump-sum credit. *Installment sales credit* is a loan that allows you to receive merchandise, usually high-priced items such as large appliances or furniture. You make a down payment and usually sign a contract to repay the balance, plus interest and service charges, in equal installments over a specified period.

Installment cash credit is a direct loan of money for personal purposes, home improvements, or vacation expenses. You make no down payment and make payments in specified amounts over a set period.

Single lump-sum credit is a loan that must be repaid in total on a specified day, usually within 30 to 90 days. Lump-sum credit is generally, but not always, used to purchase a single item. As Exhibit 5–2 shows, consumer installment credit reached over $2.5 trillion in 2008.

closed-end credit One-time loans that the borrower pays back in a specified period of time and in payments of equal amounts.

open-end credit A line of credit in which loans are made on a continuous basis and the borrower is billed periodically for at least partial payment.

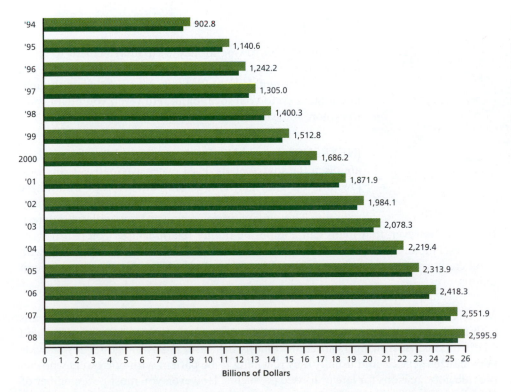

Year	Billions of Dollars
'94	902.8
'95	1,140.6
'96	1,242.2
'97	1,305.0
'98	1,400.3
'99	1,512.8
2000	1,686.2
'01	1,871.9
'02	1,984.1
'03	2,078.3
'04	2,219.4
'05	2,313.9
'06	2,418.3
'07	2,551.9
'08	2,595.9

Exhibit **5–2**

Volume of Consumer Credit

All economists now recognize consumer credit as a major force in the American economy.

Source: www.federalreserve.gov/RELEASES/g19/current accessed June 24, 2009.

Open-End Credit

Using a credit card issued by a department store, using a bank credit card (Visa, MasterCard) to make purchases at different stores, charging a meal at a restaurant, and using overdraft protection are examples of open-end credit. As you will soon see, you do not apply for open-end credit to make a single purchase, as you do with closed-end credit. Rather, you can use open-end credit to make any purchases you wish if you do not exceed your **line of credit,** the maximum dollar amount of credit the lender has made available to you. You may have to pay **interest,** a periodic charge for the use of credit, or other finance charges. Some creditors allow you a grace period of 20 to 25 days to pay a bill in full before you incur any interest charges.

Many retailers use open-end credit. Customers can purchase goods or services up to a fixed dollar limit at any time. Usually you have the option to pay the bill in full within 30 days without interest charges or to make set monthly installments based on the account balance plus interest.

Many banks extend **revolving check credit.** Also called a *bank line of credit,* this is a prearranged loan for a specified amount that you can use by writing a special check. Repayment is made in installments over a set period. The finance charges are based on the amount of credit used during the month and on the outstanding balance.

line of credit The dollar amount, which may or may not be borrowed, that a lender makes available to a borrower.

interest A periodic charge for the use of credit.

revolving check credit A prearranged loan from a bank for a specified amount; also called a *bank line of credit.*

Sources of Consumer Credit

Many sources of consumer credit are available, including commercial banks and credit unions. Exhibit 5–3 summarizes the major sources of consumer credit. Study and compare the differences to determine which source might best meet your needs and requirements.

did you know?

You can lend to micro-entrepreneurs. Kiva.org is the first microlending Web site where you can lend money to micro-entrepreneurs through a micro-finance institution.

Loans

Loans involve borrowing money with an agreement to repay it, as well as interest, within a certain amount of time. If you were considering taking out a loan, your immediate thought might be to go to your local bank. However, you might want to explore some other options first.

INEXPENSIVE LOANS Parents or other family members are often the source of the least expensive loans—loans with low interest. They may charge only interest they would have earned on the money if they had deposited it in a savings account. They may even give you a loan without interest. Be aware, however, that loans can complicate family relationships. You can borrow (or invest) money with microlending organizations, such as kiva.org. Borrowers with good credit can borrow at interest rates lower than those charged by banks and credit unions.

MEDIUM-PRICED LOANS Often you can obtain medium-priced loans—loans with moderate interest—from commercial banks, savings and loan associations, and credit unions. Borrowing from credit unions has several advantages. They provide personalized service, and usually they're willing to be patient with borrowers who can provide good reasons for late or missed payments. However, you must be a member of a credit union in order to get a loan.

Exhibit **5–3**   Sources of Consumer Credit

Credit Source	Type of Loan	Lending Policies
Commercial banks	Single-payment loan Personal installment loans Passbook loans Check-credit loans Credit card loans Second mortgages	• Seek customers with established credit history • Often require collateral or security • Prefer to deal in large loans, such as vehicle, home improvement, and home modernization, with the exception of credit card and check-credit plans • Determine repayment schedules according to the purpose of the loan • Vary credit rates according to the type of credit, time period, customer's credit history, and the security offered • May require several days to process a new credit application
Consumer finance companies	Personal installment loans Second mortgages	• Often lend to consumers without established credit history • Often make unsecured loans • Often vary rates according to the size of the loan balance • Offer a variety of repayment schedules • Make a higher percentage of small loans than other lenders • Maximum loan size limited by law • Process applications quickly, frequently on the same day the application is made
Credit unions	Personal installment loans Share draft-credit plans Credit-card loans Second mortgages	• Lend to members only • Make unsecured loans • May require collateral or cosigner for loans over a specified amount • May require payroll deductions to pay off loan • May submit large loan applications to a committee of members for approval • Offer a variety of repayment schedules
Life insurance companies	Single-payment or partial-payment loans	• Lend on cash value of life insurance policy • No date or penalty on repayment • Deduct amount owed from the value of policy benefit if death or other maturity occurs before repayment
Federal savings banks (savings and loan associations)	Personal installment loans (generally permitted by state-chartered savings associations) Home improvement loans Education loans Savings account loans Second mortgages	• Will lend to all creditworthy individuals • Often require collateral • Loan rates vary depending on size of loan, length of payment, and security involved

Consumer credit is available from several types of sources. *Which sources seem to offer the widest variety of loans?*

EXPENSIVE LOANS   The easiest loans to obtain are also the most expensive. Finance companies and retail stores that lend to consumers will frequently charge high interest rates, ranging from 12 to 25 percent. Banks also lend money to their credit card holders through cash advances—loans that are billed to the customer's credit card account. Most cards charge higher interest for a cash advance and charge interest from the day the cash advance is made. As a result, taking out a cash advance is much more expensive than charging a purchase to a credit card. Read the nearby Figure It Out box to learn why you should avoid such cash advances.

Key Web Sites for Consumer Credit

www.consumercredit.com

www.practicalmoneyskills.com

www.Bankrate.com

Figure It Out!

> Cash Advances

A cash advance is a loan billed to your credit card. You can obtain a cash advance with your credit card at a bank or an automated teller machine (ATM) or by using checks linked to your credit card account.

Most cards charge a special fee when a cash advance is taken out. The fee is based on a percentage of the amount borrowed, usually about 2 or 3 percent.

Some credit cards charge a minimum cash advance fee, as high as $5. You could get $20 in cash and be charged $5, a fee equal to 25 percent of the amount you borrowed.

Most cards do not have a grace period on cash advances. This means you pay interest every day until you repay the cash advance, even if you do not have an outstanding balance from the previous statement.

On some cards, the interest rate on cash advances is higher than the rate on purchases. Be sure you check the details on the contract sent to you by the card issuer.

Here is an example of charges that could be imposed for a $200 cash advance that you pay off when the bill arrives:

Cash advance fee = $4(2% of $200)

Interest for one month = $3(18% APR on $200)

Total cost for one month = $7($4 + $3)

In comparison, a $200 purchase on a card with a grace period could cost $0 if paid off promptly in full.

The bottom line: It is usually much more expensive to take out a cash advance than to charge a purchase to your credit card. Use cash advances only for real emergencies.

HOME EQUITY LOANS A home equity loan is a loan based on your home equity—the difference between the current market value of your home and the amount you still owe on the mortgage.

Example

Depending on your income and the equity in your home, you can apply for a line of credit for anywhere from $10,000 to $250,000 or more.

Some lenders let you borrow only up to 75 percent of the value of your home, less the amount of your first mortgage. At some banks you may qualify to borrow up to 85 percent! This higher lending limit may make the difference in your ability to get the money you need for home improvements, education, or other expenses.

Use the following chart to calculate your home loan value, which is the approximate amount of your home equity line of credit.

	Example	Your Home
Approximate market value of your home	$100,000	$ ____
Multiply by 0.75	× 0.75	× 0.75
Approximate loan value	75,000	____
Subtract balance due on mortgage(s)	50,000	____
Approximate credit limit available	$ 25,000	$ ____

Unlike interest on most other types of credit, the interest you pay on a home equity loan is tax-deductible. You should use these loans only for major items such as education, home improvements, or medical bills, and you must use them with care. If you miss payments on a home equity loan, the lender can take your home.

Credit Cards

Credit cards are extremely popular. The average cardholder has more than nine credit cards, including bank, retail, gasoline, and telephone cards. Cardholders who pay off their balances in full each month are often known as *convenience* users. Cardholders who do not pay off their balances every month are known as *borrowers*.

Most credit card companies offer a grace period, a time period during which no finance charges will be added to your account. A **finance charge** is the total dollar amount you pay to use credit. Usually, if you pay your entire balance before the due date stated on your monthly bill, you will not have to pay a finance charge. Borrowers carry balances beyond the grace period and pay finance charges.

The cost of a credit card depends on the type of credit card you have and the terms set forth by the lender. As a cardholder, you may have to pay interest or other finance charges. Some credit card companies charge cardholders an annual fee, usually about $25. However, many companies have eliminated annual fees in order to attract more customers. If you are looking for a credit card, be sure to shop around for one with no annual fee. The nearby Personal Finance in Practice box offers some other helpful hints for choosing a credit card.

finance charge The total dollar amount paid to use credit.

Key Web Sites for Credit Cards

www.cardratings.com

www.bankrate.com

DEBIT CARDS Don't confuse credit cards with debit cards. Although they may look alike, they're very different. A debit card electronically subtracts money from your savings or checking account to pay for goods and services. A credit card extends credit and delays your payment. Debit cards are most frequently used at automatic teller machines (ATMs). More and more, however, they are also used to purchase goods in stores and to make other types of payments.

Raquel Garcia is serious about avoiding debt. The 18-year-old customer representative for U-Haul recently canceled her credit card. Now she gets her entire paycheck deposited onto a prepaid debit card, which she uses for all her purchases. Since she can access only what's in the account, Garcia no longer worries about breaking her budget: "I'm spending just what I need."

did you know?

In 2010, an estimated 185 million debit card holders will use 484 million cards for 41 trillion transactions amounting to over $1.65 trillion.

SOURCE: *Statistical Abstract of the United States 2009*, Table 1147.

STORED VALUE (OR GIFT) CARDS Stored-value cards, gift cards, or prepaid cards resemble a typical debit card, using magnetic stripe technology to store information and track funds. However, unlike traditional debit cards, stored value cards are prepaid, providing you with immediate money. By the mid-1990s, large retailers began issuing stored value cards instead of traditional paper gift certificates. Over the past decade, the stored value cards have grown rapidly. Today, gift cards are being used for many purposes, including payroll, general spending, travel expenses, government benefit payments, and employee benefit and reward payments.

One market research firm estimates that holders of gift cards recently lost more than $75 million when the number of retailer bankruptcies increased sharply. Bankruptcy courts treat gift cards the same way they handle unsecured debt: If a retailer goes bankrupt, holders get pennies on the dollar at most—and in many cases nothing. Recently, American shoppers spent $26.3 billion on retailers' gift cards.

Personal Finance in Practice

> Choosing a Credit Card

When you choose a credit card, shopping around can yield big returns. Follow these suggestions to find the card that best meets your needs and to use it wisely:

1. Department stores and gasoline companies are good places to obtain your first credit card.

2. Bank credit cards are offered through banks and savings and loan associations. Annual fees and finance charges vary widely, so shop around.

3. If you plan on paying off your balance every month, look for a card that has a grace period and carries no annual fee or a low annual fee. You might have a higher interest rate, but you plan to pay little or no interest anyway.

4. Watch out for creditors that offer low or no annual fees but instead charge a transaction fee every time you use the card.

5. If you plan to carry a balance, look for a card with a low monthly finance charge. Be sure that you understand how the finance charge is calculated.

6. To avoid delays that may result in finance charges, follow the card issuer's instructions as to where, how, and when to make bill payments.

7. Beware of offers of easy credit. No one can guarantee to get you credit.

8. If your card offers a grace period, take advantage of it by paying off your balance in full each month. With a grace period of 25 days, you actually get a free loan when you pay bills in full each month.

9. If you have a bad credit history and have trouble getting a credit card, look for a savings institution that will give you a secured credit card. With this type of card, your line of credit depends on how much money you keep in a savings account that you open at the same time.

10. Travel and entertainment cards often charge higher annual fees than most credit cards. Usually, you must make payment in full within 30 days of receiving your bill, or no further purchases will be approved on the account.

11. Be aware that debit cards are not credit cards but simply a substitute for a check or cash. The amount of the sale is subtracted from your checking account.

12. Think twice before you make a telephone call to a 900 number to request a credit card. You will pay from $2 to $50 for the 900 call and may never receive a credit card.

Before you enter the world of credit, you need to understand the various options that are available to you. *Which of the preceding factors would be most important in your choice of a credit card?*

Sources: American Institute of Certified Public Accountants. U.S. Office of Consumer Affairs. Federal Trade Commission.

SMART CARDS Some lenders are starting to offer a new kind of credit card called a smart card. A smart card is a plastic card equipped with a computer chip that can store 500 times as much data as a normal credit card. Smart cards can combine credit card balances, a driver's license, health care identification, medical history, and other information all in one place. A smart card, for example, can be used to buy an airline ticket, store it digitally, and track frequent flyer miles.

TRAVEL AND ENTERTAINMENT CARDS Travel and entertainment (T&E) cards are really not credit cards because the balance is due in full each month. However, most people think of T&E cards—such as Diners Club or American Express cards—as credit cards because they don't pay for goods or service when they purchase them.

CONCEPT CHECK 5–2

1 What are two types of consumer credit? _____ _____

2 Match the following key terms with the appropriate definition.

a. closed-end credit _____ A line of credit in which loans are made on a continuous basis.

b. open-end credit _____ One-time loan paid back in a specified time in payments of equal amounts.

c. line of credit _____ The dollar amount that a lender makes available to a borrower.

d. interest _____ The total dollar amount paid to use the credit.

e. finance charge _____ A periodic charge for the use of credit.

3 What are the major sources of:

Inexpensive loans	Medium-priced loans	Expensive loans
_____	_____	_____
_____	_____	_____

4 What is the difference between a credit and a debit card?

_____

_____

Apply Yourself!

Objective 2

Research three credit card companies. List their fees and any advantages they offer. Record your findings.

Applying for Credit

Can You Afford a Loan?

The only way to determine how much credit you can assume is to first learn how to make an accurate and sensible personal or family budget.

Before you take out a loan, ask yourself whether you can meet all of your essential expenses and still afford the monthly loan payments. You can make this calculation in two ways. One is to add up all your basic monthly expenses and then subtract this total from your take-home pay. If the difference will not cover the monthly payment and still leave funds for other expenses, you cannot afford the loan.

OBJECTIVE 3

Determine whether you can afford a loan and how to apply for credit.

A second and more reliable method is to ask yourself what you plan to give up to make the monthly loan payment. If you currently save a portion of your income that is greater than the monthly payment, you can use these savings to pay off the loan. But if you do not, you will have to forgo spending on entertainment, new appliances, or perhaps even necessities. Are you prepared to make this trade-off? Although precisely measuring your credit capacity is difficult, you can follow certain rules of thumb.

General Rules of Credit Capacity

did you know?

In 2010, an estimated 181 million people used more than 1.6 billion credit cards to buy goods and services worth $2.74 trillion.

SOURCE: *Statistical Abstract of the United States 2009,* Table 1148.

DEBT PAYMENTS-TO-INCOME RATIO The debt payments-to-income ratio is calculated by dividing your monthly debt payments (not including house payment, which is long-term liability) by your net monthly income. Experts suggest that you spend no more than 20 percent of your net (after-tax) income on consumer credit payments. Thus, as Exhibit 5–4 shows, a person making $1,068 per month after taxes should spend no more than $213 on credit payments per month.

The 20 percent is the maximum; however, 15 percent or less is much better. The 20 percent estimate is based on the average family, with average expenses; it does not take major emergencies into account. If you are just beginning to use credit, you should not consider yourself safe if you are spending 20 percent of your net income on credit payments.

DEBT-TO-EQUITY RATIO The debt-to-equity ratio is calculated by dividing your total liabilities by your net worth. In calculating this ratio, do not include the value of your home and the amount of its mortgage. If your debt-to-equity ratio is about 1—that is, if your consumer installment debt roughly equals your net worth (not including your home or the mortgage)—you have probably reached the upper limit of debt obligations.

None of the above methods is perfect for everyone; the limits given are only guidelines. Only you, based on the money you earn, your obligations, and your financial plans for the future, can determine the exact amount of credit you need and can afford. You must be your own credit manager.

The Five Cs of Credit

When you're ready to apply for a loan or a credit card, you should understand the factors that determine whether a lender will extend credit to you.

When a lender extends credit to consumers, it takes for granted that some people will be unable or unwilling to pay their debts. Therefore, lenders establish policies for determining who will receive credit. Most lenders build such policies around the "five Cs of credit": character, capacity, capital, collateral, and conditions.

character The borrower's attitude toward his or her credit obligations.

CHARACTER: WILL YOU REPAY THE LOAN? Creditors want to know your **character**—what kind of person they are lending money to. They want to know that you're trustworthy and stable. They may ask for personal or professional

Monthly gross income	$1,500
Less:	
All taxes	270
Social Security	112
Monthly IRA contribution	50
Monthly net income	$1,068

Monthly installment credit payments:	
Visa	25
MasterCard	20
Discover card	15
Education loan	—
Personal bank loan	—
Auto loan	153
Total monthly payments	$ 213
Debt payments-to-income ratio ($213/$1,068)	19.94%

Exhibit 5–4

How to Calculate Debt Payments-to-Income Ratio Spend no more than 20 percent of your net (after-tax) income on credit payments.

references, and they may check to see whether you have a history of trouble with the law. Some questions a lender might ask to determine your character are:

- Have you used credit before?
- How long have you lived at your present address?
- How long have you held your current job?

CAPACITY: CAN YOU REPAY THE LOAN? Your income and the debts you already have will affect your **capacity**—your ability to pay additional debts. If you already have a large amount of debt in proportion to your income, lenders probably won't extend more credit to you. Some questions a creditor may ask about your income and expenses are:

- What is your job, and how much is your salary?
- Do you have other sources of income?
- What are your current debts?

capacity The borrower's financial ability to meet credit obligations.

CAPITAL: WHAT ARE YOUR ASSETS AND NET WORTH? Assets are any items of value that you own, including cash, property, personal possessions, and investments. Your **capital** is the amount of your assets that exceed your liabilities, or the debts you owe. Lenders want to be sure that you have enough capital to pay back a loan. That way, if you lost your source of income, you could repay your loan from your savings or by selling some of your assets. A lender might ask:

- What are your assets?
- What are your liabilities?

capital The borrower's assets or net worth.

COLLATERAL: WHAT IF YOU DON'T REPAY THE LOAN? Creditors look at what kinds of property or savings you already have, because these can be offered as **collateral** to secure the loan. If you fail to repay the loan, the creditor may take whatever you pledged as collateral. A creditor might ask:

- What assets do you have to secure the loan (such as a vehicle, your home, or furniture)?
- Do you have any other valuable assets (such as bonds or savings)?

collateral A valuable asset that is pledged to ensure loan payments.

conditions The general economic conditions that can affect a borrower's ability to repay a loan.

CONDITIONS: WHAT IF YOUR JOB IS INSECURE? General economic **conditions,** such as unemployment and recession, can affect your ability to repay a loan. The basic question focuses on security—of both your job and the firm that employs you.

The information gathered from your application and the credit bureau establishes your credit rating. A *credit rating* is a measure of a person's ability and willingness to make credit payments on time. The factors that determine a person's credit rating are income, current debt, information about character, and how debts have been repaid in the past. If you always make your payments on time, you will probably have an excellent credit rating. If not, your credit rating will be poor, and a lender probably won't extend credit to you. A good credit rating is a valuable asset that you should protect.

Creditors use different combinations of the five Cs to reach their decisions. Some creditors set unusually high standards, and others simply do not offer certain types of loans. Creditors also use various rating systems. Some rely strictly on their own instincts and experience. Others use a credit scoring or statistical system to predict whether an applicant is a good credit risk. When you apply for a loan, the lender is likely to evaluate your application by asking questions such as those included in the checklist in the Personal Finance in Practice box.

FICO AND VANTAGESCORE Typical questions in a credit application appear in Exhibit 5–5. The information in your credit report is used to calculate your FICO credit score—a number generally between 350 and 850 that rates how risky a borrower is. The higher the score, the less risk you pose to creditors. Your FICO score is available from www.myfico.com for a fee. Free credit reports do not provide your credit score. Exhibit 5–6 shows a numerical depiction of your creditworthiness and how you can improve your credit score.

VantageScore is a new scoring technique, the first to be developed collaboratively by the three credit reporting companies. This model allows for a more predictive score for consumers, even for those with limited credit histories, reducing

---

did you know?

VANTAGESCORE from Experian

VantageScore which is both used by lenders and now available to consumers, is the first credit score developed cooperatively by Experian and the other national credit reporting companies.

The VantageScore scale approximates the familiar academic scale, making it simple to associate your VantageScore number to a letter grade. You now will have clear insight into how lenders using VantageScore will view your creditworthiness.

Score	
901–990: A	601–700: D
801–900: B	501–600: F
701–800: C	

SOURCE: www.vantagescore.experian.com.

Exhibit 5–5

Sample Credit Application Questions

- Amount of loan requested.
- Proposed use of the loan.
- Your name and birth date.
- Social Security and driver's license numbers.
- Present and previous street addresses.
- Present and previous employers and their addresses.
- Present salary.
- Number and ages of dependents.
- Other income and sources of other income.

- Have you ever received credit from us?
- If so, when and at which office?
- Checking account number, institution, and branch.
- Savings account number, institution, and branch.
- Name of nearest relative not living with you.
- Relative's address and telephone number.
- Your marital status.
- Information regarding joint applicant: same questions as above.

Personal Finance in Practice

> The Five Cs of Credit

Here is what lenders look for in determining your creditworthiness.

CREDIT HISTORY

1. Character: Will you repay the loan?   Yes   No

Do you have a good attitude toward credit obligations?   _____ _____

Have you used credit before?   _____ _____

Do you pay your bills on time?   _____ _____

Have you ever filed for bankruptcy?   _____ _____

Do you live within your means?   _____ _____

STABILITY

How long have you lived at your present address?   _____ yrs.

Do you own your home?   _____ _____

How long have you been employed by your present employer?   _____ yrs.

INCOME

2. Capacity: Can you repay the loan?

Your salary and occupation? $_____ ; _____

Place of occupation?   _____

How reliable is your income?   Reliable ____ ; Not reliable ____

Any other sources of income? $_____

EXPENSES

Number of dependents?   _____

Do you pay any alimony or child support?   Yes _____ ; No _____

Current debts? $_____

NET WORTH

3. Capital: What are your assets and net worth?

What are your assets? $_____

What are your liabilities? $_____

What is your net worth? $_____

LOAN SECURITY

4. Collateral: What if you don't repay the loan?

What assets do you have to secure the loan? (Car, home, furniture?)   _____

What sources do you have besides income? (Savings, stocks, bonds, insurance?)   _____

JOB SECURITY

5. Conditions: What general economic conditions can affect your repayment of the loan?

How secure is your job?   Secure _____ ; Not secure _____

How secure is the firm you work for?   Secure _____ ; Not secure _____

Source: Adapted from William M. Pride, Robert J. Hughes, and Jack R. Kapoor, *Business*, 10th ed. (Mason, OH: South-Western Cengage Learning, 2010), p. 551.

the need for creditors to manually review credit information. VantageScore features a common score range of 501–990 (higher scores represent lower likelihood of risk). A key benefit of VantageScore is that as long as the three major credit bureaus have the same information regarding your credit history, you will receive the same score from each of them. A different score alerts you that there are discrepancies in your report.

You should also know what factors a lender cannot consider, according to the law. The *Equal Credit Opportunity Act* (ECOA) gives all credit applicants the same basic rights. It states that race, nationality, age, sex, marital status, and certain other factors may not be used to discriminate against you in any part of a credit dealing.

Exhibit **5–6**   TransUnion Personal Credit Score

The higher your FICO score, the less risk you pose to creditors.

Your Credit Score is:

Score created on:
02/18/2010

You can purchase your
credit score for $7.95
by calling 1-866-SCORE-TU
or 1-866-726-7388.

This will show a numerical depiction of your creditworthiness.

This will show how you compare to the general population.

This will show how most lenders would view your creditworthiness.

Very Poor   Poor   Fair   Good   Very Good

• How can I Improve my credit score?
A credit score is a snapshot of the contents of your credit report at the time it is calculated. The first step in improving your score is to review your credit report to ensure it is accurate. Long-term, responsible credit behavior is the most effective way to improve future scores. Pay bills on time, lower balances, and use credit wisely to improve your score over time.

Other Factors Considered in Determining Creditworthiness

did you Know?

What age group has the best credit rating in America?

According to Experian, the average credit score for Americans is 675 out of a possible 830. Credit scores are based on financial behavior (debt, credit usage, paying bills on time).

Age group	Score
70–plus	747
60–69	722
50–59	697
40–49	675
30–39	654
18–29	637

SOURCE: Experian (www.NationalScoreIndex.com), accessed January 15, 2007.

AGE The Equal Credit Opportunity Act is very specific about how a person's age may be used as a factor in credit decisions. A creditor may request that you state your age on an application, but if you're old enough to sign a legal contract (usually 18–21 years old, depending on state law), a creditor may not turn you down or decrease your credit because of your age. Creditors may not close your credit account because you reach a certain age or retire.

PUBLIC ASSISTANCE You may not be denied credit because you receive Social Security or public assistance. However, certain information related to this source of income can be considered in determining your creditworthiness.

HOUSING LOANS The ECOA also covers applications for mortgages or home improvement loans. In particular, it bans discrimination against you based on the race or nationality of the people in the neighborhood where you live or want to buy your home, a practice called *redlining*.

What If Your Application Is Denied?

If your credit application is denied, the ECOA gives you the right to know the reasons. If the denial is based on a credit report from the credit bureau, you're entitled to know the specific information in the report that led to the denial. After you receive this information, you can contact the credit bureau and ask for a copy of your credit report. The bureau cannot charge a fee for this service as long as you ask to see your files within 60 days of notification that your credit application has been denied. You're entitled to ask the bureau to investigate any inaccurate or incomplete information and correct its records (see Exhibit 5–7).

Your Credit Report

When you apply for a loan, the lender will review your credit history very closely. The record of your complete credit history is called your *credit report,* or *credit file.* Your credit records are collected and maintained by credit bureaus. Most lenders rely heavily on credit reports when they consider loan applications. Exhibit 5–8 provides a checklist for building and protecting your credit history.

CREDIT BUREAUS A credit bureau is an agency that collects information on how promptly people and businesses pay their bills. The three major credit bureaus are Experian, TransUnion, and Equifax. Each of these bureaus maintains more than 200 million credit files on individuals, based on information they receive from lenders. Several thousand smaller credit bureaus also collect credit information about consumers. These firms make money by selling the information they collect to creditors who are considering loan applications.

Credit bureaus get their information from banks, finance companies, stores, credit card companies, and other lenders. These sources regularly transmit information about

Exhibit 5–7   What If You Are Denied Credit?

Steps you can take if you are denied credit

*If a creditor receives no more than 150 applications during a calendar year, the disclosures may be oral.

SOURCE: Reprinted courtesy of Office of Public Information, Federal Reserve Bank of Minneapolis, Minneapolis, MN 55480.

Exhibit 5–8

Checklist for Building and Protecting Your Credit History

It is simple and sensible to build and protect your own credit history. Here are some steps to get you started:

- Open a checking or savings account, or both.
- Apply for a local department store credit card.
- Take out a small loan from your bank. Make payments on time.

A Creditor Must . . .	Remember that a Creditor Cannot . . .
1. Evaluate all applicants on the same basis	1. Refuse you individual credit in your own name if you are creditworthy
2. Consider income from part-time employment	2. Require your spouse to cosign a loan. Any creditworthy person can be your cosigner if one is required
3. Consider the payment history of all joint accounts, if this accurately reflects your credit history	3. Ask about your family plans or assume that your income will be interrupted to have children
4. Disregard information on accounts if you can prove that it doesn't affect your ability or willingness to repay	4. Consider whether you have a telephone listing in your name

If you want a good credit rating, you must use credit wisely. *Why is it a good idea to apply for a local department store credit card or a small loan from your bank?*

SOURCE: Reprinted by permission of the Federal Reserve Bank of Minneapolis.

CAUTION! www.annualcreditreport.com is the only online source authorized to provide a free credit report at your request. Beware of other sites that may look and sound similar.

the types of credit they extend to customers, the amounts and terms of the loans, and the customer's payment habits. Credit bureaus also collect some information from other sources, such as court records.

WHAT'S IN YOUR CREDIT FILES? A typical credit bureau file contains your name, address, Social Security number, and birth date. It may also include the following information:

- Your employer, position, and income
- Your previous address
- Your previous employer
- Your spouse's name, Social Security number, employer, and income
- Whether you rent or own your home
- Checks returned for insufficient funds

In addition, your credit file contains detailed credit information. Each time you use credit to make a purchase or take out a loan of any kind, a credit bureau is informed of your account number and the date, amount, terms, and type of credit. Your file is updated regularly to show how many payments you've made, how many payments were late or missed, and how much you owe. Any lawsuits or judgments against you may appear as well. Federal law protects your rights if the information in your credit file is incorrect.

did you know?

The Fair Credit Reporting Act requires each of the nationwide consumer reporting companies—Experian, Equifax, and TransUnion—to provide you with a free copy of your credit report annually. Call 1-877-322-8228.

FAIR CREDIT REPORTING Fair and accurate credit reporting is vital to both creditors and consumers. In 1971 the U.S. Congress enacted the Fair Credit Reporting Act, which regulates the use of credit reports. This law requires the deletion of out-of-date information and gives consumers access to their files as well as the right to correct any misinformation that the files may include. The act also places limits on who can obtain your credit report.

Five ways to boost your score and get the best rates. *By Jessica L. Anderson*

Clean Up Your Credit

With all the financial upheaval over the past year, including the subprime-mortgage mess and the rescue plan for banks toppled by risky loans, it wouldn't be surprising if you were tempted to think that *credit* is a four-letter word.

But one important lesson this crisis has driven home is that your credit is the financial equivalent of your good name. A good score is your ticket to a home, a car, a credit card or even an insurance policy and even a tiny slip-up can come back to haunt you. That's especially true now because the credit crunch has spread to other types of borrowing. For instance, banks have been forced to write off record levels of credit-card debt, so they're setting the bar higher for potential borrowers. A year ago, a score of 720 would have had lenders lining up for your business. Today, a score of 740 or 750 will get you an account but might not qualify you for the lowest interest rates, says Bill Hardekopf, of LowCards.com.

If you haven't already done so, start by taking a look at your credit report. Log on to AnnualCreditReport.com and get a free copy from each of the three credit bureaus: Equifax, Experian and TransUnion. (Note: Copycat sites often require you to purchase other services in order to get a "free" credit report.)

While you're on a bureau's Web site, you'll also have the option of buying your credit score for $6 to $8. If you've already used your once-a-year free pass on AnnualCreditReport.com, go to myFICO.com to download your reports and scores ($15.95 for the score from one credit bureau, or $47.85 for all three).

Go through your report with a fine-tooth comb and file a dispute immediately with each bureau that reports an error. The process isn't lightning-fast (you typically have to wait 30 to 45 days for the bureau to investigate any disputes you submit), but be persistent until the problems have been resolved. Big issues, such as an incorrect notation that an account has gone to collection or a home is in foreclosure, could cost you 100 points or more on your credit score.

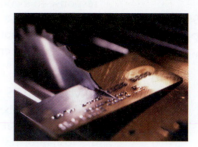

Gerri Detweiler, credit adviser for Credit.com, says it's also important to check the dates on any negative information that's being reported. Negative items, such as collections accounts, may generally be reported for seven years from when you first fell behind. Two exceptions are bankruptcies, which may be reported for ten years, and tax liens, which may stay on your record indefinitely until you pay them.

Other things to watch out for: paid-in-full accounts that still show a balance and someone else's record that appears in your file. If the credit bureau misspells your name or reports your address incorrectly, that won't affect your score.

1. How has the current economic crisis affected the consumer credit and its availability?

_____

2. What is one important lesson that this financial crisis has driven home?

_____

3. Why should you check the dates on any negative information that's being reported to your account?

_____

WHO CAN OBTAIN A CREDIT REPORT? Your credit report may be issued only to properly identified persons for approved purposes. It may be supplied in response to a court order or by your own written request. A credit report may also be provided for use in connection with a credit transaction, underwriting of insurance, or some legitimate business need. Friends, neighbors, and other individuals cannot be given access to credit information about you. In fact, if they even request such information, they may be subject to a fine, imprisonment, or both.

TIME LIMITS ON UNFAVORABLE DATA Most of the information in your credit file may be reported for only seven years. However, if you've declared personal bankruptcy, that fact may be reported for 10 years. A credit reporting agency can't disclose information in your credit file that's more than 7 or 10 years old unless you're being reviewed for a credit application of $75,000 or more, or unless you apply to purchase life insurance of $150,000 or more.

INCORRECT INFORMATION IN YOUR CREDIT FILE Credit bureaus are required to follow reasonable procedures to ensure that the information in their files is correct. Mistakes can and do occur, however. If you think that a credit bureau may be reporting incorrect data from your file, contact the bureau to dispute the information. The credit bureau must check its records and change or remove the incorrect items. If you challenge the accuracy of an item on your credit report, the bureau must remove the item unless the lender can verify that the information is accurate.

If you are denied credit, insurance, employment, or rental housing based on the information in a credit report, you can get a free copy of your report. Remember to request it within 60 days of notification that your application has been denied.

WHAT ARE YOUR LEGAL RIGHTS? You have legal rights to sue a credit bureau or creditor that has caused you harm by not following the rules established by the Fair Credit Reporting Act.

Sheet 15: Consumer Credit Usage Patterns

CONCEPT CHECK 5–3

1 What are the two general rules of measuring credit capacity? How is it calculated?

_____

_____

2 Match the following key terms with the appropriate definition.

   a. character   _____ An asset pledged to obtain a loan.

   b. capacity   _____ The borrower's attitude toward credit obligations.

   c. capital   _____ Financial ability to meet credit obligations.

   d. collateral   _____ The borrower's assets or net worth.

   e. conditions   _____ General economic conditions that affect your ability to repay a loan.

3 What are the factors a lender cannot consider according to the law?

_____

4 What is a credit bureau? _____

5 Write the steps you should take if you are denied credit.

_____

_____

Apply Yourself!

Objective 3

Talk to a person who has cosigned a loan. What experiences did this person have as a cosigner?

The Cost of Credit

If you are thinking of borrowing money or opening a credit account, your first step should be to figure out how much it will cost you and whether you can afford it. Then you should shop for the best terms. Two key concepts that you should remember are the finance charge and the annual percentage rate.

Finance Charge and Annual Percentage Rate

Credit costs vary. If you know the finance charge and the annual percentage rate you can compare credit prices from different sources. The *finance charge* is the total dollar amount you pay to use credit. It includes interest costs and sometimes other costs such as service charges, credit-related insurance premiums, or appraisal fees.

For example, borrowing $100 for a year might cost you $10 in interest. If there is also a service charge of $1, the finance charge will be $11. The **annual percentage rate (APR)** is the percentage cost (or relative cost) of credit on a yearly basis. The APR is your key to comparing costs, regardless of the amount of credit or how much time you have to repay it.

Suppose you borrow $100 for one year and pay a finance charge of $10. If you can keep the entire $100 for one year and then pay it all back at once, you are paying an APR of 10 percent.

annual percentage rate (APR) The percentage cost (or relative cost) of credit on a yearly basis. The APR yields a true rate of interest for comparisons with other sources of credit.

Amount Borrowed	Month Number	Payment Made	Loan Balance
$100	1	$ 0	$100
	2	0	100
	3	0	100
	.	.	.
	.	.	.
	.	.	.
	12	$100	0
		(plus $10 interest)	

On average, you had full use of $100 throughout the year. To calculate the average use, add the loan balance during the first and last month, then divide by 2:

$$\text{Average balance} = \frac{\$100 + \$100}{2} = \$100$$

But if you repay the $100 and the finance charge (a total of $110) in 12 equal monthly payments, you don't get use of $100 for the whole year. In fact, as shown next, you get use of increasingly less of that $100 each month. In this case, the $10 charge for credit amounts to an APR of 18.5 percent.

Amount Borrowed	Month Number	Payment Made	Loan Balance
$100	1	$ 0	$100.00
	2	8.33	91.67
	3	8.33	83.34
	4	8.33	75.01
	5	8.33	66.68
	6	8.33	58.35
	7	8.33	50.02
	8	8.33	41.69
	9	8.33	33.36
	10	8.33	25.03
	11	8.33	16.70
	12	8.33	8.37

Note that you are paying 10 percent interest even though you had use of only $91.67 during the second month, not $100. During the last month, you owed only $8.37 (and had use of $8.37), but the $10 interest is for the entire $100. As calculated in the previous example, the average use of the money during the year is $100 + $8.37 ÷ 2, or $54.18. The accompanying Figure It Out feature shows how to calculate the APR.

Tackling the Trade-Offs

When you choose your financing, there are trade-offs between the features you prefer (term, size of payments, fixed or variable interest, or payment plan) and the cost of your loan. Here are some major trade-offs you should consider.

TERM VERSUS INTEREST COSTS Many people choose longer term financing because they want smaller monthly payments, but the longer the term for a loan at a given interest rate, the greater the amount you must pay in interest charges. Consider the following analysis of the relationship between the term and interest costs.

Figure It Out!

The Arithmetic of the Annual Percentage Rate (APR)

There are two ways to calculate the APR: using an APR formula and using the APR tables. The APR tables are more precise than the formula. The formula, given below, only approximates the APR:

$$r = \frac{2 \times n \times I}{P(N + 1)}$$

where

- r = Approximate APR
- n = Number of payment periods in one year (12, if payments are monthly; 52, if weekly)
- I = Total dollar cost of credit
- P = Principal, or net amount of loan
- N = Total number of payments scheduled to pay off the loan

Let us compare the APR when the $100 loan is paid off in one lump sum at the end of the year and when the same loan is paid off in 12 equal monthly payments. The stated annual interest rate is 10 percent for both loans. Using the formula, the APR for the lump-sum loan is

$$r = \frac{2 \times 1 \times \$10}{\$100(1 + 1)} = \frac{\$20}{\$100(2)} = \frac{\$20}{\$200} = 0.10,$$

or 10 percent

Using the formula, the APR for the monthly payment loan is

$$r = \frac{2 \times 12 \times \$10}{\$100(12 + 1)} = \frac{\$240}{\$100(13)} = \frac{\$240}{\$1,300}$$

$$= 0.1846, \text{ or } 18.46 \text{ percent (rounded to 18.5 percent)}$$

Suppose you're buying a $7,500 used car. You put $1,500 down, and you need to borrow $6,000. Compare the following three credit arrangements:

	APR	Length of Loan	Monthly Payment	Total Finance Charge	Total Cost
Creditor A	14%	3 years	$205.07	$1,382.52	$7,382.52
Creditor B	14	4 years	163.96	1,870.08	7,870.08
Creditor C	15	4 years	166.98	2,015.04	8,015.04

How do these choices compare? The answer depends partly on what you need. The lowest cost loan is available from creditor A. If you are looking for lower monthly payments, you should repay the loan over a longer period of time. However, you would have to pay more in total costs. A loan from creditor B—also at a 14 percent APR, but for four years—would add about $488 to your finance charge.

If that four-year loan were available only from creditor C, the APR of 15 percent would add another $145 to your finance charges. Other terms, such as the size of the down payment, will also make a difference. Be sure to look at all the terms before you make your choice.

LENDER RISK VERSUS INTEREST RATE You may prefer financing that requires low fixed payments with a large final payment or only a minimum of up-front cash. But both of these requirements can increase your cost of borrowing because they create more risk for your lender.

If you want to minimize your borrowing costs, you may need to accept conditions that reduce your lender's risk. Here are a few possibilities:

- *Variable interest rate.* A variable interest rate is based on fluctuating rates in the banking system, such as the prime rate. With this type of loan, you share the interest rate risks with the lender. Therefore, the lender may offer you a lower initial interest rate than it would with a fixed-rate loan.

- *A secured loan.* If you pledge property or other asset as collateral, you'll probably receive a lower interest rate on your loan.
- *Up-front cash.* Many lenders believe you have a higher stake in repaying a loan if you pay cash for a large portion of what you are financing. Doing so may give you a better chance of getting the other terms you want.
- *A shorter term.* As you have learned, the shorter the period of time for which you borrow, the smaller the chance that something will prevent you from repaying and the lower the risk to the lender. Therefore, you may be able to borrow at a lower interest rate if you accept a shorter-term loan, but your payments will be higher.

In the next section, you will see how the foregoing trade-offs can affect the cost of closed-end and open-end credit.

Calculating the Cost of Credit

The most common method of calculating interest is the simple interest formula. Other methods, such as simple interest on the declining balance and add-on interest, are variations of this formula.

simple interest Interest computed on principal only and without compounding.

SIMPLE INTEREST   **Simple interest** is the interest computed on principal only and without compounding; it is the dollar cost of borrowing money. This cost is based on three elements: the amount borrowed, which is called the *principal;* the rate of interest; and the amount of time for which the principal is borrowed.

You can use the following formula to find simple interest:

$$\text{Interest} = \text{Principal} \times \text{Rate of interest} \times \text{Time}$$

or

$$I = P \times r \times T$$

Example

Suppose you have persuaded a relative to lend you $1,000 to purchase a laptop computer. Your relative agreed to charge only 5 percent interest, and you agreed to repay the loan at the end of one year. Using the simple interest formula, the interest will be 5 percent of $1,000 for one year, or $50, since you have the use of $1,000 for the entire year:

$$I = \$1,000 \times 0.05 \times 1$$
$$= \$50$$

Using the APR formula discussed earlier,

$$\text{APR} = \frac{2 \times n \times I}{P(N+1)} = \frac{2 \times 1 \times \$50}{\$1,000(1+1)} = \frac{\$100}{\$2,000} = 0.05, \text{ or 5 percent}$$

Note that the stated rate, 5 percent, is also the annual percentage rate.

Key Web Sites for Cost of Credit

www.pirg.org/consumer/credit

www.econsumer.equifax.com

SIMPLE INTEREST ON THE DECLINING BALANCE   When simple interest is paid back in more than one payment, the method of computing interest is known as the declining balance method. You pay interest only on the amount of principal that you have not yet repaid. The more often you make payments, the lower the interest you'll pay. Most credit unions use this method.

Example

Using simple interest on the declining balance to compute interest charges, the interest on a 5 percent, $1,000 loan repaid in two payments, one at the end of the first half-year and another at the end of the second half-year, would be $37.50, as follows:

First payment:

$$I = P \times r \times T$$
$$= \$1,000 \times 0.05 \times 1/2$$
$$= \$25 \text{ interest plus } \$500, \text{ or } \$525$$

Second payment:

$$I = P \times r \times T$$
$$= \$500 \times 0.05 \times 1/2$$
$$= \$12.50 \text{ interest plus the remaining balance of } \$500, \text{ or } \$512.50$$

Total payment on the loan:

$$\$525 + \$512.50 = \$1,037.50$$

Using the APR formula,

$$\text{APR} = \frac{2 \times n \times I}{P(N + 1)} = \frac{2 \times 2 \times \$37.50}{\$1,000(2 + 1)} = \frac{\$150}{\$3,000} = 0.05, \text{ or 5 percent}$$

ADD-ON INTEREST With the add-on interest method, interest is calculated on the full amount of the original principal, no matter how frequently you make payments. When you pay off the loan with one payment, this method produces the same annual percentage rate (APR) as the simple interest method. However, if you pay in installments, your actual rate of interest will be higher than the stated rate. Interest payments on this type of loan do not decrease as the loan is repaid. The longer you take to repay the loan, the more interest you'll pay.

CAUTION! Many banks will increase the interest rate because of one late payment. They'll also slap on a penalty fee, which can run as high as $50 a pop.

COST OF OPEN-END CREDIT The Truth in Lending Act requires that open-end creditors inform consumers as to how the finance charge and the APR will affect their costs. For example, they must explain how they calculate the finance charge. They must also inform you when finance charges on your credit account begin to accrue, so that you know how much time you have to pay your bills before a finance charge is added.

COST OF CREDIT AND EXPECTED INFLATION Inflation reduces the buying power of money. Each percentage point increase in inflation means a decrease of about 1 percent in the quantity of goods and services you can buy with the same amount of money. Because of this, lenders incorporate the expected rate of inflation when deciding how much interest to charge.

Remember the earlier example in which you borrowed $1,000 from your aunt at the bargain rate of 5 percent for one year? If the inflation rate was 4 percent that year, your aunt's actual rate of return on the loan would have been only 1 percent (5 percent stated interest minus 4 percent inflation rate). A professional lender who wanted to receive 5 percent interest on your loan might have charged you 9 percent interest (5 percent interest plus 4 percent anticipated inflation rate).

AVOID THE MINIMUM MONTHLY PAYMENT TRAP On credit card bills and with certain other forms of credit, the *minimum monthly payment* is the smallest amount you can pay and remain a borrower in good standing. Lenders often encourage you to make the minimum payment because it will then take you longer to pay off the loan. However, if you are paying only the minimum amount on your monthly statement, you need to plan your budget more carefully. The longer it takes for you to pay off a bill, the more interest you pay. The finance charges you pay on an item could end up being more than the item is worth.

Consider the following examples. In each example, the minimum payment is based on 1/36 of the outstanding balance or $20, whichever is greater.

Example 1

You are buying new books for college. If you spend $500 on textbooks using a credit card charging 19.8 percent interest and make only the minimum payment, it will take you more than 2½ years to pay off the loan, adding $150 in interest charges to the cost of your purchase. The same purchase on a credit card charging 12 percent interest will cost only $78 extra.

Example 2

You purchase a $2,000 stereo system using a credit card with 19 percent interest and a 2 percent minimum payment. If you pay just the minimum every month, it will take you 265 months—over 22 years—to pay off the debt and will cost you nearly $4,800 in interest payments. Doubling the amount paid each month to 4 percent of the balance owed would allow you to shorten the payment time to 88 months from 265 months—or 7 years as opposed to 22 years—and save you about $3,680.

Sheet 16 Credit Card/Charge Account Comparison

Sheet 17 Consumer Loan Comparison

CONCEPT CHECK 5–4

1 What are the two key concepts to remember when you borrow money?

_____

2 What are the three major trade-offs you should consider as you take out a loan?

_____

3 Using terms from the following list, complete the sentences below. Write the term you have chosen in the space provided.

       finance charge

       annual percentage rate

       simple interest

       minimum monthly payment

       add-on interest method

a. The _____ is the cost of credit on a yearly basis expressed as a percentage.

b. The total dollar amount paid to use credit is the _____.

c. The smallest amount a borrower can pay on a credit card bill and remain a borrower in good standing is the _____.

d. With the _____, interest is calculated on the full amount of the original principal, no matter how often you make payments.

e. _____ is the interest computed only on the principal, the amount that you borrow.

Apply Yourself!

Objective 4

Use the Internet to obtain information about the costs of closed-end and open-end credit.

Protecting Your Credit

Have you ever received a bill for merchandise you never bought or that you returned to the store or never received? Have you ever made a payment that was not credited to your account or been charged twice for the same item? If so, you are not alone.

OBJECTIVE 5

Develop a plan to protect your credit and manage your debts.

Billing Errors and Disputes

The **Fair Credit Billing Act (FCBA),** passed in 1975, sets procedures for promptly correcting billing mistakes, refusing to make credit card or revolving credit payments on defective goods, and promptly crediting your payments.

Follow these steps if you think that a bill is wrong or want more information about it. First notify your creditor in writing, and include any information that might support your case. (A telephone call is not sufficient and will not protect your rights.) Then pay the portion of the bill that is not in question.

Your creditor must acknowledge your letter within 30 days. Then, within two billing periods (but not longer than 90 days), the creditor must adjust your account or tell you why the bill is correct. If the creditor made a mistake, you don't have to pay any finance charges on the disputed amount. If no mistake is found, the creditor must promptly send you an explanation of the situation and a statement of what you owe, including any finance charges that may have accumulated and any minimum payments you missed while you were questioning the bill.

Fair Credit Billing Act (FCBA) Sets procedures for promptly correcting billing mistakes, refusing to make credit card payments on defective goods, and promptly crediting payments.

PROTECTING YOUR CREDIT RATING According to law, a creditor may not threaten your credit rating or do anything to damage your credit reputation while you're negotiating a billing dispute. In addition, the creditor may not take any action to collect the amount in question until your complaint has been answered.

Key Web Sites for Protecting Credit

www.consumer-action.org

www.ftc.gov/ogc/stats.htm

DEFECTIVE GOODS AND SERVICES Theo used his credit card to buy a new mountain bike. When it arrived, he discovered that some of the gears didn't work properly. He tried to return it, but the store would not accept a return. He asked the store to repair or replace the bike—but still he had no luck. According to the Fair Credit Billing Act, he may tell his credit card company to stop payment for the bike because he has made a sincere attempt to resolve the problem with the store.

Identity Crisis: What to Do If Your Identity Is Stolen

"I don't remember charging those items. I've never been in that store." Maybe you never charged those goods and services, but someone else did—someone who used your name and personal information to commit fraud. When imposters use your personal information for their own purposes, they are committing a crime.

The biggest problem? You may not know that your identity has been stolen until you notice that something is wrong: You may get bills for a credit card account you never opened, or you may see charges to your account for things that you didn't purchase.

If you think that your identity has been stolen and that someone is using it to charge purchases or obtain credit in some other way, the Federal Trade Commission recommends that you take the following three actions immediately:

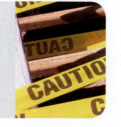

1. *Contact the credit bureaus.* Tell them to flag your file with a fraud alert, including a statement that creditors should call you for permission before they open any new accounts in your name.
2. *Contact the creditors.* Contact the creditors for any accounts that have been tampered with or opened fraudulently. Follow up in writing.
3. *File a police report.* Keep a copy of the police report in case your creditors need proof of the crime. If you're still having identity problems, stay alert to new instances of identity theft. You can also contact the Privacy Rights Clearinghouse. Call 1-619-298-3396.

Protecting Your Credit from Theft or Loss

Some thieves will pick through your trash in the hope of coming across your personal information. You can prevent this from happening by tearing or shredding any papers that contain personal information before you throw them out.

If you believe that an identity thief has accessed your bank accounts, close the accounts immediately. If your checks have been stolen or misused, stop payment on them. If your debit card has been lost or stolen, cancel it and get another with a new personal identification number (PIN).

Lost credit cards are a key element in credit card fraud. To protect your card, you should take the following actions:

- Be sure that your card is returned to you after a purchase. Unreturned cards can find their way into the wrong hands.
- Keep a record of your credit card number. You should keep this record separate from your card.
- Notify the credit card company immediately if your card is lost or stolen. Under the Consumer Credit Protection Act, the maximum amount that you must pay if someone uses your card illegally is $50. However, if you manage to inform the company before the card is used illegally, you have no obligation to pay at all.

Protecting Your Credit Information on the Internet

The Internet is becoming almost as important to daily life as the telephone and television. Increasing numbers of consumers use the Internet for financial activities, such as investing, banking, and shopping.

When you make purchases online, make sure that your transactions are secure, that your personal information is protected, and that your "fraud sensors" are sharpened. Although you can't control fraud or deception on the Internet, you can take steps to recognize it, avoid it, and report it. Here's how:

- Use a secure browser.
- Keep records of your online transactions.
- Review your monthly bank and credit card statements.
- Read the privacy and security policies of Web sites you visit.
- Keep your personal information private.
- Never give your password to anyone online.
- Don't download files sent to you by strangers.

Cosigning a Loan

If a friend or relative ever asks you to cosign a loan, think twice. *Cosigning* a loan means that you agree to be responsible for loan payments if the other party fails to make them. When you cosign, you're taking a chance that a professional lender will not take. The lender would not require a cosigner if the borrower were considered a good risk.

If you cosign a loan and the borrower does not pay the debt, you may have to pay up to the full amount of the debt as well as any late fees or collection costs. The creditor can even collect the debt from you without first trying to collect from the borrower. The creditor can use the same collection methods against you that can be used against the borrower. If the debt is not repaid, that fact will appear on your credit record.

Complaining about Consumer Credit

If you believe that a lender is not following the consumer credit protection laws, first try to solve the problem directly with the lender. If that fails, use formal complaint procedures. This section describes how to file a complaint with the federal agencies that administer credit protection laws.

Consumer Credit Protection Laws

If you have a particular problem with a bank in connection with any of the consumer credit protection laws, you can get advice and help from the Federal Reserve System. You don't need to have an account at the bank to file a complaint. You may also take legal action against a creditor. If you decide to file a lawsuit, you should be aware of the various consumer credit protection laws described below.

> *did you know?*
>
> **OPTING OUT**
> You can stop preapproved credit card offers by calling 1-888-567-8688.

TRUTH IN LENDING AND CONSUMER LEASING ACTS If a creditor fails to disclose information as required under the Truth in Lending Act or the Consumer Leasing Act, or gives inaccurate information, you can sue for any money loss you suffer. You can also sue a creditor that does not follow rules regarding credit cards. In addition, the Truth in Lending Act and the Consumer Leasing Act permit class action of all the people who have suffered the same injustice.

EQUAL CREDIT OPPORTUNITY ACT (ECOA) If you think that you can prove that a creditor has discriminated against you for any reason prohibited by the ECOA, you may sue for actual damages plus punitive damages—a payment used to punish the creditor who has violated the law—up to $10,000.

Key Web Sites for Credit Protection Laws

www.federalreserve.gov

www.uschamber.com

FAIR CREDIT BILLING ACT A creditor that fails to follow the rules that apply to correcting any billing errors will automatically give up the amount owed on the item in question and any finance charges on it, up to a combined total of $50. This is true even if the bill was correct. You may also sue for actual damages plus twice the amount of any finance charges.

FAIR CREDIT REPORTING ACT You may sue any credit bureau or creditor that violates the rules regarding access to your credit records, or that fails to correct errors in your credit file. You're entitled to actual damages plus any punitive damages the court allows if the violation is proven to have been intentional.

CONSUMER CREDIT REPORTING REFORM ACT The Consumer Credit Reporting Reform Act of 1977 places the burden of proof for accurate credit information on the credit bureau rather than on you. Under this law, the creditor must prove that disputed information is accurate. If a creditor or the credit bureau verifies incorrect data, you can sue for damages.

ELECTRONIC FUND TRANSFER ACT. If a financial institution does not follow the provisions of the Electronic Fund Transfer Act, you may sue for actual damages plus punitive damages of not less than $100 or more than $1,000. You are also entitled to court costs and attorney fees in a successful lawsuit. Class action suits are also permitted.

THE CREDIT CARD ACCOUNTABILITY RESPONSIBILITY AND DISCLOSURE ACT of 2009. President Obama signed this landmark credit-card legislation on May 22, 2009. The law, also known as the Credit Cardholders' Bill of Rights, becomes effective in February 2010. Under the law, banks can't raise interest rates on outstanding balances unless your payment is 60 days overdue. However, if you pay on time for the next six months, the company must immediately restore the lower rate. The law also eliminates fees for paying balance online and requires credit-card companies to apply payments to that part of your debts that carry the highest interest rates.

Your Rights under Consumer Credit Laws

If you believe that you've been refused credit because of discrimination, you can take one or more of the following steps:

- Complain to the creditor. Let the creditor know that you are aware of the law.
- File a complaint with the government. You can report any violations to the appropriate government enforcement agency, as shown in Exhibit 5–9.
- If all else fails, sue the creditor. If you win, you can receive actual damages and punitive damages of up to $10,000. You can also recover reasonable attorneys' fees and court costs.

Managing Your Debts

A sudden illness or the loss of your job may prevent you from paying your bills on time. If you find you cannot make your payments, contact your creditors at once and try to work out a modified payment plan with them.

Warning Signs of Debt Problems

Chris is in his late 20s. A college graduate, he has a steady job and earns an annual income of $40,000. With the latest model sports car parked in the driveway of his new home, it would appear that Chris has the ideal life.

However, Chris is deeply in debt. He is drowning in a sea of bills. Almost all his income is tied up in debt payments. The bank has already begun foreclosure proceedings

Exhibit **5-9** Federal Government Agencies that Enforce the Consumer Credit Laws

If you think you've been discriminated against by:	You may file a complaint with the following agency:
Consumer reporting agencies, creditors and others not listed below	Federal Trade Commission: Consumer Response Center - FCRA Washington, DC 20580 1-877-382-4357
National banks, federal branches/agencies of foreign banks (word "National" or initials "N.A." appear in or after bank's name)	Office of the Comptroller of the Currency Compliance Management, Mail Stop 6-6 Washington, DC 20219 800-613-6743
Federal Reserve System member banks (except national banks, and federal branches/agencies of foreign banks)	Federal Reserve Board Division of Consumer & Community Affairs Washington, DC 20551 202-452-3693
Savings associations and federally chartered savings banks (word "Federal" or initials "F.S.B." appear in federal institution's name)	Office of Thrift Supervision Consumer Complaints Washington, DC 20552 800-842-6929
Federal credit unions (words "Federal Credit Union" appear in institution's name)	National Credit Union Administration 1775 Duke Street Alexandria, VA 22314 703-519-4600
State-chartered banks that are not members of the Federal Reserve System	Federal Deposit Insurance Corporation Consumer Response Center, 2345 Grand Avenue, Suite 100 Kansas City, MO 64108-2638 1-877-275-3342

The law gives you certain rights as a consumer of credit. *What types of complaints about a creditor might you report to these government agencies?*

on his home, and several stores have court orders to repossess practically all of his new furniture and electronic gadgets. His current car payment is overdue, and he is behind in payments on all his credit cards. If he doesn't come up with a plan of action, he'll lose everything.

Chris's situation is all too common. Some people who seem to be wealthy are just barely keeping their heads above water financially. Generally, the problem they share is financial immaturity. They lack self-discipline and don't control their impulses. They use poor judgment or fail to accept responsibility for managing their money.

Chris and others like him aren't necessarily bad people. They simply haven't thought about their long-term financial goals. Someday you could find yourself in a situation similar to Chris's. Here are some warning signs that you may be in financial trouble:

- You make only the minimum monthly payment on credit cards.
- You're having trouble making even the minimum monthly payment on your credit card bills.
- The total balance on your credit cards increases every month.
- You miss loan payments or often pay late.
- You use savings to pay for necessities such as food and utilities.
- You receive second and third payment due notices from creditors.
- You borrow money to pay off old debts.
- You exceed the credit limits on your credit cards.
- You've been denied credit because of a bad credit bureau report.

If you are experiencing two or more of these warning signs, it's time for you to rethink your priorities before it's too late.

Debt Collection Practices

The Federal Trade Commission enforces the Fair Debt Collection Practices Act (FDCPA). This act prohibits certain practices by debt collectors—businesses that collect debts for creditors. The act does not erase the legitimate debts that consumers owe, but it does control the ways in which debt collection agencies may do business.

Financial Counseling Services

If you're having trouble paying your bills and need help, you have several options. You can contact your creditors and try to work out an adjusted repayment plan, or you can contact a nonprofit financial counseling program.

CONSUMER CREDIT COUNSELING SERVICES The Consumer Credit Counseling Service (CCCS) is a nonprofit organization affiliated with the National Foundation for Consumer Credit (NFCC). Local branches of the CCCS provide debt-counseling services for families and individuals with serious financial problems. The CCCS is not a charity, a lending institution, or a government agency. CCCS counseling is usually free. However, when the organization supervises a debt repayment plan, it sometimes charges a small fee to help pay administrative costs.

According to the NFCC, millions of consumers contact CCCS offices each year for help with their personal financial problems. To find an office near you, check the white pages of your local telephone directory under Consumer Credit Counseling Service, or call 1-800-388-CCCS. All information is kept confidential.

Credit counselors know that most individuals who are overwhelmed with debt are basically honest people who want to clear up their unmanageable *indebtedness,* the condition of being deeply in debt. Too often, such problems arise from the lack of planning or a miscalculation of earnings. The CCCS is concerned with preventing problems as much as it is with solving them. As a result, its activities are divided into two parts:

- Aiding families with serious debt problems by helping them to manage their money better and set up a realistic budget.
- Helping people prevent indebtedness by teaching them the importance of budget planning, educating them about the pitfalls of unwise credit buying, and encouraging credit institutions to withhold credit from people who cannot afford it.

See the accompanying Personal Finance in Practice box for help in choosing a credit counselor.

Key Web Site for Credit Counseling

www.uscourts.gov

OTHER COUNSELING SERVICES In addition to the CCCS, universities, credit unions, military bases, and state and federal housing authorities sometimes provide nonprofit credit counseling services. These organizations usually charge little or nothing for their assistance. You can also check with your bank or local consumer protection office to see whether it has a listing of reputable financial counseling services, such as the Debt Counselors of America.

Declaring Personal Bankruptcy

What if a debtor suffers from an extreme case of financial woes? Can there be any relief? The answer is bankruptcy proceedings. *Bankruptcy* is a legal process in which some or all of the assets of a debtor are distributed among the creditors because the debtor is unable to pay his or her debts. Bankruptcy may also include a plan for the debtor to repay creditors on an installment basis. Declaring bankruptcy is a last resort because it severely damages your credit rating.

Anita Singh illustrates the face of bankruptcy. A 43-year-old freelance photographer from California, she was never in serious financial trouble until she began running up big medical costs. She reached for her credit cards to pay the bills. Because Anita didn't

Personal Finance in Practice

> Choosing a Credit Counselor

Reputable credit counseling organizations employ counselors who are certified and trained in consumer credit, debt management, and budgeting. Here are a few important questions to ask when choosing a credit counselor:

1. **What services do you offer?** Look for an organization that offers a range of services, including budget counseling, savings and debt management classes, and trained certified counselors.

2. **Are you licensed to offer services in my state?** Many states require that credit counseling agencies register or obtain a license before offering their services.

3. **Do you offer free information?** Avoid organizations that charge for information about the nature of their services.

4. **Will I have a formal written agreement or contract with you?** Don't commit to participate in a debt management program over the telephone. Get all the verbal promises in writing. Read all documents carefully before you sign them. If you are told you need to act immediately, consider finding another organization.

5. **What are the qualifications of your counselors?** Are they accredited or certified by an outside organization? Which one? If not, how are they trained? Try to use an organization whose counselors are trained by an outside organization that is not affiliated with creditors.

6. **Have other consumers been satisfied with the service they received?** Once you have identified credit counseling organizations that suit your needs, check them out with your state attorney general, local consumer protection agency, and Better Business Bureau.

7. **What are your fees? Are there set-up and/or monthly fees?** Get a detailed quote in writing, and specifically ask whether all fees are covered in the quote. If an organization won't help you because you can't afford to pay, look elsewhere for help.

8. **How are your employees paid? Are the employees or the organization paid more if I sign up for certain services, pay a fee, or make a contribution to your organization?** Employees who are counseling you to purchase certain services may receive a commission if you choose to sign up for those services. Many credit counseling organizations receive additional compensation from creditors if you enroll in a debt management program.

9. **What do you do to keep personal information about your clients (for example, name, address, phone number, financial information) confidential and secure?** Credit counseling organizations handle your most sensitive financial information. The organization should have safeguards in place to protect the privacy of this information and prevent misuse.

---

have health insurance, her debt quickly mounted and soon reached $17,000—too much to pay off with her $25,000-a-year income. Her solution was to declare personal bankruptcy and enjoy the immediate freedom it would bring from creditors' demands.

THE U.S. BANKRUPTCY ACT OF 1978 Exhibit 5–10 illustrates the rate of personal bankruptcy in the United States. The vast majority of bankruptcies in the United States, like Anita Singh's, are filed under a part of U.S. bankruptcy code known as Chapter 7 . You have two choices in declaring personal bankruptcy: Chapter 7 (a straight bankruptcy) and Chapter 13 (a wage earner plan bankruptcy). Both choices are undesirable, and neither should be considered an easy way to get out of debt.

Chapter 7 Bankruptcy   In a Chapter 7 bankruptcy, an individual is required to draw up a petition listing his or her assets and liabilities. A person who files for relief under the bankruptcy code is called a *debtor*. The debtor submits the petition to a U.S. district court and pays a filing fee.

Chapter 7 is a straight bankruptcy in which many, but not all, debts are forgiven. Most of the debtor's assets are sold to pay off creditors. Certain assets, however, receive

Exhibit **5–10**   U.S. Consumer Bankruptcy Filings, 1980–2008

Consumer bankruptcies have increased significantly over the past 28 years. Consumer bankruptcy filings rose from about 287,000 in 1980 to almost 2 million in 2005. Bankruptcies decreased after the Bankruptcy Abuse Prevention and Consumer Protection Act was passed.

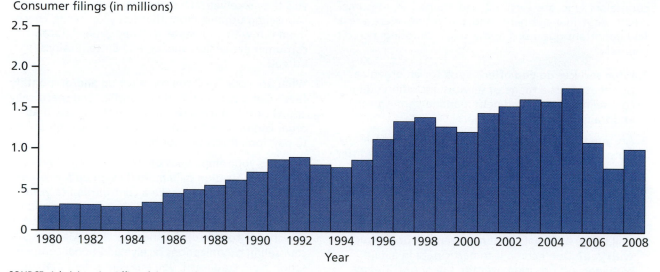

Consumer filings (in millions)

SOURCE: Administrative Office of the United States Courts; www.uscourts.gov/press-releases/bankruptcyfilingsDec2008.cfm, accessed January 24, 2009.

some protection. Among the assets usually protected are Social Security payments, unemployment compensation, and the net value of your home, vehicle, household goods and appliances, tools used in your work, and books.

The courts must charge a $245 case filing fee, a $39 miscellaneous administrative fee, and a $15 trustee fee. If the debtor is unable to pay the fees even in installments, the court may waive the fees.

In filing a petition, a debtor must provide the following information:

- A list of all creditors and the amount and nature of their claims.
- The source, amount, and frequency of the debtor's income.
- A list of all the debtor's property.
- A detailed list of the debtor's monthly expenses.

The release from debt does not affect alimony, child support, certain taxes, fines, certain debts arising from educational loans, or debts that you fail to disclose properly to the bankruptcy court. Furthermore, debts arising from fraud, driving while intoxicated, or certain other acts or crimes may also be excluded.

The Bankruptcy Abuse Prevention and Consumer Protection Act of 2005   On April 20, 2005, President George W. Bush signed the Bankruptcy Abuse Prevention and Consumer Protection Act, which is perhaps the largest overhaul of the Bankruptcy Code since it was enacted in 1978. Signing the bill, the president declared, "Bankruptcy should always be the last resort in our legal system. In recent years too many people have abused the bankruptcy laws. Under the new law, Americans who have the ability to pay will be required to pay back at least a portion of their debts. The law will help make credit more affordable, because when bankruptcy is less common, credit can be extended to more people at better rates. Debtors seeking to erase all debts will now have to wait eight years from their last bankruptcy before they can file again. The law will also allow us to clamp down on bankruptcy mills that make their money by advising abusers on how to game the system."

Among other provisions, the law requires that:

- The director of the Executive Office for U.S. Trustees develop a financial management training curriculum to educate individual debtors on how to better manage their finances; and test, evaluate, and report to Congress on the curriculum's effectiveness.
- Debtors complete an approved instructional course in personal financial management.
- The clerk of each bankruptcy district maintains a list of credit counseling agencies and instructional courses on personal financial management.

Furthermore, the law may require that states should develop personal finance curricula designed for use in elementary and secondary schools.

The bottom line: the new law made it more difficult for consumers to file a Chapter 7 bankruptcy and forces them into a Chapter 13 repayment plan.

Chapter 13 Bankruptcy   In Chapter 13 bankruptcy, a debtor with a regular income proposes a plan for using future earnings or assets to eliminate his or her debts over a period of time. In such a bankruptcy, the debtor normally keeps all or most of his or her property. A debtor must provide the same information that is required to file a Chapter 7 bankruptcy.

During the period when the plan is in effect, which can be as long as five years, the debtor makes regular payments to a Chapter 13 trustee, or representative, who then distributes the money to the creditors. Under certain circumstances, the bankruptcy court may approve a plan that permits the debtor to keep all property, even though he or she repays less than the full amount of the debts.

EFFECTS OF BANKRUPTCY People have varying experiences in obtaining credit after they file for bankruptcy. Some find the process more difficult, whereas others find it easier because they have removed the burden of prior debts or because creditors know that they cannot file another bankruptcy case for a certain period of time. Obtaining credit may be easier for people who file a Chapter 13 bankruptcy and repay some of their debts than for those who file a Chapter 7 bankruptcy and make no effort to repay any of their debts.

CONCEPT CHECK 5–5

1 What steps might you take if there is a billing error in your monthly statement?

_____

2 What steps would you take if someone stole your identity?

_____

_____

3 How might you protect your credit information on the Internet?

_____

_____

4 What are some warning signs of debt problems?

_____

_____

5 Distinguish between Chapter 7 and Chapter 13 bankruptcy.

_____

_____

Apply Yourself!

Objective 5

Use an Internet search engine to find branches of the Consumer Credit Counseling Service across the country. Choose one in your area and one in another part of the country. Visit the Web sites to find out who funds the offices.

Back to... Getting Personal

Reconsider your responses to the Getting Personal questions at the beginning of the chapter.

For more effective use of consumer credit:

- Seek information from several sources when evaluating the sources of credit, including various Web sites and Exhibit 5–3.
- Determine how you intend to use your credit card before choosing one. Follow the suggestions to find the card that best meets your needs and to use it wisely. See the Personal Finance in Practice feature on page 175.

- Get copies of your credit report, then make sure the information is correct. The only authorized online source for a free credit report is www.annualcredit report.com, or call 877-322-8228.
- Beware of credit-repair scams. The Federal Trade Commission's *Credit Repair: Self-Help May Be Best* (www.ftc.gov/bcp/online/pubs/credit/repair.shtm) explains how you can improve your creditworthiness.

What did you learn in this chapter that might affect your use of credit now or in the future?

Chapter Summary

Objective 1   Consumer credit is the use of credit by individuals and families for personal needs. Among the advantages of using credit are the ability to purchase goods when needed and pay for them gradually, the ability to meet financial emergencies, convenience in shopping, and establishment of a credit rating. Disadvantages are that credit costs money, encourages overspending, and ties up future income.

Objective 2   Closed-end and open-end credit are two types of consumer credit. With closed-end credit, the borrower pays back a one-time loan in a stated period of time and with a specified number of payments. With open-end credit, the borrower is permitted to take loans on a continuous basis and is billed for partial payments periodically.

The major sources of consumer credit are commercial banks, savings and loan associations, credit unions, finance companies, life insurance companies, and family and friends. Each of these sources has unique advantages and disadvantages.

Parents or family members are often the source of the least expensive loans. They may charge you only the interest they would have earned had they not made the loan. Such loans, however, can complicate family relationships.

Objective 3   Two general rules for measuring credit capacity are the debt payments-to-income ratio and the debt-to-equity ratio. In reviewing your creditworthiness, a creditor seeks information from one of the three national credit bureaus or a regional credit bureau.

Creditors determine creditworthiness on the basis of the five Cs: character, capacity, capital, collateral, and conditions.

Objective 4   Compare the finance charge and the annual percentage rate (APR) as you shop for credit. Under the Truth in Lending Act, creditors are required to state the cost of borrowing so that you can compare credit costs and shop for credit.

Objective 5   If a billing error occurs on your account, notify the creditor in writing within 60 days. If the dispute is not settled in your favor, you can place your version of it in your credit file. You may also withhold payment on any defective goods or services you have purchased with a credit card as long as you have attempted to resolve the problem with the merchant.

If you have a complaint about credit, first try to deal directly with the creditor. If that fails, you can turn to the appropriate consumer credit law. These laws include the Truth in Lending Act, the Consumer Leasing Act, the Equal Credit Opportunity Act, the Fair Credit Billing Act, the Fair Credit Reporting Act, the Consumer Credit Reporting Reform Act, and the Electronic Fund Transfer Act.

If you cannot meet your obligations, contact your creditors immediately. Also, contact your local Consumer Credit Counseling Service or other debt counseling organizations.

A debtor's last resort is to declare bankruptcy, permitted by the U.S. Bankruptcy Act of 1978. Consider the financial and other costs of bankruptcy before taking this extreme step. A debtor can declare Chapter 7 (straight) bankruptcy or Chapter 13 (wage earner plan) bankruptcy.

Key Terms

annual percentage rate (APR)   163
capacity   155
capital   155
character   154
closed-end credit   147
collateral   155

conditions   156
consumer credit   144
credit   143
Fair Credit Billing Act (FCBA)   169
finance charge   151
interest   148

line of credit   148
open-end credit   147
revolving check credit   148
simple interest   166

KEY FORMULAS

Page	Topic	Formula
165	Calculating annual percentage rate (APR)	$$APR = \frac{2 \times \text{Number of payment periods in one year} \times \text{Dollar cost of credit}}{\text{Loan amount (Total number of payments to pay off the loan} + 1)}$$ $$= \frac{2 \times n \times I}{P(N + 1)}$$
166	Calculating simple interest	Interest (in dollars) = Principal borrowed $\times$ Interest rate $\times$ Length of loan in years. $$I = P \times r \times T$$

Self-Test Problems

1. Suppose that your monthly net income is $1,200. Your monthly debt payments include your student loan payment and a gas credit card, and they total $180. What is your debt payments-to-income ratio?
2. Suppose you borrow $1,000 at 8 percent and will repay it in one payment at the end of one year. Use the simple interest formula to determine the amount of interest you will pay.

Solutions

1. Use the debt payments-to-income ratio formula: Monthly debt payments/Monthly net income.

$$\text{Debt payments-to-income ratio} = \frac{\$180}{\$1,200} = 0.15, \text{ or } 15\%$$

2. Using the simple interest formula (Interest = Principal $\times$ Rate of interest $\times$ Time), the interest is $80, computed as follows:

$$\$80 = \$1,000 \times 0.08 \times 1 \text{ (year)}$$

Problems

1. A few years ago, Michael Tucker purchased a home for $100,000. Today the home is worth $150,000. His remaining mortgage balance is $50,000. Assuming Michael can borrow up to 80 percent of the market value of his home, what is the maximum amount he can borrow? (Obj. 2)

2. Louise McIntyre's monthly gross income is $2,000. Her employer withholds $400 in federal, state, and local income taxes and $160 in Social Security taxes per month. Louise contributes $80 per month for her IRA. Her monthly credit payments for Visa, MasterCard, and Discover cards are $35, $30, and $20, respectively. Her monthly payment on an automobile loan is $285. What is Louise's debt payments-to-income ratio? Is Louise living within her means? Explain. (Obj. 3)

3. Robert Thumme owns a $140,000 townhouse and still has an unpaid mortgage of $110,000. In addition to his mortgage, he has the following liabilities:

Visa	$ 565
MasterCard	480
Discover card	395
Education loan	920
Personal bank loan	800
Auto loan	4,250
Total	$7,410

Robert's net worth (not including his home) is about $21,000. This equity is in mutual funds, an automobile, a coin collection, furniture, and other personal property. What is Robert's debt-to-equity ratio? Has he reached the upper limit of debt obligations? Explain.   (Obj. 3)

4. Kim Lee is trying to decide whether she can afford a loan she needs in order to go to chiropractic school. Right now Kim is living at home and works in a shoe store, earning a gross income of $820 per month. Her employer deducts a total of $145 for taxes from her monthly pay. Kim also pays $95 on several credit card debts each month. The loan she needs for chiropractic school will cost an additional $120 per month. Help Kim make her decision by calculating her debt payments-to-income ratio with and without the college loan. (Remember the 20 percent rule.)   (Obj. 3)

5. Dave borrowed $500 for one year and paid $50 in interest. The bank charged him a $5 service charge. What is the finance charge on this loan?   (Obj. 4)

6. In problem 5, Dave borrowed $500 on January 1, 2009, and paid it all back at once on December 31, 2009. What was the APR?   (Obj. 4)

7. If Dave paid the $500 in 12 equal monthly payments, what was the APR?   (Obj. 4)

8. Sidney took a $200 cash advance by using checks linked to her credit card account. The bank charges a 2 percent cash advance fee on the amount borrowed and offers no grace period on cash advances. Sidney paid the balance in full when the bill arrived. What was the cash advance fee? What was the interest for one month at an 18 percent APR? What was the total amount she paid? What if she had made the purchase with her credit card and paid off the bill in full promptly?   (Obj. 4)

9. Dorothy lacks cash to pay for a $600 dishwasher. She could buy it from the store on credit by making 12 monthly payments of $52.74. The total cost would then be $632.88. Instead, Dorothy decides to deposit $50 a month in the bank until she has saved enough money to pay cash for the dishwasher. One year later, she has saved $642—$600 in deposits plus interest. When she goes back to the store, she finds the dishwasher now costs $660. Its price has gone up 10 percent. Was postponing her purchase a good trade-off for Dorothy?   (Obj. 4)

10. What are the interest cost and the total amount due on a six-month loan of $1,500 at 13.2 percent simple annual interest?   (Obj. 4)

11. After visiting several automobile dealerships, Richard selects the used car he wants. He likes its $10,000 price, but financing through the dealer is no bargain. He has $2,000 cash for a down payment, so he needs an $8,000 loan. In shopping at several banks for an installment loan, he learns that interest on most automobile loans is quoted at add-on rates. That is, during the life of the loan, interest is paid on the full amount borrowed even though a portion of the principal has been paid back. Richard borrows $8,000 for a period of four years at an add-on interest rate of 11 percent. What is the total interest on Richard's loan? What is the total cost of the car? What is the monthly payment? What is the annual percentage rate (APR)?   (Obj. 4)

Questions

1. Vicky is trying to decide whether to finance her purchase of a used Mustang convertible. What questions should Vicky ask herself before making her decision?   (Obj. 1)

2. List advantages and disadvantages of using credit.   (Obj. 1)

3. To finance a sofa for his new apartment, Caleb signed a contract to pay for the sofa in six equal installments. What type of consumer credit is Caleb using?   (Obj. 2)

4. Alka plans to spend $5,000 on a plasma television and home theater system. She is willing to spend some of her $9,000 in savings. However, she wants to finance the rest and pay it off in small monthly installments out of the $400 a month she earns working part-time. How might she obtain a low-interest rate and make low monthly payments? (Obj. 2)

5. What factors would you consider in assessing the choices in declaring personal bankruptcy? Why should personal bankruptcy be the choice of last resort? (Obj. 5)

Case in Point

FINANCING SUE'S HYUNDAI EXCEL

After shopping around, Sue Wallace decided on the car of her choice, a used Hyundai Excel. The dealer quoted her a total price of $8,000. Sue decided to use $2,000 of her savings as a down payment and borrow $6,000. The salesperson wrote this information on a sales contract that Sue took with her when she set out to find financing.

When Sue applied for a loan, she discussed loan terms with the bank lending officer. The officer told her that the bank's policy was to lend only 80 percent of the total price of a used car. Sue showed the officer her copy of the sales contract, indicating that she had agreed to make a $2,000, or 25 percent, down payment on the $8,000 car, so this requirement caused her no problem. Although the bank was willing to make 48-month loans at an annual percentage rate of 15 percent on used cars, Sue chose a 36-month repayment schedule. She believed she could afford the higher payments, and she knew she would not have to pay as much interest if she paid off the loan at a faster rate. The bank lending officer provided Sue with a copy of the Truth-in-Lending Disclosure Statement shown here.

Truth-in-Lending Disclosure Statement (Loans)

Annual Percentage Rate	Finance Charge	Amount Financed	Total of Payments 36
The cost of your credit as a yearly rate.	The dollar amount the credit will cost you.	The amount of credit provided to you or on your behalf.	The amount you will have paid after you have made all payments as scheduled.
15%	$1,487.64	$6,000.00	$7,487.64

You have the right to receive at this time an itemization of the Amount Financed.

☐ I want an itemization.   ☐ I do not want an itemization.

Your payment schedule will be:

Number of Payments	Amount of Payments	When Payments Are Due
36	$207.99	1st of each month

Sue decided to compare the APR she had been offered with the APR offered by another bank, but the 20 percent APR of the second bank (bank B) was more expensive than the 15 percent APR of the first bank (bank A). Here is her comparison of the two loans:

	Bank A 15% APR	Bank B 20% APR
Amount financed	$6,000.00	$6,000.00
Finance charge	1,487.64	2,027.28
Total of payments	7,487.64	8,027.28
Monthly payments	207.99	222.98

The 5 percent difference in the APRs of the two banks meant Sue would have to pay $15 extra every month if she got her loan from the second bank. Of course, she got the loan from the first bank.

Questions

1. What is perhaps the most important item shown on the disclosure statement? Why?
2. What is included in the finance charge?
3. What amount will Sue receive from the bank?
4. Should Sue borrow from bank A or bank B? Why?

Continuing Case

Vikki Rococo (age 26) has been living in her apartment for three years. Her savings system is well organized and she feels comfortable about the progress she is making with her financial goals. Her credit card balance is now paid in full monthly. She is continuing to save more than 10% of her gross salary in her 401(k) plan and she stays within budget. After dating for two years, Vikki is engaged to Tim Treble (Age 28), and they are planning to be married in nine months.

Because they want to buy a house within the next 2 or 3 years, Vicky and Tim decide to meet with a mortgage lender to determine how large of a mortgage they will be able to afford and what they need to save. The mortgage lender asks them both questions about their finances that they hadn't yet considered. Although Vikki feels comfortable with the questions, Tim is nervous when he is forced to take a closer look at his finances. He discovers that he has much more debt than he realized.

Vikki and Tim's financial statistics are shown below:

Assets:
Checking account* $10,500 (Vikki), $4,000 (Tim)
   *including their emergency fund
Car $2,500 (Vikki), $15,000 (Tim)
401(k) balance $25,000 (Vikki), $8,000 (Tim)

Liabilities:
Student loan $9,000
Credit card balance $10,000 (Tim)

Income:
Gross annual salary: $50,000 (Vikki), $48,000 (Tim)
After-tax monthly salary: $2,917 (Vikki), $2,800 (Tim)

Monthly Expenses:
Rent $750 (Vikki), $450 (Tim)
Food $250 (Vikki), $350 (Tim)
Student loan $250
Credit card payments $300 (Tim)
Entertainment $300
Wedding expenses $500
Gas/repairs $350 (combined)

Retirement Savings:
401(k) $500 per month, plus 50% employer match on first 7% of pay (Vikki), $400 per month, plus 50% match on first 8% of pay (Tim)

Questions:

1. Classify Vikki and Tim's credit as open-end or closed-end.
2. Analyze the debt payments-to-income ratios for Vikki and for Tim.
3. Analyze the 5Cs of credit for Vikki and Tim.
4. What is the best way for Vikki and Tim to obtain their credit report?
5. What warning signs of debt problems do they have, if any?
6. How can they use *Your Personal Financial Plan* sheets 15–17?

Spending Diary

"I ADMIRE PEOPLE WHO ARE ABLE TO PAY OFF THEIR CREDIT CARDS EACH MONTH."

Directions

Your ability to monitor spending and credit use is a fundamental success for wise money management and long-term financial security. Use the "Daily Spending Diary" sheets provided at the end of the book to record all of your spending in the categories provided. Be sure to indicate the use of a credit card with (CR). The Daily Spending Diary sheets are located in Appendix C at the end of the book and on the student Web site at www.mhhe.com/kdh.

Questions

1. Describe any aspects of your spending habits that might indicate an overuse of credit.

2. How might your Daily Spending Diary provide information for wise credit use?

Name: _____ **Date:** _____

Consumer Credit Usage Patterns

Financial Planning Activities: Record account names, numbers, and payments for current consumer debts.

Suggested Web Sites: www.finance-center.com   www.ftc.gov

Automobile, Education, Personal, and Installment Loans

Financial institution	Account number	Current balance	Monthly payment
_____	_____	_____	_____
_____	_____	_____	_____
_____	_____	_____	_____
_____	_____	_____	_____
_____	_____	_____	_____

Charge Accounts and Credit Cards

_____	_____	_____	_____
_____	_____	_____	_____
_____	_____	_____	_____
_____	_____	_____	_____
_____	_____	_____	_____

Other Loans (overdraft protection, home equity, life insurance loan)

_____	_____	_____	_____
_____	_____	_____	_____
_____	_____	_____	_____
_____	_____	_____	_____
	Totals	_____	_____

$$\text{Debt payment-to-income ratio} = \frac{\text{Total monthly payments}}{\text{net (after-tax) income}}$$

What's Next for Your Personal Financial Plan?

- Survey three or four individuals to determine their uses of credit.
- Talk to several people to determine how they first established credit.

Credit Card/Charge Account Comparison

Financial Planning Activities: Analyze ads and credit applications and contact various financial institutions to obtain the information requested below.

Suggested Web Sites: www.bankrate.com   www.banx.com

Type of credit/charge account			
Name of company/account			
Address/phone			
Web site			
Type of purchases that can be made			
Annual fee (if any)			
Annual percentage rate (APR) (interest calculation information)			
Credit limit for new customers			
Minimum monthly payment			
Other costs: • credit report • late fee • other _____			
Restrictions (age, minimum annual income)			
Other information for consumers to consider			
Frequent flyer or other bonus points			

What's Next for Your Personal Financial Plan?

- Make a list of the pros and cons of using credit or debit cards.
- Contact a local credit bureau to obtain information on the services provided and the fees charged.

Name: _____   **Date:** _____

Consumer Loan Comparison

Financial Planning Activities: Contact or visit a bank, credit union, and consumer finance company to obtain information on a loan for a specific purpose.

Suggested Web Sites: www.eloan.com   www.centura.com

Type of financial institution			
Name			
Address			
Phone			
Web site			
Amount of down payment			
Length of loan (months)			
What collateral is required?			
Amount of monthly payment			
Total amount to be repaid (monthly amount × number of months + down payment)			
Total finance charge/ cost of credit			
Annual percentage rate (APR)			
Other costs • credit life insurance • credit report • other _____			
Is a cosigner required?			
Other information			

What's Next for Your Personal Financial Plan?

- Ask several individuals how they would compare loans at different financial institutions.
- Survey several friends and relatives to determine if they ever cosigned a loan. If yes, what were the consequences of cosigning?

6 Consumer Purchasing Strategies and Wise Buying of Motor Vehicles

Getting Personal

For each of the following shopping behaviors, circle "agree," "neutral," or "disagree" to indicate your attitude toward this action.

1. Getting very good quality is very important to me.	Agree	Neutral	Disagree
2. Well-known national brands are best for me.	Agree	Neutral	Disagree
3. I buy as much as possible at "sale" prices.	Agree	Neutral	Disagree
4. I should plan my shopping more carefully than I do.	Agree	Neutral	Disagree
5. I have favorite brands I buy over and over.	Agree	Neutral	Disagree
6. Lower priced products are usually my choice.	Agree	Neutral	Disagree

After studying this chapter, you will be asked to reconsider your responses to these items.

OBJECTIVE 1

Identify strategies for effective consumer buying.

Consumer Buying Activities

Daily buying decisions involve a trade-off between current spending and saving for the future. A wide variety of economic, social, and personal factors affect daily buying habits. These factors are the basis for spending, saving, investing, and achieving personal financial goals. In very simple terms, the only way you can have long-term financial security is to not spend all of your current income. In addition, overspending leads to misuse of credit and financial difficulties.

Practical Purchasing Strategies

Comparison shopping is the process of considering alternative stores, brands, and prices. In contrast, *impulse buying* is unplanned purchasing, which can result in

Your Personal Financial Plan Sheets

18. Consumer Purchase Comparison
19. Used-Car Purchase Comparison
20. Buying vs. Leasing an Automobile
21. Legal Services Cost Comparison

Objectives

In this chapter, you will learn to:

1. Identify strategies for effective consumer buying.
2. Implement a process for making consumer purchases.
3. Describe steps to take to resolve consumer problems.
4. Evaluate legal alternatives available to consumers.

Why is this important?

In times of economic difficulty, the number of unwise buying decisions often increases. People are tempted into scams that promise they will "earn easy money" or "get out of debt fast." Unplanned and careless buying will reduce your potential for long-term financial security. Impulse buying activities of a few dollars a week can cost you thousands in just a couple of years. Many wise buying strategies are available to avoid poor purchasing choices.

financial problems. Several buying techniques are commonly suggested for wise buying.

TIMING PURCHASES Certain items go on sale the same time each year. You can obtain bargains by buying winter clothing in mid- or late winter, or summer clothing in mid- or late summer. Many people save by buying holiday items and other products at reduced prices in late December and early January.

STORE SELECTION Your decision to use a particular retailer is probably influenced by location, price, product selection, and services available. Competition and technology have changed retailing with superstores, specialty shops, and online buying. This expanded shopping environment provides consumers with greater choice, potentially lower prices, and the need to carefully consider buying alternatives.

BRAND COMPARISON Food and other products come in various brands. *National-brand* products are highly advertised items available in many stores. *Store-brand* and *private-label* products, sold by one chain of stores, are low-cost alternatives to famous-name products. Since store-brand products are frequently manufactured by the same companies that produce brand-name items, these lower cost alternatives can result in extensive savings. The use of one or more of the many product comparison Web sites can assist you in this process.

LABEL INFORMATION Certain label information is helpful; however, other information is nothing more than advertising. Federal law requires that food labels contain certain information. Product labeling for appliances includes information about operating costs to assist you in selecting the most energy-efficient models. *Open dating* describes the freshness or shelf life of a perishable product. Phrases such as "Use before May 2009" or "Not to be sold after October 8" appear on most grocery items.

PRICE COMPARISON *Unit pricing* uses a standard unit of measurement to compare the prices of packages of different sizes. To calculate the unit price, divide the price of the item by the number of units of measurement, such as ounces, pounds, gallons, or number of sheets (for items such as paper towels and facial tissues). Then compare the unit prices for various sizes, brands, and stores.

Example

To calculate the unit price of an item, divide the cost by the number of units. For example, a 64-ounce product costing $8.32 would be calculated in this manner:

$$\text{Unit price} = \$8.32 \div 64$$
$$= \$0.13, \text{ or 13 cents an ounce}$$

Coupons and rebates also provide better pricing for wise consumers. A family saving about $8 a week on their groceries by using coupons will save $416 over a year and $2,080 over five years (not counting interest). Coupons are available online at www.coolsavings.com, www.centsoff.com, and www.couponsurfer.com. A *rebate* is a partial refund of the price of a product.

When comparing prices, remember that

- More store convenience (location, hours, sales staff) usually means higher prices.
- Ready-to-use products have higher prices.
- Large packages are usually the best buy; however, compare using unit pricing.
- "Sale" may not always mean saving money.
- The use of online sources can save time.

Exhibit 6–1 summarizes techniques that can assist you in your buying decisions.

Warranties

Most products come with some guarantee of quality. A **warranty** is a written guarantee from the manufacturer or distributor that specifies the conditions under which the product can be returned, replaced, or repaired. An *express warranty,* usually in written form, is created by the seller or manufacturer and has two forms: the full warranty and the limited warranty. A *full warranty* states that a defective product can be fixed or replaced during a reasonable amount of time.

Key Web Sites for Wise Buying

http://clarkhoward.com

www.homemoneyhelp.com

www.cheapskatemonthly.com

www.thefrugalshopper.com

warranty A written guarantee from the manufacturer or distributor of a product that specifies the conditions under which the product can be returned, replaced, or repaired.

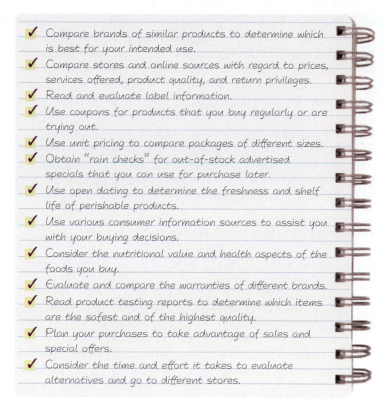

Exhibit 6–1

Wise Buying Techniques:
A Summary

The notebook checklist reads:

✔ Compare brands of similar products to determine which is best for your intended use.

✔ Compare stores and online sources with regard to prices, services offered, product quality, and return privileges.

✔ Read and evaluate label information.

✔ Use coupons for products that you buy regularly or are trying out.

✔ Use unit pricing to compare packages of different sizes.

✔ Obtain "rain checks" for out-of-stock advertised specials that you can use for purchase later.

✔ Use open dating to determine the freshness and shelf life of perishable products.

✔ Use various consumer information sources to assist you with your buying decisions.

✔ Consider the nutritional value and health aspects of the foods you buy.

✔ Evaluate and compare the warranties of different brands.

✔ Read product testing reports to determine which items are the safest and of the highest quality.

✔ Plan your purchases to take advantage of sales and special offers.

✔ Consider the time and effort it takes to evaluate alternatives and go to different stores.

A *limited warranty* covers only certain aspects of the product, such as parts, or requires the buyer to incur part of the costs for shipping or repairs. An *implied warranty* covers a product's intended use or other basic understandings that are not in writing. For example, an implied *warranty of title* indicates that the seller has the right to sell the product. An implied *warranty of merchantability* guarantees that the product is fit for the ordinary uses for which it is intended: A toaster must toast bread, and a stereo must play CDs or tapes. Implied warranties vary from state to state.

USED-CAR WARRANTIES The Federal Trade Commission (FTC) requires used cars to have a buyer's guide sticker telling whether the vehicle comes with a warranty and, if so, what protection the dealer will provide. If no warranty is offered, the car is sold "as is" and the dealer assumes no responsibility for any repairs, regardless of any oral claims. FTC used-car regulations do not apply to vehicles purchased from private owners.

While a used car may not have an express warranty, most states have implied warranties to protect used-car buyers. An implied warranty of merchantability means the product is guaranteed to do what it is supposed to do. The used car is guaranteed to run—at least for a while!

NEW-CAR WARRANTIES New-car warranties provide buyers with an assurance of quality. These warranties vary in the time, mileage, and parts they cover. The main conditions of a new-car warranty are (1) coverage of basic parts against defects; (2) power train coverage for the engine, transmission, and drive train; and (3) the corrosion warranty, which usually applies only to holes due to rust, not to surface rust. Other important conditions of a warranty are a statement regarding whether the warranty is transferable to other owners of the car and details about the charges, if any, that will be made for major repairs in the form of a *deductible*.

did you know?

When buying gifts or household items, you can make a difference in the life of an artisan in a developing country by making an online purchase from Ten Thousand Villages (www.10000villages .org). This organization works to help artisans earn a fair wage and to improve their quality of life by paying for food, education, health care, and housing. There are also more than 150 Ten Thousand Villages stores in the United States and Canada.

Key Web Sites for Warranties

www.ftc.gov

www.consumerautomotive research.com

service contract An agreement between a business and a consumer to cover the repair costs of a product.

SERVICE CONTRACTS A **service contract** is an agreement between a business and a consumer to cover the repair costs of a product. Frequently called *extended warranties,* they are not warranties. For a fee, they insure the buyer against losses due to the cost of certain repairs. Automotive service contracts can cover repairs not included in the manufacturer's warranty. Service contracts range from $400 to more than $1,000; however, they do not always include everything you might expect. These contracts usually cover failure of the engine cooling system; however, some contracts exclude coverage of such failures if caused by overheating.

Because of costs and exclusions, service contracts may not be a wise financial decision. You can minimize your concern about expensive repairs by setting aside a fund of money to pay for them. Then, if you need repairs, the money to pay for them will be available. This action could be considered "self-insurance."

Research-Based Buying

Major buying decisions should be based on a specific decision-making process, which may be viewed in four phases.

PHASE 1: PRESHOPPING ACTIVITIES Start the buying process with actions that include:

- Problem identification to set a goal and focus your purchasing activities.
- Information gathering to benefit from the buying experiences of others.

PHASE 2: EVALUATING ALTERNATIVES With every decision, consider various options:

- Attribute assessment with a comparison of product features.
- Price analysis including consideration of the costs at various buying locations.
- Comparison shopping activities to evaluate shopping locations.

PHASE 3: SELECTION AND PURCHASE When making your final choice, actions may include:

- Negotiation activities to obtain lower price or added quality.
- Payment alternatives including use of cash and various credit plans.
- Assessment of acquisition and installation that might be encountered.

PHASE 4: POSTPURCHASE ACTIVITIES After making a purchase, several actions are encouraged:

- Proper maintenance and operation.
- Identification and comparison of after-sale service alternatives.
- Resolution of any purchase concerns that may occur.

Key Web Sites for Online Comparison Shopping

www.bizrate.com

www.shopzilla.com

www.pricegrabber.com

www.pricescan.com

 Sheet 18 Consumer Purchase Comparison

CONCEPT CHECK 6–1

1 What types of brands are commonly available to consumers?

2 In what situations can comparing prices help in purchasing decisions?

_____

_____

3 How does a service contract differ from a warranty?

_____

_____

4 Match the following descriptions with the warranties listed here. Write your answer in the space provided.

express warranty   limited warranty

full warranty   service contact

implied warranty

a. _____ covers only aspects of the item purchased.

b. _____ is commonly referred to as an extended warranty.

c. _____ usually is in a written form.

d. _____ covers a product's intended use; it may not be in writing.

e. _____ covers fixing or replacement of a product for a set time period.

Apply Yourself!

Objective 1

Conduct a survey regarding brand loyalty. For what products are people most brand loyal? What factors (price, location, information) may influence their selection of another brand?

Major Consumer Purchases: Buying Motor Vehicles

As shown in Exhibit 6–2, the steps for effective purchasing can be used for wise buying of motor vehicles.

Phase 1: Preshopping Activities

First define your needs and obtain relevant product information. These activities are the foundation for buying decisions to help you achieve your goals.

PROBLEM IDENTIFICATION Effective decision making should start with an open mind. Some people always buy the same brand when another brand at a lower price would also serve their needs, or when another brand at the same price may provide better quality. A narrow view of the problem is a weakness in problem identification. You may think the problem is "I need to have a car" when the real problem is "I need transportation."

> **OBJECTIVE 2**
>
> Implement a process for making consumer purchases.

Exhibit **6–2**

A Research-Based
Approach for Purchasing
a Motor Vehicle

Purchasing a Motor Vehicle

4 Postpurchase Activities
• Automobile operation costs
• Motor vehicle maintenance

1 Preshopping Activities
• Problem identification
• Information gathering

3 Determining Purchase Price
• Used-car price negotiations
• Price bargaining for new cars
• Comparing financing alternatives

2 Evaluating Alternatives
• Selecting vehicle options
• Comparing used vehicles
• Leasing a vehicle

Key Web Sites for Consumer Product Information:

www.consumer.gov

www.consumerreports.org

www.consumerworld.org

http://clarkhoward.com

INFORMATION GATHERING Information is power. The better informed you are, the better buying decisions you will make. Some people spend very little time gathering and evaluating buying information. At the other extreme are people who spend much time obtaining consumer information. While information is necessary for wise purchasing, too much information can create confusion and frustration. The following information sources are frequently helpful:

1. *Personal contacts* allow you to learn about product performance, brand quality, and prices from others.
2. *Business organizations* offer advertising, product labels, and packaging that provide information about price, quality, and availability.
3. *Media information* (television, radio, newspapers, magazines, Web sites) can provide valuable information with purchasing advice.
4. *Independent testing organizations,* such as Consumers Union, provide information about the quality of products and services each month in *Consumer Reports.*
5. *Government agencies,* local, state, and federal, provide publications, toll-free telephone numbers, Web sites, and community programs.
6. *Online sources* offer extensive product information and shopping suggestions.

Phase 2: Evaluating Alternatives

Every purchasing situation usually has several acceptable alternatives. Ask yourself: Is it possible to delay the purchase or to do without the item? Should I pay for the item with cash or buy it on credit? Which brands should I consider? How do the price, quality, and service compare at different stores? Is it possible to rent the item instead of buying it? Considering such alternatives will result in more effective purchasing decisions.

Research shows that prices can vary for all types of products. For a camera, prices may range from under $100 to well over $500. The price of aspirin may range from less than $1 to over $3 for 100 five-grain tablets. While differences in quality and attributes may exist among the cameras, the aspirin are equivalent in quantity and quality.

We'll help with a diagnosis and a cure. *By Jessica L. Anderson*

What Kind of Spender Are You?

Want a window into your soul? Look at why you buy. Stuart Vyse, author of *Going Broke: Why Americans Can't Hold On to Their Money* (Oxford University Press, $25), says there's no question that "who we are affects the way we approach spending."

We're trained to measure ourselves by our possessions, says Dilip Soman, professor of marketing at the University of Toronto, so "we shop to find things that enhance our self-image or social status."

Seeking status is one problem, and Soman and Vyse have helped *Kiplinger's* identify two others that manifest themselves in particular types of spenders. To see if you're one (or more) of them, take our quiz.

The Overconfident Consumer

1. DO YOU SHOP TO FEEL GOOD WHEN YOU'VE HAD A BAD DAY?

2. DOES FINDING A GREAT DEAL REALLY GET YOUR BLOOD PUMPING?

3. DO YOU SHOP WHEN YOU DON'T NEED ANYTHING?

Buying makes some people feel better about themselves. They often use shopping to compensate for gaps in their lives, says Vyse. Shopping addicts often view shopping as a competition and may rationalize a purchase by saying it was a bargain.

The Shopping Addict

1. DO YOU NEGLECT TO THINK ABOUT WHERE THE MONEY'S COMING FROM BEFORE YOU BUY SOMETHING?

2. DO YOU MAKE LARGE, SPONTANEOUS PURCHASES?

3. DO YOU USE YOUR CREDIT LIMIT AS A GUIDE FOR YOUR SPENDING?

Advice: Get a life. No, really. Find other activities that offer the same feelings of accomplishment and self-worth without the cost, such as sports or volunteer work. We all try to be optimistic about the future. But overconfident consumers wear rose-colored

The Status Seeker

1. DO YOU FREQUENTLY COMPARE YOUR BELONGINGS TO THOSE OF OTHERS?

2. DO YOU HAVE TO HAVE THE LATEST "IN" THING?

3. DO YOU FEEL BAD WHEN YOU CAN'T HAVE WHAT OTHERS HAVE?

glasses when it comes to how they'll pay tomorrow for what they buy today. They have little or no savings, and Soman notes they often overestimate future earnings based on credit limits.

SOURCE: Reprinted by permission from the November issue of *Kiplinger's Personal Finance.* Copyright © 2008 The Kiplinger Washington Editors, Inc.

1. What are possible drawbacks of each of the spending groups profiled in this article?

2. Describe actions you would suggest in each of the categories described above.

3. How would you use this information to revise your spending attitudes and behaviors?

from the pages of . . . KIPLINGER'S PERSONAL FINANCE

Many people view comparison shopping as a waste of time. Although this may be true in certain situations, comparison shopping can be beneficial when (1) buying expensive or complex items; (2) buying items that you purchase often; (3) comparison shopping can be done easily, such as with advertisements, catalogs, or online; (4) different sellers offer different prices and services; and (5) product quality or prices vary greatly.

CAUTION! Every year, more than 450,000 people buy used vehicles with mileage gauges rolled back. According to the National Highway Traffic Safety Administration, consumers pay an average of $2,336 more than they should for vehicles with fraudulent mileage totals.

SELECTING VEHICLE OPTIONS Optional equipment for cars may be viewed in three categories: (1) mechanical devices to improve performance, such as a larger engine, the transmission, power steering, power brakes, and cruise control; (2) convenience options, including power seats, air conditioning, stereo systems, power locks, rear window defoggers, and tinted glass; and (3) aesthetic features that add to the vehicle's visual appeal, such as metallic paint, special trim, and upholstery.

COMPARING USED VEHICLES The average used car costs about $10,000 less than the average new car. Common sources of used cars include:

- New-car dealers, which offer late-model vehicles and may give you a warranty. Prices usually are higher than at other sources.
- Used-car dealers, which usually have older vehicles. Warranties, if offered, will be limited. However, lower prices may be available.
- Individuals selling their own cars. This can be a bargain if the vehicle was well maintained, but few consumer protection regulations apply to private-party sales. Caution is suggested.
- Auctions and dealers that sell automobiles previously owned by businesses, auto rental companies, and government agencies.
- Used-car superstores, such as CarMax, which offer a large inventory of previously owned vehicles.

Key Web Site for Used Cars

www.dealernet.com

Certified preowned (CPO) vehicles are nearly new cars that come with the original manufacturer's guarantee of quality. The rigorous inspection and repair process means a higher price than other used vehicles. CPO programs were originally created to generate demand for the many low-mileage vehicles returned at the end of a lease.

The appearance of a used car can be deceptive. A well-maintained engine may be inside a body with rust; a clean, shiny exterior may conceal major operational problems. Therefore, conduct a used-car inspection as outlined in Exhibit 6–3. Have a trained and trusted mechanic of *your* choice check the car to estimate the costs of potential repairs. This service will help you avoid surprises.

LEASING A MOTOR VEHICLE *Leasing* is a contractual agreement with monthly payments for the use of an automobile over a set time period, typically three, four, or five years. At the end of the lease term, the vehicle is usually returned to the leasing company.

Key Web Sites for Leasing

www.leasesource.com

www.leaseguide.com

Leasing offers several advantages: (1) only a small cash outflow may be required for the security deposit, whereas buying can require a large down payment; (2) monthly lease payments are usually lower than monthly financing payments; (3) the lease agreement provides detailed records for business purposes; and (4) you are usually able to obtain a more expensive vehicle, more often.

Leasing also has major drawbacks: (1) you have no ownership interest in the vehicle; (2) you must meet requirements similar to qualifying for credit; and (3) additional costs may be incurred for extra mileage, certain repairs, turning the car in early, or even a move to another state.

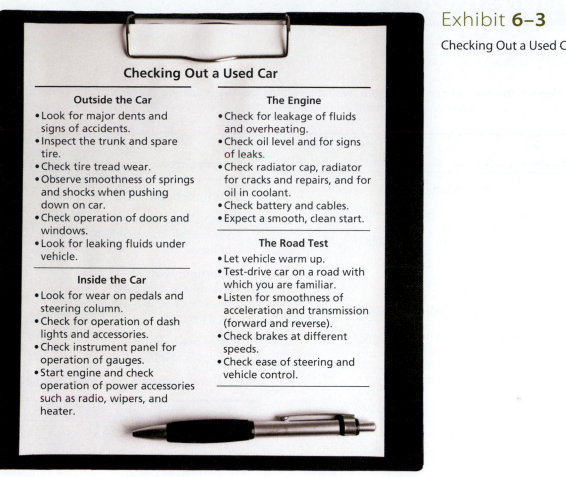

Exhibit **6–3**

Checking Out a Used Car

When leasing, you arrange for the dealer to sell the vehicle through a financing company. As a result, be sure you know the true cost, including

1. The *capitalized cost,* which is the price of the vehicle. The average car buyer pays about 92 percent of the list price for a vehicle; the average leasing arrangement has a capitalized cost of 96 percent of the list price.
2. The *money factor,* which is the interest rate being paid on the capitalized cost.
3. The *payment schedule,* which is the amount paid monthly and the number of payments.
4. The *residual value,* or the expected value of the vehicle at the end of the lease.

After the final payment, you may return, keep, or sell the vehicle. If the current market value is greater than the residual value, you may be able to sell it for a profit. If the residual value is less than the market value (which is the typical case), returning the vehicle to the leasing company is usually the best decision.

Phase 3: Determining Purchase Price

Once you've done your research and evaluations, other activities and decisions may be appropriate. Products such as real estate or automobiles may be purchased using price negotiation. Negotiation may also be used in other buying situations to obtain a lower price or additional features. Two vital factors in negotiation are (1) having all the necessary information about the product and buying situation and (2) dealing with a person who has the authority to give you a lower price or additional features, such as the owner or store manager.

Figure It Out!

> Buying versus Leasing an Automobile

To compare the costs of purchasing and leasing a vehicle, use the following framework. This analysis involves two situations based on comparable payment amounts.

Purchase Costs	Example	Your Figures
Total vehicle cost, including sales tax ($20,000)		
Down payment (or full amount if paying cash)	$ 2,000	$ _____
Monthly loan payment: $385 × 48-month length of financing (this item is zero if vehicle is not financed)	18,480	_____
Opportunity cost of down payment (or total cost of the vehicle if it is bought for cash): $2,000 × 4 years of financing/ownership × 3 percent	240	_____
Less: Estimated value of vehicle at end of loan term/ownership period	−6,000	_____
Total cost to buy	$14,720	_____

Leasing Costs	Example	Your Figures
Security deposit ($300)		
Monthly lease payments: $385 × 36-month length of lease	$13,860	$ _____
Opportunity cost of security deposit: $300 security deposit × 3 years × 3 percent	27	_____
End-of-lease charges* (if applicable)	800	_____
Total cost to lease	$14,687	_____

*Such as charges for extra mileage.

Key Web Sites for Used Car Prices

www.edmunds.com

www.kbb.com

USED-CAR PRICE NEGOTIATION Begin to determine a fair price by checking newspaper ads for the prices of comparable vehicles. Other sources of current used-car prices are *Edmund's Used Car Prices* and the *Kelley Blue Book*.

A number of factors influence the basic price of a used car. The number of miles the car has been driven, along with features and options, affect price. A low-mileage car will have a higher price than a comparable car with high mileage. The condition of the vehicle and the demand for the model also affect price.

PRICE BARGAINING FOR NEW CARS An important new-car price information source is the *sticker price* label, printed on the vehicle with the suggested retail price. This label presents the base price of the car with costs of added features. The dealer's cost, or *invoice price,* is an amount less than the sticker price. The difference between the sticker price and the dealer's cost is the range available for negotiation. This range is larger for full-size, luxury cars; subcompacts usually do not have a wide negotiation range. Information about dealer's cost is available from sources such as *Edmund's New Car Prices* and *Consumer Reports.*

Set-price dealers use no-haggling car selling with the prices presented to be accepted or rejected as stated. *Car-buying services* are businesses that help buyers obtain a specific new car at a reasonable price. Also referred to as an *auto broker,* these businesses

Key Web Sites for New Cars

www.edmunds.com

www.consumerreports.org

offer desired models with options for prices ranging between $50 and $200 over the dealer's cost. First, the auto broker charges a small fee for price information on desired models. Then, if you decide to buy a car, the auto broker arranges the purchase with a dealer near your home.

To prevent confusion in determining the true price of the new car, do not mention a trade-in vehicle until the cost of the new car has been settled. Then ask how much the dealer is willing to pay for your old car. If the offer price is not acceptable, sell the old car on your own. A typical negotiating conversation might go like this:

Customer: "I'm willing to give you $15,600 for the car. That's my top offer."

Auto salesperson: "Let me check with my manager." After returning, "My manager says $16,200 is the best we can do."

Customer (who should be willing to walk out at this point): "I can go to $15,650."

Auto salesperson: "We have the car you want, ready to go. How about $15,700?"

If the customer agrees, the dealer has gotten $100 more than the customer's "top offer."

Other sales techniques you should avoid include:

- *Lowballing,* when quoted a very low price that increases when add-on costs are included at the last moment.
- *Highballing,* when offered a very high amount for a trade-in vehicle, with the extra amount made up by increasing the new-car price.
- The question "How much can you afford per month?" Be sure to also ask how many months.
- The offer to hold the vehicle for a small deposit only. Never leave a deposit unless you are ready to buy a vehicle or are willing to lose that amount.
- Unrealistic statements, such as "Your price is only $100 above our cost." Usually, hidden costs have been added in to get the dealer's cost.
- Sales agreements with preprinted amounts. Cross out numbers you believe are not appropriate for your purchase.

did you know?

According to Bankrate.com, negotiating a lower price requires that you start by (1) determining exactly what you want, (2) researching a fair price for the item, and (3) figuring out what's most important to you and to the seller. This information will put you in a better position for bargaining.

COMPARING FINANCING ALTERNATIVES You may pay cash; however, most people buy cars on credit. Auto loans are available from banks, credit unions, consumer finance companies, and other financial institutions. Many lenders will *preapprove* you for a certain loan amount, which separates financing from negotiating the car price. Until the new-car price is set, you should not indicate that you intend to use the dealer's credit plan.

The lowest interest rate or the lowest payment does not necessarily mean the best credit plan. Also consider the loan length. Otherwise, after two or three years, the value of your car may be less than the amount you still owe; this situation is referred to as *upside-down* or *negative equity.* If you default on your loan or sell the car at this time, you will have to pay the difference.

Automobile manufacturers frequently present opportunities for low-interest financing. They may offer rebates at the same time, giving buyers a choice between a rebate and a low-interest loan. Carefully compare low-interest financing and the rebate. Special rebates are sometimes offered to students, teachers, credit union members, real estate agents, and other groups.

Phase 4: Postpurchase Activities

Maintenance and ownership costs are associated with most major purchases. Correct use can result in improved performance and fewer repairs. When you need repairs not

**Key Web Site
for Lemon Laws**

www.lemonlawamerica.com

covered by a warranty, follow a pattern similar to that used when making the original purchase. Investigate, evaluate, and negotiate a variety of servicing options.

In the past, when major problems occurred with a new car and the warranty didn't solve the difficulty, many consumers lacked a course of action. As a result, all 50 states and the District of Columbia enacted *lemon laws* that require a refund for the vehicle after the owner has made repeated attempts to obtain servicing. These laws apply when four attempts are made to get the same problem corrected or when the vehicle has been out of service for more than 30 days within 12 months of purchase or the first 12,000 miles. The terms of the state laws vary.

AUTOMOBILE OPERATION COSTS Over your lifetime, you can expect to spend more than $200,000 on automobile-related expenses. Your driving costs will vary based on two main factors: the size of your automobile and the number of miles you drive. These costs involve two categories:

Fixed Ownership Costs	Variable Operating Costs
Depreciation	Gasoline and oil
Interest on auto loan	Tires
Insurance	Maintenance and repairs
License, registration, taxes, and fees	Parking and tolls

The largest fixed expense associated with a new automobile is *depreciation,* the loss in the vehicle's value due to time and use. Since money is not paid out for depreciation, many people do not consider it an expense. However, this decreased value is a cost that owners incur. Well-maintained vehicles and certain high-quality, expensive models, such as BMW and Lexus, depreciate at a slower rate.

Costs such as gasoline, oil, and tires increase with the number of miles driven. Planning expenses is easier if the number of miles you drive is fairly constant. Unexpected trips and vehicle age will increase such costs.

MOTOR VEHICLE MAINTENANCE People who sell, repair, or drive automobiles for a living stress the importance of regular care. While owner's manuals and articles suggest mileage or time intervals for certain servicing, more frequent oil changes or tune-ups can minimize major repairs and maximize vehicle life. Exhibit 6–4 suggests maintenance areas to consider.

Exhibit 6–4

Extended Vehicle Life with Proper Maintenance

- Get regular oil changes (every 3 months or 3,000 miles).

- Check fluids (brake, power steering, transmission).

- Inspect hoses and belts for wear.

- Get a tune-up (new spark plugs, fuel filter, air filter) 12,000–15,000 miles.

- Check and clean battery cables and terminals.

- Check spark plug wires after 50,000 miles.

- Flush radiator and service transmission every 25,000 miles.

- Keep lights, turn signals, and horn in good working condition.

- Check muffler and exhaust pipes.

- Check tires for wear; rotate tires every 7,500 miles.

- Check condition of brakes.

Exhibit **6–5**

Common Automobile
Repair Frauds

The majority of automobile servicing sources are fair and honest. Sometimes, however, consumers waste dollars when they fall prey to the following tricks:

- When checking the oil, the attendant puts the dipstick only partway down and then shows you that you need oil.

- An attendant cuts a fan belt or punctures a hose. Watch carefully when someone checks under your hood.

- A garage employee puts some liquid on your battery and then tries to convince you that it is leaking and you need a new battery.

- Removing air from a tire instead of adding air to it can make an unwary driver open to buying a new tire or paying for an unneeded patch on a tire that is in perfect condition.

- The attendant puts grease near a shock absorber or on the ground and then tells you your present shocks are dangerous and you need new ones.

- You are charged for two gallons of antifreeze with a radiator flush when only one gallon was put in.

Dealing with reputable businesses and a basic knowledge of your automobile are the best methods of avoiding deceptive repair practices.

AUTOMOBILE SERVICING SOURCES The following businesses offer automobile maintenance and repair service:

- Car dealers provide a service department with a wide range of car care services. Service charges at a car dealer may be higher than those of other repair businesses.
- Service stations can provide convenience and reasonable prices for routine maintenance and repairs. However, the number of full-service stations has declined in recent years.
- Independent auto repair shops can service your vehicle at fairly competitive prices. Since the quality of these repair shops varies, talk with previous customers.
- Mass merchandise retailers, such as Sears and Wal-Mart, may emphasize sale of tires and batteries as well as brakes, oil changes, and tune-ups.
- Specialty shops offer brakes, tires, automatic transmissions, and oil changes at a reasonable price with fast service.

To avoid unnecessary expenses, be aware of the common repair frauds presented in Exhibit–6–5. Remember to deal with reputable auto service businesses. Be sure to get a written, detailed estimate in advance as well as a detailed, paid receipt for the service completed. Studies of consumer problems consistently rank auto repairs as one of the top consumer ripoffs. Many people avoid problems and minimize costs by working on their own vehicles.

CONCEPT CHECK 6–2

1 What are the major sources of consumer information?

_____

_____

Sheet 19 Used-Car Purchase Comparison

Sheet 20 Buying vs. Leasing an Automobile

2 What actions are appropriate when buying a used car?

_____

_____

3 When might leasing a motor vehicle be appropriate?

_____

_____

4 What maintenance activities could reduce the life of your vehicle?

_____

_____

5 The following abbreviations appeared in an ad for selling used cars. Interpret these abbreviations.

AC _____   pwr mrrs _____

ABS _____   P/S   _____

Apply Yourself!

Objective 2

Compare the prices charged by different automotive service locations for a battery, tune-up, oil change, and tires.

Resolving Consumer Complaints

OBJECTIVE 3

Describe steps to take to resolve consumer problems.

Most customer complaints result from defective products, low quality, short product lives, unexpected costs, deceptive pricing, and poor repairs. Federal consumer agencies estimate annual consumer losses from fraudulent business activities at $10 billion to $40 billion for telemarketing and mail order, $3 billion for credit card fraud and credit "repair" scams, and $10 billion for investment swindles. In addition, consumers commonly encounter problems with motor vehicles, mail-order purchases, work-at-home opportunities, dry cleaning, travel services, magazine subscriptions, contests, and sweepstakes.

Exhibit **6–6**

Suggested Steps for Resolving Consumer Complaints

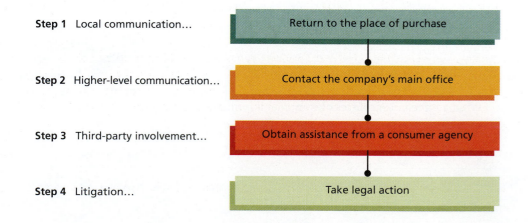

Step 1 Local communication...   Return to the place of purchase

Step 2 Higher-level communication...   Contact the company's main office

Step 3 Third-party involvement...   Obtain assistance from a consumer agency

Step 4 Litigation...   Take legal action

People do not anticipate problems with purchases but should be prepared for them. Exhibit 6–6 outlines the process for resolving differences. To help ensure success, keep a file of receipts, names of people you talked to, dates of attempted repairs, copies of letters you wrote, and costs incurred. An automobile owner kept detailed records and receipts for all gasoline purchases, oil changes, and repairs. When a warranty dispute occurred, the owner was able to prove proper maintenance and received a refund for the defective vehicle.

Step 1: Return to Place of Purchase

Most consumer complaints are resolved at the original sales location. As you talk with the salesperson, customer service person, or store manager, avoid yelling, threatening a lawsuit, or demanding unreasonable action. A calm, rational, yet persistent approach is recommended.

Key Web Site for Company Addresses

www.consumeraction.gov

Step 2: Contact Company Headquarters

Express your dissatisfaction to the corporate level if a problem is not resolved at the local store. Use a letter or e-mail such as the one in Exhibit 6–7. You can obtain addresses of companies at www.consumeraction.gov or in reference books at your library. The Web sites of companies usually provide information for contacting the organization. You can obtain a company's consumer hotline number by calling 1-800-555-1212, the toll-free information number. Many companies print the toll-free hotline number and Web site information on product packages.

did you know?

A survey by the Pew Internet & American Life Project reported that while two-thirds of the people in the study had made an online purchase, 75 percent had concerns about providing financial and personal information.

Step 3: Obtain Consumer Agency Assistance

If you do not receive satisfaction from the company, organizations are available to assist with automobiles, appliances, health care, and other consumer concerns. **Mediation** involves the use of a third party to settle grievances. In mediation, an impartial person—the *mediator*—tries to resolve a conflict between a customer and a business through discussion and negotiation. Mediation is a nonbinding process. It can save time and money compared to other dispute settlement methods.

Arbitration is the settlement of a difference by a third party—the *arbitrator*—whose decision is legally binding. After both sides agree to arbitration, each side presents its case. Arbitrators are selected from volunteers trained for this purpose. Most major automobile manufacturers and many industry organizations have arbitration programs to resolve consumer complaints.

A vast network of government agencies is available. Problems with local restaurants or food stores may be handled by a city or county health department. Every state has agencies to handle problems involving deceptive advertising, fraudulent business practices, banking, insurance companies, and utility rates. Federal agencies are available to help with consumer concerns (see Appendix B).

mediation The attempt by an impartial third party to resolve a difference between two parties through discussion and negotiation.

CAUTION! Without realizing it, many consumers sign contracts with provisions that stipulate arbitration as the method to resolve disputes. As a result, consumers face various risks, including rules vastly different from a jury trial, higher costs for the arbitrator's time, and selection of an arbitrator by the defendant.

arbitration The settlement of a difference by a third party whose decision is legally binding.

Key Web Sites for Consumer Concerns

www.consumer.gov

www.complaints.com

www.bbbonline.org/consumer/complaint.asp

Step 4: Take Legal Action

The next section considers various legal alternatives available to resolve consumer problems.

Exhibit **6–7**   Sample Complaint Letter or E-mail

Date

Appropriate Person
Company Name
Street Address
City, State, Zip Code

Dear _____ (Appropriate Name) _____ :

Name product
and serial or
model number
or service.

Include date
and location of
purchase and
other details.

Describe your
purchase.

    Last week I purchased (or had repaired) a (name of product with serial or
model number or service performed). I made this purchase at (location, date,
and other important details of the transaction).

State problem.

    Unfortunately, your product (or service) has not performed satisfactorily (or
the service was inadequate) because _____
Therefore, to solve the problem I would appreciate your (here state the
specific action you want). Enclosed are copies (copies—NOT originals) of my
records (receipts, guarantees, warranties, canceled checks, contracts, model
and serial numbers, and any other documents).

Ask for
specific action.

Give history
of problem.

Enclose copies
of documents.

    I am looking forward to your reply and resolution of my problem, and will
wait three weeks before seeking third-party assistance. Contact me at the
above address, by phone at (home and office numbers) or by e-mail (e-mail
address here).

State reasonable
time for action.

Include
your work
and home
phone numbers
and e-mail.

                Sincerely,

                Your Name
                Your Address
                Your City, State, Zip Code
                Phone
                E-mail

Note: Keep copies of your letter and all related documents and information.

Source: *Consumer's Resource Handbook* (www.pueblo.gsa.gov).

CONCEPT CHECK 6–3

1 What are common causes of consumer problems and complaints?

_____

_____

2 How can most consumer complaints be resolved?

_____

_____

3 How does arbitration differ from mediation?

_____

_____

Apply Yourself!

Objective 3

Conduct online research to determine the most frequent sources of consumer complaints.

Legal Options for Consumers

If the previous actions fail to resolve your complaint, one of the following may be appropriate.

> **OBJECTIVE 4**
>
> Evaluate legal alternatives available to consumers.

Small Claims Court

In **small claims court,** a person may file a claim involving amounts below a set dollar limit. The maximum varies from state to state, ranging from $500 to $10,000; most states have a limit of between $1,500 and $3,000. The process usually takes place without a lawyer, although in many states attorneys are allowed in small claims court. To effectively use small claims court, experts suggest that you:

- Become familiar with court procedures and filing fees (usually from $5 to $50).
- Observe other cases to learn about the process.
- Present your case in a polite, calm, and concise manner.
- Submit evidence such as photographs, contracts, receipts, and other documents.
- Use witnesses who can testify on your behalf.

small claims court A court that settles legal differences involving amounts below a set limit and employs a process in which the litigants usually do not use a lawyer.

class-action suit A legal action taken by a few individuals on behalf of all the people who have suffered the same alleged injustice.

Class-Action Suits

Occasionally a number of people have the same complaint. A **class-action suit** is a legal action taken by a few individuals on behalf of all the people who have suffered the same alleged injustice. These people are represented by one or more lawyers. Once a situation qualifies as a class-action suit, all of the affected parties must be notified. A person may decide not to participate in the class-action suit and instead file an individual lawsuit. Recent class-action suits included auto owners who were sold unneeded replacement parts for their vehicles and a group of investors who sued a brokerage company for unauthorized buy-and-sell transactions that resulted in high commission charges.

did you know?

A class-action suit can be expensive. After winning $2.19 in back interest, Dexter J. Kamilewicz also noted a $91.33 "miscellaneous deduction" on his mortgage escrow account. This charge was his portion for lawyers he never knew he hired to win a class-action suit.

Personal Finance in Practice

> Is It Legal?

The following situations are common problems for consumers. How would you respond to the question at the end of each situation?

	Yes	No
1. A store advertised a bottle of shampoo as "the $1.79 size, on sale for 99¢." If the store never sold the item for $1.79 but the manufacturer's recommended price was $1.79, was this a legitimate price comparison?	____	____
2. You purchase a stereo system for $650. Two days later, the same store offers the same item for $425. Is this legal?	____	____
3. You receive an unordered sample of flower seeds in the mail. You decide to plant them to see how well they will grow in your yard. A couple of days later, you receive a bill for the seeds. Do you have to pay for the seeds?	____	____
4. A store has a "going out of business sale—everything must go" sign in its window. After six months, the sign is still there. Is this a deceptive business practice?	____	____
5. A 16-year-old injured while playing ball at a local park is taken to a hospital for medical care. The parents refuse to pay the hospital since they didn't request the service. Can the parents be held legally responsible for the charges?	____	____
6. You purchase a shirt for a friend. The shirt doesn't fit, but when you return it to the store, you are offered an exchange since the store policy is no cash refunds. Is this legal?	____	____
7. A manufacturer refuses to repair a motorcycle that is still under warranty. The manufacturer can prove that the motorcycle was used improperly. If this is true, must the manufacturer honor the warranty?	____	____
8. An employee of a store incorrectly marks the price of an item at a lower amount. Is the store obligated to sell the item at the lower price?	____	____

Circumstances, interpretations of the law, and store policies, as well as state and local laws, can affect the above situations. The generally accepted answers are *no* for 1, 3, 7, and 8; *yes* for 2, 4, 5, and 6.

Using a Lawyer

In some situations, you may seek the services of an attorney. Common sources of lawyers are referrals from friends, advertisements, and the local division of the American Bar Association.

In general, straightforward legal situations such as appearing in small claims court, renting an apartment, or defending yourself on a minor traffic violation may not need legal counsel. More complicated matters such as writing a will, settling a real estate purchase, or suing for injury damages will likely require the services of an attorney.

When selecting a lawyer, consider several questions: Is the lawyer experienced in your type of case? Will you be charged on a flat fee basis, at an hourly rate, or on a contingency basis? Is there a fee for the initial consultation? How and when will you be required to make payment for services?

legal aid society One of a network of publicly supported community law offices that provide legal assistance to consumers who cannot afford their own attorney.

Other Legal Alternatives

Legal services can be expensive. A **legal aid society** is one of a network of publicly supported community law offices that provide legal assistance to people who cannot afford their own attorney. These community agencies provide this assistance at a minimal cost or without charge.

Prepaid legal services provide unlimited or reduced-fee legal assistance for a set fee. Some programs provide basic services, such as telephone consultation and preparation of a simple will, for an annual fee. Prepaid legal programs are designed to prevent minor troubles from becoming complicated legal problems.

**Key Web Sites
for Legal Questions**

www.nolo.com

www.smallclaimscourt.com

Sheet 21 Legal Services Cost Comparison

CONCEPT CHECK 6–4

1 In what types of situations would small claims court and class-action suits be helpful?

_____

_____

2 Describe situations in which you might use the services of a lawyer.

_____

_____

3 For the following situations, identify the legal action that would be most appropriate to take.

a. _____ A low-income person wants to obtain the services of a lawyer to file a product-liability suit.

b. _____ A person is attempting to obtain a $150 deposit for catering that was never returned.

c. _____ A consumer wants to settle a dispute out of court with the use of a legally binding third party.

d. _____ A group of telephone customers were overcharged by $1.10 a month over the past 22 months.

Apply Yourself!

Objective 4

Interview someone who has had a consumer complaint. What was the basis of the complaint? What actions were taken? Was the complaint resolved in a satisfactory manner?

Back to ... Getting Personal

Reconsider your responses to the "Getting Personal" questions at the beginning of the chapter. Learn to make better daily spending decisions by:

- Talking with experienced shoppers, such as friends, relatives, and others, to learn more about their buying habits or tips that save time and money.
- Consult Appendix B (page 510) for various sources of consumer information, government agencies, and organizations to assist you with buying decisions and to avoid potential consumer problems.

- Avoid becoming a victim of various consumer scams; these deceptions can be very creative.
- Conduct a Web search to learn about small claims court procedures and other types of consumer legal actions for your state.

What did you learn in this chapter that could help you make smarter choices when making major consumer purchases?

Chapter Summary

Objective 1 Timing purchases, comparing stores and brands, using label information, computing unit prices, and evaluating warranties are common strategies for effective purchasing.

Objective 2 A research-based approach to consumer buying involves (1) preshopping activities, such as problem identification and information gathering; (2) evaluating alternatives; (3) determining the purchase price; and (4) postpurchase activities, such as proper operation and maintenance.

Objective 3 Most consumer problems can be resolved by following these steps: (1) return to the place of purchase;

(2) contact the company's main office; (3) obtain assistance from a consumer agency; and (4) take legal action.

Objective 4 Small claims court, class-action suits, the services of a lawyer, legal aid societies, and prepaid legal services are legal means for handling consumer problems that cannot be resolved through communication with the company involved or with help from a consumer protection agency.

Key Terms

arbitration 203
class-action suit 205
legal aid society 206

mediation 203
service contract 192

small claims court 205
warranty 190

Self-Test Problems

1. An item was bought on credit with a $60 down payment and monthly payments of $70 for 36 months. What was the total cost of the item?
2. A food package with 32 ounces costs $1.76. What is the unit cost of the package?

Solutions

1. $36 \times \$70 = \$2,520$ plus the $60 down payment for a total of $2,580.
2. $\$1.76 \div 32 = 5.5$ cents an ounce.

Problems

1. An online buying club offers a membership for $175, for which you will receive a 10 percent discount on all brand-name items you purchase. How much would you have to buy to cover the cost of the membership? (Obj. 1)

2. John Walters is comparing the cost of credit to the cash price of an item. If John makes a $60 down payment and pays $32 a month for 24 months, how much more will that amount be than the cash price of $685? (Obj. 1)

3. Calculate the unit price of each of the following items: (Obj. 1)

   a. Motor oil—2.5 quarts for $1.95   _____ cents/quart
   b. Cereal—15 ounces for $2.17   _____ cents/ounce
   c. Canned fruit—13 ounces for 89 cents   _____ cents/ounce
   d. Facial tissue—300 tissues for $2.25   _____ cents/100 tissues

4. A service contract for a new video television projection system costs $120 a year. You expect to use the system for five years. Instead of buying the service contract, what would be the future value of these annual amounts after five years if you earn 4 percent on your savings? (Obj. 1)

5. A work-at-home opportunity is available in which you will receive 3 percent of the sales for customers you refer to the company. The cost of your "franchise fee" is $840. How much would your customers have to buy to cover the cost of this fee? (Obj. 1)

6. What would be the net present value of a microwave oven that costs $159 and will save you $68 a year in time and food away from home? Assume an average return on your savings of 4 percent for five years. (Hint: Calculate the present value of the annual savings, then subtract the cost of the microwave.) (Obj. 1)

7. If a person saves $63 a month by using coupons and doing comparison shopping, (a) what is the amount for a year? (b) What would be the future value of this annual amount over 10 years, assuming an interest rate of 4 percent? (Obj. 1)

8. Based on financial and opportunity costs, which of the following do you believe would be the wiser purchase? (Obj. 2)

   Vehicle 1: A three-year-old car with 45,000 miles, costing $6,700 and requiring $385 of immediate repairs.
   Vehicle 2: A five-year-old car with 62,000 miles, costing $4,500 and requiring $760 of immediate repairs.

9. Based on the following data, prepare a financial comparison of buying and leasing a motor vehicle with a $24,000 cash price:

   Down payment (to finance vehicle), $4,000   Down payment for lease, $1,200
   Monthly loan payment, $560   Monthly lease payment, $440
   Length of loan, 48 months   Length of lease, 48 months
   Value of vehicle at end of loan, $7,200   End-of-lease charges, $600

   What other factors should a person consider when choosing between buying and leasing? (Obj. 2)

10. Based on the data provided here, calculate the items requested: (Obj. 2)

Annual depreciation, $2,500   Annual mileage, 13,200
Current year's loan interest, $650   Miles per gallon, 24
Insurance, $680   License and registration fees, $65
Average gasoline price, $2.10 per gallon   Oil changes/repairs, $370
Parking/tolls, $420

a. The total annual operating cost of the motor vehicle.
b. The operating cost per mile.

11. Based on the following, calculate the costs of buying versus leasing a motor vehicle. (Obj. 2)

Purchase Costs   *Leasing Costs*
    Down payment: $1,500   Security deposit: $500
    Loan payment: $450 for 48 months   Lease payment: $450 for 36 months
    Estimated value at end of loan: $4,000   End-of-lease charges: $600
    Opportunity cost interest rate: 4 percent

12. A class-action suit against a utility company resulted in a settlement of $1.2 million for 62,000 customers. If the legal fees, which must be paid from the settlement, are $300,000, what amount will each plaintiff receive? (Obj. 4)

Questions

1. Describe how advertisements, news articles, online sources, and personal observations might be used to make wiser buying decisions.

2. When using the research-based approach for purchasing described in this chapter, which actions do you believe are overlooked by most shoppers?

3. What are potential concerns associated with obtaining furniture, appliances, and other items from a rent-to-own business?

4. What is a "certified preowned" vehicle? What are the benefits and drawbacks of this type of purchase?

5. What actions would you recommend to a person when evaluating and comparing automobile prices?

Case in Point

ONLINE CAR BUYING

With a click of the mouse, Mackenzie enters the auto "showroom." In the past few months she had realized that the repair costs for her 11-year-old car were accelerating. She thought it was time to start shopping for a new car online and decided to start her Internet search for a vehicle by looking at small and midsized SUVs.

Her friends suggested that Mackenzie research more than one type of vehicle. They reminded her that comparable models were available from various auto manufacturers.

In her online car-buying process, Mackenzie next did a price comparison. She obtained more than one price quote by using various online sources. She then prepared an overview of her online car buying experiences.

Online Car-Buying Action	Online Activities	Web Sites Consulted
Information gathering	• Review available vehicle models and options • Evaluate operating costs and safety features	http://autos.msn.com www.consumerreports.org www.caranddriver.com www.motortrend.com
Comparing prices	• Identify specific make, model, and features desired • Locate availability and specific price in your geographic area.	www.autosite.com www.edmunds.com www.kbb.com www.nada.com
Finalizing purchase	• Make payment or financing arrangements • Conduct in-person inspection • Arrange for delivery	www.autobytel.com www.autonation.com www.autoweb.com www.carsdirect.com

Mackenzie's next step was to make her final decision. After selecting what she planned to buy, she finalized the purchase online and decided to take delivery at a local dealer.

In recent years, less than 5 percent of car buyers have actually purchased vehicles over the Internet. That number is increasing; however, car buying experts strongly recommend that you make a personal examination of the vehicle before taking delivery.

Questions

1. Based on Mackenzie's experience, what benefits and drawbacks are associated with online car buying?
2. What additional actions might Mackenzie consider before buying a motor vehicle?
3. What do you consider to be the benefits and drawbacks of shopping online for motor vehicles and other items?

Continuing Case

Vikki Rococo (age 26) and Tim Treble (age 28) have been preparing for their wedding, which is now only two months away. In addition to making wedding plans, they've been talking about the the 'stuff' they'll each bring into the relationship when they get married. Of course, they need to make room for Tim's golf clubs, and Vikki's fitness equipment, but other assets like Vikki's dented coffee table and Tim's sagging sofa might need to be replaced.

One asset they plan to replace is Vikki's car. It's old, not very reliable, and soon will need new brakes and other repairs. The two of them eventually want to buy a house in a neighborhood that is close to Tim's job but unfortunately it will mean a longer commute for Vikki. They decide that getting her a new car before the move is something they need to consider.
Since gas prices have fluctuated wildly over the last few years, they want to be sure to purchase a car that gets good mileage. Safety is extremely important as well.

As much as they want to purchase a nice car for Vikki, the couple is thinking about their long-term goals, especially their goal of buying a house in the next few years. So, instead of buying a new car, they're thinking about replacing Vikki's old vehicle with a 3 or 4 year old car.

Vikki and Tim's financial statistics are shown below:

Assets:
Checking account* $12,500 (Vikki), $5,200 (Tim)
    *including emergency funds
Car $2,000 (Vikki), $14,000 (Tim)

401(k) balance $28,000 (Vikki), $12,000 (Tim)

Liabilities:
Student loan $8,000

Credit card balance $8,200 (Tim)

Income:
Gross annual salary: $50,000 (Vikki), $50,000 (Tim)

After-tax monthly salary: $2,917 (Vikki), $2,917 (Tim)

Monthly Expenses:
Rent $750 (Vikki), $450 (Tim)
Food $250 (Vikki), $350 (Tim)

Student loan $250
Credit card payments $500 (Tim)
Entertainment $300
Wedding expenses $500
Gas/repairs $450 (combined)

Retirement Savings:
401(k) $500 per month, plus 50% employer match on first 7% of pay (Vikki), $417 per month, plus 50% match on first 8% of pay (Tim)

Questions:

1. What strategies should the couple use to research and purchase big-ticket items such as new furniture or a car for Vikki?
2. What price should they pay for a car?
3. What will the car really cost to own?
4. How can they use *Your Personal Financial Plan* sheet 18?

Spending Diary

"USING THE DAILY SPENDING DIARY HAS HELPED ME CONTROL IMPULSE BUYING. WHEN I HAVE TO WRITE DOWN EVERY AMOUNT, I'M MORE CAREFUL WITH MY SPENDING. I CAN NOW PUT MORE IN SAVINGS."

Directions

Start (or continue) your Daily Spending Diary or use your own format to record and monitor spending in various categories. Most people who have participated in this activity have found it beneficial for monitoring and controlling their spending habits. The Daily Spending Diary sheets are located in Appendix C at the end of the book and on the student Web site at www.mhhe.com/kdh.

Questions

1. What daily spending items are amounts that might be reduced or eliminated to allow for higher savings amounts?

2. How might a Daily Spending Diary result in wiser consumer buying and more saving for the future?

Consumer Purchase Comparison

Financial Planning Activities: When considering the purchase of a major consumer item, use ads, catalogs, the Internet, store visits, and other sources to obtain the information below.

Suggested Web Sites: www.consumerreports.org   www.consumer.gov   http://clarkhoward.com

Product

Exact description (size, model, features, etc.)

Research the item in consumer periodicals and online for information regarding your product

article/periodical _____   **Web site** _____

date/pages _____   **date** _____

What buying suggestions are presented in the articles?

Which brands are recommended in these articles? Why?

Contact or visit two or three stores that sell the product to obtain the following information:

	Store 1	Store 2	Store 3
Company			
Address			
Phone/Web site			
Brand name/cost			
Product difference from item above			
Warranty (describe)			
Which brand and at which store would you buy this product? Why?			

What's Next for Your Personal Financial Plan?

- Which consumer information sources are most valuable for your future buying decisions?
- List guidelines to use in the future when making major purchases.

Name: _____   Date: _____

Used-Car Purchase Comparison

Financial Planning Activities: When considering a used car purchase, use advertisements, online sources, and visits to new- and used-car dealers to obtain the information below.

Suggested Web Sites: www.carbuyingtips.com   www.kbb.com

Automobile (year, make, model)			
Name			
Address			
Phone			
Web site (if applicable)			
Cost			
Mileage			
Condition of auto			
Condition of tires			
Radio			
Air conditioning			
Other options			
Warranty (describe)			
Items in need of repair			
Inspection items: • Rust, major dents?			
• Oil or fluid leaks?			
• Condition of brakes?			
• Proper operation of heater, wipers, other accessories?			
Other information			

What's Next for Your Personal Financial Plan?

- Maintain a record of automobile operating costs.
- Prepare a plan for regular maintenance of your vehicle.

Buying vs. Leasing an Automobile

Financial Planning Activities: Obtain cost information to compare leasing and buying a vehicle.

Suggested Web Sites: www.leasesource.com   www.kiplinger.com/tools

Purchase Costs

Total vehicle cost, including sales tax ($ _____)

Down payment (or full amount if paying cash) $ _____

Monthly loan payment: $ _____ times _____ month loan
(this item is zero if vehicle is not financed) $ _____

Opportunity cost of down payment (or total cost of the vehicle if bought
for cash):

$ _____ times number of years of financing/ownership times _____
percent (interest rate which funds could earn) $ _____

Less: estimated value of vehicle at end of loan term/ownership $ _____

Total cost to buy . . . . $

Leasing Costs

Security deposit $ _____

Monthly lease payments: $ _____ times _____ months $ _____

Opportunity cost of security deposit: $ _____ times years
times _____ percent $ _____

End-of-lease charges (if applicable*) $ _____

Total cost to lease . . . . $

*With a closed-end lease, charges for extra mileage or excessive wear and tear; with an open-end lease,
  end-of-lease payment if appraised value is less than estimated ending value.

What's Next for Your Personal Financial Plan?

- Prepare a list of future actions to use when buying, financing, and leasing a car.
- Maintain a record of operating costs and maintenance actions for your vehicle.

Legal Services Cost Comparison

Financial Planning Activities: Contact various sources of legal services (lawyer, prepaid legal service, legal aid society) to compare costs and available services.

Suggested Web Sites: www.nolo.com   www.abanet.org

Type of legal service			
Organization name			
Address			
Phone			
Web site			
Contact person			
Recommended by			
Areas of specialization			
Cost of initial consultation			
Cost of simple will			
Cost of real estate closing			
Cost method for other services—flat fee, hourly rate, or contingency basis			
Other information			

What's Next for Your Personal Financial Plan?

- Determine the best alternative for your future legal needs.
- Maintain a file of legal documents and other financial records.

7 Selecting and Financing Housing

Getting Personal

What are your attitudes toward housing? For each of the following statements, circle the choice that best describes your current situation.

1. When selecting a place to live, what is most important for you?
   a. Being close to work or school.
   b. The costs involved.
   c. Flexibility for moving in the future.

2. A benefit of renting for me would be
   a. Ease of mobility.
   b. Low initial costs.
   c. No benefits of renting for me.

3. The housing I would purchase that would be best for me is
   a. A house.
   b. A condominium or townhouse.
   c. A mobile home.

4. The type of mortgage I am most likely to use is
   a. A fixed-rate, 30-year mortgage.
   b. An adjustable-rate mortgage.
   c. An FHA or VA mortgage.

After studying this chapter, you will be asked to reconsider your responses to these items.

Evaluating Renting and Buying Alternatives

OBJECTIVE 1
Assess costs and benefits of renting.

As you walk around various neighborhoods, you are likely to see a variety of housing types. When assessing housing alternatives, start by identifying factors that will influence your choice.

Your Lifestyle and Your Choice of Housing

Although the concept of *lifestyle*—how you spend your time and money—may seem intangible, it materializes in consumer purchases. Every buying decision is a statement about your lifestyle. Personal preferences are the foundation of a housing decision, but financial factors may modify the final choice.

Your Personal Financial Plan Sheets

22. Renting vs. Buying Housing
23. Apartment Rental Comparison
24. Housing Affordability and Mortgage Qualification
25. Mortgage Company Comparison

Objectives

In this chapter, you will learn to:

1. Assess costs and benefits of renting.
2. Implement the home-buying process.
3. Determine costs associated with purchasing a home.
4. Develop a strategy for selling a home.

Why is this important?

With the greatest housing crisis in 70 years, home buyers are encountering a variety of deceptions. Mortgage-restructuring firms may claim an exaggerated success rate in stopping foreclosures. Consumers are warned to avoid foreclosure-prevention services that require a fee in advance. Reverse mortgages, available to homeowners 62 and older, should be used only after considering other alternatives, such as a home-equity loan. Many dishonest providers of reverse mortgages charge an extraordinary number of expensive origination fees.

Traditional financial guidelines suggest that "you should spend no more than 25 or 30 percent of your take-home pay on housing" or "your home should cost about 2½ times your annual income." Changes in various economic and social conditions have resulted in revised guidelines. Your budgeting activities and other financial records will provide information to determine an appropriate amount for your housing expenses.

Renting versus Buying Housing

The choice between renting and buying your residence should be analyzed based on lifestyle and financial factors. Mobility is a primary motivator of renters, whereas

Figure It Out!

> Renting versus Buying Your Place of Residence

Comparing the costs of renting and buying involves consideration of a variety of factors. The following framework and example provide a basis for assessing these two housing alternatives. The apartment in the example has a monthly rent of $1,250, and the home costs $200,000. A 28 percent tax rate is assumed.

Although the numbers in this example favor buying, remember that in any financial decision, calculations provide only part of the answer. You should also consider your needs and values and assess the opportunity costs associated with renting and buying.

	Example	Your Figures
Rental Costs		
Annual rent payments	$ 15,000	$ _____
Renter's insurance	210	_____
Interest lost on security deposit (amount of security deposit times after-tax savings account interest rate)	36	_____
Total annual cost of renting	$ 15,246	_____
Buying Costs		
Annual mortgage payments	$15,168	_____
Property taxes (annual costs)	4,800	_____
Homeowner's insurance (annual premium)	600	_____
Estimated maintenance and repairs (1%)	2,000	_____
After-tax interest lost on down payment and closing costs	750	_____
Less (financial benefits of home ownership):		
Growth in equity	−1,120	− _____
Tax savings for mortgage interest (annual mortgage interest times tax rate)	−3,048	− _____
Tax savings for property taxes (annual property taxes times tax rate)	−1,344	− _____
Estimated annual appreciation (1.5%)*	−3,000	− _____
Total annual cost of buying	$ 14,806	_____

*This is a nationwide average; actual appreciation of property will vary by geographic area and economic conditions.

buyers usually want permanence (see Exhibit 7–1). As you can see in the Figure It Out box, the choice between renting and buying may not be clear-cut. In general, renting is less costly in the short run, but home ownership usually has long-term financial advantages.

Exhibit **7–1**

Comparing Renting and
Buying of Housing

Advantages	Disadvantages
RENTING	
• Easy to move	• No tax benefits
• Fewer responsibilities for maintenance	• Limitations regarding remodeling
• Minimal financial commitment	• Restrictions regarding pets, other activities
BUYING	
• Pride of ownership	• Financial commitment
• Financial benefits	• Higher living expenses than renting
• Lifestyle flexibility	• Limited mobility

Rental Activities

Are you interested in a "2-bd. garden apt, a/c, crptg, mod bath, lndry, sec $850"? Not sure? Translated, this means a two-bedroom garden apartment (at or below ground level) with air conditioning, carpeting, a modern bath, and laundry facilities. An $850 security deposit is required.

At some point in your life, you are likely to rent. As a tenant, you pay for the right to live in a residence owned by someone else. Exhibit 7–2 presents the activities involved in finding and living in a rental unit.

SELECTING A RENTAL UNIT An apartment is the most common type of rental housing. Apartments range from modern, luxury units with extensive recreational

Exhibit **7–2**   Housing Rental Activities

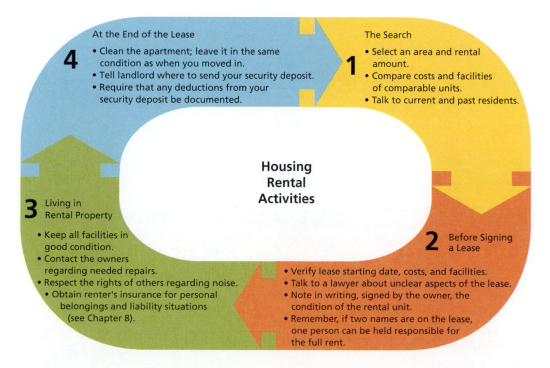

At the End of the Lease

4
• Clean the apartment; leave it in the same condition as when you moved in.
• Tell landlord where to send your security deposit.
• Require that any deductions from your security deposit be documented.

The Search

1
• Select an area and rental amount.
• Compare costs and facilities of comparable units.
• Talk to current and past residents.

Housing Rental Activities

3 Living in Rental Property

• Keep all facilities in good condition.
• Contact the owners regarding needed repairs.
• Respect the rights of others regarding noise.
• Obtain renter's insurance for personal belongings and liability situations (see Chapter 8).

2 Before Signing a Lease

• Verify lease starting date, costs, and facilities.
• Talk to a lawyer about unclear aspects of the lease.
• Note in writing, signed by the owner, the condition of the rental unit.
• Remember, if two names are on the lease, one person can be held responsible for the full rent.

did you know?

Fidelity Research Institute estimates that if renters save $300 a month (compared to making a mortgage payment), when invested at 4 percent, they would save more than $110,000 in 20 years.

facilities to simple one- and two-bedroom units in quiet neighborhoods. If you need more room, consider renting a house. If less space is needed, rent a room in a private house. The main information sources for rental units are newspaper ads, real estate and rental offices, and people you know. When comparing rental units, consider the factors in Exhibit 7–3.

ADVANTAGES OF RENTING Renting offers mobility when a location change is necessary or desirable. Renters have fewer responsibilities than homeowners since they usually do not have to be concerned with maintenance and repairs. Taking possession of a rental unit is less expensive than buying a home.

DISADVANTAGES OF RENTING Renters do not enjoy the financial advantages of homeowners. Tenants cannot take tax deductions for mortgage interest and property taxes or benefit from the increased real estate value. Renters are generally limited in the types of activities they can pursue in their place of residence. Noise from a stereo system or parties may be monitored closely. Tenants are often subject to restrictions regarding pets and decorating.

lease A legal document that defines the conditions of a rental agreement.

LEGAL DETAILS Most tenants sign a **lease,** a legal document that defines the conditions of a rental agreement. This document presents:

- A description of the property, including the address.
- The name and address of the owner/landlord (the *lessor*).
- The name of the tenant (the *lessee*).
- The effective date of the lease, and the length of the lease.
- The amount of the security deposit, and amount and due date of the monthly rent.
- The date and amount due of charges for late rent payments.

Exhibit 7–3

Selecting an Apartment

Selecting an Apartment

Location
- ✔ Schools, church, synagogue
- ✔ Shopping
- ✔ Public transportation
- ✔ Recreation

Building exterior
- ✔ Condition of building, grounds
- ✔ Parking facilities and recreation

Building interior
- ✔ Exits, security
- ✔ Hallway maintenance
- ✔ Condition of elevators
- ✔ Access to mailboxes

Financial aspects
- ✔ Rent, length of lease
- ✔ Security deposit
- ✔ Utilities, other costs

Layout and facilities
- ✔ Condition, size
- ✔ Closets, carpeting, appliances
- ✔ Type of heat, air conditioning
- ✔ Plumbing, water pressure
- ✔ Storage area
- ✔ Room size
- ✔ Doors, locks, windows

- A list of the utilities, appliances, furniture, or other facilities that are included in the rental amount.
- Restrictions regarding certain activities (pets, remodeling); tenant's right to sublet.
- Charges for damages or for moving out of the rental unit later (or earlier) than the lease expiration date.
- The conditions under which the landlord may enter the apartment.

Standard lease forms include conditions you may not want to accept. Negotiate with the landlord about lease terms you consider unacceptable. Some leases give you the right to *sublet* the rental unit. Subletting may be necessary if you must vacate the premises before the lease expires. Subletting allows you to have another person take over rent payments and live in the rental unit.

While most leases are written, oral leases are also valid. In those situations, one party must give a 30-day written notice to the other party before terminating the lease or imposing a rent increase. A lease provides protection to both landlord and tenant. The tenant is protected from rent increases unless the lease contains a provision allowing an increase. The lease gives the landlord the right to take legal action against a tenant for nonpayment of rent or destruction of property.

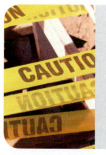

did you know?

Millions of people in the United States and around the world lack adequate housing. Habitat for Humanity (www.habitat.org) has built more than 300,000 houses, providing shelter to over 1.5 million people. The efforts of Habitat continue through local and global volunteering as well as donations of money and building supplies.

COSTS OF RENTING A *security deposit,* frequently required when you sign a lease, is usually one month's rent. This money is held by the landlord to cover the cost of any damages. Some state and local laws may require that landlords pay interest on a security deposit if they own buildings with a certain number of rental units. After you vacate the rental unit, your security deposit should be refunded within a reasonable time. If money is deducted, you have the right to an itemized list of repair costs.

As a renter, you will incur other expenses. For many apartments, water is covered by the rent; however, other utilities may not be included. If you rent a house, you will probably pay for heat, electricity, water, telephone, and cable television. When you rent, be sure to obtain insurance coverage on your personal property.

CAUTION! Renter's insurance is one of the most overlooked expenses of apartment dwellers. Damage or theft of personal property (clothing, furniture, stereo equipment, jewelry) usually is not covered by the landlord's insurance policy.

Sheet 22 Renting vs. Buying Housing

Sheet 23 Apartment Rental Comparison

CONCEPT CHECK 7–1

1 What are the main benefits and drawbacks of renting a place of residence?

_____

_____

2 Which components of a lease are likely to be most negotiable?

_____

_____

3 For the following situations, would you recommend that the person rent or buy housing? (Circle your answer)

   a. A person who desires to reduce income taxes paid.   rent   buy

   b. A person who expects to be transferred for work soon.   rent   buy

   c. A person with few assets for housing expenses.   rent   buy

Apply Yourself!

Objective 1

Interview a tenant and a landlord to obtain their views about potential problems associated with renting. How do their views on tenant–landlord relations differ?

Home-Buying Activities

> **OBJECTIVE 2**
>
> Implement the home-buying process.

Many people dream of having a place of residence they can call their own. Home ownership is a common financial goal. Exhibit 7–4 presents the process for achieving this goal.

Step 1: Determine Home Ownership Needs

In the first phase of this process, consider the benefits and drawbacks of this major financial commitment. Also, evaluate the types of housing units and determine the amount you can afford.

Exhibit **7–4**   The Home-Buying Process

5 Close the Purchase Transaction
- Arrange a closing date.
- Obtain funds and documents for closing.
- Request clarification of unclear aspects of the transaction.

1 Determine Home Ownership Needs
- Evaluate owning your place of residence.
- Assess types of housing units.
- Calculate the amount you can afford.

4 Obtain Financing
- Determine amount of down payment.
- Investigate the rates and conditions of mortgages.
- Apply for mortgage and evaluate types of mortgages.

The Home-Buying Process

2 Find and Evaluate a Property to Purchase
- Select a location.
- Consider using a real estate agent.
- Conduct a home inspection.

3 Price the Property
- Determine an appropriate market price.
- Negotiate an agreement price.

EVALUATE HOME OWNERSHIP Stability of residence and a personalized living location are important motives of many home buyers. One financial benefit is the deductibility of mortgage interest and real estate tax payments, reducing federal income taxes.

A disadvantage of home ownership is financial uncertainty. Obtaining money for a down payment and securing mortgage financing may be problems. Changing property values in an area can affect your financial investment. Home ownership does not provide ease of changing living location as does renting. If changes in your situation necessitate selling your home, doing so may be difficult.

Owning your place of residence can be expensive. The homeowner is responsible for maintenance and costs of repainting, repairs, and home improvements. Real estate taxes are a major expense of homeowners. Higher property values and increased tax rates mean higher real estate taxes.

TYPES OF HOUSING AVAILABLE Home buyers generally choose from the following options:

1. *Single-family dwellings* include previously owned houses, new houses, and custom-built houses.

2. *Multiunit dwellings* are dwellings with more than one living unit. A *duplex* is a building with separate homes. A *townhouse* may contain two, four, or six living units.

3. **Condominiums** are individually owned housing units in a building. Ownership does not include *common areas,* such as hallways, outside grounds, and recreational facilities. These areas are owned by the condominium association, which oversees the management and operation. Condominium owners pay a monthly fee for maintenance, repairs, improvements, and insurance of the building and common areas. A condominium is not the building structure; it is a legal form of home ownership.

   condominium An individually owned housing unit in a building with several such units.

4. **Cooperative housing** is a form of housing in which the units in a building are owned by a nonprofit organization. The shareholders purchase stock to obtain the right to live in a unit in the building. While the residents do not own the units, they have the legal right to occupy a unit for as long as they own stock in the cooperative association. The title for the property belongs to the co-op. This ownership arrangement is different from condominiums, in which residents own the individual living unit.

   cooperative housing A form of housing in which a building containing a number of housing units is owned by a nonprofit organization whose members rent the units.

5. *Manufactured homes* are assembled in a factory and then moved to the living site. *Prefabricated homes* have components built in a factory and then assembled at the housing site. *Mobile home* is not a completely accurate term since very few are moved from their original sites. Although typically smaller than 1,000 square feet, they can offer features such as a fully equipped kitchen, fireplace, cathedral ceiling, and whirlpool bath. The site for a mobile home may be either purchased or leased.

6. *Building a home* is for people who want certain specifications. Before starting such a project, be sure you possess the necessary knowledge, money, and perseverance. When choosing a contractor to coordinate the project, consider (*a*) the contractor's experience and reputation; (*b*) the contractor's relationship with the architect, materials suppliers, electricians, plumbers, carpenters, and other personnel; and (*c*) payment arrangements during construction. Your written contract should include a time schedule, cost estimates, a description of the work, and a payment schedule.

DETERMINE WHAT YOU CAN AFFORD The amount you spend on housing is affected by funds available for a down payment, your income, and your current living expenses. Other factors you should consider are current mortgage rates, the potential future value of the property, and your ability to make monthly payments. To determine how much you can afford to spend on a home, have a loan officer at a mortgage company or other financial institution *prequalify* you. This service is provided without charge.

You may not get all the features you want in your first home, but financial advisers suggest getting into the housing market by purchasing what you can afford. As you move up in the housing market, your second or third home can include more of the features you want.

While the home you buy should be in good condition, you may wish to buy a *handyman's special*—a home that needs work and that you are able to get at a lower price. You will then need to put more money into the house for repairs and improvements or do some of the work yourself.

Step 2: Find and Evaluate a Home

Next, select a location, consider using the services of a real estate agent, and conduct a home inspection.

zoning laws Restrictions on how the property in an area can be used.

SELECT A LOCATION Location is considered the most important factor when buying a home. You may prefer an urban, a suburban, or a rural setting. Or perhaps you want to live in a small town or in a resort area. Be aware of **zoning laws,** restrictions on how the property in an area can be used. The location of businesses and future construction projects may influence your decision.

If you have a family, assess the school system. Educators recommend that schools be evaluated on program variety, achievement level of students, percentage of students who go on to college, dedication of faculty members, facilities, school funding, and involvement of parents. Homeowners without children also benefit from strong schools, since the educational advantages of a community help maintain property values.

SERVICES OF REAL ESTATE AGENTS Real estate agents have information about housing in areas of interest to you. Their main services include (1) showing you homes to meet your needs; (2) presenting your offer to the seller based on a market analysis; (3) negotiating a settlement price; (4) assisting you in obtaining financing; and (5) representing you at the closing. A real estate agent may also recommend lawyers, insurance agents, home inspectors, and mortgage companies to serve your needs.

Since the home seller usually pays the commission, a buyer may not incur a direct cost. However, this expense is reflected in the price paid for the home. In some states, the agent could be working for the seller. In others, the agent may be working for the buyer, the seller, or as a *dual agent,* working for both the buyer and the seller. When dual agency exists, some states require that buyers sign a disclosure acknowledging that they are aware the agent is working for both buyer and seller. This agreement, however, can limit the information provided to each party. Many states have *buyer agents* who represent the buyer's interests and may be paid by either the seller or the buyer.

THE HOME INSPECTION An evaluation by a trained home inspector can minimize future problems. Being cautious will save you headaches and unplanned expenses. Exhibit 7–5 presents a detailed format for inspecting a home. Some states, cities, and

Exhibit **7–5**   Conducting a Home Inspection

CONDUCTING A HOME INSPECTION

Interior Construction
- Condition of electrical fixtures and wiring
- Condition of plumbing fixtures
- Adequate water pressure; water heater condition
- Type and condition of heating unit
- Quality/condition of walls, floors, and doors
- Cracks or potential ceiling problems
- Ease of operation of windows
- Type and condition of floor covering
- Condition, potential use of basement
- Condition of stairways

Interior Design
- Size and arrangement of rooms
- Amount of closet and storage space
- Door sizes for moving furniture
- Counter space and layout of kitchen
- Condition of kitchen appliances
- Ventilation for cooking
- Adequate laundry area
- Location of bedrooms relative to other areas
- Accessibility to attic and basement
- Adequate electrical outlets

Exterior Construction
- Material quality and condition of building
- Construction and condition of foundation
- Condition of bricks, wood, or other siding
- Condition and quality of windows
- Condition and quality of roof and gutters
- Type and condition of chimney

Exterior Facilities
- Appearance of neighborhood
- Condition of streets and sidewalks
- Location of street lights, fire hydrants
- Quality of landscaping, trees, shrubs
- Condition of driveway and garage
- Outdoor lighting
- Condition of patio or porch
- Appropriate drainage system

lenders require inspection documents for pests, radon, or mold. The mortgage company will usually conduct an *appraisal,* which is not a home inspection but an assessment of the market value of the property.

Step 3: Price the Property

After selecting a home, determine an offer price and negotiate a final buying price.

DETERMINE THE HOME PRICE The amount you offer will be affected by recent selling prices in the area, current demand for housing, the time the home has been on the market, the owner's need to sell, financing options, and features and condition of the home. Each of these factors can affect your offer price. For example, you will have to offer a higher price in times of low interest rates and high demand for homes. On the other hand, a home that has been on the market for over a year could mean an opportunity to offer a lower price. Your offer will be in the form of a *purchase agreement,* or contract, which is your legal offer to purchase the home.

did you know?

A two-story addition, a remodeled bathroom, an updated kitchen, addition of a deck, and a refinished basement are the home upgrades most likely to add value to a home.

NEGOTIATE THE PURCHASE PRICE If your initial offer is accepted, you have a valid contract. If your offer is rejected, you have several options. A *counteroffer* from the owner indicates a willingness to negotiate a price. If the counteroffer is only slightly lower than the asking price, you are expected to move closer to that price with your next offer. If the counteroffer is quite a bit off the asking price, you are closer to arriving at the purchase price. If no counteroffer is forthcoming, you may wish to make another offer to see whether

earnest money A portion of the price of a home that the buyer deposits as evidence of good faith to indicate a serious purchase offer.

the seller is willing to do any negotiating. Negotiations may involve things other than price, such as closing date or inclusion of existing items, such as appliances.

As part of the offer, the buyer must present **earnest money,** a portion of the purchase price deposited as evidence of good faith. At the closing of the home purchase, the earnest money is applied toward the down payment. This money is returned if the sale cannot be completed due to circumstances beyond the buyer's control.

Home purchase agreements may contain a *contingency clause,* stating the agreement is binding only if a certain event occurs. For example, the contract may be valid only if the buyer obtains financing for the home purchase within a certain time period, or it may make the purchase of a home contingent on the sale of the buyer's current home.

CONCEPT CHECK 7–2

1 What are the advantages and disadvantages of owning a home?

_____

_____

2 What guidelines can be used to determine the amount to spend for a home purchase?

_____

_____

3 How can the quality of a school system benefit even homeowners in a community who do not have school-age children?

_____

_____

Apply Yourself!

Objective 2

Talk with a real estate agent about the process involved in selecting and buying a home. Ask about housing prices in your area and the services the agent provides.

The Finances of Home Buying

OBJECTIVE 3

Determine costs associated with purchasing a home.

After you have decided to purchase a specific home and have agreed on a price, you will probably obtain a loan.

Step 4: Obtain Financing

THE DOWN PAYMENT The amount of cash available for a down payment affects the size of the mortgage required. If you can make a large down payment, say, 20 percent or more, you will obtain a mortgage relatively easily. Personal savings, sales of investments or other assets, and assistance from relatives are common down payment sources. Parents can help their children purchase a home by giving them a cash gift or a loan.

Private mortgage insurance (PMI) is usually required if the down payment is less than 20 percent. This protects the lender from financial loss due to default. After building up 20 percent equity in a home, a home buyer should contact the lender to cancel PMI. The Homeowners Protection Act requires that a PMI policy be terminated automatically when a homeowner's equity reaches 22 percent of the property value at the time the mortgage was executed. Homeowners can request termination earlier if they can provide proof that the equity in the home has grown to 22 percent of the current market value.

THE MORTGAGE A **mortgage** is a long-term loan on a specific piece of property such as a home or other real estate. Payments on a mortgage are usually made over 10, 15, 20, 25, or 30 years. Applying for a mortgage involves three main phases:

1. You complete the mortgage application and meet with the lender to present evidence of employment, income, ownership of assets, and amounts of existing debts.
2. The lender obtains a credit report and verifies your application and financial status.
3. The mortgage is either approved or denied, with the decision based on your financial history and an evaluation of the home you want to buy.

Today, with a strong credit score (700 or higher), a person can obtain home financing. This high credit score will also likely result in a lower mortgage rate and less required paperwork to process the loan.

This process will indicate the maximum mortgage for which you qualify. As shown in Exhibit 7–6, the major factors that affect the affordability of your mortgage are

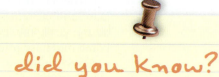

did you know?

The recent "subprime" crisis, when many mortgages were issued to borrowers with poor credit histories, resulted in numerous loan defaults. As a result, lenders are facing new regulations. To assure your creditworthiness for a home loan, pay down your credit cards, make payments on time to existing loan accounts, and accumulate funds for a down payment.

Key Web Site for Private Mortgage Insurance

www.privateemi.com

mortgage A long-term loan on a specific piece of property such as a home or other real estate.

Exhibit 7–6 Housing Affordability and Mortgage Qualification Amounts

	Example A	Example B
Step 1: Determine your monthly gross income (annual income divided by 12).	$48,000 ÷ 12	$48,000 ÷ 12
Step 2: With a down payment of at least 3 percent, lenders use 33 percent of monthly gross income as a guideline for PITI (principal, interest, taxes, and insurance) and 38 percent of monthly gross income as a guideline for PITI plus other debt payments.	$ 4,000 × 0.38 $ 1,520	$ 4,000 × 0.33 $ 1,320
Step 3: Subtract other debt payments (e.g., payments on an auto loan) and an estimate of the monthly costs of property taxes and homeowner's insurance.	−380 −300	— −300
(a) Affordable monthly mortgage payment	$ 840	$ 1,020
Step 4: Divide this amount by the monthly mortgage payment per $1,000 based on current mortgage rates—an 8 percent, 30-year loan, for example (see Exhibit 7–7)—and multiply by $1,000.	÷ $ 7.34 × $ 1,000	÷ $ 7.34 × $ 1,000
(b) Affordable mortgage amount	$114,441	$138,965
Step 5: Divide your affordable mortgage amount by 1 minus the fractional portion of your down payment (e.g., 1 − 0.1 with a 10 percent down payment).	÷ 0.9	÷ 0.9
(c) Affordable home purchase price	$127,157	$154,405

Note: The two ratios lending institutions use (step 2) and other loan requirements may vary based on a variety of factors, including the type of mortgage, the amount of the down payment, your income level, credit score, and current interest rates. For example, with a down payment of 10 percent or more and a credit score exceeding 720, the ratios might increase to 40/45 percent in this exhibit.

your income, other debts, the amount available for a down payment, the length of the loan, and current mortgage rates. The results of this calculation are (*a*) the monthly mortgage payment you can afford, (*b*) the mortgage amount you can afford, and (*c*) the home purchase price you can afford.

These sample calculations are typical of those most financial institutions use; the actual qualifications for a mortgage may vary by lender and by the type of mortgage. The loan commitment is the financial institution's decision to provide the funds needed to purchase a specific property. The approved mortgage application usually *locks in* an interest rate for 30 to 90 days.

The mortgage loan for which you can qualify is larger when interest rates are low than when they are high. For example, a person who can afford a monthly mortgage payment of $700 will qualify for a 30-year loan of

$130,354 at 5 percent	$95,368 at 8 percent
$116,667 at 6 percent	$86,956 at 9 percent
$105,263 at 7 percent	$79,726 at 10 percent

As interest rates rise, fewer people are able to afford the cost of an average-priced home.

Example

To determine the amount of your monthly mortgage payment, multiply the factor from Exhibit 7–7 by the number of thousands of the loan amount. For a 30-year, 7 percent, $223,000 mortgage:

Monthly payment amount = 223 × $6.65
= $1,482.95

When comparing mortgage companies, remember that the interest rate you are quoted is not the only factor to consider. The required down payment and the points charged will affect the interest rate. **Points** are prepaid interest charged by the lender.

points Prepaid interest charged by the lender.

Exhibit 7–7

Mortgage Payment Factors (principal and interest factors per $1,000 of loan amount)

Term Rate	30 Years	25 Years	20 Years	15 Years
5.0%	$5.37	$5.85	$ 6.60	$ 7.91
5.5	5.68	6.14	6.88	8.17
6.0	6.00	6.44	7.16	8.43
6.5	6.32	6.67	7.45	8.71
7.0	6.65	7.06	7.75	8.98
7.5	6.99	7.39	8.06	9.27
8.0	7.34	7.72	8.36	9.56
8.5	7.69	8.05	8.68	9.85
9.0	8.05	8.39	9.00	10.14
9.5	8.41	8.74	9.32	10.44
10.0	8.78	9.09	9.65	10.75
10.5	9.15	9.44	9.98	11.05
11.0	9.52	9.80	10.32	11.37

Each *discount point* is equal to 1 percent of the loan amount and should be viewed as a premium you pay for obtaining a lower mortgage rate. In deciding whether to take a lower rate with more points or a higher rate with fewer points, consider the following guidelines:

- If you plan to live in your home a long time (over five years), the lower mortgage rate is probably the best action.
- If you plan to sell your home in the next few years, the higher mortgage rate with fewer discount points may be better.

Online research may be used to compare current mortgage rates, and you can apply for a mortgage online.

FIXED-RATE, FIXED-PAYMENT MORTGAGES As Exhibit 7–8 shows, fixed-rate, fixed-payment mortgages are a major type of mortgage. The *conventional mortgage* usually has equal payments over 15, 20, or 30 years based on a fixed interest rate. Mortgage payments are set to allow **amortization** of the loan; that is, the balance owed is reduced with each payment. Since the amount borrowed is large, the payments made during the early years of the mortgage are applied mainly to interest, with only small reductions in the loan principal. As the amount owed declines, the monthly payments have an increasing impact on the loan balance. Near the end of the mortgage term, almost all of each payment is applied to the balance.

amortization The reduction of a loan balance through payments made over a period of time.

Exhibit 7–8 Types of Mortgages

Loan Type	Benefits	Drawbacks
FIXED-RATE, FIXED-PAYMENT		
1. Conventional 30-year mortgage.	• Fixed monthly payments for 30 years provide certainty of principal and interest payments.	• Higher initial rates than adjustables.
2. Conventional 15- or 20-year mortgage.	• Lower rate than 30-year fixed; faster equity buildup and quicker payoff of loan.	• Higher monthly payments.
3. FHA/VA fixed-rate mortgage (30-year and 15-year).	• Low down payment requirements and fully assumable with no prepayment penalties.	• May require additional processing time.
ADJUSTABLE-RATE, VARIABLE-PAYMENT		
4. Adjustable-rate mortgage (ARM)—payment changes on 1-, 3-, 5-, 7-, or 10-year schedules.	• Lower initial rates than fixed-rate loans, particularly on the 1-year adjustable. Generally assumable by new buyers. Offers possibility of future rate and payment decreases. Loans with rate "caps" may protect borrowers against increases in rates.	• Shifts far greater interest rate risk onto borrowers than fixed-rate loans. May push up monthly payments in future years.
5. Option ARM mortgage	• Low initial rate allows you to pay (a) interest only, (b) interest and principal, or (c) a lower payment; low down payment.	• Rate may adjust monthly and could result in mortgage balance exceeding the home value.
6. Interest-only mortgage	• Lower payments for first few years; more easily affordable.	• No decrease in amount owed; no building equity unless home value increases.

For example, a $75,000, 30-year, 10 percent mortgage would have monthly payments of $658.18. The payments would be divided as follows:

	Interest		Principal	Remaining Balance
For the first month	$625.00	($75,000 × 0.10 × 1/12)	$ 33.18	$74,966.82 ($75,000 − $33.18)
For the second month	624.72	($74,966.82 × 0.10 × 1/12)	33.46	74,933.36 ($74,966.82 − $33.46)
For the 360th month	5.41		649.54	–0–

In the past, many conventional mortgages were *assumable*. This feature allowed a home buyer to continue with the seller's original agreement. Assumable mortgages were especially attractive if the mortgage rate was lower than market interest rates at the time of the sale. Today, due to volatile interest rates, assumable mortgages are seldom offered.

GOVERNMENT-GUARANTEED FINANCING PROGRAMS
These include loans insured by the Federal Housing Authority (FHA) and loans guaranteed by the Veterans Administration (VA). These government agencies do not provide the mortgage money; rather, they help home buyers obtain low-interest, low-down-payment loans.

To qualify for an FHA-insured loan, a person must meet certain conditions related to the down payment and fees. Most low- and middle-income people can qualify for the FHA loan program. The VA-guaranteed loan program assists eligible armed services veterans with home purchases. As with the FHA program, the funds for VA loans come from a financial institution or a mortgage company, with the risk reduced by government participation. A VA loan can be obtained without a down payment.

adjustable-rate mortgage (ARM) A home loan with an interest rate that can change during the mortgage term due to changes in market interest rates; also called a *flexible-rate mortgage or a variable-rate mortgage.*

ADJUSTABLE-RATE, VARIABLE-PAYMENT MORTGAGES
The **adjustable-rate mortgage (ARM),** also referred to as a *flexible-rate mortgage* or a *variable-rate mortgage,* has an interest rate that increases or decreases during the life of the loan. ARMs usually have a lower initial interest rate than fixed-rate mortgages; however, the borrower, not the lender, bears the risk of future interest rate increases.

A *rate cap* restricts the amount by which the interest rate can increase or decrease during the ARM term. This limit prevents the borrower from having to pay an interest rate significantly higher than the one in the original agreement. A *payment cap* keeps the payments on an adjustable-rate mortgage at a given level or limits the amount to which those payments can rise. When mortgage payments do not rise but interest rates do, the amount owed can increase in months in which the mortgage payment does not cover the interest owed. This increased loan balance, called *negative amortization,* means the amount of the home equity is decreasing instead of increasing.

Consider several factors when evaluating adjustable-rate mortgages: (1) determine the frequency of and restrictions on allowed changes in interest rates; (2) consider the frequency of and restrictions on changes in the monthly payment; (3) investigate the possibility that the loan will be extended due to negative amortization, and find out if a limit exists on the amount of negative amortization; and (4) find out what index is used to set the mortgage interest rate.

did you know?

By taking out a 15-year instead of a 30-year mortgage, a home buyer borrowing $200,00 can save more than $150,000 in interest over the life of the loan. The faster equity growth with the shorter mortgage is also a benefit.

CREATIVE FINANCING
Convertible ARMs allow the home buyer to change an adjustable-rate mortgage to a fixed-rate mortgage during a certain period, such as the

time between the second and fifth year of the loan. A conversion fee, typically $500, or more must be paid to obtain a fixed rate, usually 0.50 percent higher than the current rates for conventional 30-year mortgages.

When mortgage rates are high, a *balloon mortgage,* with fixed monthly payments and a very large final payment, usually after three, five, or seven years, may be used. This financing plan is designed for people who expect to be able to refinance the loan or sell the home before or when the balloon payment is due. Most balloon mortgages allow conversion to a conventional mortgage (for a fee) if certain conditions are met.

A *growing-equity mortgage (GEM)* provides for increases in payments that allow the amount owed to be paid off more quickly. With this mortgage, a person would be able to pay off a 30-year home loan in 15 to 18 years.

An *interest-only mortgage* allows a homebuyer to have lower payments for the first few years of the loan. During that time, none of the mortgage payment goes toward the loan amount. Once the initial period ends, the mortgage adjusts to be interest only at the new payment rate. Or, a borrower may obtain a different type of mortgage to start building equity.

Remember, with an interest-only mortgage, higher payments will occur later in the loan. These are based on the amount of the original loan since no principal has been paid. Interest-only mortgages can be especially dangerous if the value of the property declines.

CAUTION! Mortgage fraud costs lenders more than $1 billion a year. These scams occur when people misrepresent their income or home value in an effort to obtain a loan. While banks and lenders are usually the victims, individual investors may also face losses. Communities are affected when the deception results in vacant buildings that are in disrepair. To avoid participating in mortgage fraud, be sure to verify that a mortgage company is property licensed and report any incorrect information in the lending process.

OTHER FINANCING METHODS A *buy-down* is an interest rate subsidy from a home builder, a real estate developer, or the borrower that reduces the mortgage payments during the first few years of the loan. This assistance is intended to stimulate sales among home buyers who cannot afford conventional financing. After the buy-down period, the mortgage payments increase to the level that would have existed without the financial assistance.

The *shared appreciation mortgage (SAM)* is an arrangement in which the borrower agrees to share the increased value of the home with the lender when the home is sold. This agreement provides the home buyer with a below-market interest rate and lower payments than a conventional loan.

A *second mortgage,* more commonly called a *home equity loan,* allows a homeowner to borrow on the paid-up value of the property. Lending institutions offer a variety of home equity loans, including a line of credit program that allows the borrower to obtain additional funds. You need to be careful when using a home equity line of credit. This revolving credit plan can keep you continually in debt as you request new cash advances. A home equity loan allows you to deduct the interest on consumer purchases on your federal income tax return. However, it creates the risk of losing the home if required payments on both the first and second mortgages are not made.

Reverse mortgages (also called *home equity conversion mortgages*) provide homeowners who are 62 or older with tax-free income in the form of a loan that is paid back (with interest) when the home is sold or the homeowner dies.

During the term of your mortgage, you may want to *refinance* your home, that is, obtain a new mortgage on your current home at a lower interest rate. Before taking this action consider the refinancing costs in relation to the savings gained with a lower monthly payment.

did you know?

Obtaining funds for a home purchase from parents can increase the value of the home you can afford. With *shared-equity financing.* parents or other relatives who provide part of the down payment share in the appreciation of the property. A contract among the parties should detail (*a*) who makes the mortgage payments and gets the tax deduction, (*b*) how much each person will pay of the real estate taxes, and (*c*) how and when the equity will be shared.

Another financing decision involves making extra payments on your mortgage. Since this amount will be applied to the loan principal, you will save interest and pay off the mortgage in a shorter time. Paying an additional $25 a month on a $75,000, 30-year, 10 percent mortgage will save you more than $34,000 in interest and enable you to pay off the loan in less than 25 years. Beware of organizations that promise to help you make additional payments on your mortgage. You can do this on your own, without the fee they are likely to charge you.

Step 5: Close the Purchase Transaction

Before finalizing the transaction, a *walk-through* allows you to inspect the condition of the home. Use a camera or video recorder to collect evidence for any last-minute items you may need to negotiate.

closing costs Fees and charges paid when a real estate transaction is completed; also called *settlement costs.*

The *closing* is a meeting of the buyer, seller, and lender of funds, or representatives of each party, to complete the transaction. Documents are signed, last-minute details are settled, and appropriate amounts are paid. A number of expenses are incurred at the closing. The **closing costs,** also referred to as *settlement costs,* are the fees and charges paid when a real estate transaction is completed; these commonly include the items listed in Exhibit 7–9.

title insurance Insurance that, during the mortgage term, protects the owner or the lender against financial loss resulting from future defects in the title and from other unforeseen property claims not excluded by the policy.

Title insurance has two phases. First, the title company defines the boundaries of the property being purchased and conducts a search to determine whether the property is free of claims such as unpaid real estate taxes. Second, during the mortgage term, the title company protects the owner and the lender against financial loss resulting from future defects in the title and from other unforeseen property claims not excluded by the policy.

Exhibit 7–9   Common Closing Costs

At the transaction settlement of a real estate purchase and sale, the buyer and seller will encounter a variety of expenses that are commonly referred to as *closing costs.*

	COST RANGE ENCOUNTERED	
	By the Buyer	By the Seller
Title search fee	$ 50–$150	—
Title insurance	$275–$500	$100–$600
Attorney's fee	$300–$700	$ 50–$700
Property survey	—	$100–$400
Appraisal fee (or nonrefundable application fee)	$100–$400	—
Recording fees; transfer taxes	$ 75–$100	$ 15–$30
Settlement fee	$300–$475+	—
Termite inspection	$ 70–$150	—
Lender's origination fee	1–3% of loan amount	—
Reserves for home insurance and property taxes	Varies	—
Interest paid in advance (from the closing date to the end of the month) and "points"	Varies	—
Real estate broker's commission	—	4–7% of purchase price

Note: The amounts paid by the buyer are in addition to the down payment.

WHAT'S THE DEAL? | Lenders want a plumper cushion against the risk of defaults.

Mortgage Fees Are on the Way up

Mortgages purchased from banks and brokers by Fannie Mae and Freddie Mac are getting a little more expensive—again. Starting in April, the latest in a series of fee adjustments—aimed at accounting for default risks—will begin to affect a wide swath of home buyers and mortgage refinancers.

Fannie Mae and Freddie Mac purchase loans of up to $417,000—and up to $625,000 in pricey markets. But gone are some discounts that borrowers once enjoyed, such as the quarter-point break for those who have credit scores of 720 or above and have less than 15% equity in their homes (such loans are considered safer because borrowers typically pay insurance). For the first time, anyone buying or refinancing a condo with less than 25% down will pay 0.75% of the loan amount, unless the term is 15 years or less.

Borrowers with less than 30% equity will pay more if their credit score is below 700; borrowers with less than 15% equity will pay more even if their credit is flawless. "Not so long ago, a credit score of 680 was considered great—you got all the good deals," says Mike Anderson, president of Essential Mortgage, in New Orleans. You can also expect a bigger hit if you've got a home-equity loan, or if you take cash out when you refinance.

Under Fannie Mae's new rubric, someone with a $250,000, 30-year loan, with 15% equity and a credit score of 699, will pay $2,500 more for a cash-out refinance than they would have before April. "Rates are so low that people want to lower their payment by $200 or $300," says Anderson. "But all these fees make it cost-prohibitive."

1. How will revised mortgage fees affect home buyers?

_____

2. What actions can be taken to reduce the fees when obtaining a mortgage?

_____

3. What information is available at www.kiplinger.com that might be of value when obtaining a mortgage?

_____

Personal Finance in Practice

> What Additional Home-Buying Information Do You Need?

For each of the following main aspects of home buying, list questions, additional information, or actions you might need to take. Locate Web sites that provide information for these areas.

- **Location.** Consider the community and geographic region. A $250,000 home in one area may be an average-priced house, while in another part of the country it may be fairly expensive real estate. The demand for homes is largely affected by the economy and the availability of jobs.

_____

- **Down payment.** While making a large down payment reduces your mortgage payments, you will also need the funds for closing costs, moving expenses, repairs, or furniture.

_____

- **Mortgage application.** When applying for a home loan, you will usually be required to provide copies of paystubs, W-2, and recent tax returns, a residence and employment history, information about bank and investment accounts, a listing of debts, and evidence of auto and any real estate ownership.

_____

- **Points.** You may need to select between a higher rate with no discount points and a lower rate requiring points paid at closing.

_____

- **Closing costs.** Settlement costs can range from 2 to 6 percent of the loan amount. This means you could need as much as $6,000 to finalize a $100,000 mortgage; this amount is in addition to your down payment.

_____

- **PITI.** Your monthly payment for principal, interest, taxes, and insurance is an important budget item. Beware of buying "too much house" and not having enough for other living expenses.

_____

- **Maintenance costs.** As any homeowner will tell you, owning a home can be expensive. Set aside funds for repair and remodeling expenses.

Web sites to consult:

_____

_____

deed A document that transfers ownership of property from one party to another.

Also due at closing time is the deed recording fee. The **deed** is the document that transfers ownership of property from one party to another. With a *warranty deed*, the seller guarantees the title is good. This document certifies that the seller is the true owner of the property, there are no claims against the title, and the seller has the right to sell the property.

The Real Estate Settlement Procedures Act (RESPA) helps home buyers understand the closing process and closing costs. This legislation requires that loan applicants be given an estimate of the closing costs before the actual closing. Obtaining this information early allows a home buyer to plan for the closing costs.

At the closing and when you make your monthly payments, you will probably deposit money to be used for home expenses. For example, the lender will require that you have property insurance. An **escrow account** is money, usually deposited with the lending institution, for the payment of property taxes and home insurance.

As a new home buyer, you might also consider purchasing an agreement that gives you protection against defects in the home. *Implied warranties* created by state laws may cover some problem areas; other repair costs can occur. Home builders and real estate sales companies offer warranties to buyers. Coverage offered usually provides protection against electrical, plumbing, heating, appliances, and other mechanical defects. Most home warranty programs have various limitations.

Home Buying: A Summary

For most people, buying a home is the most expensive decision they will undertake. As a reminder, the Personal Finance in Practice feature (on page 236) provides an overview of the major elements to consider when making this critical financial decision.

Key Web Site for RESPA

www.hud.gov

escrow account Money, usually deposited with the lending financial institution, for the payment of property taxes and homeowner's insurance.

CONCEPT CHECK 7–3

Sheet 24 Housing Affordability and Mortgage Qualification

Sheet 25 Mortgage Company Comparison

1 What are the main sources of money for a down payment?

_____

_____

2 What factors affect a person's ability to qualify for a mortgage?

_____

_____

3 How do changing interest rates affect the amount of mortgage a person can afford?

_____

_____

4 Under what conditions might an adjustable-rate mortgage be appropriate?

_____

_____

5 For the following situations, select the type of home financing action that would be most appropriate:

   a. A mortgage for a person who desires to finance a home purchase at current interest rates for the entire term of the loan. _____

b. A homebuyer who wants to reduce the amount of monthly payments since interest rates have declined over the past year. _____

c. A homeowner who wants to access funds that could be used to remodel the home. _____

d. A person who served in the military, who does not have money for a down payment. _____

e. A retired person who wants to obtain income from the value of her home. _____

Apply Yourself!

Objective 3

Conduct Web research on various types of mortgages and current rates.

A Home-Selling Strategy

> **OBJECTIVE 4**
>
> Develop a strategy for selling a home.

Most people who buy a home will eventually be on the other side of a real estate transaction. Selling your home requires preparing it for selling, setting a price, and deciding whether to sell it yourself or use a real estate agent.

Preparing Your Home for Selling

The effective presentation of your home can result in a fast and financially favorable sale. Real estate salespeople recommend that you make needed repairs and paint worn exterior and interior areas. Clear the garage and exterior areas, and keep the lawn cut and the leaves raked. Keep the kitchen and bathroom clean. Remove excess furniture and dispose of unneeded items to make the house, closets, and storage areas look larger. When showing your home, open drapes and turn on lights. Consider environmentally friendly feature such as energy-saving light bulbs and water-saving faucets. This effort will give your property a positive image and make it attractive to potential buyers.

appraisal An estimate of the current value of a property.

Determining the Selling Price

Putting a price on your home can be difficult. You risk not selling it immediately if the price is too high, and you may not get a fair amount if the price is too low. An **appraisal,** an estimate of the current value of the property, can provide a good indication of the price you should set. An asking price is influenced by recent selling prices of comparable homes in your area, demand in the housing market, and current mortgage rates.

The home improvements you have made may or may not increase the selling price. A hot tub or an exercise room may have no value for potential buyers. Among the most desirable improvements are energy-efficient features, a remodeled kitchen, an additional or remodeled bathroom, added rooms

did you know?

An appraisal is likely to cost between $250 and $500. This expense can help people selling a home on their own to get a realistic view of the property's value.

Personal Finance in Practice

> Lowering Your Property Taxes

Property taxes vary from area to area and usually range from 2 to 4 percent of the market value of the home. Taxes are based on the *assessed value*, the amount that your local government determines your property to be worth for tax purposes. Assessed values normally are lower than the market value, often about half. A home with a market value of $180,000 may be assessed at $90,000. If the tax rate is $60 per $1,000 of assessed value, this would result in annual taxes of $5,400 ($90,000 divided by $1,000 times $60). This rate is 6 percent of the assessed value but only 3 percent of the market value.

Although higher home values are desirable, this increase means higher property assessments. Quickly increasing property taxes are frustrating, but there are actions you can take:

Suggested Action	Your Action
Step 1: Know the appeal deadline. Call the local assessor's office. You will usually have between 14 and 90 days to initiate your appeal. Late requests will most likely not be accepted. Send your appeal by certified mail to have proof that you met the deadline; keep copies of all documents.	
Step 2: Check for mistakes. The assessment office may have incorrect information. Obvious mistakes may include incorrect square footage or an assessment may report a home with four bedrooms when there are only three.	
Step 3: Determine the issues to emphasize. A property tax appeal can be based on a mistake in the assessment or a higher assessment than comparable homes. Note items that negatively affect the value of your home. For example, a bridge is no longer in operation near your home, making your house much less accessible—and less valuable. Or if a garage has been taken down to increase garden space, the home's value likely would be less. Compare your assessment with homes of the same size, age, and general location. Obtain comparisons for 5 to 10 homes.	
Step 4: Prepare for the hearing. Gather your evidence and prepare an organized presentation. Use photos of comparable properties. A spreadsheet can make it easy for the hearing officials to view your evidence. Suggest a specific corrected assessment, and give your reasons. Observe the hearing of another person to become familiar with the process.	

and storage space, a converted basement, a fireplace, and an outdoor deck or patio. Daily maintenance, timely repairs, and home improvements will increase the future sales price.

Sale by Owner

Each year, about 10 percent of home sales are made by the home's owners. If you sell your home without using a real estate agent, advertise in local newspapers and create a detailed information sheet. Distribute the sheet at stores and in other public areas. When selling your home on your own, obtain information about the availability of financing and financing requirements. This will help potential buyers determine whether a sale is possible. Use the services of a lawyer or title company to assist you with the contract, the closing, and other legal matters.

Require potential buyers to provide names, addresses, telephone numbers, and background information. Show your home only by appointment and only when two or more adults are at home. Selling your own home can save several thousand dollars in commission, but an investment of your time and effort is required.

Listing with a Real Estate Agent

If you sell your home with the assistance of a real estate agent, consider the person's knowledge of the community and the agent's willingness to actively market your home. A real estate agent will provide you with various services, such as suggesting a selling price, making potential buyers and other agents aware of your home, providing advice on features to highlight, conducting showings of your home, and handling the financial aspects of the sale. Marketing efforts are likely to include presentation of your home on various Web sites.

A real estate agent can also help screen potential buyers to determine whether they will qualify for a mortgage. Discount real estate brokers are available to assist sellers who are willing to take on certain duties and want to reduce selling costs.

CONCEPT CHECK 7–4

1 What actions are recommended when planning to sell your home?

_____

_____

2 What factors affect the selling price of a home?

_____

_____

3 What should you consider when deciding whether to sell your home on your own or use the services of a real estate agent?

_____

_____

Apply Yourself!

Objective 4

Visit a couple of homes for sale. What features do you believe would appeal to potential buyers? What efforts were made to attract potential buyers to the open houses?

Back to... *Getting Personal*

Reconsider your responses to the "Getting Personal" questions at the beginning of the chapter. To make wiser decisions related to housing:

- Use various information sources when planning a housing decision, including discussions with people you know and these helpful Web sites: http://homebuying.about.com, http://realestate.msn.com, www.hud.gov/buying, and www.homefair.com.
- Before signing a lease, be sure that you understand the various elements of this legal document. For additional information on leases, go to http://apartments.about.com.

- Consider what you can afford to spend when you start the home buying process. You can prequalify for a mortgage online at www.mortgage101.com or www.erate.com. Current mortgage rate information is available at www.bankrate.com, www.hsh.com, and www.interest.com as well as from local financial institutions.
- When planning to sell a home on your own, you can find assistance at www.owners.com. Also of value is talking with people who have sold their own homes.

What did you learn in this chapter that could help you better plan your financial decisions when selecting housing?

Chapter Summary

Objective 1   Assess renting and buying alternatives in terms of their financial and opportunity costs. The main advantages of renting are mobility, fewer responsibilities, and lower initial costs. The main disadvantages of renting are few financial benefits, a restricted lifestyle, and legal concerns.

Objective 2   Home buying involves five major stages: (1) determining home ownership needs, (2) finding and evaluating a property to purchase, (3) pricing the property, (4) financing the purchase, and (5) closing the real estate transaction.

Objective 3   The costs associated with purchasing a home include the down payment; mortgage origination costs; closing costs such as a deed fee, prepaid interest, attorney's fees, payment for title insurance, and a property survey; and an escrow account for homeowner's insurance and property taxes.

Objective 4   When selling a home, you must decide whether to make certain repairs and improvements, determine a selling price, and choose between selling the home yourself and using the services of a real estate agent.

Key Terms

adjustable-rate mortgage (ARM) 232
amortization 231
appraisal 238
closing costs 234

condominium 225
cooperative housing 225
deed 236
earnest money 228
escrow account 237

lease 222
mortgage 229
points 230
title insurance 234
zoning laws 226

Self-Test Problems

1. What would be the monthly payment for a $180,000, 20-year mortgage at 6 percent?
2. What is the total amount of a 30-year mortgage with monthly payments of $850?

Solutions

1. Using Exhibit 7–7 (p. 230), multiply 180 times $7.16 to determine the monthly payment of $1,288.80
2. 360 payments (30 years × 12 months) are multiplied by $850 for a total of $306,000.

Problems

1. Based on the following data, would you recommend buying or renting? (Obj. 1)

Rental Costs	*Buying Costs*
Annual rent, $7,380	Annual mortgage payments, $9,800 ($9,575 is interest)
Insurance, $145	Property taxes, $1,780
Security deposit, $650	Down payment/closing costs, $4,500
Insurance/maintenance, $1,050	Growth in equity, $225
	Estimated annual appreciation, $1,700

Assume an after-tax savings interest rate of 6 percent and a tax rate of 28 percent.

2. When renting, various move-in costs will be encountered. Estimate the following amounts: (Obj. 1)

First month rent	$ _____
Security deposit	$ _____
Security deposit for utilities (if applicable)	$ _____
Moving truck, other moving expenses	$ _____
Household items (dishes, towels, bedding)	$ _____
Furniture and appliances (as required)	$ _____
Renter's insurance	$ _____
Refreshments for friends who helped you move	$ _____
Other items: _____	$ _____

3. Many locations require that renters be paid interest on their security deposits. If you have a security deposit of $1,150, how much would you expect a year at 3 percent? (Obj. 1)

4. Condominiums usually require a monthly fee for various services. At $160 a month, how much would a homeowner pay over a 10-year period for living in this housing facility? (Obj. 2)

5. Ben and Vicki Manchester plan to buy a condominium. They will obtain a $150,000, 30-year mortgage, at 6 percent. Their annual property taxes are expected to be $1,800. Property insurance is $480 a year, and the condo association fee is $220 a month. Based on these items, determine the total monthly housing payment for the Manchesters. (Obj. 2)

6. Estimate the affordable monthly mortgage payment, the affordable mortgage amount, and the affordable home purchase price for the following situation (see Exhibit 7–6). (Obj. 3)

   Monthly gross income, $2,950   Down payment to be made—15 percent of purchase price
   Other debt (monthly payment), $160   Monthly estimate for property taxes and insurance, $210
   30-year loan at 8 percent

7. Based on Exhibit 7–7 , what would be the monthly mortgage payments for each of the following situations? (Obj. 3)

   a. A $140,000, 15-year loan at 8.5 percent.
   b. A $215,000, 30-year loan at 7 percent.
   c. A $165,000, 20-year loan at 8 percent.

8. Which mortgage would result in higher total payments? (Obj. 3)

   Mortgage A: $985 a month for 30 years

   Mortgage B: $780 a month for 5 years and $1,056 for 25 years

9. If an adjustable-rate 30-year mortgage for $120,000 starts at 5.5 percent and increases to 6.5 percent, what is the amount of increase of the monthly payment? (Use Exhibit 7–7.) (Obj. 3)

10. Kelly and Tim Jones plan to refinance their mortgage to obtain a lower interest rate. They will reduce their mortgage payments by $56 a month. Their closing costs for refinancing will be $1,670. How long will it take them to cover the cost of refinancing? (Obj. 3)

11. In an attempt to have funds for a down payment in five years, Jan Carlson plans to save $3,000 a year for the next five years. With an interest rate of 4 percent, what amount will Jan have available for a down payment after the five years? (Obj. 3)

12. Based on Exhibit 7–9, if you were buying a home, what would be the approximate total closing costs (excluding the down payment)? As an alternative, obtain actual figures for the closing items by contacting various real estate organizations or by doing online research. (Obj. 3)

13. You estimate that you can save $3,800 by selling your home yourself rather than using a real estate agent. What would be the future value of that amount if invested for five years at 6 percent? (Obj. 4)

Questions

1. What do you believe are the most important factors a person should consider when selecting housing?

2. What are some common mistakes a person might make when renting an apartment or other housing?

3. What actions would you recommend to a person who was considering buying a home that needed several improvements?

4. Describe how knowledge of current interest rates would help you better plan when obtaining a mortgage.

5. Prepare a list of actions to take when selling a home.

Case in Point

CAN YOU BUY A HOUSE ONLINE?

When Jamie Covington bought her first home, she did so without ever meeting in person with a mortgage broker or the title insurance representative. She was one of the first home buyers to conduct her real estate transaction completely online.

Jamie started the process by viewing homes on Web sites of various real estate companies and those listed online with various newspapers in her area. Later, Jamie went out to see several of the properties she was considering. The financing process involved several online activities, including:

- The prequalification process to determine the amount of mortgage for which Jamie was eligible.
- Comparing mortgage rates among various lenders both in her area and around the country.
- The mortgage application process in which Jamie was approved for her mortgage within a few hours.

The final negotiations involved a series of e-mail exchanges. Once the buyer and seller agreed on a price, next came the closing, which was conducted completely online. The bank providing Jamie's mortgage prepared the closing documents and sent them electronically over the Internet to the closing agent, who brought them up on a specially equipped computer screen. Jamie signed the documents on the screen. The deed was scanned and delivered by computer image. All completed documents were forwarded to the appropriate parties. Jamie received a CD-ROM with copies of all of the paperwork.

The Electronic Signature in Global and National Commerce Act allowed this process to take place. This law recognizes an *electronic signature* as "an electronic sound, symbol, or process, attached to or logically associated with a contract or other record and executed or adopted by a person with the intent to sign the record."

The time needed for the postclosing process is also reduced. The recording of documents and issuing of the title insurance policy usually takes 45 days. Online, the process was complete in about three hours. This process can result in lower closing costs. Various financial experts estimate that online closings could save businesses and home buyers about $750.

Questions

1. How has technology changed the home-buying process?
2. Based on information at www.homefair.com, describe some advice that should help a person buying a home.
3. What might be some concerns with online home-buying activities? Based on a Web search to obtain additional information on electronic home buying, what other advice would you offer when using the Internet for various phases of the home- buying process?

Continuing Case

Vikki and Tim Treble (ages 27 and 29) have been married for six months, and they realize that Vikki's apartment is a tighter fit than they expected. On Sunday afternoons, they take drives around different parts of the city to look at houses. They find a beautiful neighborhood that they really like. However, to stay in their price range, they determined that the house they buy will need to be a "fixer-upper" instead of a home in "move-in condition." They want to buy a house that will grow with them since they want to have children.

Vikki and Tim hope to be able to make an offer on a house in less than one year.

Vikki and Tim's financial statistics are shown below:

Assets:
Checking account* $15,000
  *including emergency fund
House fund (for down payment) $20,000
Car $9,000 (Vikki), $13,000 (Tim)
401(k) balance $33,500 (Vikki), $17,000 (Tim)

Liabilities:
Student loan $7,500
Auto loan $4,000

Credit card balance $4,800 (Tim)

Income:
Gross annual salary: $53,000 (Vikki), $55,000 (Tim)
After-tax monthly salary: $3,091 (Vikki), $3,208 (Tim)

Monthly Expenses:
Rent $750
Food $550
Student loan $250

Auto loan $175
Credit card payments $500 (Tim)
Entertainment $300
Gas/repairs $450

Retirement Savings:
401(k) $500 per month, plus 50% employer match on first 7% of pay (Vikki), $458 per month, plus 50% match on first 8% of pay (Tim)

Questions:

1. What lifestyle and financial differences should Vikki and Tim expect living in a house compared with living in an apartment?
2. In order to get the best rate, what steps should they take before they apply for a mortgage?
3. Using Exhibit 7–6, what is the maximum mortgage Vikki and Tim can afford? Assume that property tax and homeowner's insurance will be $500/month and that the lender ratios are 40/45.
4. What are some of the tax advantages of owning rather than renting?
5. How can the couple use *Your Personal Financial Plan* sheets 22–25?

Spending Diary

"AFTER I PAY MY RENT, UTILITIES, AND RENTER'S INSURANCE, I HAVE VERY LITTLE FOR OTHER EXPENSES."

Directions

Your Daily Spending Diary will help you manage your housing expenses to create a better overall spending plan. As you record daily spending, your comments should reflect what you have learned about your spending patterns and help you consider possible changes you might want to make. The Daily Spending Diary sheets are located in Appendix C at the end of the book and on the student Web site at www.mhhe.com/kdh.

Questions

1. What portion of your daily spending involves expenses associated with housing?
2. What types of housing expenses might be reduced with more careful spending habits?

Renting vs. Buying Housing

Financial Planning Activities: To compare the cost of renting and buying your place of residence, obtain estimates for comparable housing units for the data requested below.

Suggested Web Sites: www.homefair.com   www.newbuyer.com/homes/   http://finance.move.com
www.dinkytown.net

Rental Costs

Annual rent payments (monthly rent $ _____ × 12) $ _____

Renter's insurance $ _____

Interest lost on security deposit (deposit times after-tax savings account interest rate) $ _____

Total annual cost of renting $

Buying Costs

Annual mortgage payments $ _____

Property taxes (annual costs) $ _____

Homeowner's insurance (annual premium) $ _____

Estimated maintenance and repairs $ _____

After-tax interest lost because of down payment/closing costs $ _____

Less: financial benefits of home ownership

Growth in equity $ – _____

Tax savings for mortgage interest (annual mortgage interest times tax rate) $ – _____

Tax savings for property taxes (annual property taxes times tax rate) $ – _____

Estimated annual depreciation $ – _____

Total annual cost of buying $

What's Next for Your Personal Financial Plan?

- Determine if renting or buying is most appropriate for you at the current time.
- List some circumstances or actions that might change your housing needs.

Name: _____   **Date:** _____

Apartment Rental Comparison

Financial Planning Activities: Obtain the information requested below to compare costs and facilities of three apartments.

Suggested Web Sites: www.apartments.com   www.apartmentguide.com/

Name of renting person or apartment building			
Address			
Phone			
Monthly rent			
Amount of security deposit			
Length of lease			
Utilities included in rent			
Parking facilities			
Storage area in building			
Laundry facilities			
Distance to schools			
Distance to public transportation			
Distance to shopping			
Pool, recreation area, other facilities			
Estimated utility costs: • Electric • Telephone • Gas • Water			
Other costs			
Other information			

What's Next for Your Personal Financial Plan?

- Which of these rental units would best serve your current housing needs?
- What additional information should be considered when renting an apartment?

Housing Affordability and Mortgage Qualification

Financial Planning Activities: Enter the amounts requested to estimate the amount of affordable mortgage payment, mortgage amount, and home purchase price.

Suggested Web Sites: www.realestate.com   www.kiplinger.com/tools/

Step 1

Determine your monthly gross income (annual income divided by 12) $ _____

Step 2

With a down payment of at least 10 percent, lenders use 28 percent of monthly gross income as a guideline for TIPI (taxes, insurance, principal, and interest), 36 percent of monthly gross income as a guideline for TIPI plus other debt payments (enter 0.28 or 0.36)   × _____

Step 3

Subtract other debt payments (such as payments on an auto loan), if applicable   − _____

Subtract estimated monthly costs of property taxes and homeowners insurance   − _____

Affordable monthly mortgage payment .... $ _____

Step 5

Divide this amount by the monthly mortgage payment per $1,000 based on current mortgage rates (see Exhibit 7–7, text page 230). For example, for a 10 percent, 30-year loan, the number would be $8.78.   ÷ _____

Multiply by $1,000   × _____ $1,000 _____

Affordable mortgage amount .... $ _____

Step 5

Divide your affordable mortgage amount by 1 minus the fractional portion of your down payment (for example, 0.9 for a 10 percent down payment).   ÷ _____

Affordable home purchase price .... $ _____

Note: The two ratios used by lending institutions (Step 2) and other loan requirements are likely to vary based on a variety of factors, including the type of mortgage, the amount of the down payment, your income level, and current interest rates. If you have other debts, lenders will calculate both ratios and then use the one that allows you greater flexibility in borrowing.

What's Next for Your Personal Financial Plan?

- Identify actions you might need to take to qualify for a mortgage.
- Discuss your mortgage qualifications with a mortgage broker or other lender.

Name: _____ Date: _____

Mortgage Company Comparison

Financial Planning Activities: Obtain the information requested below to compare the services and costs for different home mortgage sources.

Suggested Web Sites: www.hsh.com   www.eloan.com   www.bankrate.com

Amount of mortgage:

$ _____   Down payment: $ _____   Years: _____

Company		
Address		
Phone		
Web site		
Contact person		
Application fee, credit report, property appraisal fees		
Loan origination fee		
Other fees, charges (commitment, title, tax transfer)		
Fixed-rate mortgage		
Monthly payment		
Discount points		
Adjustable-rate mortgage		
• Time until first rate charge • Frequency of rate charge		
Monthly payment		
Discount points		
Payment cap		
Interest rate cap		
Rate index used		
Commitment period		
Other information		

What's Next for Your Personal Financial Plan?

• What additional information should be considered when selecting a mortgage?
• Which of these mortgage companies would best serve your current and future needs?

8 Home and Automobile Insurance

Getting Personal

Do you understand the importance of purchasing insurance for your home and automobile? Read the numbered list of possible perils. Then, at the appropriate point along the continuum line following the list, write the number that corresponds to how likely you feel each peril is in your life.

1. You will own a home that will need to be protected against natural disasters, theft, and other adverse occurrences.

2. Your apartment will be robbed.

3. A tornado will destroy your home and automobile.

4. Someone will trip on your sidewalk and sue you.

5. A child of yours will accidentally break a neighbor's window.

6. Your dog will bite someone.

7. Your car will be involved in an accident causing physical injuries to passengers.

8. Your car will be hit by an uninsured motorist.

Most Likely   **Less Likely**

•———————————————————————————————————————•

After studying this chapter, you will be asked to reconsider your priorities.

Your Personal Financial Plan Sheets

26. Current Insurance Policies and Needs
27. Home Inventory
28. Determining Needed Property Insurance
29. Apartment/Home Insurance Comparison
30. Automobile Insurance Cost Comparison

Objectives

In this chapter, you will learn to:

1. Identify types of risks and risk management methods and develop a risk management plan.
2. Assess the insurance coverage and policy types available to homeowners and renters.
3. Analyze the factors that influence the amount of coverage and cost of home insurance.
4. Identify the important types of automobile insurance coverage.
5. Evaluate factors that affect the cost of automobile insurance.

Why is this important?

Each year homeowners and renters in the United States lose billions of dollars from more than 3 million burglaries, 500,000 fires, and 200,000 cases of damage from other perils. The cost of injuries and property damage caused by vehicles is also enormous. By including property and liability insurance in your financial plan, you can help protect yourself from such financial loss.

Insurance and Risk Management

In today's world of the "strange but true," you can get insurance for just about anything. You might purchase a policy to protect yourself in the event that you're abducted by aliens. Some insurance companies will offer you protection if you think that you have a risk of turning into a werewolf. If you're a fast runner, you might be able to get a discount on a life insurance policy. Some people buy wedding disaster insurance

OBJECTIVE 1

Identify types of risks and risk management methods and develop a risk management plan.

insurance Protection against possible financial loss.

insurance company A risk-sharing firm that assumes financial responsibility for losses that may result from an insured risk.

insurer An insurance company.

policy A written contract for insurance.

policyholder A person who owns an insurance policy.

premium The amount of money a policyholder is charged for an insurance policy.

coverage The protection provided by the terms of an insurance policy.

insured A person covered by an insurance policy.

risk Chance or uncertainty of loss; also used to mean "the insured."

peril The cause of a possible loss.

Key Web Sites for Insurance Company Ratings

www.ambest.com

www.standardandpoors.com

hazard A factor that increases the likelihood of loss through some peril.

negligence Failure to take ordinary or reasonable care in a situation.

just in case something goes wrong on the big day. You may never need these types of insurance, but you'll certainly need insurance on your home, your vehicle, and your personal property. The more you know about insurance, the better able you will be to make decisions about buying it.

What Is Insurance?

Insurance is protection against possible financial loss. You can't predict the future. However, insurance allows you to be prepared for the worst. It provides protection against many risks, such as unexpected property loss, illness, and injury. Many kinds of insurance exist, and they all share some common characteristics. They give you peace of mind, and they protect you from financial loss when trouble strikes.

An **insurance company,** or **insurer,** is a risk-sharing business that agrees to pay for losses that may happen to someone it insures. A person joins the risk-sharing group by purchasing a contract known as a **policy.** The purchaser of the policy is called a **policyholder.** Under the policy, the insurance company agrees to take on the risk. In return the policyholder pays the company a **premium,** or fee. The protection provided by the terms of an insurance policy is known as **coverage,** and the people protected by the policy are known as the **insured.**

Types of Risk

You face risks every day. You can't cross the street without some danger that a motor vehicle might hit you. You can't own property without running the risk that it will be lost, stolen, damaged or destroyed.

"Risk," "peril," and "hazard" are important terms in insurance. In everyday use, these terms have almost the same meanings. In the insurance business, however, each has a distinct meaning.

Risk is the chance of loss or injury. In insurance it refers to the fact that no one can predict trouble. This means that an insurance company is taking a chance every time it issues a policy. Insurance companies frequently refer to the insured person or property as the risk.

Peril is anything that may possibly cause a loss. It's the reason someone takes out insurance. People buy policies for protection against a wide range of perils, including fire, windstorms, explosions, robbery, and accidents.

Hazard is anything that increases the likelihood of loss through some peril. For example, defective house wiring is a hazard that increases the chance that a fire will start.

The most common risks are personal risks, property risks, and liability risks. *Personal risks* involve loss of income or life due to illness, disability, old age, or unemployment. *Property risks* include losses to property caused by perils, such as fire or theft, and hazards. *Liability risks* involve losses caused by negligence that leads to injury or property damage. **Negligence** is the failure to take ordinary or reasonable care to prevent accidents from happening. If a homeowner doesn't clear the ice from the front steps of her house, for example, she creates a liability risk because visitors could fall on the ice.

Personal risks, property risks, and liability risks are types of *pure,* or *insurable, risk.* The insurance company will have to pay only if some event that the insurance covers actually happens. Pure risks are accidental and unintentional. Although no one can predict whether a pure risk will occur, it's possible to predict the costs that will accrue if one does.

A *speculative risk* is a risk that carries a chance of either loss or gain. Starting a small business that may or may not succeed is an example of speculative risk. Speculative risks are not insurable.

Risk Management Methods

Risk management is an organized plan for protecting yourself, your family, and your property. It helps reduce financial losses caused by destructive events. Risk management is a long-range planning process. Your risk management needs will change at various points in your life. If you understand how to manage risks, you can provide better protection for yourself and your family. Most people think of risk management as buying insurance. However, insurance is not the only way of dealing with risk. Four general risk management techniques are commonly used.

RISK AVOIDANCE You can avoid the risk of a traffic accident by not driving to work. A car manufacturer can avoid the risk of product failure by not introducing new cars. These are both examples of risk avoidance. They are ways to avoid risks, but they require serious trade-offs. You might have to give up your job if you can't get there. The car manufacturer might lose business to competitors who take the risk of producing exciting new cars.

In some cases, though, risk avoidance is practical. By taking precautions in high-crime areas, you might avoid the risk that you will be robbed.

RISK REDUCTION You can't avoid risks completely. However, you can decrease the likelihood that they will cause you harm. For example, you can reduce the risk of injury in an automobile accident by wearing a seat belt. You can reduce the risk of developing lung cancer by not smoking. By installing fire extinguishers in your home, you reduce the potential damage that could be caused by a fire. Your risk of illness might be lower if you eat properly and exercise regularly.

RISK ASSUMPTION Risk assumption means taking on responsibility for the negative results of a risk. It makes sense to assume a risk if you know that the possible loss will be small. It also makes sense when you've taken all the precautions you can to avoid or reduce the risk.

When insurance coverage for a particular item is expensive, that item may not be worth insuring. For instance, you might decide not to purchase collision insurance on an older car. If an accident happens, the car may be wrecked, but it wasn't worth much anyway. *Self-insurance* is setting up a special fund, perhaps from savings, to cover the cost of a loss. Self-insurance does not eliminate risks, but it does provide a way of covering losses as an alternative to an insurance policy. Some people self-insure because they can't obtain insurance from an insurance company.

RISK SHIFTING The most common method of dealing with risk is to shift it. That simply means to transfer it to an insurance company. In exchange for the fee you pay, the insurance company agrees to pay for your losses.

Most insurance policies include deductibles. Deductibles are a combination of risk assumption and risk shifting. A **deductible** is the set amount that the policyholder must pay per loss on an insurance policy. For example, if a falling tree damages your car, you may have to pay $200 toward the repairs. Your insurance company will pay the rest.

Exhibit 8–1 summarizes various risks and effective ways of managing them.

Planning an Insurance Program

Your personal insurance program should change along with your needs and goals. Dave and Ellen are a young couple. How will they plan their insurance program to meet their needs and goals?

did you know?

The poor of the world often lack the ability to protect their assets. However, in recent years, microinsurance has evolved to serve consumers and businesses not covered by traditional insurance programs. These low premium, low-coverage policies provide low-income households protection from losses that would have a major impact on their financial situation.

Key Web Sites for Managing Risk

www.insure.com

www.insweb.com

deductible The set amount that the policyholder must pay per loss on an insurance policy.

Exhibit **8-1**   Examples of Risks and Risk Management Strategies

RISKS		STRATEGIES FOR REDUCING FINANCIAL IMPACT		
Personal Events	Financial Impact	Personal Resources	Private Sector	Public Sector
Disability	Loss of one income Loss of services Increased expenses	Savings, investments Family observing safety precautions	Disability insurance	Disability insurance
Illness	Loss of one income Catastrophic hospital expenses	Health-enhancing behavior	Health insurance Health maintenance organizations	Military health care Medicare, Medicaid
Death	Loss of one income Loss of services Final expenses	Estate planning Risk reduction	Life insurance	Veteran's life insurance Social Security survivor's benefits
Retirement	Decreased income Unplanned living expenses	Savings Investments Hobbies, skills	Retirement and/or pensions	Social Security Pension plan for government employees
Property loss	Catastrophic storm damage to property Repair or replacement cost of theft	Property repair and upkeep Security plans	Automobile insurance Homeowner's insurance Flood insurance (joint program with government)	Flood insurance (joint program with business)
Liability	Claims and settlement costs Lawsuits and legal expenses Loss of personal assets and income	Observing safety precautions Maintaining property	Homeowner's insurance Automobile insurance Malpractice insurance	

did you know?

Deductibles are a combination of risk assumption and risk shifting. The insured person assumes part of the risk, paying the first $100, $250, or $500 of a claim. The majority of the risk for a large claim is shifted to another party, the insurance company.

Exhibit 8–2 outlines the steps in developing a personal insurance program.

STEP 1: SET INSURANCE GOALS Dave and Ellen's main goal should be to minimize personal, property, and liability risks. They also need to decide how they will cover costs resulting from a potential loss. Income, age, family size, lifestyle, experience, and responsibilities will be important factors in the goals they set. The insurance they buy must reflect those goals. Dave and Ellen should try to come up with a basic risk management plan that achieves the following:

- Reduces possible loss of income caused by premature death, illness, accident, or unemployment.
- Reduces possible loss of property caused by perils, such as fire or theft, or hazards.
- Reduces possible loss of income, savings, and property because of personal negligence.

Exhibit 8–2

Creating a Personal
Insurance Program

STEP 2: DEVELOP A PLAN TO REACH YOUR GOALS

Planning is a way of taking control of life instead of just letting life happen to you. Dave and Ellen need to determine what risks they face and what risks they can afford to take. They also have to determine what resources can help them reduce the damage that could be caused by serious risks.

Furthermore, they need to know what kind of insurance is available. The cost of different kinds of insurance and the way the costs vary among companies will be the key factors in their plan. Finally, this couple needs to research the reliability record of different insurance companies.

Dave and Ellen must ask four questions as they develop their risk management plan:

- What do they need to insure?
- How much should they insure it for?
- What kind of insurance should they buy?
- Who should they buy insurance from?

STEP 3: PUT YOUR PLAN INTO ACTION

Once they've developed their plan, Dave and Ellen need to follow through by putting it into action. During this process they might discover that they don't have enough insurance protection. If that's the case, they could purchase additional coverage or change the kind of coverage they have. Another alternative would be to adjust their budget to cover the cost of additional insurance. Finally, Dave and Ellen might expand their savings or investment programs and use those funds in the case of an emergency.

The best risk management plans will be flexible enough to allow Dave and Ellen to respond to changing life situations. Their goal should be to create an insurance program that can grow or shrink as their protection needs change.

STEP 4: CHECK YOUR RESULTS

Dave and Ellen should take the time to review their plan every two or three years, or whenever their family circumstances change.

Until recently, Dave and Ellen were satisfied with the coverage provided by their insurance policies. However, when the couple bought a house six months ago, the time had come for them to review their insurance plan. With the new house the risks became much greater. After all, what would happen if a fire destroyed part of their home?

The needs of a couple renting an apartment differ from those of a couple who own a house. Both couples face similar risks, but their financial responsibility differs

Key Web Sites for Insurance Planning Assistance

http://insweb.com

www.insure.com

Personal Finance in Practice

> How Can You Plan an Insurance Program?

Did you:	Yes	No
• Seek advice from a competent and reliable insurance adviser?	☐	☐
• Determine what insurance you need to provide your family with sufficient protection if you die?	☐	☐
• Consider what portion of the family protection is met by Social Security and by group insurance?	☐	☐
• Decide what other needs insurance must meet (funeral expenses, savings, retirement annuities, etc.)?	☐	☐
• Decide what types of insurance best meet your needs?	☐	☐
• Plan an insurance program and implement it except for periodic reviews of changing needs and changing conditions?	☐	☐
• Avoid buying more insurance than you need or can afford?	☐	☐
• Consider dropping one policy for another that provides the same coverage for less money?	☐	☐

Note: *Yes* answers reflect wise actions for insurance planning.

greatly. When you're developing or reviewing a risk management plan, ask yourself if you're providing the financial resources you'll need to protect yourself, your family, and your property. The nearby Personal Finance in Practice feature suggests several guidelines to follow in planning your insurance programs.

Property and Liability Insurance in Your Financial Plan

Major natural disasters have caused catastrophic amounts of property loss in the United States and other parts of the world. In 2005 Hurricanes Katrina, Rita, and Wilma caused $50 billion in damages. In 1992 Hurricane Andrew resulted in $22.3 billion worth of insurance **claims,** or requests for payment to cover financial losses. In the Midwest in 1993, floods caused more than $2 billion worth of damage.

claim A request for payment to cover financial losses.

Most people invest large amounts of money in their homes and motor vehicles. Therefore, protecting these items from loss is extremely important. Each year homeowners and renters in the United States lose billions of dollars from more than 3 million burglaries, 500,000 fires, and 200,000 cases of damage from other perils. The cost of injuries and property damage caused by vehicles is also enormous.

Think of the price you pay for home and motor vehicle insurance as an investment in protecting your most valuable possessions. The cost of such insurance may seem high. However, the financial losses from which it protects you are much higher.

Two main types of risk are related to your home and your car or other vehicle. One is the risk of damage to or loss of your property. The second type involves your responsibility for injuries to other people or damage to their property.

POTENTIAL PROPERTY LOSSES People spend a great deal of money on their houses, vehicles, furniture, clothing, and other personal property. Property owners face two basic types of risk. The first is physical damage caused by perils such as fire, wind, water, and smoke. These perils can damage or destroy property. For example, a windstorm might cause a large tree branch to smash the windshield of your car. You would have to find another way to get around while it was being repaired. The second type of risk is loss or damage caused by criminal behavior such as robbery, burglary, vandalism, and arson.

LIABILITY PROTECTION   You also need to protect yourself from liability. **Liability** is legal responsibility for the financial cost of another person's losses or injuries. You can be held legally responsible even if the injury or damage was not your fault. For example, suppose that Terry falls and gets hurt while playing in her friend Lisa's yard. Terry's family may be able to sue Lisa's parents even though Lisa's parents did nothing wrong. Similarly, suppose that Sanjay accidentally damages a valuable painting while helping Ed move some furniture. Ed may take legal action against Sanjay to pay the cost of the painting.

liability Legal responsibility for the financial cost of another person's losses or injuries.

Key Web Sites for State Insurance Regulatory Agencies:

www.naic.org

www.ircweb.org

Sheet 26 Current Insurance Policies and Needs

CONCEPT CHECK 8–1

1 What are the three types of risk? Give an example for each.

_____

_____

2 What are the four methods of managing risks? Give an example for each.

_____

_____

3 List the four steps in planning for your insurance program.

_____

_____

4 Give an example of each kind of risk—personal, property, and liability.

_____

Apply Yourself!

Objective 1

Using Web research and discussion with others, develop a risk management plan that best suits your present need for insurance.

Usually, if you're found liable, or legally responsible, in a situation, it's because negligence on your part caused the mishap. Examples of such negligence include letting young children swim in a pool without supervision or cluttering a staircase with things that could cause someone to slip and fall.

Home and Property Insurance

homeowner's insurance Coverage for a place of residence and its associated financial risks.

Your home and personal belongings are probably a major portion of your assets. Whether you rent your dwelling or own a home, property insurance is vital. **Homeowner's insurance** is coverage for your place of residence and its associated financial risks, such as damage to personal property and injuries to others (see Exhibit 8–3).

Homeowner's Insurance Coverages

A homeowner's insurance policy provides coverage for the following:

- The building in which you live and any other structures on the property.
- Additional living expenses.
- Personal property.
- Personal liability and related coverage.
- Specialized coverage.

BUILDING AND OTHER STRUCTURES The main purpose of homeowner's insurance is to protect you against financial loss in case your home is damaged or destroyed. Detached structures on your property, such as a garage or toolshed, are also covered. Homeowner's coverage even includes trees, shrubs, and plants.

ADDITIONAL LIVING EXPENSES If a fire or other event damages your home, additional living expense coverage pays for you to stay somewhere else. For example, you may need to stay in a motel or rent an apartment while your home is being repaired. These extra living expenses will be paid by your insurance. Some policies limit additional living expense coverage to 10 to 20 percent of the home's coverage amount. They may also limit payments to a maximum of six to nine months. Other policies may pay additional living expenses for up to a year.

PERSONAL PROPERTY Homeowner's insurance covers your household belongings, such as furniture, appliances, and clothing, up to a portion of the insured value of the home. That portion is usually 55, 70, or 75 percent. For example, a home insured

Exhibit **8–3** Home Insurance Coverage

Building and other structures

Personal property

Loss of use/additional living expenses while home is uninhabitable

Personal liability and related coverages

for $160,000 might have $112,000 (70 percent) worth of coverage for household belongings.

Personal property coverage typically limits the payout for the theft of certain items, such as $5,000 for jewelry. It provides protection against the loss or damage of articles that you take with you when you are away from home. For example, items you take on vacation or use at college are usually covered up to the policy limit. Personal property coverage even extends to property that you rent, such as a rug cleaner, while it's in your possession.

Most homeowner's policies include optional coverage for personal computers, including stored data, up to a certain limit. Your insurance agent can determine whether the equipment is covered against data loss and damage from spilled drinks or power surges.

If something does happen to your personal property, you must prove how much it was worth and that it belonged to you. To make the process easier, you can create a household inventory. A **household inventory** is a list or other documentation of personal belongings, with purchase dates and cost information. You can get a form for such an inventory from an insurance agent. Exhibit 8–4 provides a list of items you might include if you decide to compile your own inventory. For items of special value, you should have receipts, serial numbers, brand names, and proof of value.

household inventory A list or other documentation of personal belongings, with purchase dates and cost information.

Your household inventory can include a video recording or photographs of your home and its contents. Make sure that the closet and storage area doors are photographed open. On the back of the photographs, indicate the date and the value of the objects. Update your inventory, photos, and related documents on a regular basis. Keep a copy of each document in a secure location, such as a safe deposit box.

If you own valuable items, such as expensive musical instruments, or need added protection for computers and related equipment, you can purchase a personal property floater. A **personal property floater** is additional property insurance that covers the damage or loss of a specific item of high value. The insurance company will require a detailed description of the item and its worth. You'll also need to have the item appraised, or evaluated by an expert, from time to time to make sure that its value hasn't changed.

personal property floater Additional property insurance to cover the damage or loss of a specific item of high value.

PERSONAL LIABILITY AND RELATED COVERAGE Every day people face the risk of financial loss due to injuries to other people or their property. The following are examples of this risk:

- A guest falls on a patch of ice on the steps to your home and breaks his arm.
- A spark from the barbecue in your backyard starts a fire that damages a neighbor's roof.
- Your son or daughter accidentally breaks an antique lamp while playing at a neighbor's house.

In each of these situations, you could be held responsible for paying for the damage. The personal liability portion of a homeowner's policy protects you and members of your family if others sue you for injuries they suffer or damage to their property. This coverage includes the cost of legal defense.

Not all individuals who come to your property are covered by your liability insurance. Friends, guests, and babysitters are probably covered. However, if you have regular employees, such as a housekeeper, a cook, or a gardener, you may need to obtain worker's compensation coverage for them.

Exhibit **8–4**   Household Inventory Contents

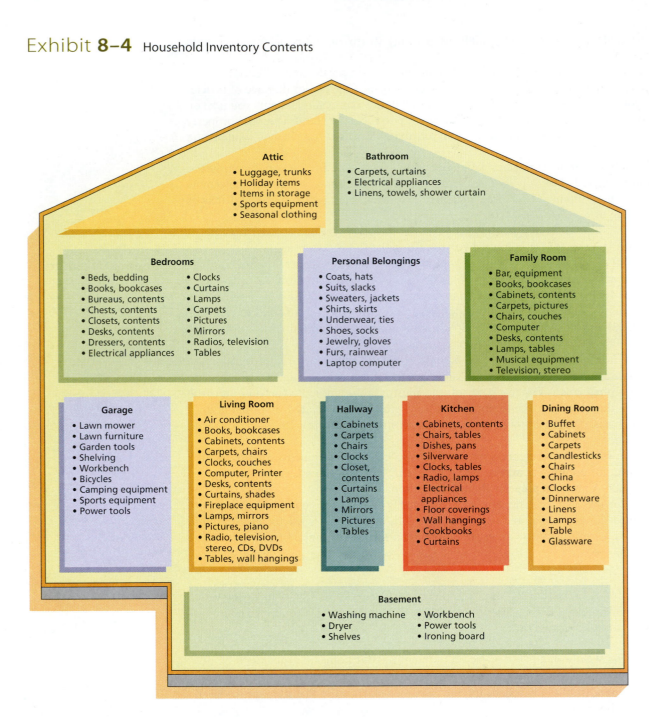

Attic
- Luggage, trunks
- Holiday items
- Items in storage
- Sports equipment
- Seasonal clothing

Bathroom
- Carpets, curtains
- Electrical appliances
- Linens, towels, shower curtain

Bedrooms
- Beds, bedding
- Books, bookcases
- Bureaus, contents
- Chests, contents
- Closets, contents
- Desks, contents
- Dressers, contents
- Electrical appliances
- Clocks
- Curtains
- Lamps
- Carpets
- Pictures
- Mirrors
- Radios, television
- Tables

Personal Belongings
- Coats, hats
- Suits, slacks
- Sweaters, jackets
- Shirts, skirts
- Underwear, ties
- Shoes, socks
- Jewelry, gloves
- Furs, rainwear
- Laptop computer

Family Room
- Bar, equipment
- Books, bookcases
- Cabinets, contents
- Carpets, pictures
- Chairs, couches
- Computer
- Desks, contents
- Lamps, tables
- Musical equipment
- Television, stereo

Garage
- Lawn mower
- Lawn furniture
- Garden tools
- Shelving
- Workbench
- Bicycles
- Camping equipment
- Sports equipment
- Power tools

Living Room
- Air conditioner
- Books, bookcases
- Cabinets, contents
- Carpets, chairs
- Clocks, couches
- Computer, Printer
- Desks, contents
- Curtains, shades
- Fireplace equipment
- Lamps, mirrors
- Pictures, piano
- Radio, television, stereo, CDs, DVDs
- Tables, wall hangings

Hallway
- Cabinets
- Carpets
- Chairs
- Clocks
- Closet, contents
- Curtains
- Lamps
- Mirrors
- Pictures
- Tables

Kitchen
- Cabinets, contents
- Chairs, tables
- Dishes, pans
- Silverware
- Clocks, tables
- Radio, lamps
- Electrical appliances
- Floor coverings
- Wall hangings
- Cookbooks
- Curtains

Dining Room
- Buffet
- Cabinets
- Carpets
- Candlesticks
- Chairs
- China
- Clocks
- Dinnerware
- Linens
- Lamps
- Table
- Glassware

Basement
- Washing machine
- Dryer
- Shelves
- Workbench
- Power tools
- Ironing board

umbrella policy Supplementary personal liability coverage; also called a *personal catastrophe policy.*

medical payments coverage Home insurance that pays the cost of minor accidental injuries on one's property.

Most homeowner's policies provide basic personal liability coverage of $100,000, but often that's not enough. An **umbrella policy,** also called a *personal catastrophe policy,* supplements your basic personal liability coverage. This added protection covers you for all kinds of personal injury claims. For instance, an umbrella policy will cover you if someone sues you for saying or writing something negative or untrue or for damaging his or her reputation. Extended liability policies are sold in amounts of $1 million or more and are useful for wealthy people. If you are a business owner, you may need other types of liability coverage as well.

Medical payments coverage pays the cost of minor accidental injuries to visitors on your property. It also covers minor injuries caused by you, members of your family, or even your pets, away from home. Settlements under medical payments coverage are made without determining who was at fault. This makes it fast and easy for the insurance company to process small claims, generally up to $5,000. If the injury is more serious, the personal liability portion of the home-owner's policy covers it. Medical payments coverage does not cover injury to you or the other people who live in your home.

If you or a family member should accidentally damage another person's property, the supplementary coverage of homeowner's insurance will pay for it. This protection is usually limited to $500 or $1,000. Again, payments are made regardless of fault. If the damage is more expensive, however, it's handled under the personal liability coverage.

SPECIALIZED COVERAGE Homeowner's insurance usually doesn't cover losses from floods and earthquakes. If you live in an area that has frequent floods or earthquakes, you need to purchase special coverage. In some places the National Flood Insurance Program makes flood insurance available. This protection is separate from a homeowner's policy. An insurance agent or the Federal Emergency Management Agency (FEMA) of the Federal Insurance Administration can give you additional information about this coverage.

You may be able to get earthquake insurance as an **endorsement**—addition of coverage—to a homeowners' policy or through a state-run insurance program. The most serious earthquakes occur in the Pacific Coast region. However, earthquakes can happen in other regions, too. If you plan to buy a home in an area that has high risk of floods or earthquakes, you may have to buy the necessary insurance in order to be approved for a mortgage loan.

endorsement An addition of coverage to a standard insurance policy.

> **did you know?**
>
> For $50 to $80 a year, homeowners can obtain $10,000 for sewage and drain backup damage. Heavy rains that clog a sewer line can cause damage to furniture and other items in a finished basement.

Renter's Insurance

For people who rent, home insurance coverage includes personal property protection, additional living expenses coverage, and personal liability and related coverage. Renter's insurance does not provide coverage on the building or other structures.

There are two standard renter's insurance policies. The *broad form* covers your personal property against perils specified in the policy, such as fires and thefts, and the *comprehensive form* protects your personal property against all perils not specifically excluded in the policy. When shopping for renter's insurance, be aware that these policies

- Normally pay only the actual cash value of your losses. Replacement cost coverage is available for an extra premium.

- Fully cover your personal property only at home. When traveling, your luggage and other personal items are protected up to a certain percentage of the policy's total amount of coverage.

- Automatically provide liability coverage if someone is injured on your premises.

- May duplicate other coverage. For instance, if you are still a dependent, your personal property may be covered by your parents' homeowner's policy. This coverage is limited, however, to an amount equal to a certain percentage of the total personal property coverage provided by the policy.

The most important part of renter's insurance is the protection it provides for your personal property. Many renters believe that they are covered under the landlord's insurance. In fact, that's the case only when the landlord is proved liable for some damage. For example, if bad wiring causes a fire and damages a tenant's property, the tenant may be able to collect money from the landlord. Renter's insurance is relatively inexpensive and provides many of the same kinds of protection as a homeowner's policy.

did you know?

While more than 9 out of 10 homeowners have property insurance, only about 4 out of 10 renters are covered.

Home Insurance Policy Forms

Home insurance policies are available in several forms. The forms provide different combinations of coverage. Some forms are not available in all areas.

The basic form (HO-1) protects against perils such as fire, lightning, windstorms, hail, volcanic eruptions, explosions, smoke, theft, vandalism, glass breakage, and riots.

The broad form (HO-2) covers an even wider range of perils, including falling objects and damage from ice, snow, or sleet.

The special form (HO-3) covers all basic- and broad-form risks, plus any other risks except those specifically excluded from the policy. Common exclusions are flood, earthquake, war, and nuclear accidents. Personal property is covered for the risks listed in the policy.

CAUTION! Computers and other equipment used in a home-based business are not usually covered by a home insurance policy. Contact your insurance agent to obtain needed coverage.

The tenant's form (HO-4) protects the personal property of renters against the risks listed in the policy. It does not include coverage on the building or other structures.

The comprehensive form (HO-5) expands the coverage of the HO-3. The HO-5 includes endorsements for items such as replacement cost coverage on contents and guaranteed replacement cost coverage on buildings.

Condominium owner's insurance (HO-6) protects personal property and any additions or improvements made to the living unit. These might include bookshelves, electrical fixtures, wallpaper, or carpeting. The condominium association purchases insurance on the building and other structures.

Manufactured housing units and mobile homes usually qualify for insurance coverage with conventional policies. However, some mobile homes may need special policies with higher rates because the way they are built increases their risk of fire and wind damage. The cost of mobile home insurance coverage depends on the home's location and the way it's attached to the ground. Mobile home insurance is quite expensive: A $40,000 mobile home can cost as much to insure as a $120,000 house.

In addition to the risks previously discussed, home insurance policies include coverage for:

- Credit card fraud, check forgery, and counterfeit money.
- The cost of removing damaged property.
- Emergency removal of property to protect it from damage.
- Temporary repairs after a loss to prevent further damage.
- Fire department charges in areas with such fees.

Not everything is covered by home insurance (see Exhibit 8–5).

Exhibit **8–5**   Not Everything Is Covered

CERTAIN PERSONAL PROPERTY IS NOT COVERED BY HOMEOWNERS INSURANCE:

- Items insured separately, such as jewelry, furs, boats, or expensive electronic equipment
- Animals, birds, or fish
- Motorized vehicles not licensed for road use, except those used for home maintenance
- Sound devices used in motor vehicles, such as radios and CD players

- Aircraft and parts
- Property belonging to tenants
- Property contained in a rental apartment
- Property rented by the homeowner to other people
- Business property

Separate coverage may be available for personal property that is not covered by a homeowners insurance policy.

Sheet 27 Home Inventory

CONCEPT CHECK 8–2

1 Define the following terms in the spaces below:

a. Homeowner's insurance _____

b. Household inventory _____

c. Personal property floater _____

d. Renter's insurance _____

2 Identify the choice that best completes the statement or answers the question:

a. The personal liability portion of a homeowner's insurance policy protects the insured against financial loss when his or her (i) house floods, (ii) jewelry is stolen, (iii) guests injure themselves, (iv) reputation is damaged.

b. Renter's insurance includes coverage for all of the following *except* (i) the building, (ii) personal property, (iii) additional living expenses, (iv) personal liability.

c. The basic home insurance policy form protects against several perils, including (i) sleet, (ii) lightning, (iii) flood, (iv) earthquake.

3 Define the following terms in the spaces below:

a. Umbrella policy _____

b. Medical payments coverage _____

c. Endorsement _____

4 List at least four personal property items that are not covered by a homeowner's insurance policy.

_____

_____

Apply Yourself!

Objective 2

You are about to rent your first apartment. You have approximately $10,000 worth of personal belongings. Contact an insurance agent to find out the cost of renter's insurance.

Home Insurance Cost Factors

How Much Coverage Do You Need?

You can get the best insurance value by choosing the right coverage amount and knowing the factors that affect insurance costs (see Exhibit 8–6). Your insurance should be based on the amount of money you would need to rebuild or repair your house, not the amount you paid for it. As construction costs rise, you should increase the amount of coverage. In fact, today most insurance policies automatically increase coverage as construction costs rise.

In the past, many homeowner's policies insured the building for only 80 percent of the replacement value. If the building were destroyed, the homeowner would have to pay for part of the cost of replacing it, which could be expensive. Today most companies recommend full coverage.

If you are borrowing money to buy a home, the lender will require that you have property insurance. Remember, too, that the amount of insurance on your home determines the coverage on your personal belongings. Coverage for personal belongings is usually from 55 to 75 percent of the insurance amount on your home.

Insurance companies base claim settlements on one or two methods. Under the **actual cash value (ACV)** method, the payment you receive is based on the replacement cost of an item minus depreciation. Depreciation is the loss of value of an item as it gets older. This means you would receive less for a five-year-old bicycle than you originally paid for it.

actual cash value (ACV) A claim settlement method in which the insured receives payment based on the current replacement cost of a damaged or lost item, less depreciation.

Under the **replacement value** method for settling claims, you receive the full cost of repairing or replacing an item. Depreciation is not considered. Many companies limit the replacement cost to 400 percent of the item's actual cash value. Replacement value coverage is more expensive than actual cash value coverage.

replacement value A claim settlement method in which the insured receives the full cost of repairing or replacing a damaged or lost item.

Factors That Affect Home Insurance Costs

The cost of your home insurance will depend on several factors, such as the location of the building and the type of building and construction materials. The amount of coverage and type of policy you choose will also affect the cost of home insurance. Furthermore, different insurance companies offer different rates.

Exhibit 8–6

Determining the Amount of Home Insurance You Need

- Replacement value of the home
- Value of the contents
- Liability coverage desired
- Protection for specific items such as jewelry, furs, cameras, silverware, or antiques

LOCATION OF HOME The location of your home affects your insurance rates. Insurance companies offer lower rates to people whose homes are close to a water supply or fire hydrant or located in an area that has a good fire department. On the other hand, rates are higher in areas where crime is common. People living in regions that experience severe weather, such as tornadoes and hurricanes, may also pay more for insurance.

TYPE OF STRUCTURE The type of home and its construction influence the price of insurance coverage. A brick house, for example, will usually cost less to insure than a similar structure made of wood. However, earthquake coverage is more expensive for a brick house than for a wood dwelling because a wooden house is more likely to survive an earthquake. Also, an older house may be more difficult to restore to its original condition. That means that it will cost more to insure.

COVERAGE AMOUNT AND POLICY TYPE The policy and the amount of coverage you select affect the premium you pay. Obviously, insuring a $300,000 home costs more than insuring a $100,000 home.

  The deductible amount in your policy also affects the cost of your insurance. If you increase the amount of your deductible, your premium will be lower because the company will pay out less in claims. The most common deductible amount is $250. Raising the deductible from $250 to $500 or $1,000 can reduce the premium you pay by 15 percent or more.

> ### Example
>
> Suppose your home insurance policy premium is $800 with a $250 deductible. If you increase the amount of your deductible to $500, you reduce the premium by 10 percent, or $80.

HOME INSURANCE DISCOUNTS Most companies offer discounts if you take action to reduce risks to your home. Your premium may be lower if you have smoke detectors or a fire extinguisher. If your home has dead-bolt locks and alarm systems, which make a break-in harder for thieves, insurance costs may be lower. Some companies offer discounts to people who don't file any claims for a certain number of years.

COMPANY DIFFERENCES You can save more than 30 percent on homeowner's insurance by comparing rates from several companies. Some insurance agents work for only one company. Others are independent agents who represent several different companies. Talk to both types of agent. You'll get the information you need to compare rates.

  Don't select a company on the basis of price alone; also consider service and coverage. Not all companies settle claims in the same way. Suppose that all homes on Evergreen Terrace are dented on one side by large hail. They all have the same kind of siding. Unfortunately, the homeowners discover that this type of siding is no longer available so all the siding on all of the houses will need to be replaced. Some insurance companies will pay to replace all the siding. Others will pay only to replace the damaged parts.

Key Web Sites for Comparing Coverage and Costs

www.insure.com

www.accuquote.com

did you know?

In some areas, a home can be automatically rejected for insurance coverage if it has had two or three claims of any sort in the past three years. Homes that have encountered water damage, storm damage, and burglaries are most vulnerable to rejection.

Key Web Site for Flood Insurance

www.fema.gov

Personal Finance in Practice

> How to Lower the Cost of Insurance

How can you lower your cost of homeowner's and renter's insurance? Shop around and compare the cost. Here are a few tips that can save you hundreds of dollars annually.

1. *Consider a higher deductible.* Increasing your deductible by just a few hundred dollars can make a big difference in your premium.

2. *Ask your insurance agent about discounts.* You may be able to secure a lower premium if your home has safety features such as dead-bolt locks, smoke detectors, an alarm system, storm shutters, or fire retardant roofing material. Persons over 55 years of age or long-term customers may also be offered discounts.

3. *Insure your house, **not** the land under it.* After a disaster, the land is still there. If you don't subtract the value of the land when deciding how much homeowner's insurance to buy, you will pay more than you should.

4. *Make certain you purchase enough coverage to replace what is insured.* "Replacement" coverage gives you the money to rebuild your home and replace its contents. An actual cash-value policy is cheaper but pays only what your property is worth at the time of the loss—your cost minus depreciation.

5. *Ask about special coverage you might need.* You may have to pay extra for computers, cameras, jewelry, art, antiques, musical instruments, stamp collections, and other items.

6. *Remember that flood and earthquake damage are not covered by a standard homeowner's policy.* The cost of a separate earthquake policy will depend on the likelihood of earthquakes in your area. Homeowners who live in areas prone to flooding should take advantage of the National Flood Insurance Program. Call 1-888-CALLFLOOD or visit www.floodalert.fema.gov.

7. *If you are a renter do **NOT** assume your landlord carries insurance on your personal belongings.* Purchase a special policy for renters.

Key Web Sites for Home and Auto Insurance

www.independentagent.com

www.trustedchoice.com

State insurance commissions and consumer organizations can give you information about different insurance companies. *Consumer Reports* rates insurance companies on a regular basis.

Read the accompanying Personal Finance in Practice box to learn how you can lower the cost of homeowner's and renter's insurance.

Sheet 28 Determining Needed Property Insurance

Sheet 29 Apartment/Home Insurance Comparison

CONCEPT CHECK 8–3

1 In the space provided, write "T" if you believe the statement is true, "F" if the statement is false.

a. Today most insurance policies automatically increase coverage as construction costs rise. _____

b. In the past, many homeowner's policies insured the building for only 50 percent of the replacement value. _____

c. Most mortgage lenders do not require that you buy home insurance. _____

d. Coverage for personal belongings is usually from 55 to 75 percent of the insurance amount on your home. _____

2 What are the two methods insurance companies use in settling claims?

_____

3 List the five factors that affect home insurance costs.

_____

_____

_____

Apply Yourself!

Objective 3

Research the Web to learn about the natural disasters that occur most frequently in your part of the country. How would you protect your home from such natural disasters?

Automobile Insurance Coverages

Motor vehicle crashes cost over $150 billion in lost wages and medical bills every year. Traffic accidents can destroy people's lives physically, financially, and emotionally. Buying insurance can't eliminate the pain and suffering that vehicle accidents cause. It can, however, reduce the financial impact.

Every state in the United States has a **financial responsibility law,** a law that requires drivers to prove that they can pay for damage or injury caused by an automobile accident. Nearly all states have laws requiring people to carry motor vehicle insurance. In the remaining states, most people buy motor vehicle insurance by choice. Very few people have the money they would need to meet financial responsibility requirements on their own.

The coverage provided by motor vehicle insurance falls into two categories. One is protection for bodily injury. The other is protection for property damage (see Exhibit 8–7).

OBJECTIVE 4
Identify the important types of automobile insurance coverage.

financial responsibility law State legislation that requires drivers to prove their ability to cover the cost of damage or injury caused by an automobile accident.

Exhibit **8–7**   Two Major Categories of Automobile Insurance

Buying bodily injury and property damage coverage can reduce the financial impact of an accident. _What type of expenses would be paid for by bodily injury liability coverage?_

Motor Vehicle Bodily Injury Coverages

Most of the money that motor vehicle insurance companies pay out in claims goes for legal expenses, medical expenses, and other costs that arise when someone is injured. The main types of bodily injury coverage are bodily injury liability, medical payments, and uninsured motorist's protection.

bodily injury liability Coverage for the risk of financial loss due to legal expenses, medical costs, lost wages, and other expenses associated with injuries caused by an automobile accident for which the insured was responsible.

BODILY INJURY LIABILITY **Bodily injury liability** is insurance that covers physical injuries caused by a vehicle accident for which you were responsible. If pedestrians, people in other vehicles, or passengers in your vehicle are injured or killed, bodily injury liability coverage pays for expenses related to the crash.

Liability coverage is usually expressed by three numbers, such as 100/300/50. These amounts represent thousands of dollars of coverage. The first two numbers refer to bodily injury coverage. In the example above, $100,000 is the maximum amount that the insurance company will pay for the injuries of any one person in any one accident. The second number, $300,000, is the maximum amount the company will pay all injured parties (two or more) in any one accident. The third number, $50,000, indicates the limit for payment for damage to the property of others (see Exhibit 8–8).

medical payments coverage Automobile insurance that covers medical expenses for people injured in one's car.

MEDICAL PAYMENTS COVERAGE **Medical payments coverage** is insurance that applies to the medical expenses of anyone who is injured in your vehicle, including you. This type of coverage also provides additional medical benefits for you and members of your family; it pays medical expenses if you or your family members are injured while riding in another person's vehicle or if any of you are hit by a vehicle.

UNINSURED MOTORIST'S PROTECTION Unfortunately, you cannot assume that everyone who is behind the wheel is carrying insurance. How can you guard yourself and your passengers against the risk of getting into an accident with someone who has no insurance? The answer is uninsured motorist's protection.

uninsured motorist's protection Automobile insurance coverage for the cost of injuries to a person and members of his or her family caused by a driver with inadequate insurance or by a hit-and-run driver.

Uninsured motorist's protection is insurance that covers you and your family members if you are involved in an accident with an uninsured or hit-and-run driver. In most states it does not cover damage to the vehicle itself. Penalties for driving uninsured vary by state, but they generally include stiff fines and suspension of driving privileges.

Underinsured motorist's coverage protects you when another driver has some insurance, but not enough to pay for the injuries he or she has caused.

Exhibit 8–8

Automobile Liability Insurance Coverage

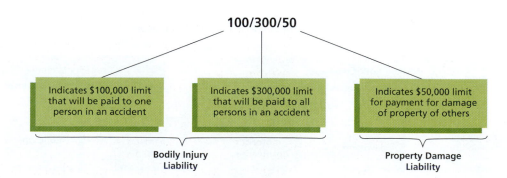

The three numbers used to describe liability coverage refer to the limits on different types of payments. *Why do you think the middle number is the highest?*

Motor Vehicle Property Damage Coverage

One afternoon, during a summer storm, Carrie was driving home from her job as a hostess at a pancake house. The rain was coming down in buckets, and she couldn't see very well. As a result, she didn't realize that the car in front of her had stopped to make a left turn, and she hit the car. The crash totaled Carrie's new car. Fortunately, she had purchased property damage coverage. Property damage coverage protects you from financial loss if you damage someone else's property or if your vehicle is damaged. It includes property damage liability, collision, and comprehensive physical damage.

PROPERTY DAMAGE LIABILITY **Property damage liability** is motor vehicle insurance that applies when you damage the property of others. In addition, it protects you when you're driving another person's vehicle with the owner's permission. Although the damaged property is usually another car, the coverage also extends to buildings and to equipment such as street signs and telephone poles.

property damage liability Automobile insurance coverage that protects a person against financial loss when that person damages the property of others.

COLLISION **Collision** insurance covers damage to your vehicle when it is involved in an accident. It allows you to collect money no matter who was at fault. However, the amount you can collect is limited to the actual cash value of your vehicle at the time of the accident. If your vehicle has many extra features, make sure that you have a record of its condition and value.

collision Automobile insurance that pays for damage to the insured's car when it is involved in an accident.

COMPREHENSIVE PHYSICAL DAMAGE Comprehensive physical damage coverage protects you if your vehicle is damaged in a nonaccident situation. It covers your vehicle against risks such as fire, theft, falling objects, vandalism, hail, floods, tornadoes, earthquakes, and avalanches.

No-Fault Insurance

To reduce the time and cost of settling vehicle injury cases, various states are trying a number of alternatives. Under the **no-fault system,** drivers who are involved in accidents collect money from their own insurance companies. It doesn't matter who caused the accident. Each company pays the insured up to the limits of his or her coverage. Because no-fault systems vary by state, you should investigate the coverage of no-fault insurance in your state.

no-fault system An automobile insurance program in which drivers involved in accidents collect medical expenses, lost wages, and related injury costs from their own insurance companies.

Other Automobile Insurance Coverages

Several other kinds of motor vehicle insurance are available to you. *Wage loss insurance* pays for any salary or income you might have lost because of being injured in a vehicle accident. Wage loss insurance is usually required in states with a no-fault insurance system. In other states it's available by choice.

Towing and emergency road service coverage pays for mechanical assistance in the event that your vehicle breaks down. This can be helpful on long trips or during bad weather. If necessary, you can get your vehicle towed to a service station. However, once your vehicle arrives at the repair shop, you are responsible for paying the bill. If you belong to an automobile club, your membership may include towing coverage. If that's the case, paying for emergency road service coverage could be a waste of money. *Rental reimbursement coverage* pays for a rental car if your vehicle is stolen or being repaired.

CONCEPT CHECK 8–4

1 List the three main types of bodily injury coverage.

_____

_____

2 In the space provided, write "T" if the statement is true, "F" if it is false.

    a. Financial responsibility law requires drivers to prove that they can pay for damage or injury caused by an automobile accident. _____

    b. Insurance that covers physical injuries caused by a vehicle accident for which you were responsible is called uninsured motorist's protection. _____

    c. Automobile liability coverage is usually expressed by three numbers 100/300/50. _____

    d. The first two numbers in 100/300/50 refer to the limit for payment for damage to the property of others. _____

    e. Uninsured motorist's protection is insurance that covers you and your family members if you are involved in an accident with an uninsured motorist or hit-and-run driver. _____

    f. Collision insurance covers damage to your vehicle when it is involved in an accident. _____

3 What is no-fault insurance? What is its purpose?

_____

_____

4 List at least three other kinds of automobile insurance that are available to you.

_____

_____

Apply Yourself!

Objective 4

Research the make and model of vehicles that are most frequently stolen, consequently resulting in higher insurance rates.

Automobile Insurance Costs

OBJECTIVE 5

Evaluate factors that affect the cost of automobile insurance.

Motor vehicle insurance is not cheap. The average household spends more than $1,200 for motor vehicle insurance yearly. The premiums are related to the amount of claims insurance companies pay out each year. Your automobile insurance cost is directly related to coverage amounts and factors such as the vehicle, your place of residence, and your driving record. (See accompanying Kiplinger's Personal Finance feature.)

AUTOMOBILE INSURANCE | *By Kimberly Lankford*

The New Math of Auto Coverage

Auto insurers are making big changes in the way they price policies, and that can mean big savings for you. When Nick Scarafile received his policy-renewal notice last December, his premium had dropped 26%—and he hadn't changed his cars or his coverage.

Scarafile's insurer, New York Central Mutual, had started to take a much closer look at the driving records and credit histories of its policyholders. Because he has an excellent credit rating, Scarafile ended up with "the most significant decrease" he'd ever seen.

In the past, most insurers based their premiums on only a handful of variables—type of car, place of residence, age, marital status and driving record. Now they focus on 30 or more factors. "I predict that the 14 companies I work with will all change their pricing within the next few years," says Tom Minkler, an independent agent in Keene, N.H.

Pinpointing Risk. Insurers have been taking your credit history into consideration for some time (in states where that's legal) because they've found a strong correlation between credit history and insurance claims. Now they study credit reports in even more detail, noting, for example, if you've made payments 30 or 60 days late.

Insurance companies are also looking more closely at the type of car you drive. In addition to studying damage and theft claims for that model, they're examining passenger injury claims and the amount of damage done to other vehicles and their occupants.

Because they now have the computing power to pinpoint risk and match it to specific prices, insurers no longer have to cram a variety of people into a wide pricing tier. Allstate, for example, has gone from using seven pricing tiers to 384. As a result, drivers with the best records saw their rates drop as much as 25%. "If you're a better driver, your rates are likely to fall because the subsidies that you've provided to worse drivers will be reduced," says Bob Hartwig, president of the Insurance Information Institute.

Even people with poor driving records are likely to benefit, however. In the past, those drivers were relegated to high-risk insurers that charged hefty premiums. That's because mainstream companies didn't have a system for pricing high-risk policies for drivers with multiple accidents or major violations. Now mainstream companies are offering to cover

riskier drivers, often at lower rates than those of high-risk insurers.

Special Perks. The company that offered you the lowest price under the old rules may no longer have the best deal. Even under the new pricing structures, "the difference in premiums can be several hundred dollars," says Minkler.

You might benefit from working with an agent to find the best price. Scarafile, who is himself an agent in Utica, N.Y., uses a rating service that immediately checks a client's credit, insurance claims and driving record to get price quotes from several companies. (You can find an agent in your area through www.iiaba.net; also contact agents who sell for a single company, such as Allstate or State Farm.)

SOURCE: Reprinted with permission from the June issue of *Kiplinger's Personal Finance*. Copyright © 2007 The Kiplinger Washington Editors, Inc.

Questions

1. Why did Nick Scarafile's automobile insurance premium drop by 26 percent even though he had not changed his cars or his coverage?

2. How do insurers pinpoint their risks in determining your automobile insurance premium?

3. What can you do to lower your automobile insurance premium?

Amount of Coverage

The amount you will pay for insurance depends on the amount of coverage you require. You need enough coverage to protect yourself legally and financially.

LEGAL CONCERNS   As discussed earlier, most people who are involved in motor vehicle accidents cannot afford to pay an expensive court settlement with their own money. For this reason, most drivers buy liability insurance.

In the past, bodily injury liability coverage of 10/20 was usually enough. However, some people have been awarded millions of dollars in recent cases, so coverage of 100/300 is usually recommended.

did you know?

Foods and drinks that were reported as the most common distractions in auto accidents: coffee, hot soup, tacos, chili-covered foods, hamburgers, chicken, jelly- or cream-filled doughnuts, and soft drinks.

PROPERTY VALUES   Just as medical expenses and legal settlements have increased, so has the cost of vehicles. Therefore, you should consider a policy with a limit of $50,000 or even $100,000 for property damage liability.

Motor Vehicle Insurance Premium Factors

Vehicle type, rating territory, and driver classification are three other factors that influence insurance costs.

VEHICLE TYPE   The year, make, and model of a vehicle will affect insurance costs. Vehicles that have expensive replacement parts and complicated repairs will cost more to insure. Also, premiums will probably be higher for vehicle makes and models that are frequently stolen.

RATING TERRITORY   In most states your rating territory is the place of residence used to determine your vehicle insurance premium. Different locations have different costs. For example, rural areas usually have fewer accidents and less frequent occurrences of theft. Your insurance would probably cost less there than if you lived in a large city.

DRIVER CLASSIFICATION   Driver classification is based on age, sex, marital status, driving record, and driving habits. In general, young drivers (under 25) and elderly drivers (over 70) have more frequent and more serious accidents. As a result these groups pay higher premiums. Your driving record will also influence your insurance premiums. If you have accidents or receive tickets for traffic violations, your rates will increase.

assigned risk pool   Consists of people who are unable to obtain automobile insurance due to poor driving or accident records and must obtain coverage at high rates through a state program that requires insurance companies to accept some of them.

The cost and number of claims that you file with your insurance company will also affect your premium. If you file expensive claims, your rates will increase. If you have too many claims, your insurance company may cancel your policy. You will then have more difficulty getting coverage from another company. To deal with this problem, every state has an assigned risk pool. An **assigned risk pool** includes all the people who can't get motor vehicle insurance. Some of these people are assigned to each insurance company operating in the state. These policyholders pay several times the normal rates, but they do get coverage. Once they establish a good driving record, they can reapply for insurance at regular rates.

Insurance companies may also consider your credit score when deciding whether to sell, renew, or cancel a policy and what premium to charge. However, an insurer cannot refuse to issue you a home or auto insurance policy solely based on your credit report. Read the accompanying Personal Finance in Practice box to understand how insurance companies use credit information.

Personal Finance in Practice

> How Insurance Companies Use Credit Information

The Fair Credit Reporting Act (FCRA, discussed in Chapter 5) allows insurance companies to examine your credit report without your permission. These companies believe that consumers who are financially responsible have fewer and less costly losses and therefore should pay less for their insurance. Insurance companies use credit scores in two ways:

- *Underwriting*—deciding whether to issue you a new policy or to renew your existing policy. Some state laws prohibit insurance companies from refusing to issue you a new policy or from renewing your existing policy based solely on information obtained from your credit report. In addition, some state laws prohibit insurance companies from using your credit information as the sole factor in accepting you and placing you into a specific company within their group of companies.

- *Rating*—deciding what price to charge you for your insurance, either by placing you into a specific rating tier, or level, or by placing you into a specific company within their group of companies. Some insurance companies use credit information along with other more traditional rating factors such as motor vehicle records and claims history. Where permitted by state law, some insurance companies may use credit reports only to determine your rate.

The FCRA requires an insurance company to tell you if it has taken "adverse action" against you because of your credit report information. If the company tells you that you have been adversely affected, it must also tell you the name of the national credit bureau that supplied the information so you can get a free copy of your credit report. The best way to know for sure if your credit score is affecting your acceptance with an insurer for the best policy at the best rate is to ask.

Reducing Vehicle Insurance Premiums

Two ways in which you can reduce your vehicle insurance costs are by comparing companies and taking advantage of discounts.

COMPARING COMPANIES Rates and services vary among motor vehicle insurance companies. Even among companies in the same area, premiums can vary by as much as 100 percent. You should compare the service and rates of local insurance agents. Most states publish this type of information. Furthermore, you can check a company's reputation with sources such as *Consumer Reports* or your state insurance department.

PREMIUM DISCOUNTS The best way for you to keep your rates down is to maintain a good driving record by avoiding accidents and traffic tickets. In addition, most insurance companies offer various discounts. If you are under 25, you can qualify for reduced rates by taking a driver training program or maintaining good grades in college.

Furthermore, installing security devices will decrease the chance of theft and lower your insurance costs. Being a non-smoker can qualify you for lower motor vehicle insurance premiums as well. Discounts are also offered for insuring two or more vehicles with the same company.

did you know?

An automobile insurance company once paid $3,600 for damages to a car in an accident caused by a mouse. The critter apparently got into the car while it was parked and then crawled up the driver's pants leg while the car was on an interstate highway. The driver lost control of the vehicle and crashed into a roadside barrier. Another claim resulted when a barbecued steak fell off a 17th-floor balcony and dented a car.

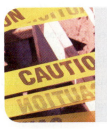

CAUTION! Your insurance company may charge an extra fee if you are involved in an accident or cited for a serious traffic violation. Worse, the insurer may not renew your insurance policy.

273

Chapter Summary

Objective 1   The main types of risk are personal risk, property risk, and liability risk. Risk management methods include avoidance, reduction, assumption, and shifting.

Planning an insurance program is a way to manage risks.

Property and liability insurance protect your homes and motor vehicles against financial loss.

Objective 2   A homeowner's policy provides coverage for buildings and other structures, additional living expenses, personal property, personal liability and related coverages, and specialized coverages.

Renter's insurance provides many of the same kinds of protection as homeowner's policies.

Objective 3   The factors that affect home insurance coverage and costs include the location, the type of structure, the coverage amount and policy type, discounts, and the choice of insurance company.

Objective 4   Motor vehicle bodily injury coverages include bodily injury liability, medical payments coverage, and uninsured motorist's protection.

Motor vehicle property damage coverages include property damage liability, collision, and comprehensive physical damage.

Objective 5   Motor vehicle insurance costs depend on the amount of coverage you need as well as vehicle type, rating territory, and driver classification.

Key Terms

Self-Test Problems

1. Eric Fowler and his wife, Susan, just purchased their first home, which cost $130,000. They purchased a homeowner's policy to insure the home for $120,000 and personal property for $75,000. They declined any coverage for additional living expenses. The deductible for the policy is $500.

   Soon after Eric and Susan moved into their new home, a strong windstorm caused damage to their roof. They reported the roof damage to be $17,000. While the roof was under repair, the couple had to live in a nearby hotel for three days. The hotel bill amounted to $320. Assuming the insurance company settles claims using the replacement value method, what amount will the insurance company pay for the damages to the roof?

2. Eric's Ford Mustang and Susan's Toyota Prius are insured with the same insurance agent. They have 50/100/15 vehicle insurance coverage. The very week of the windstorm, Susan had an accident. She lost control of her car, hit a parked car, and damaged a storefront. The damage to the parked car was $4,300 and the damage to the store was $15,400. What amount will the insurance company pay for Susan's car accident?

Solutions

1. Home damages:

Home value: $130,000
Insured amount: $120,000
Damage amount reported: $17,000
Additional living expenses incurred: $320
Total expenses incurred from windstorm: $17,320
Deductible on the policy: $500
Insurance company covered amount ($17,000 − $500 deductible): $16,500
Eric and Susan's costs ($500 + $320 hotel bill): $820

2. Car accident:

Store damage amount: $15,400
Parked car damage amount: $4,300
Total damages: $19,700
Insurance company covered amount (50/100/15): $15,000
Eric and Susan's costs ($19,700 − $15,000): $4,700

Problems

1. Most home insurance policies cover jewelry for $1,000 and silverware for $2,500 unless items are covered with additional insurance. If $3,500 worth of jewelry and $3,800 worth of silverware were stolen from a family, what amount of the claim would not be covered by insurance? (Obj. 2)

2. What amount would a person with actual cash value (ACV) coverage receive for two-year-old furniture destroyed by a fire? The furniture would cost $1,000 to replace today and had an estimated life of five years. (Obj. 2)

3. What would it cost an insurance company to replace a family's personal property that originally cost $18,000? The replacement costs for the items have increased 15 percent. (Obj. 2)

4. If Carissa Dalton has a $130,000 home insured for $100,000, based on the 80 percent coinsurance provision, how much would the insurance company pay on a $5,000 claim? (Obj. 2)

5. For each of the following situations, what amount would the insurance company pay? (Obj. 2)

   a. Wind damage of $785; the insured has a $500 deductible.
   b. Theft of a stereo system worth $1,300; the insured has a $250 deductible.
   c. Vandalism that does $375 of damage to a home; the insured has a $500 deductible.

6. Becky Fenton has 25/50/10 automobile insurance coverage. If two other people are awarded $35,000 each for injuries in an auto accident in which Becky was judged at fault, how much of this judgment would the insurance cover? (Obj. 4)

7. Kurt Simmons has 50/100/15 auto insurance coverage. One evening he lost control of his vehicle, hitting a parked car and damaging a storefront along the street. Damage to the parked car was $5,400, and damage to the store was $12,650. What amount will the insurance company pay for the damages? What amount will Kurt have to pay? (Obj. 4)

8. Beverly and Kyle Nelson currently insure their cars with separate companies, paying $450 and $375 a year. If they insured both cars with the same company, they would save 10 percent on the annual premiums. What would be the future value of the annual savings over 10 years based on an annual interest rate of 6 percent? (Obj. 4)

9. When Carolina's house burned down, she lost household items worth a total of $25,000. Her house was insured for $80,000 and her homeowner's policy provided coverage for personal belongings up to 55 percent of the insured value of the house. Calculate how much insurance coverage Carolina's policy provides for her personal possessions and whether she will receive payment for all of the items destroyed in the fire. (Obj. 2)

10. Matt and Kristin are newly married and living in their first house. The yearly premium on their homeowner's insurance policy is $450 for the coverage they need. Their insurance company offers a 5 percent discount if they install dead-bolt locks on all exterior doors. The couple can also receive a 2 percent discount if they install smoke detectors on each floor. They have contacted a locksmith, who will provide and install dead-bolt locks on the two exterior doors for $60 each. At the local hardware store, smoke detectors cost $8 each, and the new house has two floors. Kristin and Matt can install them themselves. What discount will Matt and Kristin receive if they install the dead-bolt locks? If they install smoke detectors? (Obj. 2)

11. In the preceding example, assuming their insurance rates remain the same, how many years will it take Matt and Kristin to earn back in discounts the cost of the dead-bolts? The cost of the smoke detectors? Would you recommend Matt and Kristin invest in the safety items? Why or why not? (Obj. 2)

Questions

1. Survey friends and relatives to determine the types of insurance coverages they have. Also, obtain information about the process used to select these coverages. (Obj. 1)

2. Outline a personal insurance plan with the following phases: *(a)* identify personal, financial, and property risks; *(b)* set goals you might achieve when obtaining needed insurance coverages; and *(c)* describe actions you might take to achieve these insurance goals. (Obj. 1)

3. Talk to a financial planner or an insurance agent about the financial difficulties faced by people who lack adequate home and auto insurance. What common coverages do many people overlook? (Obj. 2)

4. Contact two or three insurance agents to obtain information about home or renter's insurance. Use *Your Personal Financial Plan* sheet 29 to compare the coverages and costs. (Obj. 2)

5. Examine a homeowner's or renter's insurance policy. What coverages does the policy include? Does the policy contain unclear conditions or wording? (Obj. 3)

Case in Point

WE RENT, SO WHY DO WE NEED INSURANCE?

"Have you been down in the basement?" Nathan asked his wife, Erin, as he entered their apartment.

"No, what's up?" responded Erin.

"It's flooded because of all that rain we got last weekend!" he exclaimed.

"Oh no! We have the extra furniture my mom gave us stored down there. Is everything ruined?" Erin asked.

"The couch and coffee table are in a foot of water; the loveseat was the only thing that looked OK. Boy, I didn't realize the basement of this building wasn't waterproof. I'm going to call our landlady to complain."

As Erin thought about the situation, she remembered that when they moved in last fall, Kathy, their landlady, had informed them that her insurance policy covered the building but not the property belonging to each tenant. Because of this, they had purchased renter's insurance. "Nathan, I think our renter's insurance will cover the damage. Let me give our agent a call."

When Erin and Nathan purchased their insurance, they had to decide whether they wanted to be insured for cash value or for replacement costs. Replacement was more expensive, but it meant they would collect enough to go out and buy new household items at today's prices. If they had opted for cash value, the couch for which Erin's mother had paid $1,000 five years ago would be worth less than $500 today.

Erin made the call and found out their insurance did cover the furniture in the basement, and at replacement value after they paid the deductible. The $300 they had invested in renter's insurance last year was well worth it!

Not every renter has as much foresight as Erin and Nathan. Fewer than 4 in 10 renters have renter's insurance. Some aren't even aware they need it. They may assume they are covered by the landlord's insurance, but they aren't. This mistake can be costly.

Think about how much you have invested in your possessions and how much it would cost to replace them. Start with your stereo equipment or the flat screen television and DVD player that you bought last year. Experts suggest that people who rent start thinking about these things as soon as they move into their first apartment. Your policy should cover your personal belongings and provide funds for living expenses if you are dispossessed by a fire or other disaster.

Questions

1. Why is it important for people who rent to have insurance?
2. Does the building owner's property insurance ever cover the tenant's personal property?
3. What is the difference between cash value and replacement value?
4. When shopping for renter's insurance, what coverage features should you look for?

Continuing Case

Vikki and Tim Treble (ages 30 and 32) have been married for two years. They bought and moved into their first house within the last six months and have been decorating and making minor renovations ever since. The first room they concentrated on was the baby's room. Their daughter Molly was born only two months ago.

Vikki is on maternity leave and will soon return to work full-time. Due to all of the changes within their family and home, Vikki and Tim are re-evaluating their insurance coverage. Even Vikki's parents, who just lowered their premium with new auto insurance coverage, advise Vikki and Tim to review their home and auto policies annually. The young couple knows that they haven't paid much attention to insurance before. It is time they ask themselves: do we have the right coverage for our home and autos?

Vikki and Tim's financial statistics are shown below:

Assets:
Checking/savings account $15,000
Emergency fund $20,000
House $250,000
Car $6,000 (Vikki), $7,000 (Tim)
Household possessions $5,000
401(k) balance $45,000 (Vikki), $30,000 (Tim)
College savings $300 (from baby gifts)

Liabilities:
Mortgage $200,000

Income:
Gross Salary: $58,000 per year (Vikki), $62,000 (Tim)
After-tax monthly salary: $3,383 (Vikki), $3,617 (Tim)

Monthly Expenses:
Mortgage $1,200
Property tax/Insurance $500
Daily living expenses (including utilities, food, child care, diapers) $2,100
Student loan $250

Entertainment $300
Gas/repairs $450

Retirement Savings:
401(k) 10% of gross monthly salary

Questions

1. What insurance goals and risk management plan should Vikki and Tim have?
2. Discuss the home insurance policy Vikki and Tim should have.
3. What types of auto insurance coverage should they consider? What can affect their premium?
4. How can they use *Your Personal Financial Plan* sheets 26–30?

Spending Diary

"MY SPENDING TAKES MOST OF MY MONEY. SO AFTER PAYING FOR CAR INSURANCE, MY BUDGET IS REALLY TIGHT."

Directions

As you continue (or start using) Your Daily Spending Diary sheets, you should be able to make better choices for your spending priorities. The financial data you develop will help you better understand your spending patterns and help you plan for achieving financial goals. The Daily Spending Diary sheets are located in Appendix C at the end of the book and on the Student Web site at www.mhhe.com/kdh.

Questions

1. What information from your Daily Spending Diary might encourage you to use your money differently?

2. How can your spending habits be developed to ensure that you will be able to afford appropriate home and auto insurance coverage?

Current Insurance Policies and Needs

Financial Planning Activities: Establish a record of current and needed insurance coverage. List current insurance policies and areas where new or additional coverage is needed.

Suggested Web Sites: www.insure.com   www.insweb.com

Current Coverage	Needed Coverage
Property	
Company _____	
Policy No. _____	
Coverage amounts _____	
Deductible _____	
Annual premium _____	
Agent _____	
Address _____	
Phone _____	
Web site _____	
Automobile Insurance	
Company _____	
Policy No. _____	
Coverage amounts _____	
Deductible _____	
Annual premium _____	
Agent _____	
Address _____	
Phone _____	
Web site _____	
Disability Income Insurance	
Company _____	
Policy No. _____	
Coverage _____	
Contact _____	
Phone _____	
Web site _____	
Health Insurance	
Company _____	
Policy No. _____	
Policy provisions _____	
Contact _____	
Phone _____	
Web site _____	
Life Insurance	
Company _____	
Policy No. _____	
Type of policy _____	
Amount of coverage _____	
Cash value _____	
Agent _____	
Phone _____	
Web site _____	

What's Next for Your Personal Financial Plan?

- Talk with friends and relatives to determine the types of insurance coverage they have.
- Locate Web sites that provide additional useful information for various insurance coverages.

Name: _____   **Date:** _____

Home Inventory

Financial Planning Activities: Create a record of personal belongings for use when settling home insurance claims. For areas of the home, list your possessions including a description (model, serial number), cost, and date of acquisition.

Suggested Web Sites: www.ireweb.com   http://money.com

Item, Description	Cost	Date Acquired
Attic		
Bathroom		
Bedrooms		
Family room		
Living room		
Hallways		
Kitchen		
Dining room		
Basement		
Garage		
Other items		

What's Next for Your Personal Financial Plan?

- Survey others about the areas of insurance they have and other coverages they are considering.
- Talk to a local insurance agent to point out the areas of protection that many people tend to overlook.

Determining Needed Property Insurance

Financial Planning Activities: Determine property insurance needed for a home or apartment. Estimate the value and your needs for the categories below.

Suggested Web Sites: www.iii.org   www.quicken.com

Real Property (this section not applicable to renters)

Current replacement value of home $ _____

Personal Property

Estimated value of appliances, furniture, clothing and other household $ _____
items (conduct an inventory)

Type of coverage for personal property (check one)

    Actual cash value   ☐

    Replacement value   ☐

Additional coverage for items with limits on standard personal property coverage such as jewelry, firearms, silverware, and photographic, electronic, and computer equipment

Item	Amount
_____	_____
_____	_____
_____	_____

Personal Liability

Amount of additional personal liability coverage desired for $ _____
possible personal injury claims

Specialized Coverages

If appropriate, investigate flood or earthquake coverage excluded from $ _____
home insurance policies

Note: Use Sheet 29 to compare companies, coverages, and costs for apartment or home insurance.

What's Next for Your Personal Financial Plan?

- Outline the steps involved in planning an insurance program.
- Outline special types of property and liability insurance such as personal computer insurance, trip cancellation insurance, and liability insurance.

Name: _____   Date: _____

Apartment/Home Insurance Comparison

Financial Planning Activities: Research and compare companies, coverages, and costs for apartment or home insurance. Contact three insurance agents to obtain the information requested below.

Suggested Web Sites: www.freeinsurancequotes.com   www.insure.com

Type of building: ☐ apartment   ☐ home   ☐ condominium

Location: _____

Type of construction _____ Age of building _____

Company name			
Agent's name, address, and phone			
Coverage: Dwelling $ Other structure $ (does not apply to apartment/condo coverage)	Premium	Premium	Premium
Personal property $			
Additional living expenses $			

Personal liability
    Bodily injury
    $
    Property damage
    $			

Medical payments
    Per person
    $
    Per accident
    $			

Deductible amount			
Other coverage $			
Service charges or fees			
Total Premium			

What's Next for Your Personal Financial Plan?

- Talk to an insurance agent or claim adjuster to determine the type of documentation required for a claim settlement.
- List the reasons most commonly given by renters for not having renter's insurance.

Automobile Insurance Cost Comparison

Financial Planning Activities: Research and compare companies, coverages, and costs for auto insurance. Contact three insurance agents to obtain the information requested below.

Suggested Web Sites: www.autoinsuranceindepth.com   www.progressive.com

Automobile (year, make, model, engine size) _____

Driver's age _____ Sex _____   Total miles driven in a year _____

Full- or part-time driver? _____   Total miles driven in a year _____

Driver's education completed? _____

Accidents or violations within the past three years? _____

Company name			
Agent's name, address, and phone			
Policy length (6 months, 1 year)			

Coverage:
Bodily injury liability
  Per person
  $
  Per accident
  $
	Premium	**Premium**	**Premium**

Property damage liability per accident $			
Collision deductible $			
Comprehensive deductible $			
Medical payments per person $			

Uninsured motorist liability
  Per person
  $
  Per accident
  $			

Other coverage			
Service charges			
Total Premium			

What's Next for Your Personal Financial Plan?

- Make a list of some arguments in favor of and against mandatory auto insurance.
- Talk to friends, relatives, and insurance agents to determine methods of reducing the cost of auto insurance.

9 Health and Disability Income Insurance

Getting Personal

Should you be concerned about health insurance? Disability income insurance? For each of the following statements, select "yes" or "no" to indicate your behavior regarding these health insurance and disability insurance statements.

	Yes	No
1. Since I am a young adult, I don't really need health insurance.	____	____
2. Since I am a healthy adult, I don't need to worry about disability income insurance.	____	____
3. If my employer does not provide health insurance, I can easily and inexpensively purchase my own insurance.	____	____
4. I am aware of some of the trade-offs of different health insurance policies.	____	____
5. I am aware of health care plans offered by private companies and by the government.	____	____

After studying this chapter, you will be asked to reassess health and disability income insurance and to reconsider your responses to these items.

Your Personal Financial Plan Sheets

31. Assessing Current and Needed Health Care Insurance
32. Disability Income Insurance Needs

Objectives

In this chapter, you will learn to:

1. Recognize the importance of health insurance in financial planning.
2. Analyze the costs and benefits of various types of health insurance coverage as well as major provisions in health insurance policy.
3. Assess the trade-offs of different health insurance plans.
4. Evaluate the differences among health care plans offered by private companies and by the government.
5. Explain the importance of disability income insurance in financial planning and identify its sources.
6. Explain why the costs of health insurance and health care have been increasing.

Why is this important?

Nearly 48 million Americans lack health insurance, and those who have it are struggling with coverage cutbacks, higher copayments for doctor's office visits, and rising deductibles for out-of-pocket expenses before a policy begins. Only 11 percent of consumers feel they can handle upcoming bills. Meanwhile, hospitals and doctors are being squeezed by rising costs and cutbacks on reimbursements from insurers. This chapter can help you meet your financial goals even when dealing with unexpected medical costs and inability to work.

Health Insurance and Financial Planning

What Is Health Insurance?

Health insurance is a form of protection that eases the financial burden people may experience as a result of illness or injury. You pay a *premium,* or fee, to the insurer. In return the company pays most of your medical costs. Although plans vary in what they cover, they may reimburse you for hospital stays, doctors' visits, medications, and sometimes vision and dental care.

Health insurance includes both medical expense insurance, as discussed above, and disability income insurance. *Medical expense insurance* typically pays only the actual medical costs. *Disability income insurance* provides payments to make up for some of the income of a person who cannot work as a result of injury or illness. In this chapter the term "health insurance" refers to medical expense insurance.

Health insurance plans can be purchased in several different ways: group health insurance, individual health insurance, and COBRA.

GROUP HEALTH INSURANCE Most people who have health insurance are covered under group plans. Typically, these plans are employer sponsored. This means that the employer offers the plans and usually pays some or all of the premiums. However, not all employers provide health insurance to their employees. President Obama's plan would require large employers to provide health insurance coverage for all employees. Other organizations, such as labor unions and professional associations, also offer group plans. Group insurance plans cover you and your immediate family. The Health Insurance Portability and Accountability Act of 1996 set new federal standards to ensure that workers would not lose their health insurance if they changed jobs. As a result, a parent with a sick child, for example, can move from one group health plan to another without a lapse in coverage. Moreover, the parent will not have to pay more for coverage than other employees do.

The cost of group insurance is relatively low because many people are insured under the same *policy*—a contract with a risk-sharing group, or insurance company. However, group insurance plans vary in the amount of protection that they provide. For example, some plans limit the amount that they will pay for hospital stays and surgical procedures. If your plan does not cover all of your health insurance needs, you have several choices.

If you are married, you may be able to take advantage of a coordination of benefits (COB) provision, which is included in most group insurance plans. This provision allows you to combine the benefits from more than one insurance plan. The benefits received from all the plans are limited to 100 percent of all allowable medical expenses. For example, a couple could use benefits from one spouse's group plan and from the other spouse's plan up to 100 percent.

If this type of provision is not available to you, or if you are single, you can buy individual health insurance for added protection.

INDIVIDUAL HEALTH INSURANCE Some people do not have access to an employer-sponsored group insurance plan because they are self-employed. Others are simply dissatisfied with the coverage that their group plan provides. In these cases individual health insurance may be the answer. You can buy individual health insurance directly from the company of your choice. Plans usually cover you as an individual or cover you and your family. Individual plans can be adapted to meet your own needs. You should comparison shop, however, because rates vary.

COBRA Hakeem had a group insurance plan through his employer, but he was recently laid off. He wondered how he would be able to get medical coverage until he found a new job. Fortunately for Hakeem, the Consolidated Omnibus Budget Reconciliation Act of 1986, known as COBRA, allowed him to keep his former employer's group coverage for a set period of time. He had to pay the premiums himself, but at least the coverage wasn't canceled. When he found a new job, he was then able to switch to that employer's group plan with no break in coverage.

Not everyone qualifies for COBRA. You have to work for a private company or state or local government to benefit.

Key Web Sites for Health Insurance Information

www.insure.com
www.life-line.org

CONCEPT CHECK 9–1

1 What is health insurance?

_____

2 What are the three ways of purchasing health insurance?

_____

3 For each of the following statements, circle "T" for true or "F" for false.

   a. Health insurance is available only as a benefit from an employer.   T   F

   b. You can continue your health insurance even if you leave a job.   T   F

Apply Yourself!

Objective 1

Ask someone in a human resources office of an organization to obtain information on the health insurance provided as an employee benefit.

Health Insurance Coverage

Several types of health insurance coverage are available, either through a group plan or through individual purchase. Some benefits are included in nearly every health insurance plan; other benefits are seldom offered.

Types of Health Insurance Coverage

BASIC HEALTH INSURANCE COVERAGE **Basic health insurance coverage** includes hospital expense coverage, surgical expense coverage, and physician expense coverage.

Hospital Expense **Hospital expense coverage** pays for some or all of the daily costs of room and board during a hospital stay. Routine nursing care, minor medical supplies, and the use of other hospital facilities are covered as well. For example, covered

OBJECTIVE 2

Analyze the costs and benefits of various types of health insurance coverage as well as major provisions in health insurance policy.

basic health insurance coverage Hospital expense insurance, surgical expense insurance, and physician expense insurance.

hospital expense insurance Pays part or all of hospital bills for room, board, and other charges.

expenses would include anesthesia, laboratory fees, dressings, X-rays, local ambulance service, and the use of an operating room.

Be aware, though, that most policies set a maximum amount they will pay for each day you are in the hospital. They may also limit the number of days they will cover. Recall from Chapter 8 that many policies require a deductible. A **deductible** is a set amount that the policyholder must pay toward medical expenses before the insurance company pays benefits.

deductible An amount the insured must pay before benefits become payable by the insurance company.

Surgical Expense   **Surgical expense coverage** pays all or part of the surgeon's fees for an operation, whether it is done in a hospital or in the doctor's office. Policies often have a list of the services that they cover, which specifies the maximum payment for each type of operation. For example, a policy might allow $500 for an appendectomy. If the entire surgeon's bill is not covered, the policyholder has to pay the difference. People often buy surgical expense coverage in combination with hospital expense coverage.

surgical expense insurance Pays part or all of the surgeon's fees for an operation.

Physician Expense   **Physician expense coverage** meets some or all the costs of physician care that do not involve surgery. This form of health insurance covers treatment in a hospital, a doctor's office, or even a patient's home. Plans may cover routine doctor visits, X-rays, and lab tests. Like surgical expense, physician expense specifies maximum benefits for each service. Physician expense coverage is usually combined with surgical and hospital coverage in a package called basic health insurance.

physician expense insurance Provides benefits for doctors' fees for nonsurgical care, X-rays, and lab tests.

Major Medical Expense Insurance Coverage   Most people find that basic health insurance meets their usual needs. The cost of a serious illness or accident, however, can quickly go beyond the amounts that basic health insurance will pay. Chen had emergency surgery, which meant an operation, a two-week hospital stay, a number of lab tests, and several follow-up visits. He was shocked to discover that his basic health insurance paid less than half of the total bill, leaving him with debts of more than $10,000.

Chen would have been better protected if he had had major medical expense insurance. This coverage pays the large costs involved in long hospital stays and multiple surgeries. In other words, it takes up where basic health insurance coverage leaves off. Almost every type of care and treatment prescribed by a physician, in and out of a hospital, is covered. Maximum benefits can range from $5,000 to more than $1 million per illness per year.

Of course, this type of coverage isn't cheap. To control premiums, most major medical plans require a deductible. Some plans also include a coinsurance provision. **Coinsurance** is the percentage of the medical expenses the policyholder must pay in addition to the deductible amount. Many policies require policyholders to pay 20 or 25 percent of expenses after they have paid the deductible.

coinsurance A provision under which both the insured and the insurer share the covered losses.

Example

Ariana's policy includes an $800 deductible and a coinsurance provision requiring her to pay 20 percent of all bills. If her bill total is $3,800, for instance, the company will first exclude $800 from coverage, which is Ariana's deductible. It will then pay 80 percent of the remaining $3,000, or $2,400. Therefore, Ariana's total costs are $1,400 ($800 for the deductible and $600 for the coinsurance).

stop-loss A provision under which an insured pays a certain amount, after which the insurance company pays 100 percent of the remaining covered expenses.

Some major medical policies contain a stop-loss provision. **Stop-loss** is a provision that requires the policyholder to pay all costs up to a certain amount, after which the insurance company pays 100 percent of the remaining expenses, as long as they are covered in the policy. Typically, the policyholder will pay between $3,000 and $5,000 in out-of-pocket expenses before the coverage begins.

A Break on Health Insurance

Children are generally dropped from their parents' health insurance when they turn 18 or 19 or graduate from college. But 16 states now require insurers to cover dependent children on their parents' policies until the kids are in their mid twenties—and sometimes up to age 30.

The new rules can help cover adult children who don't have health insurance through their jobs—or don't have jobs. To qualify, grown kids must be unmarried and live in the same state as their parents. But they don't need to live with their parents or even be considered dependents for tax purposes.

This can be an attractive option for adult children who have health problems and could have trouble qualifying for affordable insurance on their own. But other young adults might

be better off declining the deal. In many states, healthy people in their twenties can purchase insurance on their own for less than $100 per month (go to www.ehealthinsurance.com or find an insurance agent through www.nahu.org). That could be less than the cost of keeping a child on your family policy.

In most states (other than New Jersey), insurers don't charge extra specifically to keep older children on your policy. But your rate might drop if you remove your child, especially if you're insuring only one child and can switch from family coverage to rates for a single person or a couple. You'd have to compare the price with what it would cost for your child to purchase individual insurance.

If you still have other children on your policy, you may be able to insure older kids at no extra

charge (as long as your insurer doesn't base premiums on the number of children). That would be the best deal.

For a list of each state's age requirements for dependent coverage, see the National Conference of State Legislatures' Web site (www.ncsl.org). Note that these laws don't apply to employers who self-insure.

SOURCE: Reprinted by permission from the August issue of *Kiplinger's Personal Finance.* Copyright © 2008 The Kiplinger Washington Editors, Inc.

1. How can new rules help cover adult children who don't have health insurance through their jobs—or don't have jobs? —————————————————————————————

—————————————————————————————

2. Where can healthy people in their twenties purchase insurance on their own for less than $100 per month? —————————————————————————————

—————————————————————————————

Major medical expense insurance may be offered as a single policy with basic health insurance coverage, or it can be bought separately. Comprehensive major medical insurance is a type of complete insurance that helps pay hospital, surgical, medical, and other bills. It has a low deductible, usually $400 to $800. Many major medical policies set limits on the benefits they will pay for certain expenses, such as surgery and hospital room and board.

HOSPITAL INDEMNITY POLICIES   A hospital indemnity policy pays benefits when you're hospitalized. Unlike most of the other plans mentioned, however, these policies don't directly cover medical costs. Instead you are paid in cash, which you can spend on medical or nonmedical expenses as you choose. Hospital indemnity policies are used as a supplement to—and not a replacement for—basic health or major medical policies. The average person who buys such a policy, however, usually pays much more in premiums than he or she receives in payments.

DENTAL EXPENSE INSURANCE   Dental expense insurance provides reimbursement for the expenses of dental services and supplies. It encourages preventive dental care. The coverage normally provides for oral examinations (including X-rays and cleanings), fillings, extractions, oral surgery, dentures, and braces. As with other insurance plans, dental insurance may have a deductible and a coinsurance provision, stating that the policyholder pays from 20 to 50 percent after the deductible.

VISION CARE INSURANCE   An increasing number of insurance companies are including vision care insurance as part of group plans. Vision care insurance may cover eye examinations, glasses, contact lenses, eye surgery, and the treatment of eye diseases.

DREAD DISEASE POLICIES   Dread disease, trip accident, death insurance, and cancer policies are usually sold through the mail, in newspapers and magazines, or by door-to-door salespeople. These kinds of policy play upon unrealistic fears, and they are illegal in many states. They cover only specific conditions, which are already fully covered if you are insured under a major medical plan.

long-term care insurance (LTC) Provides day-in, day-out care for long-term illness or disability.

Key Web Site for Long-Term Care

www.longtermcareinsurance.org

LONG-TERM CARE INSURANCE   **Long-term care insurance (LTC)** provides coverage for the expense of daily help that you may need if you become seriously ill or disabled and are unable to care for yourself. It is useful whether you require a lengthy stay in a nursing home or just need help at home with daily activities such as dressing, bathing, and household chores. Annual premiums range from less than $1,000 to over $16,000, depending on your age and extent of the coverage. The older you are when you enroll, the higher your annual premium. Typically, individual insurance plans are sold to the 50-to-80 age group, pay benefits for a maximum of two to six years, and carry a dollar limit on the total benefits they will pay. The nearby Personal Finance in Practice box can help you compare the features of long-term care policies.

Explore services available in your community to help meet long-term care needs. Care given by family members can be supplemented by visiting nurses, home health aides, friendly visitor programs, home-delivered meals, chore services, adult day care centers, and respite services for caregivers who need a break from daily responsibilities.

These services are becoming more widely available. Some or all of them may be found in your community. Your local area Agency on Aging or Office on Aging can help you locate the services you need. Call the Eldercare Locator at 1-800-677-1116 to locate your local office.

Personal Finance in Practice

> Long-Term Care Policy Checklist

The following checklist will help you compare LTC policies you may be considering:

	Policy A	Policy B		Policy A	Policy B
1. What services are covered?			**8. Are Alzheimer's disease and other organic mental and nervous disorders covered?**	_____	_____
Skilled care	_____	_____			
Intermediate care	_____	_____	**9. Does this policy require:**		
Custodial care	_____	_____	Physician certification of need?	_____	_____
Home health care	_____	_____	An assessment of activities of daily living?	_____	_____
Adult day care	_____	_____	A prior hospital stay for:		
Other	_____	_____	Nursing home care?	_____	_____
2. How much does the policy pay per day?			Home health care?	_____	_____
For skilled care	_____	_____	A prior nursing home stay for home health care coverage?	_____	_____
For intermediate care	_____	_____	**Other?**	_____	_____
For custodial care	_____	_____	**10. Is the policy guaranteed renewable?**	_____	_____
For home health care	_____	_____	**11. What is the age range of enrollment?**	_____	_____
For adult day care	_____	_____	**12. Is there a waiver-of-premium provision:**		
3. How long will benefits last?			**For nursing home care?**	_____	_____
In a nursing home for:			**For home health care?**	_____	_____
Skilled nursing care	_____	_____	**13. How long must I be confined before premiums are waived?**	_____	_____
Intermediate nursing care	_____	_____	**14. Does the policy offer an inflation adjustment feature? If so:**		
Custodial care	_____	_____	What is the rate of increase?	_____	_____
At home:	_____	_____	How often is it applied?	_____	_____
4. Does the policy have a maximum lifetime benefit? If so, what is it?			For how long?	_____	_____
For nursing home care	_____	_____	Is there an additional cost?	_____	_____
For home health care	_____	_____	**15. What does the policy cost: Per year?**	_____	_____
5. Does the policy have a maximum length of coverage for each period of confinement? If so, what is it?			With inflation feature	_____	_____
			Without inflation feature	_____	_____
For nursing home care	_____	_____	Per month?	_____	_____
For home health care	_____	_____	With inflation feature	_____	_____
6. How long must I wait before preexisting conditions are covered?	_____	_____	Without inflation feature	_____	_____
7. How many days must I wait before benefits begin?			**16. Is there a 30-day free look?**	_____	_____
For nursing home care	_____	_____			
For home health care	_____	_____			

Source: *Guide to Long-Term Care Insurance* (Washington, DC: Health Insurance Association of America, 1994), pp. 11–12.

Major Provisions in a Health Insurance Policy

All health insurance policies have certain provisions in common. You have to be sure that you understand what your policy covers. What are the benefits? What are the limits? The following are details of provisions that are usually found in health insurance policies:

- *Eligibility:* The people covered by the policy must meet specified eligibility requirements, such as family relationship and, for children, a certain age.
- *Assigned benefits:* You are reimbursed for payments when you turn in your bills and claim forms. When you assign benefits, you let your insurer make direct payments to your doctor or hospital.
- *Internal limits:* A policy with internal limits sets specific levels of repayment for certain services. Even if your hospital room costs $400 a day, you won't be able to get more than $250 if an internal limit specifies that maximum.
- *Copayment:* A **copayment** is a flat fee that you pay every time you receive a covered service. The fee is usually between $15 and $25, and the insurer pays the balance of the cost of the service. This is different from coinsurance, which is the percentage of your medical costs for which you are responsible after paying your deductible.
- *Service benefits:* Policies with this provision list coverage in terms of services, not dollar amounts: You're entitled to X-rays, for instance, not $40 worth of X-rays per visit. Service benefits provisions are always preferable to dollar amount coverage because the insurer will pay all the costs.
- *Benefit limits:* This provision defines a maximum benefit, either in terms of a dollar amount or in terms of number of days spent in the hospital.
- *Exclusions and limitations:* This provision specifies services that the policy does not cover. It may include preexisting conditions (a condition you were diagnosed with before your insurance plan took effect), cosmetic surgery, or more.
- *Guaranteed renewable:* This provision means that the insurer can't cancel the policy unless you fail to pay the premiums. It also forbids insurers to raise premiums unless they raise all premiums for all members of your group.
- *Cancellation and termination:* This provision explains the circumstances under which the insurer can cancel your coverage. It also explains how you can convert your group contract into an individual contract.

copayment A provision under which the insured pays a flat dollar amount each time a covered medical service is received after the deductible has been met.

CONCEPT CHECK 9–2

1 What three types of coverage are included in the basic health insurance?

_____

2 What benefits are provided by

_____

  a. Hospital expense coverage?_____

_____

b. Surgical expense coverage?_____

_____

c. Physician expense coverage?_____

_____

3 Match the following terms with an appropriate statement.

coinsurance   *a.* Requires the policyholder to pay all costs up to a certain amount. _____

stop-loss   *b.* The percentage of the medical expenses you must pay. _____

hospital indemnity policy *c.* A policy used as a supplement to basic health or major medical policies.

_____

exclusion and limitations *d.* Defines who is covered by the policy. _____

copayment   *e.* Specifies services that the policy does not cover. _____

eligibility   *f.* A flat fee that you pay every time you receive a covered service. _____

Apply Yourself!

Objective 2

Raj is thinking about buying major medical insurance to supplement his basic health insurance from work. Describe a situation in which Raj would need major medical.

OBJECTIVE 3

Assess the trade-offs of different health insurance plans.

Health Insurance Trade-Offs

Different health insurance policies may offer very different benefits. As you decide which insurance plan to buy, consider the following trade-offs.

REIMBURSEMENT VERSUS INDEMNITY A reimbursement policy pays you back for actual expenses. An indemnity policy provides you with specific amounts, regardless of how much the actual expenses may be.

Example

Katie and Seth are both charged $200 for an office visit to the same specialist. Katie's reimbursement policy has a deductible of $300. Once she has met the deductible, the policy will cover the full cost of such a visit. Seth's indemnity policy will pay him $125, which is what his plan provides for a visit to any specialist.

INTERNAL LIMITS VERSUS AGGREGATE LIMITS A policy with internal limits will cover only a fixed amount for an expense, such as the daily cost of room and board during a hospital stay. A policy with aggregate limits will limit only the total amount of coverage (the maximum dollar amount paid for all benefits in a year), such as $1 million in major expense benefits, or it may have no limits.

DEDUCTIBLES AND COINSURANCE The cost of a health insurance policy can be greatly affected by the size of the deductible (the set amount that the policyholder must pay toward medical expenses before the insurance company pays benefits). It can also be affected by the terms of the *coinsurance provision* (which states what percentage of the medical expenses the policyholder must pay in addition to the deductible amount).

OUT-OF-POCKET LIMITS Some policies limit the amount of money you must pay for the deductible and coinsurance. After you have reached that limit, the insurance company covers 100 percent of any additional costs. Out-of-pocket limits help you lower your financial risk, but they also increase your premiums.

BENEFITS BASED ON REASONABLE AND CUSTOMARY CHARGES Some policies consider the average fee for a service in a particular geographical area. They then use the amount to set a limit on payments to policyholders. If the standard cost of a certain procedure is $1,500 in your part of the country, then your policy won't pay more than that amount.

> ### did you know?
>
> The Employee Benefits Security Administration (EBSA) provides *Health Benefits Education for Consumers* and *Health Insurance Tips.* Call toll-free 866-444-3272 or visit www.dol.gov/ebsa.

Which Coverage Should You Choose?

Now that you are familiar with the available types of health insurance and some of their major provisions, how do you choose one? The type of coverage you choose will be affected by the amount you can afford to spend on the premiums and the level of benefits that you feel you want and need. It may also be affected by the kind of coverage your employer offers, if you are covered through your employer.

You can buy basic health coverage, major medical coverage, or both basic and major medical coverage. Any of these three choices will take care of at least some of your medical expenses. Ideally, you should get a basic plan and a major medical supplement. Another option is to purchase a comprehensive major medical policy that combines the value of both plans in a single policy. Exhibit 9–1 describes the most basic features you should look for.

Exhibit 9–1

Health Insurance Must-Haves

A health insurance plan should:
• Offer basic coverage for hospital and doctor bills
• Provide at least 120 days' hospital room and board in full
• Provide at least a $1 million lifetime maximum for each family member
• Pay at least 80 percent for out-of-hospital expenses after a yearly deductible of $500 per person or $1,000 per family
• Impose no unreasonable exclusions
• Limit your out-of-pocket expenses to no more than $3,000 to $5,000 a year, excluding dental, vision care, and precription costs

Although health insurance plans vary greatly, all plans should have the same basic features. *Would you add anything to this list of must-haves?*

Sheet 31 Assessing Current and Needed Health Care Insurance.

CONCEPT CHECK 9–3

1 As you decide which health insurance plan to buy, what trade-offs would you consider?

_____

_____

2 Match the following terms with an appropriate statement.

reimbursement   *a.*   A policy that will cover only a fixed amount of an expense. _____

indemnity   *b.*   A policy that pays you back for actual expenses. _____

internal limits   *c.*   A policy that provides you with specific amounts, regardless of how much the actual expenses may be. _____

deductible   *d.*   After you have reached a certain limit, the insurance company covers 100 percent of any additional cost. _____

out-of-pocket limit   *e.*   The set amount that you must pay toward medical expenses before the insurance company pays benefits. _____

3 What basic features should be included in your health insurance plan?

_____

_____

Apply Yourself!

Objective 3

Prepare a list of trade-offs that are important to you in a health insurance policy.

Private Health Care Plans and Government Health Care Programs

Private Health Care Plans

Most health insurance in the United States is provided by private organizations rather than by the government. Private health care plans may be offered by a number of sources: private insurance companies; hospital and medical service plans; health maintenance organizations; preferred provider organizations; home health care agencies; and employer self-funded health plans.

PRIVATE INSURANCE COMPANIES Several hundred private insurance companies are in the health insurance business. They provide mostly group health plans to employers, which in turn offer them to their employees as a benefit. Premiums may

> **OBJECTIVE 4**
>
> Evaluate the differences among health care plans offered by private companies and by the government.

Blue Cross An independent membership corporation that provides protection against the cost of hospital care.

Blue Shield An independent membership corporation that provides protection against the cost of surgical and medical care.

be fully or partially paid by the employer, with the employee paying any remainder. These policies typically pay you for medical costs you incur, or they send the payment directly to the doctor, hospital, or lab that provides the services.

HOSPITAL AND MEDICAL SERVICE PLANS Blue Cross and Blue Shield are statewide organizations similar to private health insurance companies. Each state has its own Blue Cross and Blue Shield. The "Blues" provide health insurance to millions of Americans. **Blue Cross** provides hospital care benefits. **Blue Shield** provides benefits for surgical and medical services performed by physicians.

HEALTH MAINTENANCE ORGANIZATIONS Rising health care costs have led to an increase in managed care plans. According to a recent industry survey, 23 percent of employed Americans are enrolled in some form of managed care. **Managed care** refers to prepaid health plans that provide comprehensive health care to their members. Managed care is designed to control the cost of health care services by controlling how they are used. Managed care is offered by health maintenance organizations (HMOs), preferred provider organizations (PPOs), and point-of-service plans (POSs).

Health maintenance organizations are an alternative to basic health insurance and major medical expense insurance. A **health maintenance organization (HMO)** is a health insurance plan that directly employs or contracts with selected physicians and other medical professionals to provide health care services in exchange for a fixed, prepaid monthly premium.

HMOs are based on the idea that preventive services will minimize future medical problems. Therefore, these plans typically cover routine immunizations and checkups, screening programs, and diagnostic tests. They also provide customers with coverage for surgery, hospitalization, and emergency care. If you have an HMO, you will usually pay a small copayment for each covered service. Supplemental services may include vision care and prescription services, which are typically available for an additional fee.

When you first enroll in an HMO, you must choose a plan physician from a list of doctors provided by the HMO. The physician provides or arranges for all of your health care services. You must receive care through your plan physician; if you don't, you are responsible for the cost of the service. The only exception to this rule is in the case of a medical emergency. If you experience a sudden illness or injury that would threaten your life or health if not treated immediately, you may go to the emergency room of the nearest hospital. All other care must be provided by hospitals and doctors under contract with the HMO.

HMOs are not for everyone. Many HMO customers complain that their HMO denies them necessary care. Others feel restricted by the limited choice of doctors.

Exhibit 9–2 provides some tips on using and choosing an HMO: Because HMOs require you to use only certain doctors, you should make sure that these doctors are near your home or office. You should also be able to change doctors easily if you don't like your first choice. Similarly, second opinions should always be available at the HMO's expense, and you should be able to appeal any case in which the HMO denies care. Finally, look at the costs and benefits: Will you incur out-of-pocket expenses or copayments? What services will the plan provide?

did you know?

Hundreds of millions of people must walk long distances each day to obtain their water, which is often not suitable for drinking. WaterPartners International (www.water.org) helps people obtain safe drinking water to prevent disease and water-related deaths in more than 200 communities around the world. WaterPartners does not build water systems *for* people, but *with* people to ensure long-term community sustainability.

managed care Prepaid health plans that provide comprehensive health care to members.

health maintenance organization (HMO) A health insurance plan that provides a wide range of health care services for a fixed, prepaid monthly premium.

Key Web Sites for Health Insurance Articles

www.money.cnn.com
www.kiplinger.com

preferred provider organization (PPO) A group of doctors and hospitals that agree to provide health care at rates approved by the insurer.

PREFERRED PROVIDER ORGANIZATIONS A variation on the HMO is a **preferred provider organization (PPO)**, a group of doctors and hospitals that agree to provide specified medical services to members at prearranged fees. PPOs offer these discounted services to employers either directly or indirectly through an insurance company. The premiums for PPOs are slightly higher than the premiums for HMOs.

Exhibit 9–2   Tips on Using and Choosing an HMO

How to Use an HMO

When you first enroll in an HMO, you must choose a plan physician (family practitioner, internist, pediatrician, or obstetrician-gynecologist) who provides or arranges for all of your health care services. It is extremely important that you receive your care through the plan physician. If you don't, you are responsible for the cost of the service rendered.

The only exceptions to the requirement that care be received through the plan physician are medical emergencies. A medical emergency is a sudden onset of illness or a sudden injury that would jeopardize your life or health if not treated immediately. In such instances, you may use the facilities of the nearest hospital emergency room. All other care must be provided by hospitals and doctors under contract with the HMO.

How to Choose an HMO

If you decide to enroll in an HMO, you should consider these additional factors:

1. *Accessibility.* Since you must use plan providers, it is extremely important that they be easily accessible from your home or office.

2. *Convenient office hours.* Your plan physician should have convenient office hours.

3. *Alternative physicians.* Should you become dissatisfied with your first choice of a physician, the HMO should allow you the option to change physicians.

4. *Second opinions.* You should be able to obtain second opinions.

5. *Type of coverage.* You should compare the health care services offered by various HMOs, paying particular attention to whether you will incur out-of-pocket expenses or copayments.

6. *Appeal procedures.* The HMO should have a convenient and prompt system for resolving problems and disputes.

7. *Price.* You should compare the prices various HMOs charge to ensure that you are getting the most services for your health care dollar.

What to Do When an HMO Denies Treatment or Coverage

- *Get it in writing.* To better defend your case, ask for a letter detailing the clinical reasons your claim was denied and the name and medical expertise of the HMO staff member responsible.

- *Know your rights.* The plan document or your HMO's member services department will tell you how experimental treatments are defined and covered and how the appeals process works.

- *Keep records.* Make copies of any correspondence, including payments and any reimbursements. Also, keep a written log of all conversations relevant to your claim.

- *Find advocates.* Enlist the help of your doctor, employer, and state insurance department to lobby your case before the HMO.

SOURCE: Reprinted from the May 18, 1997, issue of *BusinessWeek* by special permission. © 1999 McGraw-Hill Companies, Inc.

PPO plan members often pay no deductibles and may make minimal copayments. Whereas HMOs require members to receive care from HMO providers only, PPOs allow members greater flexibility. Members can either visit a preferred provider (a physician whom you select from a list, as in an HMO) or go to their own physicians. Patients who decide to use their own doctors do not lose coverage as they would with an HMO. Instead they must pay deductibles and larger copayments.

Increasingly, the difference between PPOs and HMOs is becoming less clear. A **point-of-service (POS) plan** combines features of both HMOs and PPOs. POSs use a network of participating physicians and medical professionals who have contracted to provide services for certain fees. As with your HMO, you choose a plan physician who manages your care and controls referrals to specialists. As long as you receive care from a plan provider, you pay little or nothing, just as you would with an HMO. However, you're allowed to seek care outside the network at a higher charge, as with a PPO.

point-of-service (POS) plan A network of selected contracted, participating providers; also called an *HMO-PPO hybrid or open-ended HMO.*

HOME HEALTH CARE AGENCIES

Rising hospital costs, new medical technology, and the increasing number of elderly people have helped make home care one of the fastest growing areas of the health care industry. Home health care consists of home health agencies; home care aide organizations; and hospices, facilities that care for the terminally ill. These providers offer medical care in a home setting in agreement with a medical order, often at a fraction of the cost hospitals would charge for a similar service.

Personal Finance in Practice

> HSAs: How They Work in 2009

1. Your company offers a health insurance policy with an annual deductible of at least $1,150.

2. You can put pretax dollars into an HSA each year, up to the amount of the deductible—but no more than $5,950 for family coverage or $3,000 for individual coverage, plus a $1,000 catch up contribution for those who are over 55.

3. You withdraw the money from your HSA tax-free, but it can be used only for your family's medical expenses. After the deductible and copays are met, insurance still typically covers 80 percent of health costs.

4. HSA plans are required to have maximum out-of-pocket spending limits, $5,800 for individuals, $11,600 for families. That's when your company's insurance kicks in again at 100 percent coverage.

5. Your company can match part or all of your HSA contributions if it wishes, just as it does with 401(k)s.

6. You can invest your HSA in stocks, bonds, or mutual funds. Unused money remains in your account at the end of the year and grows tax free.

7. You can also take your HSA with you if you change jobs or retire.

8. To help you shop for health care now that you're spending your own money, employers say they will give you detailed information about prices and quality of doctors and hospitals in your area.

Source: U.S. Department of the Treasury, www.ustreas.gov/press/releases/hp975.htm accessed February 7, 2009.

Key Web Site for Health Insurance Information

www.healthfinders.gov

EMPLOYER SELF-FUNDED HEALTH PLANS Some companies choose to self-insure. The company runs its own insurance plan, collecting premiums from employees and paying medical benefits as needed. However, these companies must cover any costs that exceed the income from premiums. Unfortunately, not all corporations have the financial assets necessary to cover these situations, which can mean a financial disaster for the company and its employees.

CAUTION!

HSA versus FSA

Don't confuse an HSA with the more familiar flexible-spending account (FSA), or flex account. Like an HSA, a flex account lets you set aside tax-free dollars you can use to pay for medical expenses that aren't covered by insurance. Unlike an HSA, a flex account isn't tied to a high-deductible policy. Also unlike an HSA, money left over in a flex account can't be carried over—if you don't use it, you lose it.

Source: *Kiplinger's Personal Finance,* October 2006, p. 90.

NEW HEALTH CARE ACCOUNTS Health savings accounts (HSAs), which Congress authorized in 2003, are the newest addition to the alphabet soup of health insurance available to American workers. Now you and your employer must sort through HSAs, health reimbursement accounts (HRAs), and flexible spending accounts (FSAs). Each has its own rules about how money is spent, how it can be spent, and how it is taxed.

How do FSAs, HRAs, and HSAs differ? FSAs allow you to contribute pretax dollars to an account managed by your employer. You use the money for health care spending but forfeit anything left over at the end of the year.

HRAs are tied to high-deductible policies. They are funded *solely* by your employer and give you a pot of money to spend on health care. You can carry over unspent money from year to year, but you lose the balance if you switch jobs. Premiums tend to be lower than for traditional insurance but higher than for HSAs. You can invest the funds in stocks, bonds, and mutual funds. The money grows tax-free but can be spent only on health care.

HSAs allow you to contribute money to a tax-free account that can be used for out-of-pocket health care expenses if you buy high-deductible health insurance policies to cover catastrophic expenses. Read the accompanying Personal Finance in Practice feature to learn how HSAs work in 2009.

Personal Finance in Practice

> A Brief Look at Medicare

Medicare is health insurance for people age 65 or older, under age 65 with certain disabilities, and any age with end-stage renal disease (permanent kidney failure requiring dialysis or a kidney transplant).

Most people get their Medicare health care coverage in one of two ways. Your costs vary depending on your plan, coverage, and the services you use.

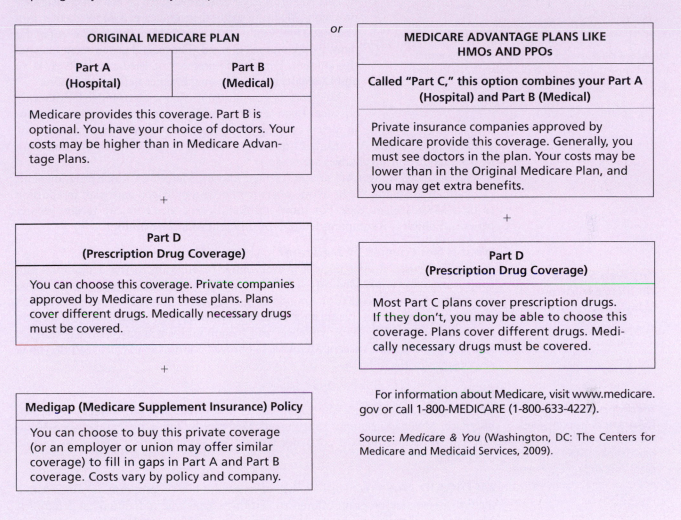

ORIGINAL MEDICARE PLAN	
Part A (Hospital)	Part B (Medical)
Medicare provides this coverage. Part B is optional. You have your choice of doctors. Your costs may be higher than in Medicare Advantage Plans.	

or

MEDICARE ADVANTAGE PLANS LIKE HMOs AND PPOs
Called "Part C," this option combines your Part A (Hospital) and Part B (Medical)
Private insurance companies approved by Medicare provide this coverage. Generally, you must see doctors in the plan. Your costs may be lower than in the Original Medicare Plan, and you may get extra benefits.

+

Part D (Prescription Drug Coverage)
You can choose this coverage. Private companies approved by Medicare run these plans. Plans cover different drugs. Medically necessary drugs must be covered.

+

Part D (Prescription Drug Coverage)
Most Part C plans cover prescription drugs. If they don't, you may be able to choose this coverage. Plans cover different drugs. Medically necessary drugs must be covered.

+

Medigap (Medicare Supplement Insurance) Policy
You can choose to buy this private coverage (or an employer or union may offer similar coverage) to fill in gaps in Part A and Part B coverage. Costs vary by policy and company.

For information about Medicare, visit www.medicare.gov or call 1-800-MEDICARE (1-800-633-4227).

Source: *Medicare & You* (Washington, DC: The Centers for Medicare and Medicaid Services, 2009).

In addition to the private sources of health insurance and health care discussed in this section, government health care programs cover over 46 million people. The next section discusses these programs.

Government Health Care Programs

The health insurance coverage discussed thus far is normally purchased through private companies. Some consumers, however, are eligible for health insurance coverage under programs offered by federal and state governments.

MEDICARE   Perhaps the best-known government health program is Medicare. *Medicare* is a federally funded health insurance program available mainly to people over 65 and to people with disabilities. Medicare has four parts: hospital insurance (Part A), medical insurance (Part B) Medicare Advantage Plan (Part C), and Prescription Drug Coverage (Part D). Medicare hospital insurance is funded by part of the Social Security payroll tax. Part A helps pay for inpatient hospital care, inpatient care in a skilled nursing facility, home health care, and hospice care. Program participants pay a single annual deductible.

Part B helps pay for doctors' services and a variety of other medical services and supplies not covered or not fully covered by Part A. Part B has a deductible and a 20 percent coinsurance provision. Medicare medical insurance is a supplemental program paid for by individuals who feel that they need it. A regular monthly premium is charged. The federal government matches this amount. For a brief summary of Medicare Parts A, B, C, and D, see the nearby Personal Finance in Practice feature.

Medicare is constantly in financial trouble. Health care costs continue to grow, and the proportion of senior citizens in society is rising. This situation puts Medicare in danger of running out of funds. According to recent projections, the program will be bankrupt by the year 2019 if no changes are made.

The Balanced Budget Act of 1997 created the new Medicare Choice program. This program allows many Medicare members to choose a managed care plan in addition to their Medicare coverage. For some additional costs, members can receive greater benefits. Exhibit 9–3 compares features of different Medicare options.

What Is Not Covered by Medicare?   Although Medicare is very helpful for meeting medical costs, it does not cover everything. In addition to the deductibles and coinsurance payments, Medicare will not cover some medical expenses at all. These are certain types of skilled or long-term nursing care, out-of-hospital prescription drugs, routine checkups, dental care, and most immunizations. Medicare also severely limits the types of services it will cover and the amount it will pay for those services. If your doctor does not accept Medicare's approved amount as payment in full, you're responsible for the difference.

Medigap

Those eligible for Medicare who would like more coverage may buy **medigap (MedSup) insurance.** Medigap insurance supplements Medicare by filling the gap between Medicare payments and medical costs not covered by Medicare. It is offered by private companies.

MEDICAID   The other well-known government health program is *Medicaid,* a medical assistance program offered to certain low-income individuals and families. Medicaid is administered by states, but it is financed by a combination of state and federal funds. Unlike Medicare, Medicaid coverage is so comprehensive that people with Medicaid do not need supplemental insurance. Typical Medicaid benefits include physicians' services, inpatient and outpatient hospital services, lab services, skilled nursing and home health services, prescription drugs, eyeglasses, and preventive care for people under the age of 21.

GOVERNMENT CONSUMER HEALTH INFORMATION WEB SITES   The Department of Health and Human Services operates more than 60 Web sites with a wealth of reliable information related to health and medicine. For example,

- *Healthfinder:* Healthfinder includes links to more than 1,000 Web sites operated by government and nonprofit organizations. It lists topics according to subject (www.hhs.gov).
- *MedlinePlus:* Medline Plus is the world's largest collection of published medical information. It was originally designed for health professionals and

did you know?

Medicare pays over $377 billion a year to more than 1 million health care providers to help more than 45 million elderly.

Key Web Site for Medicare Information

www.ssa.gov

medigap (MedSup) insurance   Supplements Medicare by filling the gap between Medicare payments and medical costs not covered by Medicare.

Exhibit **9-3**   A Comparison of Various Medicare Plans

	Current Options	New Options (Medicare and Choice)	Plan Description
Original Medicare	✔	✔	• You choose your health care providers.
			• Medicare pays your providers for covered services.
			• Most beneficiaries choose Medicare supplemental insurance to cover deductible and copayments.
Medicare health maintenance organization (HMO)	✔	✔	• You must live in the plan's service area.
			• You agree to use the plan network of doctors, hospitals, and other health providers, except in an emergency.
			• Medicare pays the HMO to provide all medical services.
Preferred provider organization (PPO)		✔	• Works like an HMO, except you have the choice to see a health provider out of the network.
			• If you do see an out-of-network provider, you will pay a higher cost.
Provider-sponsored organization (PSO)		✔	• Works like a Medicare HMO, except the networks are managed by health care providers (doctors and hospitals) rather than an insurance company.
Private fee for service		✔	• Medicare pays a lump sum to a private insurance health plan.
			• Providers can bill more than what the plan pays; you are responsible for paying the balance.
			• The plan may offer more benefits than original Medicare.
Medical savings account (MSA)		✔	• Medicare MSAs are a special type of savings account that can be used to pay medical bills.
			• Centers for Medicare and Medicaid Services (CMS) will make an annual lump-sum deposit into enrollee's account (only Medicare can deposit funds into this account).
			• MSAs work with a special private insurance company and carry a very high deductible.
			• Funds withdrawn for nonmedical purposes are taxable and subject to a penalty.

SOURCE: *Medicare & You* (Washington, DC: The Centers for Medicare and Medicaid Services, 2009).

researchers, but it's also valuable for students and others who are interested in health care and medical issues (www.nlm.nih.gov/medlineplus).

- *NIH Health Information Page:* The National Institutes of Health (NIH) operates a Web site called the NIH Health Information Page, which can direct you to the consumer health information in NIH publications and on the Internet (www.nih.gov).
- *FDA:* The Food and Drug Administration (FDA) also runs a Web site. This consumer protection agency's site provides information about the safety of various foods, drugs, cosmetics, and medical devices (www.fda.gov).

CONCEPT CHECK 9–4

1 What are the six sources of private health plans?

_____

_____

2 Match the following terms with an appropriate statement.

Blue Cross

a. A medical assistance program offered to certain low-income individuals and families. _____

Blue Shield

b. Combines features of both HMOs and PPOs. _____

HMOs

c. A statewide organization that provides hospital care benefits.

PPOS

d. A federally funded health insurance program available mainly to people over 65 and to people with disabilities._____

point of service (POS)

e. A health insurance plan that directly employs or contracts with selected physicians to provide health services in exchange for a fixed, prepaid monthly premium. _____

Medicare

f. A statewide organization that provides benefits for surgical and medical services performed by physicians. _____

Medicaid

g. A group of doctors and hospitals that agree to provide specified medical services to members at prearranged fees. _____

3 What health care services are not covered by Medicare?

_____

_____

Apply Yourself!

Objective 4

Talk to several people covered by Medicare and Medicaid to obtain information on the coverage provided and the difficulties sometimes faced.

OBJECTIVE 5

Explain the importance fo disability income insurance in financial planning and identify its sources

Disability Income Insurance

The Need for Disability Income

Before disability insurance existed, people who were ill lost more money from missed paychecks than from medical bills. Disability income insurance was set up to protect against such loss of income. This kind of coverage is very common today, and several hundred insurance companies offer it.

Disability income insurance provides regular cash income when you're unable to work because of a pregnancy, a non-work-related accident, or an illness. It protects your earning power, your most valuable resource.

The exact definition of a disability varies from insurer to insurer. Some insurers will pay you when you are unable to work at your regular job. Others will pay only if you are so ill or badly hurt that you can't work at any job. A violinist with a hand injury, for instance, might have trouble doing his or her regular work but might be able to perform a range of other jobs. A good disability income insurance plan pays you if you can't work at your regular job. A good plan will also pay partial benefits if you are able to work only part-time.

Many people make the mistake of ignoring disability insurance, not realizing that it's very important insurance to have. Disability can cause even greater financial problems than death. Disabled persons lose their earning power but still have to meet their living expenses. In addition, they often face huge costs for the medical treatment and special care that their disabilities require.

disability income insurance Provides payments to replace income when an insured person is unable to work.

Sources of Disability Income

Before you buy disability income insurance from a private insurance company, remember that you may already have some form of insurance of this kind. This coverage may be available through worker's compensation if you're injured on the job. Disability benefits may also be available through your employer or through Social Security in case of a long-term disability.

WORKER'S COMPENSATION If your disability is a result of an accident or illness that occurred on the job, you may be eligible to receive worker's compensation benefits in your state. Benefits will depend on your salary and your work history.

EMPLOYER PLANS Many employers provide disability income insurance through group insurance plans. In most cases your employer will pay part or all of the cost of such insurance. Some policies may provide continued wages for several months only, whereas others will give you long-term protection.

did you know?

Nearly one in five Americans will become disabled for one year or more before the age of 65, according to the Life Foundation, a nonprofit organization dedicated to helping consumers make smart financial decisions. The number of workers who become disabled has risen by 35 percent since 2000, according to the Social Security Administration.

SOCIAL SECURITY Social Security may be best known as a source of retirement income, but it also provides disability benefits. If you're a worker who pays into the Social Security system, you're eligible for Social Security funds if you become disabled. How much you get depends on your salary and the number of years you've been paying into Social Security. Your dependents also qualify for certain benefits. However, Social Security has very strict rules. Workers are considered disabled if they have a physical or mental condition that prevents them from working and that is expected to last for at least 12 months or to result in death. Benefits start at the sixth full month the person is disabled. They stay in effect as long as the disability lasts.

PRIVATE INCOME INSURANCE PROGRAMS Privately owned insurance companies offer many policies to protect people from loss of income resulting from illness or disability. Disability income insurance gives weekly or monthly cash payments to people who cannot work because of illness or accident. The amount paid is usually 40 to 60 percent of a person's normal income. Some plans, however, pay as much as 75 percent.

Disability Income Insurance Trade-Offs

As with the purchase of health insurance, you must make certain trade-offs when you decide among different private disability insurance policies. Keep the following in mind as you look for a plan that is right for you.

WAITING OR ELIMINATION PERIOD Benefits won't begin the day you become disabled. You'll have to wait anywhere between one and six months before you can begin collecting. The span of time is called an elimination period. Usually a policy with a longer elimination period charges lower premiums.

DURATION OF BENEFITS Every policy names a specified period during which benefits will be paid. Some policies are valid for only a few years. Others are automatically canceled when you turn 65. Still others continue to make payments for life. You should look for a policy that pays benefits for life. If your policy stops payments when you turn 65, then permanent disability could be a major financial as well as physical loss.

AMOUNT OF BENEFITS You should aim for a benefit amount that, when added to other sources of income, will equal 70 to 80 percent of your take-home pay. Of course, the greater the benefit, the greater the cost, or premium.

ACCIDENT AND SICKNESS COVERAGE Some disability policies pay only for accidents. Coverage for sickness is important, though. Accidents are not the only cause of disability.

GUARANTEED RENEWABILITY If your health becomes poor, your disability insurer may try to cancel your coverage. Look for a plan that guarantees coverage as long as you continue to pay your premiums. The cost may be higher, but it's worth the extra security and peace of mind. You may even be able to find a plan that will stop charging the premiums if you become disabled, which is an added benefit.

Your Disability Income Needs

Once you have found out what your benefits from the numerous public and private sources would be, you should determine whether those benefits would meet your disability income needs. Ideally, you'll want to replace all the income you otherwise would have earned. This should enable you to pay your day-to-day expenses while you're recovering. You won't have work-related expenses and your taxes will be lower during the time you are disabled. In some cases you may not have to pay certain taxes at all. Use Exhibit 9–4 to determine how much income you will have available if you become disabled.

OBJECTIVE 6

Explain why the costs of health insurance and health care have been increasing.

High Medical Costs

Affordable health care has become one of the most important social issues of our time. News broadcasts abound with special reports on "America's health care crisis" or politicians demanding "universal health insurance."

What do an aging and overweight population, the cost of prescription drugs, the growing number of uninsured, and advancements in medical technology have in common? These and other factors all add up to rising health costs. The United States has

	Monthly Amount	After Waiting:	For a Period of:
Sick leave or short-term disability	_____	_____	_____
Group long-term disability	_____	_____	_____
Social Security	_____	_____	_____
Other government programs	_____	_____	_____
Individual disability insurance	_____	_____	_____
Credit disability insurance	_____	_____	_____
Other income:	_____	_____	_____
Savings	_____	_____	_____
Spouse's income	_____	_____	_____
Total monthly income while disabled:	$ _____		

Exhibit 9–4

Calculating Disability Income

How much income will you have available if you become disabled?

Sheet 32: Disability Income Insurance Needs.

CONCEPT CHECK 9–5

1 What is the purpose of disability income insurance?

_____

_____

2 What are the four sources of disability income?

_____

_____

3 Match the following terms with an appropriate statement. _____

waiting or elimination period

duration of benefits

guaranteed renewability

a. A specified period during which benefits are paid.

b. A plan that guarantees coverage as long as you continue to pay your premiums. _____

c. A period of one to six months that must elapse before benefits can be collected. _____

Apply Yourself!

Objective 5

Contact an insurance agent to obtain cost information for an individual disability income insurance policy.

Exhibit 9-5   U.S. National Health Expenditures, 1960–2017

Billions of dollars

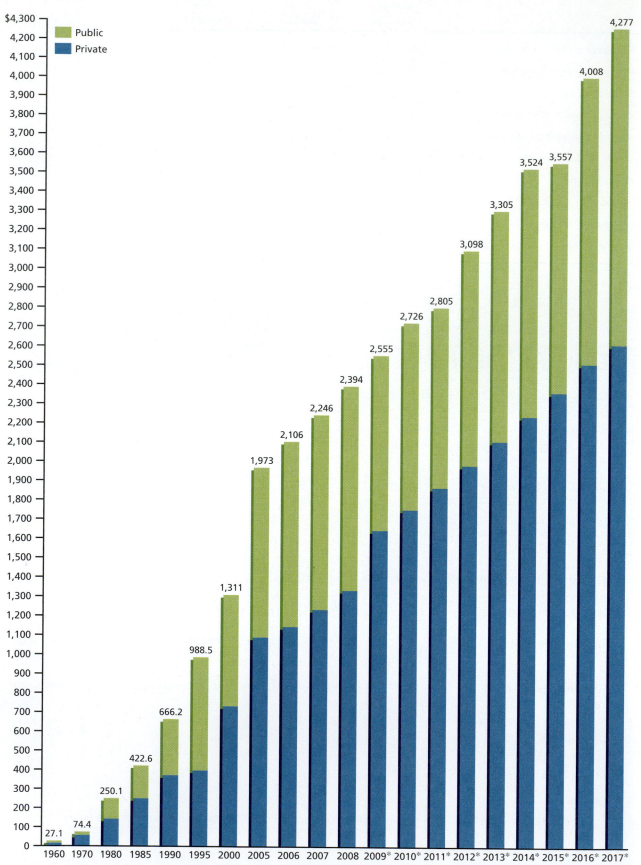

* Projected

SOURCES: U.S. Department of Health and Human Services. The Centers for Medicare and Medicaid Services. http://www.cms.hhs.gov/nationalhealthexpenddata/03_nationalhealthaccountsprojected.asp, accessed February 5, 2009.

the highest per capita medical expenditures of any country in the world. We spend twice as much on health care as the average for the 24 industrialized countries in Europe and North America. The average per employee cost for health care was more than $8,000 in 2008. It seems that, year after year, U.S. citizens can be sure of one thing besides death and taxes: higher health costs.

Health care costs were estimated at $2.56 trillion in 2009 (see Exhibit 9–5). Since 1993, health care spending as a percentage of gross domestic product (GDP) has remained relatively constant at 13.6 percent, except in 1997, when it fell to 13.4 percent, and in 2009, when it increased to 16.9 percent. The latest projections from The Centers of Medicare and Medicaid Services show that over the next 8 years annual health care spending is expected to grow to over $4.3 trillion, or 19.5 percent of GDP. Yet 48 million people, or 15.7 percent of our population, have no health insurance.

RAPID INCREASE IN MEDICAL EXPENDITURES Since federally sponsored health care began in 1965, U.S. health care expenditures rose from $41.6 billion, or about 6 percent of GDP, to $2.56 trillion in 2009, about 16.9 percent of GDP.

HIGH ADMINISTRATIVE COSTS In the United States, administrative costs consume nearly 26 percent of health care dollars, compared to 1 percent under Canada's socialized system. These costs include activities such as enrolling beneficiaries in a health plan, paying health insurance premiums, checking eligibility, obtaining authorizations for specialist referrals, and filing reimbursement claims. More than 1,100 different insurance forms are now in use in the United States.

Why Does Health Care Cost So Much?

The high and rising costs of health care are attributable to many factors, including

- The use of sophisticated, expensive technologies.
- Duplication of tests and sometimes duplication of technologies that yield similar results.
- Increases in the variety and frequency of treatments, including allegedly unnecessary tests.
- The increasing number and longevity of elderly people.
- Regulations that result in cost shifting rather than cost reduction.
- The increasing number of accidents and crimes that require emergency medical services.
- Limited competition and restrictive work rules in the health care delivery system.
- Labor intensiveness and rapid average earnings growth for health care professionals and executives.
- Using more expensive medical care than necessary, such as going to an emergency room with a bad cold.
- Built-in inflation in the health care delivery system.
- Aging baby boomers use of more health care services, whether they're going to the doctor more often, or snapping up pricier drugs, from Celebrex to Viagra.
- Other major factors that cost billions of dollars each year, including fraud, administrative waste, malpractice insurance, excessive surgical procedures, a wide range of prices for similar services, and double health coverage.

According to the Government Accountability Office, fraud and abuse account for nearly 10 percent of all dollars spent on health care. In 2008, that was a loss of more than $28 billion to Medicare.

Key Web Site for Medicare Fraud
www.hhs.gov/ stopmedicarefraud

Personal Finance in Practice

>Medical ID Theft

How to find out where you stand:

- Most patients toss out those "Explanation of Benefits" letters unopened. You should read them carefully to make sure no unauthorized treatment was performed in your name.

- Each year, ask your insurer for a "history of disclosures" from your doctor or insurer. This lists what medical information of yours was disclosed, as well as when, why, and to whom it was given, and can help spot fraud.

- Check your credit report periodically. Some victims learn of ID theft from collection notices for care they didn't get.

What to do if you're a victim:

- File theft reports with both the police and your insurer.

- Contact the Federal Trade Commission, which provides helpful resources on resolving identity theft (877-438-4338 or consumer.gov/idtheft/).

- Request a copy of your medical records from your doctor or hospital. If either refuses, file a complaint with the Office of Civil Rights at Health & Human Services (800-368-1019 or hhs.gov/ocr/privacyhowtofile.htm).

Source: Dean Foust, "Diagnosis: Identity Theft," *BusinessWeek*, January 8, 2007, p. 32.

Because third parties—private health insurers and government—pay such a large part of the nation's health care bill, hospitals, doctors, and patients often lack the incentive to make the most economical use of health care services.

What Is Being Done about the High Costs of Health Care?

In the private sector, concerned groups such as employers, labor unions, health insurers, health care professionals, and consumers have undertaken a wide range of innovative activities to contain the costs of health care. These activities include

CAUTION! For $60, a thief can buy your health records— and use them to get costly care. Guess who gets the bill? *You!*

Source: *BusinessWeek*, January 8, 2007, p. 30.

- Programs to carefully review health care fees and charges and the use of health care services.
- The establishment of incentives to encourage preventive care and provide more services out of hospitals, where this is medically acceptable.
- Involvement in community health planning to help achieve a better balance between health needs and health care resources.
- The encouragement of prepaid group practices and other alternatives to fee-for-service arrangements.
- Community health education programs that motivate people to take better care of themselves.
- Physicians encouraging patients to pay cash for routine medical care and lab tests.

President Obama maintains that improving health information technology could lower costs; setting up electronic medical records would be a smart investment and could reduce medical errors. According to Karen Davis, president of Commonwealth Fund, a health policy research organization, "Improvements in health information technology could save $88 billion over 10 years, though no gains will be realized in the first few years."

What Can You Do to Reduce Personal Health Care Costs?

The best way to avoid the high cost of illness is to stay well. The prescription is the same as it has always been:

1. Eat a balanced diet and keep your weight under control.
2. Avoid smoking and don't drink to excess.
3. Get sufficient rest, relaxation, and exercise.
4. Drive carefully and watch out for accident and fire hazards in the home.
5. Protect yourself from medical ID theft. (Read the accompanying Personal Finance in Practice box.)

did you know?

On June 22, 2009, President Obama signed the Family Smoking Prevention and Tobacco Control Act. The goal is to reduce health care costs, save lives, reduce heart and lung diseases, and other tobacco-related illnesses

Sheet 32 Disability Income Insurance Needs

CONCEPT CHECK 9–6

1 What are the reasons for rising health care expenditures?

_____

_____

2 What are various groups doing to curb the high costs of health care?

_____

_____

3 What can individuals do to reduce health care costs?

_____

_____

Apply Yourself!

Objective 6

Create a list of personal actions that you can take to reduce the costs of health care.

Back to... *Getting Personal*

Reconsider your responses to the "Getting Personal" statements at the beginning of the chapter. For more effective health and disability insurance planning, consider the following:

- Premiums are lower on employer-provided health insurance plans. Take advantage of the lower costs, but expect to pay part of the premium out of your paycheck. Many employers offer dental and vision plans, often at low cost.
- Consider participating in a flexible spending account (FSA) if it is offered, but remember that on March 15 every year, money left in an FSA from the previous year is forfeited.
- Consider a health savings account (HSA) if you do not have health insurance or you need more affordable health insurance. This high-deductible health plan provides medical insurance coverage and a tax-free opportunity to save for future medical needs. For more information about HSAs, visit www.treasury. gov/offices/public-affairs/hsa.
- Every state provides free or low-cost health insurance for children in low-to-moderate-income families. For more information, contact the U.S. Department of Health and Human Services at 877-Kids Now (877-543-7669) or go to www.insurekidsnow.gov.
- Statistics show that you have a higher risk of becoming disabled than of dying before age 65. If your employer offers disability insurance, consider buying this protection even if you have to pay part of the premium.

Finally, what did you learn in this chapter that could help you make better health insurance and disability income insurance decisions?

Chapter Summary

Objective 1 Health insurance is protection that provides payments of benefits for a covered sickness or injury. Health insurance should be a part of your overall insurance program to safeguard your family's economic security. Health insurance plans can be purchased through group health insurance, individual health insurance, and COBRA.

Objective 2 Four basic types of health insurance are available under group and individual policies: hospital expense insurance, surgical expense insurance, physician's expense insurance, and major medical expense insurance.

Major provisions of a health insurance policy include eligibility requirements, assigned benefits, internal limits, copayment, service benefits, benefit limits, exclusions and limitations, guaranteed renewability, and cancellation and termination.

Objective 3 Health insurance policy trade-offs include reimbursement versus indemnity, internal limits versus aggregate limits, deductibles and coinsurance, out-of-pocket limits, and benefits based on reasonable and customary charges.

Objective 4 Health insurance and health care are available from private insurance companies, hospital and medical service plans such as Blue Cross/Blue Shield, health maintenance organizations (HMOs), preferred provider organizations (PPOs), point-of-service plans (POSs), home health care agencies, and employer self-funded health plans.

The federal and state governments offer health coverage in accordance with laws that define the premiums and benefits. Two well-known government health programs are Medicare and Medicaid.

Objective 5 Disability income insurance provides regular cash income lost by employees as the result of an accident, illness, or pregnancy. Sources of disability income insurance include the employer, Social Security, worker's compensation, and private insurance companies.

Objective 6 Health care costs, except during 1994–1996, have gone up faster than the rate of inflation. Among the reasons for high and rising health care costs are the use of expensive technologies, duplication of tests and sometimes technologies, increases in the variety and frequency of treatments, unnecessary tests, the increasing number and longevity of elderly people, regulations that shift rather than reduce costs, the increasing number of accidents and crimes requiring emergency services, limited competition and restrictive work rules in the health care delivery system, rapid earnings growth among health care professionals, and built-in inflation in the health care delivery system.

Key Terms

Self-Test Problems

1. The MacDonald family of five has health insurance coverage that pays 75 percent of out-of-hospital expenses after a $600 deductible per person. Mrs. MacDonald incurred doctor and prescription medication expenses of $1,380. What amount would the insurance company pay?
2. Under Rose's PPO, emergency room care at a network hospital is 80 percent covered after the member has met a $300 annual deductible. Assume that Rose went to a hospital within her PPO network and that she had not met her annual deductible yet. Her total emergency room bill was $850. What amount did Rose have to pay? What amount did the PPO cover?
3. Gene, an assembly line worker at an automobile manufacturing plant, has take-home pay of $900 a week. He is injured in an accident that kept him off work for 18 weeks. His disability insurance coverage replaces 65 percent of his earnings after a six-week waiting period. What amount would he receive in disability benefits?

Solutions

1.
Total Expenses	=	$1,380
Deductible	=	− 600
		$ 780

Insurance company will pay 75 percent of $780 or $780 × 0.75 = $585.

2.
Total bill	=	$ 850
Deductible	=	− 300
		$ 550

Rose pays $550 × 0.20 = $110 + $300 = $410.

3. Insurance will replace 65 percent of $900, or $900 × 0.65 = $585 per week. Insurance will pay for 18 − 6, or 12 weeks, or $585 × 12 = $7,020.

Problems

1. The Kelleher family has health insurance coverage that pays 80 percent of out-of-hospital expenses after a $500 deductible per person. If one family member has doctor and prescription medication expenses of $1,100, what amount would the insurance company pay? (Obj. 2)

2. A health insurance policy pays 65 percent of physical therapy costs after a $200 deductible. In contrast, an HMO charges $15 per visit for physical therapy. How much would a person save with the HMO if he or she had 10 physical therapy sessions costing $50 each? (Obj. 2)

3. Sarah's comprehensive major medical health insurance plan at work has a deductible of $750. The policy pays 85 percent of any amount above the deductible. While on a hiking trip, Sarah contracted a rare bacterial disease. Her medical costs for treatment, including medicines, tests, and a six-day hospital stay, totaled $8,893. A friend told her that she would have paid less if she had a policy with a stop-loss feature that capped her out-of-pocket expenses at $3,000. Was her friend correct? Show your computations. Then determine which policy would have cost Sarah less and by how much. (Obj. 2)

4. Georgia Braxton, a widow, has take-home pay of $600 a week. Her disability insurance coverage replaces 70 percent of her earnings after a four-week waiting period. What amount would she receive in disability benefits if an illness kept Georgia from work for 16 weeks? (Obj. 5)

5. Stephanie was injured in a car accident and was rushed to the emergency room. She received stitches for a facial wound and treatment for a broken finger. Under Stephanie's PPO plan, emergency room care at a network hospital is 80 percent covered after the member has met a $300 annual deductible. Assume that Stephanie went to a hospital within her PPO network. Her total emergency room bill was $850. What amount did Stephanie have to pay? What amount did the PPO cover? (Obj. 2)

Questions 6, 7, and 8 are based on the following scenario:

Ronald Roth started his new job as controller with Aerosystems today. Carole, the employee benefits clerk, gave Ronald a packet that contains information on the company's health insurance options. Aerosystems offers its employees the choice between a private insurance company plan (Blue Cross/Blue Shield), an HMO, and a PPO. Ronald needs to review the packet and make a decision on which health care program fits his needs. The following is an overview of that information.

a. *Blue Cross/Blue Shield plan:* The monthly premium cost to Ronald will be $42.32. For all doctor office visits, prescriptions, and major medical charges, Ronald will be responsible for 20 percent and the insurance company will cover 80 percent of covered charges. The annual deductible is $500.

b. The HMO is provided to employees free of charge. The copayment for doctors' office visits and major medical charges is $10. Prescription copayments are $5. The HMO pays 100 percent after the Ronald's copayment. No annual deductible.

c. The POS requires that the employee pay $24.44 per month to supplement the cost of the program with the company's payment. If Ron uses health care providers within the plan, he pays the copayments as described above for the HMO. He can also choose to use a health care provider out of the service and pay 20 percent of all charges after he pays a $500 deductible. The POS will pay for 80 percent of those covered visits. No annual deductible.

Ronald decided to review his medical bills from the previous year to see what costs he had incurred and to help him evaluate his choices. He visited his general physician four times during the year at a cost of $125 for each visit. He also spent $65 and $89 on prescriptions during the year. Using these costs as an example, what would Ron pay for each of the plans described above? (For the purposes of the POS computation, assume that Ron visited a physician outside of the network plan. Assume he had his prescriptions filled at a network-approved pharmacy).

6. What annual medical costs will Ronald pay using the sample medical expenses provided if he were to enroll in the Blue Cross/Blue Shield plan? (Obj. 2)

7. What total costs will Ronald pay if he enrolls in the HMO plan?

8. If Ronald selects the POS plan, what would annual medical costs be?

9. In 1999, Joelle spent $3,600 on her health care. If this amount increased by 5 percent per year, what would be the amount Joelle spent in 2009 for the same health care? (Hint: Use the time value of money table in Chapter 1 .) (Obj. 6)

10. As of 2009, per capita spending on health care in the United States was about $8,000. If this amount increased by 5 percent a year, what would be the amount of per capita spending for health care in 10 years? (Hint: Use the time value of money table in Chapter 1 .) (Obj. 6)

Questions

1. Larry and Liz are a young couple both working full time and earning about $50,000 a year. They recently purchased a house and took out a large mortgage. Since both of them work, they own two cars and are still making payments on them. Liz has major medical health insurance through her employer, but Larry's coverage is inadequate. They have no children, but they hope to start a family in about three years. Liz's employer provides disability income insurance, but Larry's employer does not. Analyze the need for health and disability insurance for Liz and Larry. (Obj.2)

2. Pam is 31 and recently divorced, with children ages 3 and 6. She earns $28,000 a year as a secretary. Her employer provides her with basic health insurance coverage. She receives child support from the children's father, but he misses payments often and is always behind in payments. Her ex-husband, however, is responsible for the children's medical bills. Analyze the need for health and disability insurance for Pam. (Obj.2)

3. List the benefits included in your employee benefit package, such as health insurance, disability income insurance, and life insurance. Discuss the importance of such a benefit package to the consumer. (Obj.3)

4. Visit the Social Security Administration's Web page to determine your approximate monthly Social Security disability benefits should you become disabled in the current year. Or call your Social Security office to request the latest edition of *Social Security: Understanding the Benefits*. (Obj. 5)

5. Obtain sample health insurance policies from insurance agents or brokers, and analyze the policies for definitions, coverage, exclusions, limitations on coverage, and amounts of coverage. In what ways are the policies similar? In what ways do they differ? (Obj. 3)

Case in Point

BUYING ADEQUATE HEALTH INSURANCE COVERAGE

Kathy Jones was a junior at Glenbard High School. She had two younger brothers. Her father, the assistant manager of a local supermarket, had take-home pay of $3,000 a month. He had a group health insurance policy and a $30,000 life insurance policy. He said that he could not afford to buy additional insurance. All of his monthly salary was used to meet current expenses, including car and house payments, food, clothing, transportation, children's allowances, recreation and entertainment, and vacation trips.

One evening, Kathy was talking with her father about insurance, which she was studying in an economics course. She asked what kind of insurance program her father had for their family. The question started Mr. Jones thinking about how well he was planning for his wife and children. Since the family had always been in good health, Mr. Jones felt that additional health and life insurance was not essential.

Maybe after he received a raise in his salary and after his daughter was out of high school, he could afford to buy more insurance.

Questions

1. Do you think Kathy's father was planning wisely for the welfare of his family? Can you suggest ways in which this family could have cut monthly expenses and thus set aside some money for more insurance?

2. Although Mr. Jones's salary was not big enough to buy insurance for all possible risks, what protection do you think he should have had at this time?

3. Suppose Mr. Jones had been seriously injured and unable to work for at least one year. What would his family have done? How might this situation have affected his children?

Continuing Case

Vikki Treble (age 35) recently changed jobs because she wants the opportunity to work part-time. At her orientation, she is presented with several health plans; however, she can not immediately choose an option because she needs to think about her family's needs and compare the coverage and cost with the plan offered at her husband Tim's employer.

Tim (age 37) is feeling the effects of high school football and running with Tutti, the pet dog. His doctor suggests he go to physical therapy to strengthen his knees.

Tim and Vikki's daughter Molly (5 years old) is in kindergarten and, as a follow up to a vision screening at school, visited an optometrist who determined that she needs glasses. Molly also has allergies that require her to take medication.

During a recent get-together, Vikki's parents, Dave and Amy, ages 60 and 58, mentioned that they are thinking about retiring next year. However, Dave has been cautioned that only part of his health insurance premium would be covered if he retired before age 65. Since neither of them likes to procrastinate, Dave and Tim challenged each other to get aggressive about finding the best coverage for their families.

Vikki and Tim's financial statistics are shown below:

Assets:
Checking/savings account $20,000
Emergency fund $30,000
House $275,000
Cars $20,000 and $4,000
Household possessions $10,000
401(k) balance $75,000 (Vikki), $65,000 (Tim)
College savings $8,500

Monthly Expenses:
Mortgage $1,200
Property tax/Insurance $500
Daily living expenses (including utilities, food) $2,300
Child care $10,000
Car loan $450
Entertainment $300
Gas/repairs $500

Liabilities:
Mortgage $185,000

Savings:
401(k) 10% of gross monthly salary
College savings $200

Income:
Gross Salary: $65,000 per year (Vikki), $78,000 (Tim)
After-tax monthly salary: $3,792 (Vikki), $4,550 (Tim)

Questions:

1. What should Vikki and Tim consider when choosing their health care plan? What do you recommend for their coverage?
2. Why might Dave and Amy consider purchasing long-term care?
3. What are some steps that Vikki and Tim can take to minimize their family's after-tax medical costs?
4. What should determine Vikki and Tim's disability insurance needs and coverage?
5. How can Vikki and Tim use *Your Personal Financial Plan* sheets 31–32?

Spending Diary

"SOME OF MY EATING HABITS NOT ONLY WASTE MONEY BUT ARE ALSO NOT BEST FOR MY HEALTH."

Directions

Continue your Daily Spending Diary to record and monitor spending in various categories. Your comments should reflect what you have learned about your spending patterns and help you consider possible changes you might want to make in your spending habits. The Daily Spending Diary sheets are located in Appendix C at the end of the book and on the student Web site at www.mhhe.com/kdh.

Questions

1. What spending actions might directly or indirectly affect your health and physical well-being?
2. What amounts (if any) are currently required from your spending for the cost of health and disability insurance?

Assessing Current and Needed Health Care Insurance

Financial Planning Activities: Assess current and needed medical and health care insurance. Investigate your existing medical and health insurance, and determine the need for additional coverages.

Suggested Web Sites: www.insure.com   www.life-line.org

Insurance company

Address

Type of coverage   ☐ individual health policy   ☐ group health policy

☐ HMO   ☐ PPO   ☐ other

Premium amount (monthly/quarter/semiannual/annual)

Main coverages

Amount of coverage for

• Hospital costs

• Surgery costs

• Physicians' fees

• Lab tests

• Outpatient expenses

• Maternity

• Major medical

Other items covered/amounts

Policy restrictions (deductible, coinsurance, maximum limits)

Items not covered by this insurance

Of items not covered, would supplemental coverage be appropriate for your personal situation?

What actions related to your current (or proposed additional) coverage are necessary?

What's Next for Your Personal Financial Plan?

• Talk to others about the impact of their health insurance on other financial decisions.
• Contact an insurance agent to obtain cost information for an individual health insurance plan.

Name: _____   **Date:** _____

Disability Income Insurance Needs

Financial Planning Activities: Determine financial needs and insurance coverage related to employment disability situations. Use the categories below to determine your potential income needs and disability insurance coverage.

Suggested Web Sites: www.ssa.gov   www.insweb.com

Monthly Expenses

	Current	When Disabled
Mortgage (or rent)	$ _____	$ _____
Utilities	$ _____	$ _____
Food	$ _____	$ _____
Clothing	$ _____	$ _____
Insurance payments	$ _____	$ _____
Debt payments	$ _____	$ _____
Auto/transportation	$ _____	$ _____
Medical/dental care	$ _____	$ _____
Education	$ _____	$ _____
Personal allowances	$ _____	$ _____
Recreation/entertainment	$ _____	$ _____
Contributors, donations	$ _____	$ _____
Total monthly expenses when disabled		$ _____

Substitute Income   Monthly Benefit*

Substitute Income	Monthly Benefit*
Group disability insurance	$ _____
Social Security	$ _____
State disability insurance	$ _____
Worker's compensation	$ _____
Credit disability insurance (in some auto loan or home mortgages)	$ _____
Other income (investments, etc.)	$ _____
Total projected income when disabled	$ _____

If projected income when disabled is less than expenses, additional disability income insurance should be considered.

*Most disability insurance programs have a waiting period before benefits start, and they may have a limit as to how long benefits are received.

What's Next for Your Personal Financial Plan?

- Survey several people to determine if they have disability insurance.
- Talk to an insurance agent to compare the costs of disability income insurance available from several insurance companies.

10 Financial Planning with Life Insurance

Getting Personal

Should you be concerned about life insurance? For each of the following statements, select "yes" or "no" to indicate your behavior regarding these life insurance statements.

	Yes	No
1. I need life insurance because someone depends on me for financial support.	____	____
2. My survivors can use the life insurance benefits to cover my funeral expenses or other financial obligations.	____	____
3. I should start budgeting for my life insurance premiums while I am still young and healthy.	____	____
4. My life insurance premiums will be lower if I buy a policy at a younger age.	____	____
5. I can determine my average life expectancy with some certainty.	____	____
6. I am aware of several different types of life insurance.	____	____
7. I can decide who receives the benefits of my life insurance policy.	____	____

After studying this chapter, you will be asked to use what you learned about the purpose of life insurance and types of life insurance policies and to reconsider your responses to these items.

Your Personal Financial Plan Sheets

33. Determining Life Insurance Needs
34. Life Insurance Policy Comparison

Objectives

In this chapter, you will learn to:

1. Define life insurance and determine your life insurance needs.
2. Distinguish between the types of life insurance companies and analyze various life insurance policies these companies issue.
3. Select important provisions in life insurance contracts and create a plan to buy life insurance.
4. Recognize how annuities provide financial security.

Why is this important?

If history is any guide, you will live longer than your ancestors lived. In 1900, the life expectancy of an American male was 46.3 years, and it was 48.3 years for an American female. In contrast, by the year 2004, the life expectancy increased to about 75 years for men and 80 years for women. Deciding whether you need life insurance and choosing the right policy take time, research, and careful thought.

What Is Life Insurance?

Even though putting a price on your life is impossible, you probably own some life insurance—through a group plan where you work, as a veteran, or through a policy you bought. Life insurance is one of the most important and expensive purchases you may ever make; therefore, it is important that you budget for this need. Deciding whether you need it and choosing the right policy from dozens of options take time, research, and careful thought. This chapter will help you make decisions about life insurance. It describes what life insurance is and how it works, the major types of life insurance coverage, and how you can use life insurance to protect your family.

OBJECTIVE 1

Define life insurance and determine your life insurance needs.

beneficiary A person designated to receive something, such as life insurance proceeds, from the insured.

When you buy life insurance, you're making a contract with the company issuing the policy. You agree to pay a certain amount of money—the premium—periodically. In return the company agrees to pay a death benefit, or a stated sum of money upon your death, to your beneficiary. A **beneficiary** is a person named to receive the benefits from an insurance policy.

The Purpose of Life Insurance

Most people buy life insurance to protect the people who depend on them from financial losses caused by their death. Those people could include a spouse, children, an aging parent, or a business partner or corporation. Life insurance benefits may be used to:

- Pay off a home mortgage or other debts at the time of death.
- Provide lump-sum payments through an endowment for children when they reach a specified age.
- Provide an education or income for children.
- Make charitable donations after death.
- Provide a retirement income.
- Accumulate savings.
- Establish a regular income for survivors.
- Set up an estate plan.
- Pay estate and gift taxes.

The Principle of Life Insurance

No one can say with any certainty how long a particular person will live. Still, insurance companies are able to make some educated guesses. Over the years they've compiled tables that show about how long people live. Using these tables, the company will make a rough guess about a person's life span and charge him or her accordingly. The sooner a person is likely to die, the higher the premiums he or she will pay.

did you know?

Japan spends more per capita on life insurance than any other nation. Next: Switzerland, the United States, Great Britain, and the Netherlands.

How Long Will You Live?

If history is a guide, you'll live longer than your ancestors did. In 1900 an American male could be expected to live 46.3 years. By 2004, in contrast, life expectancy had risen to 74.8 years for men and 80 for women. Exhibit 10–1 shows about how many years a person can be expected to live today. For instance, a 30-year-old woman can be expected to live another 51 years. That doesn't mean that she has a high probability of dying at age 81. This just means that 51 is the average number of additional years a 30-year-old woman may expect to live.

Do You Need Life Insurance?

Before you buy life insurance, you'll have to decide whether you need it at all. Generally, if your death would cause financial hardship for somebody, then life insurance is a wise purchase. Households with children usually have the greatest need for life insurance. Single people who live alone or with their parents, however, usually have little or no need for life insurance unless they have a great deal of debt or want to provide for their parents, a friend, relative, or charity.

Exhibit **10–1**   Life Expectancy Tables, All Races, 2004

This table helps insurance companies determine insurance premiums. *Use the table to find the average number of additional years a 15-year-old male and female are expected to live.*

EXPECTATION OF LIFE IN YEARS			EXPECTATION OF LIFE IN YEARS		
Age	Male	Female	Age	Male	Female
0	74.8	80.0	50	28.5	32.3
1	74.4	79.5	55	24.3	27.8
5	70.5	75.5	60	20.4	23.5
10	65.6	70.6	65	16.7	19.5
15	60.6	65.6	70	13.3	15.7
20	55.9	60.8	75	10.3	12.3
25	51.3	55.9	80	7.6	9.2
30	46.6	51.0	85	5.5	6.6
35	41.9	46.2	90	3.8	4.6
40	37.3	41.5	95	2.7	3.2
45	32.8	36.8	100	2.1	2.5

SOURCE: Social Security Administration, www.ssa.gov/OACT/STATS/table4c6.html, accessed April 28, 2009.

Estimating Your Life Insurance Requirements

In estimating your life insurance requirements, consider the insurance coverage that your employer offers you as a fringe benefit. Most employers provide employees with life insurance coverage equal to their yearly salary. For example, if you earn $35,000 per year, you may receive $35,000 of insurance coverage. Some employers offer insurance of two or more times the salary with increased contributions from employees. The premiums are usually lower than premiums for individual life insurance policies, and you don't have to pass a physical exam.

There are four general methods for determining the amount of insurance you may need: the easy method, the DINK method, the "nonworking" spouse method, and the "family need" method.

THE EASY METHOD Simple as this method is, it is remarkably useful. It is based on the insurance agent's rule of thumb that a "typical family" will need approximately 70 percent of your salary for seven years before they adjust to the financial consequences of your death. In other words, for a simple estimate of your life insurance needs, just multiply your current gross income by 7 (7 years) and 0.70 (70 percent).

Example

$30,000 current income × 7 = $210,000 × 0.70 = $147,000

Example From Your Life

$ _____ current income × 7 = $ _____ × 0.70 = $ _____

This method assumes your family is "typical." You may need more insurance if you have four or more children, if you have above-average family debt, if any member of your family suffers from poor health, or if your spouse has poor employment potential. On the other hand, you may need less insurance if your family is smaller.

THE DINK (DUAL INCOME, NO KIDS) METHOD If you have no dependents and your spouse earns as much or more than you do, you have very simple insurance needs. Basically, all you need to do is ensure that your spouse will not be unduly burdened by debts should you die. Here is an example of the DINK method:

Example

	Example	Your Figures
Funeral expenses	$ 5,000	$ _____
One-half of mortgage	60,000	_____
One-half of auto loan	7,000	_____
One-half of credit card balance	1,500	_____
One-half of personal debt	1,500	_____
Other debts	1,000	_____
Total insurance needs	$76,000	$ _____

This method assumes your spouse will continue to work after your death. If your spouse suffers poor health or is employed in an occupation with an uncertain future, you should consider adding an insurance cushion to see him or her through hard times.

THE "NONWORKING" SPOUSE METHOD Insurance experts have estimated that extra costs of up to $10,000 a year may be required to replace the services of a homemaker in a family with small children. These extra costs may include the cost of a housekeeper, child care, more meals out, additional carfare, laundry services, and so on. They do not include the lost potential earnings of the surviving spouse, who often must take time away from the job to care for the family.

To estimate how much life insurance a homemaker should carry, simply multiply the number of years before the youngest child reaches age 18 by $10,000:

Example

Youngest child's age = 8 years
10 years $\times$ $10,000 = $100,000

Example From Your Life

_____ years $\times$ $10,000 = $ _____

If there are teenage children, the $10,000 figure can be reduced. If there are more than two children under age 13, or if anyone in the family suffers poor health or has special needs, the $10,000 figure should be adjusted upward.

THE "FAMILY NEED" METHOD The first three methods assume you and your family are "typical" and ignore important factors such as Social Security and your liquid assets. The nearby Figure It Out box provides a detailed worksheet for making a thorough estimate of your life insurance needs.

Figure It Out!

> A Worksheet to Calculate Your Life Insurance Needs

1. Five times your personal yearly income _____ (1)

2. Total approximate expenses above and beyond your daily living costs for you and your dependents (e.g. tuition, care for a disabled child or parent) amount to = _____ (2)

3. Your emergency fund (3 to 6 months of living expenses) amounts to = _____ (3)

4. Estimated amount for your funeral expenses (U.S. average is $5,000 to $10,000) + _____ (4)

5. Total estimate of your family's financial needs (add lines 1 through 4) = _____ (5)

6. Your total liquid assets (e.g., savings accounts, CDs, money market funds, existing life insurance both individual and group, pension plan death benefits, and Social Security benefits) – _____ (6)

7. Subtract line 6 from line 5 and enter the difference here. = _____ (7)

The net result (line 7) is an estimate of the shortfall your family would face upon your death. Remember, these are just rules of thumb. For a complete analysis of your needs, consult a professional.

Sources: *About Life Insurance,* Metropolitan Life Insurance Company, February 1997, p. 3; *The TIAA Guide to Life Insurance Planning for People in Education* (New York: Teachers Insurance and Annuity Association, January 1997), p. 3.

Although this method is quite thorough, if you believe it does not address all of your special needs, you should obtain further advice from an insurance expert or a financial planner.

As you determine your life insurance needs, don't forget to consider the life insurance you may already have. You may have ample coverage through your employer and through any mortgage and credit life insurance you purchased.

Before you consider types of life insurance policies, you must decide what you want your life insurance to do for you and your dependents. First, how much money do you want to leave to your dependents should you die today? Will you require more or less insurance protection to meet their needs as time goes on? Second, when would you like to be able to retire? What amount of income do you believe you and your spouse would need then? Third, how much will you be able to pay for your insurance program? Are the demands on your family budget for other living expenses likely to be greater or lower as time goes on?

When you have considered these questions and developed some approximate answers, you are ready to select the types and amounts of life insurance policies that will help you accomplish your objectives.

Key Web Sites for Life Insurance Planning

www.ircweb.org

www.iiaa.com

Sheet 33 Determining Life Insurance Needs

CONCEPT CHECK 10–1

1 What is life insurance? What is its purpose?

_____

_____

2 For each of the following statements, indicate your response by writing "T" or "F."

  a. Life insurance is one of the least important and inexpensive purchases. _____

  b. A beneficiary is a person named to receive the benefits from the insurance policy. _____

  c. Life insurance benefits may be used to pay off a home mortgage or other debts at the time of death. _____

  d. The sooner a person is likely to die, the higher the premiums he or she will pay. _____

  e. All people need to purchase a life insurance policy. _____

3 What are the four methods of determining life insurance needs?

_____

_____

Apply Yourself!

Objective 1

Interview relatives and friends to determine why they purchased life insurance. Summarize your findings.

Types of Life Insurance Companies and Policies

Types of Life Insurance Companies

OBJECTIVE 2

Distinguish between the types of life insurance companies and analyze various life insurance policies these companies issue.

nonparticipating policy Life insurance that does not provide policy dividends; also called a *nonpar policy.*

participating policy Life insurance that provides policy dividends; also called a *par policy.*

You can purchase the new or extra life insurance you need from two types of life insurance companies: stock life insurance companies, owned by shareholders, and mutual life insurance companies, owned by policyholders. About 95 percent of the U.S. life insurance companies are stock companies, and about 5 percent are mutual.

Stock companies generally sell **nonparticipating** (or *nonpar*) **policies,** while mutual companies specialize in the sale of **participating** (or *par*) **policies.** A participating policy has a somewhat higher premium than a nonparticipating policy, but a part of the premium is refunded to the policyholder annually. This refund is called the *policy dividend.*

A long debate about whether stock companies or mutual companies offer less expensive life insurance has been inconclusive. You should check with both stock and mutual companies to determine which type offers the best policy for your particular needs at the lowest price.

If you wish to pay exactly the same premium each year, you should choose a nonparticipating policy with its guaranteed premiums. However, you may prefer life insurance whose annual price reflects the company's experience with its investments, the health of its policyholders, and its general operating costs, that is, a participating policy.

Nevertheless, as with other forms of insurance, price should not be your only consideration in choosing a life insurance policy. You should consider the financial stability of and service provided by the insurance company.

Types of Life Insurance Policies

Both mutual insurance companies and stock insurance companies sell two basic types of life insurance: temporary and permanent insurance. Temporary insurance can be term, renewable term, convertible term, or decreasing term insurance. Permanent insurance is known by different names, including whole life, straight life, ordinary life, and cash value life insurance. As you will learn in the next section, permanent insurance can be limited payment, variable, adjustable, or universal life insurance. Other types of insurance policies—group life and credit life insurance—are generally temporary forms of insurance. Exhibit 10–2 lists major types and subtypes of life insurance.

TERM LIFE INSURANCE **Term insurance,** sometimes called *temporary life insurance,* provides protection against loss of life for only a specified term, or period of time. A term insurance policy pays a benefit only if you die during the period it covers, which may be 1, 5, 10, or 20 years, or up to age 70. If you stop paying the premiums, your coverage stops. Term insurance is often the best value for customers. You need insurance coverage most while you are raising children. As your children become independent and your assets increase, you can reduce your coverage. Term insurance comes in many different forms. Here are some examples.

term insurance Life insurance protection for a specified period of time; sometimes called *temporary life insurance.*

Renewable Term   The coverage of term insurance ends at the conclusion of the term, but you can continue it for another term—five years, for example—if you have a renewable option. However, the premium will increase because you will be older. It also usually has an age limit; you cannot renew after you reach a certain age.

Multiyear Level Term   A multiyear level term, or *straight term,* policy guarantees that you will pay the same premium for the duration of your policy.

Conversion Term   This type of policy allows you to change from term to permanent coverage. This will have a higher premium.

Decreasing Term   Term insurance is also available in a form that pays less to the beneficiary as time passes. The insurance period you select might depend on your age or on how long you decide that the coverage will be needed. For example, if you have a mortgage on a house, you might buy a 25-year decreasing term policy as a way to make sure that the debt could be paid if you died. The coverage would decrease as the balance on the loan decreased.

Return-of-Premium Term   Recently, insurance companies began to sell return-of-premium term life policies. These policies return all the premiums if you survive to the

Term (temporary)	Whole, Straight, or Ordinary Life	Other Types
• Renewable term	• Limited payment	• Group life
• Multiyear level term	• Variable life	• Credit life
• Convertible term	• Adjustable life	• Endowment life
• Decreasing term	• Universal life	
• Return of premium		

Exhibit 10–2

Major Types and Subtypes of Life Insurance

end of the policy term. Premiums are higher than the regular term policy but you do get all your money back.

whole life insurance An insurance plan in which the policyholder pays a specified premium each year for as long as he or she lives; also called a *straight life policy,* a *cash-value life policy,* or an *ordinary life policy.*

cash value The amount received after giving up a life insurance policy.

WHOLE LIFE INSURANCE   The other major type of life insurance is known as whole life insurance (also called a *straight life policy,* a *cash-value policy,* or an *ordinary life policy*). **Whole life insurance** is a permanent policy for which you pay a specified premium each year for the rest of your life. In return the insurance company pays your beneficiary a stated sum when you die. The amount of your premium depends mostly on the age at which you purchase the insurance.

Whole life insurance can also serve as an investment. Part of each premium you pay is set aside in a savings account. When and if you cancel the policy, you are entitled to the accumulated savings, which is known as the **cash value.** Whole life policies are popular because they provide both a death benefit and a savings component. You can borrow from your cash value if necessary, although you must pay interest on the loan. Cash-value policies may make sense for people who intend to keep the policies for the long term or for people who want a more structured way to save. However, the Consumer Federation of America Insurance Group suggests that you explore other savings and investment strategies before investing your money in a permanent policy.

The premium of a term insurance policy will increase each time you renew your insurance. In contrast, whole life policies have a higher annual premium at first, but the rate remains the same for the rest of your life. Several types of whole life policies have been developed to meet the needs of different customers. These include the limited payment policy, the variable life policy, the adjustable life policy, and universal life insurance.

did you know?

A Harris interactive poll reported 8 percent of Americans bought more disability insurance and 6 percent bought or increased their life insurance within one month of September 11, 2001.

Limited Payment Policy   Limited payment policies charge premiums for only a certain length of time, usually 20 or 30 years or until the insured reaches a certain age. At the end of this time, the policy is "paid up," and the policyholder remains insured for life. When the policyholder dies, the beneficiary receives the full death benefit. The annual premiums are higher for limited payment policies because the premiums have to be paid within a shorter period of time.

Variable Life Policy   With a variable life policy, your premium payments are fixed. As with a cash value policy, part of your premium is placed in a separate account; this money is invested in a stock, bond, or money market fund. The death benefit is guaranteed, but the cash value of the benefit can vary considerably according to the ups and downs of the stock market. Your death benefit can also increase, depending on the earnings of that separate fund.

Adjustable Life Policy   An adjustable life policy allows you to change your coverage as your needs change. For example, if you want to increase or decrease your death benefit, you can change either the premium payments or the period of coverage.

universal life insurance A whole life policy that combines term insurance and investment elements.

Universal Life   **Universal life insurance** is essentially a term policy with a cash value. Part of your premium goes into an investment account that grows and earns interest. You are able to borrow or withdraw your cash value. Unlike a traditional whole life policy, a universal life policy allows you to change your premium without changing

INSURANCE | Safe driving and healthy living will lower your premiums.
By Cameron Huddleston

Life Insurance for Less

Count life insurance among the many products and services that are on sale. A 40-year-old male nonsmoker can buy a $500,000, 20-year term-life policy for as little as $345 per year if he's in perfect health, or $455 if he's slightly overweight or has an elevated cholesterol level. So it's a great time to buy if you need coverage or to reshop if you have a policy.

But not everyone gets the best rates. Some factors that determine premiums are beyond your control—your age and gender, for example. Younger people pay less, and so do women, whose longer life expectancies give insurers more time to collect premiums. But there are plenty of ways to lower your rates.

Check with your doctor. A condition such as high blood pressure, high cholesterol or diabetes doesn't automatically mean you'll pay exorbitant premiums, as long as the condition is under control, says Jim Davis, vice-president of underwriting at Phoenix Cos. For instance, a diabetic who is not insulin-dependent and is otherwise in good health could get the standard rate.

Watch your weight. Poundage is a factor because obesity goes hand-in-hand with other health conditions. For example, a man who is 6 feet tall and weighs 205 pounds can usually qualify for the best rate, says Byron Udell, chief executive of AccuQuote (www.accuquote.com), a Web site that compares term-insurance rates among providers. But adding just a few more pounds could mean paying a higher premium. Women who are overweight should apply to insurers that use unisex weight tables, which are geared more toward men's higher weight ranges.

Drive carefully. "If you're breaking traffic laws, you're more likely to be involved in a life-threatening situation," says Udell, and that makes you a higher risk. Most companies want to know if you've had a moving violation in the past three years, or a DUI conviction in the past five or ten years. Accidents won't raise your premium unless you were cited for a moving violation.

Play it safe. Working in a high-risk profession (think driving a fuel truck in Iraq), participating in hazardous sports (flying planes or scuba diving) or traveling to sketchy parts of the world will

all result in higher premiums. But company standards vary. Genworth, for example, becomes concerned only if you'll be in a high-risk country for at least four weeks, says Ray Dinstel, chief underwriter for Genworth's life and long-term-care insurance.

Protect your credit history. Your credit history comes into play even when you apply for health insurance. If you've filed for bankruptcy in the past five years, that may be a strike against you.

Seek expert advice. Despite the general guidelines, standards vary from company to company. If you have a medical condition, you can get personalized help from Accu-Quote by calling 800-442-9899.

SOURCE: Reprinted by permission from the February issue of *Kiplinger's Personal Finance*. Copyright © 2009 The Kiplinger Washington Editors, Inc.

1. Why is it a great time to buy a term life insurance?

_____

2. What factors determine whether or not you get the best rates?

_____

3. What can you do to lower your life insurance premiums?

_____

Exhibit 10–3   Comparing the Major Types of Life Insurance

	Term Life	Whole Life	Universal Life
Premium	Lower initially, increasing with each renewal.	Higher initially than term; normally doesn't increase.	Flexible premiums.
Protects for	A specified period.	Entire life if you keep the policy.	A flexible time period.
Policy benefits	Death benefits only.	Death benefits and eventually a cash and loan value.	Flexible death benefits and eventually a cash and loan value.
Advantages	Low outlay. Initially, you can purchase a larger amount of coverage for a lower premium.	Helps you with financial discipline. Generally fixed premium amount. Cash value accumulation. You can take loan against policy.	More flexibility. Takes advantages of current interest rates. Offers the possibility of improved mortality rates (increased life expectancy because of advancements in medicine, which may lower policy costs).
Disadvantages	Premium increases with age. No cash value.	Costly if you surrender early. Usually no cash value for at least three to five years. May not meet short-term needs.	Same as whole life. Greater risks due to program flexibility. Low interest rates can affect cash value and premiums.
Options	May be renewable or convertible to a whole life policy.	May pay dividends. May provide a reduced paid-up policy. Partial cash surrenders permitted.	May pay dividends. Minimum death benefit. Partial cash surrenders permitted.

your coverage. Exhibit 10–3 compares the important features of term life, whole life, and universal life insurance.

OTHER TYPES OF LIFE INSURANCE POLICIES Other types of life insurance policies include group life insurance, credit life insurance, and endowment life insurance.

Group Life Insurance   Group life insurance is basically a variation of term insurance. It covers a large number of people under a single policy. The people included in the group do not need medical examinations to get the coverage. Group insurance is usually offered through employers, who pay part or all of the costs for their employees, or through professional organizations, which allow members to sign up for the coverage. Group plans are easy to enroll in, but they can be much more expensive than similar term policies.

Credit Life Insurance   Credit life insurance is used to pay off certain debts, such as auto loans or mortgages, in the event that you die before they are paid in full. These types of policies are not the best buy for the protection that they offer. Decreasing term insurance is a better option.

Endowment Life Insurance   Endowment is life insurance that provides coverage for a specific period of time and pays an agreed-upon sum of money to the policyholder if he or she is still living at the end of the endowment period. If the policyholder dies before that time, the beneficiary receives the money.

Key Web Sites for Life Insurance Information

www.iii.org

www.insweb.com

CONCEPT CHECK 10–2

1 What are the two types of life insurance companies?

_____

2 For each of the following statements, indicate your response by writing "T" or "F."

    a. Stock life insurance companies generally sell participating (or par) policies. _____

    b. Mutual life insurance companies specialize in the sale of nonparticipating (nonpar) policies. _____

    c. If you wish to pay exactly the same premium each year, you should choose a nonpar policy. _____

    d. Permanent insurance is known as whole life, straight life, ordinary life, and cash-value life insurance. _____

    e. Term life insurance is the most expensive type of policy. _____

3 What are the five forms of term insurance?

_____

_____

4 What are the four forms of whole life insurance?

_____

_____

5 Define the following types of life insurance policies:

    a. Group life insurance _____

    b. Credit life insurance _____

    c. Endowment life insurance _____

Apply Yourself!

Objective 2

Choose one stock and one mutual life insurance company. Obtain and compare premiums for $50,000 term, whole life, and universal life insurance.

Selecting Provisions and Buying Life Insurance

Key Provisions in a Life Insurance Policy

Study the provisions in your policy carefully. The following are some of the most common features.

OBJECTIVE 3

Select important provisions in life insurance contracts and create a plan to buy life insurance.

NAMING YOUR BENEFICIARY You decide who receives the benefits of your life insurance policy: your spouse, your child, or your business partner, for example. You can also name contingent beneficiaries, those who will receive the money if your primary beneficiary dies before or at the same time as you do. Update your list of beneficiaries as your needs change.

INCONTESTABILITY CLAUSE The incontestability clause says that the insurer can't cancel the policy if it's been in force for a specified period, usually two years. After that time the policy is considered valid during the lifetime of the insured. This is true even if the policy was gained through fraud. The incontestability clause protects the beneficiaries from financial loss in the event that the insurance company refuses to meet the terms of the policy.

THE GRACE PERIOD When you buy a life insurance policy, the insurance company agrees to pay a certain sum of money under specified circumstances and you agree to pay a certain premium regularly. The *grace period* allows 28 to 31 days to elapse, during which time you may pay the premium without penalty. After that time, the policy lapses if you have not paid the premium.

POLICY REINSTATEMENT A lapsed policy can be put back in force, or reinstated, if it has not been turned in for cash. To reinstate the policy, you must again qualify as an acceptable risk, and you must pay overdue premiums with interest. There is a time limit on reinstatement, usually one or two years.

NONFORFEITURE CLAUSE One important feature of the whole life policy is the **nonforfeiture clause.** This provision prevents the forfeiture of accrued benefits if you choose to drop the policy. For example, if you decide not to continue paying premiums, you can exercise specified options with your cash value.

nonforfeiture clause A provision that allows the insured not to forfeit all accrued benefits.

MISSTATEMENT OF AGE PROVISION The misstatement of age provision says that if the company finds out that your age was incorrectly stated, it will pay the benefits your premiums would have bought if your age had been correctly stated. The provision sets forth a simple procedure to resolve what could otherwise be a complicated legal matter.

POLICY LOAN PROVISION A loan from the insurance company is available on a whole life policy after the policy has been in force for one, two, or three years, as stated in the policy. This feature, known as the *policy loan provision,* permits you to borrow any amount up to the cash value of the policy. However, a policy loan reduces the death benefit by the amount of the loan plus interest if the loan is not repaid.

SUICIDE CLAUSE In the first two years of coverage, beneficiaries of someone who dies by suicide receive only the amount of the premiums paid. After two years beneficiaries receive the full value of death benefits.

RIDERS TO LIFE INSURANCE POLICIES An insurance company can change the conditions of a policy by adding a rider to it. A **rider** is a document attached to a policy that changes its terms by adding or excluding specified conditions or altering its benefits.

rider A document attached to a policy that modifies its coverage.

Waiver of Premium Disability Benefit One common rider is a waiver of premium disability benefit. This clause allows you to stop paying premiums if you're totally and

---

did you know?

LEED (Leadership in Energy and Environmental Design) is an international certification used to measure how well a building or community performs. LEED is used to assess energy savings, water efficiency, CO_2 emissions reduction, and improved indoor air quality. The program provides a guide for developing environmentally-friendly building design, construction, operations, and maintenance.

permanently disabled before you reach a certain age, usually 60. The company continues to pay the premiums at its own expense.

Accidental Death Benefit   Another common rider to life insurance is an accidental death benefit, sometimes called **double indemnity.** Double indemnity pays twice the value of the policy if you are killed in an accident. Again, the accident must occur before a certain age, generally 60 to 65. Experts counsel against adding this rider to your coverage. The benefit is very expensive, and your chances of dying in an accident are slim.

double indemnity
A benefit under which the company pays twice the face value of the policy if the insured's death results from an accident.

Guaranteed Insurability Option   A third important rider is known as a guaranteed insurability option. This rider allows you to buy a specified additional amount of life insurance at certain intervals without undergoing medical exams. This is a good option for people who anticipate needing more life insurance in the future.

Cost-of-Living Protection   This special rider is designed to help prevent inflation from eroding the purchasing power of the protection your policy provides. A *loss, reduction,* or *erosion of purchasing power* refers to the impact inflation has on a fixed amount of money. As inflation increases the cost of goods and services, that fixed amount will not buy as much in the future as it does today. Exhibit 10–4 shows the effects of inflation on a $100,000 life insurance policy. However, your insurance needs are likely to be smaller in later years.

Accelerated Benefits   *Accelerated benefits,* also known as *living benefits,* are life insurance policy proceeds paid to the policyholder who is terminally ill before he or she dies. The benefits may be provided for directly in the policies, but more often they are added by riders or attachments to new or existing policies. A representative list of insurers that offer accelerated benefits is available from the National Insurance Consumer Helpline (NICH) at 800-942-4242. Although more than 150 companies offer some form of accelerated benefits, not all plans are approved in all states. NICH cannot tell you whether a particular plan is approved in any given state. For more information, check with your insurance agent or your state department of insurance.

Assumed Annual Inflation Rate: 3%
Purchasing Power After:

5 years
$86,261

10 years
$74,409

15 years
$64,186

20 years
$55,368

Exhibit **10–4**

Effects of Inflation on a $100,000 Life Insurance Policy

Source: *The TIAA Guide to Life Insurance Planning for People in Education* (New York: Teachers Insurance and Annuity Association, January 1997), p. 8.

Second-to-Die Option   A *second-to-die life insurance policy,* also called *survivorship life,* insures two lives, usually husband and wife. The death benefit is paid when the second spouse dies. Usually a second-to-die policy is intended to pay estate taxes when both spouses die. However, some attorneys claim that with the right legal advice, you can minimize or avoid estate taxes completely.

Now that you know the various types of life insurance policies and the major provisions of and riders to such policies, you are ready to make your buying decisions.

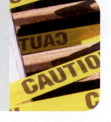

CAUTION! Each rating agency uses its own criteria to determine financial ratings. Even though all use an "A," "B," or "C" grading system, what is "A" for one might be "AA+" or "Aa1" for another.

Buying Life Insurance

You should consider a number of factors before buying life insurance. As discussed earlier in this chapter, these factors include your present and future sources of income, other savings and income protection, group life insurance, group annuities (or other pension benefits), Social Security, and, of course, the financial strength of the company.

FROM WHOM TO BUY?   Look for insurance coverage from financially strong companies with professionally qualified representatives. It is not unusual for a relationship with an insurance company to extend over a period of 20, 30, or even 50 years. For that reason alone you should choose carefully when deciding on an insurance company or an insurance agent. Fortunately, you have a choice of sources.

Sources   Protection is available from a wide range of private and public sources, including insurance companies and their representatives; private groups such as employers, labor unions, and professional or fraternal organizations; government programs such as Medicare and Social Security; and financial institutions and manufacturers offering credit insurance.

did you know?

Life insurance salespeople who pass examinations and meet other requirements are awarded the Chartered Life Underwriter (CLU) designation.

Rating Insurance Companies   Some of the strongest, most reputable insurance companies in the nation provide excellent insurance coverage at reasonable costs. In fact, the financial strength of an insurance company may be a major factor in holding down premium costs for consumers.

Locate an insurance company by checking the reputations of local agencies. Ask members of your family, friends, or colleagues about the insurers they prefer. Exhibit 10–5 describes the rating systems used by A. M. Best and the other big four rating agencies.

Choosing Your Insurance Agent   An insurance agent handles the technical side of insurance. However, that's only the beginning. The really important part of the agent's job is to apply his or her knowledge of insurance to help you select the proper kind of protection within your financial boundaries.

Choosing a good agent is among the most important steps in building your insurance program. How do you find an agent? One of the best ways to begin is by asking your parents, friends, neighbors, and others for their recommendations. The Personal Finance in Practice feature on page 336 offers guidelines for choosing an insurance agent.

Key Web Sites for Insurance Company Ratings

www.standardandpoors.com

http://infoseek.go.com/

www.ambest.com

www.moodys.com

COMPARING POLICY COSTS   Each life insurance company designs the policies it sells to make them attractive and useful to many policyholders. One policy may have features another policy doesn't; one company may be more selective than another company; one company may get a better return on its investments than another company. These and other factors affect the prices of life insurance policies.

Exhibit 10–5

Rating Systems of Major Rating Agencies: You Should Deal with Companies Rated Superior or Excellent

	A. M. Best	Standard & Poor's Duff & Phelps	Moody's	Weiss Research
Superior	A++	AAA	Aaa	A+
	A+			
Excellent	A	AA+	Aa1	A
	A−	AA	Aa2	A−
		AA−	Aa3	B+
Good	B++	A+	A1	B
	B+	A	A2	B−
		A−	A3	C+
Adequate	B	BBB+	Baa1	C
	B−	BBB	Baa2	C−
		BBB−	Baa3	D+
Below average	C++	BB+	Ba1	D
	C+	BB	Ba2	D−
		BB−	Ba3	E+
Weak	C	B+	B1	E
	C−	B	B2	E−
	D	B−	B3	
Nonviable	E	CCC	Caa	F
	F	CC	Ca	
		C, D	C	

In brief, five factors affect the price a company charges for a life insurance policy: the company's cost of doing business, the return on its investments, the mortality rate it expects among its policyholders, the features the policy contains, and competition among companies with comparable policies.

Ask your agent to give you interest-adjusted indexes. An **interest-adjusted index** is a method of evaluating the cost of life insurance by taking into account the time value of money. Highly complex mathematical calculations and formulas combine premium payments, dividends, cash-value buildup, and present value analysis into an index number that makes possible a fairly accurate cost comparison among insurance companies. The lower the index number, the lower the cost of the policy. The Figure It Out box on page 337 shows how to use an interest-adjusted index to compare the costs of insurance.

interest-adjusted index A method of evaluating the cost of life insurance by taking into account the time value of money.

OBTAINING AND EXAMINING A POLICY A life insurance policy is issued after you submit an application for insurance and the insurance company accepts the application. The company determines your insurability by means of the information in your application, the results of a medical examination, and the inspection report. When you receive a life insurance policy, read every word of the contract and, if necessary, ask your agent for a point-by-point explanation of the language. Many insurance companies have rewritten their contracts to make them more understandable.

Key Web Sites for Comparing Rates

www.accuquote.com

www.iquote.com

Personal Finance in Practice

> Ten Golden Rules of Buying Life Insurance

Remember that your need for life insurance coverage will change over time. Your income may go up or down, or your family size might change. Therefore, it is wise to review your coverage periodically to ensure that it keeps up with your changing needs.

Follow these rules when buying life insurance	Done
1. Understand and know what your life insurance needs are before you make any purchase, and make sure the company you choose can meet those needs.	☐
2. Buy your life insurance from a company that is licensed in your state.	☐
3. Select an agent who is competent, knowledgeable, and trustworthy.	☐
4. Shop around and compare costs.	☐
5. Buy only the amount of life insurance you need and can afford.	☐
6. Ask about lower premium rates for nonsmokers.	☐
7. Read your policy and make sure you understand it.	☐
8. Inform your beneficiaries about the kinds and amount of life insurance you own.	☐
9. Keep your policy in a safe place at home, and keep your insurance company's name and your policy number in a safe deposit box.	☐
10. Check your coverage periodically, or whenever your situation changes, to ensure that it meets your current needs.	☐

Source: American Council of Life Insurance, 1001 Pennsylvania Avenue NW, Washington, DC 20004-2599.

Concept Check 10–3 (continued)

continued from page 337

(continued from page 337)

6 Match the following terms with the appropriate definition:

endowment

a. A person named to receive the benefits from an insurance policy. _____

beneficiary

b. Provides coverage for a specific period of time and pays an agreed-upon sum of money to the policyholder if he or she is still living at the end of the period.

_____

whole life insurance

c. A permanent policy for which the policyholder pays a specified premium for the rest of his or her life. _____

double indemnity

d. A rider to a life insurance policy that pays twice the value of the policy if the policyholder is killed in an accident. _____

Apply Yourself!

Objective 3

Examine your life insurance policies and the policies of other members of your family. Note the contractual provisions of each policy. What does the company promise to do in return for premiums?

338

Financial Planning with Annuities

As you have seen so far, life insurance provides a set sum of money at your death. However, if you want to enjoy benefits while you are still alive, you might consider annuities. An annuity protects you against the risk of outliving your assets.

An **annuity** is a financial contract written by an insurance company that provides you with regular income. Generally, you receive the income monthly, often with payments arranged to continue for as long as you live. The payments may begin at once (*immediate annuity*) or at some future date (*deferred annuity*).

As with the life insurance principle, discussed earlier, the predictable mortality experience of a large group of individuals is fundamental to the annuity principle. By determining the average number of years a large number of persons in a given age group will live, the insurance company can calculate the annual amounts to pay to each person in the group over his or her entire life.

Because the annual payouts per premium amount are determined by average mortality experience, annuity contracts are more attractive for people whose present health, living habits, and family mortality experience suggest that they are likely to live longer than average. As a general rule, annuities are not advisable for people in poor health, although exceptions to this rule exist.

> **OBJECTIVE 4**
> Recognize how annuities provide financial security.

annuity A contract that provides a regular income for as long as the person lives.

Why Buy Annuities?

A primary reason for buying an annuity is to give you retirement income for the rest of your life. You should fully fund your IRAs, Keoghs, and 401(k)s before considering annuities. We discuss retirement income in Chapter 14.

Although people have been buying annuities for many years, the appeal of variable annuities increased during the mid-1990s due to a rising stock market. A *fixed annuity* states that the annuitant (the person who is to receive the annuity) will receive a fixed amount of income over a certain period or for life. With a *variable annuity,* the monthly payments vary because they are based on the income received from stocks or other investments.

Some of the growth in the use of annuities can be attributed to the passage of the Employee Retirement Income Security Act (ERISA) of 1974. Annuities are often purchased for individual retirement accounts (IRAs), which ERISA made possible. They may also be used in Keogh-type plans for self-employed people. As you will see in Chapter 14 , contributions to both IRA and Keogh plans are tax deductible up to specified limits.

Tax Considerations

When you buy an annuity, the interest on the principal, as well as the interest compounded on that interest, builds up free of current income tax. The Tax Reform Act of 1986 preserves the tax advantage of annuities (and insurance) but curtails deductions for IRAs. With an annuity, there is no maximum annual contribution. Also, if you die during the accumulation period, your beneficiary is guaranteed no less than the amount invested.

Exhibit 10–6 shows the difference between an investment in an annuity and an investment in a certificate of deposit (CD). Remember, federal income tax on an annuity is deferred, whereas the tax on interest earned on a CD must be paid currently.

As with any other financial product, the advantages of annuities are tempered by drawbacks. In the case of variable annuities, these drawbacks include reduced flexibility and fees that lower investment return.

Exhibit 10–6

Tax-Deferred Fixed
Annuity versus Taxable
CD (a 30-year projection
of performance; single
deposit of $30,000)

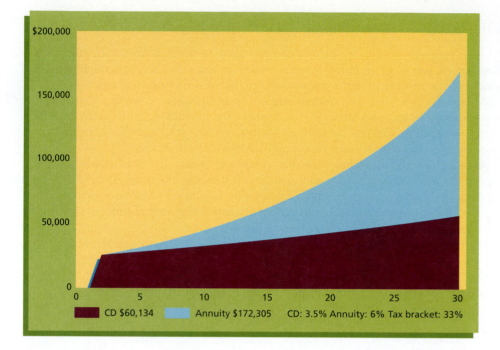

CD $60,134　　Annuity $172,305　　CD: 3.5% Annuity: 6% Tax bracket: 33%

CONCEPT CHECK 10–4

1 What is an annuity?

_____

2 What is the difference between an immediate and a deferred annuity?

_____

3 As a general rule, are annuities advisable for people in poor health?

_____

Why or why not? _____

4 What are fixed and variable annuities?

_____

Apply Yourself!

Objective 4

Interview friends, relatives, and others who have bought annuities. Which type of annuity did they purchase, and why?

Back to... *Getting Personal*

Reconsider your responses to the "Getting Personal" statements at the beginning of the chapter. For more effective personal financial planning and assessment of life insurance needs:

- Before you buy life insurance, you will have to decide whether you need it at all. Single people who live alone or with their parents usually have little or no need for life insurance. Consider information from several sources when determining life insurance needs, including friends, relatives, and various Web sites.
- Have specific life insurance goals in writing and review them as your life situation changes. What type of life insurance is best for your life situation? Use Exhibit 10–3, which distinguishes between temporary and permanent life insurance.

- Assess the pros and cons of key provisions in a life insurance policy. Who will receive the benefits of your life insurance policy—your spouse, your child, or your business partner? More information is available from www.iii.org and www.insweb.com.
- Purchase your life insurance from one of the strongest and most reputable insurance companies. Ask members of your family, friends, or colleagues about the insurers they prefer. Use Exhibit 10–5, which describes the rating systems used by major rating agencies. Also visit key Web sites for insurance company ratings such as www.ambest and www.standardandpoors.com.

What did you learn in this chapter that could help you make better decisions in purchasing life insurance?

Chapter Summary

Objective 1   Life insurance protects the people who depend on you from financial losses caused by your death. You can use the easy method, the DINK method, the "nonworking" spouse method, or the "family need" method to determine your life insurance need.

Objective 2   Two types of insurance companies—stock and mutual—sell nonparticipating and participating policies. Both sell two basic types of insurance: term life and whole life. Many variations and combinations of these types are available.

Objective 3   Most life insurance policies have standard features. An insurance company can change the conditions of a policy by adding a rider to it.

Before buying life insurance, consider all your present and future sources of income, then compare the costs and choose appropriate settlement options.

Objective 4   An annuity pays while you live, whereas life insurance pays when you die. With a fixed annuity, you receive a fixed amount of income over a certain period or for life. With a variable annuity, the monthly payments vary because they are based on the income received from stocks or other investments.

Key Terms

annuity 339

beneficiary 322

cash value 328

double indemnity 333

interest-adjusted index 335

nonforfeiture clause 332

nonparticipating policy 326

participating policy 326

rider 332

term insurance 327

universal life insurance 328

whole life insurance 328

Self-Test Problems

1. Suppose that yours is a typical family. Your annual income is $60,000. Use the easy method to determine your need for life insurance.
2. Using the "nonworking" spouse method, what should be the life insurance needs for a family whose youngest child is two years old?
3. Suppose your annual premium for a $20,000, twenty-year limited-payment policy is $420 over the twenty-year period. The cash value of your policy at the end of 20 years is $9,200. Assume that you could have invested the annual premium in a mutual fund yielding 7 percent annually. What is the net cost of your insurance for the 20-year period?

Solutions

1. Current gross income = $60,000
   Multiply gross income by 7 years = $420,000
   Take 70 percent of $420,000 = $420,000 × 0.70
   Approximate insurance needed = $294,000
2. Youngest child's age = 2 years
   16 years before the child is 18 years old
   Insurance needed 16 × $10,000 = $160,000
3. Premiums paid over 20 years = $420 × 20 = $8,400
   Time value of 20-year annual payments of $420 at 7 percent yield.
   (See Exhibit 1–B; use a factor of 40.995) = 40.995 × $420 = $17,218
   Cash value = $9,200
   Net cost of insurance = $17,218 − 9,200 = $8,018

Problems

1. You are the wage earner in a "typical family," with $40,000 gross annual income. Use the easy method to determine how much insurance you should carry. (Obj. 1)

2. You and your spouse are in good health and have reasonably secure careers. Each of you makes about $28,000 annually. You own a home with an $80,000 mortgage, and you owe $10,000 on car loans, $5,000 in personal debts, and $3,000 on credit card loans. You have no other debts. You have no plans to increase the size of your family in the near future. Estimate your total insurance needs using the DINK method. (Obj. 1)

3. Tim and Allison are married and have two children, ages 4 and 7. Allison is a "nonworking" spouse who devotes all of her time to household activities. Estimate how much life insurance Tim and Allison should carry. (Obj. 1)

4. Obtain premium rates for $25,000 whole life, universal life, and term life policies from local insurance agents. Compare the costs and provisions of these policies. (Obj. 2)

5. Use the Figure It Out worksheet on page 325 to calculate your own life insurance needs. (Obj. 1)

6. Use Exhibit 10–1 to find the average number of additional years a 20-year-old male and female were expected to live, based on the statistics gathered by the U.S. government as of 2004. (Obj. 1)

7. Mark and Parveen are the parents of three young children. Mark is a store manager in a local supermarket. His gross salary is $65,000 per year. Parveen is a full-time stay-at-home mom. Use the easy method to estimate the family's life insurance needs. (Obj. 1)

8. You are a dual-income, no-kids family. You and your spouse have the following debts (total): mortgage, $180,000; auto loan, $10,000; credit card balance, $2,000; and other debts of $6,000. Further, you estimate that your funeral will cost

$4,000. Your spouse expects to continue to work after your death. Using the DINK method, what should be your need for life insurance? (Obj. 1)

9. Using the "nonworking" spouse method, what should be the life insurance needs for a family whose youngest child is seven years old? (Obj. 1)

10. Using the "nonworking" spouse method, what should be the life insurance needs for a family whose youngest child is 10 years old? (Obj. 1)

11. Your variable annuity charges administrative fees at an annual rate of 0.15 percent of account value. Your average account value during the year is $50,000. What is the administrative fee for the year? (Obj. 4)

Questions

1. Choose a current issue of *Money, Kiplinger's Personal Finance Magazine, Consumer Reports,* or *Worth* and summarize an article that provides information on human life expectancy and how life insurance may provide financial security. (Obj. 1)

2. Analyze the four methods of determining life insurance requirements. Which method is best, and why? (Obj. 1)

3. Visit a few Web sites of companies such as Metropolitan Life, New York Life, Transamerica Life, Lincoln Benefit Life, or others of your choice. Then summarize the various types of insurance coverage available from these companies. (Obj. 2)

4. Contact your state insurance department to get information about whether your state requires interest-adjusted cost disclosure. Summarize your findings. (Obj. 3)

5. Review the settlement options on your family's life insurance policies, and discuss with your family which option would be the best choice for them at this time. (Obj. 3)

Case in Point

LIFE INSURANCE FOR THE YOUNG MARRIED

Jeff and Ann are both 28 years old. They have been married for three years, and they have a son who is almost 2. They expect their second child in a few months.

Jeff is a teller in a local bank. He has just received a $30-a-week raise. His income is $480 a week, which, after taxes, leaves him with $1,648 a month. His company provides $20,000 of life insurance, a medical/hospital/surgical plan, and a major medical plan. All of these group plans protect him as long as he stays with the bank.

When Jeff received his raise, he decided that part of it should be used to add to his family's protection. Jeff and Ann talked to their insurance agent, who reviewed the insurance Jeff obtained through his job. Under Social Security, they also had some basic protection against the loss of Jeff's income if he became totally disabled or if he died before the children were 18.

But most of this protection was only basic, a kind of floor for Jeff and Ann to build on. For example, monthly Social Security payments to Ann would be approximately $1,250 if Jeff died leaving two children under age 18. Yet the family's total expenses would soon be higher after the birth of the second baby. Although the family's expenses would be lowered if Jeff died, they would be at least $250 a month more than Social Security would provide.

Questions

1. What type of policy would you suggest for Jeff and Ann? Why?

2. In your opinion do Jeff and Ann need additional insurance? Why or why not?

Continuing Case

Vikki and Tim Treble (ages 36 and 38) own a home, have one daughter, Molly, and have just found out that Vikki is expecting twins. Vikki returned home from a doctor's appointment one evening to a sad message from her mother. Her Uncle Joe had died unexpectedly at the age of 56.

Later that evening, after Molly is asleep, Vikki asks Tim if they can talk. Of course she hopes they will both be healthy until they're 95 but worries about something happening to one of them. Do they have enough life insurance? Will they have enough insurance even if Vikki doesn't go back to work after the twins are born?

Vikki and Tim's financial statistics are shown below:

Assets:
Checking/savings account $23,000
Emergency fund $30,000
House $275,000
Cars $18,000 and $4,000
Household possessions $10,000
401(k) balance $78,000 (Vikki), $73,000 (Tim)
College savings $10,000

Liabilities:
Mortgage $182,000
Car loan $16,000

Income:
Gross Salary: $22,000 per year (Vikki), $82,000 (Tim)
After-tax monthly salary: $1,284 (Vikki), $4,783 (Tim)

Monthly Expenses:
Mortgage $1,200
Property tax/Insurance $500
Daily living expenses (including utilities, food) $2,500
Child-care (including after-school care and summer camps) $6,000
Car loan $450
Entertainment/vacations $350
Gas/repairs $500

Savings:
401(k) 10% of gross monthly salary
College savings $200

Questions:

1. How much life insurance do Vikki and Tim need? Use the Easy method and the Nonworking Spouse method.
2. What do they need to consider if they use the Family Need method to determine the life insurance coverage needed?
3. What types of policies are available for the Trebles? What are the benefits of each?
4. If Tim's employer offers life insurance coverage of one times his salary at no cost to him, how does this affect their potential life insurance purchases? Should they depend entirely on the policy available through his employer?
5. How can the Trebles use *Your Personal Financial Plan* sheets 33–34?

Spending Diary

"I'M NOT SURE SPENDING FOR LIFE INSURANCE IS NECESSARY FOR MY LIFE SITUATION."

Directions

As you continue to record and monitor spending in various categories, be sure to consider how various decisions will affect your long-term financial security. Various comments you record might remind you to consider possible changes you might want to make in your spending habits. The Daily Spending Diary sheets are located in Appendix C at the end of the book and on the student Web site at www.mhhe.com/kdh.

Questions

1. Are there any spending amounts or items that you might consider reducing or eliminating?

2. What actions might you consider now or in the future regarding spending on life insurance?

Determining Life Insurance Needs

Financial Planning Activities: Estimate life insurance coverage needed to cover expected expenses and future family living costs.

Suggested Web Sites: www.insure.com   www.kiplinger.com/tools/

Household expenses to be covered

Final expenses (funeral, estate taxes, etc.)	1	$ _____
Payment of consumer debt amounts	2	$ _____
Emergency fund	3	$ _____
College fund	4	$ _____

Expected living expenses:

Average living expense	$ _____
Spouse's income after taxes	$ − _____
Annual Social Security benefits	$ − _____
Net annual living expenses	$ _____
Years until spouse is 90	$ _____
Investment rate factor (see below)	$ _____

Total living expenses

(net annual expenses times investment rate factor)	5	$ _____
Total monetary needs (1 + 2 + 3 + 4 + 5)		$ _____
Less: Total current investments		$ _____
Life insurance needs		$ _____

Investment rate factors

Years until spouse is 90	25	30	35	40	45	50	55	60
Conservative investment	20	22	25	27	30	31	33	35
Aggressive investment	16	17	19	20	21	21	22	23

Note: Use Sheet 34 to compare life insurance policies.

What's Next for Your Personal Financial Plan?

- Survey several people to determine their reasons for buying life insurance.
- Talk to an insurance agent to compare the rates charged by different companies and for different age categories.

Name: _____   **Date:** _____

Life Insurance Policy Comparison

Financial Planning Activities: Research and compare companies, coverages, and costs for different life insurance policies. Analyze ads and contact life insurance agents to obtain the information requested below.

Suggested Web Sites: www.quotesmith.com   www.accuquote.com

Age:			
Company			
Agent's name, address, and phone			
Type of insurance (term, straight/whole, limited payment, endowment, universal)			
Type of policy (individual, group)			
Amount of coverage			
Frequency of payment (monthly, quarterly, semiannual, annual)			
Premium amount			
Other costs: • Service charges • Physical exam			
Rate of return (annual percentage increase in cash value; not applicable for term policies)			
Benefits of insurance as stated in ad or by agent			
Potential problems or disadvantages of this coverage			

What's Next for Your Personal Financial Plan?

- Talk to a life insurance agent to obtain information on the methods he or she suggests for determining the amount of life insurance a person should have.
- Research the differences in premium costs between a mutual and a stock company.

11 Investing Basics and Evaluating Bonds

Getting Personal

Why invest? For each of the following statements, select "yes" or "no" to indicate your behavior regarding these investing activities:

	Yes	No
1. My investment goals are written down.	____	____
2. I have performed a financial checkup.	____	____
3. I have taken actions to maintain my financial security during an economic crisis.	____	____
4. When making investment decisions, I understand how asset allocation can affect the choice of investments.	____	____
5. I know why people invest in bonds and other conservative investments.	____	____

After studying this chapter, you will be asked to reconsider your responses to these items.

Preparing for an Investment Program

OBJECTIVE 1

Explain why you should establish an investment program.

Many people ask the question: Why begin an investment program now? At the time of this book's publication, this is a very important question given the recent financial and banking crisis. Many investors have lost a great deal of money as a result of the crisis, yet the experts still agree that the best investment program is one that stresses long-term growth over a 20- to 40-year period. This chapter, along with the material on the time value of money presented in Chapter 1 and

Your Personal Financial Plan Sheets

35. Establishing Investment Goals
36. Assessing Risk for Investments
37. Evaluating Corporate Bonds

objectives

In this chapter, you will learn to:

1. Explain why you should establish an investment program.
2. Describe how safety, risk, income, growth, and liquidity affect your investment program.
3. Identify the factors that can reduce investment risk.
4. Understand why investors purchase government bonds.
5. Recognize why investors purchase corporate bonds.
6. Evaluate bonds when making an investment.

Why is this important?

If you begin an investment program when you are 25 and invest $2,000 each year, you could be a millionaire by the time you retire. While many people dream of being the world's next millionaire, dreaming doesn't make anything happen. You must also learn how to become a smart investor. That's what this chapter is all about—introducing you to investment concepts that can make a *real* difference.

the material on retirement planning in Chapter 14, will help you understand the importance of beginning an investment program as soon as you can. Remember, the sooner you start an investment program, the more time your investments have to work for you.

Like other decisions, the decision to start an investment plan is one you must make for yourself. No one is going to make you save the money you need to fund an investment plan. In fact, the *specific* goals you want to accomplish must be the driving force behind your investment plan.

Establishing Investment Goals

Some financial planners suggest that investment goals be stated in terms of money: By December 31, 2018, I will have total assets of $120,000. Other financial planners believe investors are more motivated to work toward goals that are stated in terms of the particular things they desire: By January 1, 2020, I will have accumulated enough money to purchase a second home in the mountains. To be useful, investment goals must be specific and measurable. They must also be tailored to your particular financial needs. The following questions will help you establish valid investment goals:

1. What will you use the money for?
2. How much money do you need to satisfy your investment goals?
3. How will you obtain the money?
4. How long will it take you to obtain the money?
5. How much risk are you willing to assume in an investment program?
6. What possible economic or personal conditions could alter your investment goals?
7. Considering your economic circumstances, are your investment goals reasonable?
8. Are you willing to make the sacrifices necessary to ensure that you meet your investment goals?
9. What will the consequences be if you don't reach your investment goals?

Your investment goals are always oriented toward the future. In Chapter 1, we classified goals as short term (less than two years), intermediate (two to five years), or long term (over five years). These same classifications are also useful in planning your investment program. For example, you may establish a short-term goal of accumulating $3,000 in a savings account over the next 18 months. You may then use the $3,000 to purchase stocks or mutual funds to help you obtain your intermediate or long-term investment goals.

Performing a Financial Checkup

Before beginning an investment program, your personal financial affairs should be in good shape. In this section, we examine several factors you should consider before making your first investment.

WORK TO BALANCE YOUR BUDGET Many individuals regularly spend more than they make. They purchase items on credit and then must make monthly installment payments and pay finance charges ranging between 12 and 18 percent or higher. With this situation, investing in certificates of deposit, bonds, stocks, mutual funds, or other investments that might earn 2 to 10 percent makes no sense until credit card and installment purchases, along with the accompanying finance charges, are reduced or eliminated. A good rule of thumb is to limit consumer credit payments to 20 percent of your net (after-tax) income. Eventually, the amount of cash remaining after the bills are paid will increase and can be used to start a savings program or finance investments.

OBTAIN ADEQUATE INSURANCE PROTECTION We discussed insurance in detail in Chapters 8 , 9 , and 10 and will not cover that topic again here. However, it is essential that you consider insurance needs. Before you start investing, examine the amount of your insurance coverage for life insurance, hospitalization, your home, automobiles, and any other assets that may need coverage.

START AN EMERGENCY FUND Before you begin an investment program, most financial planners suggest that you establish an emergency fund. An **emergency fund** is an amount of money you can obtain quickly in case of immediate need. This money should be deposited in a savings account paying the highest available interest rate or in a money market mutual fund that provides immediate access to cash if needed.

Most financial planners agree that an amount equal to at least three months' living expenses is reasonable.

emergency fund An amount of money you can obtain quickly in case of immediate need.

Example

If your monthly expenses total $1,800, you should save at least $5,400 before you can begin investing.

Minimum emergency fund = Monthly expenses × 3 months

$$= \$1,800 \times 3 \text{ months}$$

$$= \$5,400$$

Example From Your Life

$ \underline{} \times 3 \text{ months} = \$ \underline{}$
   monthly expenses

HAVE ACCESS TO OTHER SOURCES OF CASH FOR EMERGENCY NEEDS
You may also want to establish a line of credit at a commercial bank, savings and loan association, or credit union. A **line of credit** is a short-term loan that is approved before you actually need the money. Because the paperwork has already been completed and the loan has been preapproved, you can later obtain the money as soon as you need it.

The cash advance provision offered by major credit card companies can also be used in an emergency. However, both lines of credit and credit cards have a ceiling, or maximum dollar amount, that limits the amount of available credit. If you have already exhausted both of these sources of credit on everyday expenses, they will not be available in an emergency.

line of credit A short-term loan that is approved before the money is actually needed.

Surviving a Financial Crisis

The recent financial and banking crisis underscores the importance of managing your personal finances *and* your investment program. As a result of the nation's economic problems, many people were caught off guard and had to scramble to find the money to pay their monthly bills. Many of these same individuals had to borrow money or use their credit cards to survive from one payday to the next. And some individuals were forced to sell some or all of their investments at depressed prices just to buy food for the family and pay for everyday necessities.

To survive a financial crisis, many experts recommend that you take action to make sure your financial affairs are in order. Here are seven steps you can take:

1. *Establish a larger than usual emergency fund.* Under normal circumstances, an emergency fund of three months' living expenses is considered adequate, but you may want to increase your fund in anticipation of a crisis.
2. *Know what you owe.* Make a list of all your debts and the amount of the required monthly payments, then identify the debts that *must* be paid. Typically these include the mortgage or rent, medicine, utilities, food, and transportation costs.
3. *Reduce spending.* Cut back to the basics and reduce the amount of money spent on entertainment, dining at restaurants, and vacations. Although this is not pleasant, the money saved from reduced spending can be used to increase your emergency fund or pay for everyday necessities.

4. *Pay off credit cards.* Get in the habit of paying your credit card bill in full each month. If you have credit card balances, begin by paying off the balance on the credit card with the highest interest rate.

5. *Apply for a line of credit at your bank, credit union, or financial institution.* As defined earlier in this section, a line of credit is a preapproved loan and will provide access to cash for future emergencies.

6. *Notify credit card companies and lenders if you are unable to make payments.* Although not all lenders are willing to help, many will work with you and lower your interest rate, reduce your monthly payment, or extend the time for repayment.

7. *Monitor the value of your investment and retirement accounts.* Tracking the value of your stock, mutual fund, and retirement accounts, for example, will help you decide which investments to sell if you need cash for emergencies. Continued evaluation of your investments can also help you reallocate your investments to reduce investment risk.

Above all, don't panic. While financial problems are stressful, staying calm and considering all the options may help reduce the stress. Keep in mind that bankruptcy should be a last resort. The reason is simple: A bankruptcy will remain on your credit report for up to 10 years.

did you know?

The more money you make, the more challenging your investment goals can be. Here are household income levels for U.S. families.

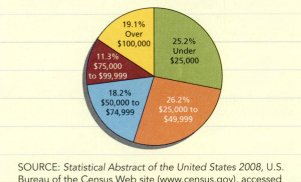

SOURCE: *Statistical Abstract of the United States 2008,* U.S. Bureau of the Census Web site (www.census.gov), accessed January 18, 2009 (Washington, DC: U.S. Government Printing Office), p. 442.

Getting the Money Needed to Start an Investment Program

Once you have established your investment goals and completed your financial checkup, it's time to start investing—assuming you have enough money to finance your investments. Unfortunately, the money doesn't automatically appear.

PRIORITY OF INVESTMENT GOALS How badly do you want to achieve your investment goals? Are you willing to sacrifice some purchases to provide financing for your investments? The answers to both questions are extremely important. Take Rita Johnson, a 32-year-old nurse in a large St. Louis hospital. As part of a divorce settlement in 2005, she received a cash payment of almost $55,000. At first, she was tempted to spend this money on a new BMW and new furniture. But after some careful planning, she decided to save $25,000 in a certificate of deposit and invest the remainder in a conservative mutual fund. On May 31, 2009, these investments were valued at $79,000.

What is important to you? What do you value? Each of these questions affects your investment goals. At one extreme are people who save or invest as much of each paycheck as they can. The satisfaction they get from attaining their intermediate and long-term financial goals is more important than the more immediate satisfaction of spending a large part of their paychecks on new clothes, a meal at an expensive restaurant, or a weekend getaway. At the other extreme are people who spend everything they make and run out of money before their next paycheck. Most people find either extreme unacceptable and take a more middle-of-the-road approach. These people often spend money on the items that make their lives more enjoyable and still save enough to fund an investment program. Suggestions to help you obtain the money you need to fund an investment program are listed in the nearby Personal Finance in Practice feature.

Personal Finance in Practice

Here are some suggestions for obtaining the money you need to fund an investment program

1. **Pay yourself first.** Each month, pay your monthly bills, save or invest a reasonable amount of money, and use whatever money is left over for personal expenses such as new clothes or entertainment.

   How could this suggestion help you?

   _____

   _____

2. **Take advantage of employer-sponsored retirement programs.** Many employers will match part or all of the contributions you make to a retirement program in accounts often referred to as 401(k)s or 403(b)s.

   How could this suggestion help you?

   _____

   _____

3. **Participate in an elective savings program.** You can elect to have money withheld from your paycheck each payday and automatically deposited in a savings or investment account.

   How could this suggestion help you?

   _____

   _____

4. **Make a special savings effort one or two months each year.** Many financial planners recommend that you cut back to the basics for one or two months each year.

   How could this suggestion help you?

   _____

   _____

5. **Take advantage of gifts, inheritances, and windfalls.** Use money from unexpected sources to fund an investment program.

   How could this suggestion help you?

   _____

   _____

EMPLOYER-SPONSORED RETIREMENT PLANS For many people, the easiest way to begin an investment program is to participate in an employer-sponsored retirement account—often referred to as a 401(k) or a 403(b) account. Many employers will match part or all of your contributions to retirement accounts. For example, an employer may contribute $0.25 for every $1.00 the employee contributes. And while the amount of the "match" varies, some employers still match $1.00 for every $1.00 employees contribute up to a certain percentage of their annual salary. More information on different types of retirement accounts is provided in Chapter 14 .

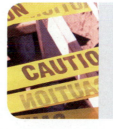

CAUTION! Because of the economic crisis and efforts to reduce expenses, many employers are reducing or eliminating matching provisions in their employee retirement plans.

The Value of Long-Term Investment Programs

Many people never start an investment program because they have only small sums of money. But even small sums grow over a long period of time. Mary and Peter Miller, for example, began their investment program by investing $2,000 *each year* when they were in their 20s; yet they expect their investment portfolio to be worth more than $1 million by the time Peter reaches age 65. How did they do it? Simple: They took advantage of the time value of money. You can achieve the same type of result. For instance, if you invest $2,000 each year for 40 years at a 6 percent annual rate of return, your investment will grow to $309,520.

Notice that the value of your investments increases each year because of two factors. First, it is assumed you will invest another $2,000 each year. At the end of 40 years, you will have invested a total of $80,000 ($2,000 × 40 years). Second, all investment earnings are allowed to accumulate and are added to your yearly deposits. In the

MY POINT OF VIEW | *By Knight Kiplinger*

TLC for your 401(k)

I can understand why, in this dismal stock market, you might be disgusted with your retirement savings account—your 401(k), your 403(b) or your IRA. Perhaps you're one of those who has scoffed that "My 401(k) is now a 201(k)." And I can understand why you might be tempted to dump your stocks and mutual funds at a loss and load up on Treasury bonds or just park everything in cash.

I can understand, too, why you might consider suspending or trimming your periodic 401(k) contributions. Maybe your household budget is pinched and you need the money right now. Or maybe you're thinking about more-drastic action: tapping your retirement account for current expenses, even though you'll have to pay income taxes on early withdrawals plus a 10% penalty.

The 401(k) Edge. Quite simply, tax-deferred retirement plans are the best gift that Washington ever gave to American workers. Yes, I know they're not as sweet a deal as were the defined-benefit pension plans once common in

the U.S. Employers funded those plans and bore all the investment risk, and there was no way that employees could raid their retirement funds early. But those pension plans aren't coming back, so there's no point in waxing nostalgic.

When I probe why people are disgusted with 401(k)s in general, I find that the real issue is not the concept. After all, what's not to like about getting an employer match to your own savings, and not having to pay taxes on the earnings inside the plan until retirement?

Instead, the issue for most people is the investments they chose for their 401(k). They are remorseful that their asset mix lacked diversity. Maybe they had too much in their employer's stock, which shouldn't represent more than 10% of the mix. Or, with retirement just a few years away, maybe they were too heavily invested in stock mutual funds.

John Bogle, the wise curmudgeon who founded Vanguard, thinks the percentage of interest-bearing investments in your

retirement accounts should equal your age—at age 55, for example, you would have 55% of your assets in bonds or cash and only 45% in stocks. That's a pretty conservative mix, but it would have prevented a massive erosion of your 401(k)'s value during this bear market.

Don't Sell Low. What about the paper losses you've already incurred in your 401(k) or IRA? Don't dump high-quality stocks and well-managed mutual funds that have been hammered. From today's depressed levels, stocks and REITs offer stronger appreciation potential over the next few years than bonds and cash.

SOURCE: Reprinted by permission from the February issue of *Kiplinger's Personal Finance.* Copyright © 2009 The Kiplinger Washington Editors, Inc.

1. Assume you have obtained a position with a firm that offers a 401(k) retirement program. You are asked if you want to participate in the firm's program. How would you answer? Explain your answer.

---

2. What factors should be considered when choosing the "right" mix of investments for your retirement account?

---

3. Often people don't monitor the value or reevaluate the investments contained in a retirement account. What steps should you take to avoid this situation?

Sheet 35 Establishing Investment Goals

CONCEPT CHECK 11–1

1 Why should an individual develop specific investment goals?

_____

_____

2 What factors should you consider when performing a financial checkup?

_____

_____

3 Describe the steps you can take to survive a financial crisis.

_____

_____

4 Why should you participate in an employer-sponsored 401(k) or 403(b) retirement plan?

_____

_____

5 In your own words, describe the time value of money concept and how it could affect your investment program.

_____

_____

Apply Yourself!

Objective 1

Visit the Consumer Credit Counseling Service Web site (www.cccs.net) and describe the services available to individuals who need help managing their finances.

---

above example, you earned $229,520 ($309,520 total return − $80,000 yearly contributions = $229,520 accumulated earnings).

Also, notice that if investments earn a higher rate of return, _total_ dollar returns increase dramatically. For example, a $2,000 annual investment that earns 10 percent a year is worth $885,180 at the end of 40 years. The rate of return and the length of time your money is invested _do_ make a difference. Exhibit 11–1 shows how much your investment portfolio will be worth at the end of selected time periods and with different rates of return. The search for higher returns is one reason many investors choose stocks, mutual funds, and other investments that offer higher potential returns compared to certificates of deposit or savings accounts.

Exhibit **11–1**

Growth Rate for $2,000 Invested at the End of Each Year at Various Rates of Return for Different Time Periods

Rate of Return	BALANCE AT END OF YEAR					
	1	5	10	20	30	40
2%	$2,000	$10,408	$21,900	$48,594	$81,176	$ 120,804
3	2,000	10,618	22,928	53,740	95,150	150,802
4	2,000	10,832	24,012	59,556	112,170	190,052
5	2,000	11,052	25,156	66,132	132,878	241,600
6	2,000	11,274	26,362	73,572	158,116	309,520
7	2,000	11,502	27,632	81,990	188,922	399,280
8	2,000	11,734	28,974	91,524	226,560	518,120
9	2,000	11,970	30,386	102,320	272,620	675,780
10	2,000	12,210	31,874	114,550	328,980	885,180
11	2,000	12,456	33,444	128,406	398,040	1,163,660
12	2,000	12,706	35,098	144,104	482,660	1,534,180

OBJECTIVE 2

Describe how safety, risk, income, growth, and liquidity affect your investment program.

Factors Affecting the Choice of Investments

Millions of Americans buy stocks, bonds, or mutual funds or make similar investments. And they all have reasons for investing their money. Some people want to supplement their retirement income when they reach age 65, while others want to become millionaires before age 40. Although each investor may have specific, individual goals for investing, all investors must consider a number of factors before choosing an investment alternative.

Safety and Risk

The safety and risk factors are two sides of the same coin. Safety in an investment means minimal risk or loss. On the other hand, risk in an investment means a measure of uncertainty about the outcome. Investments range from very safe to very risky. At one end of the investment spectrum are very safe investments. Investments in this category include government bonds, savings accounts, certificates of deposit, and certain corporate bonds, stocks, and mutual funds. Real estate may also be a very safe investment. Investors pick such investments because they know there is very little chance that investments of this kind will become worthless.

Many investors choose conservative investments because of the individual life situations in which they find themselves. As people approach retirement, for example, they usually choose more conservative investments with less chance of losing a large part of their nest egg. Finally, some investors simply dislike the risk associated with investments that promise larger returns.

At the other end of the investment spectrum are speculative investments. A **speculative investment** is a high-risk investment made in the hope of earning a relatively large profit in a short time. Such investments offer the possibility of a larger dollar return, but if they are unsuccessful, you may lose most or all of your initial investment. Speculative stocks, certain bonds, some mutual funds, some real estate,

speculative investment A high-risk investment made in the hope of earning a relatively large profit in a short time.

commodities, options, precious metals, precious stones, and collectibles are risk-oriented investments.

From an investor's standpoint, one basic rule sums up the relationship between the factors of safety and risk: *The potential return on any investment should be directly related to the risk the investor assumes.* For example, Ana Luna was injured in a work-related accident three years ago. After a lengthy lawsuit, she received a great deal of money that could be invested to provide a steady source of income for the remainder of her life. Having never invested before, she quickly realized her tolerance for risk was minimal. She had to conserve her $420,000 settlement. Eventually, after much discussion with professionals and her own research, she chose to save about half of her money in certificates of deposit. For the remaining half, she chose three stocks that offered a 2 percent average dividend, a potential for increased value, and a high degree of safety because of the financial stability of the corporations that issued the stocks.

Often beginning investors are afraid of the risk associated with many investments. But remember that without the risk, obtaining the larger returns that really make an investment program grow is impossible. The key is to determine how much risk you are willing to assume, and then choose quality investments that offer higher returns without an unacceptably high risk. To help you determine how much risk you are willing to assume, take the test for risk tolerance presented in Exhibit 11–2.

Exhibit 11–2   A Quick Test to Measure Investment Risk

The following quiz, adapted from one prepared by the T. Rowe Price group of mutual funds, can help you discover how comfortable you are with varying degrees of risk.

1. You're the winner on a TV game show. Which prize would you choose?
   - ☐ $2,000 in cash (1 point).
   - ☐ A 50 percent chance to win $4,000 (3 points).
   - ☐ A 20 percent chance to win $10,000 (5 points).
   - ☐ A 2 percent chance to win $100,000 (9 points).

2. You're down $500 in a poker game. How much more would you be willing to put up to win the $500 back?
   - ☐ More than $500 (8 points).
   - ☐ $500 (6 points).
   - ☐ $250 (4 points).
   - ☐ $100 (2 points).
   - ☐ Nothing—you'll cut your losses now (1 point).

3. A month after you invest in a stock, it suddenly goes up 15 percent. With no further information, what would you do?
   - ☐ Hold it, hoping for further gains (3 points).
   - ☐ Sell it and take your gains (1 point).
   - ☐ Buy more—it will probably go higher (4 points).

4. Your investment suddenly goes down 15 percent one month after you invest. Its fundamentals still look good. What would you do?
   - ☐ Buy more. If it looked good at the original price, it looks even better now (4 points).
   - ☐ Hold on and wait for it to come back (3 points).
   - ☐ Sell it to avoid losing even more (1 point).

5. You're a key employee in a start-up company. You can choose one of two ways to take your year-end bonus. Which would you pick?
   - ☐ $1,500 in cash (1 point).
   - ☐ Company stock options that could bring you $15,000 next year if the company succeeds, but will be worthless if it fails (5 points).

Your total score : _____

Scoring

5–18 points You are a more conservative investor. You prefer to minimize financial risks. The lower your score, the more cautious you are. When you choose investments, look for high credit ratings, and financial stability. In stocks, bonds, and real estate, look for a focus on income.

19–30 points You are a less conservative investor. You are willing to take more chances in pursuit of greater returns. The higher your score, the bolder you are. You may want to consider bonds with higher yields and lower credit ratings, the stocks of newer companies, real estate investments that use mortgage debt, or aggressive mutual funds.

A primer on the ABCs of investing is available from T. Rowe Price, 100 E. Pratt St., Baltimore, MD 21202 (800-638-5660).

Components of the Risk Factor

When choosing an investment, you must carefully evaluate changes in the risk factor. In fact, the overall risk factor can be broken down into four components.

INFLATION RISK As defined in Chapter 1 , inflation (an economic condition that is common for most economies) is a rise in the general level of prices. During periods of high inflation, there is a risk that the financial return on an investment will not keep pace with the inflation rate. To see how inflation reduces your buying power, let's assume you have deposited $10,000 in a certificate of deposit at 2 percent interest. At the end of one year, your money will have earned $200 in interest ($10,000 × 2% = $200). Assuming an inflation rate of 3 percent, it will cost you an additional $300 ($10,000 × 3% = $300), or a total of $10,300, to purchase the same amount of goods you could have purchased for $10,000 a year earlier. Thus, even though you earned $200, you lost $100 in purchasing power. And after paying taxes on the $200 interest, your loss of purchasing power is even greater.

INTEREST RATE RISK The interest rate risk associated with preferred stocks or government or corporate bonds is the result of changes in the interest rates in the economy. The value of these investments decreases when overall interest rates increase. In contrast, the value of these same investments rises when overall interest rates decrease.

To reduce the effects of interest-rate risk, both the federal government and corporations are now issuing inflation-protected bonds. Adjustments are made to the amount of interest the investor receives and in some cases to the principal and are based on changes in the consumer price index (CPI). Typically maturities for corporate inflation-protected bonds are 5, 7, or 10 years. The maturities for inflation-protected securities issued by the federal government are 5, 10, or 20 years.

BUSINESS FAILURE RISK The risk of business failure is associated with investments in stock and corporate bonds. With each of these investments, you face the possibility that bad management, unsuccessful products, competition, or a host of other factors will cause the business to be less profitable than originally anticipated. Lower profits usually mean lower dividends or no dividends at all. If the business continues to operate at a loss, even interest payments and repayment of corporate bonds may be questionable. The business may even fail and be forced to file for bankruptcy, in which case your investment may become totally worthless. Before ignoring the possibility of business failure, consider the plight of investors who owned stock in Lehman Brothers and Washington mutual—two financial firms that failed during the recent financial crisis. Investors in both firms lost millions!

Of course, the best way to protect yourself against such losses is to carefully evaluate the companies that issue the stocks and bonds you purchase and then continue to evaluate your investment after the purchase. Purchasing stock or bonds in more than one company or purchasing shares in a mutual fund can also help diversify your investments and protect against losses.

MARKET RISK Economic growth is not as systematic and predictable as most investors might believe. Generally, a period of rapid expansion is followed by a period of recession. For instance, the business cycle—the recurring time period between economic expansion and recession—has lasted an average of three to five years since World War II.[1] At the time of publication, many business leaders and politicians are debating how long the current recession will last. Despite efforts by the federal government, the

---

[1] The Investopedia Web site at (www.investopedia.com), accessed January 12, 2009.

Federal Reserve, and the U.S. Department of the Treasury, the nation is still experiencing economic problems that are affecting the value of investments.

During periods of recession, it may be difficult to sell investments such as real estate. Fluctuations in the market price for stocks and bonds may have nothing to do with the fundamental changes in the financial health of corporations. Such fluctuations may also be caused by political or social conditions. For example, the price of petroleum stocks may increase or decrease as a result of political activity in the Middle East.

Investment Income

Investors sometimes purchase certain investments because they want a predictable source of income. The most conservative investments—passbook savings accounts, certificates of deposit, and securities issued by the United States government—are also the most predictable sources of income. With these investments, you know exactly how much income will be paid on a specific date.

If investment income is a primary objective, you can also choose municipal bonds, corporate bonds, preferred stocks, utility stocks, or selected common stock issues. Other investments that may provide income potential are mutual funds and real estate rental property.

Investment Growth

To investors, *growth* means their investments will increase in value. Often the greatest opportunity for growth is an investment in common stock. During the 1990s, investors found that stocks issued by corporations in the electronics, technology, energy, and health care industries provided the greatest growth potential. And yet, many corporations in those same industries encountered financial problems, lower profits, or even losses during the first part of the 21st century. In 2003, the economy began to rebound and growth investing became popular (and profitable) for a two- to three-year period. Unfortunately, many investors watched their investments in growth companies or growth mutual funds begin to slow in 2006. By 2008, the financial crisis had become a major economic problem and many growth investments stopped growing and began to decrease in value. Still, one factor is certain: Investors still like the potential that is offered by growth investments.

Companies with earnings potential, sales revenues that are increasing, and managers who can solve the problems associated with rapid expansion are often considered to be growth companies. These same companies generally pay little or no dividends. The money the companies keep can provide at least part of the financing they need for future growth and expansion and control the cost of borrowing money. As a result, they grow at an even faster pace.

Other investments that may offer growth potential include mutual funds and real estate. For example, many mutual funds are referred to as growth funds or aggressive growth funds because of the growth potential of the individual securities included in the fund.

Investment Liquidity

Liquidity is the ability to buy or sell an investment quickly without substantially affecting the investment's value. Investments range from near-cash investments to frozen

CAUTION! Every year, thousands of people are ripped off because they respond to a phone call or an e-mail offering an investment that is too good to be true. To avoid investment scams, the experts suggest you watch out for sales pitches that begin with any of the following:

- Your profit is guaranteed.
- There's no risk.
- You would be a fool to pass this by.
- This offer is available today only.

Above all, take your time and check out any investment offer before you invest.

SOURCE: "Investment Fraud," AARP Web site (www.aarp.org), accessed January 10, 2009.

liquidity The ability to buy or sell an investment quickly without substantially affecting the investment's value.

Sheet 36 Assessing Risk for Investments

CONCEPT CHECK 11–2

1 Why are safety and risk two sides of the same coin?

_____

_____

2 In your own words, describe each of the four components of the risk factor.

Inflation risk:	
Interest rate risk:	
Business failure risk:	
Market risk:	

3 How do income, growth, and liquidity affect the choice of an investment?

_____

_____

Apply Yourself!

Objective 2

In this section, information was provided about how income and growth can affect an individual's choice of investments. Assume you are the investor in each of the following situations. Then choose either income or growth investments and justify your choice.

Life Situation	Income or Growth	Justification
An unemployed, single parent who has just received a $300,000 divorce settlement		
A 25-year-old single investor with a full-time job that pays $36,000 a year		
A retired couple with $650,000 in retirement savings		

investments from which it is virtually impossible to get your money. Interest-bearing checking and savings accounts are very liquid because they can be quickly converted to cash. Certificates of deposit impose penalties for withdrawing money before the maturity date. With other investments, you may be able to sell quickly, but market conditions, economic conditions, or many other factors may prevent you from regaining the amount you originally invested.

Type of Investment	FACTORS TO BE EVALUATED					
	Safety	Risk	Income	Growth	Liquidity
Common stock	Average	Average	Average	High	Average
Preferred stock	Average	Average	High	Average	Average
Corporate bonds	Average	Average	High	Low	Average
Government bonds	High	Low	Low	Low	High
Mutual funds	Average	Average	Average	Average	Average
Real estate	Average	Average	Average	Average	Low

Exhibit 11–3

Factors Used to Evaluate Traditional Investment Alternatives

Factors that Reduce Investment Risk

By now, you are probably thinking, how can I choose the right investment for me? Good question. To help answer that question, consider the following: Since 1926—more than 80 years—stocks have returned just over 10 percent a year. During the same period, U.S. government securities earned about 6 percent.[2] These facts suggest that everyone should invest in stocks because they offer the largest returns. In reality, stocks may have a place in your investment portfolio, but establishing an investment program is more than just picking a bunch of stocks or mutual funds that invest in stocks. Before making the decision to purchase stocks, consider the factors of portfolio management and asset allocation.

OBJECTIVE 3

Identify the factors that can reduce investment risk.

Portfolio Management and Asset Allocation

Earlier in this chapter, we examined how safety, risk, income, growth, and liquidity affect your investment choices. Now let's compare the factors that affect the choice of investments with some typical investment alternatives. Exhibit 11–3 ranks each alternative in terms of safety, risk, income, growth, and liquidity. More information on each investment alternative is provided later in this chapter and in Chapters 12 and 13.

ASSET ALLOCATION **Asset allocation** is the process of spreading your assets among several different types of investments to lessen risk. The term *asset allocation* is a fancy way of saying you need to diversify and avoid the pitfall of putting all your eggs in one basket. Asset allocation is often expressed in percentages. For example, what percentage of my assets do I want to put in stocks and mutual funds? What percentage do I want to put in bonds or certificates of deposit? To help answer these questions, many brokerage firms construct model portfolios like those illustrated in Exhibit 11–4 Some brokerage firms take the next step and suggest specific bonds, stocks, or mutual funds that are contained in each portfolio. In fact, some brokerage firms even allow you to purchase the securities in the portfolio as a package—a concept often referred to as *portfolio investing*.

Take a moment and look at each portfolio illustrated in Exhibit 11–4 . Then ask yourself: Which portfolio is the best one for me? The answer to that question is often tied to your tolerance for risk. Remember the basic rule presented earlier in this chapter: *The potential return on any investment should be directly related to the risk the investor assumes.* While investors often say they want larger returns, they must be willing to

asset allocation The process of spreading your assets among several different types of investments to lessen risk.

---

[2]"Money 101 Lesson 4: Basics of Investing," the CNN/Money Web site (http://money.cnn.com/magazines/moneymag/money101/lesson4), accessed January 13, 2009.

Exhibit 11–4

Three Different Investment Portfolios That Range from Very Conservative to Very Aggressive

Model Name	Asset Allocation	
Conservative portfolio	Stocks and mutual funds Bonds and CDs Cash and equivalents	15 to 20% 70 to 75% 5 to 15%
Aggressive portfolio	Stocks and mutual funds Bonds and CDs Cash and equivalents	65 to 70% 20 to 25% 5 to 15%
Very aggressive portfolio	Stocks and mutual funds Bonds and CDs Cash and equivalents	80 to 100% 0 to 10% 0 to 10%

SOURCE: The Investopedia.com Web site (www.investopedia.com), accessed January 12, 2009.

assume larger risks to obtain larger returns. For example, the very aggressive growth portfolio illustrated in Exhibit 11–4 promises the largest return because most or all of your money is invested in stocks or mutual funds. While stocks and mutual funds may offer the largest potential investment returns, these investments also have more risk when compared to bonds, certificates of deposit, and cash or cash equivalents. Thus, the very aggressive portfolio has more potential risk when compared to the other portfolios. In addition to asset allocation, other factors you should consider before investing are the time your investments will work for you and your age.

THE TIME FACTOR The amount of time that your investments have to work for you is another important factor when managing your investment portfolio. Recall the investment returns presented earlier in this section. Since 1926, stocks have returned just over 10 percent a year and returned more than other investment alternatives. And yet, during the same period, there were years when stocks decreased in value.[3] The point is that if you invested at the wrong time and then couldn't wait for the investment to recover, you would lose money. For instance, during the recent financial crisis, many retirees who were forced to sell stocks and mutual funds to pay everyday living expenses lost money. On the other hand, many younger investors with long-term investment goals could afford to hold their investments until the price of their securities recovered.

The amount of time you have before you need your investment money is crucial. If you can leave your investments alone and let them work for you for 5 to 10 years or more, then you can invest in stocks and mutual funds. On the other hand, if you need your investment money in two years or less, you should probably invest in short-term government bonds, highly rated corporate bonds, or certificates of deposit. By taking a more conservative approach for short-term investments, you reduce the possibility of having to sell your investments at a loss because of depressed market value or a staggering economy.

YOUR AGE A final factor to consider when choosing an investment is your age. Younger investors tend to invest a large percentage of their nest egg in growth-oriented investments. If their investments take a nosedive, they have time to recover. On the other hand, older investors tend to be more conservative and invest in government bonds, high-quality corporate bonds, and very safe corporate stocks or mutual funds. As a result, a smaller percentage of their nest egg is placed in growth-oriented investments.

[3]"Money 101 Lesson 4: Basics of Investing," the CNN/Money Web site (http://money.cnn.com/magazines/moneymag/money101/lesson4), accessed January 13, 2009.

For example, younger investors might choose the aggressive or very aggressive portfolio illustrated in Exhibit 11–4 because they are willing to take more risks in order to obtain the larger returns that will help their investment portfolio grow. On the other hand, older investors might choose the conservative portfolio illustrated in Exhibit 11–4 because they want the safety provided by more conservative investments.

Financial experts like Suze Orman, author of *The Road to Wealth* and other personal finance self-help books, suggest that you subtract your age from 110, and the difference is the percentage of your assets that should be invested in growth investments. For example, if you are 40 years old, subtract 40 from 110, which gives you 70. Therefore, 70 percent of your assets should be invested in growth-oriented investments while the remaining 30 percent should be kept in safer, conservative investments.[4]

Your Role in the Investment Process

Successful investors continually evaluate their investments. They never sit back and let their investments manage themselves. Some factors to consider when choosing different investments are described next.

EVALUATE POTENTIAL INVESTMENTS Let's assume you have $25,000 to invest. Also assume your investment will earn a 10 percent return the first year. At the end of one year, you will have earned $2,500 and your investment will be worth $27,500. Not a bad return on your original investment! Now ask yourself: How long would it take to earn $2,500 if I had to work for this amount of money at a job? For some people, it might take a month; for others, it might take longer. The point is that if you want this type of return, you should be willing to work for it, but the work takes a different form than a job. When choosing an investment, the work you invest is the time needed to research different investments so that you can make an informed decision.

Did You Know

If you really want to be socially responsible, then prove it by choosing green investments. To begin,

- Learn what socially responsible investing is.
- Research socially responsible companies and mutual funds.
- Pick your investments and then monitor both their financial performance and social responsibility record.

For more information, visit The Social Investment Forum at www.socialinvest.org.

MONITOR THE VALUE OF YOUR INVESTMENTS Would you believe that some people invest large sums of money and don't know if their investments have increased or decreased in value. They don't know if they should sell their investments or continue to hold them. A much better approach is to monitor the value of your investments. If you choose to invest in stocks, bonds, mutual funds, commodities, or options, you can determine the value of your holdings by looking at the price quotations reported on the Internet and in newspapers. Your real estate holdings may be compared with similar properties currently for sale in the surrounding area. Finally, you can determine the value of your precious metals, gemstones, and collectibles by checking with reputable dealers and investment firms. The nearby Figure It Out box presents further information on monitoring the value of your investments.

KEEP ACCURATE RECORDS Accurate recordkeeping can help you spot opportunities to maximize profits or reduce dollar losses when you sell your investments. Accurate recordkeeping can also help you decide whether you want to invest additional funds in a particular investment. At the very least, you should keep purchase records for each of your investments that include the actual dollar cost of the investment, plus any commissions or fees you paid. It is also useful to keep a list of the sources of information (Internet addresses, business periodicals, research publications, etc.), along with copies of the material you used to evaluate each investment. Then, when it is time to reevaluate an existing investment, you will know where to begin your

---

[4]Suze Orman, *The Road to Wealth* (New York: Riverbend Books, 2001), p. 371.

Figure It Out!

Charting the Value of Your Investment

To monitor the value of their investments, many investors use a simple chart like the one illustrated here. To construct a chart like this one, place the original purchase price of your investment in the middle on the side of the chart. Then use price increments of a logical amount to show increases and decreases in dollar value. *It is also possible to use computer software to chart the value of your investments.*

Place individual dates along the bottom of the chart. For stocks, bonds, mutual funds, and similar investments, you may want to graph every two weeks and chart current values on, say, a Friday. For longer term investments like real estate, you can chart current values every six months.

A WORD OF CAUTION
If an investment is beginning to have a large increase or decrease in value, you should watch that investment more closely. You can still continue to chart at regular intervals, but you may want to check dollar values more frequently— in some cases, daily.

PRACTICE MAKES PERFECT!
Using the dates and dollar amounts below, construct a graph to illustrate the price movements for a share of stock issued by Chesapeake Manufacturing.

Date	Price
June 1	$19
June 15	$16
June 29	$17
July 13	$20
July 27	$24
August 10	$25
August 24	$23

search for current information. Finally, accurate recordkeeping is also necessary for tax purposes.

OTHER FACTORS THAT IMPROVE INVESTMENT DECISIONS To achieve their financial goals, many people seek professional help. In many cases, they turn to stockbrokers, lawyers, accountants, bankers, or insurance agents. However, these professionals are specialists in one specific field and may not be qualified to provide the type of advice required to develop a thorough financial plan. Another source of investment help is a financial planner who has had training in securities, insurance, taxes, real estate, and estate planning.

Whether you are making your own decisions or have professional help, you must consider the tax consequences of selling your investments. Taxes were covered in Chapter 3 , and it is not our intention to cover them again. And yet, it is your responsibility to determine how taxes affect your investment decisions. You may want to review the material on dividend, interest, and rental income and on capital gains and capital losses that result from selling an investment. You may also want to read the material on tax-deferred investment income and retirement planning presented in Chapter 14. To find more information about how investments are taxed, visit the Internal Revenue Service Web site at www.irs.gov.

CONCEPT CHECK 11–3

1 Assume you must choose an investment that will help you obtain your investment goals. Rank the following investments from 1 (low) to 6 (high) and then justify your choice for your investment portfolio. (See Exhibit 11–3 for help evaluating each investment.)

Investment	Rank (1 = low; 6 = high)	Justification
Common stocks		
Preferred stocks		
Corporate bonds		
Government bonds		
Mutual funds		
Real estate		

2 Why should investors be concerned with asset allocation and the time their investments have to work for them?

_____

_____

3 Why should you monitor the value of your investments?

_____

_____

Apply Yourself

Objective 3

Use the Suze Orman method to determine the percentage of your investments that should be invested in growth investments.

Conservative Investment Options: Government Bonds

OBJECTIVE 4

Understand why investors purchase government bonds.

As noted in the last section, stocks have outperformed other investment alternatives over the past 80 years. Nevertheless, smart investors sometimes choose other investments. Answer the following questions to see if more conservative investments may be right for you:

Question	Yes	No
1. Stocks seem to be overpriced and will probably go down in the next 12 to 18 months.	_____	_____
2. I need to convert my investments to cash in a short period of time.	_____	_____
3. I'm afraid I will lose the money invested in speculative investments.	_____	_____

If you answered yes to any of these questions, you may want to consider the more conservative investments described in this section and the next section.

As discussed in Chapter 4 , savings accounts, certificates of deposit, money market accounts, and savings bonds provide a safe place to invest your money. Unfortunately, they don't offer a lot of growth or income potential. Other conservative investments that may offer more potential include bonds and debt securities issued by the U.S. government and state and local governments.

Government Bonds and Debt Securities

The U.S. government and state and local governments issue bonds to obtain financing. A **government bond** is a written pledge of a government or a municipality to repay a specified sum of money, along with interest. In this section, we discuss bonds issued by each level of government and look at why investors purchase these bonds.

government bond The written pledge of a government or a municipality to repay a specified sum of money, along with interest.

U.S. TREASURY BILLS, NOTES, AND BONDS The main reason investors choose U.S. government securities is that most investors consider them risk free. Because they are backed by the full faith and credit of the U.S. government and carry a decreased risk of default, they offer lower interest rates than corporate bonds. In this section, we discuss four principal types of securities issued by the U.S. Treasury: Treasury bills, Treasury notes, Treasury bonds, and Treasury inflation-protected securities (TIPS). These securities can be purchased through Treasury Direct at www.treasury-direct.gov. Treasury Direct conducts auctions to sell Treasury securities, and buyers interested in purchasing these securities at such auctions may bid competitively or noncompetitively. If they bid competitively, they must specify the rate or interest yield they are willing to accept. If they bid noncompetitively, they are willing to accept the interest rate determined at auction. Treasury securities may also be purchased through banks or brokers, which charge a commission.

U.S. government securities can be held until maturity or sold or redeemed before maturity. Interest paid on U.S. government securities is taxable for federal income tax purposes but is exempt from state and local taxation.

Treasury Bills A *Treasury bill,* sometimes called a *T-bill,* is sold in a minimum unit of $100 with additional increments of $100 above the minimum. Currently the Treasury Department sells T-bills with 4-week, 13-week, 26-week, and 52-week maturities only. T-bills are discounted securities, and the actual purchase price you pay is less than the maturity value of the T-bill. At maturity, the government repays the face value.

Treasury Notes A *Treasury note* is issued in $100 units with a maturity of more than 1 year but not more than 10 years. Typical maturities are 2, 3, 5, 7, and 10 years. Interest rates for Treasury notes are slightly higher than those for Treasury bills, because investors must wait longer to get their money back and therefore demand higher interest. Interest for Treasury notes is paid every six months.

Treasury Bonds A *Treasury bond* is issued in minimum units of $100 and has a 30-year maturity. Interest rates for Treasury bonds are generally higher than those for either Treasury bills or Treasury notes. Again, the primary reason for the higher interest rates is the length of time investors must hold Treasury bonds. Like interest on Treasury notes, interest on Treasury bonds is paid every six months.

Treasury Inflation-Protected Securities (TIPS) *Treasury inflation-protected securities (TIPS)* are sold in minimum units of $100 with additional increments of $100 above the minimum. Currently, TIPS are sold with 5-, 10-, or 20-year maturities. The principal of TIPS securities increases with inflation and decreases with deflation, as measured by the consumer price index. When TIPS mature, you are paid the adjusted principal or original principal, whichever is greater. TIPS also pay interest twice a year, at a fixed rate applied to the adjusted principal. Interest income and growth in principal are exempt from state and local income taxes, but are subject to federal income tax.

FEDERAL AGENCY DEBT ISSUES In addition to the bonds and securities issued by the Treasury Department, debt securities are issued by federal agencies and quasi-federal agencies. Although these debt issues are, for practical purposes, risk free, they offer a slightly higher interest rate than government securities issued by the Treasury Department. The minimum investment may be as high as $10,000 to $25,000. Securities issued by federal agencies usually have maturities ranging from 1 to 30 years, with an average life of about 12 years.

STATE AND LOCAL GOVERNMENT SECURITIES A **municipal bond** is a debt security issued by a state or local government. Such securities are used to finance the ongoing activities of state and local governments and major projects such as airports, schools, toll roads, and toll bridges, and may be purchased directly from the government entity that issued them or through account executives.

> **municipal bond** A debt security issued by a state or local government.

State and local securities are classified as either general obligation bonds or revenue bonds. A **general obligation bond** is backed by the full faith, credit, and unlimited taxing power of the government that issued it. A **revenue bond** is repaid from the income generated by the project it is designed to finance. Although both general obligation and revenue bonds are relatively safe, defaults have occurred in recent years.

> **general obligation bond** A bond backed by the full faith, credit, and unlimited taxing power of the government that issued it.

If the risk of default worries you, you can purchase insured municipal bonds. A number of states offer to guarantee payments on selected securities. Three large private insurers—MBIA, Inc.; the Financial Security Assurance Corporation (FSA); and AMBAC, Inc. (American Municipal Bond Assurance Corporation)—also insure municipal bonds. Even if a municipal bond issue is insured, however, financial experts worry about the insurer's ability to pay off in the event of default on a large bond issue. Most advise investors to determine the underlying quality of a bond whether or not it is insured.

> **revenue bond** A bond that is repaid from the income generated by the project it is designed to finance.

One of the most important features of municipal bonds is that the interest on them may be exempt from federal taxes. Whether or not the interest on municipal bonds is tax exempt often depends on how the funds obtained from their sale are used. *You are responsible, as an investor, to determine whether or not interest on municipal bonds is taxable.* Municipal bonds exempt from federal taxation are generally exempt from state and local taxes only in the state where they are issued. Although the interest on municipal bonds may be exempt from taxation, a *capital gain* that results when you sell a municipal bond before maturity *and* at a profit may be taxable just like capital gains on other investments sold at a profit.

Because of their tax-exempt status, the interest rates on municipal bonds are lower than those on taxable bonds. By using the following formula, you can calculate the *taxable equivalent yield* for a municipal security:

$$\text{Taxable equivalent yield} = \frac{\text{Tax-exempt yield}}{1.0 - \text{Your tax rate}}$$

Example

For example, the taxable equivalent yield on a 5 percent, tax-exempt municipal bond for a person in the 28 percent tax bracket is 6.94 percent, as follows:

$$\text{Taxable equivalent yield} = \frac{0.05}{1.0 - 0.28}$$

$$= 0.0694, \text{ or } 6.94 \text{ percent}$$

Once you have calculated the taxable equivalent yield, you can compare the return on tax-exempt securities with the return on taxable investments. Exhibit 11–5 illustrates the yields for tax-exempt investments and their taxable equivalent yields.

CONCEPT CHECK 11–4

1 What is the difference between a Treasury bill, a Treasury note, a Treasury Bond and TIPS?

_____

_____

2 Explain the difference between a general obligation bond and a revenue bond.

_____

_____

3 What are the risks involved when investing in state and local securities?

_____

_____

Apply Yourself

Objective 4

Using the formula presented in this section, calculate the taxable equivalent yields for the following tax-exempt bonds.

Tax-Exempt Yield	Equivalent Yield for a Taxpayer in the 25% Tax Bracket	Equivalent Yield for a Taxpayer in the 28% Tax Bracket	Equivalent Yield for a Taxpayer in the 33% Tax Bracket
4.5%			
5.5%			
6.5%			

Exhibit 11–5

Yields for Tax-Exempt Investments

The following information can be used to compare the return on tax-exempt investments with the returns offered by taxable investments.

	EQUIVALENT YIELDS FOR TAXABLE INVESTMENTS				
Tax-Exempt Yield	15% Tax Rate	25% Tax Rate	28% Tax Rate	33% Tax Rate	35% Tax Rate
4%	4.71%	5.33%	5.56%	5.97%	6.15%
5	5.88	6.67	6.94	7.46	7.69
6	7.06	8.0	8.33	8.96	9.23
7	8.24	9.33	9.72	10.45	10.77

Conservative Investment Options: Corporate Bonds

A **corporate bond** is a corporation's written pledge to repay a specified amount of money with interest. The face value is the dollar amount the bondholder will receive at the bond's maturity. The usual face value of a corporate bond is $1,000. Between the time of purchase and the maturity date, the corporation pays interest to the bondholder.

OBJECTIVE 5
Recognize why investors purchase corporate bonds.

corporate bond A corporation's written pledge to repay a specified amount of money with interest.

Example

Assume you purchase a $1,000 bond issued by Boeing that pays 5.8 percent interest each year. Using the following formula, you can calculate the annual interest amount.

Amount of annual interest = Face value × Interest rate

= $1,000 × 5.8 percent

= $1,000 × 0.058

= $58.00

Typically, the interest is paid semiannually, or every six months. In the preceding example, this would be in $29 ($58 ÷ 2 = $29) installments until the bond matures.

The **maturity date** of a corporate bond is the date on which the corporation is to repay the borrowed money. On the maturity date, the bondholder returns the bond to the corporation and receives cash equal to the bond's face value. Maturity dates for bonds generally range from 1 to 30 years after the date of issue.

The actual legal conditions for a corporate bond are described in a bond indenture. A **bond indenture** is a legal document that details all of the conditions relating to a bond issue. Since corporate bond indentures are very difficult for the average person to read and understand, a corporation issuing bonds appoints a trustee. The **trustee** is a financially independent firm that acts as the bondholders' representative. Usually the trustee is a commercial bank or some other financial institution. If the corporation fails to live up to all the provisions in the indenture agreement, the trustee may bring legal action to protect the bondholders' interests.

maturity date For a corporate bond, the date on which the corporation is to repay the borrowed money.

bond indenture A legal document that details all of the conditions relating to a bond issue.

trustee A financially independent firm that acts as the bondholders' representative.

Why Corporations Sell Corporate Bonds

Corporations borrow when they don't have enough money to pay for major purchases—much as individuals do. Bonds can also be used to finance a corporation's ongoing business activities. In addition, corporations often sell bonds when it is difficult or impossible to sell stock. The sale of bonds can also improve a corporation's financial leverage—the use of borrowed funds to increase the corporation's return on investment. Finally, the interest paid to bond owners is a tax-deductible expense and thus can be used to reduce the taxes the corporation must pay to the federal and state governments.

Corporate bonds are a form of *debt financing*. Bond owners must be repaid at a future date, and interest payments on bonds are required. Finally, in the event of bankruptcy, bondholders have a claim to the assets of the corporation prior to that of stockholders. Before issuing bonds, a corporation must decide what type of bond to issue and how the bond issue will be repaid.

TYPES OF BONDS Most corporate bonds are debentures. A **debenture** is a bond that is backed only by the reputation of the issuing corporation. If the corporation

debenture A bond that is backed only by the reputation of the issuing corporation.

fails to make either interest payments or repayment at maturity, debenture bondholders become general creditors, much like the firm's suppliers.

To make a bond issue more appealing to conservative investors, a corporation may issue a mortgage bond. A **mortgage bond** (sometimes referred to as a *secured bond*) is a corporate bond secured by various assets of the issuing firm. Because of this added security, interest rates on mortgage bonds are usually lower than interest rates on unsecured debentures.

mortgage bond A corporate bond secured by various assets of the issuing firm.

CONVERTIBLE BONDS A special type of bond a corporation may issue is a convertible bond. A **convertible bond** can be exchanged, at the owner's option, for a specified number of shares of the corporation's common stock. This conversion feature allows investors to enjoy the lower risk of a corporate bond but also take advantage of the speculative nature of common stock. For example, assume you purchase a Medtronic $1,000 bond issue that is convertible. Each bond can be converted to 16.18 shares of the company's common stock. This means you could convert the bond to common stock whenever the price of the company's common stock is $61.80 ($1,000 ÷ 16.18 = $61.80) or higher.

convertible bond A bond that can be exchanged, at the owner's option, for a specified number of shares of the corporation's common stock.

In reality, there is no guarantee that Medtronic bondholders will convert to common stock even if the market value of the common stock does increase to $61.80 or higher. The reason for choosing not to exercise the conversion feature in this example is quite simple. As the market value of the common stock increases, the market value of the convertible bond *also* increases. By not converting to common stock, bondholders enjoy the added safety of the bond and interest income in addition to the increased market value of the bond caused by the price movement of the common stock. Generally, the interest rate on a convertible bond is 1 to 2 percent lower than that on traditional bonds. Convertible bonds, like all potential investments, must be carefully evaluated. Remember, not all convertible bonds are quality investments.

PROVISIONS FOR REPAYMENT Today most corporate bonds are callable. A **call feature** allows the corporation to call in, or buy, outstanding bonds from current bondholders before the maturity date. In most cases, corporations issuing callable bonds agree not to call them for the first 5 to 10 years after the bonds have been issued. The money needed to call a bond may come from the firm's profits, the sale of additional stock, or the sale of a new bond issue that has a lower interest rate.

call feature A feature that allows the corporation to call in, or buy, outstanding bonds from current bondholders before the maturity date.

A corporation may use one of two methods to ensure that it has sufficient funds available to redeem a bond issue at maturity. First, the corporation may establish a sinking fund. A **sinking fund** is a fund to which annual or semiannual deposits are made for the purpose of redeeming a bond issue. To repay a $250 million bond issue, J.C. Penney agreed to make $12.5 million annual sinking fund payments prior to the bond issue's maturity in 2021.

sinking fund A fund to which annual or semiannual deposits are made for the purpose of redeeming a bond issue.

Second, a corporation may issue serial bonds. **Serial bonds** are bonds of a single issue that mature on different dates. For example, Seaside Productions used a 20-year, $100 million bond issue to finance its expansion. None of the bonds mature during the first 10 years. Thereafter, 10 percent of the bonds mature each year until all the bonds are retired at the end of the 20-year period.

serial bonds Bonds of a single issue that mature on different dates.

Detailed information about provisions for repayment, along with other vital information (including maturity date, interest rate, bond rating, call provisions, trustee, and details about security) is available from Moody's Investors Service, Standard & Poor's Corporation, Fitch Ratings Service, and Mergent, Inc. Take a look at the information provided by Mergent's *Industrial Manual* for a bond issued

Personal Finance in Practice

The "How To" of Researching a Bond

How do you find out whether or not a corporate bond is callable? Where can you find out who the trustee for a specific bond issue is? These are only two of the multitude of questions that concern investors who are trying to evaluate bond investments. Fortunately, the answers are easy to obtain if you know where to look.

Today the most readily available source of detailed information about a corporation, including information about its bond issues, is Mergent's *Manuals*. Individual subscriptions to this series of publications are too expensive for most investors, but the series is available at both college and public libraries. It includes individual manuals on industrial companies, public utilities, banks and financial institutions, and transportation companies. Each manual contains detailed information on major companies, including the company's history, operations, products, and bond issues.

The following data on a corporate bond issued by Halliburton Company will give you an idea of the contents of the "Long-Term Debt" section of a Mergent's report.

Company name	**1. Halliburton Co. 8.75% debs, due 2021:**	Interest rate
	AUTHORIZED – $200,000,000.	
	OUTSTANDING– Dec. 31, 2002, $200,000,000.	
	DATED– Feb. 20, 1991.	
Maturity date	DUE– Feb. 15, 2021.	
	INTEREST– F&A 15 to holders registered F&A 15.	
	TRUSTEE– Texas Commerce Bank National Association.	Trustee
	DENOMINATION– Fully registered, $1,000 or any integral multiple thereof.	
	CALLABLE– Not callable prior to maturity.	
Details about security, if any	SECURITY– Not secured. Ranks pari passu with all other unsecured and unsubordinated debt of Co.	Call provision
	INDENTURE MODIFICATION – Indenture may be modified, except as provided, with consent of a majority of debs. outstg.	
	RIGHTS ON DEFAULT – Trustee, or 25% of debs. outstg., may declare principal due and payable (30 day's grace for payment of interest).	
	PURPOSE – Proceeds will be used to redeem $33,250,000 of its outstanding 10.20% Sinking Fund Debentures due June 1, 2005 and $20,000,000 of its outstanding 9 1/4% Sinking Fund Debentures Due April 1, 2000, and for general corporate purposes.	Purpose
Information about original issue	OFFERED – ($200,000,000) at 99.159% plus accrued interest, if any, (proceeds to Co., 98.284%) on Feb. 12, 1991 thru Lehman Brothers, and Lazard Freres & Co.	
	PRICE RANGE –	

	2002	2001	2000	1999	
High	110/10	120.09	117 3/4	127 5/8	Price history
Low	80.58	88.12	103 3/4	110 5/8	

SOURCE: The information for the Halliburton Company corporate bond was taken from Mergent's *Industrial Manual* (New York: Mergent, 2008), p. 1443.

by the Halliburton Company—a global engineering and construction company—in the nearby Personal Finance in Practice feature.

Why Investors Purchase Corporate Bonds

Investors often consider many corporate and government bonds a safer investment when compared to stocks or mutual funds. Bonds are also considered a "safe harbor" in troubled economic times. For example, many investors lost money during the period from 2007 to 2009 because of the banking and financial crisis. As an alternative to leaving your money in stocks and mutual funds, assuming that you thought the financial markets were headed for a period of decline, you could have moved money into corporate or government bonds. That's exactly what Joe Goode did before the 2008 financial crisis. Although his friends thought he was crazy for taking such a conservative approach, he actually avoided a downturn in the stock market. Now many of his friends wish they had made the same decision. According to Joe, he earned interest on his corporate and government bonds while preserving his investment funds for a return to the stock market when the economy rebounds. Investors sometimes purchase bonds as a way to diversify their investment portfolio. Instead of purchasing individual bonds, some investors prefer to purchase bond funds. Bond funds are an indirect way of owning bonds and other securities issued by the U.S. Treasury; city, state, and local governments; and corporations. Many financial experts recommend bond funds for small investors because they offer diversification and professional management. The advantages and disadvantages of bond funds are discussed in more detail in Chapter 13.

Basically, investors purchase corporate bonds for three reasons: (1) interest income, (2) possible increase in value, and (3) repayment at maturity.

INTEREST INCOME As mentioned earlier in this section, bondholders normally receive interest payments every six months. Because interest income is so important to bond investors, let's review this calculation.

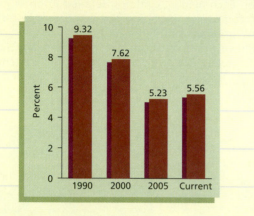

Example

Assume you purchase a $1,000 bond issued by IBM that pays 7 percent interest each year. Using the following formula, you can calculate the annual interest amount.

Amount of annual interest = Face value × Interest rate

= $1,000 × 7 percent

= $1,000 × 0.07

= $70

Note: Yearly interest of $70 will be paid in two installments of $35 at the end of each six-month period.

The method used to pay bondholders their interest depends on whether they own registered bonds, registered coupon bonds, or zero-coupon bonds. A **registered bond** is registered in the owner's name by the issuing company. Most registered bonds are now tracked electronically, using computers to record the owners' information. Interest checks for registered bonds are mailed directly to the bondholder of record. A variation of a registered bond is the registered coupon bond. A **registered coupon bond** is registered for principal only, not for interest. To collect interest payments on a registered coupon bond, the owner must present one of the detachable coupons to the issuing corporation or the paying agent.

registered bond A bond that is registered in the owner's name by the issuing company.

registered coupon bond A bond that is registered for principal only, and not for interest.

A **zero-coupon bond** is sold at a price far below its face value, makes no annual or semiannual interest payments, and is redeemed for its face value at maturity. With a zero-coupon bond, the buyer receives a return based on the bond's increased market value as its maturity date approaches. For example, assume you purchased a General Mills zero-coupon bond for $690 in 2006. When General mills redeemed these zero-coupon bonds in August 2008, you received $1,000.

Before investing in zero-coupon bonds, you should consider at least two factors. First, even though all of the interest on these bonds is paid at maturity, the IRS requires you to report interest each year—that is, as you earn it, not when you actually receive it. Second, zero-coupon bonds may be more volatile than other types of bonds.

zero-coupon bond A bond that is sold at a price far below its face value, makes no annual or semiannual interest payments, and is redeemed for its face value at maturity.

DOLLAR APPRECIATION OF BOND VALUE

Most beginning investors think that a $1,000 bond is always worth $1,000. In reality, the price of a corporate bond may fluctuate until the maturity date. Changes in overall interest rates in the economy are the primary cause of most bond price fluctuations. Changing bond prices that result from changes in overall interest rates in the economy are an example of interest rate risk, discussed earlier in this chapter. When IBM issued the bond mentioned earlier, the 7 percent interest rate was competitive with the interest rates offered by other corporations issuing bonds at that time. If overall interest rates fall, your IBM bond will go up in market value due to its higher, 7 percent, interest rate. On the other hand, if overall interest rates rise, the market value of your IBM bond will fall due to its lower, 7 percent, interest rate.

It is possible to approximate a bond's market value using the following formula:

$$\text{Approximate market value} = \frac{\text{Dollar amount of annual interest}}{\text{Comparable interest rate}}$$

Example

Assume you purchase a Verizon New Jersey bond that pays 5.875 percent or annual interest of $58.75 and has a face value of $1,000. Also assume new corporate bond issues of comparable quality are currently paying 5 percent. The approximate market value is $1,175, as follows:

$$\text{Approximate market value} = \frac{\text{Dollar amount of annual interest}}{\text{Comparable interest rate}} = \frac{\$58.75}{5\%}$$

$$= \$1,175$$

The market value of a bond may also be affected by the financial condition of the company or government unit issuing the bond, the factors of supply and demand, an upturn or downturn in the economy, and the proximity of the bond's maturity date.

BOND REPAYMENT AT MATURITY

Corporate bonds are repaid at maturity. After you purchase a bond, you have two options: You may keep the bond until maturity and then redeem it, or you may sell the bond to another investor. In either case, the value of your bond is closely tied to the corporation's ability to repay its bond indebtedness. For example, the value of bonds issued by cable giant Charter Communications dropped in value when the prospects for bond repayment at maturity came into question. Then the value of bonds dropped even further when the corporation

CONCEPT CHECK 11–5

1 Calculate the annual interest and the semiannual interest payment for corporate bond issues with a face value of $1,000.

Annual Interest Rate	Annual Interest	Semiannual Interest Payment
6%		
6.5%		
7%		
7.5%		

2 In your own words, describe why corporations issue corporate bonds.

_____

_____

3 List the three reasons investors purchase corporate bonds.

_____

_____

Apply Yourself!

Objective 5

Historically, the dollar return for bonds is less than the return for stocks. Still, investors often choose corporate and government bonds for their investment portfolio. In the chart below, describe the advantages and disadvantages of bond investments.

Type of Bond	Advantages	Disadvantages
Corporate		
Government		

could not pay interest payments totaling $73.7 million on its existing bonds, and the company filed for bankruptcy.[5]

A Typical Bond Transaction

Most bonds are sold through full-service brokerage firms, discount brokerage firms, or the Internet. If you use a full-service brokerage firm, your account executive should provide both information and advice about bond investments. As with other investments, the chief advantage of using a discount brokerage firm or trading online is lower commissions, but you must do your own research.

---

[5]Kelly Riddell, "Charter Misses Bond Interest Payments, Risks Default," Bloomberg.com Web site (www.bloomberg.com), accessed January 16, 2009.

Generally, if you purchase a $1,000 corporate bond through an account executive or brokerage firm, you should expect to pay a minimum commission of between $5 and $35. If you purchase more bonds, the commission usually drops to $2 to $20 per bond. You should also expect to pay commissions when you sell bonds.

The Decision to Buy or Sell Bonds

One basic principle we have stressed throughout this chapter is the need to evaluate any potential investment. Certainly corporate *and* government bonds are no exception. As you will see in this section, a number of sources of information can be used to evaluate bond investments.

The Internet

By accessing a corporation's Web page and locating the topics "financial information," "annual report," or "investor relations," you can find many of the answers to the questions asked in Your Personal Financial Plan Sheet 37.

When investing in bonds, you can use the Internet in three other ways. First, you can obtain price information on specific bond issues to track your investments. Especially if you live in a small town or rural area without access to newspapers that provide bond coverage, the Internet can be a welcome source of current bond prices. Second, it is possible to trade bonds online and pay lower commissions than you would pay a full-service or discount brokerage firm. Third, you can get research about a corporation and its bond issues (including recommendations to buy or sell) by accessing specific bond Web sites. *Be warned:* Bond Web sites are not as numerous as Web sites that provide information on stocks, mutual funds, or other investment alternatives. And many of the better bond Web sites charge a fee for their research and recommendations.

You may want to visit the Moody's Web site (www.moodys.com) and the Standard & Poor's Web site (www2.standardandpoors.com) to obtain detailed information about both corporate and government bonds.

Financial Coverage for Bond Transactions

In bond quotations, prices are given as a percentage of the face value, which is usually $1,000. Thus, to find the actual current price for a bond, you must multiply the face value ($1,000) by the bond quotation.

> ### Example
>
> To calculate the current price for a bond, you multiply the bond price quotation by the face value—usually $1,000. If the bond price quotation is 84, the current price is $840, as shown below.
>
> Current price = Bond price quotation × Face value
>
> = 84 percent × $1,000
>
> = 0.84 × $1,000
>
> = $840

While *The Wall Street Journal, Barron's,* and some metropolitan newspapers publish information on bonds, most bond investors use the Internet to obtain detailed information on bond issues. Detailed information obtained from the Yahoo! Finance Web site (http://bonds.yahoo.com) for a $1,000 AT & T Corporation bond, which pays 6.40 percent interest and matures in 2038, is provided in Exhibit 11–6.

OBJECTIVE 6
Evaluate bonds when making an investment

Web Sites for Bond Investor Information

www.bondsonline.com

www.bondsearch123.com

http://bonds.yahoo.com

Exhibit 11–6

Bond Information Available by Accessing the Yahoo! Bond Web Site

AT & T Inc.	
Overview	
1. Price:	110.60
2. Coupon (%):	6.400
3. Maturity Date:	15-May-2038
4. Yield to Maturity (%):	5.655
5. Current Yield (%):	5.787
6. Fitch Ratings:	A
7. Coupon Payment Frequency:	Semi-Annual
8. First Coupon Date:	15-Nov-2008
9. Type:	Corporate
10. Callable:	No

1. Price quoted as a percentage of the face value: $1,000 × 110.60% = $1,106

2. Coupon (%) is the rate of interest: 6.400 percent

3. Maturity Date is the date when bondholders will receive repayment of the face value: May 15, 2038

4. Yield to Maturity (%) takes into account the relationship among a bond's maturity value, the time to maturity, the current price, and the amount of interest: 5.655 percent

5. Current Yield (%) is determined by dividing the dollar amount of annual interest by the current price of the bond: $64 ÷ $1,106 = 5.787 percent

6 Fitch Ratings is issued by Fitch Bond Ratings and is used to assess the risk associated with this bond: A

7. Coupon Payment Frequency tells bondholders how often they will receive interest payments: Semi-Annual

8. First Coupon Date: November 15, 2008

9. Type: Corporate

10. Callable tells the bondholder if the bond is callable or not: No

SOURCE: The Yahoo! Finance bond Web site (http://bonds.yahoo.com), accessed January 16, 2009.

Bond Ratings

To determine the quality and risk associated with bond issues, investors rely on the bond ratings provided by Moody's Investors Service, Inc., Standard & Poor's Corporation, and Fitch Ratings. All three companies rank thousands of corporate and municipal bonds.

As Exhibit 11–7 illustrates, bond ratings range from AAA (the highest) to D (the lowest) for Standard & Poor's and Aaa (the highest) to C (the lowest) for Moody's. Fitch ratings are similar to the bond ratings provided by Standard & Poor's and Moody's. For both Moody's and Standard & Poor's, the first four individual categories represent investment-grade securities. Investment-grade securities are suitable for conservative investors who want a safe investment that provides a predictable source of income. Bonds in the next two individual categories are considered speculative in nature. Finally, the C and D categories are used to rank bonds where there are poor prospects of repayment or even continued payment of interest. Bonds in these categories may be in default.

Exhibit **11–7**   Description of Bond Ratings Provided by Moody's Investors Service and Standard & Poor's Corporation

Quality	Moody's	Standard & Poor's	Description
High-grade	Aaa	AAA	Bonds that are judged to be of the best quality.
	Aa	AA	Bonds that are judged to be of high quality by all standards. Together with the first group, they comprise what are generally known as *high-grade* bonds.
Medium-grade	A	A	Bonds that possess many favorable investment attributes and are to be considered upper-medium-grade obligations.
	Baa	BBB	Bonds that are considered medium-grade obligations; i.e., they are neither highly protected nor poorly secured.
Speculative	Ba	BB	Bonds that are judged to have speculative elements; their future cannot be considered well assured.
	B	B	Bonds that generally lack characteristics of the desirable investment.
Poor prospects or Default	Caa	CCC	Bonds that are of poor standing.
	Ca	CC	Bonds that represent obligations that are highly speculative.
	C		Bonds that are regarded as having extremely poor prospects of attaining any real investment standing.
		C	Standard & Poor's rating given to bonds where a bankruptcy petition has been filed.
		D	Bond issues in default.

SOURCE: Mergent, Inc., *Mergent Bond Record* (New York: Mergent, 2008), pp. 3–4, and Standard & Poor's Corporation, *Standard & Poor's Bond Guide*, September 2008, p. 4.

Generally, U.S. government securities issued by the Treasury Department and various federal agencies are not graded because they are risk free for practical purposes. The rating of municipal bonds is similar to that of corporate bonds.

Bond Yield Calculations

For a bond investment, the **yield** is the rate of return earned by an investor who holds a bond for a stated period of time. The **current yield** is determined by dividing the annual interest amount by the bond's current price. The following formula may help you complete this calculation:

$$\text{Current yield} = \frac{\text{Annual interest amount}}{\text{Current price}}$$

yield The rate of return earned by an investor who holds a bond for a stated period of time.

current yield Determined by dividing the yearly dollar amount of interest by the bond's current price.

Example

Assume you own a D. R. Horton corporate bond that pays 6.5 percent interest on an annual basis. This means that each year you will receive $65 ($1,000 × 6.5% = $65). Also assume the current market price of the D. R. Horton bond is $908. Because the current price is less than the bond's face value, the current yield increases to 7.16 percent, as follows:

$$\text{Current yield} = \frac{\$65}{\$908}$$

$$= 0.0716, \text{ or } 7.16 \text{ percent}$$

Sheet 37 Evaluating Corporate Bonds

CONCEPT CHECK 11–6

1 What type of information about bonds is available on the Internet?

_____

_____

2 Calculate the current market value for the following bonds:

Face Value	Bond Quotation	Current Market Value
$1,000	103	
$1,000	92	
$1,000	77.5	

3 Explain what the following bond ratings mean for investors.

Bond Rating	Explanation
Aaa	
BBB	
B	
CC	

Apply Yourself!

Objective 6

Visit one of the bond Web sites listed in this section and describe how this type of information could help you evaluate a bond investment.

This calculation allows you to compare the yield on a bond investment with the yields of other investment alternatives, which include savings accounts, certificates of deposit, common stock, preferred stock, and mutual funds. Naturally, the higher the current yield, the better! A current yield of 8 percent is better than a current yield of 7.16 percent.

Key Web Sites for Economic Information for Bond Investors

www.federalreserve.gov

www.treasury.gov

www.commerce.gov

www.sec.gov

Other Sources of Information

Investors can use two additional sources of information to evaluate potential bond investments. First, business periodicals can provide information about the economy and interest rates and detailed financial information about a corporation or government entity that issues bonds. You can locate many of these periodicals at your college or public library or on the Internet.

Second, a number of federal agencies provide information that may be useful to bond investors in either printed form or on the Internet. Reports and research published by the Federal Reserve System, the U.S. Treasury, and the Department of Commerce may be used to assess the nation's economy. You can also obtain information that corporations have reported to the Securities and Exchange Commission by accessing the SEC Web site. Finally, state and local governments will provide information about specific municipal bond issues.

Reconsider your responses to the "Getting Personal" questions at the beginning of the chapter. For more effective personal financial planning and investment planning:

- Reevaluate your short-term, intermediate, and long-term financial goals to make sure they reflect what is important to you.
- Perform a financial checkup to determine if you have the financial resources needed to weather an economic crisis.

- Visit the Motley Fool Web site at www.fool.com to learn why people invest in government or corporate bonds.

Finally, describe what you learned in this chapter that will help you develop an investment plan designed to accomplish your financial goals and objectives.

Chapter Summary

Objective 1 Investment goals must be specific and measurable. In addition to developing investment goals, you must make sure your personal financial affairs are in order. The next step is the accumulation of an emergency fund equal to at least three months' living expenses. In fact, you may want to increase the amount in your emergency fund if you think you may lose your job or the nation is experiencing an economic or financial crisis. Then, and only then, is it time to save the money needed to establish an investment program.

Objective 2 Although each investor may have specific, individual reasons for investing, all investors must consider the factors of safety, risk, income, growth, and liquidity. Especially important is the relationship between safety and risk. Basically, this relationship can be summarized as follows: The potential return for any investment should be directly related to the risk the investor assumes. In addition to safety and risk, investors choose investments that provide income, growth, or liquidity.

Objective 3 Before making the decision to purchase an investment, you should consider the factors of asset allocation, the time your investments will work for you, and your age. Asset allocation is the process of spreading your assets among several different types of investments to lessen risk. In addition to asset allocation, the amount of time before you need your money is a critical component in the type of investments you choose. Finally, your age is a factor that influences investment choices. Younger investors tend to invest a large percentage of their nest egg in growth-oriented investments. On the other hand, older investors tend to be more conservative. You can also improve your investment returns by evaluating all potential investments, monitoring the value of your investments, and keeping accurate and current records.

Objective 4 Conservative investments include savings accounts, certificates of deposit, money market accounts, savings bonds, and government securities. Generally, U.S. government securities are chosen because most investors consider them risk free. Although the level of risk can be higher for federal agency debt issues and municipal bonds, they are also chosen as a conservative investment. Municipal bonds may also provide tax-exempt income.

Objective 5 Bonds are issued by corporations to raise capital. Investors purchase corporate bonds for three reasons: (1) interest income, (2) possible increase in value, and (3) repayment at maturity. Bonds also can be an excellent way to diversify a portfolio. The method used to pay bondholders interest depends on whether they own registered bonds, registered coupon bonds, or zero-coupon bonds. Most corporate bonds are bought and sold through full-service brokerage firms, discount brokerage firms, or the Internet. Investors pay commissions when bonds are bought and sold.

Objective 6 Today it is possible to obtain information and trade bonds online via the Internet. In addition to the

Internet, *The Wall Street Journal, Barron's* , and some local newspapers provide investors with information they need to evaluate a bond issue. To determine the quality of a bond issue, most investors study the ratings provided by Standard & Poor's, Moody's, and Fitch Ratings. Investors can also calculate a current yield to evaluate a decision to buy or sell bond issues. Finally, business periodicals and government sources can be used to evaluate bonds and the economy.

Key Terms

asset allocation 361	general obligation bond 367	registered coupon bond 372
bond indenture 369	government bond 366	revenue bond 367
call feature 370	line of credit 351	serial bonds 370
convertible bond 370	liquidity 359	sinking fund 370
corporate bond 369	maturity date 369	speculative investment 356
current yield 377	mortgage bond 370	trustee 369
debenture 369	municipal bond 367	yield 377
emergency fund 351	registered bond 372	zero-coupon bond 373

Key Formulas

Page	Topic	Formula
351	Emergency fund	Minimum emergency fund = Monthly expenses × 3 months
367	Taxable equivalent yield	$\text{Taxable equivalent yield} = \dfrac{\text{Tax-exempt yield}}{1.0 - \text{Your tax rate}}$
369	Interest calculation for a bond	Amount of annual interest = Face value × Interest rate
373	Approximate market value	$\text{Approximate market value} = \dfrac{\text{Dollar amount of annual interest}}{\text{Comparable interest rate}}$
375	Current price for a bond	Current price = Bond price quotation × Face value
377	Current yield for a bond	$\text{Current yield} = \dfrac{\text{Annual interest amount}}{\text{Current price}}$

Self-Test Problems

1. For Ned Masterson, the last few years have been a financial nightmare. It all started when he lost his job. Because he had no income, he began using his credit cards to obtain the cash needed to pay everyday living expenses. Finally, after an exhaustive job search, he has a new job that pays $42,000 a year. While his take-home pay is $2,450 a month, he must now establish an emergency fund, pay off his $6,200 credit card debt, and start saving the money needed to begin an investment program.

   a. If monthly expenses are $1,750, how much money should Ned save for an emergency fund?

   b. What steps should Ned take to pay the $6,200 credit card debt?

   c. Ned has decided that he will save $2,000 a year for the next five years in order to establish a long-term investment program. If his savings earn 4 percent each year, how much money will he have at the end of five years? (Use Exhibit 11–1 to answer this question.)

2. Betty Forrester is 55 years old and wants to diversify her investment portfolio and must decide if she should invest in tax-free municipal bonds or corporate bonds. The tax-free bonds are highly rated and pay 5.25 percent. The corporate bonds are more speculative and pay 7.5 percent.

   a. If Betty is in the 33 percent tax bracket, what is the taxable equivalent yield for the municipal bond?
   b. If you were Betty, would you choose the municipal bonds or corporate bonds? Justify your answer.

3. Mary Glover purchased ten $1,000 corporate bonds issued by JCPenney. The annual interest rate for the bonds is 6.375 percent.

   a. What is the annual interest amount for each JCPenney bond?
   b. If the bonds have a current bond price quotation of 73, what is the current price of the bond?
   c. Given the above information, what is the current yield for a JCPenney bond?

Solutions

1. a. The minimum emergency fund is $5,250.

$$\text{Minimum emergency fund} = \text{Monthly expenses} \times 3 \text{ months}$$

$$= \$1,750 \times 3$$

$$= \$5,250$$

   b. To pay his $6,200 credit card debt, Ned should take the following actions: (1) talk to the credit card companies and ask if they can lower the interest rate he is paying; (2) pay at least the minimum balance on all credit cards to ensure that he does not get behind on any payments; and (3) pay off the credit card with the highest interest rates first, then work on the remaining credit cards.
   c. Based on the information in Exhibit 11–1, Ned will have invested $10,000 at the end of five years. If his savings are invested at 4 percent, he will have $10,832 at the end of five years that can be used to fund an investment program.

2. a. The tax-equivalent yield for the municipal bond is

$$\text{Taxable equivalent yield} = \frac{\text{Tax-exempt yield}}{1.0 - \text{Your tax rate}}$$

$$= \frac{0.0525}{1.0 - 0.33}$$

$$= 0.078, \text{ or } 7.8 \text{ percent}$$

   b. The taxable equivalent yield for the municipal bonds is 7.8 percent; the yield for the corporate bonds is 7.5 percent. Also, it should be noted that the corporate bonds are "speculative." In this case, Betty should choose the tax-free municipal bonds because the yield is higher and they are more conservative.

3. a. The annual interest rate is $63.75.

$$\text{Amount of annual interest} = \text{Face value} \times \text{Interest rate}$$

$$= \$1,000 \times 0.06375$$

$$= \$63.75$$

   b. The current price is $730.

$$\text{Current price} = \text{Bond price quotation} \times \text{Face value}$$

$$= 73\% \times \$1,000$$

$$= 0.73 \times \$1,000$$

$$= \$730$$

   c. The current yield is

$$\text{Current yield} = \frac{\text{Annual interest amount}}{\text{Current price}}$$

$$= \frac{\$63.75}{\$730}$$

$$= 0.087, \text{ or } 8.7 \text{ percent}$$

Problems

1. Jane and Bill Collins have total take-home pay of $3,900 a month. Their monthly expenses total $2,800. Calculate the minimum amount this couple needs to establish an emergency fund. (Obj. 1)

2. Using Exhibit 11–1, complete the following table. (Obj. 1)

Annual Deposit	Rate of Return	Number of Years	Investment Value at the End of Time Period	Total Amount of Investment	Total Amount of Interest
$2,000	3%	10			
$2,000	9%	10			
$2,000	5%	30			
$2,000	11%	30			

3. Based on the following information, construct a graph that illustrates price movement for a Washington Utilities bond fund. (Obj. 3)

January	$16.50	July	$14.00
February	$15.50	August	$13.10
March	$17.20	September	$15.20
April	$18.90	October	$16.70
May	$19.80	November	$18.40
June	$16.50	December	$19.80

4. Use the following table to compare U.S. Treasury bills, notes, bonds, and TIPS. (Obj. 4)

	Minimum Amount	Maturity	How Interest Is Paid
Treasury bill			
Treasury note			
Treasury bond			
TIPS			

5. Assume you are in the 35 percent tax bracket and purchase a 4.25 percent municipal bond. Use the formula presented in this chapter to calculate the taxable equivalent yield for this investment. (Obj. 4)

6. Assume you are in the 28 percent tax bracket and purchase a 3.75 percent municipal bond. Use the formula presented in this chapter to calculate the taxable equivalent yield for this investment. (Obj. 4)

7. Assume that three years ago you purchased a corporate bond that pays 6.5 percent. The purchase price was $1,000. What is the annual dollar amount of interest that you receive from your bond investment? (Obj. 5)

8. Twelve months ago, you purchased a 30-year bond with a face value of $1,000. The interest rate is 3.0 percent. What is the annual dollar amount of interest you will receive each year? (Obj. 5)

9. Assume that you purchased a $1,000 convertible corporate bond. Also assume the bond can be converted to 35.714 shares of the firm's stock. What is the dollar value that the stock must reach before investors would consider converting to common stock? (Obj. 5)

10. Five years ago, you purchased a $1,000 corporate bond issued by General Electric. The interest rate for the bond was 5 percent. Today comparable bonds are paying 7 percent. (Obj. 5)

    a. What is the approximate dollar price for which you could sell your General Electric bond?
    b. In your own words, describe why your bond decreased in value.

11. In 1990, you purchased a 30-year, $1,000 corporate bond issued by AMR, the parent company of American Airlines. At the time, the interest rate for the bond was 9 percent. Today, comparable bonds are paying 7 percent. (Obj. 5)

    a. What is the approximate dollar price for which you could sell your AMR bond?
    b. In your own words, describe why your bond increased in value.

12. Determine the current yield on a corporate bond investment that has a face value of $1,000, pays 6 percent interest, and has a current price of $820. (Obj. 6)

13. Determine the current yield on a corporate bond investment that has a face value of $1,000, pays 5.5 percent, and has a current price of $1,080. (Obj. 6)

14. Choose a corporate bond that you would consider purchasing. Then, using information obtained on the Internet or in the library, answer the questions in *Your Personal Financial Plan* Sheet 37. Based on your research, would you still purchase this bond? (Obj. 6)

Questions

1. After performing a financial checkup, you realize that you have too much credit card debt. What steps can you take to reduce the amount of money you owe on your credit cards? (Obj. 1)

2. Choose a current issue of *Kiplinger's Personal Finance Magazine, Money,* or *Consumer Reports* and summarize an article that provides suggestions on how you could use your money more effectively. (Obj. 1)

3. Many people would like to start investing, but they never have enough money to begin. What steps can you take to get the money needed to start an investment program? (Obj. 1)

4. Explain the following statement: The potential return on any investment should be directly related to the risk the investor assumes. (Obj. 2)

5. List three personal factors that might lead some investors to emphasize income rather than growth in their investment planning. (Obj. 2)

6. List three personal factors that might lead some investors to emphasize growth rather than income in their investment planning. (Obj. 2)

7. Choose one of the model portfolios illustrated in Exhibit 11–4 and explain how it could help you obtain your investment goals. (Obj. 3)

8. Assume that you are choosing an investment for your retired parents. Would you choose a bond issued by the federal government or a bond issued by a state or local government? Justify your answer. (Obj. 4)

9. What is the difference between a debenture bond, a mortgage bond, and a convertible bond? (Obj. 5)

10. Why would investors care if a bond is callable or not? (Obj. 5)

11. In what circumstances would a $1,000 corporate bond be worth more than $1,000? In what circumstances would the corporate bond be worth less than $1,000? (Obj. 5)

12. You are considering two different corporate bonds. One is rated AAA by Standard & Poor's and pays 5.8 percent annual interest. The other bond is rated B by Standard & Poor's and pays 7.5 percent annual interest. What do these ratings mean? Which bond would you choose and why? (Obj. 6)

Case in Point

YOU'D BE A FOOL IF YOU DIDN'T USE THE MOTLEY FOOL WEB SITE!

Fifteen years ago, Penny and Jim Tilson opened a brokerage account, and each month they contributed what they could afford. Over the years, they had managed to invest almost $30,000 in high-tech companies. Because their investments increased in value, the value of their investment portfolio had grown to just over $100,000 by January 2000. And yet, by January 2005, the value of their investments had dropped to a little less than $55,000. They had lost almost half the value of their investments in just five years. What happened?

To answer that question, you must understand that the Tilsons were like a lot of people investing in the high-tech surge. They chose high-tech stocks because they offered great returns. Computers were popular, and who would even dream that the bubble would eventually burst and the nation would experience a financial crisis? Now the Tilsons admit that they didn't know how to research stocks, mutual funds, or other potential investments. In fact, they didn't even bother to open the statements that their brokerage firm sent out each month. They just assumed that their investments would keep increasing in value. Unfortunately, their wake-up call came when they opened their January 2005 statement in order to obtain some information they needed to file their tax return. That's when they realized how much money they had lost. That's also when they decided that if they were going to continue to invest their money, they needed to learn how to invest.

The Tilsons began their search for educational materials by using their home computer to find investment Web sites. According to Penny, many sites offered investment information, but they chose the Motley Fool Web site because they felt pretty foolish after losing so much money. Started by David and Tom Gardner, the goal of the Motley Fool is to help average people make the best decisions about every dollar that they spend, save, and invest. Although just one of many investment Web sites, the Motley Fool is an excellent choice for beginning investors like the Tilsons as well as more experienced investors.

While the Tilsons looked at other Web sites, they kept coming back to the Motley Fool because this site offered investment advice that the average person could understand. According to Jim, learning about the investments was not only rewarding, but also fun. For the first time since they began their investment program, they actually knew how to evaluate their investment options. Penny adds that over the last few years they really have learned how to evaluate investments before investing their money. It must be working because at the beginning of 2010, their investment portfolio was worth more than $125,000—despite the financial crisis that occurred during 2008 and 2009.

Questions

1. The Tilsons lost almost half of the value of their investment portfolio in just five years. What did they do wrong?

2. Visit the Motley Fool Web site at www.fool.com . Describe the type of investment information that is available.

3. If you were beginning an investment program, would you use the information provided by the Motley Fool or similar Web sites? Explain your answer.

Continuing Case

Vikki Treble just celebrated a milestone birthday: 40. She and her husband Tim (age 42) are the busy parents of 10-year old Molly and 3-year old twins Caleb and Tyler. Vikki is teaching night classes, so they can minimize their childcare costs; she and Tim call it "tag-team parenting."

Even though Vikki's salary has decreased since taking the teaching job, the couple is saving up for their children's college funds. They hope to be able to pay $10,000 per year of college for each of their children. Other expenses have cropped up as well. Molly recently started taking cello lessons and already is planning to go to a two-week music camp when she starts high school (cost: $2,100). The family has lived in their house over 10 years, and Vikki and Tim are thinking about making some updates.

Ever since Dave and Amy (Vikki's parents) retired, they have been meeting with a financial planner annually to check their financial condition. Their birthday gift for Vikki was a paid meeting for Vikki and Tim with their planner. The focus of the meeting was short-term savings and long-term investing.

Vikki and Tim's financial statistics are shown below:

Assets:
Checking/savings account $25,000
Emergency fund $25,000
House $300,000
Cars $11,000 and $2,000
Household possessions $12,000
401(k) balance $86,000 (Vikki), $110,000 (Tim)
College savings $25,000
Life insurance cash value $1,500

Liabilities:
Mortgage $167,000
Car loan $10,000

Income:
Gross Salary: $18,000 per year (Vikki), $97,000 (Tim)
After-tax monthly salary: $875 (Vikki), $5,658 (Tim)

Monthly Expenses:
Mortgage $1,200
Property tax/Insurance $550
Daily living expenses (including utilities, food, child care) $2,200
Car loan $350
Entertainment/vacations $350

Gas/repairs $500
Term & whole life insurance $400

Savings:
401(k) 8% of gross monthly salary
College savings $600

Questions

1. What do you think Vikki and Tim's investment goals are? How are they different from Vikki's parents' goals?
2. Assume that Vikki and Tim have been investing since they started working after college. What steps should they have taken before they began investing?
3. What type of investment portfolio would you recommend for Vikki and Tim? How would this portfolio be different from one for Vikki's parents? Who would be more interested in investing in bonds?
4. How can the Trebles use *Your Personal Financial Plan* sheets 35–37?

Spending Diary

"WHILE I HAVE A FAIRLY LARGE AMOUNT IN A SAVINGS ACCOUNT, I SHOULD THINK ABOUT INVESTING SOME OF THIS MONEY IN OTHER WAYS."

Directions The use of your Daily Spending Diary can provide an important foundation for monitoring and controlling spending. This will allow the possibility of wiser use of money now and in the future. The Daily Spending Diary sheets are located in Appendix C at the end of the book and on the student Web site at www.mhhe.com/kdh.

Questions

1. Explain how the use of a Daily Spending Diary could result in starting an investment program.
2. Based on your Daily Spending Diary, describe actions that you might take to identify and achieve various financial goals.

Name: _____   Date: _____

Establishing Investment Goals

Financial Planning Activities: Determine specific goals for an investment program. Based on short- and long-term objectives for your investment efforts, enter the items requested below.

Suggested Web Sites: www.fool.com   www.money.cnn.com

Description of investment goal	Dollar amount	Date needed	Level of acceptable risk (high, medium, low)	Possible investments to achieve this goal

Note: Sheets 37, 38, and 41 may be used to implement specific investment plans to achieve these goals.

What's Next for Your Personal Financial Plan?

• Use the suggestions listed in this chapter to perform a financial checkup.
• Discuss the importance of investment goals and financial planning with other household members.

Name: _____ **Date:** _____

Assessing Risk for Investments

Financial Planning Activities: Assess the risk of various investments in relation to your personal risk tolerance and financial goals. List various investments you are considering based on the type and level of risk associated with each.

Suggested Web Sites: http://moneycentral.msn.com/investor/calcs/n_riskq/main.asp.   www.fool.com

Type of investment	Loss of market value (market risk)	Type of Risk		
		Inflation risk	Interest rate risk	Liquidity risk
High risk				
Moderate risk				
Low risk				

What's Next for Your Personal Financial Plan?

- Identify current economic trends that might increase or decrease the risk associated with your choice of investments.
- Based on the risk associated with the investments you chose, which investment would you choose to obtain your investment goals?

Name: _____   Date: _____

Evaluating Corporate Bonds

Financial Planning Activities: No checklist can serve as a foolproof guide for choosing a corporate bond. However, the following questions will help you evaluate a potential bond investment.

Suggested Web Sites: http://bonds.yahoo.com   www.bondsonline.com

Category 1: Information about the Corporation

1. What is the corporation's name, address, and phone number? _____
   _____

2. What type of products or services does this firm provide? _____
   _____

3. Briefly describe the prospects for this company. (Include significant factors like product development, plans for expansion, plans for mergers, etc.)
   _____
   _____
   _____

Category 2: Bond Basics

4. What type of bond is this? _____

5. What is the face value for this bond? _____

6. What is the interest rate for this bond? _____

7. What is the dollar amount of annual interest for this bond? _____

8. When are interest payments made to bondholders?
   _____

9. Is the corporation currently paying interest as scheduled? ☐ Yes ☐ No

10. What is the maturity date for this bond? _____

11. What is Moody's rating for this bond? _____

12. What is Standard & Poor's rating for this bond?
    _____

13. What do these ratings mean? _____
    _____
    _____

14. What was the original issue date? _____
    _____

15. Who is the trustee for this bond issue? _____
    _____

16. Is the bond callable? If so, when? _____
    _____

17. Is the bond secured with collateral? If so, what?
    ☐ Yes ☐ No
    _____

Category 3: Financial Performance

18. What are the firm's earnings per share for the last year? _____

19. Have the firm's earnings increased over the past five years? _____

20. What are the firm's projected earnings for the next year? _____

21. Do the analysts indicate that this is a good time to invest in this company?
    _____
    _____

22. Briefly describe any other information that you obtained from Moody's, Standard & Poor's, or other sources of information.
    _____
    _____

A Word of Caution

The above checklist is not a cure-all, but it does provide some very sound questions that you should answer before making a decision to invest in bonds. If you need other information, *you* are responsible for obtaining it and for determining how it affects your potential investment.

What's Next for Your Personal Financial Plan?

- Talk with various people who have invested in government, municipal, or corporate bonds.
- Discuss with other household members why bonds might be a logical choice for your investment program.

12 Investing in Stocks

Getting Personal

Why invest in stocks? For each of the following statements, select "yes" or "no" to indicate your behavior regarding these investing activities:

	Yes	No
1. I understand the three ways investors can profit from stock investments.	____	____
2. I know how to evaluate a stock issue.	____	____
3. I know how to buy and sell stock investments.	____	____
4. I know the difference between long-term and short-term investment techniques.	____	____

After studying this chapter, you will be asked to reconsider your responses to these questions.

Common and Preferred Stock

OBJECTIVE 1

Identify the most important features of common and preferred stock.

The Standard & Poor's 500 Stock Index—a benchmark of stock market performance often reported on financial news programs—reached record highs in 2007. And yet this same index lost over 40 percent of its value by the beginning of January 2009. Given this information and the nation's depressed economy, many investors ask the question: Why invest in stocks? To answer this question, consider the returns provided by stocks over a long period of time. Since 1926, the average annual return for stocks is just over 10 percent as measured by the Standard & Poor's 500 stock index—substantially

Your Personal Financial Plan Sheets

38. Evaluating Corporate Stocks
39. Investment Broker Comparison

Objectives

In this chapter, you will learn to:

1. Identify the most important features of common and preferred stock.
2. Explain how you can evaluate stock investments.
3. Analyze the numerical measures that cause a stock to increase or decrease in value.
4. Describe how stocks are bought and sold.
5. Explain the trading techniques used by long-term investors and short-term speculators.

Why is this important?

Although many investors have watched the value of their investments decline over the last few years, the fact is that since 1926 the average annual return for stocks is just over 10 percent. As a result, many financial experts recommend stock investments for investors who are establishing a long-term investment program.

more than the returns provided by more conservative investments.[1] Simply put, investors who want larger returns choose stocks. Certainly, there have been periods when stocks declined in value. For proof, just ask any long-term investor what happened to the value of his or her stock investments during the recent economic crisis. Still, the key to success with any investment program often is allowing your investments to work for you over a long period of time. A long-term investment program allows you

---

[1] "Money 101 Lesson 4: Basics of Investing," the CNN/Money Web site (http://money.cnn.com/magazines/moneymag/money101lesson4), accessed January 13, 2009.

to ride through the rough times and enjoy the good times. However, before you decide to invest your money, you should realize the importance of evaluating a potential stock investment.

Many investors face two concerns when they begin an investment program. First, they don't know where to get the information they need to evaluate potential investments. In reality, more information is available than most investors can read. Yet, as crazy as it sounds, some investors invest in stocks without doing any research at all. As we begin this chapter, *you should know that there is no substitute for researching a potential investment.*

Second, beginning investors sometimes worry that they won't know what the information means when they do find it. Yet common sense goes a long way when evaluating potential investments. For example, consider the following questions:

1. Is an increase in sales revenues a healthy sign for a corporation? (Answer: yes)
2. Should a firm's net income increase or decrease over time? (Answer: increase)
3. Should a corporation's earnings per share increase or decrease over time? (Answer: increase)

Although the answers to these questions are obvious, you will find more detailed answers to these and other questions in this chapter. In fact, that's what this chapter is all about. We want you to learn how to evaluate a stock and to make money from your investment decisions.

Since common stockholders are the actual owners of the corporation, they share in its success. But before investing your money, it helps to understand why corporations issue common stock and why investors purchase that stock.

Why Corporations Issue Common Stock

common stock The most basic form of corporate ownership.

Common stock is the most basic form of ownership for a corporation. Corporations issue common stock to finance their business start-up costs and help pay for expansion and their ongoing business activities. Corporate managers prefer selling common stock as a method of financing for several reasons.

equity financing Money received from the owners or from the sale of shares of ownership in a business.

A FORM OF EQUITY *Important point:* Stock is equity financing. **Equity financing** is money received from the sale of shares of ownership in a business. One reason corporations prefer selling stock is because the money obtained from equity financing doesn't have to repaid and the company doesn't have to buy back shares from the stockholders. On the other hand, a stockholder who buys common stock may sell his or her stock to another individual. The selling price is determined by how much a buyer is willing to pay for the stock. The price for a share of stock changes when information about the firm or its future prospects is released to the general public. For example, information about expected sales revenues, earnings, expansions or mergers, or other important developments within the firm can increase or decrease the price for the firm's stock.

dividend A distribution of money, stock, or other property that a corporation pays to stockholders.

DIVIDENDS NOT MANDATORY *Important point:* Dividends are paid out of profits, and dividend payments must be approved by the corporation's board of directors. A **dividend** is a distribution of money, stock, or other property that a corporation pays to stockholders. Dividend policies vary among corporations, but most firms distribute between 30 and 70 percent of their earnings to stockholders. However, some corporations follow a policy of smaller or no dividend distributions to stockholders. In general, these are rapidly growing firms, like Amazon (online sales) or Bankrate, Inc. (online banking), that retain a large share of their earnings for research and development, expansion, or major projects. On the other hand, utility companies, such as Duke Energy, and other financially secure enterprises may distribute 80 to 90 percent of their earnings. Always remember that if a corporation has had a bad year, dividend payments may be reduced or omitted.

VOTING RIGHTS AND CONTROL OF THE COMPANY In return for the financing provided by selling common stock, management must make concessions to stockholders that may restrict corporate policies. For example, corporations are required by law to have an annual meeting at which stockholders have a right to vote, usually casting one vote per share of stock. Stockholders may vote in person or by proxy. A **proxy** is a legal form that lists the issues to be decided at a stockholders' meeting and requests that stockholders transfer their voting rights to some individual or individuals. The common stockholders elect the board of directors and must approve major changes in corporate policies.

Why Investors Purchase Common Stock

How do you make money by buying common stock? Basically, there are three ways: income from dividends, dollar appreciation of stock value, and the *possibility* of increased value from stock splits.

INCOME FROM DIVIDENDS While the corporation's board members are under no legal obligation to pay dividends, most board members like to keep stockholders happy (and prosperous). Few things will unite stockholders into a powerful opposition force more rapidly than omitted or lowered dividends. Therefore, board members usually declare dividends if the corporation's after-tax profits are sufficient for them to do so. Since dividends are a distribution of profits, investors must be concerned about future after-tax profits.

Dividends for common stock may take the form of cash, additional stock, or company products. However, the last type of dividend is extremely unusual. If the board of directors declares a cash dividend, each common stockholder receives an equal amount per share. Although dividend policies vary, most corporations pay dividends on a quarterly basis.

Notice in Exhibit 12–1 that CMS Energy declared a quarterly dividend of $0.125 per share to stockholders who own the stock on the record date of February 6, 2009. The **record date** is the date on which a stockholder must be registered on the corporation's books in order to receive dividend payments. When a stock is traded around the record date, the company must determine whether the buyer or the seller is entitled to the dividend. To solve this problem, this rule is followed: *Dividends remain with the stock until two business days before the record date.* On the second day before the record date, the stock begins selling *ex-dividend*. Investors who purchase an ex-dividend stock are not entitled to receive dividends for that quarter, and the dividend is paid to the previous owner of the stock.

For example, CMS Energy declared a quarterly dividend of $0.125 per share to stockholders who owned its stock on Friday, February 6, 2009. The stock went ex-dividend on Wednesday, February 4, 2009, *two business days* before the February 6 date. A stockholder who purchased the stock on Wednesday, February 4 or after was not entitled to this quarterly dividend payment. The actual dividend payment was paid on February 27 to stockholders who owned the stock on the record date. Investors are generally very conscious of the date on which a stock

proxy A legal form that lists the issues to be decided at a stockholders' meeting and requests that stockholders transfer their voting rights to some individual or individuals.

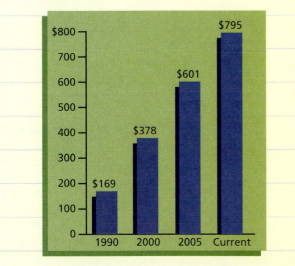

did you know?

One reason investors purchase stocks is because corporation's pay investors dividends. (amounts in billions)

Source: *Statistical Abstract of the United States, 2009*, U.S. Bureau of the Census Web site (www.census.gov), accessed February 1, 2009 (Washington, DC: U.S. Government Printing Office), p. 506.

record date The date on which a stockholder must be registered on the corporation's books in order to receive dividend payments.

Exhibit 12–1

Typical Information on Corporate Dividends as Presented in *The Wall Street Journal*

The numbers above each of the columns correspond to the numbered entries in the list of explanations that appear at the bottom of the exhibit.

1	2	3	4
Company/Symbol	Yield (%)	Amount New/Old	Payable/Record
Increased			
CMS Energy Corp CMS	4.2	.125/.09 Q	Feb 27/Feb 06
Genuine Parts Co GPC	5.0	.40/.39 Q	Apr 01/Mar 06
Heritage Fin'l HBOS	3.8	.08/.07 Q	Feb 20/Feb 06

1. The name of the company paying the dividend is CMS Energy and its stock ticker is CMS.

2. The current yield is 4.2 percent and is based on the dividend amount and the current price of the stock.

3. The amount of the new dividend is $0.125 and the old dividend is $0.09.

4. The dividend will be paid on the payable date (February 27) to stockholders who own the stock on the record date (February 6).

Source: Republished with permission of Dow Jones, Inc., from *The Wall Street Journal,* January 24, 2009; permission conveyed through Copyright Clearance Center, Inc.

goes ex-dividend, and the dollar value of the stock may go down by the value of the dividend.

DOLLAR APPRECIATION OF STOCK VALUE In most cases, you purchase stock and then hold onto that stock for a period of time. If the market value of the stock increases, you must decide whether to sell the stock at the higher price or continue to hold it. If you decide to sell the stock, the dollar amount of difference between the purchase price and the selling price represents your profit.

Let's assume that on January 20, 2006, you purchased 100 shares of General Mills stock at a cost of $49 a share. Your cost for the stock was $4,900 plus $55 in commission charges, for a total investment of $4,955. (Note: Commissions, a topic covered later in this chapter, are charged when you purchase stock *and* when you sell stock.) Let's also assume you held your 100 shares until January 20, 2009, and then sold them for $60 a share. During the investment period you owned General Mills, the company paid dividends totaling $4.64 a share. Exhibit 12–2 shows your return on the investment. In this case, you made money because of dividend distributions and through an increase in stock value from $49 to $60 per share. As Exhibit 12–2 shows, your total return is $1,454. Of course, if the stock's value should decrease, or if the firm's board of directors reduces or votes to omit dividends, your return may be less than the original investment. For help in deciding if it's time to sell stock, read the nearby Personal Finance in Practice feature.

POSSIBILITY OF INCREASED VALUE FROM STOCK SPLITS Investors can also increase potential profits through a stock split. A **stock split** is a procedure in which the shares of stock owned by existing stockholders are divided into a larger number of shares. In 2009, for example, the board of directors of Village Super Market, Inc., the parent company of Shop Rite supermarkets, approved a 2-for-1 stock split. After the stock split, a stockholder who had previously owned 100 shares now owned 200 shares. The most common stock splits are 2-for-1 or 3-for-1.

Why do corporations split their stock? In many cases, a firm's management has a theoretical ideal price range for the firm's stock. If the market value of the stock rises above the ideal range, a stock split brings the market value back in line. In the case of Village Super Market, the 2-for-1 stock split reduced the market value to one-half of

stock split A procedure in which the shares of stock owned by existing stockholders are divided into a larger number of shares.

> When Should You Sell a Stock?

Here are some suggestions for deciding when you should sell a stock.

1. *Follow your stock's value.* Too often, investors purchase a stock and then forget about it. A much better approach is to graph the dollar value of your stock every two weeks.

2. *Watch the company's financials.* Smart investors evaluate a stock investment before they make it. The smartest investors use all the available information to continuously evaluate their stocks.

3. *Track the firm's product line.* If the firm's products become obsolete and the company fails to introduce state-of-the-art new products, its sales—and, ulti-mately, profits—may take a nosedive.

4. *Monitor economic developments.* An economic re-cession or an economic recovery may cause the value of a stock investment to increase or decrease. Also, watch the unemployment rate, inflation rate, inter-est rates, productivity rates, and similar economic indicators.

5. *Be patient.* The secret of success for making money with stocks is time. As pointed out earlier in this chapter, stocks have returned just over 10 percent before adjusting for inflation each year since 1926. Assuming you purchase *quality* stocks, your invest-ments will eventually increase in value.

the stock's value on the day prior to the split. The lower market value for each share of stock was the result of dividing the dollar value of the company by a larger number of shares of common stock. Also, a decision to split a company's stock and the result-ing lower market value make the stock more attractive to the investing public. This attraction is based on the belief that most corporations split their stock only when their financial future is improving and on the upswing.

Be warned: There are no guarantees that a stock's market value will go up after a split. This is important to understand, because investors often think that a stock split leads to immediate profits. Nothing could be further from the truth. Here's why. The total market capitalization—the value of the company's stock multiplied by the number of

Exhibit 12–2

Sample Stock Transaction for General Mills

Assumptions			
100 shares of common stock purchased January 20, 2006, sold January 20, 2009; dividends of $4.64 per share for the investment period.			

Costs when Purchased		Return when Sold	
100 shares @ $49 =	$4,900	100 shares @ $60 =	$6,000
Plus commission	+ 55	Minus commission	− 55
Total investment	$4,955	Total return	$5,945

Transaction Summary	
Total return	$5,945
Minus total investment	− 4,955
Profit from stock sale	$ 990
Plus dividends	+ 464
Total return for the transaction	$1,454

shares outstanding—does not change because a corporation splits its stock. A company that has a market capitalization of $100 million before a 2-for-1 stock split is still worth $100 million after the split. Simply put, there is twice as much stock, but each share is worth half of its previous value before the stock split occurred. If a stock's value does increase after a stock split, it increases because of the firm's financial performance after the split and not just because there are more shares of stock.

Preferred Stock

preferred stock A type of stock that gives the owner the advantage of receiving cash dividends before common stockholders are paid any dividends.

In addition to or instead of purchasing common stock, you may purchase preferred stock. **Preferred stock** is a type of stock that gives the owner the advantage of receiving cash dividends before common stockholders are paid any dividends. This is the most important priority an investor in preferred stock enjoys. Unlike the amount of the dividend on common stock, the dollar amount of the dividend on preferred stock is known before the stock is purchased.

Preferred stocks are often referred to as "middle" investments because they represent an investment midway between common stock (an ownership position for the stockholder) and corporate bonds (a creditor position for the bondholder). When compared to corporate bonds, the yield on preferred stocks is often smaller than the yield on bonds. When compared to common stocks, preferred stocks are safer investments that offer more secure dividends. They are often purchased by individuals who need a predictable source of income greater than offered by common stock investments. They are also purchased by other corporations, because corporations receive a tax break on the dividend income. For all other investors, preferred stocks lack the growth potential that common stocks offer and the safety of many corporate bond issues.

When compared to corporations selling common stock, preferred stock is issued less often by only a few corporations. Yet it is an alternative method of financing that may attract investors who do not wish to buy common stock. Preferred stock, like common stock, is equity financing that does not have to be repaid. And dividends on preferred stock, as on common stock, may be omitted by action of the board of directors. While preferred stock does not represent a legal debt that must be repaid, if the firm is dissolved or declares bankruptcy, preferred stockholders do have first claim to the corporation's assets after creditors (including bondholders). To make preferred stock issues more attractive, some corporations may offer two additional features.

One way preferred stockholders can protect themselves against omitted dividends is to purchase cumulative preferred stock. *Cumulative preferred stock* is stock whose unpaid dividends accumulate and must be paid before any cash dividend is paid to the common stockholders. If a corporation does not pay dividends to the cumulative preferred stockholders during one dividend period, the amount of the missed dividends is added to the following period's preferred dividends. If you own noncumulative preferred stock, an omitted dividend will not be made up later.

The second feature that makes preferred stock attractive is the conversion feature. *Convertible preferred stock* can be exchanged, at the stockholder's option, for a specified number of shares of common stock. The conversion feature provides the investor with the added safety of preferred stock and the possibility of greater speculative gain through conversion to common stock. For example, assume Martin & Martin Manufacturing has issued a convertible preferred stock. Each share of preferred stock is convertible into two shares of common stock. Assume the market price of Martin & Martin's convertible preferred stock is $24 and the stock pays an annual preferred dividend of $1.60 a share. Also assume the market price of the company's common stock is $9 and the common stock currently pays an annual dividend of $0.54 a share. Under these circumstances, you would keep the preferred stock. If the market price of the common stock increased to above $12 a share, however, you would have an incentive to exercise the conversion option.

The decision to convert preferred stock to common stock is complicated by three factors. First, the dividends paid on preferred stock are more secure than the dividends paid on common stock. Second, the amount of the dividend for preferred stock is generally higher than the amount of the dividend for common stock. Third, because of the conversion option, the market value of convertible preferred stock usually increases as the market value of common stock increases.

CONCEPT CHECK 12–1

1 Why do corporations sell stock? Why do investors purchase stock?

_____

_____

2 Why do corporations split their stock? Is a stock split good or bad for investors?

_____

_____

3 From an investor's viewpoint, what is the difference between common stock and preferred stock?

_____

_____

Apply Yourself!

Objective 1

Use the Internet or library research to identify a corporation that has split its stock. Then graph the price of the stock each day for a week before the split and each day for a week after the split. Describe your findings.

Evaluating a Stock Issue

Many investors expect to earn a 10 percent or higher return on their investments, yet they are unwilling to spend the time required to become a good investor. In fact, many people purchase investments without doing *any* research. They wouldn't buy a car without a test drive or purchase a home without comparing different houses, but for some unknown reason they invest without doing their homework. The truth is that there is no substitute for a few hours of detective work when choosing an investment. This section explains how to evaluate a potential stock investment. In reality, it is important to evaluate not only the corporation that issues the individual stock you are interested in purchasing, but also the industry in which the corporation operates. For example, when the automobile industry encountered problems, most companies within this industry found that increasing sales and profits was difficult if not impossible. Also, keep in mind that the nation's and even the world's economy—the big picture—may impact the way a corporation operates and cause a corporate stock to increase or decrease in value.

> **OBJECTIVE 2**
>
> Explain how you can evaluate stock investments.

Exhibit **12–3**

Classification of Stock Investments

When evaluating a stock investment, investors often classify stocks into the following ten categories.

Type of Stock	Characteristics of This Type of Investment
Blue chip	A safe investment that generally attracts conservative investors.
Cyclical	A stock that follows the business cycle of advances and declines in the economy.
Defensive	A stock that remains stable during declines in the economy.
Growth	A stock issued by a corporation that has the potential of earning profits above the average profits of all firms in the economy.
Income	An investment that pays higher-than-average dividends.
Large cap	A stock issued by a corporation that has a large amount of capitalization in excess of $10 billion.
Micro cap	A stock issued by a company that has a capitalization of $250 million or less.
Midcap	A stock issued by a corporation that has capitalization of between $2 billion and $10 billion.
Penny	A stock that typically sells for less than $1 per share.
Small cap	A stock issued by a company that has a capitalization of between $250 million and $2 billion.

A wealth of information is available to stock investors, and a logical place to start the evaluation process for stock is with the classification of different types of stock investments described in Exhibit 12–3. Once you have identified a type of stock that may help you obtain your investment goals, you may want to use the Internet to evaluate a potential investment.

did you know?

Saving the Planet One Investment at a Time!

Experts predict that the next "great" investments will be companies that produce alternative fuels, fuel cells, hybrid vehicles, and organic foods. To obtain information about investing in the companies that are developing environmentally friendly products and services, go to

www.sustainablebusiness.com
www.greenchipstocks.com
www.ecobusinesslinks.com

The Internet

In this section, we examine some Web sites that are logical starting points when evaluating a stock investment, but there are many more than those described. Let's begin with information about the corporation that is available on the Internet.

Today most corporations have a Web site, and the information these pages provide is especially useful. First, it is easily accessible. All you have to do is type in the corporation's URL address or use a search engine to locate the corporation's home page. Second, the information on the Web site may be more up to date and thorough than printed material obtained from the corporation or outside sources. Look at the financial information on the investor page for Walt Disney displayed in Exhibit 12–4. By clicking on a button, you can access information on the firm's earnings and other financial factors that could affect the value of the company's stock.

You can also use Web sites like Yahoo! and other search engines to obtain information about stock investments. Take a look at Exhibit 12–5, which illustrates a portion of the summary page taken from Yahoo! Finance for Boeing, a leading aerospace manufacturer. In addition to the current price, the Yahoo! Finance Web site provides even more specific information about a particular

Exhibit 12–4   Financial Information Available on Walt Disney's Investor Relations Web Page

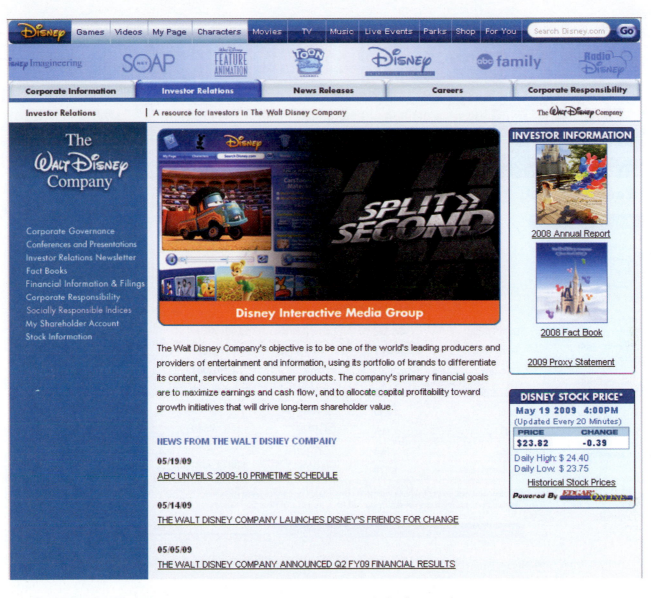

Source: The Walt Disney Web site (http://corporate.disney.go.com/investors/index.html), accessed May 19, 2009.

company like Boeing. By clicking on the buttons under the headings for the quotes, charts, news and info, company, analyst coverage, ownership, and financials that are part of the screen for each corporation, you can obtain even more information. How about picking a company like Johnson & Johnson (symbol JNJ) or Coca-Cola (symbol KO) and going exploring on the Internet? To begin, enter the Web address for Yahoo! Finance (http://finance.yahoo.com). Then enter the symbol for one of the above corporations in the Quotes section and click Get Quotes. You'll be surprised at the amount of information you can obtain with a click of your mouse.

You can also use professional advisory services like Standard & Poor's Financial Services (www2.standardandpoors.com), Mergent Online (www.mergentonline.com), and Value Line (www.valueline.com). While some of the information provided by these services is free, there is a charge for the more detailed information you may need to evaluate a stock investment. For more information about professional advisory services and the type of information they provide, read the next section.

Exhibit 12–5 A Portion of the Opening Page for the Yahoo! Finance Web Site

Source: Reproduced with permission of Yahoo! Inc. © 2009 by Yahoo! Inc. Yahoo! and Yahoo! logo are trademarks of Yahoo! Inc.

Key Web Sites for Stock Information

www.thestreet.com

http://money.cnn.com

http://moneycentral.msn.com/investor

In addition to Internet search engines and professional advisory services, you can access personal finance Web sites like *SmartMoney* (www.smartmoney.com) and *Kiplinger's Personal Finance* (www.kiplinger.com). Both Web sites provide a wealth of information for the stock investor. Additional Web sites that can help you learn more about investing in stocks are included in the nearby Key Web Sites for Stock Information feature.

Stock Advisory Services

In addition to the Internet, sources of information you can use to evaluate potential stock investments are the printed materials provided by stock advisory services. The information ranges from simple alphabetical listings to detailed financial reports.

Standard & Poor's reports, Value Line, and Mergent are three widely used advisory services that provide detailed research for stock investors. Here we will examine a detailed report for PepsiCo, the global beverage company, that is published in *Mergent's Handbook of Common Stocks* (see Exhibit 12–6).

Exhibit **12–6**   Mergent's Report for PepsiCo, Inc.

PEPSICO INC.

Exchange	Symbol	Price	52Wk Range
NYS	PEP	$68.30 (5/30/2008)	79.57–64.65

*7 Year Price Score 99.84   *NYSE Composite Index = 100   *12 Month Price Score 99.96

	Yield	P/E	Div Acheiver.
	2.49	19.63	36 Years

Interim Earnings (Per Share)

Qtr.	Mar	Jun	Aug	Dec
2005	0.53	0.70	0.51	0.65
2006	0.60	0.80	0.88	1.06
2007	0.65	0.94	1.06	0.77
2008	0.70			

Interim Dividends (Per Share)

Amt	Deci	Ex	Rec	Pay
0.375Q	07/19/2007	09/05/2007	09/07/2007	09/28/2007
0.375Q	11/16/2007	12/05/2007	12/07/2007	01/02/2008
0.375Q	02/01/2008	03/05/2008	03/07/2008	03/31/2008
0.425Q	05/07/2008	06/04/2008	06/06/2008	06/30/2008

Indicated Div: $1.70 (Div. Reinv. Plan)

Valuation Analysis **Institutional Holding**

Forecast EPS	$3.73	No of Institutions
	(06/20/2008)	1557
Market Cap	$108.6 Billion	Shares
Book Value	16.8 Billion	1,260,247,040
Price/Book	6.46	%Held
Price/Sales	2.68	67.02

Business Summary: Food (MIC: SIC: 2086 NAIC: 312111)

Pepsico is engaged in manufacturing, marketing and selling a range of salty, sweet and grain-based snacks as well as carbonated and non-carbonated beverages and foods. Co. is organized into four divisions: Frito-Lay North America (FLNA); PepsiCo Beverages North America (PBNA); PepsiCo International (PI); and Quaker Foods North America (QFNA). FLNA branded snacks include Lay's potato chips, Doritos tortilla chips and Rold Gold pretzels. PBNA's brands include Pepsi, Mountain Dew, Gatorade, Tropicana Pure Premium, and Dole. PI's brands include Lay's, Walkers, Cheetos; Doritos, Ruffles, Gamesa and Sabritas. QFNA's brands include Quaker oatmeal, Rice-A-Roni and Near East side dishes.

Recent Developments: For the quarter ended Mar 22 2008, net income increased 4.7% to US$1.15 billion from US$1.10 billion in the year-earlier quarter. Revenues were US$8.33 billion, up 13.4% from US$7.35 billion the year before. Operating income was US$1.55 billion versus US$1.42 billion in the prior-year quarter, an increase of 9.4%. Direct operating expenses rose 16.7% to US$3.83 billion from US$3.29 billion in the comparable period the year before. Indirect operating expenses increased 11.3% to US$2.95 billion from US$2.65 billion in the equivalent prior-year period.

Prospects: For full-year 2008; Co. expects 3.0% to 5.0% volume growth, high-single-digit net revenue growth and earnings per share of at least $3.72. Meanwhile, on May 6 2008. The Pepsi Bottling Group, Inc. and Co. announced that, through their PR Beverages Limited joint venture in Russia, they have completed their acquisition of Sobol-Aqua JSC, a beverage manufacturing company based in Novosibirsk. Russia Separately, on Apr 30 2008. Co. announced the acquisition of V Water, a vitamin water brand in the U.K. This acquisition reflects Co.'s strategy to transforming its portfolio of products and extending its range of healthier beverages, and should provide Co. with significant opportunities.

Financial Data

(US$ in Thousands)	3 Mos	12/29/2007	12/30/2006	12/31/2005	12/25/2004	12/27/2003	12/28/2002	12/29/2001
Earnings Per Share	3.48	3.41	3.34	2.39	2.44	2.05	1.85	1.47
Cash Flow Per Share	4.27	4.29	3.70	3.45	2.99	2.53	2.65	2.39
Tang Book Value Per Share	6.01	6.30	5.50	5.20	4.84	3.82	4.93	2.17
Dividends Per Share	1.500	1.425	1.160	1.010	0.850	0.630	0.595	0.575
Dividend Payout %	43.13	41.79	34.73	42.26	34.84	30.73	32.16	39.12
Income Statement								
Total Revenue	8,333,000	39,474,000	35,137,000	32,562,000	29,261,000	26,971,000	25,112,000	26,935,000
EBITDA	1,926,000	9,092,000	8,399,000	7,732,000	6,848,000	6,269,000	6,077,000	5,189,000
Depn & Amortn	303,000	1,362,000	1,344,000	1,253,000	1,209,000	1,165,000	1,067,000	1,008,000
Income Before Taxes	1,566,000	7,631,000	6,989,000	6,382,000	5,546,000	4,992,000	4,868,000	4,029,000
Income Taxes	418,000	1,973,000	1,347,000	2,304,000	1,372,000	1,424,000	1,555,000	1,367,000
Net Income	1,148,000	5,658,000	5,642,000	4,078,000	4,212,000	3,568,000	3,313,000	2,662,000
Average Shares	1,632,000	1,658,000	1,687,000	1,706,000	1,729,000	1,739,000	1,789,000	1,807,000
Balance Sheet								
Current Assets	11,065,000	10,151,000	9,130,000	10,454,000	8,639,000	6,930,000	6,413,000	5,853,000
Total Assets	35,699,000	34,628,000	29,930,000	31,727,000	27,987,000	25,327,000	23,474,000	21,695,000
Current Liabilities	8,587,000	7,753,000	6,860,000	9,406,000	6,752,000	6,415,000	6,052,000	4,998,000
Long-Term Obligations	4,884,000	4,203,000	2,550,000	2,313,000	2,397,000	1,702,000	2,187,000	2,651,000
Total Liabilities	18,985,000	17,394,000	14,562,000	17,476,000	14,464,000	13,453,000	14,183,000	13,021,000
Stockholders' Equity	16,806,000	17,325,000	15,447,000	14,320,000	13,572,000	11,896,000	9,298,000	8,648,000
Shares Outstanding	1,590,000	1,605,000	1,638,000	1,656,000	1,679,000	1,705,000	1,722,000	1,756,000
Statistical Record								
Return on Assets %	17.47	17.58	18.35	13.44	15.84	14.66	14.71	13.34
Return on Equity %	35.51	34.62	38.01	28.77	33.17	33.76	37.02	33.58
EBITDA Margin %	23.11	23.03	23.90	23.75	23.40	23.24	24.20	19.26
Net Margin %	13.78	14.33	16.06	12.52	14.39	13.23	13.19	9.88
Asset Turnover	1.24	1.23	1.14	1.07	1.10	1.11	1.11	1.35
Current Ratio	1.29	1.31	1.33	1.11	1.28	1.08	1.06	1.17
Debt to Equity	0.29	0.24	0.16	0.16	0.18	0.14	0.24	0.31
Price Range	79.57–62.89	78.69–62.16	65.91–56.77	59.90–51.57	55.55–45.39	48.71–37.30	53.12–35.50	50.28–41.26
P/E Ratio	22.86–18.07	23.08–18.23	19.73–17.00	25.06–21.58	22.77–18.60	23.76–18.20	28.71–19.19	34.20–28.07
Average Yield %	2.15	2.09	1.90	1.82	1.66	1.43	1.29	1.25

Address: 700 Anderson Hill Road, Purchase, NY 10577-1444 Telephone: 914-253-2000 Fax: 914-253-2070	Web Site: www.pepsico.com Officers: Indra K. Nooyi - Chairman, President, Chief Executive Officer Michael D. White - Vice-Chairman	Auditors: KPMG LLP Investor Contact: 914-253-3035 Transfer Agents: The Bank of New York

Source: *Mergent's Handbook of Common Stocks,* Summer 2008 (New York: Mergent, 2008).

The basic report illustrated in Exhibit 12–6 consists of six main sections. The top section provides information about stock prices, earnings, and dividends. The Business Summary describes the company's major operations in detail. The next section, Recent Developments, provides current information about the company's net income and sales revenue. The Prospects section describes the company's outlook. The Financial Data section provides important data on the company for the past 7 years plus the last 3-month reporting period. Among the topics included in this section are total revenues, earnings per share, dividends per share, return on equity, and net income. The final section of the report states, among other things, who its auditors are, where its principal office is located, who its transfer agent is, and who its main corporate officers are. While other stock advisory services provide basically the same types of information as that in Exhibit 12–6, it is the investor's job to interpret such information and decide whether the company's stock is a good investment.

How to Read the Financial Section of the Newspaper

Although some newspapers have eliminated or reduced the amount of financial coverage, *The Wall Street Journal* and most metropolitan newspapers still contain some information about stocks. Although not all newspapers print exactly the same information, they usually provide the basic information. Stocks are listed alphabetically, so your first task is to move down the table to find the stock you're interested in. Then, to read the stock quotation, you simply read across the table. The third line in Exhibit 12–7 provides information about Aflac.

Corporate News

The federal government requires corporations selling new issues of securities to disclose in a prospectus information about corporate earnings, assets and liabilities, products or services, and the qualifications of top management. In addition to a prospectus, all publicly owned corporations send their stockholders an annual report that contains detailed financial data. In addition, an electronic version of a corporation's annual report is available on its Internet Web site. Even if you're not a stockholder,

Exhibit 12–7

Financial Information about Common Stocks

Reproduced at the top of the exhibit is an enlarged portion of the stock quotations reported in *The Wall Street Journal.* The numbers above each of the columns correspond to the numbered entries in the list of explanations that appear at the bottom of the exhibit.

1 STOCK	2 SYMBOL NYSE	3 CLOSE	4 NET CHG
ACE Ltd	ACE	48.82	3.44
AES Cp	AES	8.67	–
Aflac	AFL	25.06	2.92

1. Name (often abbreviated) of the company: Aflac

2. Ticker symbol or letters that identify a stock for trading: AFL

3. Price paid in the last transaction of the day: $25.06

4. Difference between the price paid for the last share sold today and the price paid for the last share sold on the previous day: $2.92 (In Wall Street terms, Aflac "closed up $2.92" on this day.)

Source: Republished with permission of Dow Jones, Inc., from *The Wall Street Journal,* January 29, 2009; permission conveyed through Copyright Clearance Center, Inc.

you can obtain an annual report from the corporation. For most corporations, all it takes to obtain the print version is a call to a toll-free phone number, a written request to the corporation's headquarters, or a visit to a corporation's Web site.

In addition to corporate publications, you can access the Securities and Exchange Commission Web site (www.sec.gov) to obtain financial and other important information that a corporation has supplied to the federal government.

Finally, many periodicals, including *Business Week, Fortune, Forbes, Money, Kiplinger's Personal Finance Magazine,* and similar publications contain information about stock investing.

CONCEPT CHECK 12–2

1 Describe how each of the following sources of investment information could help you evaluate a stock investment.

Source of Information	Type of Information	How Could This Help
The Internet		
Stock advisory services		
A newspaper		
Government publications		
Business periodicals		

2 What is the difference between a prospectus and an annual report?

_____

_____

3 Using Exhibit 12–6, pick three financial measures and describe how they could help you evaluate a corporate stock.

_____

_____

Apply Yourself!

Objective 2

Go to the library and use Standard & Poor's, Value Line, or Mergent to research a stock that you think would help you obtain your investment goals.

Numerical Measures That Influence Investment Decisions

OBJECTIVE 3

Analyze the numerical measures that cause a stock to increase or decrease in value.

How do you determine whether the time is right to buy or sell a particular stock? Good question! Unfortunately, there is no simple answer. In addition to the material in the last section, Evaluating a Stock Issue, many investors rely on numerical measures to decide when to buy or sell a stock. We begin this section by examining the relationship between a stock's price and a corporation's earnings.

Why Corporate Earnings Are Important

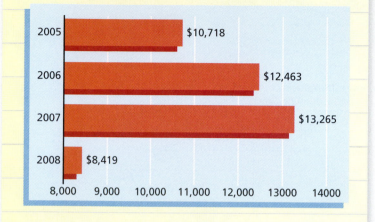
Many analysts believe that a corporation's ability or inability to generate earnings in the future may be one of the most significant factors that account for an increase or decrease in the value of a stock. Simply put, higher earnings generally equate to higher stock value. Unfortunately, the reverse is also true. If a corporation's earnings decline, generally the stock's value will also decline. Corporate earnings are reported in the firm's annual report. You can also obtain information about a corporation's current earnings by using a professional advisory service or accessing the Yahoo! Finance Web site or one of the other Web sites described in the last section.

EARNINGS PER SHARE Many investors calculate earnings per share to evaluate the financial health of a corporation. **Earnings per share** are a corporation's after-tax earnings divided by the number of outstanding shares of a firm's common stock.

earnings per share A corporation's after-tax earnings divided by the number of outstanding shares of a firm's common stock.

Example

Assume XYZ Corporation's 2009 after-tax earnings were $5,000,000. Also assume that XYZ has 10,000,000 shares of common stock. Earnings per share are $0.50, as illustrated below.

$$\text{Earnings per share} = \frac{\text{After-tax earnings}}{\text{Number of shares outstanding}}$$

$$= \frac{\$5,000,000}{10,000,000} = \$0.50$$

Most stockholders consider the amount of earnings per share important because it is a measure of the company's profitability. No meaningful average for this measure exists, mainly because the number of shares of a firm's stock is subject to change via stock splits and stock dividends. *As a general rule, however, an increase in earnings per share is a healthy sign for any corporation and its stockholders.*

price-earnings (PE) ratio The price of a share of stock divided by the corporation's earnings per share of stock.

PRICE-EARNINGS RATIO Another calculation, the price-earnings ratio, can be used to evaluate a potential stock investment. The **price-earnings (PE) ratio** is the price of a share of stock divided by the corporation's earnings per share of stock.

Example

Assume XYZ Corporation's common stock is selling for $10 a share. As determined above, XYZ's earnings per share are $0.50. The corporation's price-earnings ratio is 20, as illustrated below.

$$\text{Price-earnings (PE) ratio} = \frac{\text{Price per share}}{\text{Earnings per share}}$$

$$= \frac{\$10}{\$0.50} = 20$$

The price-earnings ratio is a key factor that serious investors use to evaluate stock investments. Generally, a price-earnings ratio gives investors an idea of how much they are paying for a company's earning power. The higher the price-earnings ratio, the more investors are paying for earnings. A high price-earnings ratio (over 20) often indicates investor optimism because of the expectation of higher earnings in the future. Always remember the relationship between earnings and stock value. If future earnings do increase, the stock usually becomes more valuable in the future. On the other hand, a low price-earnings ratio (under 20) indicates that investors have lower earnings expectations. If future earnings decrease or don't maintain the same level of growth, the stock will become less valuable in the future.

Like earnings per share, a corporation's PE ratio is often reported on investment Web sites. When researching a stock, comparing the P/E ratios of one company to other companies in the same industry, to the market in general, or against the company's own historical P/E ratios is usually useful. Keep in mind that the PE ratio calculation is just another piece of the puzzle when researching a stock for investment purposes.

PROJECTED EARNINGS Both earnings per share and the price-earnings ratio are based on historical numbers. In other words, this is what the company has done in the past. With this fact in mind, many investors will also look at earnings estimates for a corporation. The Yahoo! Finance Web site or similar financial Web sites provide earnings estimates for major corporations. At the time of publication, for example, Yahoo! Finance provided the following earnings estimates for Apple, Inc., one of the most innovative technology companies in the United States.[2]

Apple, Inc.	This Year	Next Year
Yearly earnings estimates	$5.21 per share	$6.04 per share

From an investor's standpoint, a projected increase in earnings from $5.21 per share to $6.04 per share is a good sign. In the case of Apple, these estimates were determined by surveying different analysts who track Apple, Inc. By using the same projected earnings amount, it is possible to calculate a projected price-earnings ratio or a projected price per share of stock. Of course, you should remember that these are estimates and are not "etched in stone." An increase or decrease in interest rates, higher or lower unemployment rates, terrorist attacks, and changes that affect the economy, industry, or company's sales and profit amounts could cause analysts to revise the above estimates.

---

[2]Yahoo! Finance Web site (http://finance.yahoo.com), accessed January 28, 2009, Yahoo!, Inc., 701 First Avenue, Sunnyvale, CA 94089.

Figure It Out!

Other Factors That Influence the Price of a Stock

One of the calculations investors use most frequently to monitor the value of their investments is the dividend yield. *Note:* The dividend yield described below is very similar to the current yield calculation presented in Chapter 11. The difference is that the term "annual interest amount" used in the current yield calculation has been changed to "annual dividend amount" because stocks often pay dividends to investors and provide dividend income. The **dividend yield** is the yearly dollar amount of dividend generated by an investment divided by the investment's current price per share.

dividend yield The yearly dollar amount of dividend generated by an investment divided by the investment's current price per share.

Example

Assume you own McDonald's stock. A share of stock pays an annual dividend of $2.00 and is currently selling for $59 a share. The current dividend yield is 3.4 percent, as illustrated below.

$$\text{Dividend yield} = \frac{\text{Annual dividend amount}}{\text{Price per share}}$$

$$= \frac{\$2}{\$59} = 0.034 = 3.4 \text{ percent}$$

As a general rule, an increase in dividend yield is a healthy sign for any investment. A dividend yield of 4 percent is better than a 3.4 percent dividend yield.

Although the dividend yield calculation is useful, you should also consider whether the investment is increasing or decreasing in dollar value. **Total return** is a calculation that includes not only the yearly dollar amount of dividend but also any increase or decrease in the original purchase price of the investment. While this concept may be used for any investment, let's illustrate it by using the assumptions for the McDonald's stock presented in the preceding example.

total return A calculation that includes the yearly dollar amount of dividend as well as any increase or decrease in the original purchase price of the investment.

Example

Assume you own 100 shares of McDonald's stock that you purchased for $49.50 a share and hold your stock for one year before deciding to sell it at the current market price of $59 a share. Your total return is $1,150, as illustrated below.

Total return = Dividends + Capital gain

= $200 + $950 = $1,150

The dividend of $200 results from the payment of dividends for one year ($2.00 per-share dividend × 100 shares). The capital gain of $950 results from the increase in the stock price from $49.50 a share to $59 a share ($9.50 per-share increase × 100 shares = $950). (Of course, commissions to buy and sell your stock, a topic covered in the next section, would reduce your total return.)

Although little correlation may exist between the market value of a stock and its book value, book value is widely reported in financial publications. Therefore, it deserves mention. The **book value** for a share of stock is determined by deducting all liabilities from the corporation's assets and dividing the remainder by the number of outstanding shares of common stock.

book value Determined by deducting all liabilities from the corporation's assets and dividing the remainder by the number of outstanding shares of common stock.

Example

Assume ABC Corporation has assets of $60 million and liabilities of $20 million. The company has also issued 5,000,000 shares of stock. The book value is $8 per share, as illustrated below.

$$\text{Book value} = \frac{\text{Assets} - \text{Liabilities}}{\text{Number of shares outstanding}}$$

$$= \frac{\$60,000,000 - \$20,000,000}{5,000,000 \text{ shares}} = \$8 \text{ per share}$$

Some investors believe they have found a bargain when a stock's market value is about the same as or lower than its book value. *Be warned:* Book value calculations may be misleading, because the dollar amount of assets used in the above formula may be understated or overstated on the firm's financial statements. From a practical standpoint, most financial experts suggest that book value is just another piece of the puzzle and you must consider other factors along with book value when evaluating a possible stock investment.

Sheet 38 Evaluating Corporate Stocks

CONCEPT CHECK 12–3

1 Explain the relationship between corporate earnings and a stock's market value.

_____

_____

2 Why are earnings per share and price-earnings ratios important?

_____

_____

3 Write the formula for the following stock calculations, and then describe how this formula could help you make a decision to buy or sell a stock.

Calculation	What Is the Formula?	Why Is This Calculation Useful?
Earnings per share		
Price-earnings (PE) ratio		
Dividend yield		
Total return		
Book value		

Apply Yourself!

Objective 3

Use an Internet Web site to locate the current price for a share of stock and earnings per share for Microsoft (symbol MSFT), 3M Company (symbol MMM), and Colgate-Palmolive (symbol CL).

OBJECTIVE 4

Describe how stocks are bought and sold.

Buying and Selling Stocks

To purchase common or preferred stock, you generally have to work through a brokerage firm. In turn, your brokerage firm must buy the stock in either the primary or secondary market. In the **primary market,** you purchase financial securities, via an investment bank or other representative, from the issuer of those securities. An **investment bank** is a financial firm that assists corporations in raising funds, usually by helping to sell new security issues.

New security issues sold through an investment bank can be issued by corporations that have sold stocks and bonds before and need to sell new issues to raise additional financing. The new securities can also be initial public offerings. An **initial public offering (IPO)** occurs when a corporation sells stock to the general public for the first time. At the time of publication, the three largest IPOs were Visa ($17.9 billion), AT&T

primary market A market in which an investor purchases financial securities, via an investment bank or other representative, from the issuer of those securities.

Wireless Group ($10.6 billion), and Kraft Foods ($8.7 billion).[3] Because these companies used the financing obtained through IPOs wisely, they have grown and prospered, and investors have profited from their IPO investments.

Be warned: The promise of quick profits often lures investors to purchase IPOs. An IPO is generally classified as a high-risk investment—one made in the hope of earning a relatively large profit in a short time. Depending on the corporation selling the new security, IPOs are usually too speculative for most people.

Once stocks are sold in the primary market, they can be sold time and again in the secondary market. The **secondary market** is a market for existing financial securities that are currently traded among investors. The fact that stocks can be sold in the secondary market improves the liquidity of stock investments because the money you pay for stock goes to the seller of the stock.

Secondary Markets for Stocks

To purchase common or preferred stock, you usually have to work with an employee of a brokerage firm who will buy or sell for you at a securities exchange or through the over-the-counter market.

SECURITIES EXCHANGES A **securities exchange** is a marketplace where member brokers who represent investors meet to buy and sell securities. The securities sold at a particular exchange must first be listed, or accepted for trading, at that exchange. Generally, the securities issued by nationwide corporations are traded at the New York Stock Exchange or regional exchanges. The securities of very large corporations may be traded at more than one exchange. American firms that do business abroad may also be listed on foreign securities exchanges—in Tokyo, London, or Paris, for example.

The New York Stock Exchange (NYSE), now owned by the NYSE Euronext holding company, is one of the largest securities exchanges in the world. This exchange lists stocks for nearly 4,000 corporations with a total market value of about $30 trillion.[4] Most of the NYSE members represent brokerage firms that charge commissions on security trades made by their representatives for their customers. Other members are called *specialists* or *specialist firms.* A **specialist** buys *or* sells a particular stock in an effort to maintain a fair and orderly market.

Before a corporation's stock is approved for listing on the NYSE, the corporation must meet specific listing requirements. The various regional exchanges also have listing requirements, but typically these are less stringent than the NYSE requirements. The stock of corporations that cannot meet the NYSE requirements, find it too expensive to be listed on the NYSE, or choose not to be listed on the NYSE is often traded on one of the regional exchanges, or through the over-the-counter market.

THE OVER-THE-COUNTER MARKET Not all securities are traded on organized exchanges. Stocks issued by several thousand companies are traded in the over-the-counter market. The **over-the-counter (OTC) market** is a network of dealers who buy and sell the stocks of corporations that are not listed on a securities exchange. Today these stocks are not really traded over the counter. The term was coined more than 100 years ago when securities were sold "over the counter" in stores and banks.

Most over-the-counter securities are traded through Nasdaq (pronounced "nazzdack"). **Nasdaq** is an electronic marketplace for stocks issued by approximately

investment bank A financial firm that assists corporations in raising funds, usually by helping to sell new security issues.

initial public offering (IPO) Occurs when a corporation sells stock to the general public for the first time.

secondary market A market for existing financial securities that are currently traded among investors.

securities exchange A marketplace where member brokers who represent investors meet to buy and sell securities.

specialist Buys or sells a particular stock in an effort to maintain an orderly market.

over-the-counter (OTC) market A network of dealers who buy and sell the stocks of corporations that are not listed on a securities exchange.

Nasdaq An electronic marketplace for stocks issued by approximately 3,200 different companies.

---

[3]The Renaissance Capital IPO Home Web site (www.ipohome.com), accessed January 30, 2009.
[4]New York Stock Exchange Web site (www.nyse.com), accessed January 30, 2009.

3,200 different companies.[5] In addition to providing price information, this computerized system allows investors to buy and sell shares of companies traded on Nasdaq. When you want to buy or sell shares of a company that trades on Nasdaq—say, Microsoft—your account executive sends your order into the Nasdaq computer system, where it shows up on the screen with all the other orders from people who want to buy or sell Microsoft. Then a Nasdaq dealer (sometimes referred to as a *market maker*) sitting at a computer terminal matches buy and sell orders for Microsoft. Once a match is found, your order is completed.

Begun in 1971, Nasdaq is known for its innovative, forward-looking growth companies. Although many securities are issued by smaller companies, some large firms, including Intel, Microsoft, and Cisco Systems, also trade on Nasdaq.

Brokerage Firms and Account Executives

account executive A licensed individual who buys or sells securities for clients; also called a *stockbroker*.

An **account executive,** or *stockbroker,* is a licensed individual who buys or sells investments for his or her clients. While all account executives can buy or sell stock and other investments for clients, most investors expect more from their account executives. Ideally, an account executive should provide information and advice to be used in evaluating potential investments.

Before choosing an account executive, you should have already determined your short-term and long-term financial objectives. Then you must be careful to communicate those objectives to the account executive so that he or she can do a better job of advising you. Needless to say, account executives may err in their investment recommendations. To help avoid a situation in which your account executive's recommendations are automatically implemented, you should be *actively* involved in the decisions related to your investment program and you should never allow your account executive to use his or her discretion without your approval. Watch your account for signs of churning. **Churning** is excessive buying and selling of securities to generate commissions. Churning is illegal under the rules established by the Securities and Exchange Commission; however, it may be difficult to prove. Finally, keep in mind that account executives generally are not liable for client losses that result from their recommendations. In fact, most brokerage firms require new clients to sign a statement in which they promise to submit any complaints to an arbitration board. This arbitration clause generally prevents a client from suing an account executive or a brokerage firm.

churning Excessive buying and selling of securities to generate commissions.

Should You Use a Full-Service or a Discount Brokerage Firm?

Today a healthy competition exists between full-service, discount, and online brokerage firms. While the most obvious difference between full-service, discount, and online firms is the amount of the commissions they charge when you buy or sell stock and other securities, there are at least three other factors to consider. First, consider how much research information is available and how much it costs. All three types of brokerage firms offer excellent research materials, but you are more likely to pay extra for information if you choose a discount or online brokerage firm.

Second, consider how much help you need when making an investment decision. Many full-service brokerage firms argue that you need a professional to help you make important investment decisions. While this may be true for some investors, most account executives employed by full-service brokerage firms are too busy to spend unlimited time with you on a one-on-one basis, especially if you are investing a small amount. On the other side, many discount and online brokerage firms argue that you

---

[5]The Nasdaq Web site (www.nasdaq.com), accessed January 30, 2009.

alone are responsible for making your investment decisions. They are quick to point out that the most successful investors are the ones involved in their investment programs. And they argue that they have both personnel and materials dedicated to helping you learn how to become a better investor. Although there are many exceptions, the information below may help you decide whether to use a full-service, discount, or online brokerage firm.

- Full service

  Beginning investors with little or no experience.

  Individuals who are uncomfortable making investment decisions.

  Individuals who are uncomfortable trading stocks online.

- Discount

  People who understand the "how to" of researching stocks and prefer to make their own decisions.

  Individuals who are uncomfortable trading stocks online.

- Online

  People who understand the "how to" of researching stocks and prefer to make their own decisions.

  Individuals who are comfortable trading stocks online.

Finally, consider how easy it is to buy and sell stock and other securities when using a full-service, discount, or online brokerage firm. Questions to ask include:

1. Can I buy or sell stocks over the phone?
2. Can I trade stocks online?
3. Where is your nearest office located?
4. Do you have a toll-free telephone number for customer use?
5. How often do I get statements?
6. Is there a charge for statements, research reports, and other financial reports?
7. Are there any fees in addition to the commissions I pay when I buy or sell stocks?

Computerized Transactions

Many people still prefer to use telephone orders to buy and sell stocks, but a growing number are using computers to complete security transactions. To meet this need, online, discount, and many full-service brokerage firms allow investors to trade online.

As a rule of thumb, the more active the investor is, the more sense it makes to use computers to trade online. Other reasons that justify using a computer include the size of your investment portfolio, the ability to manage your investments closely, and the capability of your computer and the software package.

While buying and selling stock online can make the investment process easier and faster, you should realize that *you* are still responsible for analyzing the information and making the final decision to buy or sell a security.

CAUTION! Whether you are a beginner or have been investing for many years doesn't matter; it's never too early or too late to ask questions—especially about

- Specific stocks and other investment products.
- An account executive.
- A brokerage firm.

To find out if other investors have lodged complaints about an account executive or a brokerage firm and for information about investment frauds, go to the Securities and Exchange Commission Web site at www.sec.gov.

A Sample Stock Transaction

Once you and your account executive have decided on a particular transaction, it is time to execute an order to buy or sell. Let's begin by examining three types of orders used to trade stocks.

market order A request to buy or sell a stock at the current market value.

A **market order** is a request to buy or sell a stock at the current market value. Since the stock exchange is an auction market, the account executive's representative will try to get the best price available and the transaction will be completed as soon as possible. Payment for stocks is generally required within three business days after the transaction. Then, in about four to six weeks, a stock certificate is sent to the purchaser of the stock, unless the securities are left with the brokerage firm for safekeeping. Today it is common practice for investors to leave stock certificates with a brokerage firm. Because the stock certificates are in the broker's care, transfers when the stock is sold are much easier. The phrase "left in the street name" is used to describe investor-owned securities held by a brokerage firm.

limit order A request to buy or sell a stock at a specified price.

A **limit order** is a request to buy or sell a stock at a specified price. When you purchase stock, a limit order ensures that you will buy at the best possible price but not above a specified dollar amount. When you sell stock, a limit order ensures that you will sell at the best possible price, but not below a specified dollar amount. For example, if you place a limit order to buy Amazon stock for $58 a share, the stock will not be purchased until the price drops to $58 a share or lower. Likewise, if your limit order is to sell Amazon for $58 a share, the stock will not be sold until the price rises to $58 a share or higher. *Be warned:* Limit orders are executed if and when the specified price or better is reached and *all* other previously received orders have been fulfilled.

Many stockholders are certain they want to sell their stock if it reaches a specified price. A limit order does not guarantee this will be done. With a limit order, as mentioned above, orders by other investors may be placed ahead of your order. If you want to guarantee that your order will be executed, you place a special type of limit order known as a stop order. A **stop order** (sometimes called a *stop-loss order*) is an order to sell a particular stock at the next available opportunity after its market price reaches a specified amount. This type of order is used to protect an investor against a sharp drop in price and thus stop the dollar loss on a stock investment. For example, assume you purchased Amazon stock at $58 a share. Two weeks after you made that investment, Amazon reports lower-than-expected sales revenues and profits. Fearing that the market value of your stock will decrease, you enter a stop order to sell your Amazon stock at $40. This means that if the price of the stock decreases to $40 or lower, the account executive will sell it. While a stop order does not guarantee that your stock will be sold at the price you specified, it does guarantee that it will be sold at the next available opportunity. Both limit and stop orders may be good for one day, one week, one month, or good until canceled (GTC).

stop order An order to sell a particular stock at the next available opportunity after its market price reaches a specified amount.

Commission Charges

Most brokerage firms have a minimum commission ranging from $7 to $35 for buying and selling stock. Additional commission charges are based on the number of shares and the value of stock bought and sold.

Exhibit 12–8 shows typical commissions charged by discount and online brokerage firms. Generally, full-service and discount brokerage firms charge higher commissions than those charged by online brokerage firms. As a rule of thumb, full-service brokers may charge as much as 1 to 2 percent of the transaction amount. In return for charging higher commissions, full-service brokers usually spend more time with each client, help make investment decisions, and provide free research information.

Although full-service brokerage firms usually charge higher commissions, on some occasions a discount brokerage firm may charge higher commissions. This generally

Exhibit **12–8**

Typical Commission Charges for Online Stock Transactions in Which 1,000 Shares Are Bought or Sold

Source: TD Ameritrade Web site (www.tdameritrade.com), accessed January 30, 2009, TD Ameritrade, Inc., 4211 South 102nd Street, Omaha, NE 68127.

occurs when the transaction is small, involving a total dollar amount of less than $1,000, and the investor is charged the discount brokerage firm's minimum commission charge.

Sheet 39 Investment Broker Comparison

CONCEPT CHECK 12–4

1 What is the difference between the primary market and the secondary market? What is an initial public offering (IPO)?

_____

_____

2 Assume you want to purchase stock. Would you use a full-service broker or a discount broker? Would you ever trade stocks online?

_____

_____

3 Explain the important characteristics of each of the following types of stock transaction orders:

Market order:	
Limit order:	
Stop order:	

Apply Yourself!

Objective 4

Prepare a list of at least five questions that could help you interview a prospective account executive.

OBJECTIVE 5

Explain the trading techniques used by long-term investors and short-term speculators.

Long-Term and Short-Term Investment Strategies

Once you purchase stock, the investment may be classified as either long term or short term. Generally, individuals who hold an investment for a year or longer are referred to as *investors*. Individuals who routinely buy and then sell stocks within a short period of time are called *speculators* or *traders*.

Long-Term Techniques

In this section, we discuss the long-term techniques of buy and hold, dollar cost averaging, direct investment programs, and dividend reinvestment programs.

BUY-AND-HOLD TECHNIQUE   Many long-term investors purchase stock and hold onto it for a number of years. When they do this, their investment can increase in value in three ways. First, they are entitled to dividends if the board of directors approves dividend payments to stockholders. Second, the price of the stock may go up, or appreciate in value. Third, the stock may be split. Although there are no guarantees, stock splits may increase the future value of a stock investment over a long period of time.

dollar cost averaging A long-term technique used by investors who purchase an equal dollar amount of the same stock at equal intervals.

DOLLAR COST AVERAGING   **Dollar cost averaging** is a long-term technique used by investors who purchase an equal dollar amount of the same stock at equal intervals. Assume you invest $2,000 in Johnson & Johnson's common stock each year for a period of three years. The results of your investment program are illustrated in Exhibit 12–9. Notice that when the price of the stock increased in 2007, you purchased fewer shares. The average cost for a share of stock, determined by dividing the total investment ($6,000) by the total number of shares, is $61.73 ($6,000 ÷ 97.2 = $61.73). Other applications of dollar cost averaging occur when employees purchase shares of their company's stock through a payroll deduction plan or as part of an employer-sponsored retirement plan over an extended period of time.

The two goals of dollar cost averaging are to minimize the average cost per share and to avoid the common pitfall of buying high and selling low. In the situation shown in Exhibit 12–9, you would lose money only if you sold your stock at less than the average cost of $61.73. Thus, with dollar cost averaging, you can make money if the stock is sold at a price higher than the average cost for a share of stock.

Exhibit **12–9**

Dollar Cost Averaging for Johnson & Johnson

Year	Investment	Stock Price	Shares Purchased
2006	$2,000	$60	33.3
2007	2,000	$68	29.4
2008	2,000	$58	34.5
Total	$6,000		97.2

Average cost = Total investment ÷ Total shares

= $6,000 ÷ 97.2

= $61.73

The Second Time Around

I love buying exciting new stocks. But sometimes the best stocks to own are *old* stocks, former holdings you've sold off. It's a joy to buy Home Depot at $18 after selling it seven years ago at $36. Trust me, I know. I just did it. But before we discuss the pros and cons of this nostalgic approach, let's address the elephant in the living room. (There have been so many elephants in my living room lately that I may soon have to move.)

Tricks with yourself. This elephant is your ego and the tricks it can play on investment decisions. I felt good buying Home Depot at 50% off the price at which I'd sold it, but it's not as if I could take that to the bank. Yet I felt richer, even mildly euphoric. *Why?* Because I thought I had gotten a bargain on a great item. My ego told me I had done something smart, but who knows? The market will inform me eventually. In June 2000, you could have bought Yahoo at half price, for just $60, and now you'd be down 80%. Remember: The worst stocks in history always trade at tantalizingly low prices before they plunge to oblivion.

But repurchasing a stock you know can have some real benefits. For one thing, you understand the business. You may know and trust the company's managers. You may be more aware than the average investor that an excellent company has been in the toilet for transitory reasons.

Speaking of toilets, let's revisit Home Depot. The housing blight has torpedoed the stock, and customer-service problems haven't helped. I don't know when Home Depot will recover, but I can imagine it earning $3 a share in 2013. Put a 15 multiple on that and you have a $45 stock, or a 150% gain. Will the company improve customer service? I hope so, but it is not an essential part of my investment thesis. Note: I also bought rival Lowe's, which has better growth opportunities and sharper customer service.

I also recently returned to Intrepid Potash, which produces fertilizer. I bought it in May at $43 soon after it went public, sold weeks later at $60, for a 40% profit, then watched it soar and then do a death dive.

I bought Intrepid back at $18. Why? Because it may earn $5 a share next year. Because people in emerging markets have to keep eating. And, finally, because it had been bludgeoned as if it were a steel or copper stock and I believed that, in today's world, agriculture would prove less of a boom-and-bust business.

When doing this, however, beware of assuming that you know more than you do. Companies change, times change, and just because you sold General Motors at $50 doesn't make it a gem at $25—or, for that matter, at $5.

1. What are the real benefits of repurchasing a stock that you owned and sold in the past?

_____

2. Mr. Feinberg describes three stock investments in this article: Home Depot, Lowe's, and Intrepid Potash. What factors did he consider before making the decisions to purchase these stocks?

_____

3. What Factors can help you decide to buy or sell a stock?

_____

direct investment plan A plan that allows stockholders to purchase stock directly from a corporation without having to use an account executive or a brokerage firm.

dividend reinvestment plan A plan that allows current stockholders the option to reinvest or use their cash dividends to purchase stock of the corporation.

Key Web Sites for Direct Investing and Dividend Reinvestment

www.directinvesting.com

www.dripcentral.com

margin A speculative technique whereby an investor borrows part of the money needed to buy a particular stock.

DIRECT INVESTMENT AND DIVIDEND REINVESTMENT PLANS Today a large number of corporations offer direct investment plans. A **direct investment plan** allows you to purchase stock directly from a corporation without having to use an account executive or a brokerage firm. Similarly, a **dividend reinvestment plan** (often called a DRIP) allows you the option to reinvest your cash dividends to purchase stock of the corporation. For stockholders, the chief advantage of both types of plans is that these plans enable them to purchase stock without paying a commission charge to a brokerage firm. (*Note:* A few companies may charge a small fee for direct and dividend reinvestment plans, but the fee is less than the commissions most brokerage firms charge.) The fees, minimum investment amounts, rules, and features for both direct investment and dividend reinvestment vary from one corporation to the next. Also, with the direct investment and dividend reinvestment plans, you can take advantage of dollar cost averaging, discussed in the last section. For corporations, the chief advantage of both types of plans is that they provide an additional source of capital. As an added bonus, they are providing a service to their stockholders.

Short-Term Techniques

In addition to the long-term techniques presented in the preceding section, investors sometimes use more speculative, short-term techniques. In this section, we discuss buying stock on margin, selling short, and trading in options. *Be warned:* The methods presented in this section are risky; do not use them unless you fully understand the underlying risks. Also, you should not use them until you have experienced success using the more traditional long-term techniques described above.

BUYING STOCK ON MARGIN When buying stock on **margin,** you borrow part of the money needed to buy a particular stock. The margin requirement is set by the Federal Reserve Board and is subject to periodic change. The current margin requirement is 50 percent. This requirement means you may borrow up to half of the total stock purchase price. Although margin is regulated by the Federal Reserve, specific requirements and the interest charged on the loans used to fund margin transactions may vary among brokers and dealers. Usually the brokerage firm either lends the money or arranges the loan with another financial institution.

Investors buy on margin because the financial leverage created by borrowing money can increase the return on an investment. Because they can buy up to twice as much stock by buying on margin, they can earn larger returns. Suppose you expect the market price of a share of ExxonMobil to *increase* in the next three to four months. Let's say you have enough money to purchase 100 shares of the stock. However, if you buy on margin, you can purchase an additional 100 shares for a total of 200 shares.

Example

If the price of ExxonMobil's stock increases by $7 a share, your profit will be:

Without margin: $ 700 = $7 increase per share × 100 shares

With margin: $1,400 = $7 increase per share × 200 shares

In the preceding example, buying more shares on margin enables you to earn double the profit (less the interest you pay on the borrowed money and customary commission charges).

If the value of a margined stock decreases to approximately 60 percent of the original price, you will receive a *margin call* from the brokerage firm. After the margin call, you must pledge additional cash or securities to serve as collateral for the loan. If you don't have acceptable collateral or cash, the margined stock is sold and the proceeds are used to repay the loan. The exact price at which the brokerage firm issues the margin call is determined by the amount of money you borrowed when you purchased the stock. Generally, the more money you borrow, the sooner you will receive a margin call if the value of the margined stock drops.

In addition to facing the possibility of larger dollar losses because you own more shares, you must pay interest on the money borrowed to purchase stock on margin. Most brokerage firms charge 1 to 3 percent above the prime rate. Normally, economists define the prime rate as the interest rate that the best business customers must pay. Interest charges can absorb the potential profits if the value of margined stock does not increase rapidly enough and the margined stocks must be held for long periods of time.

SELLING SHORT   Your ability to make money by buying and selling securities is related to how well you can predict whether a certain stock will increase or decrease in market value. Normally, you buy stocks and assume they will increase in value, a procedure referred to as *buying long*. But not all stocks increase in value. In fact, the value of a stock may decrease for many reasons, including lower sales, lower profits, reduced dividends, product failures, increased competition, product liability lawsuits, and labor strikes. In addition, the health of a nation's economy can make a difference. At the time of publication, the nation was in the midst of an economic crisis. As a result, individual stock prices had fallen and most stock investors had watched as the value of their investment portfolio and retirement plans also dropped in value.

When stock prices are declining, you may use a procedure called *selling short* to make money. **Selling short** is selling stock that has been borrowed from a brokerage firm and must be replaced at a later date. When you sell short, you sell today, knowing you must buy or *cover* your short transaction at a later date. To make money in a short transaction, you must take these steps:

selling short   Selling stock that has been borrowed from a brokerage firm and must be replaced at a later date.

1. Arrange to *borrow a stock certificate* for a certain number of shares of a particular stock from a brokerage firm.
2. *Sell the borrowed* stock, assuming it will drop in value in a reasonably short period of time.
3. *Buy the stock at a lower price* than the price it sold for in step 2.
4. Use the stock purchased in step 3 to *replace the stock borrowed from the brokerage firm* in step 1.

When selling short, your profit is the difference between the amount received when the stock is sold in step 2 and the amount paid for the stock in step 3. For example, assume that you think Wells Fargo stock is overvalued at $19 a share. You also believe the stock will *decrease* in value over the next four to six months because of the problems banks have experienced during the recent economic crisis. You call your broker and arrange to borrow 100 shares of Wells Fargo stock (step 1). The broker then sells your borrowed stock for you at the current market price of $19 a share (step 2). Also assume that four months later Wells Fargo stock drops to $11 a share. You instruct your broker to purchase 100 shares of Wells Fargo stock at the current lower price (step 3). The newly purchased stock is given to the brokerage firm to repay the borrowed stock (step 4).

> ## Example
>
> Your profit from the Wells Fargo short transaction was $800 because the price declined from $19 to $11.
>
> $1,900 Selling price = $19 price per share × 100 shares (Step 2)
>
> −1,100 Purchase price = $11 price per share × 100 shares (Step 3)
>
> $ 800 Profit from selling short

There is usually no special or extra brokerage charge for selling short, since the brokerage firm receives its regular commission when the stock is bought and sold. Before selling short, consider two factors. First, since the stock you borrow from your broker is actually owned by another investor, you must pay any dividends the stock earns before you replace the stock. After all, you borrowed the stock and then sold the borrowed stock. Eventually, dividends can absorb the profits from your short transaction if the price of the stock does not decrease rapidly enough. Second, to make money selling short, you must be correct in predicting that a stock will decrease in value. If the value of the stock increases, you lose.

option The right to buy or sell a stock at a predetermined price during a specified period of time.

TRADING IN OPTIONS An **option** gives you the right—but not the obligation—to buy or sell a stock at a predetermined price during a specified period of time. Options are usually available for three-, six-, or nine-month periods. If you think the market price of a stock will increase during a short period of time, you may decide to purchase a call option. A *call option* is sold by a stockholder and gives the purchaser the right to *buy* 100 shares of a stock at a guaranteed price before a specified expiration date. With a call option, the purchaser is betting that the price of the stock will increase in value before the expiration date.

It is also possible to purchase a put option. A *put option* is the right to sell 100 shares of a stock at a guaranteed price before a specified expiration date. With a put option, the purchaser is betting that the price of the stock will decrease in value before the expiration date. If these price movements do not occur before the expiration date, you lose the money you paid for your call or put option.

Because of the increased risk involved in option trading, a more detailed discussion of how you profit or lose money with options is beyond the scope of this book. *Be warned:* Amateurs and beginning investors should stay away from options unless they fully understand all of the risks involved. For the rookie, the lure of large profits over a short period of time may be tempting, but the risks are real.

CONCEPT CHECK 12–5

1 In your own words, describe the difference between an investor and a speculator.

_____

_____

2 In the space provided, describe each of the following investment techniques.

Buy and hold:	
Dollar cost averaging:	
Direct investment:	
Dividend reinvestment:	
Margin:	
Selling short:	
Options:	

Apply Yourself!

Objective 5

In a short paragraph, describe why you would use a long-term technique or a short-term technique to achieve your investment goals.

Back to … Getting Personal

Reconsider your responses to the "Getting Personal" questions at the beginning of the chapter. To help reinforce your understanding of the material on stocks:

- Review the reasons why people invest in stocks.
- Choose a specific stock and use the Internet or library research to complete Your Personal Financial Plan sheet 38 located at the end of this chapter.

- Describe the types of orders you can use to buy or sell stocks.

Finally, describe what you learned in this chapter about stock investing that will help you obtain your financial goals.

Chapter Summary

Objective 1 Corporations sell stock (a form of equity) to finance their business start-up costs and help pay for their ongoing business activities. In return for providing the money needed to finance the corporation, stockholders have the right to elect the board of directors. They must also approve major changes to corporate policies.

People invest in stock because of dividend income, appreciation of value, and the *possibility* of gain through stock splits. In addition to common stock, a few corporations may issue preferred stock. The most important priority an investor in preferred stock enjoys is receiving cash dividends before any cash dividends are paid to common stockholders. Still, dividend distributions to both preferred and common stockholders must be approved by the board of directors.

Objective 2 A wealth of information is available to stock investors. A logical place to start the evaluation process is with the classification of different types of stock investments that range from very conservative to very speculative—see Exhibit 12–3. Today, many investors use the information available on the Internet to evaluate individual stocks. Information is also available from stock advisory services, the newspaper, business and personal finance periodicals, and government publications.

Objective 3 Many analysts believe that a corporation's ability or inability to generate earnings in the future may be one of the most significant factors that account for an increase or decrease in the value of a stock. Generally, higher earnings equate to higher stock value, and lower earnings equate to lower stock value. In addition to the total amount of earnings reported by the corporation, investors can calculate earnings per share and a price-earnings ratio to evaluate a stock investment. Whereas both earnings per share and price-earnings ratio are historical numbers based on what a corporation has already done, investors can obtain earnings estimates for most corporations. Other calculations that help evaluate stock investments include dividend yield, total return, and book value.

Objective 4 A corporation may sell a new stock issue with the help of an investment banking firm. Once the stock has been sold in the primary market, it can be sold time and again in the secondary market. In the secondary market, investors purchase stock listed on a securities exchange or traded in the over-the-counter market. Many securities transactions are made through an account executive who works for a full-service brokerage firm, but a growing number of investors are using a discount brokerage firm or are completing security transactions online. Whether you trade online or not, you must decide if you want to use a market, limit, or stop order to buy or sell stock. Most brokerage firms charge a minimum commission for buying or selling stock. Additional commission charges are based on the number and value of the stock shares bought or sold and if you use a full-service or discount broker or trade online.

Objective 5 Purchased stock may be classified as either a long-term investment or a speculative investment. Long-term investors typically hold their investments for at least a year or longer; speculators (sometimes referred to as traders) usually sell their investments within a shorter time period. Traditional trading techniques long-term investors use include the buy-and-hold technique, dollar cost averaging, direct investment plans, and dividend reinvestment plans. More speculative techniques include buying on margin, selling short, and trading in options.

Key Terms

account executive 410
book value 407
churning 410
common stock 392
direct investment plan 416
dividend 392
dividend reinvestment plan 416
dividend yield 406
dollar cost averaging 414
earnings per share 404
equity financing 392

initial public offering (IPO) 409
investment bank 409
limit order 412
margin 416
market order 412
Nasdaq 409
option 418
over-the-counter (OTC) market 409
preferred stock 396
price-earnings (PE) ratio 404
primary market 408

proxy 393
record date 393
secondary market 409
securities exchange 409
selling short 417
specialist 409
stock split 394
stop order 412
total return 407

Key Formulas

Page	Topic	Formula
404	Earnings per share	$\text{Earnings per share} = \dfrac{\text{After-tax earnings}}{\text{Number of shares outstanding}}$
405	Price-earnings (PE) ratio	$\text{Price-earnings (PE) ratio} = \dfrac{\text{Price per share}}{\text{Earnings per share}}$
406	Dividend yield	$\text{Dividend yield} = \dfrac{\text{Annual dividend amount}}{\text{Price per share}}$
407	Total return	$\text{Total return} = \text{Dividends} + \text{Capital gain}$
407	Book value	$\text{Book value} = \dfrac{\text{Assets} - \text{Liabilities}}{\text{Number of shares outstanding}}$

Self-Test Problems

1. Four years ago, Ken Guessford purchased 200 shares of Mountain View Manufacturing. At the time, each share of Mountain View was selling for $30. He also paid a $24 commission when the shares were purchased. Now, four years later, he has decided it's time to sell his investment. The Mountain View share price when sold was $32.50. In addition, he paid a $36 commission to sell his shares. He also received dividends of $1.80 per share over the four-year investment period.

   a. What is the total amount of dividends Mr. Guessford received over the four-year period?
   b. What was the total return for Mr. Guessford's investment?

2. Karen Newton is trying to decide between two different stock investments, and she asks for your help. Information about each investment is below.

Company	Price per Share	Annual Dividend	After-Tax Income This Year	Projected Earnings Next Year	Number of Shares Outstanding
Jackson Utility Construction	$22	$0.30	$34 million	$39 million	20 million shares
West Coast Homes	$46	$0.52	$182 million	$142 million	130 million shares

   a. Calculate the dividend yield for each company.
   b. Calculate the earnings per share for each company.
   c. Based on this information, which company would you recommend?

Solutions

1. a. Total dividends = $1.80 per share dividends × 200 shares = $360.
   b. Dividends = $1.80 per share dividends × 200 shares = $360.
      Purchase price = $30 per share × 200 shares = $6,000 + $24 commission = $6,024.
      Selling price = $32.50 per share × 200 shares = $6,500 − $36 commission = $6,464.

Capital gain = $6,464 selling price − $6,024 purchase price = $440.
Total return = $360 dividends + $440 capital gain = $800.

2. *a.* The dividend yield for each company is

Jackson: Dividend yield = $\dfrac{\$0.30 \text{ annual dividend}}{\$22 \text{ current price}}$

$= 0.014 = 1.4$ percent

West Coast: Dividend yield = $\dfrac{\$0.52 \text{ annual dividend}}{\$46 \text{ current price}}$

$= 0.011 = 1.1$ percent

b. The earnings per share for each company are

Jackson: Earnings per share = $\dfrac{\$34,000,000 \text{ income}}{20,000,000 \text{ shares}}$

$= \$1.70$

West Coast: Earnings per share = $\dfrac{\$182,000,000 \text{ income}}{130,000,000 \text{ shares}}$

$= \$1.40$

c. Sometimes the dollar amounts reported on a firm's financial statements are only part of the picture when choosing an investment. On the surface, the financial amounts for West Coast are impressive because they are larger than the amounts for Jackson Utility Construction. But as the calculations for dividend yield and earnings per share illustrate, Jackson Utility Construction may be the better investment. Jackson's dividend yield (1.4 percent) is higher than West Coast's dividend yield (1.1 percent). Also, the earnings per share for Jackson are higher ($1.70) when compared to the earnings per share for West Coast ($1.40). Before making your choice, two other factors should be noted. Look at the projected earnings for next year. Jackson's earnings are increasing; West Coast's earnings are projected to decline. Finally, think about the industries represented by these two companies. Because of the economic crisis, home sales are at record lows. On the other hand, people always need utilities and this company is involved in construction for utility companies. Given just the above information, Jackson Utility Construction may be the better choice. What do you think?

Problems

1. Jamie and Peter Dawson own 250 shares of IBM common stock. IBM's quarterly dividend is $0.50 per share. What is the amount of the dividend check the Dawson couple will receive for this quarter? (Obj. 1)

2. During the four quarters for 2009, the Browns received two quarterly dividend payments of $0.18, one quarterly payment of $0.20, and one quarterly payment of $0.22. If they owned 200 shares of stock, what was their total dividend income for 2009? (Obj. 1)

3. Jim Johansen noticed that a corporation he is considering investing in is about to pay a quarterly dividend. The record date is March 15. In order for Jim to receive this quarterly dividend what is the last date that he could purchase stock in this corporation and receive this quarter's dividend payment? (Obj. 1)

4. Sarah and James Hernandez purchased 100 shares of Cisco Systems stock at $18.50 a share. One year later, they sold the stock for $26.35 a share. They paid a broker a $32 commission when they purchased the stock and a $40 commission when they sold the stock. During the 12-month period the couple owned the stock, Cisco Systems paid no dividends. Calculate the Hernandez's total return for this investment. (Obj. 1)

5. Wanda Sotheby purchased 150 shares of Home Depot stock at $21.25 a share. One year later, she sold the stock for $31.10 a share. She paid her broker a $34 commission when she purchased the stock and a $42 commission when she sold it. During the 12 months she owned the stock, she received $90 in dividends. Calculate Wanda's total return on this investment. (Obj. 1)

6. Wallace Davis purchased 200 shares of Dell stock at $9.50 a share. One year later, he sold the stock for $8.42 a share. He paid his broker a $22 commission when he purchased the stock and a $24 commission when he sold it. During the 12 months he owned the stock, the company paid no dividends. Calculate Wallace's total return on this investment. (Obj. 1)

7. In September, stockholders of Chaparral Steel approved a 2-for-1 stock split. After the split, how many shares of Chaparral Steel stock will an investor have if he or she owned 360 shares before the split? Obj. 1)

8. As a stockholder of Kentucky Gas and Oil, you receive its annual report. In the financial statements, the firm reported after-tax earnings of $1,200,000 and has issued 1,500,000 shares of common stock. The stock is currently selling for $24 a share. (Obj. 3)

   a. Calculate the earnings per share for Kentucky Gas and Oil.
   b. Calculate the price-earnings (PE) ratio for Kentucky Gas and Oil.

9. Michelle Townsend owns stock in National Computers. Based on information in its annual report, National Computers reported after-tax earnings of $4,850,000 and has issued 3,500,000 shares of common stock. The stock is currently selling for $32 a share. (Obj. 3)

   a. Calculate the earnings per share for National Computers.
   b. Calculate the price-earnings (PE) ratio for National Computers.

10. Analysts that follow JPMorgan Case, one of the nation's largest providers of financial services, estimate that the corporation's earnings per share will increase from $1.78 in the current year to $2.93 next year. (Obj. 3)

    a. What is the amount of the increase?
    b. What effect, if any, should this increase have on the value of the corporation's stock?

11. Currently, Johnson & Johnson pays an annual dividend of $1.84. If the stock is selling for $58, what is the dividend yield? (Obj. 3)

12. Casper Energy Exploration reports that the corporation's assets are valued at $185,000,000, its liabilities are $80,000,000, and it has issued 6,000,000 shares of stock. What is the book value for a share of Casper stock? (Obj. 3)

13. For four years, Marty Campbell invested $4,000 each year in Newsome Golf Apparel. The stock was selling for $32 in 2006, $45 in 2007, $35 in 2008, and $50 in 2009. (Obj. 5)

    a. What is Marty's total investment in Newsome Golf?
    b. After four years, how many shares does Marty own?
    c. What is the average cost per share of Marty's investment?

14. Bob Orleans invested $3,000 and borrowed $3,000 to purchase shares in Verizon Communications. At the time of his investment, Verizon was selling for $30 a share. (Obj. 5)

    a. If Bob paid a $30 commission, how many shares could he buy if he used *only* his own money and did not use margin?
    b. If Bob paid a $60 commission, how many shares could he buy if he used his $3,000 and borrowed $3,000 on margin to buy Verizon stock?
    c. Assuming Bob did use margin, paid a $60 total commission to buy his Verizon stock and another $60 to sell his stock, and sold the stock for $39 a share, how much profit did he make on his Verizon stock investment?

15. After researching Valero Energy common stock, Sandra Pearson is convinced the stock is overpriced. She contacts her account executive and arranges to sell short 200 shares of Valero Energy. At the time of the sale, a share of common stock has a value of $25. Three months later, Valero Energy is selling for $16 a share, and Sandra instructs her broker to cover her short transaction. Total commissions to buy and sell the stock were $65. What is her profit for this short transaction? (Obj. 5)

Questions

1. Why would a corporation sell common or preferred stock to raise equity financing? (Obj. 1)

2. In your own words, describe how an investment in common stock could help you obtain your investment goals. (Obj. 1)

3. What is the difference between common and preferred stock? What type of investor would invest in preferred stock? (Obj. 1)

4. Assume you have $5,000 to invest and that you are trying to decide between investing in Procter & Gamble or Coca-Cola. Describe how the Internet could help you decide which investment is the right one for you. What other sources of information could help you evaluate these companies? (Obj. 2)

5. Explain the relationship between earnings per share, projected earnings, and the market value for a stock. (Obj. 3)

6. What is the difference between the dividend yield and total return calculations that were described in this chapter? (Obj. 3)

7. Stock can be sold in the primary market or the secondary market. What is the difference between these two markets? (Obj. 4)

8. Explain the difference between a securities exchange and the over-the-counter market. (Obj. 4)

9. Prepare a list of questions you could use to interview an account executive about career opportunities in the field of finance and investments. (Obj.4)

10. Today, you can use a full-service brokerage firm, a discount brokerage firm, or trade online to buy and sell stocks. Which type of brokerage firm would you use? Justify your answer. (Obj. 4)

11. Prepare a chart that describes the similarities and differences among the buy-and-hold investment technique, dollar cost averaging, direct investment, and dividend reinvestment. (Obj. 5)

12. Why would a speculator use margin? Why would a speculator sell short? (Obj. 5)

Case in Point

RESEARCH INFORMATION AVAILABLE FROM MERGENT

This chapter stressed the importance of evaluating potential investments. Now it's your turn to try your skill at evaluating a potential investment in PepsiCo, Inc. Assume you could invest $10,000 in the common stock of this company. To help you evaluate this potential investment, carefully examine Exhibit 12–6, which reproduces the research report on PepsiCo from *Mergent's Handbook of Common Stocks.* The report was published in the summer of 2008.

Questions

1. Based on the research provided by Mergent, would you buy PepsiCo stock? Justify your answer.

2. What other investment information would you need to evaluate PepsiCo common stock? Where would you obtain this information?

3. On January 29, 2009, PepsiCo common stock was selling for $50.23 a share. Using the Internet or a newspaper, determine the current price for a share of PepsiCo. Based on this information, would your PepsiCo investment have been profitable? (*Hint:* PepsiCo stock is listed on the New York Stock Exchange and its stock symbol is PEP.)

4. Assuming you purchased PepsiCo stock on January 29, 2009, and based on your answer to question 3, how would you decide if you want to hold or sell your PepsiCo stock? Explain your answer.

Continuing Case

Vikki and Tim Treble (ages 48 and 50) are planning to take their daughter Molly on a college tour next week during her spring break. Molly is most interested in attending a public school on the other side of the state. Molly's younger twin brothers, Caleb and Tyler (11 years old), will also be coming on the trip. They are excited to see the dorms and the campus even though they won't be heading to college for another 7 years.

Recently, for a class assignment, Molly interviewed her parents about their investing philosophy and resources. Vikki and Tim explained to Molly that they began investing for retirement as soon as they had their first full-time job, and that even her college fund began shortly after she was born. Because they planned ahead, Vikki and Tim were able to invest for the long term, and the balances in the accounts showed that it was a smart decision. Tim briefly discussed their portfolio, and shared that most of their long-term investments were in stocks and mutual funds.

As part of the conversation, Vikki and Tim decided it was a good time to discuss not only their financial plan, but also the plan for Molly to pay for her college education. Molly reminded her parents of the $10,000 per year promise they made, and her parents reminded her that she was expected to get a job to earn some money for tuition and room and board. Molly agreed and plans to look into loan and scholarship opportunities to help supplement the cost of school.

Vikki and Tim's financial statistics are shown below:

Assets:
Checking/savings account $25,000
Emergency fund $25,000
House $375,000
Cars $5,000 and $32,000
Household possessions $25,000
401(k) balance $160,000 (Vikki), $280,000 (Tim)
College savings $52,000
Life insurance cash value $28,000

Monthly Expenses:
Mortgage $1,200
Property tax/Insurance $650
Daily living expenses (including utilities, food, child expenses) $4,000
Car loan $450
Entertainment/vacations $400
Gas/repairs $500
Term & whole life insurance $400

Liabilities:
Mortgage $122,000
Car loan $17,000

Savings:
401(k) 8% of gross monthly salary
College savings $600

Income:
Gross Salary: $25,000 per year (Vikki), $125,000 (Tim)
After-tax monthly salary: $1,458 (Vikki), $7,291 (Tim)

Questions

1. Why do you think Vikki and Tim use stocks in their portfolio?
2. How can Vikki and Tim use the Internet to assist with their stock portfolio?
3. What are some investing techniques they can use?
4. If Vikki and Tim wanted to manage their own stocks, how should they set up an online account?
5. What advice would you give Molly about investing in stocks?
6. How can they use *Your Personal Financial Plan* sheets 38–39?

Spending Diary

"INVESTING IN STOCK IS NOT POSSIBLE. I'M BARELY ABLE TO PAY MY VARIOUS LIVING EXPENSES."

Directions

Your Daily Spending Diary will help you manage your expenses to create a better overall spending plan. Once you know and try to control your spending, you will likely be able to have funds available for various types of investments. The Daily Spending Diary sheets are located in Appendix C at the end of the text and on the student Web site at www.mhhe.com/kdh.

Questions

1. What information from your daily spending records could help you achieve your financial goals?
2. Based on your observations of our society and the economy, what types of stocks might you consider for investing now or in the near future?

Name: _____   Date: _____

Evaluating Corporate Stocks

Financial Planning Activities: No checklist can serve as a foolproof guide for choosing a common or preferred stock. However, the following questions will help you evaluate a potential stock investment. Use stock Web sites on the Internet and/or use library materials to answer these questions about a corporate stock that you believe could help you obtain your investment goals.

Suggested Web Sites: http://finance.yahoo.com   www.smartmoney.com

Category 1: The Basics

1. What is the corporation's name? _____
_____

2. What are the corporation's address and telephone number? _____
_____

3. Have you requested the latest annual report and quarterly report? ☐ Yes ☐ No

4. What information about the corporation is available on the Internet? _____
_____

5. Where is the stock traded? _____
_____

6. What types of products or services does this firm provide? _____
_____

7. Briefly describe the prospects for this company. (Include significant factors like product development, plans for expansion, plans for mergers, etc.)
_____

Category 2: Dividend Income

8. Is the corporation currently paying dividends? If so, how much? _____
_____

9. What is the dividend yield for this stock? _____
_____

10. Has the dividend payout increased or decreased over the past three years? _____
_____

11. How does the yield for this investment compare with those for other potential investments?
_____

Category 3: Financial Performance

12. What are the firm's earnings per share for the last year? _____
_____

13. Have the firm's earnings increased over the past three years? _____
_____

14. What is the firm's current price-earnings ratio? _____

15. How does the firm's current price-earnings ratio compare with firms in the same industry?
_____

16. Describe trends for the firm's price-earnings ratio over the past three years. Do these trends show improvement or decline in investment value?
_____

17. What are the firm's projected earnings for the next year? _____
_____

18. Have sales increased over the last five years? _____
_____

19. What is the stock's current price? _____
_____

20. What are the 52-week high and low for this stock?
_____

21. Do the analysts indicate that this is a good time to invest in this stock? _____
_____

22. Briefly describe any other information that you obtained from Mergent, Value Line, Standard & Poor's, or other sources of information.
_____
_____

A Word of Caution

When you use a checklist, there is always a danger of overlooking important relevant information. Quite simply, it is a place to start. If you need other information, *you* are responsible for obtaining it and for determining how it affects your potential investment.

What's Next for Your Personal Financial Plan?

- Identify additional factors that may affect your decision to invest in this corporation's stock.
- Develop a plan for monitoring an investment's value once a stock(s) is purchased.

Investment Broker Comparison

Financial Planning Activities: To compare the benefits and costs of different investment brokers, compare the services of an investment broker based on the factors listed below.

Suggested Web Sites: www.scottrade.com   www.placeatrade.com

	Broker Number 1	Broker Number 2
Broker's name		
Brokerage firm		
Address		
Phone		
Web site		
Years of experience		
Education and training		
Areas of specialization		
Certifications and licenses held		
Employer's stock exchange and financial market affiliations		
Information services offered		
Minimum commission charge		
Commission on 100 shares of stock at $50 per share		
Fees for other investments: • Corporate bonds • Government bonds • Mutual funds		
Other fees: • Annual account fee • Inactivity fee • Other		

What's Next for Your Personal Financial Plan?

- Using the information you obtained, choose a broker and a brokerage firm that you feel will help you attain your investment goals.
- Access the Web site for the brokerage firm you have chosen and answer the questions on page 411 in your text.

13 Investing in Mutual Funds

Getting Personal

Why invest in mutual funds? For each of the following statements, select "yes" or "no" to indicate your behavior regarding these investment activities.

	Yes	No
1. I understand the reasons investors choose mutual funds.	____	____
2. I understand the different charges and fees associated with mutual fund investments.	____	____
3. I can identify the types of mutual funds that will help me achieve my investment goals.	____	____
4. I know how to evaluate a mutual fund.	____	____
5. I am aware of the purchase and withdrawal options for mutual funds.	____	____

After studying this chapter, you will be asked to reconsider your responses to these questions.

mutual fund An investment company that pools the money of many investors—its shareholders—to invest in a variety of securities.

If you ever thought about buying stocks or bonds but decided not to, your reasons were probably like most other people's: You didn't know enough to make a good decision, and you lacked enough money to diversify your investments among several choices. These same two reasons explain why people invest in mutual funds. By pooling your money with money from other investors, a mutual fund can do for you what you can't do on your own. Specifically, a **mutual fund** is an investment company that pools the money of many investors—its shareholders—to invest in a variety of securities.[1] For a fee, an investment company invests money from investors in stocks, bonds,

---

[1]The Mutual Fund Education Alliance Web site (www.mfea.com), accessed February 6, 2009.

Your Personal Financial Plan Sheets

40. Evaluating Mutual Fund Investment Information
41. Evaluation of a Mutual Fund

Objectives

In this chapter, you will learn to:

1. Explain the characteristics of mutual fund investments.
2. Classify mutual funds by investment objective.
3. Evaluate mutual funds.
4. Describe how and why mutual funds are bought and sold.

Why is this important?

For many investors, mutual funds have become the investment of choice. In fact, you can choose from more than 9,300 different funds in the United States. So how do you choose the right fund to help you obtain your long-term investment goals? To help answer that question, read the material in this chapter.

money market securities, or some combination of these securities appropriate to a fund's investment objective.

Mutual funds are an excellent choice for many individuals. In many cases, they can also be used for retirement accounts, including traditional individual retirement accounts, Roth IRAs, and 401(k) and 403(b) retirement accounts. For example, many employees contribute a portion of their salary to a 401(k) retirement account. And in some cases, the employer matches the employee's contribution. A common match would work like this: For every $1.00 the employee invests, the employer contributes an additional $0.50. All monies—both the employee's and employer's contributions— are often invested in mutual funds that are selected by the employee.

An investment in mutual funds is based on the concept of opportunity costs, which we have discussed throughout this text. Simply put, you have to be willing to take some chances if you want to get larger returns on your investments. But a "real risk" is associated with investing in funds because they can decrease in value. For example, ask any investor what happened to the value of his or her fund investments during the economic crisis that began in October 2007. The fact is that many funds decreased in value—sometimes as much as 20 percent, 30 percent, or more. Fortunately, we don't often experience an economic crisis like this one, but the crisis does underscore the need to understand the risk associated with all investments, including mutual funds. Before deciding whether mutual funds are the right investment for you, read the material presented in the next section.

Why Investors Purchase Mutual Funds

> **OBJECTIVE 1**
>
> Explain the characteristics of mutual fund investments.

The following statistics illustrate how important mutual fund investments are to both individuals and the nation's economy:

1. An estimated 88 million individuals own mutual funds in the United States.[2]
2. The number of funds grew from 361 in 1970 to over 9,300 in 2008.[3]
3. The combined value of assets owned by investment companies in the United States totals $13 trillion.[4]

No doubt about it, the mutual fund industry is big business. And yet you may be wondering why so many people invest in mutual funds.

The major reasons investors purchase mutual funds are *professional management* and *diversification.* Most investment companies do everything possible to convince you that they can do a better job of picking securities than you can. Sometimes these claims are true, and sometimes they are just so much hot air. Still, investment companies do have professional fund managers with years of experience who devote large amounts of time to picking just the "right" securities for their funds' portfolios. *Be warned:* Even the best portfolio managers make mistakes. So you, the investor, must be careful!

The diversification mutual funds offer spells safety, because a loss incurred with one investment contained in a fund may be offset by gains from other investments in the fund. For example, consider the diversification provided in the portfolio of the AIM Basic Value Fund, shown in Exhibit 13–1. An investment in the $1.3 billion AIM Basic Value Fund represents ownership in at least 10 different industries, as seen at the top of Exhibit 13–1. In addition, the fund's largest investments are listed at the bottom of Exhibit 13–1. With a total of almost 50 different companies included in the fund's investment portfolio, investors enjoy diversification coupled with AIM's stock-selection expertise. For beginning investors or investors without a great deal of money to invest, the diversification offered by funds is especially important because there is no other practical way to purchase the individual stocks issued by a large number of corporations. A mutual fund like the AIM Basic Value fund, on the other hand, can provide a practical way for investors to obtain diversification because the fund can use the pooled funds of a large number of investors to purchase a large number of shares of many different companies.

Characteristics of Funds

Today funds may be classified as closed-end funds, exchange-traded funds, or open-end funds.

---

[2]The Investment Company Institute Web site (www.ici.org), accessed February 5, 2009.
[3]Ibid.
[4]Ibid.

Exhibit **13–1**

Types of Securities
Included in the Portfolio
of the AIM Basic Value
Fund

Top Industries	
Managed health care	9.34
Semiconductor equipment	7.41
Other diversified financial services	6.19
Advertising	5.16
Consumer finance	4.49
Systems software	4.07
Specialized finance	3.78
Investment banking & brokerage	3.12
Industrial machinery	2.90
Home improvement	2.88

Top Equity Holdings	% of Total Net Assets
UnitedHealth Group Inc.	5.81
ASML Holding N.V.	4.92
Robert Half International Inc.	3.97
Moody's Corp.	3.78
Aetna Inc.	3.53
JPMorgan Chase & Co.	3.36
Omnicom Group Inc.	3.16
Illinois Tool Works Inc.	2.90
Home Depot Inc.	2.88
Molson Coors Brewing Co.	2.86

Holdings are subject to change.

SOURCE: The InvescoAim Web site (www.invescoaim.com), accessed February 8, 2009.

CLOSED-END, EXCHANGE-TRADED, OR OPEN-END MUTUAL FUNDS

Approximately 650, or about 7 percent, of all mutual funds are closed-end funds offered by investment companies. A **closed-end fund** is a mutual fund whose shares are issued by an investment company only when the fund is organized. As a result, only a certain number of shares are available to investors. After all the shares originally issued have been sold, an investor can purchase shares only from another investor who is willing to sell. Closed-end funds are actively managed by professional fund managers and shares are traded on the floors of stock exchanges, including the New York Stock Exchange, or in the over-the-counter market (Nasdaq). Like the prices of stocks, the prices of shares for closed-end funds are determined by the factors of supply and demand, by the value of stocks and other investments contained in the fund's portfolio, and by investor expectations.

An **exchange-traded fund (ETF)** is a fund that invests in the stocks or other securities contained in a specific stock or securities index. While most investors think of an ETF as investing in the stocks contained in the Standard & Poor's 500 stock index, the Dow Jones Industrial Average, or the Nasdaq 100 Index, many different types of ETFs available today attempt to track all kinds of indexes, including

- Midcap stocks.
- Small-cap stocks.

closed-end fund A mutual fund whose shares are issued by an investment company only when the fund is organized.

exchange-traded fund (ETF) A fund that invests in the stocks or other securities contained in a specific stock or securities index, and whose shares are traded on a securities exchange or over the counter.

PORTFOLIO DOCTOR | Don't let regrets over last year's mutual fund losses dictate your investment strategy.
By Jeffrey R. Kosnett

You can do better than break even

• Our reader **Sandy ST. John, 54 Owner of a micro-wave path-surveying business Forney, Tex. Wants to recoup last year's losses, then return to safety of cds.**

If her one-woman business goes bust because of the recession, Sandy's investing mishaps will be just a footnote to her life story. For now, it looks as if the business will survive. Sandy, who responds to client emergencies in her own airplane, is more concerned about insurance costs and delays in getting paid than about losing customers.

But those investment losses are irksome for someone like Sandy, who is single and the sole source of her long-term financial security. A year ago, Sandy moved $51,000 from a maturing certificate of deposit in her IRA to some Hartford mutual funds that are now worth only $30,000. Yields on CDs were pitiful at the time, but she now thinks that she and the broker she consulted

should have anticipated the market crash.

Sandy would like to wait for her funds to break even and then return to CDs. She also holds a few dividend-paying stocks, mainly in oil and gas, that are way down, too. She's leaving them alone.

The idea of recouping your losses and then quitting the game is hardly unheard of, and not just in poker. "I used to be a currency trader, and it was common to say that if you had a bad position, you would hold it until it was flat," says Morris Armstrong, of Armstrong Financial Strategies, in Danbury, Conn. "But if things are turning around in your favor, why sell then?"

If Sandy's funds recover their losses within a reasonable length of time, says Armstrong, it means that the economy and the markets are getting healthier, so it wouldn't make sense to sell. Eventually, after stocks have recovered and become pricey, Sandy will want to

pare her holdings. But right now her plan seems arbitrary.

With stocks behaving better, this is also a good time to face up to your emotions over last year's losses. "The best money managers got this one wrong," says Connie Stone, of Stepping Stone Financial, in Chagrin Falls, Ohio. Stone says people who are self-employed, single, widowed or divorced are particularly frightened by losses and often react by wrapping both arms around what's left. Stone would prefer that Sandy increase her IRA contributions in 2009 or set up an individual 401(k), with an emphasis on stocks.

Sandy's mutual funds are decent. She holds Hartford Capital Appreciation, which has a fine long-term record; a fund that tracks the S&P 500; a small-company fund; and some bond funds. To ask her broker to select different funds (and possibly generate a fresh set of sales charges) won't help Sandy much, if at all.

1. In 2008, Ms. St. John watched the value of her investment in Hartford mutual funds drop from $51,000 to $30,000. Now she is trying to decide if she should sell, hold, or buy more mutual funds and stocks. What would you recommend?

2. Sandy St. John, 54, is a single, self-employed business owner planning for retirement. She is the sole source of her long-term financial security. What steps should she take now to prepare for eventual retirement?

- Fixed-income securities.
- Stocks issued by companies in specific industries.
- Stocks issued by corporations in different countries.

Like a closed-end fund, shares of an exchange-traded fund are traded on a securities exchange or in the over-the-counter market. With both types of funds, an investor can purchase as little as one share of a fund. Also like a closed-end fund, prices for shares in an ETF are determined by supply and demand, the value of stocks and other investments contained in the fund's portfolio, and by investor expectations.

Although exchange-traded funds are similar to closed-end funds, there is an important difference. Most closed-end funds are actively managed, with portfolio managers making the selection of stocks and other securities contained in a closed-end fund. An exchange-traded fund, on the other hand, invests in the securities included in a specific index. Exchange-traded funds tend to mirror the performance of the index, moving up or down as the individual securities contained in the index move up or down. Therefore, there is less need for a portfolio manager to make investment decisions. Because of passive management, fees associated with owning shares are generally lower than those of both closed-end and open-end funds. In addition to lower fees, other advantages to investing in ETFs include.

- No minimum investment amount, because shares are traded on an exchange and not purchased from an investment company.
- Shares can be bought or sold through a broker or online any time during regular market hours at the current price.
- You can use limit orders and the more speculative techniques of selling short and margin—all discussed in Chapter 12—to buy and sell ETF shares.

Although increasing in popularity, approximately 600, or about 6 percent of all funds, are exchange-traded funds.

Approximately 8,000, or about 87 percent of all mutual funds, are open-end funds. An **open-end fund** is a mutual fund whose shares are issued and redeemed by the investment company at the request of investors. Investors are free to buy and sell shares at the net asset value. The **net asset value (NAV)** per share is equal to the current market value of securities contained in the mutual fund's portfolio minus the mutual fund's liabilities divided by the number of shares outstanding.

open-end fund A mutual fund whose shares are issued and redeemed by the investment company at the request of investors.

net asset value (NAV) The current market value of the securities contained in the mutual fund's portfolio minus the mutual fund's liabilities divided by the number of shares outstanding.

Example

The investments contained in the New American Frontiers Mutual Fund have a current market value of $980 million. The fund also has liabilities that total $10 million. If this mutual fund has 40 million shares, the net asset value per share is $24.25, as shown below.

$$\text{Net asset value} = \frac{\text{Value of the fund's portfolio} - \text{Liabilities}}{\text{Number of shares outstanding}}$$

$$= \frac{\$980 \text{ million} - \$10 \text{ million}}{40 \text{ million shares}} = \$24.25 \text{ NAV per share}$$

For most open-end funds, the net asset value is calculated at the close of trading each day.

In addition to buying and selling shares on request, most open-end funds provide their investors with a wide variety of services, including payroll deduction programs, automatic reinvestment programs, automatic withdrawal programs, and the option to change shares in one fund to another fund within the same fund family—all topics discussed later in this chapter.

load fund A mutual fund in which investors pay a commission (as high as 8.5 percent) every time they purchase shares.

COSTS: LOAD FUNDS COMPARED TO NO-LOAD FUNDS Before investing in mutual funds, you should compare the cost of this type of investment with the cost of other investment alternatives, such as stocks or bonds. With regard to cost, mutual funds are classified as load funds or no-load funds. A **load fund** (sometimes referred to as an *A fund*) is a mutual fund in which investors pay a commission every time they purchase shares. The commission, often referred to as the *sales charge*, may be as high as 8.5 percent of the purchase price for investments.

Example

The Davis Opportunity mutual fund charges a sales load of 4.75 percent. If you invest $10,000, you must pay a $475 commission to purchase shares. After paying the commission, the amount available for investment is $9,525, as shown below.

Load charge = Dollar amount of investment × Load stated as a percentage

= $10,000 × 4.75 percent = $475

Amount available for investment = Investment amount − Load charge

= $10,000 − $475 = $9,525

Many exceptions exist, but the average load charge for mutual funds is between 3 and 5 percent. Typically, load funds are purchased through brokerage firms or registered representatives. The "stated" advantage of a load fund is that the fund's sales force (account executives, financial planners, or brokerage divisions of banks and other financial institutions) will explain the mutual fund, help determine which fund will help you achieve your financial objective, and offer advice as to when shares of the fund should be bought or sold.

no-load fund A mutual fund in which the individual investor pays no sales charge.

A **no-load fund** is a mutual fund in which the individual investor pays no sales charge. No-load funds don't charge commissions when you buy shares because they have no salespeople. If you want to buy shares of a no-load fund, you must make your own decisions and deal directly with the investment company. The usual means of contact is by telephone, the Internet, or mail. You can also purchase shares in a no-load fund from many discount brokers, including Charles Schwab, TD Ameritrade, and E*Trade.

As an investor, you must decide whether to invest in a load fund or a no-load fund. Some investment salespeople have claimed that load funds outperform no-load funds. But many financial analysts suggest there is generally no significant difference between mutual funds that charge commissions and those that do not.[5] *Since no-load funds offer the same investment opportunities load funds offer, you should investigate them further before deciding which type of mutual fund is best for you.* Although the sales commission should not be the decisive factor, the possibility of saving a sales commission of up to 8.5 percent is a factor to consider.

contingent deferred sales load A 1 to 5 percent charge that shareholders pay when they withdraw their investment from a mutual fund.

Instead of charging investors a fee when they purchase shares in a mutual fund, some mutual funds charge a **contingent deferred sales load** (sometimes referred to as a *back-end load,* a *B fund,* or a *redemption fee*). These fees range from 1 to 5 percent, depending on how long you own the mutual fund before making a withdrawal. Typically, you will pay a 5 percent contingent deferred sales load if you withdraw money the first year after your initial investment. This fee declines every year until it disappears if you own shares in the fund for more than five years.

Example

Assume you withdraw $6,000 from B shares that you own in the Oppenheimer Tax-Free Municipal Bond Fund within a year of your purchase date. You must

---

[5]Bill Barker, "Loads," the Motley Fool Web site (www.fool.com), accessed February 9, 2009.

pay a 5 percent contingent deferred sales fee. Your fee is $300. After deducting the fee, you will receive $5,700, as shown below.

Contingent deferred sales fee = Amount of withdrawal
$$\times \text{ Fee stated as a percentage}$$
$$= \$6,000 \times 5 \text{ percent} = \$300$$

Amount you receive = Amount of withdrawal − Contingent deferred sales fee
$$= \$6,000 - \$300 = \$5,700$$

COSTS: MANAGEMENT FEES AND OTHER CHARGES Fees are important because they reduce your investment return and are a major factor to consider when choosing a mutual fund. For example, the investment companies that sponsor mutual funds charge management fees. This fee, which is disclosed in the fund's prospectus, is a fixed percentage of the fund's net asset value on a predetermined date. Today annual management fees range between 0.25 and 1.5 percent of the fund's net asset value. While fees vary considerably, the average is 0.5 to 1 percent of the fund's net asset value.

The investment company may also levy a **12b-1 fee** (sometimes referred to as a *distribution fee*) to defray the costs of advertising and marketing a mutual fund and commissions paid to a broker who sold you shares in the mutual fund. Approved by the Securities and Exchange Commission, annual 12b-1 fees are calculated on the value of a fund's net assets and cannot exceed 1 percent of a fund's assets per year. *Note:* For a fund to be called a "no-load" fund, its 12b-1 fee must not exceed 0.25 percent of its assets.

Unlike the one-time sales load fees that mutual funds charge to purchase or sell shares, the 12b-1 fee is often an ongoing fee that is charged on an annual basis. Note that 12b-1 fees can cost you a lot of money over a period of years. Assuming there is no difference in performance offered by two different mutual funds, one of which charges a 12b-1 fee while the other doesn't, choose the latter fund. The 12b-1 fee is so lucrative for investment companies that a number of them have begun selling Class C shares that charge a higher 12b-1 fee and no sales load or contingent deferred sales fee to attract new investors. When compared to Class A shares (commissions charged when shares are purchased) and Class B shares (commissions charged when withdrawals are made over the first five years), Class C shares, with their ongoing, higher 12b-1 fees, may be more expensive over a long period of time.

By now, you are probably asking yourself, "Should I purchase Class A shares, Class B shares, or Class C shares?" There are no easy answers, but your professional financial adviser or broker can help you determine which class of shares of a particular mutual fund best suits your financial needs. You can also do your own research to determine which fund is right for you. Factors to consider include whether you want to invest in a load fund or no-load fund, management fees, and expense ratios. As you will see later in this chapter, a number of sources of information can help you evaluate investment decisions.

Together, all the different management fees and fund operating costs are often referred to as an **expense ratio.** Since it is important to keep fees and costs as low as possible, you should examine a fund's expense ratio as one more fact to consider when evaluating a mutual fund.

The investment company's prospectus must provide all details relating to management fees, sales fees, 12b-1 fees, and other expenses. Exhibit 13–2 reproduces the summary of expenses (sometimes called a *fee table*) taken from the Davis Opportunity Fund. Notice that this fee table has two separate parts. The first part describes shareholder transaction expenses. For this fund, the maximum sales charge is 4.75 percent. The second part describes the fund's annual operating expenses. For this fund, the expense ratio is 1.06 percent for Class A shares.

12b-1 fee A fee that an investment company levies to defray the costs of advertising and marketing a mutual fund.

CAUTION! Many financial planners recommend that you choose a mutual fund with an expense ratio of 1 percent or less.

expense ratio The amount that investors pay for all of a mutual fund's management fees and operating costs.

Exhibit 13-2

Summary of Expenses Paid to Invest in the Davis Opportunity Fund

	Class A Shares	Class B Shares	Class C Shares
Fees You May Pay as a Davis Funds Shareholder *paid directly from your investment*			
Maximum sales charge (load) imposed on purchases *as a percentage of offering price*	4.75%	None	None
Maximum deferred sales charge (load) imposed on redemptions *as a percentage of the lesser of the net asset value of the shares redeemed or the total cost of such shares*	0.50%	4.00%	1.00%
Maximum sales charge (load) imposed on reinvested dividends	None	None	None
Redemption fee	None	None	None
Exchange fee	None	None	None
Davis Opportunity Fund Annual Operating Expenses *deducted from the Fund's assets*			
Management fees	0.61%	0.61%	0.61%
Distribution (12b-1) fees	0.25%	1.00%	1.00%
Other expenses	0.20%	0.24%	0.20%
Total annual operating expenses	1.06%	1.85%	1.81%

Expenses may vary in future years.

SOURCE: Excerpted from the Davis Opportunity Fund Prospectus, Davis Funds Web site (www.davisfunds .com), accessed February 9, 2009, Davis Funds, P.O. Box 8406, Boston, MA 02266.

Exhibit 13-3

Typical Fees Associated with Mutual Fund Investments

Type of Fee or Charge	Customary Amount
Load fund	Up to 8.5 percent of the purchase.
No-load fund	No sales charge.
Contingent deferred sales load	1 to 5 percent of withdrawals, depending on how long you own shares in the fund before making a withdrawal.
Management fee	0.25 to 1.5 percent per year of the fund's net asset value on a predetermined date.
12b-1 fee	Cannot exceed 1 percent of the fund's assets per year.
Expense ratio	The amount investors pay for all fees and operating costs.
Class A shares	Commission charge when shares are purchased.
Class B shares	Commission charge when money is withdrawn during the first five years.
Class C shares	No commission to buy or sell shares of a fund, but higher, ongoing 12b-1 fees.

CONCEPT CHECK 13–1

1 Closed-end, exchange-traded, and open-end mutual funds are available today. Describe the differences between each type of fund.

Closed-end fund:	
Exchange-traded fund:	
Open-end fund:	

2 What is the net asset value (NAV) for a mutual fund that has assets totaling $730 million, liabilities totaling $10 million, and 24 million shares outstanding?

_____

_____

3 In the table below, indicate the typical charges for each type of mutual fund fee and when the fee is assessed.

Fee	Typical Charge
Load fund	
Contingent deferred sales load	
Management fee	
12b-1 fee	

4 What is an expense ratio? Why is it important?

_____

_____

Apply Yourself!

Objective 1

Use the Internet or library research to find a fund you think will help you obtain a long-term investment goal. Then determine the fund's load charge (if any), management fee, and expense ratio.

To reinforce the material on the costs of investing in funds, Exhibit 13–3 summarizes information for load charges, no-load charges, and Class A, Class B, and Class C shares. In addition, it reports typical management fees, contingent deferred sales loads, and 12b-1 charges.

Classifications of Mutual Funds

The managers of mutual funds tailor their investment portfolios to the investment objectives of their customers. Usually a fund's objectives are plainly disclosed in its prospectus. For example, the objective and strategy of the Fidelity Capital Appreciation Mutual Fund are described as follows:

OBJECTIVE 2

Classify mutual funds by investment objective.

Objective
Seeks capital appreciation

Strategy

Normally invests primarily in common stocks of domestic and foreign issuers. Invests in either "growth" stocks or "value" stocks or both. Uses fundamental analysis of each issuer's financial condition and industry position and market and economic conditions to select instruments.[6]

Although categorizing over 9,300 funds may be helpful, note that different sources of investment information may use different categories for the same mutual fund. In most cases, the name of the category gives a pretty good clue to the types of investments included within the category. The *major* fund categories are described in alphabetical order as follows:

did you know?

Number of different types of mutual funds

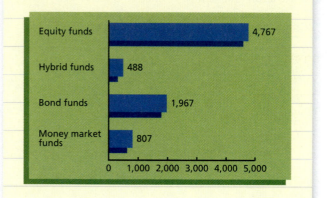

Source: U.S. Bureau of the Census. *Statistical Abstract of the United States, 2009* (Washington, DC: U.S. Government Printing Office, 2009), p. 735.

Stock Funds

- *Aggressive growth funds* seek rapid growth by purchasing stocks whose prices are expected to increase dramatically in a short period of time. Turnover within an aggressive growth fund is high because managers are buying and selling stocks of small, growth companies. Investors in these funds experience wide price swings because of the underlying speculative nature of the stocks in the fund's portfolio.

- *Equity income funds* invest in stocks issued by companies with a long history of paying dividends. The major objective of these funds is to provide income to shareholders. These funds are attractive investment choices for conservative or retired investors.

- *Global stock funds* invest in stocks of companies throughout the world, including the United States.

- *Growth funds* invest in companies expecting higher-than-average revenue and earnings growth. While similar to aggressive growth funds, growth funds tend to invest in larger, well-established companies. As a result, the prices for shares in a growth fund are less volatile compared to aggressive growth funds.

- *Index funds* invest in the same companies included in an index like the Standard & Poor's 500 stock index or Russell 3000 Index. Since fund managers pick the stocks issued by the companies included in the index, an index fund should provide approximately the same performance as the index. Also, since index funds are cheaper to manage, they often have lower management fees and expense ratios.

- *International funds* invest in foreign stocks sold in securities markets throughout the world; thus, if the economy in one region or nation is in a slump, profits can still be earned in others. Unlike global funds, which invest in stocks issued by companies in both foreign nations and the United States, a true international fund invests outside the United States.

- *Large-cap funds* invest in the stocks of companies with total capitalization of $10 billion or more. Large-capitalization stocks are generally stable, well-established companies and are likely to have minimal fluctuation in their value.

---

[6]Fidelity Investments Web site (www.fidelity.com), accessed February 9, 2009, Fidelity Investments, Inc., 82 Devonshire St., Boston, MA 02109.

- *Midcap funds* invest in companies with total capitalization of $2 billion to $10 billion whose stocks offer more security than small-cap funds and more growth potential than funds that invest in large corporations.

- *Regional funds* seek to invest in stock traded within one specific region of the world, such as the European region, the Latin American region, and the Pacific region.

- *Sector funds* invest in companies within the same industry. Examples of sectors include Health and Biotech, Science & Technology, and Natural Resources.

- *Small-cap funds* invest in smaller, lesser-known companies with a total capitalization of less than $2 billion. Because these companies are small and innovative, these funds offer higher growth potential. They are more speculative than funds that invest in larger, more established companies.

- *Socially responsible funds* avoid investing in companies that may cause harm to people, animals, and the environment. Typically, these funds do not invest in companies that produce tobacco, nuclear energy, or weapons or in companies that have a history of discrimination.

did you know?

Socially responsible investing (SRI) is becoming more popular because . . .

- Today there are more than 250 SRI funds.
- Fifteen percent of SRI funds outperform traditional funds.
- SRI funds help you align your investments with your personal values.

For more information on socially responsible investing, go to www.socialinvest.org.

Bond Funds

- *High-yield (junk) bond funds* invest in high-yield, high-risk corporate bonds.

- *Intermediate corporate bond funds* invest in investment-grade corporate debt with maturities between 5 and 10 years.

- *Intermediate U.S. government bond funds* invest in U.S. Treasury securities with maturities between 5 and 10 years.

- *Long-term corporate bond funds* invest in investment-grade corporate bond issues with maturities in excess of 10 years.

- *Long-term (U.S.) government bond funds* invest in U.S. Treasury securities with maturities in excess of 10 years.

- *Municipal bond funds* invest in municipal bonds that provide investors with tax-free interest income.

- *Short-term corporate bond funds* invest in investment-grade corporate bond issues with maturities that are less than 5 years.

- *Short-term (U.S.) government bond funds* invest in U.S. Treasury issues with maturities that are less than 5 years.

Other Funds

- *Asset allocation funds* invest in various asset classes, including stocks, bonds, fixed-income securities, and money market instruments. These funds seek high total return by maintaining precise amounts within each type of asset.

- *Balanced funds* invest in both stocks and bonds with the primary objectives of conserving principal, providing income, and providing long-term growth. Often the percentage of stocks, bonds, and other securities is stated in the fund's prospectus.

- *Fund of funds* invest in shares of other mutual funds. The main advantage of a fund of funds is increased diversification and asset allocation, because this type of fund purchases shares in many different funds. Higher expenses and extra fees are common with this type of fund.

- *Lifecycle funds* (sometimes referred to as *lifestyle funds*) are popular with investors planning for retirement by a specific date. Typically, these funds initially invest in risk-oriented securities (stocks) and become increasingly conservative and income oriented (bonds and CDs) as the specified date approaches and investors are closer to retirement.

- *Money market funds* invest in certificates of deposit, government securities, and other safe and highly liquid investments.

family of funds A group of mutual funds managed by one investment company.

A **family of funds** exists when one investment company manages a group of mutual funds. Each fund within the family has a different financial objective. For instance, one fund may be a long-term government bond fund and another a growth stock fund. Most investment companies offer exchange privileges that enable shareholders to switch among the mutual funds in a fund family. For example, if you own shares in the Franklin growth fund, you may, at your discretion, switch to the Franklin balance sheet investment fund. Generally, investors may give instructions to switch from one fund to another within the same family in writing, over the telephone, or via the Internet. The family-of-funds concept allows shareholders to conveniently switch their investments among funds as different funds offer more potential, financial reward, or security. Charges for exchanges, if any, generally are small for each transaction. For funds that do charge, the fee may be as low as $5 per transaction.

CONCEPT CHECK 13–2

1 How important is the investment objective as stated in a mutual fund's prospectus?

_____

_____

2 Identify one mutual fund in each of the three categories (stocks, bonds, and other) and describe the characteristics of the fund you select and the type of investor who would invest in that type of fund.

General Fund Type	Fund Name	Characteristics of Fund	Typical Investor
Stock			
Bond			
Other			

3 Explain the family-of-funds concept. How is it related to shareholder exchanges?

_____

_____

Apply Yourself!

Objective 2

Using the information in this section, pick a mutual fund category that you consider suitable for each of the following investors and justify your choice:

1. A 24-year-old single investor with a new job that pays $32,000 a year.
2. A single parent with two children who has just received a $400,000 inheritance, has no job, and has not worked outside the home for the past five years.
3. A husband and wife who are both in their mid-60s and retired.

How to Make a Decision to Buy or Sell Mutual Funds

Often the decision to buy or sell shares in mutual funds is "too easy" because investors assume they do not need to evaluate these investments. Why question what the professional portfolio managers decide to do? Yet professionals do make mistakes. And sometimes, economic and financial conditions beyond the control of a fund manager cause a fund's value to decrease. During the recent economic crisis, for instance, most stock funds decreased in value. As an alternative to leaving your money in stock funds that are declining in value, you could have switched to more conservative corporate and government bond funds. That's exactly what Allison Campbell did in November 2007. Although her friends thought she was crazy for taking such a conservative approach, her strategy helped her avoid the recent economic crisis. Now many of her friends wish they had made the same decision. According to Allison, she earned interest on her bond investments while preserving her investment funds for a return to more aggressive funds when the economy rebounds. The responsibility for choosing the right mutual fund rests with *you*. After all, you are the only one who knows how much risk you are willing to assume and how a particular mutual fund can help you achieve your goals.

Fortunately, a lot of information is available to help you evaluate a specific mutual fund. Unfortunately, you can get lost in all the facts and figures and forget your ultimate goal: to choose a mutual fund that will help you achieve your financial goals. To help you sort out all the research, statistics, and information about mutual funds and give you some direction as to what to do first, answer the questions in the nearby Personal Finance in Practice feature. Then answer one basic question: Do you want a managed fund or an index fund?

> **OBJECTIVE 3**
> Evaluate mutual funds.

Managed Funds versus Index Funds

Most mutual funds are managed funds. In other words, there is a professional fund manager (or team of managers) who chooses the securities that are contained in the fund. The fund manager also decides when to buy and sell securities in the fund. To help evaluate a fund, you may want to determine how well a fund manager manages during both good and bad economic times. The benchmark for a good fund manager is the ability to increase share value when the economy is good and retain that value when the economy is bad. For example, most funds increased in value during the first part of 2007. Yet only a few funds were able to retain those gains during the economic crisis that occurred during the last part of 2007 and continued through 2008. One

Personal Finance in Practice

Mutual Funds: Getting Started

Here are some suggestions for beginning a mutual fund investment program.

1. *Perform a financial checkup.* Before investing, you should make sure your budget is balanced, you have adequate insurance protection, and you have established an emergency fund.

   How could this suggestion help you prepare for an investment program?

   _____

   _____

2. *Obtain the money you need to purchase mutual funds.* Although the amount will vary, $250 to $3,000 or more is usually required to open an account with a brokerage firm or an investment company.

   How can I obtain the money needed to fund my investment program?

   _____

   _____

3. *Determine your investment goals.* Without investment goals, you cannot know what you want to accomplish. For more information on the importance of goals, review the material in Chapter 11.

How could this suggestion help you establish a mutual fund investment program?

   _____

   _____

4. *Find a fund with an objective that matches your objective. The Wall Street Journal, Barron's,* and personal finance magazines may help you identify funds with objectives that match your investment objectives.

   Why is a "match" between your investment objective and a fund's objective important?

   _____

   _____

5. *Evaluate, evaluate, and evaluate any mutual fund before buying or selling.* Possible sources of information include the Internet, professional advisory services, the fund's prospectus, the fund's annual report, financial publications, and newspapers—all sources described in the remainder of this section.

   Since mutual funds provide professional management, why is evaluation important?

   _____

   _____

CAUTION! Don't forget the role of the fund manager in determining a fund's success.

important consideration is how long the present fund manager has been managing the fund. If a fund has performed well under its present manager over a 5-year, 10-year, or longer period, there is a strong likelihood that it will continue to perform well under that manager in the future. On the other hand, if the fund has a new manager, his or her decisions may affect the performance of the fund. The decisions made by a new manager are often untested and may or may not stand the test of time. Managed funds may be open-end funds or closed-end funds.

Instead of investing in a managed fund, some investors choose to invest in an index fund. Why? The answer to that question is simple: Over many years, the majority of managed mutual funds fail to outperform the Standard & Poor's 500 stock index. The exact statistics vary, depending on the year, but a common statistic often found in mutual fund research is that the Standard & Poor's 500 stock index outperforms 80 percent of all mutual funds.[7]

---

[7]"The Lowdown on Index Funds," the Investopedia Web site (www.investopedia.com), accessed February 13, 2009.

Because an index mutual fund is a mirror image of a specific index like the Standard & Poor's 500, the Nasdaq Composite, the Russell 2000, or similar Indexes, the dollar value of a share in an index fund also increases when the index increases. Unfortunately, the reverse is true. If the index goes down, the value of a share in an index fund goes down. Index funds, sometimes called "passive" funds, have managers, but they simply buy the stocks or bonds contained in the index. A second and very important reason why investors choose index funds is the lower expense ratio charged by these passively managed funds. As mentioned earlier in this chapter, the total fees charged by a mutual fund is called the expense ratio. If a fund's expense ratio is 1.25 percent, then the fund has to earn at least that amount on its investment holdings just to break even each year. With very few exceptions, typical expense ratios for an index fund are 0.50 percent or less. Index funds may be open-end funds, closed-end funds, or exchange-traded funds.

Which type of fund is best? Good question. The answer depends on which managed mutual fund you choose. If you pick a managed fund that has better performance than an index, then you made the right choice. If, on the other hand, the index (and the index fund) outperforms the managed fund—which happens as often as 80 percent of the time—an index fund is a better choice. With both investments, the key is how well you can research a specific investment alternative using the sources of information that are described in the remainder of this section.

The Internet

Many investors have found a wealth of information about mutual fund investments on the Internet. Basically, you can access information three ways. First, you can obtain current market values for mutual funds by using one of the Internet search engines, such as Yahoo! The Yahoo! Finance page (http://finance.yahoo.com) has a box where you can enter the symbol of the mutual fund you want to research. If you don't know the symbol, you can enter in the name of the mutual fund in the Get Quotes box. The Yahoo! Finance Web site will respond with the correct symbol. In addition to current market values, you can obtain a price history for a mutual fund, a profile including information about current holdings, performance data, comparative data, risk, and purchase information.

Second, most investment companies that sponsor mutual funds have a Web page. To obtain information, all you have to do is access one of the Internet search engines and type in the name of the fund or enter the investment company's Internet address (URL) in your computer. Generally, statistical information about performance of individual funds, procedures for opening an account, promotional literature, and different investor services are provided. *Be warned:* Investment companies want you to become a shareholder. As a result, the Web sites for *some* investment companies read like a sales pitch. Read between the glowing descriptions and look at the facts before investing your money.

Finally, professional advisory services, covered in the next section, offer online research reports for mutual funds. A sample of the information available from the Morningstar Web site for the Dodge and Cox Balanced Fund is illustrated in Exhibit 13–4. Note that information about the fund symbol, Morningstar Rating, and past returns is provided. You can also obtain more detailed information by clicking on the appropriate button on the left side of the Web site. In many cases, more detailed information is provided by professional advisory services like Morningstar, Inc. (www.morningstar.com), and Lipper Analytical Services, Inc. (www.lipperweb.com) for a small fee. While the information is basically the same as that in the printed reports described later in this section, the ability to obtain up-to-date information quickly without having to wait for research materials to be mailed or to make a trip to the library is a real selling point.

Key Web Sites for Investing Advice

www.morningstar.com
www.valueline.com
www.lipperweb.com

Exhibit **13–4** Information about the Dodge and Cox Balanced Fund Available from the Morningstar Web Site

| Join | Home | Portfolio | Stocks | Options | **Funds** | ETFs | Hedge Funds | Markets | Tools | Per |

Morningstar Svs Idx	Morningstar Info Idx	DJIA	Morningstar Mfg Idx	Nasdaq
2336.93 -26.03(-1.10%)	2379.79 11.30(0.47%)	8474.85 -29.22(-0.34%)	2503.78 16.55(0.66%)	1734.54 2

New Beta   Preview our new Fund Snapshot.

Snapshot

- Performance
- Chart beta
- Analyst Research
- Stewardship Grade
- Morningstar Rating
- Portfolio
- Fees & Expenses
- Management
- Tax Analysis
- Risk Measures
- Purchase Info
- SEC Filings

Fund Report	🗎
Add to Portfolio	🗀
Email Alert	⏰
Print	🖨
Data Question	?

Video Reports

Dodge & Cox Balanced DODBX

See Fund Family Data ▶▶

Information from dodgeandcox.com   DODGE & COX FUNDS

Performance more ▶▶

Growth of $10,000   04-30-09
● Fund   ● Current Category   ● Index

	2005	2006	2007	2008	2009
Fund	6.6	13.9	1.7	-33.6	-0.1
+/- DJ Moderate Portfolio TR USD	-0.7	2.0	-6.3	-8.8	-1.6
+/- Cat	1.5	2.6	-4.3	-5.6	-1.0
Fund Category	MA	MA	MA	MA	MA

Trailing Returns % ⓘ   05-18-09

	YTD	3 year	5 year
Fund	5.23	-7.94	-0.53
+/- Cat	0.90	-3.23	-1.05
+/- DJ Moderate Portfolio TR USD (change index)	0.70	-5.13	-3.85

Should you be buying or selling Dodge & Cox Balanced?
Morningstar has the answer.

Sign up for Premium Membership to get our fund recommendations.

▶ **Join Now**   close ☒

Yield % (TTM) ▲   Min Investment
3.63 $2,500

Manager ⓘ   **Start Date**

Source: Morningstar Web site (www.morningstar.com), accessed May 19, 2009, Morningstar, Inc., 225 W. Wacker Drive, Chicago, IL 60606.

Professional Advisory Services

A number of subscription services provide detailed information on mutual funds. Lipper Analytical Services, Morningstar, Inc., and Value Line are three widely used sources of such information. Exhibit 13–5 illustrates the type of information provided by Morningstar, Inc., for the T. Rowe Price Equity Income Fund. Although the

Exhibit 13–5   Mutual Fund Research Information Provided by Morningstar, Inc.

T. Rowe Price Eq Inc

	Ticker	Status	NAV	Yeild	Total Assets	Master Category
Analyst Pick ✓	PRFDX	Open	$18.39	2.9%	$15,324 mil	Large Value

Governance and Management

Stewardship Grade: A

Portfolio Manager(s)

Seasoned, Brian Rogers has managed this fund since its 1985 inception. He is backed by T. Rowe Price's deep bench of analysts. In January 2004. Rogers became T. Rowe Price's chief investment officer and he also serves as the chairman of the company's board. He says he invests a large portion of his assets in the fund.

Strategy

This fund employs a true-blue approach to value investing. Longtime manager Brian Rogers strives to keep the fund's yield at least 25% higher than that of the S&P 500 Index, and he looks for companies trading cheaply relative to their historic price multiples. This strategy often leads him to load up on traditional value sectors, such as energy and industrial cyclicals, although he is willing to delve into growth-oriented areas such as health care, technology, and telecom when the price is right.

Performance 10-31-08

	1st Qtr	2nd Qtr	3rd Qtr	4th Qtr	Total
2004	1.91	2.59	0.72	9.25	15.05
2005	−0.62	0.34	2.88	1.63	4.26
2006	5.36	−0.29	5.57	7.42	19.14
2007	1.26	6.76	−1.34	−3.14	3.30
2008	−8.08	−5.89	−4.61	—	—

Trailing	Total Return %	+/− S&P 500	+/− Russ 1000 VI	% Rank Cat	Growth of $10,000
3 Mo	−20.97	2.14	1.11	27	7,903
6 Mo	−28.28	1.00	1.63	36	7,172
1 Yr	−34.66	1.44	2.14	30	6,534
3 Yr Avg	−4.39	0.82	0.85	30	8,740
5 Yr Avg	1.68	1.42	−0.22	31	10,869
10 Yr Avg	3.29	2.89	0.50	24	13,822
15 Yr Avg	7.94	1.01	0.03	18	31,458

Tax Analysis	Tax-Adj Rtn %	% Rank Cat	Tax-Cost Rat	% Rank Cat
3 Yr (estimated)	−5.87	26	1.55	43
5 Yr (estimated)	0.33	31	1.33	51
10 Yr (estimated)	1.59	25	1.65	65

Potential Capital Gain Exposure: −23% of assets

Historical Profile

Return Above Avg
Risk Average
Rating ★★★★ Above Avg

94%	95%	96%	96%	94%	95%	94%	95%	95%	

Investment Style: Equity / Stock %

▼ Manager Change
▽ Partial Manager Chanage

Growth of $10,000
— Investment Values of Fund
— Investment Values of S&P 500

26.0 / 22.0 / 18.0 / 14.0 / 10.0

Performance Quartile (within Category)

	1997	1998	1999	2000	2001	2002	2003	2004	2005	2006	2007	10.08	History
	26.07	26.32	24.81	24.67	23.65	19.79	24.16	26.59	25.92	29.55	28.10	18.39	NAV
	28.82	9.23	3.82	13.12	1.64	−13.04	25.78	15.05	4.26	19.14	3.30	−31.49	Total Return %
	−4.54	−19.35	−17.22	22.22	13.53	9.06	−2.90	4.17	−0.65	3.35	−2.19	1.35	+/− S&P 500
	−6.36	−6.40	−3.53	6.11	7.23	2.48	−4.25	−1.44	−2.79	−3.11	3.47	1.41	+/− Russ 1000 VI
	2.99	2.40	2.04	2.12	1.49	1.54	1.99	1.76	1.75	1.91	2.00	1.57	Income Return %
	25.83	6.83	1.78	11.00	0.15	−14.58	23.79	13.29	2.51	17.23	1.30	−33.06	Capital Return %
	34	70	60	23	16	10	69	23	68	37	36	31	Total Rtn % Rank Cat
	0.66	0.61	0.53	0.51	0.36	0.36	0.39	0.42	0.46	0.49	0.58	0.43	Income $
	2.14	1.49	1.97	2.64	1.01	0.45	0.27	0.72	1.33	0.69	1.83	0.71	Capital Gains $
	0.79	0.77	0.77	0.78	0.80	0.79	0.78	0.74	0.71	0.69	0.67	—	Expense Ratio %
	2.67	2.26	1.95	2.01	1.53	1.72	1.80	1.69	1.73	1.77	1.89	—	Income Ratio %
	24	23	22	22	17	15	12	16	21	17	26	—	Turnover Rate %
	12,771	13,495	12,321	10,187	10,128	8,954	12,167	15,947	17,878	20,999	20,521	13,467	Net Assets $mil

Rating and Risk

Time Period	Load-Adj Return %	Morningstar Rtn vs Cat	Morningstar Risk vs Cat	Morningstar Risk-Adj Rating
1 Yr	−34.66			
3 Yr	−4.39	+Avg	Avg	★★★★
5 Yr	1.68	+Avg	Avg	★★★★
10 Yr	3.29	+Avg	Avg	★★★★
Incept	10.53			

Other Measures	Standard Index S&P 500	Best Fit Index Russ 1000 VI
Alpha	0.5	0.4
Beta	0.96	0.95
R-Squared	97	98
Standard Deviation	14.63	
Mean	−4.39	
Sharpe Ratio	−0.51	

Portfolio Analysis, 09-30-09

Share change since 06-08 Total Stocks: 12T

Share change		Sector	PE	Tot Ret %	% Assets
⊕	J.P. Morgan Chase & Co.	Financial	13.6	−2.05	3.58
⊕	General Electric Company	Ind Mtrls	9.3	−45.62	3.15
	Chevron Corporation	Energy	7.9	−18.35	2.55
	ExxonMobil Corporation	Energy	9.2	−19.78	2.50
⊕	Wells Fargo Company	Financial	15.6	16.42	2.02
⊕	AT&T. Inc.	Telecom	12.1	−32.38	1.80
⊖	Marsh & McLennan Compani	Financial		13.96	1.79
⊕	US Bancorp	Financial	13.0	−2.33	1.65
	Royal Dutch Shell PLC AD	Energy		−31.57	1.58
⊖	Hershey Company	Goods	38.3	−3.17	1.54
	Microsoft Corporation	Software	11.8	−36.54	1.47
	International Paper Co.	Ind Mtrls	7.8	−45.33	1.41
⊕	3M Company	Ind Mtrls	12.4	−22.22	1.38
⊕	Bank of America Corporat	Financial	13.3	−38.05	1.37
⊕	Home Depot, Inc.	Consumer	12.3	−10.24	1.36
⊕	Eli Lilly & Company	Health	9.7	−34.80	1.35
⊖	Amgen. Inc.	Health	20.9	28.96	1.27
⊕	SunTrust Banks, Inc.	Financial	11.3	−32.81	1.21
⊕	Bank of New York Mellon	Financial	15.8	−30.52	1.12
⊖	Johnson & Johnson	Health	14.9	−6.18	1.12

Current Investment Style

Value Bind Growth — Large Mid Small

Market Cap	%
Giant	40.1
Large	33.0
Mid	26.7
Small	0.2
Micro	0.0

Avg $mil: 30,710

Value Measures		Rel Category
Price/Earnings	12.25	1.06
Price/Book	1.53	0.92
Price/Sales	0.93	0.92
Price/Cash Flow	5.28	0.80
Dividend Yield %	3.67	1.17

Growth Measure	%	Rel Category
Long-Term Erngs	9.28	0.91
Book Value	4.46	0.64
Sales	5.11	0.79
Cash Flow	5.97	0.64
Historical Erngs	4.91	0.59

Profitability	%	Rel Catagory
Return on Equity	16.24	0.88
Return on Assets	6.16	0.88
Net Margin	9.68	0.85

Sector Weightings	% of Stocks	Rel S&P 500	3 Year High	Low
⟳ Info	15.17	0.78		
Software	2.23	0.56	3	1
Hardware	3.23	0.34	7	3
Media	6.00	2.29	8	6
Telecom	3.71	1.12	6	4
⟳ Service	40.14	0.98		
Health	8.99	0.65	11	8
Consumer	6.21	0.81	6	3
Business	1.15	0.24	3	1
Financial	23.79	1.62	24	18
⟳ Mfg	44.69	1.13		
Goods	12.18	1.11	14	12
Ind Mtrls	15.34	1.32	17	14
Energy	11.57	0.88	15	8
Utilities	5.60	1.49	6	4

Composition

	%
● Cash	4.3
● Stocks	94.9
○ Bonds	0.8
○ Other	0.0
Foreign	4.0
(% of Stock)	

Morningstar's Take by Hilary Fazzone 10-28-08

Shareholders are in good hands at T. Rowe Price Equity Income.

This fund benefits from manager Brian Rogers* depth of experience and ability to maintain perspective in challenging times. In addition to filling the roles of chief investment officer and chairman of T. Rowe Price's board. Rogers has managed this fund since its 1985 inception, meaning he's seen his sound strategy through a gamut of market cycles. Rogers targets tried-and-true companies that have come under pressure from the market. His picks must demonstrate solid financial health; Rogers gauges this in part by looking at companies* dividend yield which boosts shareholders* returns in the form of current income. Finally, Rogers must be confident that investor's perception of the company will improve in the years after he buys it.

Given this approach, Rogers sees opportunities surfacing as a result of the recent financial crisis. He is looking to pick up companies with depressed

equity prices that can emerge from this period in good standing. True to form, Rogers has been finding value among out-of-favor sectors. For example, he's added financials such as American Express. Goldman Sachs, and Wells Fargo to the portfolio because he's confident that they will survive the crisis and continue to be strong performers. Along the same lines, Rogers also has been carefully adding to the fund's energy and industrials sectors because he likes their attractive current values and strong long-term prospects.

Rogers has a history of getting such calls right. Although the fund has suffered steep absolute losses over the past 12 months, they're slimmer than most large value funds'. And over the trailing 15 years through Oct. 27, 2008, the fund's annualized returns outpace those of 83% of its peers and have come amid below-average volatility. The fact that investors can access Rogers' skill for a low 0.67% annual fee is icing on the cake.

Address:	100 East Pratt Street Baltimore, MD 21202 800-638-5660	Minimum Purchase:	$2500	Add: $100	IRA: $1000
		Min Auto Inv Plan	$0	Add: $50	
		Sales Fees:	No load		
Web Address:	www.troweprice.com	Management Fee:	0.56%		
Inception:	10-31-85	Actual Fees:	Mgt: 0.55%	Dist: —	
Advisor	T. Rowe Price Associates, Inc.	Expense Projections:	3 Yr: $214	5Yr: $373	10 Yr: $835
Subadvisor	None	Income Distrib			
NTF Plans	N/A				

M⊙RNINGSTAR® Mutual Funds   89

Source: *Morningstar Mutual Funds* December 6, 2008, p. 89, Morningstar, Inc., 225 W. Wacker Drive, Chicago, IL 60606.

Morningstar report is just one page long, it provides a wealth of information designed to help you decide if this is the right fund for you. Notice that the information is divided into various sections. At the top, a small box entitled "Historical Profile" contains information about financial return, risk, and rating. Notice that T. Rowe Price Equity Income Fund is rated four stars, Morningstar's next to highest rating. The report also provides statistical information over the past 12 years. The middle section of the report provides information about the fund's performance, risk analysis, and portfolio analysis. The last section at the very bottom describes the investment philosophy of the fund. Generally, the "Morningstar's Take" section summarizes the analyst's research.

As you can see, the research information for this fund is pretty upbeat. However, other research firms like Lipper Analytical Services and Value Line, as well as Morningstar, Inc., will also tell you if a fund is a poor performer that offers poor investment potential.

In addition, various mutual fund newsletters provide financial information to subscribers for a fee. All of these sources are rather expensive, but their reports may be available from brokerage firms or libraries.

The Mutual Fund Prospectus

An investment company sponsoring a mutual fund must give potential investors a prospectus. You can also request a prospectus by mail, by calling a toll-free phone number, or by accessing the investment company Web site.

According to financial experts, the prospectus is usually the first piece of information investors receive, and they should read it completely before investing. Although it may look foreboding, a commonsense approach to reading a fund's prospectus can provide valuable insights. In fact, most investors find that a fund's prospectus offers a wealth of information. As pointed out earlier, the prospectus summarizes the fund's objective. Also, the fee table summarizes the fees a fund charges. In addition to information about objectives and fees, the prospectus should provide the following:

- A statement describing the risk factor associated with the fund.
- A description of the fund's past performance.
- A statement describing the type of investments contained in the fund's portfolio.
- Information about dividends, distributions, and taxes.
- Information about the fund's management.
- Information on limitations or requirements, if any, the fund must honor when choosing investments.
- The process investors can use to buy or sell shares in the fund.
- A description of services provided to investors and fees for services, if any.
- Information about how often the fund's investment portfolio changes (sometimes referred to as its *turnover ratio*).

Finally, the prospectus provides information about how to open a mutual fund account with the investment company.

The Mutual Fund Annual Report

If you are a prospective investor, you can request an annual report by mail, a toll-free telephone number, or the Internet. A fund's annual report contains a letter from the president of the investment company, from the fund manager, or both. The annual report also contains detailed financial information about the fund's assets and liabilities, statement of operations, and statement of changes in net assets. Next, the annual report includes a schedule of investments. Finally, the fund's annual report should include a letter from the fund's independent auditors that provides an opinion as to the accuracy of the fund's financial statements.

Financial Publications

Investment-oriented magazines like *BusinessWeek, Forbes, Kiplinger's Personal Finance Magazine,* and *Money* are excellent sources of information about mutual funds. Depending on the publication, coverage ranges from detailed articles that provide in-depth information to simple listings of which funds to buy or sell. And many investment-oriented magazines now provide information on the Internet about mutual funds. The material in Exhibit 13–6 was obtained from the *BusinessWeek* "Mutual Fund Scoreboard." Although the information seems complicated at first glance, much of the information is self-explanatory for an investor who takes the time to evaluate the information supplied in each column. For example, information is provided about

- The fund type.
- The fund name.

Exhibit 13–6   Information Provided by the "Mutual Fund Scoreboard" on the *BusinessWeek* Web Site

Fund Name	BW Overall Rating ▲	Fund Category	BW Category Rating	Assets ($ Mil.)	1 Yr. Assets Change (%)	Sales Charge	Expense Ratio	1- Mo.	3- Mo.	Year-to-date	12- Mo.	3-Yr.	5-Yr.	10-Yr.	Turnover	Cash (%)	12-Mo. Yield (%)	Risk	Foreign (%)	P-E Ratio	Untaxed Gains (%)
Aegis Value (AVALX)	A	Small Value	A	85.3	-60.8	No load	1.44	31.7	19.1	11.7	-47.8	-18.2	-7.6	5.1	Average	0.3	5.5	High	3.3	15.4	-174.1
AIM Basic Balanced A (BBLAX)	A	Moderate Allocation	A	345.4	-44.0	5.5	1.20	14.3	11.9	4.9	-32.6	-11.2	-4.2	NA	Average	5.9	4.6	High	48.8	9.9	-127.8
AIM Basic Value A (GTVLX)	A	Large Blend	A	804.5	-60.2	5.5	1.26	22.3	20.1	11.0	-42.5	-16.7	-6.8	0.0	Average	3.2	0.3	High	18.2	10.1	-54.8
AIM Constellation A (CSTGX)	A	Large Growth	A	2,496.4	-48.3	5.5	1.26	5.8	-0.7	-3.8	-38.8	-14.9	-5.1	-3.4	Very High	2.1	0.0	Average	13.5	8.8	-61.0
AIM Financial Services Inv (FSFSX)	A	Financial	B+	105.3	-64.5	No load	1.31	21.6	17.4	-10.3	-61.3	-33.2	-18.2	-8.4	Low	7.3	2.0	High	10.0	12.6	-207.6
AIM Large Cap Basic Value Inst (LCBIX)	A	Large Blend	A	71.5	-45.9	No load	0.71	21.5	17.5	8.4	-43.7	-17.4	-7.2	NA	Average	2.1	2.5	High	16.3	10.1	-58.9
AIM Select Equity A (AGWFX)	A	Large Blend	B+	147.6	-39.5	5.5	1.52	9.8	10.6	-0.2	-32.7	-13.3	-4.2	-3.5	Very High	1.6	0.0	Above Average	4.8	9.4	-74.7

Source: The *BusinessWeek* Web site (www.businessweek.com), accessed May 19, 2009. Used by special permission © 2009 McGraw-Hill Companies, Inc.

- *BusinessWeek* overall rating.
- Fund category.
- *BusinessWeek* category rating.
- Value of assets in the fund.
- Percentage of one-year change in asset value.
- Sales charge, if any.
- Expense ratio.
- Returns for 1 month, 3 months, year-to-date, 12 months, 3-year, 5-year, and 10-year periods.
- Turnover of investments in the fund.
- Percentage of cash in the fund.
- The 12-month yield for the fund.
- The risk level associated with the fund.

An investor can also compare the information for one fund with the same data for other funds. In most cases, all you have to do to get started is to enter the name of the fund or the trading symbol for the fund.

In addition to mutual fund information in financial publications, a number of mutual fund guidebooks are available at your local bookstore or public library.

Newspapers

Most large metropolitan newspapers, *The Wall Street Journal,* and *Barron's* provide information about mutual funds. Typical coverage includes information about the fund family and fund name, the net asset value, net change, and year-to-data percentage of return. The highlighted line in Exhibit 13–7 provides detailed information for

Exhibit 13–7

Financial Information about Mutual Funds Available in *The Wall Street Journal*

1 FUND	2 NAV	3 NET CHG	4 YTD % RET
A B C			
American Century Inv			
Ultra	14.53	. . .	0.6
American Funds Cl A			
BalA p	13.47	0.02	−2.2
Amcp Ap	12.01	0.03	−0.5
AMutl Ap	18.60	0.01	−2.5

1. **FUND:** The name of the fund is the American Balanced fund.

2. **NAV:** Net asset value. For the American Balanced fund, the NAV is $13.47 per share.

3. **NET CHG:** Net change is the difference between the price paid for the last share today and the price paid for the last share on the previous trading day. The American Balanced fund closed $0.02 higher than yesterday's closing price.

4. **YTD % RET:** The year-to-date percentage of increase or decrease for a fund. This American fund has lost 2.2 percent of its value since January 1.

SOURCE: Republished by permission of Dow Jones Inc. from *The Wall Street Journal,* February 10, 2009, p. C14; permission conveyed through the Copyright Clearance Center, Inc.

the American Balanced fund. Each numbered entry in the list below the exhibit refers to a numbered column in the mutual fund table. Much of this same information is also available on the Internet.

The letters beside the name of a specific fund can be very informative. You can find out what they mean by looking at the footnotes that accompany the newspaper's mutual fund quotations. Generally, "p" means a 12b-1 distribution fee is charged, "r" means a redemption charge may be made, and "t" means both the p and r footnotes apply.

The newspaper coverage described in this section is a good means of monitoring the value of your mutual fund investments. However, other sources of information provide a more complete basis for evaluating mutual fund investments.

CONCEPT CHECK 13–3

> **Sheet 40** Evaluating Mutual Fund Investment Information
>
> **Sheet 41** Evaluation of Mutual Fund

1 In your own words, describe the difference between a managed fund and an index fund. Which one do you think could help you achieve your investment goals?

_____

_____

2 Describe how each of the following sources of investment information could help you evaluate a mutual fund investment.

Source of Information	Type of Information	How This Could Help
The Internet		
Professional advisory services		
Mutual fund prospectus		
Mutual fund annual report		
Financial publications		
Newspapers		

3 Describe the type of information contained in the *BusinessWeek* Mutual Fund Scoreboard.

_____

_____

Apply Yourself!

Objective 3

Choose either the Alger Capital Appreciation fund (symbol ACAAX) or the Gabelli Asset fund (symbol GATAX) and use the Internet or library sources to report the type of fund, year-to-date (YTD) return, net asset value, and Morningstar rating for the fund.

The Mechanics of a Mutual Fund Transaction

For many investors, mutual funds have become the investment of choice. In fact, you probably either own shares or know someone who owns shares in a mutual fund—they're that popular! They may be part of a 401(k) or 403(b) retirement account, a SEP IRA, a Roth IRA, or a traditional IRA retirement account, all topics discussed in Chapter 14. They can also be owned outright in a taxable account by purchasing shares through a registered sales representative who works for a bank or brokerage firm or an investment company that sponsors a mutual fund. As you will see later in this section, it's easy to purchase shares in a mutual fund. For $250 to $3,000 or more, you can open an account and begin investing. And there are other advantages that encourage investors to purchase shares in funds. Unfortunately, there are also disadvantages. Exhibit 13–8 summarizes the advantages and disadvantages of fund investments.

One advantage of any investment is the opportunity to make money on the investment. In the next section, we examine how you can make money by investing in closed-end funds, exchange-traded funds, or open-end funds. We consider how taxes affect your fund investments. Then we look at the options used to purchase shares in a mutual fund. Finally, we examine the options used to withdraw money from a mutual fund.

Return on Investment

income dividends The earnings a fund pays to shareholders from its dividend and interest income.

capital gain distributions The payments made to a fund's shareholders that result from the sale of securities in the fund's portfolio.

As with other investments, the purpose of investing in a closed-end fund, exchange-traded fund, or open-end fund is to earn a financial return. Shareholders in such funds can receive a return in one of three ways. First, all three types of funds pay income dividends. **Income dividends** are the earnings a fund pays to shareholders from its dividend and interest income. Second, investors may receive capital gain distributions. **Capital gain distributions** are the payments made to a fund's shareholders that result

Exhibit 13–8

Advantages and Disadvantages of Investing in Mutual Funds

Advantages
• Diversification.
• Professional management.
• Ease of buying and selling shares.
• Multiple withdrawal options.
• Distribution or reinvestment of dividends and capital gains.
• Switching privileges within the same fund family.
• Services that include toll-free telephone numbers, complete records of all transactions, and savings and checking accounts.

Disadvantages
• Purchase/withdrawal costs.
• Ongoing management fees and 12b-1 fees.
• Poor performance that may not match the Standard & Poor's 500 stock index or some other index.
• Inability to control when capital gain distributions occur and complicated tax-reporting issues.
• Potential market risk associated with all investments.
• Some sales personnel are aggressive and/or unethical.

Figure It Out!

> Calculating Total Return for Mutual Funds

In Chapter 12, we defined total return as a calculation that includes not only the yearly dollar amount of income but also any increase or decrease in market value. For mutual funds, you can use the following calculation to determine the dollar amount of total return:

> Income dividends
> + Capital gain distributions
> + Change in share market value when sold
> _____
> Dollar amount of total return

For example, assume you purchased 100 shares of Majestic Growth Fund for $12.20 per share for a total investment of $1,220. During the next 12 months, you received income dividends of $0.45 a share and capital gain distributions of $0.90 a share. Also, assume you sold your investment at the end of 12 months for $13.40 a share. As illustrated below, the dollar amount for total return is $255:

Income dividends = 100 × $0.45 =	$ 45
Capital gain distributions = 100 × $0.90 =	+ 90
Change in share value = $13.40 − $12.20	
= $1.20 × 100 =	+ 120
Dollar amount of total return	$ 255

To calculate the percentage of total return, divide the dollar amount of total return by the original cost of your mutual fund investment. The percentage of total return for the above example is 20.9 percent, as follows:

$$\text{Percent of total return} = \frac{\text{Dollar amount of total return}}{\text{Original cost of your investment}}$$

$$= \frac{\$255}{\$1,220}$$

$$= 0.209, \text{ or } 20.9\%$$

Now it's your turn. Use the following financial information for the Northeast Utility fund to calculate the dollar amount of total return and percent of total return over a 12-month period.

> Number of shares, 100
> Purchase price, $14.00 a share
> Income dividends, $0.30 a share
> Capital gain distribution, $0.60 a share
> Sale price, $15.25 a share

Calculation	Calculation Formula	Your Answer
Dollar amount of total return		
Percent of total return		

Answers: The total return is $215 and the percent of total return is 15.4%.

---

from the sale of securities in the fund's portfolio. Both amounts generally are paid once a year. Note: Exchange-traded funds often pay dividends on a monthly or quarterly basis. Third, as with stock and bond investments, you can buy shares in funds at a low price and then sell them after the price has increased. For example, assume you purchased shares in the Fidelity Stock Selector Fund at $16.00 per share and sold your shares two years later at $20.50 per share. In this case, you made $4.50 ($20.50 selling price minus $16.00 purchase price) per share. With this financial information and the dollar amounts for income dividends and capital gain distributions, you can calculate a total return for your mutual fund investment. Before completing this section, you may want to examine the actual procedure used to calculate the dollar amount of total return and percentage of total return in the nearby Figure It Out box.

When shares in a fund are sold, the profit that results from an increase in value is referred to as a *capital gain*. Note the

did you know?

CHARACTERISTICS OF MUTUAL FUND OWNERS	
4	The median number of funds owned
76	The percentage of shareholders who own funds in their retirement accounts
91	The percentage of shareholders who are saving for retirement

Source: The Investment Company Institute Web site (www.ici.org), accessed February 16, 2009.

difference between a capital gain distribution and a capital gain. A capital gain distribution occurs when *the fund* distributes profits that result from *the fund* selling securities in the portfolio at a profit. On the other hand, a capital gain is the profit that results when *you* sell your shares in the mutual fund for more than you paid for them. Of course, if the price of a fund's shares goes down between the time of your purchase and the time of sale, you incur a capital loss.

Taxes and Mutual Funds

Taxes on reinvested income dividends, capital gain distributions, and profits from the sale of shares can be deferred if mutual fund investments are held in your retirement account. Assuming all qualifications are met, you can even eliminate taxes on reinvested income, capital gain distributions, and profits from the sale of shares for mutual funds held in a Roth individual retirement account. For mutual funds held in taxable accounts, income dividends, capital gain distributions, and financial gains and losses from the sale of closed-end, exchange-traded, or open-end funds are subject to taxation. At the end of each year, investment companies are required to send each shareholder a statement specifying how much he or she received in dividends and capital gain distributions. Although investment companies may provide this information as part of their year-end statement, most funds use IRS Form 1099 DIV. The following information provides general guidelines on how mutual fund transactions are taxed when held in a taxable account:

- Income dividends are reported, along with all other dividend amounts you have received, on your federal tax return and are taxed as income.
- Capital gain distributions that result from the fund selling securities in the fund's portfolio at a profit are reported on Schedule D as part of your federal tax return and on the 1040. Capital gain distributions are taxed as long-term capital gains regardless of how long you own shares in the fund.
- Capital gains or losses that result from your selling shares in a mutual fund are reported on Schedule D and the 1040. How long you hold the shares determines if your gains or losses are taxed as a short-term or long-term capital gain. (See Chapter 3 for more information on capital gains and capital losses.)

Two specific problems develop with taxation of mutual funds. First, almost all investment companies allow you to reinvest income dividends and capital gain distributions from the fund to purchase additional shares instead of receiving cash. Even though you didn't receive cash because you chose to reinvest such distributions, they are still taxable and must be reported on your federal tax return as current income. Second, when you purchase shares of stock, corporate bonds, or other investments and use the buy-and-hold technique described in Chapter 12, you decide when you sell. Thus, you can pick the tax year when you pay tax on capital gains or deduct capital losses. Mutual funds, on the other hand, buy and sell securities within the fund's portfolio on a regular basis during any 12-month period. At the end of the year, profits that result from the mutual fund's buying and selling activities are paid to shareholders in the form of capital gain distributions. Because income dividends and capital gain distributions are taxable, one factor to consider when choosing a mutual fund is its turnover. For a mutual fund, the **turnover ratio** measures the percentage of a fund's holdings that have changed or "been replaced" during a 12-month period of time. Simply put, it is a measure of a fund's trading activity. *Caution:* Unless you are using the fund in a 401(k) or 403(b) retirement account, or some type of individual retirement account, a mutual fund with a high turnover ratio can result in higher income tax bills. A higher turnover ratio can also result in higher transaction costs and fund

turnover ratio A ratio that measures the percentage of a fund's holdings that have changed or "been replaced" during a 12-month period of time.

expenses. Unlike the investments that you manage, you have no control over when the mutual fund sells securities and when you will be taxed on capital gain distributions.

To ensure having all of the documentation you need for tax reporting purposes, it is essential that *you* keep accurate records. The same records will help you monitor the value of your mutual fund investments and make more intelligent decisions with regard to buying and selling these investments.

Purchase Options

You can buy shares of a closed-end fund or exchange-traded fund through a stock exchange or in the over-the-counter market. You can purchase shares of an open-end, no-load fund by contacting the investment company that manages the fund, through a salesperson who is authorized to sell them, or through an account executive of a brokerage firm.

You can also purchase both no-load and load funds from mutual fund supermarkets available through brokerage firms. A mutual fund supermarket offers at least two advantages. First, instead of dealing with numerous investment companies that sponsor mutual funds, you can make one toll-free phone call or use the Internet to obtain information, purchase shares, and sell shares in a large number of mutual funds. Second, you receive one statement from one brokerage firm instead of receiving a statement from each investment company or brokerage firm you deal with. One statement can be a real plus because it provides the information you need to monitor the value of your investments in one place and in the same format.

Because of the unique nature of open-end fund transactions, we will examine how investors buy and sell shares in this type of mutual fund. To purchase shares in an open-end mutual fund, you may use four options:

- Regular account transactions.
- Voluntary savings plans.
- Contractual savings plans.
- Reinvestment plans.

The most popular and least complicated method of purchasing shares in an open-end fund is through a regular account transaction. When you use a regular account transaction, you decide how much money you want to invest and when you want to invest, and simply buy as many shares as possible.

The chief advantage of the voluntary savings plan is that it allows you to make smaller purchases than the minimum purchases required by the regular account method described above. At the time of the initial purchase, you declare an intent to make regular minimum purchases of the fund's shares. Although there is no penalty for not making purchases, most investors feel an "obligation" to make purchases on a periodic basis, and, as pointed out throughout this text, small monthly investments are a great way to save for long-term objectives. For most voluntary savings plans, the minimum purchase ranges from $25 to $100 for each purchase after the initial investment. Funds try to make investing as easy as possible. Most offer payroll deduction plans, and many will deduct, upon proper shareholder authorization, a specified amount from a share holder's bank account. Also, many investors can choose mutual funds as a vehicle to invest money that is contributed to a 401(k), 403(b), or individual retirement account. As mentioned earlier, Chapter 14 provides more information on the tax advantages of different types of retirement accounts.

Not as popular as they once were, contractual savings plans require you to make regular purchases over a specified period of time, usually 10 to 15 years. These plans are sometimes referred to as *front-end load plans* because almost all of the commissions are paid in the first few years of the contract period. Also, you may incur penalties if you do not fulfill the purchase requirements. For example, if you drop out of a contractual savings plan before completing the purchase requirements, you sacrifice the prepaid commissions. In some cases, contractual savings plans combine mutual fund shares and life insurance to make these plans more attractive. Many financial experts and government regulatory agencies are critical of contractual savings plans. As a result, the Securities and Exchange Commission and many states have imposed new rules on investment companies offering contractual savings plans.

reinvestment plan A service provided by an investment company in which shareholder income dividends and capital gain distributions are automatically reinvested to purchase additional shares of the fund.

You may also purchase shares in an open-end fund by using the fund's reinvestment plan. A **reinvestment plan** is a service provided by an investment company in which income dividends and capital gain distributions are automatically reinvested to purchase additional shares of the fund. Most reinvestment plans allow shareholders to use reinvested money to purchase shares without having to pay additional sales charges or commissions. *Reminder:* When your dividends or capital gain distributions are reinvested, you must still report these transactions as taxable income.

All four purchase options allow you to buy shares over a long period of time. As a result, you can use the principle of *dollar cost averaging,* which was explained in Chapter 12. Dollar cost averaging allows you to average many individual purchase prices over a long period of time. This method helps you avoid the problem of buying high and selling low. With dollar cost averaging, you can make money if you sell your fund shares at a price higher than their *average* purchase price.

Withdrawal Options

Because closed-end funds and exchange-traded funds are listed on stock exchanges or traded in the over-the-counter market, an investor may sell shares in such a fund to another investor. Shares in an open-end fund can be sold on any business day to the investment company that sponsors the fund. In this case, the shares are redeemed at their net asset value. All you have to do is give proper notification and the fund will send you a check. With some funds, you can even write checks to withdraw money from the fund.

In addition, most funds have provisions that allow investors with shares that have a minimum asset value (usually at least $5,000) to use four options to systematically withdraw money. First, you may withdraw a specified, fixed dollar amount each investment period until your fund has been exhausted. Normally, an investment period is three months.

A second option allows you to liquidate or "sell off" a certain number of shares each investment period. Since the net asset value of shares in a fund varies from one period to the next, the amount of money you receive will also vary.

A third option allows you to withdraw a fixed percentage of asset growth. If no asset growth occurs, no payment is made to you. Under this option, your principal remains untouched.

Example

You arrange to receive 60 percent of the asset growth of your mutual fund investment. In one investment period, the asset growth amounts to $3,000. For that period, you will receive a check for $1,800, as shown below.

Amount you receive = Investment growth × Percentage of growth withdrawn

= $3,000 × 60 percent = $1,800

A final option allows you to withdraw all income dividends and capital gain distributions earned by the fund during an investment period. Under this option, your principal remains untouched.

CONCEPT CHECK 13–4

1 In your own words, describe the advantages and disadvantages of mutual fund investments.

_____

_____

2 In the table below indicate how each of the key terms affects a mutual fund investment and how each would be taxed.

Key Term	Effect on a Mutual Fund Investment	Type of Taxation
Income dividends		
Capital gain distributions		
Capital gains		

3 How would you purchase a closed-end fund? An exchange-traded fund?

_____

_____

4 What options can you use to purchase shares in or withdraw money from an open-end mutual fund?

_____

_____

Apply Yourself!

Objective 4

Use the Internet to obtain a prospectus for a specific mutual fund that you believe would be a quality long-term investment. Then describe the purchase and withdrawal options described in the fund's prospectus.

Back to ... Getting Personal

Reconsider your responses to the "Getting Personal" questions at the beginning of the chapter. For more effective personal investment planning using mutual funds:

- Visit the Mutual Fund Education Alliance at www.mfea.com or a similar Web site to learn why people invest in funds.
- Determine which type or types of mutual funds could help you obtain your investment goals.

- Choose a specific closed-end fund, exchange-traded fund, or open-end fund and use the Internet or library research to complete Your Personal Financial Plan sheet 41 located at the end of this chapter.

Finally, describe what you learned in this chapter that may help you use mutual funds to build a long-term investment program.

Chapter Summary

Objective 1   The major reasons investors choose mutual funds are professional management and diversification. Mutual funds are also a convenient way to invest money—especially for retirement accounts. There are three types of funds: closed-end funds, exchange-traded funds, and open-end funds. A closed-end fund is a fund whose shares are issued only when the fund is organized. An exchange-traded fund (ETF) is a fund that invests in the stocks contained in a specific stock index like the Standard & Poor's 500 stock index, the Dow Jones Industrial Average, or the Nasdaq 100 Index. Both closed-end and exchange-traded funds are traded on a stock exchange or in the over-the-counter market. An open-end fund is a mutual fund whose shares are sold and redeemed by the investment company at the net asset value (NAV) at the request of investors.

Mutual funds can also be classified as A shares (commissions charged when shares are purchased), B shares (commissions charged when money is withdrawn during the first five years), and C shares (no commission to buy or sell shares, but higher, ongoing fees). Other possible fees include management fees and 12b-1 fees. Together all the different management fees and operating costs are referred to as an expense ratio.

Objective 2   The major categories of stock mutual funds, in terms of the types of securities in which they invest, are aggressive growth, equity income, global, growth, index, international, large cap, midcap, regional, sector, small cap, and socially responsible. There are also bond funds that include high-yield (junk), intermediate corporate, intermediate U.S.

government, long-term corporate, long-term U.S. government, municipal, short-term corporate, and short-term U.S. government. Finally, other funds invest in a mix of different stocks, bonds, and other investment securities that include asset allocation funds, balanced funds, fund of funds, lifecycle funds, and money market funds. Today many investment companies use a family-of-funds concept, which allows shareholders to switch among funds as different funds offer more potential, financial reward, or security.

Objective 3   The responsibility for choosing the "right" mutual fund rests with you, the investor. Fortunately, a lot of information is available to help you evaluate a specific mutual fund. Often, the first question investors must answer is whether they want a managed fund or an index fund. With a managed fund, a professional fund manager (or team of managers) chooses the securities that are contained in the fund. Some investors choose to invest in an index fund, because over many years, index funds have outperformed the majority of managed funds. If the individual securities included in an index increase in value, the index goes up. On the other hand, if the securities included in the index go down, the index goes down. Because an index mutual fund is a mirror image of a specific index, the dollar value of a share in an index fund also increases or decreases when the index increases or decreases. To help evaluate different mutual funds, investors can use the information on the Internet, from professional advisory services, from the fund's prospectus and annual report, in financial publications, and in newspapers.

Objective 4 The advantages and disadvantages of mutual funds have made mutual funds the investment of choice for many investors. For $250 to $3,000 or more, you can open an account and begin investing. The shares of a closed-end fund or exchange-traded fund are bought and sold on organized stock exchanges or the over-the-counter market. The shares of an open-end fund may be purchased through a salesperson who is authorized to sell them, through an account executive of a brokerage firm, from a mutual fund supermarket, or from the investment company that sponsors the fund. The shares in an open-end fund can be sold to the investment company that sponsors the fund. Shareholders in mutual funds can receive a return in one of three ways: income dividends, capital gain distributions when the fund buys and sells securities in the fund's portfolio at a profit, and capital gains when the shareholder sells shares in the mutual fund at a higher price than the price paid. Income dividends, capital gain distributions, and capital gains are subject to taxation. A number of purchase and withdrawal options are available for mutual fund investors.

Key Terms

capital gain distributions 450
closed-end fund 431
contingent deferred sales load 434
exchange-traded fund (ETF) 431
expense ratio 435

family of funds 440
income dividends 450
load fund 434
mutual fund 428
net asset value (NAV) 433

no-load fund 434
open-end fund 433
reinvestment plan 454
turnover ratio 452
12b-1 fee 435

Key Formulas

Page	Topic	Formula
433	Net asset value	$\text{Net asset value} = \dfrac{\text{Value of the fund's portfolio} - \text{Liabilities}}{\text{Number of shares outstanding}}$
451	Total return	Income dividends + Capital gain distributions + Changes in share value when sold Dollar amount of total return
451	Percent of total return	$\text{Percent of total return} = \dfrac{\text{Dollar amount of total return}}{\text{Original cost of your investment}}$

Self-Test Problems

1. Two years ago, Mary Applegate's mutual fund portfolio was worth $410,000. Now, because of the recent economic crisis, the total value of her investment portfolio has decreased to $296,000. Even though she has lost a significant amount of money, she has not changed her investment holdings, which consist of either aggressive growth funds or growth funds.

   a. How much money has Ms. Applegate lost in the last two years?
   b. Given the above information, calculate the percentage of lost value.
   c. What actions would you take to get her investment back in shape if you were Mary Applegate?

2. Twelve months ago, Gene Peterson purchased 400 shares in the no-load Black Rock Equity Dividend I fund—a Morningstar 5-star fund that seeks long-term total return and current income. His rationale for choosing this fund was that he wanted a fund that was conservative and highly rated. Each share in the fund cost $18.60. At the end of the year, he received dividends of $0.11 a share and a capital gain distribution of $0.08 a share. At the end of 12 months, the shares in the fund were selling for $12.18.

   a. How much did Mr. Peterson invest in this fund?
   b. At the end of 12 months, what is the total return for this fund?
   c. What is the percentage of total return?
   d. Despite the fact that this fund is a 5-star fund, it decreased in value. What factors led to the decrease in value?

Solutions

1. a. Dollar loss = $410,000 Value two years ago − $296,000 Current value
      = $114,000

   b. Percent of dollar loss = $114,000/$410,000 Value two years ago
      = 0.278 = 27.8 percent

   c. While Ms. Applegate has several options, any decision should be based on careful research and evaluation. First, she could do nothing. While she has lost a substantial portion of her investment portfolio ($114,000, or 27.8 percent), it may be time to hold on to her investments if she believes the economy is improving. Second, she could sell (or exchange) some or all of her shares in the aggressive growth or growth funds and move her money into more conservative money market or government bond funds, or even certificates of deposit. Finally, she could buy more shares if she believes the economy is beginning to improve. Because of depressed prices for quality funds, this may be a real buying opportunity. Deciding which option for Ms. Applegate to take may depend on the economic conditions at the time you answer this question.

2. a. Total investment = Price per share × Number of shares
      = $18.60 × 400 = $7,440

   b. Income dividends = $0.11 Dividend per share × 400 shares = $44.00
      Capital gain distributions = $0.08 capital gain distribution × 400 shares = $32
      Change in share value = $18.60 beginning value − $12.18 ending value = $6.42 (loss)
      Total decline in value = $6.42 loss per share × 400 shares = $2,568 (loss)
      Total return = $ 44 Income dividends
                      + $ 32 Capital gain distributions
                      − $2,568 Total decline in value
                      ($2,492 loss) Dollar amount of total return

   c. Percent of dollar loss = $\dfrac{\$2,492 \text{ loss}}{\$7,440 \text{ invesment (loss of negative amount)}}$

      = 0.335 = 33.5 percent

   d. Even a fund with a 5-star Morningstar rating is not guaranteed to increase in value. Ratings are just one piece of the puzzle, and other factors should be considered when evaluating a fund. For example, the economic crisis undoubtedly could be a major reason why this fund decreased in value over this 12-month period. While it would be nice to have a positive total return at the end of every 12-month period, investors are not guaranteed dividend income, capital gain distributions, or increasing share values—especially during an economic crisis.

Problems

1. Given the following information, calculate the net asset value for the Boston Equity mutual fund: (Obj. 1)
   Total assets, $225,000,000
   Total liabilities, 5,000,000
   Total number of shares, 4,400,000

2. The Western Capital Growth mutual fund has
   Total assets, $750,000,000
   Total liabilities, 7,200,000
   Total number of shares, 24,000,000
   What is the fund's net asset value (NAV)? (Obj. 1)

3. Jan Throng invested $15,000 in the AIM Charter Mutual Fund. The fund charges a 5.50 percent commission when shares are purchased. Calculate the amount of commission Jan must pay. (Obj. 1)

4. As Bill Salvatore approached retirement, he decided the time had come to invest some of his nest egg in a conservative bond fund. He chose the American Century Municipal Bond Fund. If he invests $80,000 and the fund charges a 4.50 percent load when shares are purchased, what is the amount of commission that Bill must pay? (Obj. 1)

5. Mary Canfield purchased the New Dimensions Global Growth Fund. This fund doesn't charge a front-end load, but it does charge a contingent deferred sales load of 4 percent for any withdrawals during the first five years. If Mary withdraws $6,000 during the second year, how much is the contingent deferred sales load? (Obj. 1)

6. Mike Jackson invested a total of $8,500 in the ABC Mutual Fund. The management fee for this particular fund is 0.70 percent of the total asset value. Calculate the management fee Mike must pay this year. (Obj. 1)

7. Betty and James Holloway invested $34,000 in the Financial Vision Social Responsibility Fund. The management fee for this fund is 0.60 percent of the total asset value. Calculate the management fee the Holloways must pay. (Obj. 1)

8. As part of his 401(k) retirement plan at work, Ken Lowery invests 5 percent of his salary each month in the Capital Investments Lifecycle Fund. At the end of the year, Ken's 401(k) account has a dollar value of $21,800. If the fund charges a 12b-1 fee of 0.80 percent, what is the amount of the fee? (Obj. 1)

9. When Jill Thompson received a large settlement from an automobile accident, she chose to invest $120,000 in the Vanguard 500 Index Fund. This fund has an expense ratio of 0.18 percent. What is the amount of the fees that Jill will pay this year? (Obj. 1)

10. The Yamaha Aggressive Growth Fund has a 2.13 percent expense ratio. (Obj. 1)

    a. If you invest $25,000 in this fund, what is the dollar amount of fees that you would pay this year?
    b. Based on the information in this chapter and your own research, is this a low, average, or high expense ratio?

11. Jason Mathews purchased 250 shares of the Hodge & Mattox Energy fund. Each share cost $13.66. Fifteen months later, he decided to sell his shares when the share value reached $17.10. (Obj. 4)

    a. What the amount of his total investment?
    b. What was the total amount Mr. Mathews received when he sold his shares in the Hodge & Mattox fund?
    c. How much profit did he make on his investment?

12. Three years ago, James Matheson bought 200 shares of a mutual fund for $21 a share. During the three-year period, he received total income dividends of 0.70 per share. He also received total capital gain distributions of $1.40 per share. At the end of three years, he sold his shares for $25 a share. What was his total return for this investment? (Obj.4)

13. Assume that one year ago, you bought 100 shares of a mutual fund for $15 a share, you received a $0.55 per-share capital gain distribution during the past 12 months, and the market value of the fund is now $17 a share. (Obj.4)

   a. Calculate the total return for your $1,500 investment.
   b. Calculate the percentage of total return for your $1,500 investment.

14. Over a three-year period, LaKeisha Thompson purchased shares in the Oakmark I Fund. Using the following information, answer the questions that follow. You may want to review the concept of dollar cost averaging in Chapter 12 before completing this problem. (Obj. 4)

Year	Investment Amount	Price per Share	Number of Shares*
February 2007	$1,500	$45.80	
February 2008	$1,500	$37.70	
February 2009	$1,500	$23.30	

*Carry your answer to two decimal places.

   a. At the end of three years, what is the total amount invested?
   b. At the end of three years, what is the total number of shares purchased?
   c. At the end of three years, what is the average cost for each share?

Questions

1. For many investors, mutual funds have become the investment of choice. In your own words, describe why investors purchase mutual funds. (Obj. 1)

2. Describe the type of fees that you would pay to purchase a load fund. What annual fees would you typically pay for your mutual fund investment? (Obj. 1).

3. This chapter explored a number of different classifications of mutual funds. (Obj. 2)

   a. Based on your age and current financial situation, which type of mutual fund seems appropriate for your investment needs? Explain your answer.
   b. As people get closer to retirement, their investment goals often change. Assume you are now 45 and have accumulated $110,000 in a retirement account. In this situation, what type of mutual funds would your choose? Why?
   c. Assume you are now 60 years of age and have accumulated $400,000 in a retirement account. Also assume you would like to retire when you are 65. What type of mutual funds would you choose to help you reach your investment goals? Why?

4. Choose either the AIM Charter (symbol CHTRX) mutual fund or the Fidelity Fifty (symbol FFTYX) mutual fund. Then describe how each of the following sources of information could help you evaluate one of these funds. (Obj. 3)

   a. The Internet.
   b. Professional advisory services.
   c. The fund's prospectus.
   d. The fund's annual report.
   e. Financial publications.
   f. Newspapers.

5. Visit the Yahoo! Finance Web site and evaluate one of the following mutual funds. To complete this activity, follow these steps: (Obj. 3)

   a. Go to http://finance.yahoo.com.
   b. Choose one of the following three funds, enter its symbol, and click on the "Get Quotes" button: Oppenheimer Balanced (OPASX), Janus Enterprise fund (JAENX), and American Funds Washington Mutual fund (AWSHX).

c. Print out the information for the mutual fund that you chose to evaluate.

d. Based on the information included in this research report, would you invest in this fund? Explain your answer.

6. Obtain a mutual fund prospectus to determine the options you can use to purchase and redeem shares. (Obj. 4)

a. Which purchase option would appeal to you? Why?

b. Assuming you are now of retirement age, which withdrawal option would appeal to you?

Case in Point

RESEARCH INFORMATION AVAILABLE FROM MORNINGSTAR

This chapter stressed the importance of evaluating potential investments. Now it is your turn to try your skill at evaluating a potential investment in the T. Rowe Price Equity Income Fund. Assume you could invest $10,000 in shares of this fund. To help you evaluate this potential investment, carefully examine Exhibit 13–5 , which reproduces the Morningstar research report for the T. Rowe Price Equity Income Fund. The report was published December 6, 2008.

Questions

1. Based on the research provided by Morningstar, would you buy shares in the T. Rowe Price Equity Income Stock Fund? Justify your answer.

2. What other investment information would you need to evaluate this fund? Where would you obtain this information?

3. On February 13, 2009, shares in the T. Rowe Price Equity Income Fund were selling for $14.86 per share. Using the Internet or a newspaper, determine the current price for a share of this fund. Based on this information, would your investment have been profitable? (*Hint:* The symbol for this fund is PRFDX.)

4. Assuming you purchased shares in the T. Rowe Price Equity Income Fund on February 13, 2009, and based on your answer to question 3, how would you decide if you want to hold or sell your shares? Explain your answer.

Continuing Case

Vikki and Tim Treble (ages 50 and 52) have been busy cleaning out Tim's parents' house since his mom passed away and his dad moved to an apartment complex for seniors. Their daughter, Molly (age 20), and their 13 year old twins, Caleb and Tyler, are helping out and setting aside keepsakes from their grandparents. The extra furniture and knick knacks will be sold in an estate sale. Tim met with his father and his parents' attorney to discuss his mother's will. He was surprised and touched to learn that his parents, living frugally, had amassed a portfolio to allow Vikki and Tim a $175,000 inheritance.

Vikki and Tim decide this is a good time to sit down with a financial planner to discuss their goals for investing the inheritance. They want to use $100,000 to boost the college savings for all three children, and, in accordance with the stipulations of the will, they plan to save $75,000 to distribute equally among their children as each reaches the age of 25.

Vikki and Tim want to invest this inheritance wisely to be able to meet their objectives. Their financial statistics are shown below:

Assets:

Checking/savings account $25,000

Emergency fund $25,000

House $385,000

Cars $3,000 and $28,000

Household possessions $25,000

401(k) balance $167,000 (Vikki), $305,000 (Tim)

College savings $57,000

Life insurance cash value $33,000

Liabilities:

Mortgage $108,000

Car loan $14,000

Income:

Gross Salary:

$25,000 per year (Vikki), $131,000 (Tim)

After-tax monthly salary:

$1,458 (Vikki), $7,641 (Tim)

Monthly Expenses:
Mortgage $1,200
Property tax/Insurance $700
Daily living expenses (including utilities, food, child expenses) $4,500
Car loan $450
Entertainment/vacations $400

Gas/repairs $500
Term & whole life insurance $400

Savings:
401(k) 8% of gross monthly salary
College savings $600

Questions:

1. How can Vikki and Tim use mutual funds or ETFs to meet their goals?
2. What concerns might they have about loads or other fees?
3. How can we tell if Vikki and Tim are well diversified?
4. What types of mutual funds would you recommend for Vikki and Tim at this stage in their life? Would you recommend the same funds for their college financing goals and their retirement goals? What type of mutual fund should they choose for their inheritance money?
5. How can they use *Your Personal Financial Plan* sheets 40–41?

Spending Diary

"I MUST CHOOSE BETWEEN SPENDING MONEY ON SOMETHING NOW OR INVESTING FOR THE FUTURE."

Directions

Monitoring your daily spending will allow you to better consider financial planning alternatives. You will have better information and the potential for better control if you use your spending information for making wiser choices. The Daily Spending Diary sheets are located in Appendix C at the end of the book and on the student Web site at www.mhhe.com/kdh.

Questions

1. Are there any spending items that you might consider revising to allow you to increase the amount you invest?

2. Based on your investment goals and the amount available to invest, what types of mutual funds would you consider?

Evaluating Mutual Fund Investment Information

Financial Planning Activities: To identify and assess the value of various sources of information about funds, obtain samples of several items of information that you might consider to guide you in your investment decisions.

Suggested Web Sites: www.morningstar.com   www.kiplinger.com

Criteria Evaluation	Item 1	Item 2	Item 3
Name location, and phone			
Web site			
Overview of information provided (main features)			
Cost, if any			
Ease of access			
Evaluation • Reliablility • Clarity • Value of information compared to cost			

What's Next for Your Personal Financial Plan?

• Talk with friends and relatives to determine what sources of information they use to evaluate mutual funds.
• Choose one source of information and describe how the information could help you obtain your investment goals.

Name: _____ Date: _____

Evaluation of a Mutual Fund

Financial Planning Activities: No checklist can serve as a foolproof guide for choosing a mutual fund. However, the following questions will help you evaluate a potential investment in a specific fund. Use mutual fund Web sites and/or library materials to answer these questions about a mutual fund that you believe could help you obtain your investment goals.

Suggested Web Sites: www.morningstar.com   http://finance.yahoo.com

Category 1: Fund Characteristics

1. What is the fund's name?
   _____

2. What is this fund's Morningstar rating?
   _____

3. What is the minimum investment?
   _____

4. Does the fund allow telephone or Internet exchanges? ☐ Yes ☐ No

5. Is there a fee for exchanges? ☐ Yes ☐ No

Category 2: Costs

6. Is there a front-end load charge? If so, how much is it?
   _____

7. Is there a redemption fee? If so, how much is it?
   _____

8. How much is the annual management fee?
   _____

9. Is there a 12b-1 fee? If so, how much is it?
   _____

10. What is the fund's expense ratio?
    _____

Category 3: Diversification

11. What is the fund's objective?
    _____

12. What types of securities does the fund's portfolio include?
    _____

13. How many different securities does the fund's portfolio include?
    _____

14. How many types of industries does the fund's portfolio include?
    _____

15. What are the fund's five largest holdings?
    _____

Category 4: Fund Performance

16. How long has the fund manager been with the fund?
    _____

17. How would you describe the fund's performance over the past 12 months?
    _____

18. How would you describe the fund's performance over the past five years?
    _____

19. How would you describe the fund's performance over the past 10 years?
    _____

20. What is the current net asset value for this fund?
    _____

21. What is the high net asset value for this fund over the last 12 months?
    _____

22. What is the low net asset value for this fund over the last 12 months?
    _____

23. What do the experts say about this fund?
    _____

Category 5: Conclusion

24. Based on the above information, do you think an investment in this fund will help you achieve your investment goals? ☐ Yes ☐ No

25. Explain your answer to question 24.

A Word of Caution

When you use a checklist, there is always a danger of overlooking important relevant information. This checklist is not a cure-all, but it does provide some very sound questions that you should answer before making a mutual fund investment decision. Quite simply, it is a place to start. If you need other information, *you* are responsible for obtaining it and for determining how it affects your potential investment.

What's Next for Your Personal Financial Plan?

- Identify additional factors that may affect your decision to invest in this fund.
- Develop a plan for monitoring an investment's value once a mutual fund(s) is purchased.

14 Retirement and Estate Planning

Getting Personal

What are your attitudes toward retirement and estate planning? For each of the following statements, select "agree" or "disagree" to indicate your behavior regarding the following statements:

	Agree	Disagree
1. I have plenty of time to start saving for retirement.	____	____
2. My living expenses will drop when I retire.	____	____
3. I can depend on Social Security and my company pension to pay for my retirement living expenses.	____	____
4. Since I am not married now, I don't need a will.	____	____
5. I believe estate planning is only for the rich and famous.	____	____
6. I can free myself from managing my assets by setting up a trust.	____	____

After studying this chapter, you will be asked to reconsider your responses to these questions.

OBJECTIVE 1

Analyze your current assets and liabilities for retirement and estimate your retirement living costs.

Planning for Retirement: Start Early

Your retirement years may seem a long way off right now. However, the fact is, it's never too early to start planning for retirement. Planning can help you cope with sudden changes that may occur in your life and give you a sense of control over your future.

Your Personal Financial Plan Sheets

Objectives

In this chapter, you will learn to:

1. Analyze your current assets and liabilities for retirement and estimate your retirement living costs.
2. Determine your planned retirement income and develop a balanced budget based on your retirement income.
3. Analyze the personal and legal aspects of estate planning.
4. Distinguish among various types of wills and trusts.

Why is this important?

While Social Security replaces about 30 percent of the average worker's preretirement earnings, most financial advisers suggest that you will need 70 to 90 percent of preretirement earnings to live comfortably. Even with a company pension, you will still need to save.

According to a recent American Association of Retired Persons (AARP) survey, over 40 percent of Americans age 45 or older have not drawn up a will. Creating an effective estate plan will allow you to prosper during retirement and provide for your loved ones when you die.

If you haven't done any research on the subject of retirement, you may hold some outdated beliefs about your "golden years." Some common mistaken beliefs include:

- You have plenty of time to start saving for retirement.
- Saving just a little bit won't help.

- You'll spend less money when you retire.
- Your retirement will only last about 15 years.
- You can depend on Social Security and a company pension plan to pay your basic living expenses.
- Your pension benefits will increase to keep pace with inflation.
- Your employer's health insurance plan and Medicare will cover all your medical expenses when you retire.

Some of these statements were once true but are no longer true today. You may live for many years after you retire. If you want your retirement to be a happy and comfortable time of your life, you'll need enough money to suit your lifestyle. You can't count on others to provide for you. That's why you need to start planning and saving as early as possible. It's never too late to start saving for retirement, but the sooner you start, the better off you'll be. (See Exhibit 14–1.)

Example

Suppose that you want to have at least $1 million when you retire at age 65. If you start saving for retirement at age 25, you can meet that goal by putting about $127 per month into investment funds that grow at a rate of about 11 percent each year. If you wait until you're 50, the monthly amount skyrockets to $2,244.

Key Web Sites for Retirement Planning

www.isrplan.org/

www.asec.org

As you think about your retirement years, consider your long-range goals. What does retirement mean to you? Maybe it will simply be a time to stop working, sit back, and relax. Perhaps you imagine traveling the world, developing a hobby, or starting a second career. Where do you want to live after you retire? What type of lifestyle would you like to have? Once you've pondered these questions, your first step in retirement planning is to determine your current financial situation. That requires you to analyze your current assets and liabilities.

Conducting a Financial Analysis

As you learned in Chapter 2, an asset is any item of value that you own—cash, property, personal possessions, and investments—including cash in checking and savings accounts, a house, a car, a television, and so on. It also includes the current value of any stocks, bonds, and other investments that you may have as well as the current value of any life insurance and pension funds.

Your liabilities, on the other hand, are the debts you owe: the remaining balance on a mortgage or automobile loan, credit card balances, unpaid taxes, and so on. If you subtract your liabilities from your assets, you get your net worth. Ideally, your net worth should increase each year as you move closer to retirement.

It's a good idea to review your assets on a regular basis. You may need to make adjustments in your saving, spending, and investment in order to stay on track. As you review your assets, consider the following factors: housing, life insurance, and other investments. Each will have an important effect on your retirement income.

HOUSING   A house will probably be your most valuable asset. However, if you buy a home with a large mortgage that prevents you from saving, you put your ability to meet your retirement goal at risk. In that case you might consider buying a smaller, less

Exhibit **14–1**   Tackling the Trade-Offs: Saving Now versus Saving Later

Get an early start on your plan for retirement.

	SAVER ABE (THE EARLY SAVER)				SAVER BEN (THE LATE SAVER)		
Age	Years	Contributions	Year-End Value	Age	Years	Contributions	Year-End Value
25	1	$ 2,000	$ 2,188	25	1	$ 0	$ 0
26	2	2,000	4,580	26	2	0	0
27	3	2,000	7,198	27	3	0	0
28	4	2,000	10,061	28	4	0	0
29	5	2,000	13,192	29	5	0	0
30	6	2,000	16,617	30	6	0	0
31	7	2,000	20,363	31	7	0	0
32	8	2,000	24,461	32	8	0	0
33	9	2,000	28,944	33	9	0	0
34	10	2,000	33,846	34	10	0	0
35	11	0	37,021	35	11	2,000	2,188
36	12	0	40,494	36	12	2,000	4,580
37	13	0	44,293	37	13	2,000	7,198
38	14	0	48,448	38	14	2,000	10,061
39	15	0	52,992	39	15	2,000	13,192
40	16	0	57,963	40	16	2,000	16,617
41	17	0	63,401	41	17	2,000	20,363
42	18	0	69,348	42	18	2,000	24,461
43	19	0	75,854	43	19	2,000	28,944
44	20	0	82,969	44	20	2,000	33,846
45	21	0	90,752	45	21	2,000	39,209
46	22	0	99,265	46	22	2,000	45,075
47	23	0	108,577	47	23	2,000	51,490
48	24	0	118,763	48	24	2,000	58,508
49	25	0	129,903	49	25	2,000	66,184
50	26	0	142,089	50	26	2,000	74,580
51	27	0	155,418	51	27	2,000	83,764
52	28	0	169,997	52	28	2,000	93,809
53	29	0	185,944	53	29	2,000	104,797
54	30	0	203,387	54	30	2,000	116,815
55	31	0	222,466	55	31	2,000	129,961
56	32	0	243,335	56	32	2,000	144,340
57	33	0	266,162	57	33	2,000	160,068
58	34	0	291,129	58	34	2,000	177,271
59	35	0	318,439	59	35	2,000	196,088
60	36	0	348,311	60	36	2,000	216,670
61	37	0	380,985	61	37	2,000	239,182
62	38	0	416,724	62	38	2,000	263,807
63	39	0	455,816	63	39	2,000	290,741
64	40	0	498,574	64	40	2,000	320,202
65	41	0	545,344	65	41	2,000	352,427
		$20,000				$62,000	
Value at retirement*			$545,344	Value at retirement*			$352,427
Less total contributions			−20,000	Less total contributions			−62,000
Net earnings			$525,344	Net earnings			$290,427

*The table assumes a 9 percent fixed rate of return, compounded monthly, and no fluctuation of the principal. Distributions from an IRA are subject to ordinary income taxes when withdrawn and may be subject to other limitations under IRA rules.

SOURCE: *The Franklin investor* (San Mateo, CA: Franklin Distributors Inc., January 1989).

expensive place to live. Remember that a smaller house is usually easier and cheaper to maintain. You can use the money you save to increase your retirement fund.

LIFE INSURANCE At some point in the future, you may buy life insurance to provide financial support for your children in case you die while they are still young. As you near retirement, though, your children will probably be self-sufficient. When that time comes, you might reduce your premium payments by decreasing your life insurance coverage. This would give you extra money to spend on living expenses or to invest for additional income.

OTHER INVESTMENTS When you review your assets, you'll also want to evaluate any other investments you have. When you originally chose these investments, you may have been more interested in making your money grow than in getting an early return from them. When you are ready to retire, however, you may want to use the income from those investments to help cover living expenses instead of reinvesting it.

Estimating Retirement Living Expenses

Next you should estimate how much money you'll need to live comfortably during your retirement years. (See the nearby Personal Finance in Practice feature.) You can't predict exactly how much money you'll need when you retire. You can, however, estimate what your basic needs will be. To do this, you'll have to think about your spending patterns and how your living situation will change when you retire. For instance, you probably will spend more money on recreation, health insurance, and medical care in retirement than you do now. At the same time, you may spend less on transportation and clothing. Your federal income taxes may be lower. Also, some income from various retirement plans may be taxed at a lower rate or not at all. As you consider your retirement living expenses, remember to plan for emergencies. Look at Exhibit 14–2 for an example of retirement spending patterns.

Exhibit 14–2

How an "Average" Older (65+) Household Spends Its Money
Retired families spend a greater share of their income for food, housing, and medical care than nonretired families.

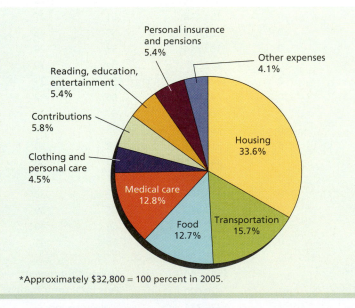

*Approximately $32,800 = 100 percent in 2005.

SOURCE: U.S. Bureau of Labor Statistics.

Personal Finance in Practice

> Your Retirement Housing

The place where you choose to live during retirement can have a significant impact on your financial needs. Use vacations in the years before you retire to explore areas you think you might enjoy. If you find a place you really like, go there at different times of the year. That way you'll know what the climate is like. Meet people who live in the area and learn about activities, transportation, and taxes.

Consider the downside of moving to a new location. You may find yourself stuck in a place you really don't like after all. Moving can also be expensive and emotionally draining. You may miss your children, your grandchildren, and the friends and relatives you leave behind. Be realistic about what you'll have to give up as well as what you'll gain if you move after you retire.

AVOIDING RETIREMENT RELOCATION PITFALLS

Some retired people move to the location of their dreams and then discover that they've made a big mistake financially. Here are some tips from retirement specialists on how to uncover hidden taxes and other costs before you move to a new area:

- Contact the local chamber of commerce to get details on area property taxes and the local economy.

- Contact the state tax department to find out about income, sales, and inheritance taxes as well as special exemptions for retirees.

- Read the Sunday edition of the local newspaper of the city where you're thinking of moving.

- Check with local utility companies to get estimates on energy costs.

- Visit the area in different seasons, and talk to local residents about the various costs of living.

- Rent for a while instead of buying a home immediately.

What are your findings?

_____

_____

Don't forget to take inflation into account. Estimate high when calculating how much the prices of goods and services will rise by the time you retire (see Exhibit 14–3). Even a 3 percent rate of inflation will cause prices to double every 24 years.

Exhibit 14–3

The Effects of Inflation over Time

This chart shows you what $10,000 today will be worth in 10, 20, and 30 years assuming a fairly conservative 4 percent rate of inflation.

The prices of goods and services rarely remain the same for any significant period of time because of inflation. *How much will $10,000 be worth in 30 years, assuming a 4 percent rate of inflation? What can you do to counteract the effects of inflation?*

471

CONCEPT CHECK 14–1

1 The three assets you should review on a regular basis during retirement are:

_____

_____

2 What expenses are likely to increase during retirement?

_____

_____

3 What expenses are likely to decrease during retirement?

_____

_____

Apply Yourself!

Objective 1

Survey friends, relatives, and other people to get their views on retirement planning. Prepare a written report of your findings.

Your Retirement Income

OBJECTIVE 2

Determine your planned retirement income and develop a balanced budget based on your retirement income.

The four major sources of retirement income are employer pension plans, public pension plans, personal retirement plans, and annuities.

Employer Pension Plans

A pension plan is a retirement plan that is funded, at least in part, by an employer. With this type of plan, your employer contributes to your retirement benefits, and sometimes you contribute too. (See the nearby Figure It Out feature.) These contributions and earnings remain tax-deferred until you start to withdraw them in retirement.

Private employer pension plans vary. If the company you work for offers one, you should know when you become eligible to receive pension benefits. You'll also need to know what benefits you'll receive. Ask these questions during your interview with a prospective employer and start participating in the plan as soon as possible. (Read the accompanying *Kiplingers* Personal Finance Feature.) Most employer plans are one of two basic types: defined-contribution plans or defined-benefit plans.

defined-contribution plan A plan—profit sharing, money purchase, Keogh, or 401(k)—that provides an individual account for each participant; also called an *individual account plan.*

DEFINED-CONTRIBUTION PLAN A **defined-contribution plan,** sometimes called an *individual account plan,* consists of an individual account of each employee to which the employer contributes a specific amount annually. This type of retirement

Figure It Out!

> Saving for Retirement

Calculate how much you would have in 10 years if you saved $2,000 a year at an annual compound interest rate of 10 percent, with the company contributing $500 a year.

	Contributions	10% Interest	Total
Annual contribution of 10% of a $20,000 salary	$2,000.00		
Company annual contribution matching $0.50 of 5% of the salary	500.00		
1st Year			
2nd Year			
3rd Year			
4th Year			
5th Year			
6th Year			
7th Year			
8th Year			
9th Year			
10th Year			
Total			

plan does not guarantee any particular benefit. When you retire and become eligible for benefits, you simply receive the total amount of funds (including investment earnings) that have been placed in your account.

Several types of defined-contribution plans exist. With a money-purchase plan, your employer promises to set aside a certain amount of money for you each year. The amount is generally a percentage of your earnings. Under a stock bonus plan, your employer's contribution is used to buy stock in the company for you. The stock is usually held in trust until you retire. Then you can either keep your shares or sell them. Under a profit-sharing plan, you employer's contribution depends on the company's profits.

In a **401(k) plan,** also known as a *salary-reduction plan,* you set aside a portion of your salary from each paycheck to be deducted from your gross pay and placed in a special account. Your employer will often match your contribution up to a specific dollar amount or percentage of your salary. For example, as one of the retirement benefits, the McGraw-Hill Companies (the publisher of your textbook) offers its employees a 401(k) savings plan. Under this plan, employees

401(k) plan A plan under which employees can defer current taxation on a portion of their salary; also called a *salary-reduction plan.*

did you know?

Many employers, including Federal Express, Eastman Kodak, General Motors, Frontier Airlines, Motorola, Sears, and Unisys, have suspended their matching contributions to employee 401(k) plans.

WHEN YOU'RE LEFT OUT IN THE COLD

When some of the country's biggest employers and industry trade associations pleaded with Congress for temporary funding relief, several key unions and employee groups supported their request, hoping it would prevent companies from freezing their pension plans. (A pension freeze means employees keep the retirement benefits they have already earned but do not accrue any further benefits. That minimizes employers' future costs, but it doesn't relieve them from having to make up current shortfalls in the plan's funding.) But pension freezes seem to be picking up steam since last year's stock-market meltdown.

More than a dozen major corporations, from aircraft-manufacturing giant Boeing to publishing icon Random House, have announced pension freezes effective this year. Because a freeze reduces future retirement benefits for employees, companies often introduce a new 401(k) plan or enhance their existing plan by boosting employer contributions.

That can be a boon for younger workers. Most of them probably wouldn't stick around long enough to benefit from a traditional defined-benefit plan, which typically generates the greatest benefits toward the end of a long career. And older workers nearing retirement are often unscathed by pension freezes because they have already accrued the bulk of their benefits, which are based on a formula that includes years of service and the average of your highest three or five years of salary.

But for mid-career workers in their fifties, a pension freeze can be devastating. Future raises and years of service won't be factored into their pension calculation, causing them to miss out on the most lucrative part of the back-loaded retirement benefit. And they have less time to make up the loss by saving in a 401(k).

For example, the Center for Retirement Research at Boston College found that a pension for an employee who joins a company's pension plan at age 35 and continues to earn benefits until he retires at 62 would replace about 43% of his final earnings. But if the pension is frozen when the employee is 50 and replaced with a 401(k), the worker's retirement-income replacement rate drops to just 28% of final earnings. Even with 401(k) enhancements, retirement benefits decline.

In both cases, Social Security benefits would supplement retirement income. But the worker whose pension was frozen would have to rely more heavily on personal savings to maintain his preretirement income or cut expenses after he leaves his job. Plus, the investment risk shifts from employer to retiree. What can you do? Financial planner David Kudla says you should focus on the things you can control, such as contributions to your 401(k) and other personal savings. Although he sympathizes with retirement savers who may want to walk away from the stock market forever, he says that's "wrong thinking at the wrong time for long-term investors."

SOURCE: Reprinted by permission from the March issue of *Kiplinger's Personal Finance*. Copyright © 2009 The Kiplinger Washington Editors, Inc.

1. When employers and industry-trade associations pleaded with Congress for funding relief, why did several key unions and employee groups support their request?

_____

2. Why have many major corporations announced pension freezes effective in 2009?

_____

3. Why can a pension freeze for midcareer workers in their fifties be devastating?

_____

4. What is financial planner David Kudla's advice about your 401(k)s and other personal savings?

_____

can contribute up to 25 percent of their pay with a maximum contribution limit of $16,500 in 2009. The company matches up to 4.5 percent of the first 6 percent of the employee's pretax contributions.

The funds in 401(k) plans are invested in stocks, bonds, and mutual funds. As a result you can accumulate a significant amount of money in this type of account if you begin contributing to it early in your career. In addition, the money that accumulates in your 401(k) plan is tax-deferred, meaning that you don't have to pay taxes on it until you withdraw it.

If you're employed by a tax-exempt institution, such as a hospital or a nonprofit organization, the salary-reduction plan is called a Section 403(b) plan. As in 401(k) plan, the funds in a 403(b) plan are tax-deferred. The amount that can be contributed annually to 401(k) and 403(b) plans is limited by law, as is the amount of annual contributions to money-purchase plans, stock bonus plans, and profit-sharing plans.

Employee contributions to a pension plan belong to you, the employee, regardless of the amount of time that you are with a particular employer. What happens to the contributions that the employer has made to your account if you change jobs and move to another company before you retire? One of the most important aspects of such plans is vesting. **Vesting** is the right to receive the employer's pension plan contributions that you've gained, even if you leave the company before retiring. After a certain number of years with the company, you will become *fully vested,* or entitled to receive 100 percent of the company's contributions to the plan on your behalf. Under some plans, vesting may occur in stages. For example, you might become eligible to receive 20 percent of your benefits after three years and gain another 20 percent each year until you are fully vested.

vesting An employee's right to at least a portion of the benefits accrued under an employer pension plan, even if the employee leaves the company before retiring.

DEFINED-BENEFIT PLAN Λ **defined-benefit plan** specifies the benefits you'll receive at retirement age, based on your total earnings and years on the job. The plan does not specify how much the employer must contribute each year. Instead your employer's contributions are based on how much money will be needed in the fund as each participant in the plan retires. If the fund is inadequate, the employer will have to make additional contributions.

defined-benefit plan Λ plan that specifies the benefits the employee will receive at the normal retirement age.

CARRYING BENEFITS FROM ONE PLAN TO ANOTHER Some pension plans allow *portability,* which means that you can carry earned benefits from one pension plan to another when you change jobs. Workers are also protected by the Employee Retirement Income Security Act of 1974 (ERISA), which sets minimum standards for pensions plans. Under this act the federal government insures part of the payments promised by defined-benefit plans.

Public Pension Plans

Another source of retirement income is Social Security, a public pension plan established by the U.S. government in 1935. The government agency that manages the program is called the Social Security Administration.

SOCIAL SECURITY Social Security is an important source of retirement income for most Americans. The program covers 97 percent of all workers, and almost one out of every six Americans currently collects some

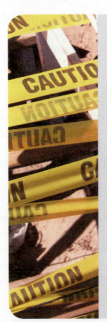

CAUTION! This chart shows the percentage of final earnings Social Security is estimated to replace. Will you have enough to make up the difference?

Your Retirement "Gap"		
Preretirement Salary	Percent of income replaced by Social Security	The "Gap" You and Your Employer Must Fill
$20,000	45%	35%
30,000	40	40
40,000	33	47
60,000	25	55
$100,000	15	65

Source: TIAA-CREF.

form of Social Security benefit. Social Security is actually a package of protection that provides benefits to retirees, survivors, and disabled persons. The package protects you and your family while you are working and after you retire. Nevertheless, you should not rely on Social Security to cover all of your retirement expenses. Social Security was never intended to provide 100 percent of your retirement income.

Who Is Eligible for Social Security Benefits?   The amount of retirement benefits you receive from Social Security is based on your earnings over the years. The more you work and the higher your earnings, the greater your benefits, up to a certain maximum amount.

The Social Security Administration provides you an annual history of your earnings and an estimate of your future monthly benefits. The statement includes an estimate, in today's dollars, of how much you will get each month from Social Security when you retire—at age 62, 65, or 70—based on your earnings to date and your projected future earnings.

To qualify for retirement benefits you must earn a certain number of credits. These credits are based on the length of time you work and pay into the system through the Social Security tax, or contribution, on your earnings. You and your employer pay equal amounts of the Social Security tax. Your credits are calculated on a quarterly basis. The number of quarters you need depends on your year of birth. People born after 1928 need 40 quarters to qualify for benefits.

Certain dependents of a worker may receive benefits under the Social Security program. They include a wife or dependent husband aged 62 or older; unmarried children under 18 (or under 19 if they are full-time students no higher than grade 12); and unmarried, disabled children aged 18 or older. Widows or widowers can receive Social Security benefits earlier.

did you know?

Estimated average monthly Social Security benefit payable to retirees in 2009 was $1,153.

Social Security Retirement Benefits   Most people can begin collecting Social Security benefits at age 62. However, the monthly amount at age 62 will be less than it would be if the person waits until full retirement age. This reduction is permanent.

In the past, people could receive full retirement benefits at age 65. However, because of longer life expectancies, the full retirement age is being increased in gradual steps. For people born in 1960 and later, the full retirement age will be 67. If you postpone applying for benefits beyond your full retirement age, your monthly payments will increase slightly for each year you wait, but only up to age 70.

Social Security Information   For more information about Social Security, you can visit the Social Security Web site. It provides access to forms and publications and gives links to other valuable information. To learn more about the taxability of Social Security benefits, contact the Internal Revenue Service at 800-829-3676 and ask for Publication 554, *Social Security and Equivalent Railroad Retirement Benefits.*

Key Web Sites for Retirement Income

www.quicken.com/retirement

www.moneymag.com

OTHER PUBLIC PENSION PLANS   Besides Social Security, the federal government provides several other special retirement plans for federal government workers and railroad employees. Employees covered under these plans are not covered by Social Security. The Veterans Administration provides pensions for survivors of people who died while in the armed forces. It also offers disability pensions for eligible veterans. Many state and local governments provide retirement plans for their employees as well.

Personal Retirement Plans

In addition to public and employer retirement plans, many people choose to set up personal retirement plans. Such plans are especially important to self-employed people and other workers who are not covered by employer pension plans. Among the most popular personal retirement plans are individual retirement accounts (IRAs) and Keogh accounts.

INDIVIDUAL RETIREMENT ACCOUNTS An **individual retirement account (IRA)** is a special account in which the person sets aside a portion of income for retirement. Several types of IRAs are available:

- **Regular IRA:** A regular (traditional or classic) IRA lets you make annual contributions until age 70½. The contribution limit was $5,000 per year in 2009 and after ($6,000 if 50 or over). Depending on your tax filing status and income, the contribution may be fully or partially tax-deductible. The tax deductibility of a traditional IRA also depends on whether you belong to an employer-provided retirement plan.

- **Roth IRA:** Annual contributions to a Roth IRA are not tax-deductible, but the earnings accumulate tax-free. You may contribute the amounts discussed above if you're a single taxpayer with an adjusted gross income (AGI) of less than $120,000. For married couples the combined AGI must be less than $176,000. You can continue to make annual contributions to a Roth IRA even after age 70½. If you have a Roth IRA, you can withdraw money from the account tax-free and penalty-free after five years if you are at least 59½ 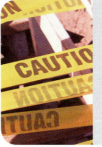 years old or plan to use the money to help buy your first home. You may convert a regular IRA to a Roth IRA. Depending on your situation, one type of account may be better for you than the other.

- **Simplified Employee Pension (SEP) Plan:** A simplified employee pension (SEP) plan, also known as a SEP IRA, is an individual retirement account funded by an employer. Each employee sets up an IRA account at a bank or other financial institution. Then the employer makes an annual contribution of up to $49,000. The employee's contributions, which can vary from year to year, are fully tax-deductible, and earnings are tax-deferred. The SEP IRA is the simplest type of retirement plan if a person is self-employed.

- **Spousal IRA:** A spousal IRA lets you make contributions on behalf of your nonworking spouse if you file a joint tax return. The contributions are the same as for the traditional and Roth IRAs. As with a traditional IRA, this contribution may be fully or partially tax-deductible, depending on your income. This also depends on whether you belong to an employer-provided retirement plan.

- **Rollover IRA:** A rollover IRA is a traditional IRA that lets you roll over, or transfer, all or a portion of your taxable distribution from a retirement plan or other IRA. You may move your money from plan to plan without paying taxes on it. To avoid taxes, however, you must follow certain rules about transferring the money from one plan to another. If you change jobs or retire before age 59½, a rollover IRA may be just what you need. It will let you avoid the penalty you would otherwise have to pay on early withdrawals.

Key Web Sites for Retirement Plans

www.financialengines.com

http://401k.com

individual retirement account (IRA) A special account in which the employee sets aside a portion of his or her income; taxes are not paid on the principal or interest until money is withdrawn from the account.

CAUTION! Withdrawals from a regular IRA prior to age 59½ may be subject to a 10 percent penalty. From a Roth IRA, contributions may be withdrawn at any age without penalty if the account has been open for five years.

- **Education IRA:** An education IRA, also known as a Coverdell Education Savings Account, is a special IRA with certain restrictions. It allows individuals to contribute up to $2,000 per year toward the education of any child under age 18. The contributions are not tax-deductible. However, they do provide tax-free distributions for education expenses. Exhibit 14–4 summarizes the various types of IRA.

Whether or not you're covered by another type of pension plan, you can still make IRA contributions that are not tax-deductible. All of the income your IRA earns will compound tax-deferred, until you begin making withdrawals. Remember, the biggest benefit of an IRA lies in its tax-deferred earnings growth. The longer the money accumulates tax-deferred, the bigger the benefit.

IRA Withdrawals   When you retire, you can withdraw the money from your IRA by one of several methods. You can take out all of the money at one time, but the entire amount will be taxed as income. If you decide to withdraw the money from your IRA in installments, you will have to pay tax only on the amount that you withdraw. A final alternative would be to place the money that you withdraw in an annuity that guarantees payments over your lifetime. See the discussion of annuities later in this section for further information about this option.

KEOGH PLANS   A **Keogh plan,** also known as an *H.R. 10 plan* or a *self-employed retirement plan,* is a retirement plan specially designed for self-employed people and their employees. Keogh plans have limits on the amount of annual tax-deductible

Keogh plan A plan in which tax-deductible contributions fund the retirement of self-employed people and their employees; also called an *H.R. 10 plan* or a *self-employed retirement plan.*

Exhibit **14–4**

Various Types of IRA

Type of IRA	IRA Features
Regular IRA	• Tax-deferred interest and earnings • Annual limit on individual contributions • Limited eligibility for tax-deductible contributions • Contributions do not reduce current taxes
Roth IRA	• Tax-deferred interest and earnings • Annual limit on individual contributions • Withdrawals are tax-free in specific cases • Contributions do not reduce current taxes
Simplified Employee Pension Plan (SEP IRA)	• "Pay yourself first" payroll reduction contributions • Pretax contributions • Tax-deferred interest and earnings
Spousal IRA	• Tax-deferred interest and earnings • Both working spouse and nonworking spouse can contribute up to the annual limit • Limited eligibility for tax-deductible contributions • Contributions do not reduce current taxes
Rollover IRA	• Traditional IRA that accepts rollovers of all or a portion of your taxable distribution from a retirement plan • You can roll over to a Roth IRA
Education IRA	• Tax-deferred interest and earnings • 10% early withdrawal penalty is waived when money is used for higher-education expenses • Annual limit on individual contributions • Contributions do not reduce current taxes

IRAs can be a good way to save money for retirement. *What are the features of the Education IRA?*

contributions as well as various other restrictions. Keogh plans can be complicated to administer, so you should get professional tax advice before using this type of personal retirement plan.

LIMITS ON PERSONAL RETIREMENT PLANS With the exception of Roth IRAs, you cannot keep money in most tax-deferred retirement plans forever. When you retire, or by age 70½ at the latest, you must begin to receive "minimum lifetime distributions," withdrawals from the funds you accumulated in the plan. The amount of the distributions is based on your life expectancy at the time the distributions begin. If you don't withdraw the minimum distributions from a retirement account, the IRS will charge you a penalty.

Annuities

What do you do if you have funded your 401(k), 403(b), Keogh, and profit-sharing plans up to the allowable limits and you want to put away more money for retirement? The answer may be an annuity. You will recall from Chapter 10, an *annuity* is a contract purchased from an insurance company that provides for a sum of money to be paid to a person at regular intervals for a certain number of years or for life.

You might purchase an annuity with the money you receive from an IRA or company pension. You can simply buy an annuity to supplement the income you'll receive from either of these types of plans.

You can choose to purchase an annuity that has a single payment or installment payments. You will also need to decide whether you want the insurance company to send the income from your annuity to you immediately or begin sending it to you at a later date. The payments you receive from an annuity are taxed as ordinary income. However, the interest you earn from the annuity accumulates tax-free until payments begin.

did you know?

Social Security provides only 27 percent of the average retiree's annual income. On average, pension income accounts for about 18 percent, less than that provided by Social Security.

SOURCES OF INCOME IN RETIREMENT

Living on Your Retirement Income

As you plan for retirement, you'll estimate a budget or spending plan. When the time to retire arrives, however, you may find that your expenses are higher than you expected. If that's the case, you'll have some work to do.

First, you'll have to make sure that you're getting all the income to which you're entitled. Are there other programs or benefits for which you might qualify? You'll also need to think about any assets or valuables you might be able to convert to cash or sources of income.

You may have to confront the trade-off between spending and saving again. For example, perhaps you can use your skills and time instead of money. Instead of spending money on an expensive vacation, take advantage of free and low-cost recreation opportunities, such as public parks, museums, libraries, and fairs. Retirees often receive special discounts on movie tickets, meals, and more.

WORKING DURING RETIREMENT Some people decide to work part-time after they retire. Some even take new full-time jobs. Work can provide a person with a greater sense of usefulness, involvement, and self-worth. It may also be a good way to add to your retirement income.

DIPPING INTO YOUR NEST EGG When should you take money out of your savings during retirement? The answer depends on your financial circumstances, your age, and how much you want to leave to your heirs. (Your *heirs* are the people who will have the legal right to your assets when you die.) Your savings may be large enough to allow you to live comfortably on the interest alone. On the other hand, you may need to make regular withdrawals to help finance your retirement. Dipping into savings isn't wrong. However, you must do so with caution.

If you dip into your retirement nest egg, you should consider one important question: How long will your savings last if you make regular withdrawals?

Example

If you have $10,000 in savings that earns 5.5 percent interest, compounded quarterly, you could take out $68 every month for 20 years before reducing those savings to zero. If you have $40,000, you could withdraw $224 every month for 30 years.

Whatever your situation is, once your nest egg is gone, it's gone. As shown in Exhibit 14–5, dipping into your nest egg is not wrong, but do so with caution.

Exhibit 14–5

Dipping into Your Nest Egg

Dipping into savings isn't wrong; however, you must do so with caution.

Starting Amount of Nest Egg	YOU CAN REDUCE YOUR NEST EGG TO ZERO BY WITHDRAWING THIS MUCH EACH MONTH FOR THE STATED NUMBER OF YEARS . . .					Or You Can Withdraw This Much Each Month and Leave Your Nest Egg Intact
	10 Years	15 Years	20 Years	25 Years	30 Years	
$ 10,000	$ 107	$ 81	$ 68	$ 61	$ 56	$ 46
15,000	161	121	102	91	84	69
20,000	215	162	136	121	112	92
25,000	269	202	170	152	140	115
30,000	322	243	204	182	168	138
40,000	430	323	272	243	224	184
50,000	537	404	340	304	281	230
60,000	645	485	408	364	337	276
80,000	859	647	544	486	449	368
100,000	1,074	808	680	607	561	460

Note: Based on an interest rate of 5.5 percent per year, compounded quarterly.

SOURCE: Select Committee on Aging, U.S. House of Representatives.

Sheet 42 Retirement Plan Comparison
Sheet 43 Forecasting Retirement Income

CONCEPT CHECK 14–2

1 What are four major sources of retirement income?

_____

_____

2 What are the two basic types of employer pension plans?

_____

_____

3 What are the most popular personal retirement plans?

_____

_____

4 What is the major difference between a regular IRA and a Roth IRA?

_____

_____

5 What might you do if your expenses during retirement are higher than you expected?

_____

_____

Apply Yourself!

Objective 2

Read newspaper or magazine articles to determine what expenses are likely to increase and decrease during retirement. How might this information affect your retirement-planning decisions?

Estate Planning

The Importance of Estate Planning

Many people think of estates as belonging only to the rich or elderly. The fact is, however, everyone has an estate. Simple defined, your **estate** consists of everything you own. During your working years your financial goal is to acquire and accumulate

> **OBJECTIVE 3**
>
> Analyze the personal and legal aspects of estate planning.

estate Everything one owns.

money for both your current and future needs. Many years from now, as you grow older, your point of view will change. Instead of working to acquire assets, you'll start to think about what will happen to your hard-earned wealth after you die. In most cases you'll want to pass that wealth along to your loved ones. That is where estate planning becomes important.

What Is Estate Planning?

estate planning A definite plan for the administration and disposition of one's property during one's lifetime and at one's death.

Estate planning is the process of creating a detailed plan for managing your assets so that you can make the most of them while you're alive and ensure that they're distributed wisely after your death. It's not pleasant to think about your own death. However, it is a part of estate planning. Without a good estate plan, the assets you accumulate during your lifetime might be greatly reduced by various taxes when you die.

Estate planning is an essential part of both retirement planning and financial planning. It has two phases. First, you build your estate through savings, investments, and insurance.

Second, you ensure that your estate will be distributed as you wish at the time of your death. If you're married, your estate planning should take into account the needs of your spouse and children. If you are single, you still need to make sure that your financial affairs are in order for your beneficiaries. Your *beneficiary* is a person you've named to receive a portion of your estate after your death.

When you die, your surviving spouse, children, relatives, and friends will face a period of grief and loneliness. At the same time, one or more of these people will probably be responsible for settling your affairs. Make sure that important documents are accessible, understandable, and legally proper.

Legal Documents

An estate plan typically involves various legal documents, one of which is usually a will. When you die, the person who is responsible for handling your affairs will need access to these and other important documents. The documents must be reviewed and verified before your survivors can receive the money and other assets to which they're entitled. If no one can find the necessary documents, your heirs may experience emotionally painful delays. They may even lose part of their inheritance. The important papers you need to collect and organize include:

- Birth certificates for you, your spouse, and your children.
- Marriage certificates and divorce papers.
- Legal name changes (especially important to protect adopted children).
- Military service records.
- Social Security documents.
- Veteran's documents.
- Insurance policies.
- Transfer records of joint bank accounts.
- Safe-deposit box records.
- Automobile registration.
- Titles to stock and bond certificates.

CONCEPT CHECK 14–3

1 What is estate planning?

_____

_____

2 What are the two stages in planning your estate?

_____

_____

3 List some important documents you will need to collect and organize.

_____

_____

Apply Yourself!

Objective 3

Contact several lawyers in your area to find out how much they would charge to prepare your simple will. Are their fees about the same?

Legal Aspects of Estate Planning

Wills

One of the most important documents that every adult should have is a written will. A **will** is the legal document that specifies how you want your property to be distributed after your death. If you die **intestate** —without a valid will—your legal state of residence will step in and control the distribution of your estate without regard for any wishes you may have had.

You should avoid the possibility of dying intestate. The simplest way to do that is to make sure that you have a written will. By having an attorney help you draft your will, you may forestall many difficulties for your heirs. Legal fees for drafting a will vary with the size of your estate and your family situation. A standard will costs between $300 and $400. Make sure that you find an attorney who has experience with wills and estate planning.

Types of Wills

You have several options in preparing a will. The four basic types of wills are the simple will, the traditional marital share will, the exemption trust will, and the stated amount will. The differences among them can affect how your estate will be taxed.

> **OBJECTIVE 4**
> Distinguish among various types of wills and trusts.

will The legal declaration of a person's mind as to the disposition of his or her property after death.

intestate Without a valid will.

Key Web Sites for Estate Planning

www.law.cornell.edu

www.nolo.com

SIMPLE WILL A simple will leaves everything to your spouse. Such a will is generally sufficient for people with small estates. However, if you have a large or complex estate, a simple will may not meet your objectives. It may also result in higher overall taxation, since everything you leave to your spouse will be taxed as part of his or her estate.

TRADITIONAL MARITAL SHARE WILL The traditional marital share will leaves one-half of the adjusted gross estate (the total value of the estate minus debts and costs) to the spouse. The other half of the estate may go to children or other heirs. It can also be held in trust for the family. A **trust** is an arrangement by which a designated person, known as a *trustee,* manages assets for the benefit of someone else. A trust can provide a spouse with a lifelong income and would not be taxed at his or her death.

trust A legal arrangement through which one's assets are held by a trustee.

EXEMPTION TRUST WILL With an exemption trust will, all of your assets go to your spouse except for a certain amount, which goes into a trust. This amount, plus any interest it earns, can provide your spouse with lifelong income that will not be taxed. The tax-free aspect of this type of will may become important if your property value increases considerably after you die.

STATED AMOUNT WILL The stated amount will allows you to pass on to your spouse any amount that satisfies your family's financial goals. For tax purposes you could pass the exempted amount of $3.5 million (in 2009). However, you might decide to pass on a stated amount related to your family's future income needs or to the value of personal items.

> **did you know?**
>
> According to a recent American Association of Retired Persons (AARP) survey, over 40 percent of Americans age 45 or older have not drawn up a will.

WILLS AND PROBATE The type of will that is best for your particular needs depends on many factors, including the size of your estate, inflation, your age, and your objectives. No matter what type of will you choose, it's best to avoid probate. **Probate** is the legal procedure of proving a valid or invalid will. It's the process by which your estate is managed and distributed after your death, according to the provisions of your will. A special probate court generally validates wills and makes sure that your debts are paid. You should avoid probate because it's expensive, lengthy, and public. As you will read later, a living trust avoids probate and is also less expensive, quicker, and private.

probate The legal procedure of proving a valid or invalid will.

Formats of Wills

Wills may be either holographic or formal. A *holographic will* is a handwritten will that you prepare yourself. It should be written, dated, and signed entirely in your own handwriting. No printed or typed information should appear on its pages. Some states do not recognize holographic wills as legal.

A *formal will* is usually prepared with the help of an attorney. It may be typed, or it may be a preprinted form that you fill out. You must sign the will in front of two witnesses; neither person can be a beneficiary named in the will. The witnesses must then sign the will in front of you.

A *statutory will* is prepared on a preprinted form, available from lawyers or stationery stores. Using preprinted forms to prepare your will presents serious risks. The form may include provisions that are not in the best interests of your heirs. Therefore, it is best to seek a lawyer's advice when you prepare your will.

Writing Your Will

Writing a will allows you to express exactly how you want your property to be distributed to your heirs. If you're married, you may think that all the property owned jointly by you and your spouse will automatically go to your spouse after your death. This is true of some assets, such as your house. Even so, writing a will is the only way to ensure that all of your property will end up where you want it.

SELECTING AN EXECUTOR   An **executor** is someone who is willing and able to perform the tasks involved in carrying out your will. These tasks include preparing an inventory of your assets, collecting any money due, and paying off your debts. Your executor must also prepare and file all income and estate tax returns. In addition, he or she will be responsible for making decisions about selling or reinvesting assets to pay off debt and provide income for your family while the estate is being settled. Finally, your executor must distribute the estate and make a final accounting to your beneficiaries and to the probate court.

executor Someone willing and able to perform the tasks involved in carrying out your will.

SELECTING A GUARDIAN   If you have children, your will should also name a guardian to care for them in the event that you and your spouse die at the same time and the children cannot care for themselves. A **guardian** is a person who accepts the responsibility of providing children with personal care after their parents' death and managing the parents' estate for the children until they reach a certain age.

did you know?

Who can be an executor? Any U.S. citizen over 18 who has not been convicted of a felony can be named the executor of a will.

ALTERING OR REWRITING YOUR WILL   Sometimes you'll need to change the provisions of your will because of changes in your life or in the law. Once you've made a will, review it frequently so that it remains current. Here are some reasons to review your will:

- You've moved to a new state that has different laws.
- You've sold property that is mentioned in the will.
- The size and composition of your estate have changed.
- You've married, divorced, or remarried.
- Potential heirs have died, or new ones have been born.

guardian A person who assumes responsibility for providing children with personal care and managing the deceased's estate for them.

Don't make any written changes on the pages of an existing will. Additions, deletions, or erasures on a will that has been signed and witnessed can invalidate the will. If you want to make only a few minor changes, adding a codicil may be the best choice. A **codicil** is a document that explains, adds, or deletes provisions in your existing will.

codicil A document that modifies provisions in an existing will.

A Living Will

At some point in your life you may become physically or mentally disabled and unable to act on your own behalf. If that happens, you'll need a living will. A **living will** is a document in which you state whether you want to be kept alive by artificial means if you become terminally ill and unable to make such a decision. Many states recognize living wills. Exhibit 14–6 is an example of a typical living will.

To ensure the effectiveness of a living will, discuss your intention of preparing such a will with the people closest to you. You should also discuss this with your family doctor. Sign and date your document before two witnesses. Witnessing shows that you signed of your own free will.

Give copies of your living will to those closest to you, and have your family doctor place a copy in your medical file. Keep the original document readily accessible, and look it over periodically—preferably once a year—to be sure your wishes have remained unchanged. To verify your intent, redate and initial each subsequent endorsement.

Most lawyers will do the paperwork for a living will at no cost if they are already preparing your estate plan. You can also get the necessary forms from nonprofit advocacy groups. Partnership for Caring: America's Voices for the Dying is a national

living will A document that enables an individual, while well, to express the intention that life be allowed to end if he or she becomes terminally ill.

Exhibit **14–6** A Living Will

Living Will Declaration

Declaration made this _____ day of _____ (month, year)

I, _____, being of sound mind, willfully and voluntarily make known my desire that my dying shall not be artificially prolonged under the circumstances set forth below, do hereby declare

If at any time I should have an incurable injury, disease, or illness regarded as a terminal condition by my physician and if my physician has determined that the application of life-sustaining procedures would serve only to artificially prolong the dying process and that my death will occur whether or not life-sustaining procedures are utilized, I direct that such procedures be withheld or withdrawn and that I be permitted to die with only the administration of medication or the performance of any medical procedure deemed necessary to provide me with comfort care.

In the absence of my ability to give directions regarding the use of such life-sustaining procedures, it is my intention that this declaration shall be honored by my family and physician as the final expression of my legal right to refuse medical or surgical treatment and accept the consequences from such refusal. I understand the full import of this declaration, and I am emotionally and mentally competent to make this declaration.

Signed   _____

City, County, and State of Residence   _____

The declarant has been personally known to me, and I believe him or her to be of sound mind.

Witness   _____

Witness   _____

Some people who become terminally ill cannot make decisions on their own behalf.
What is the basic purpose of a living will?

nonprofit organization that operates the only national crisis and information hotline dealing with end-of-life issues. It also provides living wills, medical powers of attorney, and similar documents geared to specific states. You may download these documents free at www.partnershipforcaring.org. Working through end-of-life issues is difficult, but it can help avoid forcing your family to make a decision in a hospital waiting room—or worse, having your last wishes ignored.

POWER OF ATTORNEY Related to the idea of a living will is power of attorney. A **power of attorney** is a legal document that authorizes someone to act on your behalf. If you become seriously ill or injured, you'll probably need someone to take care of your needs and personal affairs. This can be done through a power of attorney.

power of attorney A legal document authorizing someone to act on one's behalf.

LETTER OF LAST INSTRUCTION In addition to a traditional will, it is a good idea to prepare a letter of last instruction. This document is not legally binding, but it can provide your heirs with important information. It should contain your wishes for your funeral arrangements as well as the names of the people who are to be informed of your death.

Trusts

Basically, a trust is a legal arrangement that helps manage the assets of your estate for your benefit or that of your beneficiaries. The creator of the trust is called the *trustor,* or *grantor.* The *trustee* might be a person or institution, such as a bank, that administers the trust. A bank charges a small fee for its services in administering a trust. The fee is usually based on the value of the assets in the trust.

Individual circumstances determine whether establishing a trust makes sense. Some of the common reasons for setting up a trust are to:

- Reduce or otherwise provide payment of estate taxes.
- Avoid probate and transfer your assets immediately to your beneficiaries.
- Free yourself from managing your assets while you receive a regular income from the trust.
- Provide income for a surviving spouse or other beneficiary.
- Ensure that your property serves a desired purpose after your death.

Key Web Sites for Trusts

www.webtrust.com

http://the.nnepa.com

Types of Trusts

There are many types of trusts, some of which are described in detail below. You'll need to choose the type of trust that's most appropriate for your particular situation. An estate attorney can advise you about the right type of trust for your personal and family needs.

All trusts are either revocable or irrevocable. A *revocable trust* is one in which you have the right to end the trust or change its terms during your lifetime. An *irrevocable trust* is one that cannot be changed or ended. Revocable trusts avoid the lengthy process of probate, but they do not protect assets from federal or state estate taxes. Irrevocable trusts avoid probate and help reduce estate taxes. However, by law you cannot remove any assets from an irrevocable trust, even if you need them at some later point in your life.

CREDIT-SHELTER TRUST A credit-shelter trust is one that enables the spouse of a deceased person to avoid paying federal taxes on a certain amount of assets left to him or her as part of an estate. Perhaps the most common estate planning trust, the credit-shelter trust has many other names: bypass trust, "residuary" trust, A/B trust, exemption equivalent trust, or family trust. It is designed to allow married couples, who can leave everything to each other tax free, to take full advantage of the exemption that allows $2 million (in 2006, 2007, and 2008) in every estate to pass free of federal estate taxes.

The Economic Growth and Tax Relief Reconciliation Act of 2001 (EGTRRA) increased the exemption amounts to $3.5 million by the year 2009 as follows:

2006–2008	$2,000,000
2009	$3,500,000
2010	Repeal (no estate tax)
2011	$1,000,000

DISCLAIMER TRUST A disclaimer trust is appropriate for couples who do not yet have enough assets to need a credit-shelter trust but may have in the future. With a disclaimer trust, the surviving spouse is left everything, but he or she has the right to disclaim, or deny, some portion of the estate. Anything that is disclaimed goes into a credit-shelter trust. This approach allows the surviving spouse to protect wealth from estate taxes.

LIVING TRUST A living trust, also known as an inter vivos trust, is a property management arrangement that goes into effect while you're alive. It allows you, as a trustor, to receive benefits during your lifetime. To set up a living trust, you simply transfer some of your assets to a trustee. Then you give the trustee instructions for managing the trust while you're alive and after your death. A living trust has several advantages:

- It ensures privacy. A will is a public record; a trust is not.
- The assets held in trust avoid probate at your death. This eliminates probate costs and delays.
- It enables you to review your trustee's performance and make changes if necessary.
- It can relieve you of management responsibilities.
- It's less likely than a will to create arguments between heirs upon your death.
- It can guide your family and doctors if you become terminally ill or unable to make your own decisions.

Setting up a living trust costs more than creating a will. However, depending on your particular circumstances, a living trust can be a good estate planning option.

TESTAMENTARY TRUST A testamentary trust is one established by your will that becomes effective upon your death. Such a trust can be valuable if your beneficiaries are inexperienced in financial matters. It may also be your best option if your estate taxes will be high. A testamentary trust provides many of the same advantages as a living trust.

did you know?

President Obama proposed extending the 2009 federal estate tax law into 2010 and beyond, maintaining the $3.5 million estate tax exemption with a 45 percent estate tax rate.

Taxes and Estate Planning

Federal and state governments impose various types of taxes that you must consider in estate planning. The four major types of taxes are estate taxes, estate and trust federal income taxes, inheritance taxes, and gift taxes.

ESTATE TAXES An estate tax is a federal tax collected on the value of a person's property at the time of his or her death. The tax is based on the fair market value of the deceased person's investments, property, and bank accounts, less an exempt amount of $3.5 million in 2009; this tax is due nine months after a death.

ESTATE AND TRUST FEDERAL INCOME TAXES In addition to the federal estate tax return, estates and certain trusts must file federal income tax returns with the Internal Revenue Service. Taxable income for estates and trusts is computed in the same manner as taxable income for individuals. Trusts and estates must pay quarterly estimated taxes.

did you know?

Charitable gifts can be an important tool in estate planning. Giving to charity supports a cause and offers benefits such as reduced taxes and increased interest income. The National Philanthropic Trust is an independent public charity dedicated to increasing philanthropy in our society. For more information, visit www.nptrust.org.

INHERITANCE TAXES Your heirs might have to pay a tax for the right to acquire the property that they have inherited. An inheritance tax is a tax collected on the property left by a person in his or her will.

Only state governments impose inheritance taxes. Most states collect an inheritance tax, but state laws differ widely as to exemptions and rates of taxation. A reasonable average for state inheritance taxes would be 4 to 10 percent of whatever the heir receives.

GIFT TAXES Both the state and federal governments impose a gift tax, a tax collected on money or property valued at more than $13,000 given by one person to another in a single year. One way to reduce the tax liability of your estate is to reduce the size of the estate while you're alive by giving away portions of it as gifts. You're free to make such gifts to your spouse, children, or anyone else at any time. (Don't give away assets if you need them in your retirement!)

Sheet 45 Will Planning Sheet
Sheet 46 Trust Comparison Sheet

CONCEPT CHECK 14–4

1 What is a will?

_____

_____

2 What are the four basic types of wills?

_____

_____

3 What are the responsibilities of an executor?

_____

_____

4 Why should you name a guardian?

_____

_____

5 What is the difference between a revocable and an irrevocable trust?

_____

_____

6 What are the four major types of trusts?

_____

_____

7 What are the four major types of taxes to consider in estate planning?

_____

_____

Apply Yourself!

Objective 4

Discuss with your attorney the possibility of establishing a trust as a means of managing your estate.

Back to... **Getting Personal**

Reconsider your responses to the Getting Personal questions at the beginning of the chapter. For more effective personal financial planning and retirement and estate planning:

- Reevaluate your retirement and estate planning goals to make sure they reflect what is important to you and your family.
- Consider information from several sources when making retirement and estate planning decisions. Consult older friends and relatives, bankers, and tax advisers.
- Use future value and present value computations to help you achieve your retirement and estate planning goals. Calculators are available at www .dinkytown.net, www.moneychimp.com/calculator, and www.rbccentura.com/tools.

- In the first column of the following table, list items you'd like to include in your will. Include all financial assets, like cash, savings, stocks, bonds, mutual funds, and other investments you imagine having. Then think about items that may have cost a good deal: a car or bike, computer, stereo system, musical instrument, or sports and hobby equipment. Finally, consider inexpensive items that may have sentimental or other special value to a friend or relative, such as a piece of jewelry, an old letter or photograph, or a favorite memento. In the second column, write to whom you'd like to give the item. In the third column, explain why you've decided to give that item to that particular person. Use extra paper if you need more space.

Financial Assets	To Whom?	Why?
Major possessions		
Items of sentimental or special value		

What did you learn in this chapter that could help you make better retirement and estate planning decisions?

Chapter Summary

Objective 1   The difference between your assets and your liabilities is your net worth. Review your assets to ensure they are sufficient for retirement. Then estimate your living expenses. Some expenses are likely to decrease while others will increase.

Objective 2   Your possible sources of income during retirement include employer pension plans, public pension plans, personal retirement plans, and annuities. If your income approximates your expenses, you are in good shape; if not, determine additional income needs and sources.

Objective 3   The personal aspects of estate planning depend on whether you are single or married. Never having been married does not eliminate the need to organize your financial affairs. Every adult should have a written will. A will is a way to transfer your property according to your wishes after you die.

Objective 4   The four basic types of wills are the simple will, the traditional marital share will, the exemption trust will, and the stated amount will. Types of trusts include the credit-shelter trust, the disclaimer trust, the living trust, and the testamentary trust.

Federal and state governments impose various types of estate taxes; you can prepare a plan for paying these taxes.

Key Terms

codicil 485

defined-benefit plan 475

defined-contribution plan 472

estate 481

estate planning 482

executor 485

401(k) plan 473

guardian 485

individual retirement account
    (IRA) 477

intestate 483

Keogh plan 478

living will 485

power of attorney 486

probate 484

trust 484

vesting 475

will 483

Self-Test Problems

1. Beverly Foster is planning for her retirement. She has determined that her car is worth $10,000, her home is worth $150,000, her personal belongings are worth $100,000, and her stocks and bonds are worth $300,000. She owes $50,000 on her home and $5,000 on her car. Calculate her net worth.

2. Calculate how much money an average older (65+) household with an annual income of $32,800 spends on food each year. (*Hint:* Use Exhibit 14–2.)

3. On December 31, 2009, George gives $13,000 to his son and $13,000 to his son's wife. On January 1, 2010, George gives another $13,000 to his son and another $13,000 to his son's wife. George made no other gifts to his son or his son's wife in 2009 and 2010. What is the gift tax?

Solutions

1. *Assets*   *Liabilities*

Car	$ 10,000	Mortgage	$50,000
Home	$150,000	Car	5,000
Personal belongings	$100,000	Total liabilities	$55,000
Stocks and bonds	$300,000		
Total assets	$560,000		

Net worth	=	Assets	−	Liabilities		
	=	$560,000	−	$55,000	=	$505,000

2. Average older household with an annual income of $32,800 spends about 12.7 percent of the income on food. Thus $32,800 × 12.7 percent = $4,166.

3. There is no gift tax in 2009 or in 2010 since George gifted $13,000 to his son and son's wife in each of the two years.

Problems

1. Shelly's assets include money in the checking and saving accounts, investments in stocks and mutual funds, and personal property, such as furniture, appliances, an automobile, a coin collection, and jewelry. Shelly calculates that her total assets are $108,800. Her current unpaid bills, including an auto loan, credit card balances, and taxes, total $16,300. Calculate Shelly's net worth.   (Obj. 1)

2. Prepare your net worth statement using the Assets – Liabilities = Net worth equation.   (Obj. 1)

3. Ted Riley owns a 2008 Lexus worth $25,000. He owns a home worth $225,000. He has a checking account with $500 in it and a savings account with $1,500 in it. He has a mutual fund worth $85,000. His personal assets are worth $90,000. He still owes $10,000 on his car and $100,000 on his home, and he has a balance on his credit card of $1,000. What is Ted's net worth?   (Obj. 1)

4. Calculate how much money an older household with an annual income of $32,800 spends on housing each year. (*Hint:* Use Exhibit 14–2.)   (Obj. 1)

5. Using Exhibit 14–2, calculate how much money the household from problem 3 spends on medical care.   (Obj. 1)

6. Janine is 25 and has a good job at a biotechnology company. She currently has $5,000 in an IRA, an important part of her retirement nest egg. She believes her IRA will grow at an annual rate of 8 percent, and she plans to leave it untouched until she retires at age 65. Janine estimates that she will need $875,000 in her *total* retirement nest egg by the time she is 65 in order to have retirement income of $20,000 a year (she expects that Social Security will pay her an additional $15,000 a year).   (Obj. 2)

    a. How much will Janine's IRA be worth when she needs to start withdrawing money from it when she retires? (*Hint:* Use Exhibit 1–A in the appendix to Chapter 1.)
    b. How much money will she have to accumulate in her company's 401(k) plan over the next 40 years in order to reach her retirement income goal?

7. Gene and Dixie, husband and wife (ages 45 and 42), both work. They have an adjusted gross income of $40,000, and they are filing a joint income tax return. What is the maximum IRA contribution they can make? How much of that contribution is tax deductible?   (Obj. 2)

8. You have $50,000 in your retirement fund that is earning 5.5 percent per year, compounded quarterly. How many dollars in withdrawals per month would reduce this nest egg to zero in 20 years? How many dollars per month can you withdraw for as long as you live and still leave this nest egg intact? (*Hint:* Use Exhibit 14–5.)   (Obj. 2)

9. In 2009, Joshua gave $13,000 worth of Microsoft stock to his son. In 2010, the Microsoft shares are worth $23,000.   (Obj. 4)

    a. What was the gift tax in 2009?
    b. What is the total amount removed from Joshua's estate in 2010?
    c. What will be the gift tax in 2010?

10. In 2009, you gave a $13,000 gift to a friend. What is the gift tax?   (Obj. 4)

11. Barry and his wife Mary have accumulated over $4 million during their 45 years of marriage. They have three children and five grandchildren. How much money can they gift to their children and grandchildren in 2009 without any gift tax liability?   (Obj. 4)

12. The date of death for a widow was 2008. If the estate was valued at $2,129,000 and the estate was taxed at 47 percent, what was the heir's tax liability?   (Obj. 4)

13. Joe and Rachel are both retired. Married for 50 years, they've amassed an estate worth $2.4 million. The couple has no trusts or other types of tax-sheltered assets. If Joe or Rachel dies in 2009, how much federal estate tax would the surviving spouse have to pay, assuming that the estate is taxed at the 47 percent rate?   (Obj. 4)

Questions

1. How will your spending patterns change during your retirement years? Compare your spending patterns with those shown in Exhibit 14–2. (Obj. 1)

2. Obtain Form SSA-7004 from your local Social Security office. Complete and mail the form to receive a personal earnings and benefits statement. Use the information in this statement to plan your retirement. (Obj. 2)

3. Prepare a written report of personal information that would be helpful to you and your heirs. Be sure to include the location of family records, your military service file, and other important papers; medical records; bank accounts; charge accounts; location of your safe-deposit box; U.S. savings bonds, stocks, bonds, and other securities; property owned; life insurance; annuities; and Social Security information. (Obj. 3)

4. Visit Metropolitan Life Insurance Company's Web page at http://www.lifeadvice.com. Using this information, prepare a report on the following: (*a*) Who needs a will? (*b*) What are the elements of a will (naming a guardian, naming an executor, preparing a will, updating a will, estate taxes, where to keep your will, living will, etc.)? (*c*) How is this report helpful in preparing your own will? (Obj. 3)

5. Make a list of the criteria you will use in deciding who will be the guardian of your minor children if you and your spouse die at the same time. (Obj. 3)

Case in Point

PLANNING FOR RETIREMENT

Is a bad day fishing better than a good day at the office? Yes, according to a retired dad, Chuck. With his company pension, at least he didn't have to worry about money. In the good old days, if you had a decent job, you'd hang on to it, and then your company's pension combined with Social Security payments would be enough to live comfortably. Chuck's son, Rob, does not have a company pension and is not sure whether Social Security will even exist when he retires. So when it comes to retirement, the sooner you start saving, the better.

Take Maureen, a salesperson for a computer company, and Therese, an accountant for a lighting manufacturer. Both start their jobs at age 25. Maureen starts saving for retirement right away by investing $300 a month at 9 percent until age 65. But Therese does nothing until age 35. At 35 she begins investing the same $300 a month at 9 percent until age 65. What a shocking difference! Maureen has accumulated $1.4 million, while Therese has only $553,000 in her retirement fund. The moral? The sooner you start, the more you'll have for your retirement. Women especially need to start sooner, because they typically enter the workforce later, have lower salaries, and, ultimately, have lower pensions.

Laura Tarbox, owner and president of Tarbox Equity, explains how to determine your retirement needs and how your budget might change when you retire. Tarbox advises that the old rule of thumb that you need 60 to 70 percent of preretirement income is too low an estimate. She cautions that most people will want to spend very close to what they were spending before retiring. There are some expenses that might be lower, however, such as clothing for work, dry cleaning, and commuting expenses. Other expenses, though, such as insurance, travel, and recreation, may increase during retirement.

Questions

1. In the past, many workers chose to stay with their employers until retirement. What was the major reason for employees' loyalty?
2. How did Maureen amass $1.4 million for retirement, while Therese could accumulate only $553,000?
3. Why do women need to start early to save for retirement?
4. What expenses may increase or decrease during retirement?

Continuing Case

Vikki and Tim Treble (ages 60 and 62) have met their goal of helping to finance their children's college education. Molly, Caleb, and Tyler have all graduated from college. Molly and Caleb are married and Molly has two children. Tyler is in an orchestra and travels as a viola soloist.

Tim and Vikki both remember their parents pinching pennies too much and they don't want to do the same in retirement. Instead, they want to be able to travel, donate to organizations as they wish, and spoil their grandchildren.

Knowing that they have two years before they retire, they decide it is a good time to meet with their financial planner and ask what additional steps they need to take to meet their retirement goals. Their financial situation has changed with fewer expenses, a rather large inheritance, and an increasing cash value for their life insurance policies. In fact, the life insurance coverage alone is $1,000,000 each for Vikki and for Tim.

Vikki and Tim's financial statistics are shown below:

Assets:
Checking/savings account $50,000
Emergency fund $45,000
House $500,000
Cars $15,000 and $35,000
Household possessions $50,000
401(k) balance $420,000 (Vikki), $965,000 (Tim)
Life insurance cash value $75,000

Liabilities: None

Income:
Gross Salary:
$40,000 per year (Vikki), $170,000 (Tim)
After-tax monthly salary:
$2,333 (Vikki), $9,917 (Tim)

Monthly Expenses:
Property tax/Insurance $800
Day to day living expenses (including utilities, food) $3,500

Entertainment/vacations $700
Gas/repairs $500
Term & whole life insurance $400

Savings:
401(k) 12% of gross monthly salary

Questions

1. What steps do Vikki and Tim need to take to prepare for retirement?
2. How should they finance their retirement?
3. What estate planning documents should they have in place? What estate planning documents should their children Molly, Caleb, and Tyler have?
4. What are some important decisions they need to make regarding their estate planning?
5. How can they use *Your Personal Financial Plan* sheets 42–46?

Spending Diary

"KEEPING TRACK OF MY DAILY SPENDING GETS ME TO START THINKING ABOUT SAVING AND INVESTING FOR RETIREMENT."

Directions

The consistent use of a Daily Spending Diary can provide you with ongoing information that will help you manage your spending, saving, and investing activities. Taking time to reconsider your spending habits can result in achieving better satisfaction from your available finances. The Daily Spending Diary sheets are located in Appendix C at the end of the book and on the student Web site at www.mhhe.com/kdh.

Analysis Questions

1. What portion of your available finances involve saving or investing for long-term financial security?

2. What types of retirement and estate planning activities might you start to consider at this point of your life?

Retirement Plan Comparison

Financial Planning Activities: Compare benefits and costs for different retirement plans (401k, IRA, Keogh). Analyze advertisements and articles, and contact your employer and financial institutions to obtain the information below.

Suggested Web Sites: www.lifenet.com   www.aarp.org

Type of plan			
Name of financial institution or employer			
Address			
Phone			
Web site			
Type of investments			
Minimum initial deposit			
Minimum additional deposits			
Employer contributions			
Current rate of return			
Service charges/fees			
Safety insured? By whom?			
Amount			
Payroll deduction available			
Tax benefits			
Penalty for early withdrawal: • IRS penalty (10%) • Other penalties			
Other features or restrictions			

What's Next for Your Personal Financial Plan?

- Survey local businesses to determine the types of retirement plans available to employees.
- Talk to representatives of various financial institutions to determine their suggestions for IRA investments.

Name: _____ **Date:** _____

Forecasting Retirement Income

Financial Planning Activities: Determine the amount needed to save each year to have the necessary funds to cover retirement living costs. Estimate the information requested below.

Suggested Web Sites: www.ssa.gov   www.pensionplanners.com

Estimated annual retirement living expenses

Estimated annual living expenses
if you retired today $ _____

Future value for _____ years until
retirement at expected annual
income of _____ % (use future
value of $1, Exhibit 1–A of
Appendix A)   × _____

**Projected annual retirement living expenses
adjusted for inflation** . . . . (A) $ _____

Estimated annual income at retirement

Social Security income $ _____

Company pension, personal
retirement account income $ _____

Investment and other income $ _____

Total retirement income . . . . (B) $ _____

Additional retirement plan contributions (if B is less than A)

Annual shortfall of income after
retirement (A – B) $ _____

Expected annual rate of return on
invested funds after retirement,
percentage expressed as a decimal $ _____

Needed investment fund after retirement (A – B) . . . . (C) $ _____

Future value factor of a series of deposits for _____ years until
retirement and an expected annual rate of return before
retirement of _____ % (Use Exhibit 1–B in Appendix A)   (D) $ _____

**Annual deposit to achieve needed investment fund
(C ÷ D)** . . . . $ _____

What's Next for Your Personal Financial Plan?

- Survey retired individuals or people close to retirement to obtain information on their main sources of retirement income.
- Make a list that suggests the best investment options for an individual retirement account.

Estate Planning Activities

Financial Planning Activities: Develop a plan for estate planning and related financial activities. Respond to the following questions as a basis for making and implementing an estate plan.

Suggested Web Sites: www.nolo.com   www.webtrust.com

Are your financial records, including recent tax forms, insurance policies, and investment and housing documents, organized and easily accessible?	
Do you have a safe-deposit box? Where is it located? Where is the key?	
Location of life insurance policies. Name and address of insurance company and agent.	
Is your will current? Location of copies of your will. Name and address of your lawyer.	
Name and address of your executor	
Do you have a listing of the current value of assets owned and liabilities outstanding?	
Have any funeral and burial arrangements been made?	
Have you created any trusts? Name and location of financial institution.	
Do you have any current information on gift and estate taxes?	
Have you prepared a letter of last instruction? Where is it located?	

What's Next for Your Personal Financial Plan?

- Talk to several individuals about the actions they have taken related to estate planning.
- Create a list of situations in which a will would need to be revised.

Name: _____ **Date:** _____

Will Planning Sheet

Financial Planning Activities: Compare costs and features of various types of wills. Obtain information for the various areas listed based on your current and future situation; contact attorneys regarding the cost of these wills.

Suggested Web Sites: www.netplanning.com   www.estateplanninglinks.com

Type of will	Features that would be appropriate for my current or future situation	Cost Attorney, Address, Phone

What's Next for Your Personal Financial Plan?

- Create a list of items that you believe would be desirable to include in a will.
- Obtain the cost of a will from a number of different lawyers.

Trust Comparison Sheet

Financial Planning Activities: Identify features of different types of trusts. Research features of various trusts to determine their value to your personal situation.

Suggested Web Sites: www.webtrust.com   www.lifenet.com

Type of trust	Benefits	Possible value for my situation

What's Next for Your Personal Financial Plan?

- Talk to legal and financial planning experts to contrast the cost and benefits of wills and trusts.
- Talk to one or more lawyers to obtain information about the type of trust recommended for your situation.

A

Developing a Career Search Strategy

The average person changes jobs seven times during a lifetime. Most likely, you will reevaluate your work situation on a regular basis. The following information will help you plan and manage your career.

The Career Planning Process

Career planning activities may be viewed using the following steps:

1} *Personal assessment*—to determine interests and values, and to identify talents and abilities.
2} *Employment market analysis*—to assess geographic, economic, technological, and social influences on employment opportunities.
3} *Application process*—in which you prepare a résumé and create a cover letter.
4} *Interview process*—in which you practice your interview skills, research the organization, and send a follow-up message to the organization.
5} *Employment acceptance*—when you assess the salary and other financial factors as well as the organizational environment of your potential employer.
6} *Career development and advancement*—in which you develop plans to enhance career success behaviors and build strong work relationships.

Career Activity 1

For each of the six steps of the career planning process, write: (*a*) a goal you have now or might have in the future and (*b*) an action you might take regarding this career planning area.

did you know?

More and more employers are using credit reports as hiring tools. Federal law requires that job applicants be told if credit histories are being used in the hiring process. You can check your credit report at www.annualcreditreport.com.

Using Career Information Sources to Identify Career Trends

Whereas careers have dwindled in some sectors of our economy, opportunities in other sectors have grown. Service industries that are expected to have the greatest employment potential in the 21st century include computer technology, health care, business services, social and government services, sales and retailing, hospitality and food services, management and human resources, education, and financial services.

Many career information sources are available; these include:

1} *Print and other media sources,* such as the *Occupational Outlook Handbook,* which provides detailed information on many occupations. The employment and business sections of newspapers also publish articles on various career topics.

2} *Online sources* are available to assist you with all aspects of career planning. Consider a Web search to gather information about résumés, effective interviewing, or creating a career portfolio.

3} *Informational interviews* are very effective for obtaining career information. A planned discussion with a person in a field of interest to you will help you learn about the job duties, required training, and the person's feelings about the career. Most people like to talk about their work experiences. Before the interview, plan to ask questions such as:

- How did you get your current position? Did other jobs lead to this one?
- In what ways do you find your work most satisfying? What are your main frustrations?
- What tasks and activities are required in your work?
- What are the most important qualifications for working in this field? What training and education are needed?
- What advice would you give a person who is considering this type of work?

Career Activity 2

Locate a career information source. Prepare a brief summary of key ideas that could be valuable to you in the future.

Obtaining Employment Experience

Most people possess more career skills than they realize. Your involvement in school, community, and work activities provides a foundation for employment experiences. The following opportunities offer work-related training:

1} *Part-time employment* can provide experience and knowledge for a career field.

2} *Volunteer work* in community organizations or agencies can help you acquire skills, establish good work habits, and make contacts.

3} *Internships* allow you to gain experience needed to obtain employment in a field.

4} *Campus projects* offer work-related experiences to help you obtain career skills through campus organizations, course assignments, and research projects.

did you know?

Résumés often include vague words such as "competent," "creative," "flexible," "motivated," or "team player." Instead, give specific examples of your experiences and achievements to better communicate these capabilities.

Career Activity 3

Create a list of your work, volunteer, and school activities. Describe how each could apply to a future work situation.

Identifying Job Opportunities

Some of the most valuable sources of job information include:

1} *Job advertisements* in newspapers and professional periodicals are a common source. However, since over 60 percent of jobs may not be advertised to the public, use other job search activities as well.

2} *Career fairs,* on campus and at convention centers, allow you to contact several firms in a short time. At a career fair, you will be asked a couple of questions to determine if you qualify for a longer interview. Prepare for job fairs by being ready to quickly communicate your potential contributions to an organization. Knowing something about the organization will help distinguish you from other applicants.

3} *Employment agencies* match job hunters with employers. Often the hiring company pays the fee. Be wary when asked to pay a fee in advance. Government employment services may be contacted through your state employment service or state department of labor.

4} *Business contacts* advise people about careers. Friends, relatives, and others are potential business contacts. *Networking* is the process of making and using contacts to obtain and update career information.

5} *Job creation* involves developing a position that matches your skills with organizational needs. As you develop skills you enjoy, you may be able to create a demand for yourself.

6} *Other job search sources* include (*a*) visits to companies to make face-to-face contacts; (*b*) business directories and Web sites to obtain names of organizations that employ people with your qualifications; and (*c*) alumni who work in your field.

Career Activity 4

Using one or more of the sources of available jobs, select a position that you might apply for in the future. How well do your qualifications match those required for the job?

Developing a Résumé

Marketing yourself to prospective employers usually requires a résumé, or personal information sheet.

Résumé Elements

This summary of your education, training, experience, and other qualifications has these main components:

1} *The personal data section* presents your name, address, telephone number, and e-mail address. Do not include your birth date, sex, height, and weight unless this information applies to a specific job qualification.

2} *A career objective* is designed to clearly focus you to a specific employment situation. Your career objective may be omitted from the résumé and communicated in your cover letter. Also, consider a summary section with a synopsis of your main skills and capabilities.

3} *The education section* should include dates, schools attended, fields of study, and degrees earned.

4} *The experience section* lists organizations, dates of involvement, and responsibilities for previous employment, relevant school activities, and community service. Highlight computer skills, technical abilities, and other specific competencies. Use action verbs to connect your experience to the needs of the organization. Focus this information on results and accomplishments.

5} *The related information section* may include honors, awards, and other activities related to your career field.

6} *The references section* lists people who can verify your skills. These individuals may be teachers, past employers, supervisors, or business colleagues. References are usually not included in a résumé; however, have this information available when requested.

did you know?

A combination résumé blends the chronological and functional types. With this format, you first highlight skills and experience relevant to the position. This is followed by your employment history section which reports specific experiences that match the requirements for the job.

Résumé Preparation

An effective résumé must be presented in a professional manner. Many candidates are disqualified by poor résumés. Limit your résumé to one page. Send a two-page résumé only if you have enough material to fill three pages; then use the most valid information to prepare an impressive two-page presentation.

Exhibit **A–1**

Sample Résumé

CHAD BOSTWICK

SCHOOL ADDRESS
234B University Drive
Jasper, MO 54321
(316) 555-7659
bostwc@unsoark.edu

HOME ADDRESS
765 Cannon Lane
Benton, KS 67783
(407) 555-1239

CAREER OBJECTIVE
An entry-level position in medical or health care administration.

EDUCATION
Bachelor of Science in Business Administration and Health Care Marketing, University of South Arkansas, June 2009.
Associate of Arts, Medical Technician Assistant, Arrow Valley Community College, Arlington, Kansas, June 2007.

EXPERIENCE
Patient account clerk, University Hospital, Jasper, Missouri, November 2007-present. Researched overdue accounts, created collection method for faster accounts receivable turnover, assisted in training billing clerks.
Sales data clerk, Jones Medical Supply Company, Benton, Kansas, January-August 2005. Maintained inventory records, processed customer records.

CAMPUS ACTIVITIES
Newsletter editor, University of South Arkansas chapter of Financial Management Association, January-June 2007.
Tutor for business statistics and computer lab, 2006–2007.

HONORS
College of Business Community Service Award, University of South Arkansas, June 2008.
Arrow Valley Health Care Society Scholarship, June 2006.

REFERENCES
Furnished upon request.

One key to successful résumé writing is the use of action words to demonstrate what you have accomplished or achieved. Examples of strong action words include:

- Achieved
- Administered
- Coordinated
- Created
- Designed
- Developed
- Directed

- Edited
- Facilitated
- Initiated
- Implemented
- Managed
- Monitored
- Organized

- Planned
- Produced
- Researched
- Supervised
- Trained
- Updated

Other words and phrases that commonly impress prospective employers include foreign language skills, computer experience, achievement, research experience, flexible, team projects, and overseas study or experience. Instead of just listing your ability to use various software packages (such as Excel or PowerPoint), describe how these tools were used to research information or to present findings for a specific project. For best results, seek assistance from counselors, the campus placement office, and friends to find errors and suggest improvements.

Career Activity 5

Outline the main sections of a résumé that you might create for a job offer the next couple of years. Conduct a Web search to find a résumé format that you might use.

Creating a Cover Letter

A *cover letter,* designed to express your interest in a specific job, accompanies your résumé and consists of three main sections:

did you know?

The *Q letter* (Q for qualifications) provides a side-by-side comparison of your experiences and abilities with the job requirements. The two coordinated lists allow you to be quickly rated as a viable candidate for the position.

1} The *introductory paragraph* gets the reader's attention. Indicate your reason for writing by referring to the employment position. Communicate what you have to offer the organization. If applicable, mention the name of the person who referred you.

2} The *development paragraphs* highlight aspects of your background that specifically qualify you for the position. At this point, elaborate on experiences and training. Connect your skills and competencies to specific organizational needs.

3} The *concluding paragraph* should request action. Ask for an interview to discuss your qualifications in detail. Include your contact information, such as telephone numbers and the times when available. Close your letter by summarizing your benefits to the organization.

Create a personalized cover letter for each position addressed to the appropriate person in the organization. A poorly prepared cover letter guarantees rejection.

In recent years, job applicants are increasingly using a *targeted application letter* instead of a résumé and cover letter. After researching a position and company, you can communicate how your specific skills and experiences will benefit the organization. Once again, your goal is to emphasize achievements and accomplishments so you will be invited for an interview.

May 23, 2010

Ms. Hanna Cabral
Human Resources Director
Global Translation Services
3400 Superior Boulevard
Jamestown, NY 13456

Dear Ms. Cabral:

Based on my background and studies in international relations, this is to express my interest in the position available with your organization. Brenda Kelly in your accounting department recommended that I contact you. My studies have included courses in global business practices along with an internship with the exporting department of an electronics company.

My ability to work in a cross-cultural environment provides your organization with a person who can adapt to varied business settings. As a result of my work with companies in other countries, I am able to meet the diverse needs of your clients. My language skills have allowed me to handle customer relations activities with international customers.

I look forward to the opportunity to discuss my qualifications with you in further detail. You may contact me at 501–963–4556 or at jhopkinsl@internet.com. I believe my training and background will allow me to contribute to the continued success of your organization.

Sincerely,

Jerry Hopkins

Jerry Hopkins
5678 Collins Road
West Barrington, NY 14332
jhopkinsl@internet.com

Career Activity 6

Select a potential job. Create a cover letter for that position. Conduct an online search to obtain additional suggestions for effective cover letters.

Career Portfolios

In addition to a résumé, many job applicants prepare a *career portfolio.* This collection of documents and other items provides tangible evidence of your ability and skills. A career portfolio may include the following items:

1} *Documentation*—a résumé, sample interview answers, a competency summary, and letters of recommendation.

2} *Creative works*—ads, product designs, packages, brand, promotions, and video clips on DVD.

3} *Research project samples*—research findings, PowerPoint presentation, Web site designs, marketing plans, and photos of project activities.

4} *Employment accomplishments*—published articles, sales results data, financial charts, and news articles of community activities.

A career portfolio can present your abilities and experiences in a tangible manner. In addition, these materials will communicate your initiative and uniqueness. The cover page of your portfolio should connect your ability to the needs of the organization.

An electronic portfolio can be developed on a Web site, with graphics and links. Be sure your home page is not cluttered and is organized to quickly find desired information. Consider sending a CD with your Web site files along with your résumé.

Online Application Process

Many organizations require online applications involving some of these activities:

1} *Online applications*—in addition to the basic application, you may also be asked to answer some preliminary questions to determine your suitability for the position available.

2} *E-résumés*—when posting your résumé online or sending it by e-mail, be sure to (*a*) use a simple format, avoiding bold, underlines, italics, and tabs; and (*b*) attach no files that may be difficult to open. Remember that an Internet résumé is impersonal, so do not overlook other job search methods—phone calls, ads, job fairs, and personal contacts.

3} *Cyber interviewing*—many organizations conduct screening interviews using video conferencing. Others require that you post preliminary interview responses online. These "e-interviews" may involve questions such as: "Would you rather have structure or flexibility in your work?" and "What approach do you use to solve difficult problems?" Online interviewing may also be used to test a person's ability in job-related situations. For example, an applicant may be asked to respond to tasks such as those that an investment broker or customer service representative might encounter.

The Job Interview

The interview phase is limited to candidates who possess the desired qualifications.

Preparing for the Interview

Prepare by obtaining additional information about the organization. The best sources include the library, the Internet, observations during company visits, analysis of company products, informal conversations with employees, and discussions with people knowledgeable about the company or industry. Research the company's operations, competitors, recent successes, planned expansion, and personnel policies to help you discuss your potential contributions to the company.

Another preinterview activity is preparing questions you will ask during the interview, such as:

- What do employees like most about your organization's working environment?
- What challenges might be encountered by new employees?

Education and Training Questions

What education and training qualify you for this job?

Why are you interested in working for this company?

In addition to going to school, what activities have helped you to expand your interests and knowledge?

What did you like best about school?

What did you like least?

Work and Other Experience Questions

In what types of situations have you done your best work?

Describe the supervisors who motivated you most.

Which of your past accomplishments are you proud of?

Have you ever had to coordinate the activities of several people?

Describe some people whom you have found difficult to work with.

Describe a situation in which your determination helped you achieve a specific goal.

What situations frustrate you?

Other than past jobs, what experiences have helped prepare you for this job?

What methods do you consider best for motivating employees?

Personal Qualities Questions

What are your major strengths?

What are your major weaknesses? What have you done to overcome your weaknesses?

What do you plan to be doing 5 or 10 years from now?

Which individuals have had the greatest influence on you?

What traits make a person successful?

How well do you communicate your ideas orally and in writing?

How would your teachers and your past employers describe you?

What do you do in your leisure time?

How persuasive are you in presenting ideas to others?

- What training opportunities are available to employees who desire advancement?
- What qualities do your most successful employees possess?
- What actions of competitors are likely to affect the company in the near future?

Successful interviewing requires practice. Use a video or work with friends to develop confidence when interviewing. Organize ideas, speak clearly and calmly, and communicate enthusiasm. Prepare specific answers regarding your strengths. Campus organizations and career placement offices may offer opportunities for interview practice.

When interviewing, keep in mind that proper dress and grooming are vital. Dress more conservatively than current employees. A business suit is usually appropriate. Avoid trendy and casual styles, and don't wear too much jewelry.

Confirm the time and location of the interview. Take copies of your résumé, your reference list, and paper for notes. Arrive about 10 minutes earlier than your appointed time.

The Interview Process

Interviews may include situations or questions to determine how you react under pressure. Answer clearly in a controlled manner. Career counselors suggest having a "theme" for interview responses to focus your key qualifications. Throughout the interview come back to the central idea that communicates your potential contributions to the organization.

Behavioral interviewing, also called *competency-based interviewing,* is frequently used to evaluate an applicant's on-the-job potential. In these questions, you might be asked how you would handle various work situations. Behavioral interview questions typically begin with "Describe . . ." or "Tell me about . . ." to encourage interviewees to better explain their work style.

In *situational interviewing,* you are asked to participate in role-playing, similar to what may be encountered on the job. For example, you might be asked to resolve a complaint with a customer or negotiate with a supplier. This interview experience is used to evaluate your ability to work in various organizational environments.

Avoid talking too much, but answer each question completely maintaining good eye contact. Stay calm during the interview. Remember, you are being asked questions about a subject about which you are the world's expert—YOU! Finally, thank the interviewer for the opportunity to discuss the job and your qualifications.

did you know?

In *situational interviewing,* candidates for a sales position may be asked to interact with a potential customer. Prospective employees for Southwest Airlines participate in a "job audition." This starts the moment they apply, with extensive notes from the initial phone call. During the flight to the interview, gate agents, flight attendants, and other company employees are instructed to pay special attention to the candidate's behaviors. Thus, the candidate is being observed constantly, in situations similar to the job setting. The process also includes giving a talk to a large group. Bored or distracted audience members are disqualified. This selection process has been shown to reduce employee turnover and increase customer satisfaction.

After the Interview

Most interviewers conclude by telling you when you can expect to hear from them. While waiting, do two things. First, send a follow-up letter or e-mail within a day or two expressing your appreciation for the opportunity to interview. If you don't get the job, this thank-you letter can make a positive impression to improve your chances for future consideration.

Second, do a self-evaluation of your interview performance. Write down the areas to improve. Try to remember the questions you were asked that differed from your expected questions. Remember, the more interviews you have, the better you will present yourself and the better the chance of being offered a job.

Career Activity 9

Have someone ask you sample interview questions and then point out the strengths and weaknesses of your interview skills.

Job Offer Comparison

The financial aspects of a job should be assessed along with some organization factors.

1} *Salary and financial factors*—your rate of pay will be affected by the type of work and your experience. The position may also include employee benefits. These include insurance, retirement plans, vacation time, and other special benefits for employees. Many organizations offer recreational facilities, discounts, and other advantages for workers.

2} *Organizational environment*—while the financial elements of a job are very important, also consider the working environment. Leadership style, dress code, and the social atmosphere should be investigated. Talk with people who have worked in the organization. Advancement potential might also be evaluated. Training programs may be available. These opportunities can be very beneficial for your long-term career success.

did you know?

The main factors college graduates consider when choosing an employer are enjoyment of the work, integrity of the organization, potential for advancement, benefits, and job location.

Career Activity 10

Prepare a list of factors that you would consider when accepting a job. Talk to other people about what they believe to be important when accepting a job.

Career Strategies in a Weak Job Market

In recent years, obtaining employment has been more difficult for many job seekers due to the economic downturn. What actions would be useful to take when attempting to seek employment or maintain your current position? Consider the following:

- Acknowledge stress, anxiety, frustration, and fear. Eat properly and exercise to avoid health problems.
- Assess your financial situation. Determine sources of emergency funds to pay needed expenses. Cut unnecessary spending.
- Evaluate your current and future employment potential. Consider work and community experiences that you have which are not on your résumé.
- Maintain a focus with a positive outlook. Your ability to communicate confidence and competency will result in more job offers.
- Connect with others in professional and social settings.
- Consider part-time work, consulting, and volunteering to exercise your skills, develop new contacts, and expand your career potential.

An ability to obtain and maintain employment in difficult economic times will serve you in every type of job market.

Key Web Sites for Career Planning

www.careerjournal.com	www.rileyguide.com
www.ajb.dni.us	www.careerbuilder.com
www.monster.com	www.careerfairs.com
www.bls.gov/oco	www.businessweek.com/careers

B Consumer Agencies and Organizations

The following government agencies and private organizations can offer information and assistance on various financial planning and consumer purchasing areas. These groups can serve your needs when you want to

- Research a financial or consumer topic area.
- Obtain information for planning a purchase decision.
- Seek assistance to resolve a consumer problem.

Section 1 provides an overview of federal, state, and local agencies and other organizations you may contact for information related to various financial planning and consumer topic areas. Section 2 covers state consumer protection offices that can assist you in local matters.

Section 1

Most federal agencies may be contacted through the Internet; several Web sites are noted. In addition, consumer information from several federal government agencies may be accessed at www.consumer.gov.

Information on additional government agencies and private organizations available to assist you may be obtained in the *Consumer Action Handbook,* available at no charge from the Consumer Information Center, Pueblo, CO 81009 or online at www. pueblo.gsa.gov.

Exhibit **B–1**   Federal, State, and Local Agencies and Other Organizations

Topic Area	Federal Agency	State, Local Agency; Other Organizations
Advertising False advertising Product labeling Deceptive sales practices Warranties	Federal Trade Commission 600 Pennsylvania Avenue, NW Washington, DC 20580 1-877-FTC-HELP (www.ftc.gov)	State Consumer Protection Office c/o State Attorney General or Governor's Office National Fraud Information Center Box 65868 Washington, DC 20035 1-800-876-7060 (www.fraud.org)
Air Travel Air safety Airport regulation Airline route	Federal Aviation Administration 800 Independence Avenue, SW Washington, DC 20591 1-800-FAA-SURE (www.faa.gov)	International Airline Passengers Association Box 660074 Dallas, TX 75266 1-800-527-5888 (www.iapa.com)

Exhibit **B–1** (*continued*)

Topic Area	Federal Agency	State, Local Agency; Other Organizations
Appliances/Product Safety Potentially dangerous products Complaints against retailers, manufacturers	Consumer Product Safety Commission Washington, DC 20207 1-800-638-CPSC (www.cpsc.gov)	Council of Better Business Bureaus 4200 Wilson Boulevard Arlington, VA 22203 1-800-955-5100 (www.bbb.org)
Automobiles New cars Used cars Automobile repairs Auto safety	Federal Trade Commission (see above) National Highway Traffic Safety Administration 400 Seventh Street, SW Washington, DC 20590 1-800-424-9393 (www.nhtsa.gov)	AUTOCAP/National Automobile Dealers Association 8400 Westpark Drive McLean, VA 22102 1-800-252-6232 (www.nada.org) Center for Auto Safety 2001 S Street, NW Washington, DC 20009 (202) 328-7700 (www.autosafety.org)
Banking and Financial Institutions Checking accounts Savings accounts Deposit insurance Financial services	Federal Deposit Insurance Corporation 550 17th Street, NW Washington, DC 20429 1-877-275-3342 (www.fdic.gov) Comptroller of the Currency 15th Street and Pennsylvania Avenue, NW Washington, DC 20219 (202) 447-1600 (www.occ.treas.gov) Federal Reserve Board Washington, DC 20551 (202) 452-3693 (www.federalreserve.gov) National Credit Union Administration 1775 Duke Street Alexandria, VA 22314 (703) 518-6300 (www.ncua.gov)	State Banking Authority Credit Union National Association Box 431 Madison, WI 53701 (608) 232-8256 (www.cuna.org) American Bankers Association 1120 Connecticut Avenue, NW Washington, DC 20036 (202) 663-5000 (www.aba.com) U.S. savings bond rates 1-800-US-BONDS (www.savingsbonds.gov)
Career Planning Job training Employment information	Coordinator of Consumer Affairs Department of Labor Washington, DC 20210 (202) 219-6060 (www.dol.gov)	State Department of Labor or State Employment Service

Exhibit B–1 (continued)

Topic Area	Federal Agency	State, Local Agency; Other Organizations
Consumer Credit Credit cards Deceptive credit advertising Truth-in-Lending Act Credit rights of women, minorities	Federal Trade Commission 600 Pennsylvania Avenue, NW Washington, DC 20580 (202) 326-2222 (www.ftc.gov)	100 Edgewood Avenue (#1800) Atlanta, GA 30303 1-800-251-2227 (www.cccsatl.org) National Foundation for Credit Counseling 801 Roeder Road (#900) Silver Spring, MD 20910 (301) 589–5600 (www.nfcc.org)
Environment Air, water pollution Toxic substances	Environmental Protection Agency Washington, DC 20024 1-800-438-4318 (indoor air quality) 1-800-426-4791 (drinking water safety) (www.epa.gov)	Clean Water Action 4455 Connecticut Avenue, NW Washington, DC 20008 (202) 895-0420 (www.cleanwater.org)
Food Food grades Food additives Nutritional information	U.S. Department of Agriculture Washington, DC 20250 1-800-424-9121 (www.usda.gov) Food and Drug Administration 5600 Fishers Lane Rockville, MD 20857 1-888-463-6332 (www.fda.gov)	Center for Science in the Public Interest 1875 Connecticut Avenue, NW, Suite 300 Washington, DC 20009 (202) 332-9110 (www.cspinet.org)
Funerals Cost disclosure Deceptive business practices	Federal Trade Commission (see above)	Funeral Service Help Line 13625 Bishop's Drive Brookfield, WI 53005 1-800-228-6332 (www.nfda.org)
Housing and Real Estate Fair housing practices Mortgages Community development	Department of Housing and Urban Development 451 Seventh Street, SW Washington, DC 20410 1-800-669-9777 (www.hud.gov)	National Association of Realtors (www.realtor.com) (www.move.com) National Association of Home Builders 1201 15th Street, NW Washington, DC 20005 (www.nahb.com)

Exhibit **B–1**   (*continued*)

Topic Area	Federal Agency	State, Local Agency; Other Organizations
Insurance Policy conditions Premiums Types of coverage Consumer complaints	Federal Trade Commission (see above) National Flood Insurance Program 500 C Street, SW Washington, DC 20472 1-888-CALL-FLOOD	State Insurance Regulator American Council of Life Insurance 1001 Pennsylvania Avenue, NW Washington, DC 20004-2599 (www.acli.com) Insurance Information Institute 110 William Street New York, NY 10038 1-800-331-9146 (www.iii.org)

Investments
Stocks, bonds
Mutual funds
Commodities
Investment brokers
	Securities and Exchange Commission
	100 F Street, NE
	Washington, DC 20549
	(202) 551-6551
	(www.sec.gov)
	
	Commodity Futures Trading
	  Commission
	1155 21st Street, NW
	Washington, DC 20581
	(202) 418-5000
	(www.cftc.gov)
		Investment Company Institute
		1600 M Street, NW
		Washington, DC 20036
		(202) 293-7700
		(www.ici.org)
		
		National Association of Securities
		  Dealers
		1735 K Street, NW
		Washington, DC 20006
		(202) 728-8000
		(www.nasd.com)
		
		National Futures Association
		200 West Madison Street
		Chicago, IL 60606
		1-800-621-3570
		(www.nfa.futures.org)
		
		Securities Investor Protection Corp.
		805 15th Street, NW, Suite 800
		Washington, DC 20005
		(202) 371-8300
		(www.sipc.org)

Legal Matters Consumer complaints Arbitration	Department of Justice Office of Consumer Litigation Washington, DC 20530 (202) 514-2401	American Arbitration Association 140 West 51st Street New York, NY 10020 (212) 484-4000 (www.adr.org) American Bar Association 321 North Clark Street Chicago, IL 60610 1-800-285-2221 (www.abanet.org)

Exhibit **B–1** (*continued*)

Topic Area	Federal Agency	State, Local Agency; Other Organizations
Mail Order Damaged products Deceptive business practices Illegal use of U.S. mail	U.S. Postal Service Washington, DC 20260-2202 1-800-ASK-USPS (www.usps.gov)	Direct Marketing Association 1120 Avenue of the Americas New York, NY 10036 (212) 768-7277 (www.the-dma.org)
Medical Concerns Prescription medications Over-the-counter medications Medical devices Health care	Food and Drug Administration (see above) Public Health Service 200 Independence Avenue, SW Washington, DC 20201 1-800-336-4797 (www.usphs.gov)	American Medical Association 510 North State Street Chicago, IL 60610 1-800-621-8335 (www.ama-assn.org) Public Citizen Health Research Group 1600 20th Street, NW Washington, DC 20009 (202) 588-1000
Retirement Old-age benefits Pension information Medicare	Social Security Administration 6401 Security Boulevard Baltimore, MD 21235 1-800-772-1213 (www.ssa.gov)	AARP 601 E Street, NW Washington, DC 20049 (202) 434-2277 (www.aarp.org)
Taxes Tax information Audit procedures	Internal Revenue Service 1111 Constitution Avenue, NW Washington, DC 20204 1-800-829-1040 1-800-TAX-FORM (www.irs.gov)	Department of Revenue (in your state capital city) The Tax Foundation 2001 L Street, NW (#1050) Washington, DC 20036 (202) 464-6200 (www.taxfoundation.org) National Association of Enrolled Agents 1120 Connecticut Avenue, NW (#440) Washington, DC 20036 1-800-424-4339 (www.naea.org)
Telemarketing 900 numbers	Federal Communications Commission 445 12th Street, SW Washington, DC 20554 1-888-225-5322 (www.fcc.gov)	National Consumers League 1701 K Street, NW Washington, DC 20006 (202) 835-3323 (www.nclnet.org)
Utilities Cable television Utility rates	Federal Communications Commission 445 12th Street, SW Washington, DC 20554 1-988-225-5322 (www.fcc.gov)	State utility commission (in your state capital)

Section 2

State, county, and local consumer protection offices provide consumers with a variety of services, including publications and information before buying as well as handling complaints. This section provides contact information for state consumer protection agencies. In addition to the primary offices listed here, agencies regulating banking, insurance, securities, and utilities are available in each state. These may be located through a Web search or by going to the *Consumer's Resource Handbook* at www.pueblo.gsa.gov.

Many state consumer protection offices may be accessed through the Web site of the National Association of Attorneys General at www.naag.org or with a Web search for your state consumer protection office using "*(state)* consumer protection agency."

To save time, call the office before sending in a written complaint. Ask if the office handles the type of complaint you have or if complaint forms are provided. Many offices distribute consumer materials specifically geared to state laws and local issues. Call to obtain available educational information on your problem.

State departments of insurance may be accessed online at www.naic.org/state_web_map.htm.

The Web sites of state tax departments are available at www.taxadmin.org or www.aicpa.org/yellow/yptsgus.htm.

C   Daily Spending Diary

Effective short-term money management and long-term financial security are dependent on spending less than you earn. The use of a Daily Spending Diary will provide information to better understand your spending patterns and to help you achieve desired financial goals.

The following sheets should be used to record *every cent* of your spending each day in the categories provided. Or you can create your own format to monitor your spending. You can indicate the use of a credit card with (CR). This experience will help you better understand your spending habits and identify desired changes you might want to make in your spending activities. Your comments should reflect what you have learned about your spending and can assist with changes you might want to make. Ask yourself, "What spending amounts can I reduce or eliminate?"

Many people who take on this task find it difficult at first, and may consider it a waste of time. However, nearly everyone who makes a serious effort to keep a Daily Spending Diary has found it beneficial. The process may seem tedious at first, but after a while recording this information becomes easier and faster. Most important, you will know where your money is going. Then you will be able to better decide if that is truly how you want to spend your available financial resources. A sincere effort with this activity will result in very beneficial information for monitoring and controlling your spending.

Using a Daily Spending Diary can help to:

- Reveal hidden aspects of your spending habits so you can better save for the future.
- Create and achieve financial goals.
- Revise buying habits and reduce wasted spending.
- Control credit card purchases.
- Improve recordkeeping for your measuring financial progress and filing your taxes.
- Plan for major expenditures encountered during the year.
- Start an investment program with the money you save through controlled spending.

The following Daily Spending Diary sheets are also available in an Excel® format on the student Web site www.mhhe.com/kdh.

Daily Spending Diary

Directions: Record every cent of your spending each day in the categories provided, or create your own format to monitor your spending. You can indicate the use of a credit card with (CR). Comments should reflect what you have learned about your spending patterns and desired changes you might want to make in your spending habits. (Note: As income is received, record in Date column.)

Month: _____   Amount available for spending: $ _____   Amount to be saved: $ _____

Date (Income)	Total Spending	Auto, Transportation	Housing, Utilities	Food (H) Home (A) Away	Health, Personal Care	Education	Recreation, Leisure	Donations, Gifts	Other (note item, amount)	Comments
Example	$83	$20 (gas) (CR)		$47 (H)		$2 (pen)	$4 (DVD rental)	$10 (church)		This takes time but it helps me control my spending
1										
2										
3										
4										
5										
6										
7										
8										
9										
10										
11										
12										
13										
14										
Subtotal										

(continued)

Date (Income)	Total Spending	Auto, Transportation	Housing, Utilities	Food (H) Home (A) Away	Health, Personal Care	Education	Recreation, Leisure	Donations, Gifts	Other (note item, amount)	Comments
15										
16										
17										
18										
19										
20										
21										
22										
23										
24										
25										
26										
27										
28										
29										
30										
31										
Total										

Total Income $ _____

Total Spending $ _____

Difference (+/−) $ _____

Actions: amount to savings, areas for reduced spending, other actions . . .

Daily Spending Diary

Directions: Record *every cent* of your spending each day in the categories provided, or create your own format to monitor your spending. You can indicate the use of a credit card with (CR). Comments should reflect what you have learned about your spending patterns and desired changes you might want to make in your spending habits. (Note: As income is received, record in Date column.)

Month: _____   Amount available for spending: $ _____   Amount to be saved: $ _____

Date (Income)	Total Spending	Auto, Transportation	Housing, Utilities	Food (H) Home (A) Away	Health, Personal Care	Education	Recreation, Leisure	Donations, Gifts	Other (note item, amount)	Comments
1										
2										
3										
4										
5										
6										
7										
8										
9										
10										
11										
12										
13										
14										
Subtotal										

(continued)

Date (Income)	Total Spending	Auto, Transportation	Housing, Utilities	Food (H) Home (A) Away	Health, Personal Care	Education	Recreation, Leisure	Donations, Gifts	Other (note item, amount)	Comments
15										
16										
17										
18										
19										
20										
21										
22										
23										
24										
25										
26										
27										
28										
29										
30										
31										
Total										

Total Income $ _____

Total Spending $ _____

Difference (+/−) $ _____

Actions: amount to savings, areas for reduced spending, other actions . . . .

Daily Spending Diary

Directions: Record *every cent* of your spending each day in the categories provided, or create your own format to monitor your spending. You can indicate the use of a credit card with (CR). Comments should reflect what you have learned about your spending patterns and desired changes you might want to make in your spending habits. (Note: As income is received, record in Date column.)

Month: _____   Amount available for spending: $ _____   Amount to be saved: $ _____

Date (Income)	Total Spending	Auto, Transportation	Housing, Utilities	Food (H) Home (A) Away	Health, Personal Care	Education	Recreation, Leisure	Donations, Gifts	Other (note item, amount)	Comments
1										
2										
3										
4										
5										
6										
7										
8										
9										
10										
11										
12										
13										
14										
Subtotal										

(continued)

Date (Income)	Total Spending	Auto, Transportation	Housing, Utilities	Food (H) Home (A) Away	Health, Personal Care	Education	Recreation, Leisure	Donations, Gifts	Other (note item, amount)	Comments
15										
16										
17										
18										
19										
20										
21										
22										
23										
24										
25										
26										
27										
28										
29										
30										
31										
Total										

Total Income
$ _____

Total Spending
$ _____

Difference (+/−)
$ _____

Actions: amount to savings, areas for reduced spending, other actions . . . .

Daily Spending Diary

Directions: Record *every cent* of your spending each day in the categories provided, or create your own format to monitor your spending. You can indicate the use of a credit card with (CR). Comments should reflect what you have learned about your spending patterns and desired changes you might want to make in your spending habits. (Note: As income is received, record in Date column.)

Month: _____   Amount available for spending: $ _____   Amount to be saved: $ _____

Date (Income)	Total Spending	Auto, Transportation	Housing, Utilities	Food (H) Home (A) Away	Health, Personal Care	Education	Recreation, Leisure	Donations, Gifts	Other (note item, amount)	Comments
1										
2										
3										
4										
5										
6										
7										
8										
9										
10										
11										
12										
13										
14										
Subtotal										

(continued)

Date (Income)	Total Spending	Auto, Transportation	Housing, Utilities	Food (H) Home (A) Away	Health, Personal Care	Education	Recreation, Leisure	Donations, Gifts	Other (note item, amount)	Comments
15										
16										
17										
18										
19										
20										
21										
22										
23										
24										
25										
26										
27										
28										
29										
30										
31										
Total										

Total Income	Total Spending	Difference (+/−)
$ _____	$ _____	$ _____

Actions: amount to savings, areas for reduced spending, other actions . . .

Photo Credits

CHAPTER 1

Page 22   © Royalty-Free/Corbis

CHAPTER 2

Page 62   © Brand X Pictures/PunchStock

CHAPTER 3

Page 101   Brand X Pictures

CHAPTER 4

Page 120   Digital Vision/Getty Images

CHAPTER 5

Page 161   Nick Koudis/Getty Images

CHAPTER 6

Page 195   Royalty-Free/Corbis
Page 195   PhotoLink/Getty Images
Page 195   Comstock Images

CHAPTER 7

Page 235   Brand X Pictures

CHAPTER 8

Page 271   Getty Images/Stockbyte

CHAPTER 9

Page 291   Creatas/PictureQuest

CHAPTER 10

Page 329   © Javier Pierini/Getty Images

CHAPTER 11

Page 354   © Brand X Pictures/PunchStock

CHAPTER 12

Page 415   David Arky/Corbis

Index

A page number followed by an *e* indicates an exhibit on that page; an *n*, notes.